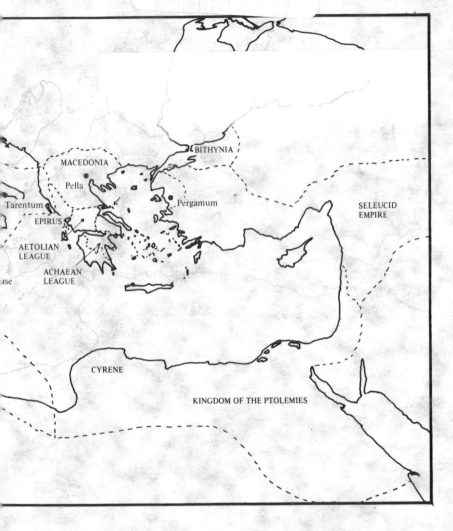

# HANNIBAL'S WAR

— To my Wife —

who first chose Hannibal, and then accepted me

"omnia aequare unus hostis Hannibal potest"
Livy 30.26.8

# HANNIBAL'S WAR

## A military history of the Second Punic War

### J. F. Lazenby

## Aris & Phillips Ltd

WARMINSTER ENGLAND

ISBN 0 85668 080 X

Published by        **Aris & Phillips Ltd**
Teddington House, Warminster, England

Printed in England by    **Biddles Ltd.**, Guildford, Surrey

# CONTENTS

## Military Book Society | ORDER FORM

**Keep this half** and make a note of the book(s) you order

*13*

*The date on the reverse of this form is the date on which your statement was prepared. Any payments, orders or book returns received after this date will appear on your NEXT statement.*

**Tear off and return this half within 10 days of receipt** with any payment due

---

The Recommended Book for **WINTER** is

**GERMANY'S ELITE PANZER FORCE**

**GROSSDEUTSCHLAND** *Pub. Price* £6.95

The Recommended **Book for WINTER** will be sent to you automatically unless you return this form with a cross (x) in this box:—

*Club Price* £4.95     2425     ☐ **13**

---

| Alternative Books | Pub. Price | Club Price Please send book(s) ticked (✓) | |
|---|---|---|---|
| THE LORE OF ARMS | £13.95 | £8.90 | ☐....5371 |
| ULTRA GOES TO WAR | £6.95 | £4.95 | ☐....2443 |
| AIRSHIPWRECK | £4.95 | £3.60 | ☐....2504 |
| HALBRITTER'S ARMOURY | £4.95 | £3.70 | ☐....2639 |
| BATTLES OF THE '45 | £5.95 | £3.95 | ☐....2393 |
| AGINCOURT | £5.95 | £3.95 | ☐....2394 |
| PRISONERS OF HONOUR | £3.95 | £2.95 | ☐....5085 |
| HISTORY OF THE BRITISH SECRET SERVICE | £7.95 | £4.95 | ☐....2545 |
| THE GUN | £7.50 | £4.95 | ☐....2546 |
| ILLUSTRATED HISTORY OF THE THIRD REICH | £7.50 | £4.95 | ☐....2344 |
| FIGHTER: THE TRUE STORY OF THE BATTLE OF BRITAIN | £4.95 | £3.85 | ☐....4514 |
| CROMWELL OUR CHIEF OF MEN | £7.95 | £4.95 | ☐....1825 |
| THE ROMAN IMPERIAL ARMY | £7.50 | £5.50 | ☐....2526 |
| BATTLES OF THE AMERICAN CIVIL WAR | £6.95 | £4.95 | ☐....5897 |
| SEVEN PILLARS OF WISDOM | £4.95 | £3.25 | ☐....1617 |
| INTO BATTLE | £5.95 | £3.95 | ☐....4869 |
| GUINNESS BOOK OF AIR FACTS AND FEATS | £6.50 | £4.45 | ☐....4563 |
| TIRPITZ: THE FLOATING FORTRESS | £6.95 | £4.95 | ☐....4583 |

*Prices do Not include post & packing*

---

**KEEP THIS HALF**     |     **RETURN THIS HALF**

# THE Military BOOK SOCIETY

## P.O. BOX 19, SWINDON SN1 5AX

**IMPORTANT** see over

## STATEMENT OF YOUR ACCOUNT AS AT THIS DATE

PAYMENTS RECEIVED AFTER THIS DATE WILL BE CREDITED ON YOUR NEXT STATEMENT

**Please note your Membership Number** and quote it on all correspondence. If address shown is not correct, please alter.

Z02147831          317          2414          15/11/78

MR R BRYANT
5 SHAFTESBURY CLOSE
MEAD PARK NAILSEA
BRISTOL
00000000          CEA

6.65

| | | Charges | Credit |
|---|---|---|---|
| BALANCE B/F | ENCLOSED | | 0.00 |
| HANNIBALS WAR | | 6.65 | |
| | AMOUNT DUE  £ | 6.65 | |

*N.B. Charges include postage and packing*

008705     15/11/78     Z02147831

# PREFACE

Unlike some of those who have written about Hannibal, I cannot claim to have been fascinated by him since childhood, although I do seem to remember insisting on doing "First Period" Roman History for Greats in order to include the Hannibalic War. But this book is mainly prompted by many years of teaching a special subject in the University of Newcastle upon Tyne, and the feeling that there is nothing really satisfactory on it in English. I am also convinced that the war is not only important in itself, as a turning-point in Roman history, but that the study of it is immensely rewarding for anyone who really wants to understand the Roman Republic. The last century of the Republic's existence benefits from the greater amount of evidence available, particularly in the writings of Cicero, but the Republic was then in decline, and the period of the Second Punic War is probably better documented than any other period of the Republic in its great days.

Writers of books on history are faced with two particular problems: what to do about references, and how much detailed argument to include in the main text. I can only say that I have always found it irritating to have to look elsewhere for the sources of statements made in the text, but at the same time one can obviously not include all references in it. I have therefore adopted the principle of putting all or most references to the ancient sources into the text, and references to modern works into the notes.

As for arguments about details, again I dislike having to break off reading a text to refer to some lengthy note or appendix at the back of the book, and so I have included most of the detailed argument in my text. In any case, I feel that it is not the business of the historian simply to make a series of bland statements, particularly on Greek and Roman history, where even so few facts are known: what a historian should be trying to do is to say what happened and why it happened, and the details are, after all, the stuff of which history is made. They have, too, their own fascination, at least for me, and I can only hope that my readers will share it. But at the same time, the general reader will not, of course, be familiar with some of the technical terms which are, as it were, the short-hand of the historian, particularly in ancient history, where not only are the sources in unfamiliar languages, but the cultures and societies are so remote in time and different from our own. So I have tried to explain such terms, and have included Appendices on the ancient writers and on most of the technical terms used. I hope, as a result, that the book will be at least intelligible to anyone who is seriously interested in the war.

Anyone who writes a book on a subject like the Hannibalic War, as indeed on most subjects in ancient history, is bound to be aware that it is difficult, if not impossible, to offer an entirely new interpretation, and I would be the last to claim any

great originality in this book, except, perhaps, on some points of detail. On most aspects of the war one has to rely heavily on one's predecessors, and essentially what I have tried to do are two things: firstly, to produce a detailed narrative, based firmly on the original sources, particularly Polybius and Livy. I may sometimes, indeed, appear to be too uncritical towards the sources, especially Polybius, for example in the matter of numbers. But if one rejects what one's principal sources have to say, one might as well give up any attempt to write history: most "reconstructions" of what "must" have happened are little better than historical novels, and may lead to the ultimate absurdity of Delbruck's remark that "certain portions of Herodotus' account (of Salamis) correspond so closely, it is true, to the nature of the matter, that we can well accept them." Thus, on numbers, I am fairly sure that what the sources say represent at best paper-strengths, but I can see no way of arriving at the truth, and it is pointless constantly to re-iterate that the numbers are probably too large. Rather, like Herodotus I would say, "ἐγὼ δὲ ὀφείλω λέγειν τὰ λεγόμενα, πείθεσθαί γε μὲν οὐ παντάπασιν ὀφείλω " (I am obliged to say what is said, but I am not at all obliged to believe it).

Secondly, I have tried to draw together the results of much detailed research often hidden away in learned tomes and articles not readily accessible to the student, let alone the general reader. I hope that my notes make clear my indebtedness to these other scholars, and even here I cannot claim to have read everything that has been written on a subject so often studied: I am fully aware that there must be many omissions from the notes and bibliography. But my debt to two of my predecessors is obvious: Professor Walbank's monumental *Historical Commentary on Polybius* should be the indispensable 'Bible' of any serious student of the war; Professor Scullard's two books on Scipio Africanus have cleared up many points, particularly topographical, on his hero's campaigns in Spain and Africa, and while I find his *Roman Politics 220-150 B.C.* less satisfactory, it is an invaluable quarry for the tangled internal politics of Rome at the time. One disagrees with both these scholars at one's peril, and one disagrees so often only because one makes so much use of their writings.

My debts to others are manifold: to generations of students who have at least forced me to try to think more clearly about the problems, and have sometimes produced illuminating ideas of their own; to my immediate colleagues in the Department of Classics at Newcastle, and other colleagues up and down the country, who have endured, with apparent interest, my habit of turning almost any conversation into Hannibalic paths. My debt to two of my colleagues is profound: Jerry Paterson and Tony Woodman have not only put up with more than their fair share of such conversations, but read the manuscript through and drew my attention to many an error: if I use the old cliche that the faults that remain are entirely my own, it is with a very real sense that - apart from anything else - this is not the kind of book either of them would have wanted to write.

My debt to my family is more personal: my wife not only designed the dust-jacket, drew many of the maps, and helped constantly with her own ideas and suggestions, but had to endure many hours of my hammering at a typewriter, and ruining her pens while I struggled to complete the maps; my children, too, more or less patiently put up with the constant injunction - "don't bother Daddy - he's doing Hannibal." I hope that they will all feel that it was worth it in the end.

I would also like to thank my publishers for their friendliness, kindness and patience - particularly Adrian and Lucinda Phillips, who even braved the climb to the Col de Clapier on a cold November's day to take the photographs which appear as Plate IV; my thanks, too, to Group Captain Peter Drury Bird for the photographs used for Plates I, III, VI & VIII, and to the French Air Force for the aerial photographs of the Rhône.

It is often claimed that history can teach us something, and this might be put forward as the reason for studying a conflict like the Hannibalic War, with all its attendant horrors and brutalities. But we, in this day and age, with photographs and films to see, as well as original documents and eye-witness accounts to read, surely do not need to be reminded of the horrors of war by studying one which took place over two thousand years ago. If I appear, sometimes, to relish the details of campaigns and battles, and to protest too little about the violence and brutality, I can only say that I do not, in fact, relish the thought of violence and slaughter. But I do not think that history can teach us anything in the sense that is often claimed: the more one studies it, the more one realises its complexities, and it is simply not the case that "the same kind of events, or ones very like them, will happen again," as Thucydides appears to have believed. The study of the Hannibalic War tells us about the Hannibalic War, and I study history because I find it interesting, not for any ulterior motive. As in so much else, I would agree with the father of all historians that the purpose of writing history is "ὡς μήτε τὰ γενόμενα ἐξ ἀνθρώπων τῷ χρόνῳ ἐξίτηλα γένηται, μήτε ἔργα μεγάλα τε καὶ θωμαστά . . . ἀκλεᾶ γένηται" (that neither what men have done may fade through time, nor great and wondrous deeds be lost to fame).

J. F. Lazenby,
Newcastle upon Tyne, May, 1978.

# SELECT BIBLIOGRAPHY

I have made most use of the following works (abbreviations used are shown in square brackets at the end of each entry):-

Badian, E.: *Foreign Clientelae (264-70 B.C.)* (Oxford 1958).

Beer, Sir Gavin de: *Hannibal's March* (London 1967).

Beer, Sir Gavin de: *Hannibal* (London 1969).

Broughton, T. R. S.: *The Magistrates of the Roman Republic* (Vol. I New York 1951, Vol. II New York 1952) [*MRR* I, *MRR* II]

Brunt, P. A.: *Italian Manpower 225 B.C. - A.D. 14* (Oxford 1971). [*IM*]

Dorey, T. A. & Dudley, D. R.: *Rome Against Carthage* (London 1968).

Picard, G. C. & C.: *The Life and Death of Carthage* (London 1968).

Proctor, Dennis: *Hannibal's March in History* (Oxford 1971). [Proctor]

Sanctis, G. de: *Storia dei Romani* (Turin-Florence 1907-23, 1953). [de Sanctis]

Scullard, H. H.: *Scipio Africanus in the Second Punic War* (Cambridge 1930). [*SAPW*]

Scullard, H. H.: *A History of Rome 753-146 B.C.* (3rd ed. London 1961). [*History*]

Scullard, H. H.: *Scipio Africanus: Soldier and Politician* (London 1970). [*SASP*]

Scullard, H. H.: *Roman Politics 220-150 B.C.* (2nd ed. Oxford 1973).

Thiel, J. H.: *Studies on the History of Roman Sea-power in Republican Times* (Amsterdam 1946). [Thiel]

Toynbee, A. J.: *Hannibal's Legacy* (2 vols., London 1965). [Toynbee]

Walbank, F. W.: *Philip V of Macedon* (Cambridge 1940).

Walbank, F. W.: *A Historical Commentary on Polybius* (Vol. I Oxford 1957, Vol. II Oxford 1967. [Walbank I, Walbank II]

*Additional Abbreviations used in the Notes*

*AJP:*   American Journal of Philology
*CAH:*   Cambridge Ancient History
*CIL:*   Corpus Inscriptionum Latinarum
*CP:*    Classical Philology
*CR:*    Classical Review
*HSCP:*  Harvard Studies in Classical Philology
*JHS:*   Journal of Hellenic Studies
*JRS:*   Journal of Roman Studies
*PBSR:*  Papers of the British School at Rome
*RE:*    Real-Encyclopädie der classischen Altertumswissenschaft

To the full bibliographies in Walbank's commentary, Toynbee and Badian, and to the works cited in the notes, may be added:

Adamesteanu, D.: *'Metaponto (Matera). Appunti fotoiinterpretavi', Notizie degli Scavi di Atichità* 19 (1965 suppl.), 179-84.

Alvisi, G.: *'Dal Trasimeno a Capua, Le marce di Annibale nel biennio 217-16 a.C.', Mélanges offerts à Roger Dion* (Paris 1974), 293-313.

Armstrong, D.: *The Reluctant Warriors. The Decline and Fall of the Carthaginian Empire* (New York 1966).

Astin, A. E.: *'Saguntum and the origins of the Second Punic War', Latomus* 26 (1967), 577-96.

Bloch, R.: *'Hannibal et les dieux de Rome', Comptes Rendus de l'Académie des Inscriptions et Belles-Lettres,* 1975, 14-25.

Brisson, J. P.: *'Les mutations de la seconde guerre punique', Problèmes de la guerre à Rome* (Paris 1969), 33-59.

Christ, K. von: *Hannibal* (Wege der Forsch. CCCLXXI, Darmstadt 1974).

Christ, K. von: *'Hannibal und Scipio Africanus', Die Grossen der Weltgeschichte* (Zurich 1971).

Corbett, J. H.: *C. Flaminius and Roman policy in north Italy* (diss. Toronto 1968).

Dawson, A.: *'Hannibal and chemical warfare', Classical Journal* 63 (1967), 117-25.

Derow, P. S.: *'The Roman Calendar, 218-191 B.C.', Phoenix* 30 (1976), 265-81.

Develin, R.: *'Prorogation of imperium before the Hannibalic War', Latomus* 34 (1975), 716-22.

Develin, R.: *'Scipio Africanus Imperator', Latomus* 36 (1977), 110-3.

Dolan, M.: *Anibal de Cartago* (Barcelona 1971).

Edlund, I.: *'Before Zama. A comparison of Polybios' and Livy's descriptions of the meeting between Hannibal and Scipio', Eranos* 65 (1967), 146-68.

Errington, R. M.: *'Rome and Spain before the Second Punic War', Latomus* 29 (1970), 25-37.

Eucken, H. C.: *Probleme der Vorgeschichte des zweiten punischen Krieges* (diss. Freiburg 1968).

Goerlitz, W.: *Hannibal. Eine politische Biographie* (Stuttgart 1970).

Gachnitzer, F.: *'Die Stellung Karthagos nach dem Frieden von 201 v.Chr.', Wiener Studien* 79 (1966), 276-89.

Hafner, G.: *'Das Bildnis Hannibals', Mitteilungen des Deutschen Archäologischen Instituts* (Abt. Madrid), 14 (1973), 143-50.

Hahn, I.: *'Appian und Hannibal', Acta Antiqua Academiae Scientarum Hungaricae* 20 (1972), 95-121.

Hammond, N. G. L.: *'Illyris, Rome and Macedon', Jornal of Roman Studies* 58 (1968), 1-21.

Horsfall, N.: *'Turnus ad portas', Latomus* 33 (1974), 80-6.

Jones, B. W.: *'Rome's relationship with Carthage. A Study in aggression', The Classical Bulletin* 49 (1972), 5-26.

Kotula, T.: *'De Carthaginiensium civitatis ordine qui putatur populari ab Hannibale novato', Eos* 57 (1967-8), 272-81.

Liebmann-Frankfort, Th.: *'Du traité de l'Ebre à la paix de Dardanos', Latomus* 30 (1971), 585-97.

Liebmann-Frankfort, Th.: *'Le traité de l'Ebre et sa valeur juridique'*, Revue *Historique de Droit français et étranger* 50 (1972), 193-204.

Lloyd, A.: *Destroy Carthage!* (London 1977).

Lovejoy, J.: *'The fides of New Carthage'*, Classical Philology 67 (1972), 110-1.

Maestre Yernes, M. A. M.: *'Una explicacion matematica del triunfo militar de Anibal en la battala de Cannas'*, Estudios Classicos 15 (1971), 7-48.

Mansel, A. M.: *'Zur Lage des Hannibalgrabes'*, Archäologischer Anzeiger 1972, 272-5.

Marchetti, P.: *'La deuxième guerre punique en Sicile. Les années 215-14 et le recit de Tite-Live'*, Bulletin de l'Institut historique Belge de Rome 42 (1972), 5-26.

Marquion, P.: *Sur le pas d'Hannibal* (Orange 1965).

Meister, K.: *'Annibale in Sileno'*, Maia 23 (1971), 3-9.

Mitchell, R. E.: *'Roman-Carthaginian treaties, 306 and 279/8 B.C.'*, Historia 20 (1971), 633-55.

Moscovich, M. J.: *'Hostage regulations in the treaty of Zama'*, Historia 23 (1974), 417-27.

Muylle, J.: *'Le traité d'amitié entre Rome et la ligue étolienne'*, L'Antiquité Classique 38 (1969), 408-29.

Pascucci, G.: *'Lo scoppio delle ostilità nella guerra annibalica secondo il racconto degli Annali di Ennio' (Poesia latina in frammenti*, Genoa 1974), 103-15.

Pédech, P.: *'Sur le pas d'Hannibal'*, Revue des Études Grecques 79 (1966), 727-9.

Pfiffig, A. J.: *'Die Haltung Etruriens in 2. punischen Krieg'*, Historia 15 (1966), 193-210.

Pfiffig, A. J.: *'Eine Nennung Hannibals in einer Inschrift des 2. Jahrhunderts v. Chr. aus Tarquinia'*, Studi Etruschi 35 (1967), 659-63.

Pelletier, A.: *'A propos de la Lex Claudia de 218 av. J.-C.'*, Rivista di Studi Liguri 35 (1969), 7-14.

Picard, G. C.: *Hannibal* (Paris 1967).

Picard, G.C.: *'Le traité romano-barcide de 226 av. J.-C.'*, Mélanges d'archéologie, d'epigraphie et /d'histoire offerts à J. Carcopino (Paris 1966), 747-62.

Radke, G.: *'Die territoriale Politik des C. Flaminius'*, Festschrift für F. Altheim (Berlin 1969), 366-86.

Ridley, R. J.: *'Was Scipio Africanus at Cannae?'*, Latomus 34 (1975), 161-5.

Seguin, R.: *'La Religion de Scipion l'Africain'*, Latomus 33 (1974), 3-21.

Stanton, G. R.: *'Cunctando restituit rem. The tradition about Fabius'*, Antichthon 5 (1971), 49-56.

Sumner, G. V.: *'The chronology of the outbreak of the Second Punic War'*, Proceedings of the African Classical Association 9 (1966), 5-30.

Sumner, G. V.: *'Roman Policy in Spain before the Hannibalic War'* Harvard Studies in Classical Philology 72 (1967), 205-46.

Sumner, G. V.: *'Rome, Spain and the Outbreak of the Second Punic War'*, Latomus 31 (1972), 469-80.

Tammler, U.: *Der römische Senat in der Zeit des zweiten punischen Krieges 218-01* (Diss. Bonn 1970).

Trankle, H.: *Livius und Polybius. Eine text vergleichende Untersuchung zur Abhangigkeit der liviarischen Ab urbe condita von den polybianischen Historien* (Basel 1976).

Tudor, D.: *Hannibal* (Bucureşti 1966).

Ungern-Sternberg, J. von: *Capua in zweiten punischen Krief: Untersuchungen zur Römischen Annalistik* (Munich 1975).

Vessey, D. W. T.: *'The Myth of Falernus in Silius, Punica 7'*, *Classical Journal* 68 (1972-3), 240-6.

Vessey, D. W. T.: *'Silius Italicus on the fall of Saguntum'*, *Classical Philology* 69 (1974), 28-36.

Walbank, F. W.: *'The Scipionic Legend'*, *Proceedings of the Cambridge Philological Society* 13 (1967), 54-69.

Xella, P.: *'A proposito del guiramento annibalico, Oriens Antiqua. Rivista de Centro per le Antichità e la Storia dell'Arte del vicino Oriente,* 10 (1971), 189-93.

Yaavetz, D.: 'The policy of Gaius Flaminius and his attitude in regard to *the plebiscitum Claudianum'* (in Hebrew), *Eškolot* 4 (1962), 113-32.

# CHAPTER ONE – ROME, CARTHAGE AND THE ORIGINS OF THE WAR.

"What man exists," Polybius[1] asks towards the beginning of his work (1.1.5), "who is so worthless or so apathetic that he would not wish to know how and by what sort of political system practically the whole of the inhabited world was conquered in not quite fifty-three years and came under the rule of the Romans?"; and although he clearly exaggerates both the extent and the speed of the Roman conquest even of the "inhabited world" that he knew, he was obviously right in thinking that the period he had in mind - 220 to 167[2] - was one of astonishing change in the Mediterranean world. Within this period it was the Hannibalic War which was the crucial turning-point, and even contemporaries appear to have realized that this was so: in 217, for example, the Aetolian leader, Agelaos of Naupaktos, warned his fellow-Greeks of "the clouds now looming from the west" (Polybius 5.104.10), and six years later the Acarnanian, Lykiskos, echoed the warning (Polybius 9.37.10). To us the outcome of the struggle may seem inevitable, but the fact remains that Rome never came nearer to total disaster again for something like six hundred years - never saw a foreign enemy at the gates, as it saw Hannibal in 211, until the coming of Alaric the Visigoth in A.D.408.[3] Conversely, whereas before the war, apart from the abortive invasion of Africa in 256/5, minor operations in Corsica between 236 and 231, and the two brief forays to Illyria (Albania) in 229 and 219, Roman forces had never set foot outside the modern confines of Italy (including Sicily and Sardinia), by the end of it Roman soldiers had fought in southern France, Spain, Albania, Greece and north Africa, and Roman warships had been seen as far west as the straits of Gibraltar and as far east as the Aegean. Thus the Second Punic War was far more than just the second round in the great struggle between Rome and Carthage: the first war had hardly affected Italy directly and in the third the issue was merely the survival of Carthage - in the second everything was at stake.

At first sight the belligerents seem evenly matched. Both had originated as city-states, but had expanded to rule considerable empires; both drew heavily on those empires for the men to man their armies and fleets; both had what Polybius, using the terminology of Greek political theory, regarded as "mixed constitutions" (cf. 6. 11.3ff., 6.51.1ff.), containing elements of monarchy, aristocracy and democracy, but in both power in reality lay with the aristocratic element - the Senate in Rome and the corresponding body or bodies in Carthage. Unfortunately, despite the interest taken in it by such scholars as Aristotle, we know too little about the constitution of Carthage to be able to follow its workings in detail, but we can probably assume from what we do know about Rome that theory and practice were not at all the same thing. It is clear, for example, from a reading of Polybius' or still more of Livy's account of the Hannibalic War, that it was the Senate which decided how large the forces raised each year were to be, where they were to operate and who among the incoming or outgoing magistrates was to command them, and that it was the Senate which controlled relations with Rome's allies, the finances of the state, religion, and no doubt multifarious other matters about which our sources say little or nothing. Yet in theory the Senate was an advisory body, there to give advice to the annually elected executive officials, in particular the two consuls, and hence a decision of the Senate was not a *lex* or a *plebiscitum,* but a *senatus consultum.*[4]

In particular, although in theory the *populus Romanus,* when met together in one or other of the various assemblies, had ultimate sovereignty in the sense that it decided on questions of policy, passed legislation, and annually elected magistrates to carry out its will, it is clear that in practice this sovereignty was severely limited: no assembly could meet unless summoned by a competent magistrate, no one could speak unless invited to do so by the presiding magistrate, voting took place in groups - "centuries" or "tribes" as the case might be - the vote of the majority within a group counting as one vote, and the distribution of citizens among the groups gave the wealthy a voting strength out of all proportion to their numbers.[5] Even after voting had started the presiding magistrate seems to have had considerable powers: at the elections for 214/3, for example, the presiding consul ordered the *centuria praerogativa* - the first century to vote - to go and think again (Livy 24.7.11ff.), and when all was over, the sovereign will of the People could be nullified by a bad omen - as happened at elections in 215 (Livy 23.31.13) - or reversed by a subsequent vote, as was the decision not to go to war with Philip V of Macedonia in 200 (Livy 31.6ff.).

Within such a system, in which the People only met from time to time and elected magistrates annually to implement its will, it was perhaps inevitable that the only semi-permanent body, the Senate, should exercise a preponderant influence, particularly since it contained everybody who was anybody in the Republic and consequently had overwhelming *auctoritas.* Theoretically the members of the Senate were chosen by the two Censors, normally elected every five years, but once chosen, a Senator retained his seat for life unless expelled by subsequent Censors for some sort of misconduct, and this happened rarely enough to excite comment: the Censors of 209/8, for example, are said to have expelled eight members (out of several hundred), and those of 204/3 seven, though none of these had held high office (Livy 27.11.12 and 29.37.1); those of 214/3 also expelled some members, but unfortunately the number is not given (Livy 24.18.1-8). Of course, the People exercised some control over the composition of the Senate in so far as it elected the Censors in the first place, and the annual magistrates from whom the Senators were probably largely chosen: Livy, for example, says of the Romans killed at Cannae that they included eighty men who were either already Senators or who "had held those magistracies through which they had a right to be enrolled in the Senate" (22.49.17), and similarly says that the Dictator, M. Fabius Buteo, in supplementing the roll of the Senate after Cannae, chose first "those who had held curule office since the censorship of L. Aemilius and C. Flaminius (220/19), and had not yet been chosen for the Senate . . . then those who had been aediles, tribunes of the plebs or quaestors" (23.23.5). But if Livy has reported the spirit of Buteo's remarks correctly - that *his* choice "would let it appear that rank was preferred to rank, not man to man" (23.23.4) - the implication is that normally not all Senators were magistrates or ex-magistrates. In any case, since those who were elected would have had to wait for anything up to five years, even in normal times, before being chosen for the

Senate, it is obvious that the composition of the Senate cannot have been altered radically year by year - indeed, even if all the magistrates were promptly chosen for the Senate in a year in which there were Censors, this would still only have meant the addition of something like twenty new members, assuming that the Consuls and Praetors at least were already members. In short, the People in practice would have had very little control over the composition of the Senate.

It is extremely doubtful, moreover, whether the Roman People as a whole can even have had much say in the elections. In the first place, all assemblies took place at Rome, which would have effectively prevented most of those who lived at a distance from casting their votes, particularly in wartime, and in the second place the whole of Roman society was permeated by the patron-client relationship so that the wealthy upper classes could normally command large numbers of votes among the lower classes, particularly in the days before the secret ballot was introduced (in 139). In the third place, as was said above, the way in which the assemblies were organized gave more weight to the votes of the wealthy than to the presumably more numerous poor: in the *comitia centuriata,* for example, which elected Consuls, Praetors and Censors, out of the 193 centuries to which citizens were assigned on the basis of property qualifications, the First Class comprised seventy centuries, and the other four Classes only had a hundred between them, while of the remaining twenty-three centuries, eighteen were assigned to the *Equites* (possibly the richest citizens of all), and one - the *fabri tignarii* - was also apparently composed of comparatively wealthy citizens. All citizens, finally, who were not wealthy enough to be assigned - by the Censors - to one of the five Classes, or who were not qualified to belong to one of the other twenty-two centuries, were relegated to the single century of the *proletarii,* which by Cicero's time, at least, was said to contain more citizens than all seventy centuries of the First Class put together (Cicero, *de re publica* 2.40). The effect of all this can be seen by an examination of the names of known magistrates: the same names recur again and again, particularly among the Consuls, and hence the same families must have effectively dominated the Senate, and so the Roman state, for generation after generation. It was these families - ones which had achieved the consulship - which collectively made up the *nobiles.* [6]

It is, thus, difficult to believe Livy when he alleges, for example, that such men as C. Flaminius (consul 217), C. Terentius Varro (consul 216/5), and M. Minucius Rufus (Master of the Horse in 217) were some sort of "Popular leaders" or to understand those modern scholars who see in the election and activities of such men "popular criticism" of the Senate's conduct of the war. [7] How could a man like Flaminius, if he really had incurred the hatred of the nobility as Livy says (21.63.2ff.), ever have succeeded in securing the votes of enough centuries in the *comitia centuriata* to become consul - for the second time - in 217? How could a man like Terentius Varro, alleged by a source quoted by Livy, but perhaps not believed by him, to have been the son of a butcher (22.25.19), have successfully stood at the elections for the different aedileships (probably in 221 and 220), for the praetorship of 218/7, and finally for the consulship itself, unless he had had the support of powerful members of the nobility? Are we to suppose that there were many butchers or similar businessmen in the eighteen centuries of Equites or the seventy centuries of the First Class, or if the remaining 105 centuries for once combined to outvote them, what had happened to the patronage of the nobility on this occasion?

It seems more likely that we should see behind the controversies surrounding such men as Flaminius, Minucius and Varro, not a conflict between the "people" - whatever that may mean - and the Senate, but rather conflicts within the senatorial class, though perhaps with one side or the other to some extent manipulating "popular" support in its own interests. That there were such conflicts within the senatorial class is obvious, but it is a controversial question how far we can talk of "parties" in this or any other period of Roman history. Clearly there were no "parties" in anything like the modern sense, with all their paraphernalia of party conferences, manifestoes and whips, and clearly too, particularly at elections, men were supported far more for personal reasons than for what they advocated - indeed, in Cicero's day, his brother advised him when standing for the consulship precisely to avoid pronouncing on controversial issues, and to try to appear "all things to all men."[8] But once elected, and particularly once chosen for the Senate, such men cannot have just sat around all day discussing their family trees: questions of policy were discussed, and even if here family ties were more important than rational agreement, groups must have formed on the various issues. In any case, the distinction between "personal ties" and "rational agreement" is probably an unreal one: however "rationally" men may think they are acting, inherent and instinctive attitudes play an important part.

But were such groups consistent, and did they have a coherent policy, over a matter of years? In the case of the Hannibalic War, for example, can we properly talk of a "Cornelian group" or of "Fabian" or "Claudio-Fulvian" groups throughout the war, or should we not rather regard the Senate as being like a collection of biological cells, each with some great man as its nucleus, sometimes coming together on a particular issue, sometimes dividing and forming other organisms? The details will be discussed at greater length in the following chapters, but in general it does seem to make sense to explain much of the political manoeuvring in terms of groups, and also to suppose that such groups had something to do with the changing strategy pursued by the Republic. It is surely significant, for example, that Roman strategy was cautious and defensive from 215 to 212, when Q. Fabius Maximus and his son held three of the consulships, and that when a new offensive note is struck with the investment of Capua in 212, it happened under consuls who do not appear to have had any links with the Fabian family.

What little we know of Carthaginian politics suggests that in practice the situation there was similar to the Roman. Again we find the same names recurring generation after generation, suggesting that family ties were important, and it is even stated in some sources[9] that if the Carthaginian senate and the two chief magistrates, the Sufets, were in agreement, they did not have to have the approval of the Carthaginian people. We do not know how the members of the senate were chosen, but it was possibly by co-option, in which case the people of Carthage would have had even less say in the composition of its senate than the people of Rome, and the existence of a

4

smaller, inner Council of Thirty and of the board of judges known as The Hundred (actually one hundred and four), suggests that Carthage was ruled by an even narrower oligarchy than Rome. The people of Carthage did have some part to play - Polybius, for example, says that the choice of Hannibal to be their general by the Carthaginian troops in Spain was confirmed by "the people" (3.13.4), and even alleges that at the time of the Hannibalic War "the people at Carthage had already acquired the greatest power in deliberations" (6.51.6). But his narrative in general does not suggest that the people of Carthage as a whole played any significant part in the direction of policy or strategy, and his account of the famous scene in 218 at which war was declared (3.20. 9-21.8, and especially 3.33.1-4), or of the almost equally dramatic scene in which Scipio's terms were accepted (15.19), does not even mention the people, whereas Livy duly notes that the question of war with Carthage was put to the people at Rome (21.17.4).

Livy several times talks in terms of "factions" at Carthage, usually in connection with the Carthaginian senate or its members, and this suggests - as one would in any case have expected - that 'party politics' there ran on much the same lines as in Rome. There was clearly some attempt, for example, to pin the blame for the war on Hannibal and his supporters: Livy alleges that the Carthaginians were divided on the question of going to war in the first place (cf.21.9.4ff), and even quotes what purports to be a speech by one Hanno advocating the surrender of Hannibal as the Romans demanded (21.10.4ff), though since the Roman embassy which is said to have given rise to the speech is probably unhistorical (see below, p. 26), one cannot put much faith in the speech: later (23.12.8ff.) Livy puts another speech into the mouth of the same Hanno, belittling Hannibal's achievements. In 203 he says that the Carthaginian envoys sent to Scipio to plead for peace after the battle of the Great Plains tried to put the blame on Hannibal and his party (30.16.5), and later that the envoys sent to Rome had the audacity to claim that the senate and people of Carthage had in fact never broken their treaty with Rome, since Hannibal had throughout acted without orders (30.22.1ff.); these accusations are said to have been repeated by the delegation which went to Rome after Zama, led by Hasdrubal the 'Kid' (Livy 30.42.11ff.). The tradition evidently goes back to the contemporary Roman annalist, Fabius Pictor (cf. Polybius 3.8.1ff.), so there may be some truth in it, though, as Polybius saw, it is absurd to imagine that Hannibal did not really enjoy the support of the government and people of Carthage. Some modern scholars have suggested that there was a fundamental cleavage between the landowning and commercial interests of Carthage, represented by Hanno and Hannibal respectively, but although there may be something in this, it does not seem to have had much effect on the Second Punic War, unless it explains the lack of support Hannibal seems to have had from the Carthaginian navy. [10]

Constitutionally, then, Rome and Carthage were much alike, but there was one important difference between them, namely that whereas in the case of Rome the annually elected magistrates were also expected to command the armies and fleets in time of war, this was not so of Carthage where generals and admirals were elected for a specific task and no time limit was placed on their appointment. In this respect Carthage was more like a modern state than Rome, but it is important not to overestimate its significance. It is true that Roman generals were 'amateurs' not merely in the sense that there was no separate career-structure for officers, but also that the Roman political system put a premium not so much on ability and experience as on family background. But one should not assume that, as a result, all the generals who faced Hannibal and other Carthaginian commanders were incompetent and inexperienced. Most, if not all, would have had some military experience as *tribuni militum* at the beginning of their careers, and many would probably have had further experience as staff-officers (*legati*) under relatives. The great Scipio, for example, although he had never commanded an army before he was appointed to the command in Spain in 210, and although he is as likely to have owed that appointment to his being the head of one of the most influential families among the nobility as to any ability he had displayed, had served under his father at the Ticinus, and later at Cannae, and had presumably also fought at the Trebbia.

Nor was annual tenure of command in practice strictly enforced, firstly because the *imperium* of consuls and praetors could be 'prorogued' (i.e. prolonged) for a further year or years, apparently at the discretion of the Senate, and secondly because re-election to office was permitted, though normally custom seems to have demanded an interval. Naturally, constant use was made of both these practices during so dangerous and prolonged a struggle as the Hannibalic War, and thus many of Rome's generals and admirals did gain considerable experience, or were already men of experience. The elder Scipios, for example, one of whom had already been consul in 222/1 and commanded an army in northern Italy, commanded continuously in Spain from 218 until their deaths in 211, apparently both with proconsular *imperium* from 217, and the younger Scipio commanded in Spain, as proconsul from 210 to 206, and in Sicily and Africa, first as consul and then as proconsul again, from 205 to 201. Such men became, to all intents and purposes, professional generals, even though none of them could match Hannibal's twenty years of continuous high command.

As for re-election, it is worth noting that in ten out of the eighteen years the Hannibalic War lasted, at least one of the consuls had held the office before, and that it was only after the defeat of Hannibal's brother, Hasdrubal, at the Metaurus in 207, that it became normal again for neither consul previously to have held the office. This might explain why this was also true of the year 211/10: with the fall of Syracuse, probably in the late autumn of 212, and the successful completion of the siege-works around Capua at about the same time, it must have appeared that the war in Italy and Sicily was going well, and the news from Spain and Greece was still good. It would then have been the shock of the defeat of the Scipios in Spain in 211 which led to a return to men of experience. It is also noticeable that two of Rome's best generals, Q. Fabius Maximus and M. Claudius Marcellus, each held three consulships during the war, and that Marcellus would have had a fourth had not a clap of thunder deprived him of it. In the direst emergencies, resort could also be had to the device of appointing a dictator with *imperium* overriding that of all other magistrates, as happened after Trasimene in 217 and after Cannae in 216, and in these circumstances it was certainly possible to secure the services of men of experience. Finally, it is worth remembering that both the generals whose incompetence is usually cited as typical of the defects in the Roman system, C. Flaminius and C. Terentius Varro, were *novi homines,* who must already have displayed some ability to have got where they did, and Flaminius' failure at Trasimene was not due to inexperience since he had been consul before, in 223/2, and had commanded an army with some success in the Po valley.

Conversely, although the Carthaginian system under which anyone was eligible for high command and no time-limit was imposed on tenure, did mean that some of Carthage's generals and admirals were 'professionals' in a sense that Rome's could never be, it would be a mistake to imagine that they were different in background or training from their Roman counterparts: Hannibal owed his command just as much as the younger Scipio did, to his family background, and although he had served under his father and brother-in-law for many years before he succeeded to command, Scipio had also had similar experience as we have seen. The separation of civil and military powers in Carthage, moreover, tended to mean that the attitude of the Carthaginian aristocracy towards their generals was one of suspicion, despite the fact that the generals were from the same class as themselves and had only very rarely used their armies against the state in the past. This in turn meant that the generals were sometimes timid and cautious, and, needless to say, the Carthaginian habit of crucifying unsuccessful generals did not help: Livy was quite right to point out that if Varro had been a Carthaginian, he would probably have been executed (22.61.15). Generals were certainly given more independence by the Carthaginians, and this undoubtedly helped good generals like Hamilcar and Hannibal to develop their own ideas, but at the same time one does get the impression that the Carthaginian government did not exercise the same overall control as the Senate, and that sometimes the conflicting claims of the various theatres of war spoilt the Carthaginian war-effort in a way the Senate did not allow.

This was possibly partly due to the fact that whereas Rome's generals were senators, and when not holding command would have been able to give the Senate the benefit of their experience, this would not have been true to anything like the same extent of the Carthaginian senate: Hannibal, for example, had been absent from Carthage for thirty-six years when he finally returned in 202 and was impatient of 'parliamentary conventions' as an anecdote related by Polybius reveals (15.19). The Roman Senate contained all men of experience in the Roman state and there was nothing "amateurish" about its collective wisdom: in 218, for example, it would have contained men who had commanded armies and fleets in northern Italy, Sardinia and Corsica, Albania, and probably Sicily, and despite the tactical blunders committed by some of its members during the Hannibalic War, it is arguable that it never made a mistake in long-term strategy.

It is also sometimes suggested that there was a significant difference between the 'amateur' forces of Rome and the 'professional' forces of Carthage, and it is certainly true that both Rome's citizen soldiers and those of her allies were essentially militia, called up for a campaign and then dismissed to their former occupations: one must assume that in periods of prolonged campaigning many gained considerable experience, but few, if any, would have been professional soldiers in the sense that they knew no other life. But although the Roman army was to suffer a series of catastrophic defeats at

Hannibal's hands, and occasionally the sources talk of the inexperience of Roman soldiers (e.g. Polybius 3.70.10), one should not underestimate their fighting qualities: it was clearly the limited ability of Rome's generals and the rigidity of her infantry tactics which let her down, and in Spain and Africa, under a general like Scipio, Rome's 'amateur' soldiers were to show themselves capable of the most complicated manoeuvres on the battlefield.

Carthaginian armies, by comparison, were partly composed of 'professional' soldiers, and their experience and training probably made possible some of the things Hannibal did with them (cf. Polybius 3.35.8). But it would be a mistake to imagine that the majority of the soldiers in Carthage's armies throughout the war were professional mercenaries: in Spain, Italy and Africa they clearly also used hurriedly-raised native levies who can hardly have been any more professional than the Roman soldiers they had to face. There was also a severe disadvantage in the use of mercenary soldiers as practised by Carthage - not that they would not have had their hearts in the matter, but that there were too few of them. Carthage's mercenaries seem to have fought at least as well as their opponents throughout the war, and there are very few instances of ill-discipline or desertion, [11] partly no doubt because most of them found themselves fighting in foreign lands where defeat meant death or slavery, and desertion was difficult or dangerous. But however loyal and well-trained the mercenaries were, the difficulty and expense of raising and training them meant that there could never be as many of them as there were of Rome's citizen and allied soldiers.

Carthage's comparative lack of manpower, which was in the end perhaps the crucial factor in her defeat, was probably not due to the fact that she had a smaller population upon which to draw, for the Carthaginian empire in 218 was, if anything, more extensive than the Roman, and its population was probably at least as large. Originally just one of the colonies founded by settlers from what is now Lebanon, [12] Carthage - i.e. 'Kart-Hadasht' or 'New City' as the Carthaginians called it - had for some three centuries been steadily assuming the leadership of the other colonies founded in the west by people from the same homeland, while at the same time expanding her own territory in the hinterland of what is now Tunisia, and founding new colonies and trading-posts of her own. At the outbreak of the Second Punic War, she ruled over approximately the northern half of Tunisia, but including the whole of the east coast, and beyond Tunisia her sway extended along the coast of what is now Libya to the Gulf of Sidra, south of Benghazi. Northwest of Carthage lay Utica which was held to be an even older Phoenician settlement, but which was now an ally, though sometimes not a very reliable one, and beyond Utica along the coast as far as the Straits of Gibraltar and further lay a string of trading-posts and anchorages in what are now Algeria and Morocco. Inland from the coast and immediately to the west of Carthaginian territory itself dwelt the Numidians, with their most important centre at Cirta (now Constantine), and beyond them the Moors (Mauretani). These peoples, and particularly the various Numidian tribes, were loosely allied to the Carthaginians and provided them with troops, including excellent light cavalry. Overseas the Carthaginians controlled most of southern and southeastern Spain (roughly corresponding to Andalusia and Murcia), the

Balearic islands, and some of the smaller islands between Africa and Sicily such as Pantellaria, Malta and Gozo. (See map on end papers).

The relationship between these various communities and Carthage differed according to their origin and their relative state of civilization. States which - like Carthage - owed their origin to settlement from the Lebanon - for example, Utica and Gades (Cadiz) in Spain - or which had been founded by Carthage herself, probably had treaties with Carthage, and their citizens possibly enjoyed something like the status of Latins in the Roman confederacy (see below, p. 10). But Carthage controlled their foreign policies as is made clear by the early treaties between Carthage and Rome quoted by Polybius (3.22-24), and exacted both direct and indirect taxes. There is also evidence that troops were levied from them, and presumably also rowers for the Carthaginian fleet. The native population of the actual territory of Carthage - referred to by Polybius as "Libyans" and by Livy as "Africans" [13] - was apparently worse off, having to make over a quarter of its produce as tribute in normal times, as well as to provide the soldiers who formed the core of Carthaginian armies. The Numidians and Moors were more or less independent allies, supplying troops and nothing more. The Spanish communities, finally, also supplied troops, and probably paid tribute.

It is clear that the ties which bound these dependencies to Carthage were in general looser than those which bound the Latins and other Italians to Rome, and there seems to have been no attempt on Carthage's part to secure the loyalty of her subjects, for example by extending Carthaginian citizenship to them. Moreover, although Carthage certainly could and did mobilize troops from among her subjects, as we have seen, such service does not seem to have been inherent in the relationship: although one doubts whether there was anything genuinely "voluntary" about the service of Africans, Numidians or Spaniards in the Carthaginian army, they do appear to have been "mercenaries" in the sense that they neither formed national contingents nor were citizens of the state they served. Indeed, since the end of the fourth century, Carthaginian citizens do not appear to have been liable for military service, at least overseas, although most of the higher officers in the Carthaginian army and fleet were, naturally, Carthaginian citizens. The only occasions during the Hannibalic War on which Carthaginian soldiers may be mentioned as serving outside Africa are in Livy's accounts of the battles of Ibera and Ilipa, in Spain. In the first, he mentions "Poeni" on the Carthaginian right wing (23.29.4), as opposed to the Africans on the left; in the second, "Carthaginienses" mixed with Africans in the centre of the Carthaginian line (28.14.4). But the "Poeni" at Ibera may have been levies from the citizen-population of Gades and Cartagena, since when Livy does undubitably refer to levies from Carthage itself, in his account of the campaigns in Africa, he invariably calls them "Carthaginienses" (cf. 30.8.6-7; 30.33.5,7,11,16; 30.34.5,7; 30.35.3), and although, by the same token, the "Carthaginienses" at Ilipa should be Carthaginian citizens - perhaps brought over the previous year (cf. 28.1.4), in view of the deteriorating situation - here, too, Livy should, perhaps, have written "Poeni", meaning citizens of Gades, which was very near Ilipa.

The situation on the Roman side was completely different: all male Roman citizens between the ages of seventeen and forty-six were liable for military service, with very few exceptions, [14] and, by Hannibal's time, this included men from a number of states which had been granted Roman citizenship, and almost certainly also men from states granted the "citizenship without the vote" (*civitas sine suffragio*), particularly Campanians and Picentes. [15] It is not certain how many citizens there were - of both categories - when the Hannibalic War broke out, but Polybius gives some figures for 225 (2.24), and assuming the totals he gives of men capable of bearing arms include the totals allegedly under arms, although he or his source appears to have added them together to give his grand totals, Rome then had 250,000 citizens available for the infantry, and 23,000 for the cavalry. [16] Of course, Rome could never have mobilized all these men at once, but they did provide an enormous reservoir of manpower.

Nor was this all, for as Polybius' figures make clear, [17] over half Rome's available manpower in 225 came from her Italian allies, comprising two broad groups, the "Allies of the Latin Name" (*socii nominis Latini*), and ordinary allies. The former included, in 218, thirty Latin colonies ranging from Placentia (Piacenza) and Cremona on the Po, to places like Brundisium (Brindisi) in the south, and six or eight old states in Latium and its immediate vicinity which had not been granted the citizenship at the end of the last war between Rome and her Latin neighbours, for example Praeneste (Palestrina). [18] These were capable of producing 80,000 infantry and 5000 cavalry between them, according to Polybius. The other allies included all the other states of peninsular Italy, and could provide a further 250,000 infantry and 26,000 cavalry.

It is, of course, obvious that not all Rome's allies were equally reliable, and, as we shall see, Hannibal's strategy was primarily based on the hope that he could seduce the allies by fear or favour, if not to fight for him, at least to remain neutral. As it turned out, however, although many of the southern allies went over to him after Cannae, he could not shake the loyalty of those in the centre and north of the peninsula. Above all, not a single Latin state went over to him, and this meant that Rome retained reliable strongholds throughout the length and breadth of Italy. Only in 209 did twelve of the thirty Latin colonies refuse to supply their quotas of soldiers, claiming that they had no men left, and even then there was no suggestion that they might side with the enemy.

Part of the reason for this Latin loyalty was undoubtedly that the Latins felt themselves to be the next best thing to Roman citizens, and indeed many of them appear to have been the descendants of Roman citizens who had presumably been prepared to join a Latin colony in the hope of a fresh start in a new home - a point made to the recalcitrant twelve in 209 (Livy 27.9.10-11). All of them, too, will have spoken Latin, worshipped the same gods as the Romans, and had the same sort of institutions, and not only enjoyed certain rights in Roman law - for example the right to enter into a legal marriage or other form of contract with a Roman citizen - but also knew that they could become Roman citizens by simply emigrating to Roman territory. Even the old non-colonial Latin states seem largely to have forgotten any bitterness they may once have felt, and one contingent from Praeneste behaved with such conspicuous gallantry that they were offered the citizenship - which they refused (Livy 23.20.2).

The inhabitants of the other Italian states allied to Rome were racially, politically and geographically distinct, and often even spoke a different language. Often too, they had only become "allies" of Rome after long and desperate resistance. But it was characteristic of Rome that when all was over she would conclude a treaty with the defeated enemy, which left them intact as a state with at least theoretical sovereignty, though often mulcted of territory and subject to considerable limitations in practice. Some of the allies, however, sided with Rome more or less voluntarily, and some scholars have sought to draw a distinction between the *foedus aequum* (treaty between equals) enjoyed by such a place as Camerinum in Umbria (cf. Livy 28.45.20), and the *foedus iniquum* allegedly imposed upon the majority. But it must be noted that the term *foedus iniquum* was in fact apparently never used by the Romans, and indeed hardly could have been since it would have constituted an unnecessary and provocative insult to the other party, and the truth of the matter is probably that all treaties were "between equals" - though some, naturally, were more "equal" than others. [19]

Thus if Hannibal had had a political map of Italy with him when he crossed the Alps in 218, it would have looked like this: in the Po valley Roman forces had been operating with some success for a number of years, and two new Latin colonies were in the process of being established at Placentia and Cremona. But any allies Rome might ostensibly have among the Celtic peoples of the area were of dubious loyalty, except perhaps the Cenomani between the Oglio and the Adige around Lake Garda, and the Veneti in the hinterland of the later site of Venice. If he marched south-eastwards through the plains, leaving the Apennines on his right, he would come to the Latin colony of Ariminum (Rimini) on the coast where the curve of the Apennines almost reaches the sea, and southwards from Ariminum, in the foothills and on the coast, stretched a block of Roman territory consisting, firstly, of the "*Ager Gallicus*", territory confiscated from the Senones early in the third century, in which a Roman citizen colony had been founded at Sena (Senigallia) shortly afterwards, and which since 232 had also partly been settled by individual Roman colonists. Secondly, beyond the river Aesis (Esino), lay the *Ager Picenus,* with Latin colonies at Firmum and Hadria, but mostly peopled by *citizens without the vote,* apart from the enclaves around Ancona and Asculum which were ordinary allied states. (See Maps 1 & 2).

If, on the other hand, he crossed the Apennines southwards from Bologna, he would enter a block of allied territory in Etruria, to the north and west of the Tiber, with a Latin colony at Cosa on the coast, and fringed by Latin colonies in the south at Sutrium, Nepet, Narnia and Spoletium. Relations between Rome and the Etruscans were peculiar - there is, for example, only one certain example of a *foedus* between Rome and an Etruscan state (Falerii) - and Rome evidently viewed the Etruscans with suspicion: Hannibal's decision to cross the Apennines into Etruria in 217 may thus have been based on the hope that they would defect. [20]

The centre of the peninsula, west of the crest of the Apennines, was now largely occupied by Roman citizens, including citizens without the vote, or by Latins, apart from some of the hill tribes like the Marsi or the Paeligni who were now loyal allies. But to the east of the Apennines and extending all over the southern part of the peninsula east of a line drawn roughly from Hadria to Naples, was a huge area of allied states. Within the area were five Latin colonies at Luceria, Venusia, Brundisium, Beneventum and Paestum, but the loyalty of the rest of it was highly questionable: the ancient Greek cities fringing the instep and toe of the peninsula had only become allies in the 270s after a bitter war, and the native tribes in the hinterland, particularly the Bruttii, Lucani and Samnites, had been amongst the Republic's most implacable foes.

The Roman confederacy, then, consisted of a variety of states bound to Rome by a network of treaties and alliances. But the common requirement on all Rome's allies was to supply men for her armed forces, and it was in her ability to mobilize vast masses of men that Rome differed most conspicuously from Carthage. The key to the strength of the confederacy lay in its very complexity: since no two states tended to have exactly the same relationship to Rome, their attitudes also tended to differ. Thus, though Hannibal came with the avowed intent of freeing the Latins and Italians from the Roman yoke, although disaffection was widespread and even included such states as Capua the citizens of which were Roman citizens, albeit without the vote, it was by no means universal: the Latins refused to make common cause with other Italians, in Campania Nola and Naples resisted all attempts to coerce them into joining him, among the Samnites the Pentri continued to side with Rome, and even in Bruttium which was long to be his base and refuge, the small town of Petelia stood an eleven months siege and only surrendered when its inhabitants were reduced to eating leather and bark.

Unfortunately, it is difficult to see in detail how the forces of Rome's allies were raised, organized and armed. Probably, in theory, the allies were obliged to aid Rome with all their forces, but in practice it is clear that by the time of the Hannibalic War their obligations were governed by what became known as the *formula togatorum* (i.e., list of adult males), which may have been some sort of sliding-scale requiring each ally to supply so many men for each legion of citizen-troops raised in any one year.[21] In total the proportion of allied soldiers to citizen-soldiers seems to have varied from campaign to campaign,[22] but in the Hannibalic War it never seems to have been less than 1:1 and was sometimes more. In practice, too, it is possible that Rome relied more heavily on the Latins than on the other allies. Livy, for example, may have thought that all the allied soldiers at the Trebbia were Latins (cf.21.55.4), and alleges that Hiero of Syracuse's envoys to the Senate in 217 declared that the king knew that the Roman people did not use infantry or cavalry "except Romans and allies of the Latin Name," but did allow "foreign auxiliaries consisting of light-armed troops" (22.27.7-8); similarly, he only records the taking of Latin troops to Africa by Scipio in 204 (29.24.14). But he also records Tarentine cavalry at Trasimene and Cannae (cf.24.13.1), Perugians at Casilinum (23.17.11), Paeligni at Beneventum (25.14.4), and Etruscan cavalry in the skirmish which led to Marcellus' death in 208 (27.16.11). Polybius, moreover, although he rarely mentions the allied contingents in Roman armies, twice mentions Italians in his summaries of Hannibal's appeals to his non-Roman prisoners (3.77.6, 3.85.4).

The infantry of the allies, whether Latin or Italian, was organized in cohorts (*cohortes*) which varied in size as one would expect, seeing that the states from which they were drawn varied in population. Thus a cohort from Camerinum sent to serve under Scipio in 205 consisted of 600 men (Livy 28.45.20), the soldiers from Praeneste at Casilinum numbered 500 (Livy 23,17.8), and the cohort from Perugia which formed part of the same garrison contained 460 men (Livy 23.17.11). One passage in Livy has been held to show that there were normally fifteen such cohorts attached to each legion (30.41.5), but this may have been exceptional. Cohorts seem to have been commanded by officers from their own states - we know the name of the commander of the Praenestines at Casilinum, Marcus Anicius (Livy 23.19.17-8), but there were also Roman officers, the Prefects of the Allies (*praefecti socium* - cf., e.g., Livy 27.26.12), who were presumably in overall command of groups of cohorts. We do not know whether the cohorts were subdivided into smaller units, nor how they were equipped, but one must presume that they were organized and equipped in much the same way as Roman citizen soldiers, since otherwise it would have been difficult for Roman generals to draw up armies of mixed citizen and allied contingents, and this may also explain why Polybius habitually omits to mention how or where the allied troops were deployed in the great battles. At the Great Plains and Zama, in particular, the interaction of his three lines was essential to Scipio's plans, and this would have been difficult if his allied troops were essentially different from his Romans. Indeed, Polybius may hint at a subdivision of each cohort into three maniples when he notes in his account of Ilipa that a Roman unit consisting of a maniple each of *hastati, principes* and *triarii* (see below, and p. 147), was known as a cohort (11.23.1). Neither Polybius nor Livy ever records any allied light infantry or skirmishers, so perhaps there was nothing corresponding to the Roman *velites* in an allied cohort. But it is, perhaps, more likely that some of the younger and poorer allied soldiers were equipped and trained as skirmishers like the *velites.* Allied states also supplied cavalry, organized in *turmae,* and presumably drawn from the upper classes, like the Roman cavalry - Livy specifically describes the Tarentine cavalrymen mentioned above as "young nobles" (24.13.1).

Rome's citizen infantry was organized into legions (*legiones*), again of varying size, but usually with at least a paper-strength of 4200 men. In battle, a legion was still tactically subdivided into three lines, the men in each being called - from front to rear - *hastati, principes* and *triarii,* with the light infantry or skirmishers (*velites*) [23] being normally flung out in front of the *hastati* at the outset of a battle. The most important small unit was the maniple (*manipulus*), of which there were thirty to the legion, ten for each of the three lines, with the *velites* equally distributed among them for organisational purposes; each maniple consisted of two centuries commanded by centurions. Above the centurions in rank came the six military tribunes (*tribuni militum*) attached to each legion, usually young men of senatorial or equestrian family "doing their military service," but there does not seem to have been an officer with a regular rank in command of each legion, though if there was more than one in any army, one must presume that the commander-in-chief usually deputed members of his staff to command them.

The *hastati, principes* and *triarii* appear to have worn more protective armour than the *velites,* and to have carried a larger shield, probably shaped like an oval with its top and bottom removed. Their chief offensive weapons, like those of the *velites,* were throwing-spears - possibly still thrusting-spears in the case of the *triarii* - and a formidable cut-and-thrust, two-edged sword. It was the use of this weapon which marked Roman infantry off from Greek infantry, for with the use of the sword rather than the thrusting-spear as the main offensive weapon went an inevitable looseness and flexibility in the infantry formations, since a swordsman needs more room than a spearman to wield his weapon. [24]

Attached to each legion, in normal circumstances, was a small cavalry detachment, between two and three hundred strong, drawn from wealthy citizens. Polybius (6.25.3ff.) seems to have thought that Roman cavalry before his day wore no protective armour and was equipped with inferior lances and shields, and they certainly made a very poor showing against Hannibal's cavalry. But one wonders whether it can be true that some of the richest Romans, well able to afford the latest thing in equipment, went into battle almost entirely unprotected as he says, and by implication he often seems to contrast them with Hannibal's light Numidian cavalry, although this might be because they were not taught to fight in the loose skirmishing order which was characteristic of Numidian battle-tactics. As in the case of the infantry, we know nothing of the equipment or training of the allied cavalry, but as we have seen, they came from the same sort of background and so were presumably equipped like the Roman cavalry.

Unfortunately, we know even less about the organization and equipment of Carthaginian armies in general and of Hannibal's army in particular. Polybius gives a vivid description of the alternating Celtic and Spanish companies in the centre of Hannibal's infantry line at Cannae, the Celts naked with long slashing swords, the Spaniards in linen tunics with purple borders, with shorter, cut-and-thrust swords (3.114.2-4), and this suggests that they were organized in units corresponding to the Roman maniple - the word he uses ($\sigma\pi\epsilon\tilde{\iota}\rho\alpha\iota$) is the word he uses for maniples - and that although they clearly wore less protective armour than Roman infantry, they were essentially swordsmen like their foes. The Africans at Cannae had been equipped with captured Roman arms (Polybius 3.114.1), and this suggests that they too had been trained as swordsmen, since unless the Roman equipment they used was purely protective, they must have used Roman swords and Hannibal would not have tried to turn spearmen into swordsmen in the midst of such a campaign. But the Africans, too, were clearly more lightly equipped than Romans before they took over their arms. However, it is important to remember that the distinction between what historians of Greece and Rome are accustomed to call "heavy" and "light" infantry, was not so much that the former were more lightly equipped than the latter, but that the "heavy" infantry were trained to fight together in lines, whereas "light" infantry was trained to fight as skirmishers, and this would have been particularly true of Hannibal's trained professionals - perhaps "infantry of the line" and "skirmishers" would be better terms to use. Hannibal certainly made extensive use of the latter, and they can hardly have been more lightly equipped than his Spaniards, or the naked Celts, though they are clearly distinguished from them. Hannibal's skirmishers certainly included slingers from the Balearic islands (Polybius 3.72.7), but were mainly what Polybius calls "spear-bearers" ($\lambda o\gamma\chi o\phi\acute{o}\rho o\iota$: cf. 3.72.7, 3.73.7, 3.83.3, 3.84.14, 3.86.4, 3.92.9, 3.94.3, 3.101.5, 3.113.6), and since he refers to the Roman *velites* - who certainly used throwing-spears-by different terms, [25] it is possible that Hannibal's skirmishers were armed with stabbing-spears, which might help to explain why they were apparently more useful than the *velites*. They may partly have been Numidians, for Polybius refers to Mago's force which carried out the ambush at the Trebbia, as Numidians (3.74.1), and it certainly included infantry as well as cavalry (Polybius 3.71.6). On the other hand, no Numidians are enumerated among the infantry with which Hannibal entered Italy (cf. Polybius 3.56.4), so Polybius may refer to Mago's force as Numidians simply because he regarded its Numidian cavalry component as the more important. Thus some of the Spaniards may have been trained as skirmishers, and later some of the Celts used in the same role.

One would particularly like to know more about Hannibal's cavalry, which played so prominent a part at the Trebbia and later at Cannae. He arrived in Italy with 6000 in all (Polybius 3.56.4), and these certainly included both Numidians and Spaniards, since at Cannae he still had some Spanish cavalry (Polybius 3.113.7), though by then he had a considerable force of Celtic cavalry in addition. At the Ticinus, before he had been joined by any appreciable number of Celts, it is presumably to the Spanish cavalry that Polybius refers as the "bridled and steady (στάσιμος) horse" (3.65.6) which formed the centre of his line, as opposed to the Numidians on either wing; similarly, at Cannae, the Spanish cavalry formed part of the left wing with the Celtic horse, while the Numidians were on the right (Polybius 3.113.7). The Numidians were certainly light cavalry, apparently partly armed with missile weapons (cf. Polybius 3.71.10), and famous for their manoeuvrability (cf. Polybius 3.72.10 and 3.116.5). But again one wonders whether the "heavy" cavalry - the Spaniards and Celts - would in fact have been more heavily armed: no ancient cavalry rode with stirrups so that their use as shock troops was limited, but the word Polybius uses to describe the Spaniards at the Ticinus - "στάσιμος" (translated "steady" above), rather suggests that here, as with the infantry, the main difference was in training: the Spaniards, and presumably the Celts, were trained to fight *en masse,* the Numidians in a much looser formation, and it is clear that the cavalry on the Roman side was much more like the former than the latter, and found it very difficult to cope with Numidian tactics.

Of Hannibal's elephants, too, one would like to know more: Appian records (*Hannibalic War,* 1.4) that he crossed the Pyrenees with thirty-seven which may be right, but unfortunately no source records how many were lost in the crossing of the Alps, although there were certainly enough left to play a significant part in the battle of the Trebbia (cf. Polybius 3.72.9, 3.74.2 & 7). However, according to Polybius (3.74.11), all but one died after the battle from the rain and snow, and although Livy (21.56.6) declares that seven initially survived, he agrees with Polybius that all save one subsequently perished: it was mounted on this one that Hannibal crossed the marshes of the Arno in 217 (Livy 22.2.10). But thereafter we hear nothing of it, and no elephants are recorded as taking part at Trasimene or Cannae. Later, however, the reinforcements landed at Locri in 215 are said to have included elephants (Livy 23.41.10), and we occasionally hear of these later, e.g. at the siege of Capua in 211 (Livy 26.5.11). It seems fairly certain that the Carthaginian war-elephants were at least predominantly African and not Indian, but that they belonged to the smaller species, known as the forest elephant (*Loxodonta africana cyclotis*) as opposed to the great bush elephants of central and southern Africa, standing about 2.4 metres high at the shoulder, as against nearly 3 metres for the Indian elephant and 3.3 metres for the African bush elephant. An interesting possibility is that the elephant called "Surus" (i.e., the Syrian), mentioned by the elder Pliny (*Naturalis Historia* 8.5.11), on the authority of Cato, as the elephant which fought most bravely in the Second Punic War, may have been of the Indian variety - the Syrians probably got their war-elephants from India - and may indeed have been the sole survivor of the winter of 218/7. The smaller, forest elephants were too small to have carried a howdah, and were usually ridden by a single mahout, apparently armed with javelins, though it was clearly the elephant itself which was the main weapon. [26]

The Second Punic War was not a great naval struggle like the First, but the relative strength of the two sides at sea was of considerable importance, as we shall see. One might have expected a nation with Carthage's great maritime tradition to have been immeasurably superior, but by the time of the Second Punic War not only was the Carthaginian fleet inferior in size, but it appears to have been lower in morale. It is true that there are some hints that Carthaginian sailors were still superior in sheer seamanship: in his account of the minor engagement fought off western Sicily in 218, for example, Livy says that the Carthaginians tried to avoid being brought to close quarters and "to make it a fight between ships rather than men and arms," though he seems to imply that this was because they had few marines on board (21.50.1-2); later (25.25.11) he alleges that in 212 the Carthaginian admiral, Bomilcar, once slipped out of Syracuse when the weather was too bad for the Roman blockading ships to remain at sea. But in general the Carthaginian navy appears to have been unwilling to run the risk of encountering Roman warships at sea, and even when it had a numerical advantage, as it did off Cape Pachynon probably late in 212, it weakly sheared away (see below, pp. 117-8). When i did encounter the Roman navy, it invariably lost, and it was almost completely ineffective in raiding Italy, in conveying supplies to Hannibal - it only once got through to him - or even in interrupting the extended supply-lines of the Roman armies - again we only hear once of Roman supply-ships being captured (Livy 22.11.6). It was typical of the Carthaginian navy's failure that Scipio could sail to Africa in 204 escorted by only 40 warships (Livy 29.25.10), despite the fact that Carthage still had far more warships available, judging from the 500 of all types which were allegedly burnt when peace was finally concluded (Livy 30.43.12).

The "battleship" of the period was the quinquereme (πεντήρης in Greek), so-called not because it was propelled by five banks of oars - the oars of the top bank would have been impossibly long - but probably because the ratio of a quinquereme's oar-power to that of the classical trireme (which certainly did have three banks of oars) was 5:3. How many banks of oars a quinquereme had, and how many men manned each oar, is not known, but their crews were much larger than those of triremes (300 to 200), and they carried more marines - up to 120 on a Roman quinquereme, when fully manned for battle, and apparently 40 as a normal complement. [27] Such vessels were formidable in battle, whether using the ram or boarding, but essentially they were designed to pack as many oarsmen as possible into the shortest possible length, with the result that their sea-keeping qualities were not good. Thus a numerically inferior fleet manned by good seamen should have had endless opportunities for the sort of hit-and-run tactics so ably demonstrated by the famous Carthaginian captain, Hannibal the Rhodian, during the First Punic War (cf. Polybius 1.46.4ff.). Part of the problem the Carthaginian navy had during the second war may, however, have been the difficulty of finding trained crews, for Polybius, for example, says (3.33.14) that eighteen of the quinqueremes Hannibal left behind in Spain in 218 were unmanned, and it appears from a passage in Livy (23. 26.4) that even some the officers in Carthage's Spanish fleet were Spaniards. The crews of Roman warships were drawn from the *proletarii,* from freedmen and from the naval allies (*socii navales*) - mainly Greek states in southern Italy and Sicily - and only very rarely were rowed by slaves or prisoners of war. [28]

The two sides in the Hannibalic War were thus superficially similar, but there were also great differences between them, and many of these can be traced back to fundamental differences in origin and outlook. Above all, the Romans were essentially a nation of farmers, the Carthaginians a nation of traders. This goes a long way towards explaining the different development of the two empires. There is hardly any evidence that economic or commercial factors entered into the motives behind the Roman conquest of Italy: no tribute was paid to Rome by her allies in Italy, for example, and although she frequently confiscated territory from her defeated foes and planted Roman settlers upon it, this seems to have been for subsequent security, not because the Republic had gone to war in order to acquire the land in the first place - indeed, *ager publicus* acquired by the Roman state in this way frequently remained undistributed for long periods; [29] nor did Rome confiscate the iron mines from the Etruscan state of Populonia, or seek to tax the trading profits of places like Tarentum or Capua. Similarly, Roman colonies, whether of citizens or Latins, were planted mainly for strategic purposes, not for commercial exploitation, and hence, too, Roman citizens remained liable for military service, like the hoplite militia of a Greek city-state.

The Carthaginians, however, although they had acquired considerable territories in Tunisia by Hannibal's time, had apparently hardly even begun this process before the fourth century - Justin even alleges (19.2.4) that Carthage was still paying the traditional tribute to the Africans for the site of Carthage itself in the fifth. But long before this they had begun to exploit the coasts of north Africa, southern and eastern Spain, Sicily and the other islands in the western Mediterranean, for commercial purposes, and this remained the basic motivation behind the expansion of the Carthaginian empire, as the first two treaties between Carthage and Rome suggest: it may be of some significance that Hannibal's wife is said to have come from Castulo in Spain (Livy 24.41.7) where there were important mines (cf. Polybius 10.38.7). Thus Carthage remained the richest city in the Mediterranean world, according to Polybius (18.35.9), even after she had twice been defeated by Rome, whereas, according to Livy (22.32.4ff.), by the end of 217, a year after the war had begun, envoys from Naples were already offering Rome gifts because "they knew that the treasury of the Roman people was exhausted by the war."

There was thus no inherent reason why powers with such differing interests should have come into conflict, and relations between them, in so far as there had been any, seem to have been reasonably friendly down to the outbreak of the first war in 264. Polybius (3.22ff.) records three treaties between them, the first two of which were probably concluded in 509 and 348, and seem mainly to have been concerned to limit the activities of Roman and Italian traders in areas which the Carthaginians regarded as their own. [30] The third, concluded in 278, had provided for mutual assistance against Pyrrhus, King of Epirus, who had come to Italy to aid the Greek states of southern Italy against Rome, and had then turned his attention to Sicily where other Greek states were threatened by Carthage. Livy seems also to have thought that there was another treaty, concluded in 306 (9.43.26), but this is probably unhistorical since Polybius does not mention it in what was clearly meant to be a careful examination of all the treaties between the two states. On the other hand, if there was a treaty in 306, and if this was the treaty recorded by Philinos but dismissed by Polybius (3.26), then it is possible that it was deliberately suppressed by the Romans. For Philinos' alleged treaty, according to Polybius, bound the Romans not to interfere in Sicily and they were clearly in breach of it when they accepted the appeal of the Mamertines of Messina in 265. However, Philinos' treaty is also said to have bound the Carthaginians not to interfere in Italy, and a treaty concluded in 306 can hardly have regarded Italy as lying wholly within the Roman sphere of influence. Thus, if Philinos' treaty is historical, it must have been concluded later than 306, and would then be yet another treaty not mentioned by Polybius - which is very improbable.

Polybius' third treaty - the pact of mutual assistance against Pyrrhus - is the most interesting from the point of view of Romano-Carthaginian relations in the years immediately preceding the first conflict between them. The Carthaginians were anxious to forestall intervention by Pyrrhus in Sicily, and so the treaty provided that if either Rome or Carthage concluded an alliance with Pyrrhus, this alliance should not preclude either from aiding the other should it be attacked, Carthage to supply the ships in either case, but each to pay its own men. It also provided that Carthage should aid Rome against Pyrrhus by sea if need be, but that the crews of her ships should not be required to disembark against their will. It is clear that both sides were already wary of the other's intentions, and that Carthage is still the dominant party, since she apparently did not have to lift her restrictions on Roman trade in order to secure Rome's help: according to Polybius (3.25.2) the treaty maintained the provisions of the two earlier ones. It is also interesting to note that the new treaty frankly recognizes Rome's weakness at sea at that time.

As it turned out, although Pyrrhus had considerable success in Sicily, he eventually returned to Italy in face of the apathy of the Sicilian Greeks towards his wider plans against Carthage, and having been fought to a standstill by the Roman army at Beneventum in 275, abandoned his Italian adventure: the last of his garrisons in Italy - at Tarentum - surrendered to Rome three years later. Rome had not rendered any assistance to Carthage while he had been in Sicily, and direct Carthaginian aid to Rome seems to have been limited to the transporting of a few troops to Rhegium. But both sides ought to have been well satisfied with Pyrrhus' departure, and certainly there were no apparent grounds for conflict between them. Yet within a decade they were to embark upon what was perhaps the longest continuous war in ancient history.

The immediate cause of the war is clear: some Campanian mercenary soldiers had seized Messina some years before and calling themselves the Mamertini (i.e. "people of Mamers" - a Campanian name for the war-god Mars), had continued to harry north-eastern Sicily until defeated by Hiero, the new ruler of Syracuse, in 265. Thereupon they asked for Carthaginian protection and Carthaginian troops were sent to their aid. But at the same time a different faction among them sent envoys to Rome asking for Roman assistance, and it was the acceptance of this appeal by Rome which led to war. The fundamental causes of the war are not so clear, but for once we have, in Polybius' account (1.10-11), some of the arguments which were supposed to have gone on in the Senate at the time, and it seems that in Polybius' view the overriding consideration in the minds of those who advocated acceptance of the appeal, was fear less the island pass finally under Carthaginian control and "allow the Carthaginians as it were to build a bridge for crossing to Italy." We have no means of knowing whether the Carthaginians had any intention of interfering in Italy, but Rome must have been sensitive about the attitude of the Greek cities of the south with which she had so recently been at war, and there is a tradition that a Carthaginian fleet had gone to the aid of Tarentum (Livy *Periocha* 14). [31] Thus Roman fears, though perhaps groundless, may have been quite genuine. It should also be noted that the acceptance of the Mamertine appeal did not mark any new departure in Roman foreign policy: it had long been characteristic of the Romans to accept such appeals - when it suited them. The Carthaginians, for their part, could have avoided war had they been prepared to accept a *fait accompli* in Messina, but they must have calculated that if the Romans were allowed to interfere there, this might lead to further interference elsewhere in Sicily. At the same time, they had every reason to expect success: their fleet could dominate the waters around Sicily and control of the island was ultimately bound to depend on seapower.

The war that followed raged for twenty-three years, mainly in Sicily and around its coasts, and was chiefly remarkable for the Roman achievement in not only building up a fleet, but in winning all the important naval engagements save one, culminating in the decisive victory off the Aegates Islands (Egadi), probably on March 10th, 241. The struggle at sea was the greatest naval war in ancient history, and at the end of it Rome emerged as the most powerful naval state in the Mediterranean, a fact which is often forgotten, but which goes far to explain her eventual domination over all the lands bordering that sea. Carthage lost Sicily and the western part of the island became the first Roman 'province' overseas. The eastern part remained under the rule of King Hiero of Syracuse until his death in 215. Carthage was also condemned to pay a war-indemnity of 3200 talents - the equivalent of more than eighty tons of silver.

Obviously a war of this length and magnitude must have left a legacy of bitterness and distrust between the two powers, and this is one of the factors to be borne in mind when considering the causes of the second war. One Carthaginian general in particular may have been left with feelings akin to those of many German soldiers in 1918: Hamilcar Barca had gone to Sicily in 247, and had successfully maintained the struggle against the Roman forces in the north-west corner of the island until the Carthaginian defeat at sea left him no alternative but to open negotations, the Carthaginian government having left the decision to him. His son, Hannibal, was born shortly before or shortly after his departure for Sicily, and probably never saw him until he returned to Carthage after the war was over.

Thus when Polybius came to analyse the causes of the second war, he may well have been right to put first what he calls the "wrath" (θυμός) of Hamilcar (3.9.6), later justifying his view that Hamilcar's attitude contributed towards the outbreak of a war which only began ten years after his death, by telling the famous story of Hannibal's oath, sworn to his father before his departure for Spain in 237, "never to show good will to the Romans" (Polybius 3.11.7). The story has inevitably been doubted, but Polybius says that Hannibal himself told it to Antiochus of Syria, and it is probably true.[32] The view that the Hannibalic War was thus a war of revenge certainly gained widespread credence among the Romans - it is, perhaps, most dramatically expressed in the splendid passage towards the end of the fourth book of Vergil's *Aeneid* (lines 622-7), in which the Carthaginian queen, Dido, heartbroken and furious at her desertion by Aeneas, curses him and his whole race and calls upon an avenger to arise and destroy them - and even if the view stems from Carthaginian attempts to pin the blame for the war on Hannibal and his supporters (see above, p. 5), there may still be some truth in it - who is to say, for example, how much the personal feelings of Adolf Hitler contributed towards the outbreak of war in 1939? It is true that neither Hamilcar himself, nor his immediate successor, his son-in-law Hasdrubal, made any overt move against Rome, but we do not know how much they influenced Hannibal, and it is his attitude which is important: his forthright attack upon Saguntum, a town that he knew to be under Rome's protection, less than two years after he succeeded to the command of the Carthaginian forces in Spain, and the bold and decisive way in which he matured his plans for the invasion of Italy in 218, at least suggest that he was not too unwilling to have a war with Rome.

But not even a dictator can make war alone, and Hannibal, even if his command was largely independent of the Carthaginian home government, was not in a position to force a war upon his fellow-countrymen: as Polybius argues (3.8) in disputing the view of the Roman historian Fabius Pictor that Hannibal was responsible for the war, the Carthaginians could have repudiated him as Rome demanded. Polybius' own account of the circumstances in which Rome declared war, leaves no room for believing that there was any hesitation or lack of resolution in the Carthaginian senate when the final Roman embassy presented its ultimatum, and earlier it appears to have given Hannibal a free hand to deal with Saguntum as he liked, though it must have known what this might entail (see below, p. 25). Thus if Hannibal's war was a war of revenge, the desire for vengeance was clearly not only felt by Hannibal.

Undoubtedly, too, there must be some truth in Polybius' suggested "second and greatest cause of the war" (3.10.4) - Carthaginian resentment at Rome's behaviour during the great mutiny of the mercenaries which broke out at the end of the first war. At first the Romans behaved with scrupulous fairness: when the Carthaginians arrested Italians trafficking with the mutineers, there was at first some annoyance, especially when a rumour got about that Roman citizens had been thrown overboard to conceal the crime (Appian, *History of Libya*, 1.5). But having recovered the prisoners by diplomatic means, Rome responded by releasing the remaining Carthaginian prisoners in her hands, and acceded to Carthaginian requests that Italian merchants be allowed to export to Carthage, but be banned from dealings with the mutineers. Subsequently, when the mutiny spread to the Carthaginian forces in Sardinia, and the mutineers there offered to hand the island over to Rome, the Senate rejected the offer, as later it refused to accept the submission of Carthage's ally, Utica, which was also in revolt (Polybius 1.83). Rome even permitted Carthage to hire more mercenaries in Italy, if we are to believe Appian, and tried to use her good offices to bring an end to the mutiny (*History of Sicily and the Islands,* 2.3). But when Carthage began to make preparations to subdue Sardinia, Rome affected to regard this as a threat to Rome herself and declared war: according to Polybius (1.88.8), there had meanwhile been a second offer on the part of the mutineers to surrender the island to Rome, which the Senate had this time decided to accept, and it is clear that by then (238) it had come to regard control of the island as desirable for the security of Italy.

Nothing can excuse this example of Rome's cynical disregard for anything but her own interest, as Polybius evidently thought (cf.3.15.10), but Carthage was in no position to fight and was compelled to cede the island and even to pay a further indemnity of 1200 talents in order to restore peaceful relations (Polybius 1.88.11-12). But Rome did not find it at all easy to take over control of Sardinia and this exacerbated relations with Carthage for years to come since she was suspicious, perhaps rightly, that Carthage was fomenting resistance on the island. There was fighting there in 238 when the consul, Tiberius Sempronius Gracchus, first tried to impose Roman rule, and in every year from 235 to 231 inclusive, one or both of the consuls were sent to the island; in 225 one of the consuls was there again. Exasperated by this resistance, in 233 the consul, Q. Fabius Maximus, who was later to play so large a part in the Hannibalic War, actually went so far as to threaten Carthage with war again, and the Roman campaigns in Liguria in these years were another source of friction: in 230, for example, the consuls commanding Roman forces there are said to have come across Carthaginian officers in suspicious circumstances (Zonaras 8.19), though they claimed they had come to aid the Romans - perhaps they were really engaged in recruiting mercenaries for the Carthaginian army in Spain.

Carthage, meanwhile, after a desperate struggle (Polybius 1.65ff), had finally crushed her mutinous mercenaries in the savage war which forms the background to Gustave Flaubert's splendidly barbaric novel *Salammbo.* Thereafter, Hamilcar Barca who had been principally responsible for the defeat of the mercenaries, had been sent to Spain (237), where, building on the footholds Carthage already had in the country, he had set about creating a considerable empire based on the valley of the river Baetis (Guadalquivir) and the fertile territory of the Contestani in what is now Murcia. It is these activities of Hamilcar and his successors which formed, for Polybius (cf. 3.10.5-6) the third underlying cause of the Hannibalic War. On Hamilcar's death in battle, probably during the winter of 229/8, he was succeeded by his son-in-law, Hasdrubal, who continued his activities, though more by diplomacy than by force of arms (Polybius 2.36.2), and founded the city of "New Carthage" (now Cartagena) [33] to serve as a centre for Carthaginian control of the southeast and, possibly, as a base for further advances up the east coast (Polybius 2.13.1-2). In the late summer or autumn of 221, Hasdrubal in turn was assassinated, and was succeeded by his brother-in-law,

Hamilcar's son Hannibal, then some twenty-six years old. Polybius says that when the Carthaginians learnt of the death of Hasdrubal, they first waited to ascertain the feelings of the army in Spain, but when the news came that the soldiers had chosen Hannibal as their general, "they gathered the people together and unanimously ratified the choice of the forces". (3.13.4).

The army's choice was immediately justified, for in his first campaign as comman-der-in-chief, probably within a month or two of Hasdrubal's death, Hannibal proceeded to crush a tribe Polybius calls the "Olkades" and to take their principal town, Althaia (3.13.5-7). Unfortunately, it is not certain where the Olkades lived: one view is that they lived around the upper waters of what is now the Guadiana, south of Madrid.[34] But Stephanus of Byzantium says that they lived near Cartagena, and unless this is a mere inference from Polybius' account of Hannibal's campaign against them, it is tempting to equate their town "Althaia" with the modern Altea, on the coast about 140 kilometres northeast of Cartagena.[35] If this is right, then Saguntum (Sagunto), some 120 kilometres further north, might well have begun to feel threatened. But Hannibal's next campaign (Polybius 3.14.1-8) took him far away from these regions to the borders of Spain and northern Portugal, where he defeated the Vaccaei and stormed their chief centres, Helmantica and Arbukale, on the sites of modern Salamanca and Toro on the Douro, and it would perhaps make more sense to see the defeat of the Olkades as a preliminary to this campaign, and therefore to locate them south of Madrid. It was on his return from this second campaign that Hannibal won his first considerable victory in the field, when he was set upon by the Carpesii or Carpetani, probably somewhere near Toledo on the Tagus.

These campaigns have been held by some to show that Hannibal did not at this time envisage an immediate war with Rome,[36] but even if the first campaign against the Olkades took him northwestwards from Cartagena rather than northeastwards, it could equally well be argued that he was merely putting his Spanish house in order before embarking on a war with Rome. At all events, whatever his own long-term plans, he had very soon to make up his mind about Rome, for on returning to Cartagena for the winter of 220-19, he found there a Roman embassy come to issue certain warnings to him (Polybius 3.15.3ff.).

Since her seizure of Sardinia in 238/7, Rome had been pre-occupied with opera-tions in Sardinia, Corsica, Liguria, the Po valley and against the pirates of Illyria, but it is clear that she had not been unaware of what was going on in Spain. Thus, in 231, she had sent envoys to Hamilcar to investigate his activities, and the Carthaginian general had blandly declared that he was endeavouring to secure the funds necessary to pay off the indemnity owed to Rome (Cassius Dio 12.48) - presumably the indemnity imposed in 238/7 was meant, since the first should have been paid off in 231. Some five or six years later, possibly in the second half of 226, a second embassy had concluded an agreement with Hasdrubal by which, according to Polybius (2.13.7), the Carthaginian general undertook not to cross a river Polybius calls the "Iber" for warlike purposes.

This agreement has caused endless controversy mainly because it is not easy to see what its purpose was: Polybius certainly thought that the river in question was the river now called the Ebro, [37] and if he was right, Rome does not appear to have been trying to impose any serious limitation upon Hasdrubal since it is very unlikely that the Carthaginian dominions extended anywhere near the Ebro at this date. Perhaps all Rome was really trying to do was to protect the interests of her ally Marseille which had colonies on the east coast of Spain north of the Ebro at Rhode (Rosas) and Emporion (Ampurias). It is often said that Marseille was behind the Roman intervention in Spain, [38] and although there is no direct evidence for it, it may well be the case: she had also established colonies south of the Ebro - for example at Hemeroskopeion (Denia) and Akra Leuke (Alicante) - which had presumably already fallen under Carthaginian domination, and if so, she would already have had a grievance against Carthage and been anxious to preserve her remaining footholds in Spain. Another theory which has gained acceptance [39] is that Rome, faced with serious trouble from the Celts of the Po valley in these years, was anxious at all costs to prevent any co-operation between Carthage and the Celts, and so tried to stop Hasdrubal from reaching the Pyrenees. But this is hard to believe: even though it was thought that Celts "living among the Alps and about the river Rhône" (Polybius 2.22.1) had taken part in the great Celtic invasion of Etruria which was defeated at Telamon in 225 (Polybius 2.23ff.), it is a long way from the Ebro to the Rhône, and to secure Hasdrubal's agreement not to cross the former seems an odd way of preventing his joining the Celts. Nevertheless, Marseille may have played upon Roman fears in this direction, and with the somewhat hazy notions the Romans had about geography, the dangers may have seemed real enough.

Polybius, however, although he evidently believed that the river Hasdrubal undertook not to cross was the Ebro, in three passages (3.21.1, 3.29.1-3, and especially 3.30.3) appears to imply that Hannibal's attack upon Saguntum was itself a breach of the agreement with Hasdrubal, despite the fact that Saguntum lies some 140 kilometres south of the Ebro, and there has been speculation that the river Hasdrubal undertook not to cross was not the Ebro, but some other river south of Saguntum.[40] This finds some support in the statement by the Byzantine scholar Tzetzes (1.718), who drew upon Diodorus and Cassius Dio in this part of his extraordinary narrative poem (cf. 1.700), that Hamilcar was drowned in a river called the "Iber", since he can hardly have been drowned as far north as the Ebro, and in Appian's statement (*History of Spain,* 7) that Saguntum lay between the Pyrenees and the "Iber". But Tzetzes was clearly hopelessly confused about other things - he says, for example, that Hannibal was general of the Sikels of Sicily (1.703) - and Appian's notions about the geography of Spain seem to have been equally confused: he seems to have thought, for example, that the "Iber" flowed into the Atlantic, and in two passages apparently confuses Saguntum with New Carthage (op.cit., 12 and 19). However, if the river specified in the agreement was some relatively obscure stream south of Saguntum, with a name similar to that of the Ebro, it is easy to see how these various confusions might have arisen, and in this case the agreement did impose a fairly severe limitation upon Hasdrubal.

But to believe this would be to convict Polybius of a serious error in thinking that the river was the Ebro, and it is best to hold that he was right: in the passages in which he appears to imply that Hannibal's attack upon Saguntum itself constituted a breach of the agreement with Hasdrubal, he may either by reproducing the Romans' own ignorance of the geography, or possibly their confused attempts to justify their declaration of war - in one of the passages referred to above (3.29.1) he does state that he is not putting the Roman case at the time, but the case they repeated afterwards. Livy, on the other hand, states that Saguntum was specifically mentioned in the agreement with Hasdrubal (21.2.7), and although this can hardly be true (see below) it would appear to indicate that by his time, or by the time of his source, the Romans had realised that geography was against them and were now trying to justify themselves in other ways. In the end, perhaps, what was important about the Ebro agreement from the Roman point of view was not so much whether or not it imposed any serious limitation on Hasdrubal, as that the Carthaginians, by accepting it, implicitly recognized Rome's right to interfere in Spain, and this may be why, according to Polybius (3.21.1), the Carthaginian senate later denied that the agreement was valid on the grounds that it had not been ratified at Carthage.

Polybius' version of the agreement (2.13.7, 3.6.2, 3.15.5, 3.29.3) makes no mention of Saguntum, unless it is implied in the passage discussed above (3.30.3) in which Polybius appears to say that Hannibal's attack on the place violated the agreement with Hasdrubal, and he seems explicitly to deny that Saguntum was mentioned when he says (2.13.7) that when the Romans approached Hasdrubal, "they made no mention of the rest of Spain." This raises the question when Rome entered into relations with Saguntum. Polybius (3.30.1) says that it was "a good many years" ($\pi\lambda\acute{\epsilon}o\sigma\iota\nu$ $\ddot{\epsilon}\tau\epsilon\sigma\iota\nu$) before Hannibal's time, and it has been suggested that it was at the time of the Roman embassy to Hamilcar in 231. [41] If so, one might have expected there to have been some mention of Saguntum in the subsequent agreement with Hasdrubal, and Livy in fact says (21.2.7) that the freedom of Saguntum was secured by that agreement. But in view of Polybius' denial that the Romans made any mention of the rest of Spain on this occasion, Livy's statement can hardly be accepted - it is part and parcel of the Roman attempts to justify their intervention on behalf of Saguntum, attempts which may even have led to their claiming that Saguntum lay north of the Ebro, as we have seen. Nevertheless, it is easier to understand how the Romans can have overlooked or disregarded Saguntum when seeking agreement with Hasdrubal, if their relationship with Saguntum was entered into some years before, and, after all, if Polybius' version of the agreement with Hasdrubal was correct and complete, they could argue that his agreement not to cross the Ebro made no difference to Saguntum's position - they were not agreeing to anything in return. If, on the other hand, they entered into relations with Saguntum after the agreement with Hasdrubal, this brings it rather nearer in time to Hannibal's succession to the command than Polybius' statement that it was "a good many years" before his time would suggest, and if it is argued [42] that Rome can have had no interest in Saguntum in 231, then equally it is difficult to believe that Rome can have been concerned with Saguntum after 226 in view of her pre-occupation with the Celtic invasion of Etruria.

We must presumably, however, accept Polybius' statement that it was some years before Hannibal's time that the people of Saguntum had "placed themselves under the protection of Rome" (Polybius 3.30.1), [43] and Hannibal had hitherto scrupulously avoided any act of aggression against Saguntine territory (Polybius 3.14.9-10). For their part, too, the Romans had hitherto ignored repeated warnings from Saguntum (Polybius 3.15.1-2), though at some point they had intervened in an internal disturbance in the town (Polybius 3.15.7). Now, however, when Hannibal returned to Cartagena for the winter of 220/19, he was confronted by Roman envoys who adjured him to keep his hands off Saguntum and not to cross the Ebro, in accordance with the agreement made with Hasdrubal (Polybius 3.15.5) - it is possible that it had been these same envoys who had intervened in the dispute in Saguntum. [44]

Hannibal is said to have replied by accusing the Romans of unjustly putting to death a number of leading Saguntine citizens, and declaring that Carthage would look after their interests since it was "a hereditary trait among the Carthaginians not to over-look any victim of injustice" (Polybius 3.15.7). This suggests that the internal disturb-ances in Saguntum which had perhaps led to the despatch of the embassy in the first place, had been due to disagreements between the supporters of Rome and the supporters of Carthage, and if this is the case, the parallel with the situation in Messina in 265/4 was exact and ominous. At the same time, however, Hannibal sent to Carthage for instruc-tions, alleging that Saguntum had been guilty of agression against some of the subjects of Carthage. Polybius (3.15.8) does not name these alleged victims of Saguntine aggression. Livy (21.6.1, 21.12.5) says that they were the Turdetani, but this does not seem possible since they lived around the Guadalquivir, and even Appian's statement (*History of Spain* 2.10) that they were the Torboletai seems unlikely, since they lived near Cartagena. [45] Possibly the tribe which had really quarelled with the Saguntines was the Edetani or Sedetani who really did live near Saguntum. [46] The reply of the Carthaginian government is not recorded by Polybius, but it probably authorized Hannibal to take what steps he saw fit, as Appian says, and thus he now had to make up his mind whether to climb down and obey the Roman ultimatum, or to go ahead and deal with Saguntum. Appian may also be right that he made a show of giving the Saguntines a chance of patching up their differences with the tribe in question, by inviting both sides to send envoys to his camp. But, as he had probably expected, the Saguntine envoys, when invited to state their case, simply replied that they preferred to refer the matter to Rome.

It was the turning point in Hannibal's life: if he chose to accept Roman interven-tion on Saguntum's behalf, he could no doubt look forward to a career like his father's and his brother-in-law's, but now with the threat of Roman interference ever before him; if on the other hand, he chose to attack Saguntum, he must have had little doubt that sooner or later this would involve war with Rome. Even if he and his family had long been planning for this moment, it was not too late to turn back now. In the event, he does not seem to have hesitated long, and, as was said above, for those who believe that the war which followed was a war of revenge, Hannibal's resolute decision not to acquiesce in Rome's intervention on Saguntum's behalf provides perhaps the best argument.

Saguntum lay a little over a kilometre from the sea, on the site of the modern Spanish town which until 1877 was called Murviedro, though now it has been renamed

Sagunto. It was said to have been founded by colonists from the island of Zakynthos, off the northwest coast of the Peloponnese, but this is probably no more than a guess based on the similarity of the names: its coins bore the name "Arse" or "Arseken" and this may have given rise to the even more improbable - though in Roman eyes useful - legend that some of its original inhabitants came from Ardea in Latium (Livy 21.7.2). In reality, it was probably a native settlement, though perhaps with some Greek admixture - it appears, in particular, to have had commercial relations with Marseille. [47] Hannibal attacked it probably in April or May, 219, and took it after a desperate eight months' resistance (Polybius 3.17), but despite the length of the siege, Rome appears to have done nothing to help, although it can probably be assumed that resistance was prolonged in the hope that help would come. It is true that both consuls of 219 and considerable forces were committed to a second round of operations against the Illyrian pirates (Polybius 3.16 & 18), but Rome could surely have spared some ships and men to help Saguntum had she really put her mind to it. Probably her leaders had complacently assumed that her warning to Hannibal - which Polybius says had also been conveyed to Carthage (3.15.12) [48] - would be enough.

Livy, however, appears to have thought that at least a Roman embassy was sent to Hannibal after he had commenced the siege (21.6), and it is just possible that he was right. But his chronology is clearly in a hopeless tangle, as he himself subsequently seems to have appreciated (cf.21.15), and it is usually thought that this embassy is the same as Polybius' embassy of winter 220/19, before Hannibal's attack on Saguntum, perhaps deliberately put later by Roman apologists to excuse Rome's failure to do anything to help Saguntum. [49] One is tempted to conjecture that there were two embassies - one Polybius' in the winter of 220/19, the other Livy's during 219 - but this would mean that Polybius has omitted the second, which is unlikely. If Livy has misplaced his embassy, we must inevitably regard with suspicion his report of the debate in the senate at Carthage, which presupposes Hannibal's attack on Saguntum, and at which the leading opponent of Hannibal and his family, Hanno, is alleged to have argued that Rome's ultimatum be accepted and Hannibal and his staff be surrendered to Rome (Livy 21.10-11).

Assuming, then, that the Senate did nothing to help Saguntum, we can well believe, with Livy (21.16), that the news of the fall of the town came as a considerable shock to its members, and despite Polybius' somewhat peevish assertions to the contrary (3.20), even now there seems to have been some debate on the course of action Rome should pursue. There is, for example, a tradition that there was a fierce argument between Q. Fabius Maximus and L. Cornelius Lentulus, who was *pontifex maximus* and the *princeps senatus* at the time (Zonaras 8.22), and there was also considerable delay before the embassy bearing a final ultimatum to Carthage was despatched: the news of the fall of Saguntum must presumably have reached Rome at latest by February, 218, yet the embassy cannot have left the city before March 15th, because two of its members were the consuls of 219/18 whose term of office did not end until March 14th, and who cannot have served as ambassadors while still in office: recently it has been argued that the embassy did not in fact leave Rome before May. [50]

According to Polybius (3.20.8), whenever they eventually left, the Roman envoys were instructed to present Carthage with a simple alternative - either Hannibal and his staff were to be surrendered - which would amount to repudiation of his action - or war would be declared. Probably, indeed, as Livy seems to have believed (21.17.4ff), the formal motion to declare war had already gone through the *comitia centuriata* in a conditional form, and thus, after the Carthaginian senate had rejected the demand to surrender Hannibal and his staff, the senior senator in the embassy - probably M. Fabius Buteo, consul in 245/4, and not Q. Fabius Maximus, consul in 233/2 and 228/7, as Livy believed - was himself empowered to declare war. [51] The scene in the Carthaginian senate is a famous one: after the Roman envoys had formally asked the Carthaginians whether they were prepared to repudiate Hannibal's action, a spokesman for Carthage attempted to justify what had happened, but this the Romans studiously ignored. Instead, their leader, gesturing to the fold of his toga, said that it held peace or war - he would let fall whichever they chose. At this the presiding sufet bade him let fall whichever they liked, and Buteo said he let fall "war" to shouts of "we accept it" from many of the assembled Carthaginians (Polybius 3.20.6-21.8, and 3.33.1-4).

The question whether Rome or Carthage in the person of Hannibal was morally responsible for the war has been debated from Polybius' day (cf.3.28ff.) to this, and has become tedious: in the discussions the fate of the wretched people of Saguntum seems to be forgotten, yet however specious the Roman claims to be justifiably intervening on their behalf, this does not justify Hannibal's attack upon them unless it was true that they had been guilty of aggression against allies of Carthage, and this is a question we cannot answer at this late date. In other words, even the legal aspects of the question really concern Carthage and Saguntum more than they concern Carthage and Rome. But what is more important for the historian to consider is why Rome chose to make an issue of Saguntum and why Hannibal chose to ignore her warning. The latter question is fairly easy to answer: if Hannibal had backed down over Saguntum, there can be little doubt that Roman interference in Spain would not have stopped there - it would have been open to any Spanish community which felt itself to be threatened by Carthage, to seek Roman protection, and this would have spelt the beginning of the end of Carthaginian dominion in Spain. Thus Hannibal's attitude is easy to understand even if he was not planning a war of revenge on Rome; if he was, it was of course essential to establish Carthaginian control in Spain as widely and as firmly as possible, and Polybius, who believed that Hannibal was bent on revenge, says that this was his main motive for attacking Saguntum (3.17.5-6).

The Roman stand on Saguntum is far more difficult to explain, let alone to justify, since the Carthaginian activities in Spain hardly threatened Roman interests. But we should not exclude the possibility that there were Romans who genuinely felt that Rome was justified in intervening on Saguntum's behalf whatever the nature of the relations between the two states - eight years later, when in a position to do so, the Roman commanders in Spain took steps to restore the survivors from the siege to their land, and to punish the tribe with whom they had originally quarrelled (Livy 24.42.9-11). At the same time there were probably many Romans who equally genuinely felt threatened by the build-up of Carthaginian power in Spain, and in this context we should not forget the legacy of bitterness, hostility and fear left by the first war - feelings which the intervening years had done little to diminish and which were no doubt played upon by the people of Marseille and others (cf. Appian, *History of Spain,* 2.7). A less excusable, but equally powerful factor may have been the positive desire of some elements in the Senate to see the Republic become embroiled in Spain. [52]

We should also not forget that there was probably an element of bluff in the Roman attitude - this would explain why, when Hannibal called it, the Senate did nothing to help Saguntum and was later slow even to send the final ultimatum to Carthage: such bluffs had, after all, come off in the recent past, for Carthage had climbed down over Sardinia, and Hasdrubal had agreed not to cross the Ebro. Furthermore, even if the bluff were called this time, as Polybius points out (3.15.13), and as the dispositions originally made by Rome in 218 prove, no Roman thought that the war would be fought in Italy. Perhaps to many Senators the succession to the command of the Carthaginian forces in Spain of a new, young general seemed a suitable time to bring pressure to bear. If so, they can hardly ever have made a greater mistake.

## CHAPTER TWO – HANNIBAL'S MARCH TO ITALY

Hannibal probably took Saguntum towards the end of 219, and the new year would have seen his victorious soldiers dispersed to winter quarters, the Africans to Cartagena, the Spaniards to their homes. He had no means of knowing for certain what the Roman reaction to his attack upon Saguntum would be, assuming that Livy was wrong to say that a Roman embassy approached him during the siege, but he seems to have assumed that war with Rome was inevitable, and almost immediately to have begun to take steps to implement the daring plan he had conceived - to lead an army overland to northern Italy and attack the Romans in their homeland. He probably did not set out on his long march until June, 218, as we shall see, but the preparations which preceded his own departure - particularly the transference of troops to and from Africa - would have taken some time, and he also apparently sent off envoys to the Celtic chiefs of the Alpine region through which he intended to pass, and even of northern Italy (cf. Polybius 3.34.4). These envoys would probably have had to travel overland on their hazardous mission, and if it is true, as Livy says (21.29.6), that Magilos, one of the Celtic chieftains who met him at the Rhône (cf. Polybius 3.44.5), was a chieftain of the Boii, then presumably the envoys travelled as far as Bologna, the main centre of the Boii. Such a journey could well have taken two or three months, and since Hannibal was still anxiously waiting the return of the envoys before he set out from Cartagena in June (Polybius 3.34.4), they must have left quite early in the year.[1]

Unfortunately, we do not know Hannibal's thoughts, since he left no memoirs to guide us, but we can probably assume that three factors were crucial in his thinking. Firstly, the obvious alternative to the strategy he adopted would have been simply to stand on the defensive and resist the inevitable Roman attacks upon Spain and Africa when they came. It is clear from the measures he took to safeguard Spain and Africa that he expected such attacks, and he could have himself remained in Spain, or returned to Africa, and at the same time have retained his best troops - the ones in the event earmarked for Italy. But he must have calculated that a war fought along these lines would soon have fallen into the pattern of the first war, with Spain now filling the role of Sicily. He might defeat successive Roman armies, but he could not be in two places at once, and he must have known that Roman resources were such that they could replace losses, and keep up a long drawn out war on several fronts, until Carthage was exhausted: the record of the first war held out no real hope of wearing the Romans down and bringing them to the conference table ready to accept the Carthaginian empire in Spain. An attack on Italy might, of course, forestall a Roman attack on Spain and Africa, and this was no doubt one of the considerations in his mind, but far more important than this, he must have known that over half the manpower at Rome's disposal was drawn from her allies in Italy, some of whom had only succumbed to her just over fifty years before, and many of whom had long and bitterly resisted her encroachments. If Carthage was ever to defeat Rome, this confederacy must be broken up and Rome isolated from a significant proportion of her allies, even if they did not come in actively on Carthage's side. But a war fought in Spain and Africa, however long drawn out, could never be expected to do more than weary Rome's allies: they might become increasingly reluctant to honour their obligations, but they could hardly be expected to turn against Rome until they had some hope that rebellion might succeed - however victorious the Carthaginians were in Spain or Africa, this could not help the Italians. If, on the other hand, a Carthaginian army invaded Italy, the case would be very different: Rome's allies might be induced to desert her cause and some of them might even come actively into the war on the Carthaginian side.

That this is the way Hannibal thought is indicated by his actions and declarations, as recorded by Polybius and Livy, after his victories at the Trebbia, Lake Trasimene and Cannae. Thus, after the battle of the Trebbia, Polybius says (3.77.4-7), he showed the greatest kindness to his non-Roman prisoners and eventually released them without ransom, declaring "that he had not come to make war on them, but on the Romans for their sakes. For this reason, if they thought rightly, they should seize his proffered friendship, for he was there, first, to win back freedom for the Italians, and at the same time to recover the cities and the land they had lost through the Romans." Similarly, after Trasimene, he released allied prisoners with the declaration that he had not come to fight the Italians but the Romans for the sake of the freedom of the Italians (Polybius 3.85.4). Finally, after Cannae, in August 216, he again released his non-Roman prisoners (Livy 22.58.1-2), and at last his gestures and, of course, his great victories, began to pay off as most of southern Italy began to go over to him. We do not know how many Italians actively served the Carthaginian cause from this point on - most of their forces were probably always concentrated in defence of their own towns - but some Italians certainly joined Hannibal's field-army, and some were to leave Italy with him in 203 and to fight and die for him on the field of Zama.

The second factor which probably entered into Hannibal's thinking was seapower. The easiest way for him to have got an army to Italy would have been by sea, and this would have avoided the losses he must have expected to sustain on the march overland, and brought him more speedily to his objective. Nor would be necessarily have had to make do with a smaller army than the one which he eventually succeeded in getting to Italy: when he reached the foot of the Alps, he had 20,000 infantry and 6000 cavalry (Polybius 3.56.4), but Scipio probably took as many men as that to Africa with him in 204 (see below, p. 203), and although he is said to have needed 400 transports (Livy 29.26.3), Carthage could probably have put even more at Hannibal's disposal in 218 - six years later she scraped together 700 merchant vessels for the relief of Syracuse (Livy 25.27.4). Nor was there apparently any problem about transporting horses and even elephants by sea, for elephants are said to have been carried to Hannibal at Locri from Carthage in 215 (Livy 23.41.10), and Mago not only took horses with him from Minorca to Liguria in 205 (Livy 28.46.7), but is later said to have received horses and elephants all the way from Carthage (Livy 29.4.6). Finally, although Hannibal would have been landing in at least potentially hostile territory, unless he landed somewhere in the north, this need not have precluded an invasion of Italy by sea, for with the exception of the British attempt to stop Caesar's first landing in 55 - and that failed - ancient landings on hostile coasts seem almost invariably to have been unopposed, and there is no reason to believe that a landing by Hannibal somewhere in southern Italy would have been any different.

The problem, then, was not one of logistics nor of the difficulty of getting ashore in enemy territory: it was Roman seapower. We know that Rome had at least 220 quinqueremes in commission in 218 (Polybius 3.41.2), of which 60 accompanied one consul, P. Cornelius Scipio, as far as the mouth of the Rhône, and then went on to Spain under his brother, while 160 went with the other consul, Ti. Sempronius Longus, to Sicily. Unfortunately we do not have equally precise figures for Carthaginian naval strength, but there were certainly 50 quinqueremes based on Spain, though eighteen of these were unmanned (Polybius 3.33.4), and Livy says that twenty more were sent to raid Italy (21.49.2), while a further thirty-five were sent to western Sicily (21.49.4). These 105 quinqueremes were probably not the only ones Carthage had available in 218, because even after losses among the small squadrons operating off Sicily in that year, she could still send 70 to Sardinia in 217 (Polybius 3.96.8). But of these seventy some were presumably from the squadrons sent to Sicilian waters in 218, so it looks as though Carthage had at least between fifty and a hundred fewer warships in commission than Rome at the beginning of the war, and the largest fleet she ever assembled during this war was the one she sent to escort the 700 transports to Syracuse late in 212, and only numbered 130 warships (Livy 25.27.4). Thus Rome had a decisive superiority in ready warships, and Livy says that the Romans knew it (21.17.8, 21.22.4): Hannibal's dispositions to protect Spain and Africa suggest that he knew it too. This is not to say, of course, that he might not have been able to slip through, as a Carthaginian fleet did to Sardinia and Pisa in 217 (Polybius 3.96.8-10), and as Bomilcar later did to Locri in 215 (Livy 23.41.10). But he really dared not risk an invasion fleet's being intercepted at sea by a superior Roman war-fleet. The Carthaginian navy probably did enter into his long-term plans - as we shall see, he later took steps to try to capture a port in Campania - but he must have known that he could not rely upon it to convey his army safely to Italy.

A third factor which undoubtedly influenced Hannibal was the knowledge that he would almost certainly find allies in northern Italy when he arrived. From 225 to 222 the Romans had fought a desperate war against the Celts of the Po valley, and although the invasion of Etruria had been bloodily defeated at Telamon in 225 by the consuls L. Aemilius Papus and C. Atilius Regulus, it had revived memories of the sack of Rome by similar Celtic peoples - the Romans called them Gauls - early in the fourth century. Since then Roman forces had crushed the Boii - or so they thought - and crossed the Po to defeat the Insubres and their allies from beyond the Alps, and take their capital Mediolanum (Milan), in 222. But in 220 Roman forces had again been operating as far as the Alps (Zonaras 8.20), and it appears that it was in this year or the next that the decision was taken to found two new Latin colonies at Placentia and Cremona on the Po (Livy *Periocha* Book 20). Hannibal probably thought that the situation in northern Italy was far from settled, and that the founding of the colonies might well stir up trouble again, as indeed turned out to be the case. We have already seen that he sent envoys as far as the valley of the Po early in 218, and if they went as far as the Boii (see above, p. 29), they are also likely to have been in touch with the Insubres - one of Hannibal's first actions on reaching Italy was to attack their enemies the Taurini and take their chief town, probably on the site of Turin (Polybius 3.60.8-9). The Celts were notoriously unreliable allies, but they were brave and ferocious fighters who could be trained - they had served in the Carthaginian army in Sicily during the First Punic War (cf. Polybius 1.17.4, 43.4). The Insubres and the Boii were their largest tribes, according to Polybius (2.22.1), and had been allied to each other in the previous war with Rome. Thus Hannibal was assured of a reasonably friendly reception when he first came down out of the Alps - just when he must have expected to be at his most vulnerable.

Hannibal's decision to invade Italy by land can thus be seen to have been based on sound strategic thinking, and the preparations he made bear all the hall-marks of careful planning. First agents were sent to the Alpine regions through which he expected to pass, and on into Cisalpine Gaul to sound out the Insubres and the Boii. They probably went overland, since landing in any port in Italy or near Marseille might have been dangerous, and in any case, if they started soon after the capture of Saguntum, as they must have done to have been back in Cartagena by June 218, the sailing season would have been closed. Livy (21.20.8) says that when Roman ambassadors subsequently approached the Gauls of Languedoc (see below, pp. 49-50), they found that they had already been won over by Hannibal, and if this is true, this may well have been another of the tasks entrusted to these same agents.

Secondly, Hannibal took steps to safeguard Spain and Africa in his absence, taking the precaution, as Polybius notes (3.33.8), of sending Spanish troops to Africa and bringing Africans to Spain. Thus, 13,850 Spanish infantry, 1200 cavalry, and 870 slingers from the Balearic islands were sent to Africa, most of them to what Polybius calls "the Metagonia area" ($\tau \grave{\alpha}$ Mεταγώνια: 3.33.12), which may have been the eastern part of what is now Morocco,[2] but some to Carthage itself, while from the towns of Metagonia 4000 foot were also sent to Carthage. His brother, Hasdrubal, who was to be entrusted with the command in Spain during his absence, was left a fleet of 50 quinqueremes with some smaller warships, 11,580 African foot, 300 Ligurians, 500 Balearic slingers, 2550 cavalry, mostly from Africa, and 21 elephants (Polybius 3.33.14-16). To counter any possible doubt as to the accuracy of his figures, Polybius here cites the bronze tablet Hannibal himself later set up on the Lacinian promontory (Capo Colonne), near Croton in southern Italy, recording these and other details (3.33.17-8).[3]

All these troop movements would have taken time, and although Polybius seems to have thought that they were carried out during the winter (3.35.1), in fact they could probably not even have begun before about March since ancient ships did not normally put to sea during the winter, and the transfers had, of course, to be made by sea. Meanwhile Hannibal must also have been anxiously awaiting the return of the agents he had sent to northern Italy, and indeed still did not know what the Roman reaction to his attack on Saguntum would be. It is usually assumed that he would have wanted to set out on his long march as soon as possible,[4] but, as we can see, there was plenty to do before he could go, and there is one good piece of evidence that he did not finally leave Cartagena until sometime in the first half of June, or the end of May at the earliest: Polybius (3.54.1) records that when he reached the summit of the pass over the Alps, it was "close to the time of the setting of the Pleiades," which for him would have meant a date in the first fortnight in November, or the end of October at the earliest.[5] Hannibal then took about another week to descend to the plains (Polybius 3.54.4 - 3.56.1), and he reached the plain five months after leaving Cartagena (Polybius 3.56.3). In short, if we take these statements by Polybius at their face value - and there is no good reason not to - Hannibal cannot have left Cartagena before the last week in May, and probably did not leave until the first or second week in June. Apart from the necessity of making all dispositions to safeguard Spain and Africa, there were probably two other reasons why a late start was not undesirable: firstly, the rivers in eastern Spain would have been in spate in the spring, and the later he left, the lower the level of water in them was likely to be; secondly, he would have to live off the land once he was beyond the Carthaginian sphere of influence, and he probably calculated that in Spain the harvest would be in by the end of May, and progressively later as he went northwards - fodder for the thousands of cavalry horses would also have been a problem.

At last all the preparations would have been completed: Africa and Spain had been safeguarded as far as possible, and the agents had returned from northern Italy with a favourable report. Probably, then, in the last weeks of May,[6] Hannibal began to reassemble his army from its winter quarters, and when he heard the news of the Carthaginian senate's response to the Roman ultimatum, he was able to make capital out of the Roman demand that he and his officers be surrendered (Polybius 3.34.8). There was nothing now to stop him, and accordingly he named a day, probably sometime in the first fortnight of June, for the start of the great march. When the day came, he set out from Cartagena with an army of about 90,000 foot and 12,000 cavalry, if we are to believe Polybius (3.35.1) - Appian (*Hannibalic War*, 1.4) adds thirty-seven elephants - his first objective the river Ebro which now, in effect, marked the boundary of the Carthaginian empire. This was his Rubicon, and although the sober Polybius has him cross the river without comment, Livy has him dream of a ghost like a young man sent to guide him on his way, and behind him "a snake of wondrous size came gliding amidst the widespread ruin of trees and bushes, and after it followed a cloud with heaven crashing about it" (Livy 21.22.8) - a not inappropriate image to herald the start of a war which was to bring such devastation in its train.

The Carthaginian army would probably have taken about five weeks to march the 462 kilometres from Cartagena to the Ebro (see Appendix III), and would thus have reached the river about the middle of July. Beyond the Ebro, however, it would have entered hostile territory for the first time, and it would no longer have been sufficient just to march through as quickly as possible: unless and until a secure base was established in Italy, with access to the sea, the line of communications would run back through southern France and north-east Spain, and even if it was possible to establish direct communications with Carthage by sea from Italy, it would still be necessary to keep communications with Spain open, particularly in view of Roman seapower. It was thus essential to reduce the tribes north of the Ebro to submission, and this may well have taken some considerable time and involved heavy fighting, although Polybius does say (3.35.3) that progress was "unexpectedly swift". Hannibal entrusted the newly conquered territory to a general named Hanno, and left him an army of 10,000 foot and 1000 cavalry (Polybius 3. 35.4-5). It is sometimes said that this Hanno was his brother,[7] but there is no ancient evidence for this, and Polybius would surely have said so had he known it. In addition to leaving Hanno troops, Hannibal is also said to have released an equal number of his Spanish troops to their homes as a conciliatory gesture (Polybius 3.35.6), but, according to Livy (21.23.4), 3000 deserted while he was crossing the Pyrenees, and he dismissed a further 7000, partly to get rid of unreliable troops, partly to cover up the desertion. Since he is said to have eventually crossed the Pyrenees with about 50,000 foot and 9000 horse (Polybius 3.35.7), he would appear to have lost about 20,000 foot and 1000 horse since leaving Cartagena, but these losses seem very high, even allowing for the fighting north of the Ebro. Perhaps most of the losses were due to the desertion of unreliable Spanish levies, but it is possible that Polybius' figures are not very reliable here: it is significant that he does not cite the Lacinian inscription for them, as he does for the dispositions made to protect Africa and southern Spain, and as he does later for the numbers with which Hannibal finally reached Italy (3.56.4).

With an army of 50,000 foot and 9000 horse, or perhaps somewhat less, Hannibal set out from Emporion to cross the Pyrenees, probably about the end of August (see Appendix III), leaving his heavy baggage behind him. Polybius gives no details of the march from here to the Rhône, but since he says that the distance from Emporion to the Rhône was 1600 stades (284 kilometres),[8] and since either he himself, just before he died, or an editor shortly afterwards, added a note that "this part of the road has now been paced out and marked carefully by the Romans at every eighth stade (i.e. at every Roman mile)" (3.39.8), it is possible that he thought that Hannibal marched along the line of the later *via Domitia*, laid down exactly a century later after the Roman conquest of this part of France. The *via Domitia* followed an ancient route, and there is no reason to doubt that Hannibal could have used it: it is now roughly represented by Routes Nationales 114, 9 and 113 from the Spanish border through Elne, Perpignan, Narbonne and Montpellier to Nîmes. Livy (21.24.1) says that the Carthaginian army camped at Iliberis (Elne) after crossing the Pyrenees, and that from there Hannibal sent messages inviting the Gauls who were gathering at Ruscino (Perpignan) to a parley. This they accepted, and were soon won over by the Carthaginian general's friendly words and gifts, promising him free passage to the Rhône. We can probably assume, then, that he would have had a fairly rapid march to that river, and would have reached it towards the end of September. Polybius later says (3.60.5) that when he eventually set out from the Rhône on the next stage of his march, he had 38,000 foot and more than 8000 horse, and this, if true, would mean that he had lost a further 12,000 foot and 1000 horse since crossing the Pyrenees, and clearly he had experienced no such losses in crossing the Rhône, though there was fighting there. It has been suggested, on the basis of archaeological evidence from Enserune and elsewhere[9] that most of these men were left in garrisons along the route from the Pyrenees to the Rhône, and this may be right, although, as was noted above, there is some doubt about Polybius's figures in this part of his narrative.

From this point on not only did Hannibal's own real difficulties begin, but so also do the difficulties of anyone who attempts to follow his route.[10] The only detailed accounts we have are those of Polybius and Livy, and Livy follows Polybius so closely - except in one passage where, as we shall see, he has almost certainly made a mistake - that it is clear that he either used Polybius as his main source, or - less probably - directly or indirectly used the same source as Polybius. The most that we can hope to do is, thus, to work out the route Polybius thought Hannibal followed, and it is at least some comfort that he claims to have questioned men who had taken part and to have followed the same route through the Alps himself (3.48.12). It is, of course, possible that he did not follow the right route - he must have made his journey at least fifty, and more probably nearly seventy years later - [11] but in that case the task is hopeless: it is difficult enough even to establish which route he thought Hannibal took, and since there would have been no adequate maps available in his day, and no signposts or kilometre stones to which he could refer, we can hardly blame him.

The first problem is to try to establish where Hannibal crossed the Rhône. Polybius (3.42.1) says he crossed "where the stream is single, being at a distance of four days' march from the sea," and this at least means that it was at or above Fourques, where the river divides into several branches before discharging into the sea. But the apparent precision of the expression "four days' march from the sea" is illusory, for we do not know how fast the army normally marched, nor where it left the sea, nor even whether Polybius literally meant that Hannibal's army took four days to reach the crossing-place from where it left the sea, or whether the expression "four days' march" is not rather a measure of distance - as we might say "a day's drive". But Polybius must have had some idea in his head of the distance from the sea to the crossing-place, and he surely cannot have believed that it was as far from the sea as some have thought. Later (3.50.1) he says that Hannibal marched a distance of 800 stades (142 kilometres) in ten days, which gives an average day's march of 80 stades or just over 14 kilometres, and as we shall see, this seems to fit what he says about times and distances elsewhere. In view of this, it would appear that when he wrote about a distance of "four days' march" from the sea, he would have been thinking in terms of something like 320 stades or 56.8 kilometres, and that the crossing-place was not too far from the sea, in his view, is confirmed by his statement that the natives who lived near the crossing-place engaged in maritime trade (3.42.2). (See Map 3).

Now, as was noted above, we do not know what he meant by "from the sea", but at the present day the last place on the coast west of the western mouth of the Rhône (the Petit Rhône) is le Grau-du-Roi, and it is about 60 kilometres from there, by modern roads, even to Fourques, if one has to keep to the right bank of the Petit Rhône. This means that Polybius can hardly have been thinking of a crossing-place even as far up the river as Avignon - nearly 90 kilometres by modern roads from le Grau-du-Roi - on any rational interpretation of his words, let alone at Roquemaure or anywhere further north, and, for what it is worth, this conclusion is confirmed by what we are told about the movements of the Roman army under P. Cornelius Scipio, which appears to have marched from its landing-place somewhere near the eastern mouth of the Rhône (Livy 21.26.4), to the crossing-place, in two or three days. [12]

There is, finally, another way of approaching the problem: if Hannibal was march-ing along the line of the ancient route later represented by the *via Domitia,* he would have made for the normal crossing-place used by those travelling along this route, and his Celtic allies from the Po would also have had to make for a definite crossing-place to meet him. It would appear that this normal crossing-place was where the river is now spanned by the bridge from Beaucaire to Tarascon,[13] and as this point is at something like the right distance from the sea - it is about 63 kilometres from le Grau-du-Roi, about 76 from Montpellier - there seems little reason to doubt that it was somewhere near here that Hannibal crossed the Rhône.

The Carthaginian army spent two days on the river bank collecting canoes, boats and logs for making canoes, but meanwhile the Gauls gathered on the farther bank to dispute the crossing (Polybius 3.42.1-4). Hannibal, realising that it would be very difficult, if not impossible, to force a crossing against such opposition, on the third night after his arrival, sent Hanno, son of Bomilcar, up river to create a diversion, probably with a detachment of cavalry (Polybius 3.42.6; Livy 21.27.2ff.). Hanno is said to have gone upstream for 200 stades (35.5 kilometres) under cover of darkness, until he reached a place where an island divided the stream (Polybius 3.42.7). The course and nature of the river has changed so much since 218 that we cannot now be certain where Hanno crossed it, but if the main crossing was at Beaucaire, then his sortie would have taken him to a point about opposite Avignon. Here he constructed rafts from the timber he found ready to hand, and crossed over, occupying a strong position on the left bank where he rested up for the remainder of the day (Polybius 3.42.8-9). Polybius says (3.43.1) that it was "on the fifth night" - i.e., presumably, the fifth since the main army had reached the Rhône - that Hanno started back down the left bank of the river "about dawn", but unless 'fifth' is a mistake for "fourth", he appears to have missed a day out of his narrative. Perhaps we should understand that Hanno reached his crossing-place too late on the third night to cross before dawn, and so hid up for the day on the right bank before crossing on the fourth night, hiding up again, now on the left bank before starting back on the fifth night.

Hannibal, meanwhile, had made his preparations for the crossing of the main army, and when he saw that Hanno was in position through a pre-arranged smoke-signal (Polybius 3.43.6), ordered the crossing to begin. With boats carrying "shield-bearing" (πελτόφοροι) cavalry upstream - presumably Spanish cavalry is meant - to break the force of the current, each towing three or four horses behind, and canoes carrying his most mobile infantry downstream, the first assault waves rapidly established a foothold on the farther bank (Polybius 3.43.2-4). The Gauls poured out of their encampment to repel the attack, but at this moment Hanno's force charged into their rear having achieved complete surprise, and they broke and fled almost immediately. Hannibal could now bring the rest of his army across in safety, and by nightfall - the sixth since he had reached the river - the job was done, except for the elephants. The skill with which Hannibal and his army accomplished the crossing of the Rhône was an earnest of things to come and bears out Polybius' comment (3.37.8) about the high state of the army's training.

Next morning - the seventh since his arrival at the river - Hannibal learned that a Roman fleet had come to anchor at its mouth, and sent 500 Numidian cavalry south to

*Pl. I:*     *The Rhône at Beaucaire/Tarascon – Hannibal's crossing place ?*

*Pl. II:*    *The confluence of the Rhône and Isère at Valence. Hannibal ascending the east bank of the Rhone, may have mistaken the Isere, the lighter stream in the photograph, for the mainstream.*

reconnoitre, while he busied himself with the task of getting his elephants across, and introduced Magilos and the other chieftains from the Po valley who had come to meet him, to his army (Polybius 3.44). Livy (21.29-30) puts the assembly at which Magilos and his fellow chiefs were introduced to the troops, after the return of the Numidian horsemen, whereas Polybius puts it before, but there is one passage in the speech Livy gives to Hannibal when he saw that his men were dispirited at the prospect of crossing the Alps, which one would like to believe came from Hannibal himself: "How do you think these envoys got here - (pointing at Magilos and the others) - on wings?"

After the assembly had broken up - if we adhere to Polybius' timetable (3.45.1) - the Numidian cavalry force returned in headlong flight, having encountered a force of 300 Roman cavalry sent north by Scipio on a similar mission. The Roman cavalry rode right up to the Carthaginian camp, and then hurried back to their general with their news, whereupon he put his heavy baggage back on board his ships, and set off up the river (Polybius 3.45.3-4). Meanwhile Hannibal, on the day after the cavalry skirmish - the eighth since he had reached the Rhône - ordered his infantry to start the march up the river, flinging his cavalry out southwards as a screen, and busied himself with getting his elephants across. Polybius has a splendid description of the methods used to ferry the elephants across the river (3.46): first a pier of rafts, lashed two by two, was built out into the stream for about 60 metres and covered with earth; then a pair of rafts, lashed together, was fastened to the end of the pier. Onto these the elephants were driven, a few at a time, with two females leading, and then the ropes attaching the rafts to the pier were cut, whereupon the rafts were towed across the river by boats. Some of the elephants panicked and fell into the river, but Polybius claims that they simply waded across with their trunks sticking out of the water, like so many snorkels, though their mahouts were drowned. Then, when everybody was across, Hannibal recalled his cavalry and himself set off upstream after his infantry, using his elephants and cavalry as a rearguard.

The Carthaginian army was now marching up the left bank of the Rhône towards Avignon and Orange, and the question arises whether this had been the plan all along, or whether Scipio's unexpected arrival at the eastern mouth of the Rhône had brought about a change of plan. Livy (21.29.6-7) alleges that Hannibal hesitated between marching on to Italy and going to meet Scipio, and was advised against the latter by Magilos and his Gallic allies. This seems improbable, but the obvious route from a crossing of the Rhône at Beaucaire-Tarascon to Italy would have been up the valley of the Durance via Sisteron and Embrun to Briançon, and then over the Col de Montgenèvre, and this - from the ancient evidence - is patently not the route Hannibal followed. He may, then, have planned to go by this route, but now decided to avoid all chance of a clash with the Roman army by marching up the river. It is equally possible, however, that he had planned to avoid the obvious route from the beginning.

Both Polybius and Livy are agreed (Polybius 3.49.5; Livy 21.31.4) that after a march of four days, Hannibal reached a district known as the "island", formed by the confluence of the Rhône and one of its tributaries. Polybius says nothing of any difficulties on the way, but the passage in Livy (21.31.10) in which he describes the crossing of the Durance, may preserve an authentic record of this stage of the march, although in that case Livy has misplaced it to his account of the march after leaving the "island" (see below, p. 41). In any case, the next problem is to locate the "island", or, more particularly, to identify the tributary of the Rhône which formed one of its sides. The manuscripts of Polybius give "Skaras" or "Skoras" as its name, those of Livy "Arar", "Sarar" or "Bisarar", but these names only "Arar" is readily intelligible. This was the Roman name for the river Saône which joins the Rhône at Lyon. But this can hardly be the river in question: it would put the "island" far too far north, and in any case the Saône flows into the Rhône from its right, whereas Hannibal was now marching up the left bank when he came to the "island". Polybius' "Skaras" or "Skoras" has been identified with the river Aygues which flows into the Rhône near Orange, on the basis of its Mediaeval names, [14] and to locate the "island" at the confluence of the Rhône and the Aygues makes perfect sense, assuming the crossing to have been at Beaucaire-Tarascon: it is about 50 kilometres from Tarascon to Orange, and this would mean that Hannibal could easily have reached an "island" here in four days from his probable crossing-place.

It is sometimes argued [15] that Polybius thought that there were 600 stades (106.5 kilometres) from the crossing-place to the "island", because in one passage (3.39.9) he says there were 1400 stades from the crossing-place to what he calls "the ascent of the Alps" ($\dot{\eta}$ $\dot{\alpha}\nu\alpha\beta o\lambda\dot{\eta}$ $\tau\tilde{\omega}\nu$ $'A\lambda\pi\epsilon\omega\nu$), and in a later one (3.50.1) implies that there were 800 stades between the "island" and what he there calls "the ascent towards the Alps" ($\dot{\eta}$ $\pi\rho\dot{o}\varsigma$ $\tau\dot{\alpha}\varsigma$ $'A\lambda\pi\epsilon\iota\varsigma$ $\dot{\alpha}\nu\alpha\beta o\lambda\dot{\eta}$). But it is difficult to believe that Polybius can have thought that Hannibal marched 600 stades in four days from the crossing-place to the "island" - an average speed of 150 stades (26.6 kilometres) a day - when he later says (3.50.1) that he marched 800 stades in *ten* days after leaving the "island", and a careful examination of his account of what happened when Hannibal "began the ascent towards the Alps" (3.50.1), reveals that this is not the same point as the one he had earlier (3.39.9) described as "the ascent of the Alps", as his use of two different phrases indicates (see p. 42 below).

Many scholars, however, have accepted the correction "Isara" for what stands in the manuscripts of Livy as the name of the river which formed one side of the "island", and have even been prepared to alter Polybius' text, accordingly, to read "Isaras", which would mean that the "island" was formed by the confluence of the Rhône and the Isère. But this view, resting, as it does, on emendations to the texts of our two most important sources, must be rejected, if, as seems likely, Hannibal crossed the Rhône near Tarascon: it is nearly 150 kilometres from Tarascon to where the Isère flows into the Rhône, and to cover this distance in four days, Hannibal would have had to be marching at the impossible rate of between 35 and 40 kilometres a day. Naturally, those who believe that the "island" did lie between the Rhône and the Isère, try to get round this difficulty by putting the crossing-place higher up the river, and indeed tend to put it at a distance of 106.5 kilometres from the confluence of the Rhône and Isère for reasons rejected above. [16] But, as we have seen, any theory which has Hannibal cross the Rhône much above Beaucaire-Tarascon, soon makes nonsense of Polybius' statement that the crossing-place was four days' march from the sea, and also, for good measure, makes it impossible to believe that Scipio reached the crossing-place in a march of two or three days from the eastern mouth of the river. If the "island" lay between the Rhône and the Isère, moreover, and Hannibal here left the Rhône to march on up the Isère, as those who believe the "island" lay here generally think he did, Polybius has been needlessly obscure in saying (3.50.1) that he marched on from there "along the river", for this would naturally mean "along the Rhône". In any case, Hannibal would now presumably, have been marching up the wrong (i.e. the right) bank of the Isère, and would have had to cross that river at some point, unless he went over the Little St. Bernard pass - and we can be fairly sure that this was not the pass he eventually used (see below, p. 43). Finally, Polybius evidently believed that it was something like 2600 stades from the crossing of the Rhône to the plains of the Po by the route Hannibal used (3.39.9-10), and this means that he believed that it was 2600 stades, less the distance from the crossing to the "island", from the "island" to the plains. Unfortunately, as we have seen, we do not know how far it was from the crossing-place to the "island", but Polybius believed it took four days (3.49.5), and that should mean that it was something like 320 stades, judging by the march of 800 stades in ten days Hannibal marched along the next part of the route. In short, Polybius must have thought that it was something like 2280 stades (404.8 kilometres) from the "island" to the plains, and the confluence of the Rhône and Isère is too near Italy by any rational route - it is only some 305 kilometres from Susa, for example, via the Mt. Cenis.

The only piece of evidence that the "island" lay between the Rhône and the Isère is that in one passage (21.31.9) Livy implies that the inhabitants of the "island" were Allobroges, for the Allobroges certainly later lived mainly north of the Isère - their main town was Vienne. But Livy contradicts himself in a slightly earlier passage (21.31.5) where he says that the Allobroges lived "near the island", and in any case Polybius' account certainly makes clear that he believed that the Allobroges lived some way beyond the "island" along the line of march (3.49.5-13). In short, everything that Polybius says about the "island" virtually precludes the possibility that it lay between the Rhône and the Isère, whereas nothing that he says is against the hypothesis that it lay between the Rhône and the Aygues, except the comparison in size with the Nile delta.

When Hannibal reached the "island", probably at the end of September, he found two brothers disputing control of the area, and helped the elder - called "Braneus" by Livy (21.31.6) - to expel the younger. In return, the grateful chief not only replenished the Carthaginians' stores, and provided warm clothing and footwear for the coming march through the mountains, but undertook to protect the rear of the army during the next stage of its march (Polybius 3.49.8-13). We do not know how long the Carthaginians spent on the "island", but it was presumably several days.

So far our two principal authorities, Polybius and Livy, have been in substantial agreement, and we have been able to follow Hannibal with some confidence as far as the "island". But at this point their accounts diverge, or at least appear to do so. Polybius (3.50.1) says simply that after a ten days' march of 800 stades (142 kilometres) "along the river" from the "island", Hannibal "began the ascent towards the Alps." The natural interpretation of the phrase "along the river" is, as was argued above, "along the Rhône", but if Hannibal had really marched 142 kilometres up the Rhône from its confluence with the Aygues, he would have reached a point about halfway between Valence and Lyon, and it is difficult to see what Polybius could have meant by saying that it was there that he "began the ascent towards the Alps". Thus it looks as though Hannibal must have left the Rhône at some point during his 800-stade march, and it would make more sense of Polybius' statement that he marched "along the river", if he diverted off up one of the Rhône's tributaries. The obvious candidate is the Isère, which is the largest river flowing into the Rhône from the left, and joins it at an easy angle, and that this is where Hannibal turned off is confirmed by Livy (21.31.9).

Livy says that after leaving the "island", Hannibal "turned to the left into (the territory of) the Tricastini, then advanced along the farthest frontier of the land of the Vocontii into (the territory of) the Tricorii," and this seems to describe exactly a route from the district between the Rhône and the Aygues along the Rhône to the Isère, and then up the latter river. Unnecessary fuss has been made of Livy's statement that Hannibal "turned to the left": these words do not mean that he turned to the left off his previous line-of-march (from the crossing to the "island"), but must be taken with the words immediately preceding them - "although he was now making for the Alps." All Livy means is that although the direct approach to the Alps from the "island" would have been more or less due east, in fact Hannibal "turned left" (i.e. north) off this line. But it is the names of the three tribes which are interesting, for the Tricastini later certainly inhabited the area still called the Tricastin, along the left bank of the Rhône between Bollène and Montélimar, and the Vocontii appear to have occupied the hilly country east of the smaller tribes along the river, from the Mt. Ventoux- Montagne de Lure hills in the south, to the Isère in the north. [17] The Tricorii are more difficult to locate, but Strabo (4.184 & 203) seems to have thought they occupied the high country somewhere behind (i.e. to east of) the Vocontii. [18]

Livy's information about the three tribes may go back to his elder contemporary, the Greek historian Timagenes of Alexandria, who was also used by Strabo in his account of Gaul (cf.4.188), for Timagenes is quoted by Ammianus Marcellinus (15.10.11) as having said that Hannibal marched through the Tricastini and along the farthest frontier of the Vocontii to the passes (*saltus*) of the Tricorii. But wherever Livy found his information, he seems either to have misunderstood it, or to have combined it with information from another source in such a way as to produce nonsense, for, having given the information about the tribes - which, as we have seen, amplifies and clarifies Polybius' narrative in a perfectly intelligible way - he goes on to say that Hannibal's "path was nowhere impeded until he came to the river Druentia" (21.31.9). But if the Druentia is the river now called the Durance, as seems to be the case, [19] then Hannibal would have passed it soon after he crossed the Rhône, assuming that he crossed from Beaucaire to Tarascon, and if he crossed higher up than Avignon, he would never have passed the Durance at all.

A recent attempt has been made to make sense of Livy here by supposing that Hannibal left the Rhône at its confluence with the Drôme, then marched up the latter river and up over the Col de Grimone and so down to the middle reaches of the Durance near Gap. [20] But there are at least four serious objections to this theory: firstly, such a route would have taken Hannibal nowhere near the Allobroges, who lived between the Rhône and the Isère, [21] yet it was with the Allobroges, according to Polybius (3.50.2-3, 3.51.9), that he had his first serious fighting since he had crossed the Rhône. Secondly, if he had marched up the Drôme, he would not have been marching "along the farthest frontier of the Vocontii" as Timagenes of Alexandria and Livy said, but right through the middle of them. Thirdly, Polybius does say that after leaving the "island", he marched "along the river" for 800 stades, and although as we have seen, he must really have left the Rhône before the end of this march, it is one thing to suppose that he went off up the Isère - which Polybius indeed may have thought was the main stream of the Rhône - quite another to suppose that he went off up the Drôme. Fourthly, it is very difficult to reconcile Livy's description of the Durance where Hannibal crossed it (21.31. 10-12), with the middle reaches of the river: Livy's description fits much better the wide flood-plain through which the Durance flows into the Rhône, and where it can rise phenomenally after a sudden storm such as Livy implies (21.31.12: *tum forte imbribus auctus*), than it does the middle reaches where the river is likely to have been confined between banks. [22] Finally, even on this theory it has to be admitted that Livy has misplaced his account of the fight with the Allobroges, for he thought it took place after the crossing of the Durance, whereas on this theory it took place before Hannibal reached the Durance.

A far more plausible theory to account for the difficulty in Livy's narrative is that either he, or his source, misplaced an account of the crossing of the Durance, putting it in his narrative after the "island" episode, when it should have come before it, [23] immediately after the crossing of the Rhône: it is noticeable that when after the Durance episode, Livy turns to the actions of the Roman consul, he refers to Hannibal's departure from the bank of the Rhône (21.32.1), thus almost confirming that he has misplaced the Durance episode. But whatever one may feel the correct solution to the problems raised by Livy's narrative to be, it is perverse to build any hypothesis on this rather than on Polybius, and as has been pointed out, [24] Livy appears to return to following Polybius when he says (21.32.6) that "from the Durance" - (he should have said "from the 'island' ") - Hannibal came to the Alps with good relations with the Gauls who inhabit the area, along a route for the most part on the flat" (cf. Polybius 3.50.2).

According to Polybius, then, Hannibal marched on "along the river" from the "island" for 800 stades (142 kilometres), until he reached a point where he "began the ascent towards the Alps" (3.50.1), and we now have to try to determine where that point was. It has already been argued that he probably turned away from the Rhône up the Isère, and a march of 142 kilometres from the confluence of the Rhône and the Aygues would in that case have brought him to somewhere near St. Nazaire-en-Royans on Route Nationale 532 up the left bank of the Isère. Here the Isère begins to swing north in a great loop round to Grenoble, and although it might seem obvious that Hannibal would simply have continued to march along the river, in fact the route along its left bank would have become increasingly difficult, and eventually probably impassable, before the construction of the modern road. He would not have wanted to face the difficulties of ferrying his army across to the right bank of the Isère, especially as he already probably had reason to fear the Allobroges who lived across the river (cf. Polybius 3.50.2), and so the only alternative would have been to "begin the ascent towards the Alps," as Polybius says - that is to try to cut across the mountains, perhaps along the route now followed by Route Nationale 531 from St. Nazaire-en-Royans to Sassenage near Grenoble. [25]

Perhaps, then, it was in the magnificent rocky ravine of the Gorges de la Bourne, along this route, that the Carthaginian army encountered its first opposition since it had crossed the Rhône. The mountains through which the route runs, rise to over 2000 metres, and the modern road burrows through three tunnels and crosses two bridges before climbing to a height of over 1000 metres at Villard-de-Lans. It is wild country and possibly then a disputed area between the Allobroges and the Vocontii. [26] But it was the Allobroges who now occupied suitable positions commanding the route the Carthaginians were bound to take, their escort of friendly Gauls from the "island" having turned back as soon as they left the river (Polybius 3.50.2-3). But Hannibal was, as usual, equal to the situation: learning of the enemy's intentions, he camped near the pass, perhaps somewhere near Pont-en-Royans, and sent some of his Gallic guides forward to reconnoitre - presumably some of the men who had accompanied Magilos, since the Gauls from the "island" had now left (Polybius 3. 50.3-6). The scouts returned with the vital information that the enemy were occupying their positions during the day, but retiring to a nearby town at nightfall - it was not to be the last time that an enemy was to learn not to assume that Hannibal would not move at night. On this occasion he remained where he was for one night - his scouts could not have been certain that the enemy was gone until after nightfall - and then next day moved forward openly and camped again near the most difficult part of the route, not far from the enemy positions, as though he intended to try to force his way through next day (Polybius 3.50.7-8). The site of this second camp was perhaps a little way beyond the modern village of Choranche, and it is Polybius' detailed account of these preliminaries to the coming fight which shows that the point at which he says Hannibal "began the ascent towards the Alps" (30.50.1), was not the same as the point described earlier (3.39.9) - for the measurements of distance given there - as "the ascent of the Alps", for even after this second camp, the Carthaginians still had to make the ascent (cf.3.50.3). The measurements may have been made from the highest point of the ascent, at Villard-de-Lans, which is about 235 kilometres from Tarascon (cf. Polybius' 1400 stades - 248.6 kilometres - 3.39.9).

When night fell, Hannibal ordered camp-fires lit to give the impression that he was remaining where he was, and then personally led forward a flying column to occupy the enemy positions. Next day, when the Allobroges realised what had happened, they at first hesitated to attack, but the long line of pack-animals and horsemen slowly winding their way up the difficult track was too much of a temptation, and they began to harass the column, causing considerable losses particularly among the animals, for some of the horses panicked and tried either to push ahead or to turn back. Then Hannibal, realising that the losses among the animals were becoming serious, came charging down from the higher ground he had occupied, and drove off the Allobroges who were attacking the head of the column, with heavy losses, before rallying as many of his men as he could and hurrying on to seize the town from which the enemy had issued that morning, while the rest of the column slowly and laboriously made its way along the difficult part of the route (Polybius 3.50.9 - 3.51.10).

It has been suggested that this town was what was later called Cularo (cf. Cicero, *ad Familiares* 10.23.7), now Grenoble, [27] but this seems a little far away, if the battle with the Gauls took place in the Gorges de la Bourne. Perhaps, rather, the town was at the site of the present Villard-de-Lans which lies at the highest point of the route and is only some fifteen kilometres from the site suggested above for Hannibal's previous camp: it is now a health resort, beautifully situated amidst broad meadows - just the place for the Carthaginian army to have a rest (cf. Polybius 3.52.1). There is also the curious fact that although Polybius says that the Allobroges fled "to their own country" (εἰς τὴν οἰκείαν 3.51.9), the Carthaginians apparently found the town deserted (Polybius 3.51.11): this would be explained if the majority of those who had joined in the attack on them, had been Allobroges from across the Isère, who had now fled back "to their own country," while the town they had been using as their immediate base had belonged to other people who had been "tempted out by the prospect of booty," as Polybius says (3.51.11), and were now too terrified to return. But Cularo was certainly later a town of the Allobroges.

In the town, wherever it was, Hannibal found some of his pack-animals and horses and the men who had been captured with them, and also a good supply of corn and cattle, enough to feed his army for two or three days. Better still, his victory so terrified the people living along the next part of his route that they did not venture to attack him (Polybius 3.51.12-13). He rested his army in the town for a day, and then set off again, presumably rejoining the Isère somewhere near where Grenoble now lies, and then marching on up that river. If he had continued to follow it all the way up to Bourg-St. Maurice, he could then have crossed the main range of the Alps by the Little St. Bernard pass, and this was the pass that the historian Coelius Antipater said he used, according to Livy (21.38.6), assuming that Livy was right to identify Coelius' expression "the pass of Cremo" (*Cremonis iugum*) with a pass leading into the territory of the Salassi in the Val d'Aosta. [28] But Livy himself expressed amazement that anyone should have thought that Hannibal came down into Italy through the territory of the Salassi, "since," he says (ibid.), "all are agreed that he came down among the Taurini (i.e. near Turin)," and we can probably dismiss Coelius Antipater's view out of hand. Apart from anything else, the Little St. Bernard would not have given the Carthaginians the view over the plains Polybius says they had from the summit of their pass (3.54.2-3). Strabo, moreover, quotes Polybius as having said - presumably in a lost part of his work - that Hannibal's pass led into the territory of the Taurini (Strabo 4.208), and this is confirmed not only by Livy's remark that "all" (i.e. all the historians he knew about, except Coelius) were agreed that Hannibal came down among the Taurini, but also by the surviving passage of Polybius (3.60.8-9) in which he says that Hannibal's first action on reaching Italy was to attack the Taurini. It may, however, have been Hannibal's intention to follow the Isère up to Bourg-St. Maurice and then go over the Little St. Bernard, and it was possibly the treachery of the natives through whose country he was now marching which led him astray.

43

It was on the fourth day's march from the town he had captured, according to Polybius (3.52.2), that Hannibal "again encountered great dangers": he was met by a deputation from those who lived along the route carrying "branches and wreaths" (Polybius 3.52.3), and making every protestation of friendship. The word Polybius uses here for "branches" ($\theta\alpha\lambda\lambda o\iota$) was frequently used by the Greeks to mean "olive branches", and it has been argued that this means that Hannibal cannot have been as far north as the Isère.[29] But the original meaning of the word is, simply, "branches", and although Polybius naturally used it because of its associations with the traditional symbol of peace in Greece, the branches on this occasion could have been from some other tree - for example, the willow.

The Carthaginian general was extremely suspicious of the proferred friendship of these tribesmen, but after they had handed over hostages and provided him with plenty of cattle, he decided to trust them at least as far as to use them as guides over the next part of the route, and this was a mistake. Four days' march from Villard-de-Lans above Grenoble would have brought the army to somewhere near Tencin on the Route Nationale 525 running northeast from Grenoble, and it is possible that the treacherous guides persuaded Hannibal to turn off the Isère at Pontcharra, some fifteen kilometres beyond Tencin, and take the apparent short-cut up to La Rochette. The natural interpretation of Polybius' account (3.52.8) is that the Carthaginians advanced for a further two days before the treachery of the Gauls became apparent,[30] and it is thus possible that the ambush occurred in the gorge between Pontcharra and La Rochette.[31]

Fearing treachery, Hannibal had taken the precaution of sending his cavalry and pack-train on ahead, keeping his infantry in the rear, and it was these who bore the brunt of the attack, though the pack-animals and cavalry also suffered severely as they struggled through the gorge, with the enemy rolling boulders down on top of them or hurling stones. As night fell, Hannibal thus found himself cut off from his cavalry, and was compelled to spend the night with his infantry at a place Polybius (3.53.5) describes as "a strong position with white (or 'bare') rocks" ($\pi\epsilon\rho\iota$ $\tau\iota$ $\lambda\epsilon\upsilon\kappa\acute{o}\pi\epsilon\tau\rho o\nu$ $\acute{o}\chi\upsilon\rho\acute{o}\nu$), covering his cavalry and pack-train as all night long they struggled through the gorge. Attempts to identify the "white rocks" have not been very successful, but it is at least clear from Polybius' account that they should be looked for before the gorge and not after it.[32]

Hannibal presumably spent the night in some anxiety, expecting that the attacks would be resumed on the morrow, but when day dawned the enemy had gone. We must remember that the Gauls were primarily out for plunder (cf. Polybius 3.51.11), not to stop Hannibal's advance, and once they realised that plunder was only to be had at heavy cost, they were naturally inclined to let the Carthaginians go. Thus Hannibal was able to rejoin his cavalry and pack-train without further trouble and resume the advance (Polybius 3.53.6). From now on he only had to contend with isolated hit-and-run attacks, and he found that his faithful elephants were of the greatest service, because their strange appearance so terrified the natives that they would not attack any part of the column where the elephants were (Polybius 3.53.8). At last, "on the ninth day" (Polybius 3.53.9), he reached the pass and camped.

There is some doubt about what Polybius meant by "on the ninth day" here, but the natural interpretation of his words is that Hannibal reached the pass on the ninth day after the battle in the gorge, just as "on the fourth day" in an earlier passage (3.52.2) clearly meant on the fourth day after the day of rest in the captured town, and as "on the third day" in a later passage (3.56.1) means on the third day after leaving the place where a landslide had carried away the track, as Polybius there says (ἀπὸ τῶν προειρημένων κρημνῶ ν). In each case, the days are to be counted from the last event mentioned. It has been argued [33] that Polybius implies that Hannibal reached the pass on the day after the battle in the gorge, but all he says is that "on the day after . . . he advanced towards the highest pass of the Alps" (3.53.6), and his statement that Hannibal was attacked "piece-meal and in various places" (3.53.6), rather implies that the march from the gorge to the top of the pass took several days.

The final problem of geography is, then, to identify the pass Hannibal used, and since it is clear that this was already the subject of controversy in Livy's day, if not in Polybius', it might seem a hopeless task. But apart from the geographical indications we have been following so far, the evidence strongly suggests that the pass led down to the vicinity of Turin, and the problem is, perhaps, simpler than the disagreements among scholars suggest. There are three crucial factors involved: the first is that Hannibal marched a considerable distance up the Rhône, but cannot have followed that river all the way round to the Great St. Bernard, since that pass does not lead down to the vicinity of Turin, and, in any case, if Hannibal had gone that way, his route would have been far longer than the distance implied by Polybius (3.39.9-10) for the whole march from the crossing of the Rhône to the plains of the Po - 2600 stades or 461.6 kilometres: it is over 700 kilometres from Tarascon to Ivrea at the foot of the Val d'Aosta via the Rhône valley and the Great St. Bernard. Secondly, the first opposition encountered by the Carthaginians after crossing the Rhône, came from the Allobroges, and this suggests that they turned off the Rhône up the valley of the Isère. Thirdly, if they had followed the Isère to its headwaters, they would have come ultimately to the Little St. Bernard, and, as we have seen, only Coelius Antipater seems to have thought that this was the pass. Thus, they must have branched off the Isère too, and here the obvious alternative was the valley of the Arc.

The main pass out of the valley of the Arc is now the Col du Mont Cenis, and this is the pass which Napoleon thought Hannibal used. [34] But it is very doubtful whether he was right, since, firstly, there is no such view as Polybius describes (3.54.1-3), from the summit of the Col du Mont Cenis, and, secondly, it is almost certainly too low at 2083 metres. Polybius, after all, does describe the pass as "the highest of the Alps" (3.53.6), and everything he says about it, implies that it was a very high pass indeed. Thus, he makes the point (3.55.9) that there was no fodder for the animals, whereas they should have been able to find some on the Mont Cenis, and, more particularly, he states (3.55.1) that after the army had begun to descend the Italian side of the pass, it encountered hard-packed snow from the previous winter, lying under snow that had recently fallen. As it happens, Polybius was probably wrong to think that the hard-packed snow was from the previous winter, since, in a normal summer, the snow clears from all the slopes below about 3000 metres, but if the pass was high enough, snow would have tended to fall earlier that winter than on a comparatively low pass, and to have hardened instead of being melted away. Thus, the higher the pass, the easier it is to understand how the phenomenon described by Polybius occurred. There is, however, a high pass leading out of the valley of the Arc which seems to fulfil all the requirements - the Col de Clapier. This is 2482 metres high, has a wonderful view of the plains of Italy from a spur below the summit, and, for good measure, has a suitable camping-ground for an army just short of the summit. [35]

We can imagine Hannibal's army, then, having fought its way through the gorge between Pontcharra and La Rochette, coming down to what it may well have thought to be the Isère again, but was in fact the Arc, a few kilometres west of Aiguebelle, then marching up the valley of the Arc through the district now known as the Maurienne, on its left the Massif de la Vanoise, and on its right, now, the Hautes Alpes. Perhaps when he reached the site of the modern village of Bramans, past Modane, Hannibal was tempted by the valley of the little river Ambin, to cut the long march short at last, and so missed the relatively easy route over the Mont Cenis. The distance between the gorge above Pontcharra and the Col de Clapier is approximately 120 kilometres, and this is just about what the Carthaginian army could have accomplished in nine days' marching, at its average speed of fourteen kilometres a-day, allowing for a certain slowing up the higher it marched.

On reaching the summit, Hannibal camped there for two days - perhaps that day and the next (see below) - to rest his weary troops and let the stragglers catch up (Polybius 3.53.9) - they included horses and pack-animals which faithfully followed the tracks of the army until they came to the camp. Then, having encouraged his men by a sight of the plains of Italy far below, he started the descent. Unfortunately, Polybius' account of the timing of even these last few days presents difficulties. He seems to imply that it took eight days to reach the plains - one day to where a landslide had carried away the track, ending in a camp on a ridge (3.54.4-55.6), a second day on which the track was built up sufficiently for the pack-animals and horses to pass, ending in a camp in a spot where the snow had cleared (3.55.7), three more days for building up the track for the elephants (3.55.8), and a further three days to reach the plains (3.56.1). But to allow eight days for the descent causes problems on any interpretation of the fifteen days Polybius says Hannibal spent on "the crossing of the Alps" (3.56.3: see below), and a case can be made out for thinking that he really meant that the descent took six days. [36] Firstly, he seems to imply that work on building up the track for the elephants began on the same day that the pack-animals and horses got across and were let out to graze (3.55.7-8), and this could mean that this day is to be included in the three days he says it took to build up the track for the elephants (3.55.8). This, after all, makes sense, since the elephants would have used the same basic track as the pack-animals and horses had used. Secondly, although he says that after collecting his whole force together, "Hannibal descended and on the third day . . . reached the plains" (3.56.1), he could well have been counting the day on which the whole force was reunited as the first of the three days. In this way, we would arrive at a total of six days for the descent.

*Pl. III:*    *The Gorges de la Bourne — the possible site of Hannibal's ambush by the Allobroges.*

*Pl. IV:*   *The Col de Clapier in Sept.* (top) *the flat area just below the lake and pass.* (bottom) *looking towards Italy — the pass is on the left & the panorama rock centre right. The lake is now dammed.*

It is, in any case, clear that Hannibal's difficulties were by no means over when he started to descend. Nearly all these Alpine passes are more precipitous on the Italian side, and this is particularly true of the high passes like the Col de Clapier. Polybius says (3.54.5ff.) that the track down was very narrow and steep, and that because of the snow men and beasts often could not tell where it was: if they stepped off the track, they were liable to go crashing down the mountain. At one point, landslides had carried the track away altogether, and after trying to make a detour and finding it impossible because the hard-packed old snow, covered in soft, powdery, new snow, was too slippery to provide a foothold, Hannibal had to call a halt and build the track up again: the Numidians were set to work, but it took a day to build one wide enough for the pack-animals, and perhaps two further days to get the elephants across (Polybius 3.55.7-8). It was here, too, according to Livy (21.36-7), that a rock had to be blasted out of the way by first heating it, and then pouring vinegar onto it - a story that has been quite unnecessarily doubted. [37] But at last it was done, and after perhaps two further days, the army reached the plains. It had marched 1500 kilometres since leaving Cartagena, and had been five months on the march (Polybius 3.56.3).

One final problem remains - Polybius' statement that "the crossing of the Alps" had taken fifteen days (3.56.3). Here the natural meaning is that the whole route from the point at which Hannibal was said to have "begun the ascent towards the Alps" (3.50.1), to the plains of Italy had taken fifteen days, and this is the way it has been taken. [38] It goes without saying that if this is what Polybius meant, then the whole of the reconstruction of this part of the route attempted above must be wrong. But Polybius cannot really have meant any such thing, firstly because it involves still further juggling with his statements about time, [39] but secondly because it just does not make sense: Polybius evidently believed that the distance involved on this part of the route was something like 1200 stades (213 kilometres: cf.3.39.10), [40] but although 1200 stades in 15 days implies an average of 80 stades a day, which is the same as for the ten days march "along the river" (3.50.1), this must be mere coincidence, for Polybius knew full well that one of the fifteen days was spent resting at the captured town (3.52.1), one or two at the summit of the pass (3.53.9), and three or four on building up the track on the way down (3.55.7-8). In short, if Polybius did intend "the crossing of the Alps" on which he says Hannibal spent fifteen days, to refer to the whole march of 1200 stades, he would be implying that the Carthaginian army maintained a much higher average rate of marching over this, the most arduous part of the route, than it had done "along the river" - at least 120 stades (21.3 kilometres) a day as compared to 80 stades a day - despite fighting two major engagements and several minor skirmishes on the way.

A much better way to interpret the fifteen days spent on "the crossing of the Alps" is to take the latter phrase to refer only to the final pass, and the fifteen days to be the nine of the approach march added to the six of the descent. This would still mean that Polybius has omitted the day or days spent at the summit of the pass, but in all probability the first of these days is the "ninth" day on which the army reached the pass (3.53.9) - Hannibal would surely not have wanted to spend long at a height of over 2400 metres - and in any case this solution involves far less juggling with his times and distances than any other. It may be objected that when Polybius describes the approach

47

of the army to the "ascent towards the Alps", he uses the same phrase - "the crossing of the Alps" (ἡ τῶν Ἀλπεων ὑπερβολή: 3.49.13) as he does for the fifteen-day march, and that in summarising the whole march from Cartagena (3.56.3), he would not have picked out just the final pass for special comment. But his use of phrases like "the crossing of the Alps" is equivocal throughout this part of his account, [41] and he may have been deliberately trying to emphasise that even after the two battles against the Allobroges and in the gorge, the Carthaginians still had immense difficulties to overcome - hence his use of the phrase "the highest pass of the Alps" (αἱ ὑπερβολαί αἱ ἀνωτάτω τῶν Ἀλπεων: 3.53.6), and the two and a half chapters (3.53.6-3.56.3) he devotes to this final section of the march. If these views are accepted, it would mean that the Carthaginians took not fifteen days to march the 1200 stades from "the ascent of the Alps" to Italy, but something like twenty-four, [42] and this makes far more sense.

Hannibal probably reached Italy during the first fortnight in November, as we saw (above, p. 33). He now had 12,000 African and 8000 Spanish foot-soldiers left, and 6000 cavalry, according to Polybius (3.56.4, referring to the Lacinian inscription),[43] and if his figures for the size of the army when it left the Rhône, 38,000 infantry and 8000 cavalry (3.60.5), are correct, Hannibal had lost, as he says (ibid.), nearly half his force. Even if the figures he gives for the army when it crossed the Pyrenees and left the Rhône are exaggerated (see above, p. 34), an army of 26,000 men seems pitifully small to challenge the might of Rome, and inevitably one wonders whether it had all been worth it. To such doubts, however, Hannibal himself gave the answer at the Trebbia, Lake Trasimene and at Cannae: his army, with the Gallic help on which he had planned, was sufficient to achieve the task not only of defeating anything the Romans threw against him, but of causing widespread revolt against Roman rule in Italy: if he lost in the end, this was not because he had brought too small a force down from the Alps, but because the task was hopeless from the start. As it was, he succeeded in throwing the Roman war-plans completely awry and in wresting the initiative from the enemy. They were not really to recover it for seven long years, and it was to be fourteen before they finally invaded Africa as they had been planning to do in 218. This is the measure of Hannibal's achievement in crossing the Alps, which still remains one of the greatest feats in the history of warfare.

# CHAPTER THREE – BLITZKRIEG

By about mid-November, at the latest, Hannibal had brought his battered army safely down into the plains of northern Italy. After briefly resting and refreshing his men, he turned immediately to making his presence felt among the Celtic tribes of the area: learning that the Taurini who lived "at the foot of the mountains", as Polybius says (3.60.8), had quarrelled with the Insubres, he first made overtures to them, but when these were rejected, attacked their chief town - probably on the site of Turin - and reduced it in three days, massacring its inhabitants. By this calculated act of terror, he soon won the submission of the neighbouring tribes, and thus rapidly lessened the chances of his being attacked while his forces were still weak through lack of allies. He thus held on to the strategic initiative which his bold march had won for him.

For this the Romans had only themselves to blame: they had done nothing to help Saguntum, despite the length of the siege, and had even been slow to respond to news of its fall, for it was certainly not until mid-March, and probably not until May, that the embassy was sent to Carthage bearing the final ultimatum, since Hannibal had only just learnt its result before he set out for Italy, probably in June (Polybius 3.34.7). It has even been suggested[1] that the embassy was not sent until after the news had reached Rome that Hannibal had crossed the Ebro, but this cannot be true: the only evidence for it occurs in a highly rhetorical passage of Livy (21.16), which he himself contradicts later on (21.20.9) when he says that there was a "fairly consistent rumour" that the Carthaginians had crossed the Ebro, when the embassy returned to Rome. Polybius confirms this later statement (3.40.2), and although in his discussion of the Carthaginian response to the ultimatum, he mentions the Ebro treaty (3.21, 29-30), in the first passage he specifically says that the Carthaginians did not mention the Ebro treaty, and in the second again specifically says that he is not giving the Roman reply at the time, but what was said "on many occasions and by many people among them" (3.29.1) - in other words, presumably, what they said to him in justification for their declaration of war. In any case, Polybius' main narrative makes it quite clear that Hannibal knew about the Carthaginian response to the ultimatum before he left Cartagena (3.34.7).

The only difficulty is the statements of Polybius (3.40.2) and Livy (21.20.9), referred to above, that the news that Hannibal had crossed the Ebro reached Rome about the time of the return of the embassy from Carthage, for the embassy should have returned about the time Hannibal heard the news of the Carthaginian response to it, and he cannot have crossed the Ebro until at least a month later (see Appendix III). There are two possible explanations: either this was another false rumour, like the one which possibly lies behind Livy's statement (cf.21.16) that the Romans thought Hannibal had crossed the Ebro before they sent the embassy, or the embassy's return was delayed and it did not in fact get back to Rome before mid-July or later. Livy does provide some evidence that it did not return directly to Rome: he says that it went to Spain and southern France, on its way back, to try to win the tribes over to the Roman side, and although this story has been doubted, it is not inconceivable in itself, and it is consistent with the tradition that the embassy's return to Rome coincided with the news that Hannibal had crossed the Ebro.[2]

But even if the embassy did not go to Carthage until May, and did not return until July, this does not mean, as some have argued,[3] that the Romans cannot have begun their preparations for war until then. At the very least, the envoys would surely have reported the failure of their mission directly to Rome, before they set out on their tour of northeastern Spain and southern France, and in any case the Romans could have begun to make some precautionary preparations against the possibility that their ultimatum would be rejected. Livy, indeed, believed (cf.21.17.1-4) that Spain and Africa had been nominated as the consular provinces before the new consuls took office on March 15th, 218, and that then it was merely a question of their drawing lots, Spain falling to Scipio, Africa (with Sicily) to Sempronius Longus; he even believed (above, p. 27) that the declaration of war had been passed by the *comitia centuriata,* presumably in a conditional form, before the final embassy was sent. Of course, the consuls could hardly have set out for their provinces before the news arrived of the failure of the final embassy, although there was nothing to prevent Sempronius Longus going to western Sicily, and with the benefit of seapower, Rome could have struck almost immediately at Spain and Africa. Roman lethargy here contrasts strongly with the speed with which Hannibal got on the move as soon as he had heard that war had been declared.

Roman preparations, whenever they were finally made, were based on the assumption that the war would be fought in Spain and in Africa. Livy, indeed, consistently with his belief that the consuls had drawn lots for their provinces before the final embassy was despatched, also appears to have believed that forces were assigned at the same time (21.17.5-9), and even when the news that Hannibal had crossed the Ebro reached Rome, probably in the second half of July, the Romans seem to have had no inkling of his plan, for Sempronius Longus certainly departed for Sicily, and Scipio, although he landed at the eastern mouth of the Rhône, seems only to have done so on the spur of the moment, when he heard that Hannibal was crossing the Pyrenees (Polybius 3.41.6) - even then,[4] after missing Hannibal at the Rhône-crossing, he sent his army on to Spain (see below). If our time-table for Hannibal's march is anything like correct, Scipio only arrived off the mouth of the Rhône about mid-September at the earliest (see Appendix III), and his lateness requires some explanation. Probably it was due to a re-assignment of Roman forces made necessary by trouble in Cisalpine Gaul. According to Livy (21.17.3ff.), it had been decided to raise six legions of Roman troops at the beginning of the consular year, with as many allied troops as the consuls saw fit, and to commission as strong a fleet as possible. The forces were then distributed as follows: to Sempronius Longus were assigned two legions of 4000 infantry and 300 cavalry each, 16,000 allied infantry, 1800 allied cavalry, and 160 quinqueremes; to Scipio went two legions with their normal cavalry contingents, but only 14,000 allied infantry, 1600 allied cavalry, and 60 quinqueremes; finally, to the *praetor peregrinus,* L. Manlius Vulso, who was to command in the Po valley, were assigned the same number of Roman troops, and 10,000 allied infantry

with 1000 allied cavalry. Polybius, however, seems to have thought that Manlius originally had only one legion of Roman troops, and that this was the Fourth legion (3.40.14),
which would normally have been under the command of one of the consuls; subsequently
he says that both Scipio's legions were sent to Cisalpine Gaul as reinforcements, and that
Scipio was ordered to levy two more, whereas Livy thought (cf. 21.26.2), that only one
of Scipio's legions was sent. Both authors are clearly somewhat muddled, since both
believed that eventually there were only four Roman legions in the north, after the
arrival of Sempronius with his two from Sicily. One possible explanation is that originally
only four legions were raised, but that when Manlius was ordered to Cisalpine Gaul, he
was given one of Scipio's legions, and subsequently the second was sent too, compelling
Scipio to raise two fresh legions as Polybius thought.[5]

At all events, it is clear that the Roman preparations were thrown awry by trouble
in the Po valley involving the Boii and the Insubres. It is possible that it had something
to do with the activities of Hannibal's agents in the first half of the year (see above,
p.31), but the immediate cause was a Roman attempt to hurry along with the foundation
of the new Latin colonies at Placentia and Cremona. The Gauls rapidly overran the
territory assigned to the new colonists, and forced them to flee to Mutina (Modena),
which Polybius also calls a colony (3.40.8), though in fact it did not become one until
183 (Livy 39.55.7-8). Manlius, who had reached Ariminum (Rimini), came hurrying up
to the rescue, and despite losing a number of men in two ambushes on the road, pressed
on to relieve Mutina. But when he continued his march towards Placentia and Cremona,
he was forced to stop at a place Livy calls Tannetum (21.25.13), probably somewhere
near Parma, and there to stand on the defensive. The news of this débâcle forced the
Senate to reappraise the situation, and it was decided to send either both Scipio's legions
to Gaul, under the *praetor urbanus,* C. Atilius Serranus, as Polybius says (3.40.14), or
one of his legions, as Livy says (21.26.2). (See Map 4).

The operations in Cisalpine Gaul and the Roman attempts to deal with the situation must have occupied at least a month, and probably another month elapsed before
Scipio was able to raise fresh troops to replace the ones sent to the north. This is probably
why he did not reach the Rhône until after Hannibal had crossed the Pyrenees and was
already marching for the Rhône. Hannibal, moreover, reached the Rhône far sooner than
Scipio had expected, and although he disembarked his troops and marched rapidly up
river to dispute the crossing, he arrived three days after the Carthaginians had gone
(Polybius 3.41.4-9, 3.49.1-3) - the only fighting, as we have seen (above, p. 37), was
between scouting parties of cavalry from both armies. But Scipio must now have realised
Hannibal's objective, and had to decide whether to return to Italy, or to continue on to
Spain. The decision he took was to have crucial consequences for the war as a whole: it
would have been natural to have decided to hurry back to the defence of the homeland,
but instead he decided to send his elder brother. Cn. Cornelius Scipio (consul in 222/1)
on to Spain, with most of his army, and only himself to return to Italy, with presumably
a small escort, to take command of the Roman forces in northern Italy (Polybius 3.49.4).

Neither Polybius nor Livy elaborates on the reasons for Scipio's decision, beyond
Livy's saying that he thought that Spain should not be denied Roman aid, and that his

intention was that his brother should "not only protect old allies and win over new ones, but should also drive Hasdrubal from Spain" (21.32.4). Of course, Scipio had been allotted Spain as his *provincia,* as Livy says (21.32.3), and his decision to send most of his army to Spain may have been no more than playing safe by adhering to the strategy laid down by the Senate. But his own return to Italy shows that he was not merely acting in accordance with the Senate's wishes. He surely must have at least considered taking his army back to Italy with him, and that he did not do so is the first example of the grasp of essential long-term strategy which was to be the hall-mark of Roman conduct of the war. By sending his army to Spain, Scipio ensured at least that the Carthaginians would not have a free hand there, and opened up the possibility that some part of their war-effort would have to be concentrated away from the main struggle - in 215, for example, considerable reinforcements under Hannibal's younger brother, Mago, which had been destined for Italy, were to be diverted to Spain instead (Livy 23.32.5-12). At the same time, the presence of Roman forces in Spain would at least make it less easy for reinforcements to be sent to Hannibal by the route he himself had followed, though there is no reason to doubt that this had been the intention. Thus, in 216, for example, Hannibal's other brother, Hasdrubal, was sent orders from Carthage to march on Italy (Livy 23.27.9), and it was only his defeat at the mouth of the Ebro late in 216, or early in 215, which prevented him from doing so (see below, p. 128). As far as we know, no reinforcements ever did reach Hannibal from Spain, and this was probably mainly due to Scipio's decision to send his army there in 218, and the Senate's later decision to support him and his brother. Scipio's decision, finally, illustrates the flexibility in strategy which Roman seapower and her resources made possible: it is significant that the first serious engagement of the war in Spain was a battle at sea off the mouth of the Ebro in 217, in which the Romans were successful (Polybius 3.95-96.6); thereafter Rome's control of the coastal waters off eastern Spain and southern France was never challenged.

But for the time being, Spain was a side-issue, and Scipio clearly recognized that the main threat was Hannibal's coming descent on northern Italy. According to Polybius (3.49.4), Scipio's intention was to meet Hannibal at the pass over the Alps, but in the event, after returning to Pisa (Polybius 3.56.5),[6] marching rapidly through Etruria and taking over the forces under the praetors then engaged with the Boii, he did not move up into the area where Hannibal was likely to descend: to have done so would have been to put himself and his army in hostile territory, cut off from regions solidly under Roman control, and might have led to an even worse disaster than the Trebbia. Thus it was that Hannibal was able to descend unmolested into the territory of the Taurini and to storm their chief town, winning over many of the Gauls in the immediate vicinity, as a result.

Meanwhile, Scipio crossed the Po, probably by the raft-bridge Livy mentions later (21.47.2), near Placentia, and advancing westwards, had also bridged the Ticinus (Ticino), his presence immediately having a deterrent effect on the local tribes (cf. Polybius 3.60. 11-12). Hannibal, who was just as surprised by Scipio's sudden appearance on the scene, according to Polybius (3.61.1-6), as Scipio was by his, determined to bring on a battle as soon as possible, and thus both armies approached each other along the Po, the

Carthaginians having it on their right, the Romans on their left. Somewhere to the west of the Ticinus, the first engagement of the war in Italy took place: Polybius does not say exactly where, but Livy (21.45.3) says it was near Victumulae. This place is, however, usually located at Biella, which is too far to the west and north; either then, this location of Victumulae is wrong, and it lay somewhere to the west of Pavia, or Livy has got the name wrong. The battle was probably fought somewhere near Lomello, halfway between Pavia and Casale Montferrato.[7]

The battle of the Ticinus, as it is usually called, was really no more than a cavalry skirmish, only the Romans having any infantry present, and this only consisting of skirmishers. But the result immediately illustrated one advantage which Hannibal was to enjoy until the situation was reversed on the field of Zama, superiority in cavalry. Scipio placed the cavalry supplied by his Gallic allies in the van with his skirmishers, his Roman and Italian cavalry in the rear, Hannibal his heavier cavalry in the centre, his Numidians on either wing (Polybius 3.65.5-6). But the onset was so sudden that the Roman infantry skirmishers had no time to throw their spears, before Hannibal's force was upon them, and had to retire behind their own cavalry. Despite this, the Roman cavalry held its own for some time, until the Numidians, sweeping round on either flank, annihilated the skirmishers and charged into its rear, whereupon it broke and fled (Polybius 3.65.7-11). Scipio himself was wounded in the fight (Livy 21.46.7; cf. Polybius 3.66.2), and according to one tradition (Polybius 10.3.3-7; Livy 21.46.7-8), his life was saved by his son, later to become Hannibal's conqueror at Zama.[8]

Although the engagement near the Ticinus was only a skirmish, it illustrated Hannibal's favourite tactic of pinning the enemy's centre and attacking his flanks and rear, and also gave the Romans due warning that his superiority in cavalry could be very dangerous in the right conditions. For the moment, however, the remnants of Scipio's cavalry and infantry skirmishers retired on their main body, taking their wounded commander with them, and the whole army fell back on the Ticinus. There it crossed by the bridge it had already constructed, and leaving 600 men to destroy the bridge, presumably with orders to retreat as soon as the job was done, continued its withdrawal to Placentia, where it crossed by the raft-bridge already mentioned, and encamped on the southern bank (Polybius 3.66.1, cf. Livy 21.47.2).

Hannibal had at first anticipated a full-scale battle, but when he saw that the Romans had moved out of their camp west of the Ticinus, he pursued them rapidly as far as the river, taking prisoner the 600 men who had been left to destroy the bridge, although he found the bridge itself largely destroyed (Polybius 3.66.3-4). Then, when he learned from his prisoners that the main Roman army was now well ahead, he swung round and marched eastwards up the Po for two days until he reached a convenient place to bridge it. Here he constructed a bridge of river boats, and leaving an officer named Hasdrubal to see to bringing the main body across, himself crossed immediately to meet the Gallic envoys from the surrounding area, his success having persuaded the Gauls to throw in their lot with him. When he had reached agreement with them, and been rejoined by his main forces, he began the march down the right bank of the Po to meet Scipio (Polybius 3.66.5-8).

Both Polybius and Livy are in substantial agreement about these operations, although Livy (21.47.3) says that Hannibal captured the 600 at the Po.[9] But although both authors imply that Scipio's camp was near Placentia (Polybius 3.66.9, Livy 21.47.3 & 7), it seems likely that it was really some distance to the west, for when Hannibal's army appeared and after offering battle camped about nine kilometres away, Scipio is said to have withdrawn across the river Trebbia, which flows into the Po from the south a short distance west of Placentia (Polybius 3.67.9 and 68.4), and this makes no sense unless the original Roman camp had been west of the Trebbia: since Hannibal was advancing from the west, if Scipio had originally been encamped east of the Trebbia, and had crossed it on Hannibal's approach, he would have put himself on the same side of the river as his enemy, and would have placed the river between himself and his colleague, Sempronius Longus, whose arrival he was anxiously expecting.[10] (See Map 5).

The immediate cause of Scipio's withdrawal was the desertion of some of his Celtic allies, amounting in all to about 2000 infantry and a few less than 200 cavalry, who burst out of his camp one night after attacking the Romans bivouacked near them (Polybius 3.67.1-3). Thinking that this would be the signal for most of the surrounding Gauls openly to espouse the Carthaginian cause, he decided to withdraw eastwards across the Trebbia, and also southwards towards the foothills of the Apennines where he hoped to find a position where he could wait in safety for his colleague's arrival (Polybius 3.67.8-9). As it was, he only just got away in time, for Hannibal immediately sent his Numidian cavalry in pursuit, and had the Numidians not stopped to plunder the deserted Roman camp, they were bound to have caught up with the retreating Romans, encumbered as they were with their baggage; even then those in the rear of the Roman column suffered some casualties in killed and captured (Polybius 3.68.1-4). But the main body of the Roman army got safely away to the foothills across the Trebbia, where it proceeded to fortify its usual camp, possibly near Pieve-Dugliara, about eighteen kilometres south-west of Piacenza on the road that leads to Genoa, while Hannibal, following closely, took up a position about seven kilometres away, possibly near the site of the modern village of Sarturano.[11] He had already been encouraged by the desertion of Scipio's Celtic allies, and by the accession of the Boii (Polybius 3.67.4-7), and now he found the Gauls living around his camp-site ready and willing to keep him supplied and to take part in his operations (Polybius 3.68.8).

Meanwhile, the Senate had ordered the other consul, Ti. Sempronius Longus, to abandon his projected plans for the invasion of Africa, and to return to defend Italy. Both Polybius (3.61.7-9) and Livy (21.51.5) seem to have thought that this only happened after Hannibal had reached Italy, but if that had been the case, there would not have been time for Sempronius to reach the Trebbia in time for a battle fought probably about December 22nd or 23rd (cf. Polybius 3.72.3), and in reality he was probably recalled as soon as Scipio returned to Pisa with the news that Hannibal was on his way, about mid-October. Polybius and Livy differ as to how Sempronius then proceeded: Polybius (3.61.10) says that he collected the crews of his ships and ordered them to return to Italy, while from the soldiers of his army he exacted an oath that they would all be at Ariminum by a certain day at bed-time; later Polybius says (3.69.9-14) that the consul and his army passed through Rome on its way to Ariminum shortly after the news of the Ticinus had reached the city, and that the march to Ariminum took forty days. Livy (21.51.6-7) says that Sempronius sent his army to Ariminum by sea, after assigning 25 quinqueremes to protect the Italian coast around Vibo, and after making up the fleet of the praetorian governor of western Sicily to 50 quinqueremes, taking 10 quinqueremes with him to Ariminum. Here Polybius is probably to be preferred: if the consul had received his orders sometime in the last fortnight of October, it would have been very late in the year for him to have risked either his army or himself on the dangerous sea-passage up the Adriatic, and Polybius' story, improbable as it may seem at first sight, is circumstantial. As has recently been pointed out, [12] the oath, the statement that the soldiers "gathered" at Ariminum and that they "travelled on foot" to the rendez-vous, combine to suggest that Sempronius did not lead his army in regular formation, constructing a marching-camp each night, but sent them off on their honour to be at Ariminum on a certain day. Thus the problems of feeding and lodging so large a body of men would have been reduced. But even then the time Polybius gives for a march of something like 1300 kilometres seems very short, and it may be that he was mistaken in thinking that the march from Lilybaeum (Marsala), on the western tip of Sicily, took forty days, and should have said that it was from Rhegium (Reggio Calabria), for example, on the Italian side of the straits of Messina. But however it was done, Sempronius' army probably reached Ariminum early in December, and would have joined Scipio on the Trebbia about mid-December or a little later.

Thus the events of this momentous year drew to their climax. Scipio was still nursing his wound, but Sempronius' arrival injected fresh vigour into the Roman army as well as doubling its strength. At about the time of his arrival, Polybius says (3.69.1), the town of Clastidium (Casteggio), forty-eight kilometres west of Placentia, was betrayed to Hannibal by the commander of its garrison, a Latin from Brundisium - Livy (21.48.9) calls him Dasius - together with all its stores, and this enabled the Carthaginian general to fire the first shots in his propaganda war by treating the prisoners well - presumably they were Latins like Dasius - and by honouring their commander. But Carthage's new allies between the Trebbia and the Po seemed to be having dealings with the enemy, and when Hannibal despatched a force of 2000 infantry and 1000 cavalry to raid their territory, Sempronius responded by sending out his own cavalry, supported by some infantry skirmishers. The result was a scrambling fight ranging backwards and forwards between the two camps, in which the Romans had rather the better of it (Polybius 3.69.5-11), since Hannibal refused to be drawn into a pitched battle not of his own choosing, an attitude which Polybius commends (3.69.13). But Sempronius was elated by what he interpreted as a success, particularly as it had been achieved by the cavalry, the arm in which the Romans were supposed to be weakest. He was also anxious to achieve a victory while his colleague was still incapacitated, and before new consuls took office in about three months time, and thus everything conspired to make him determined to fight a full-scale action, though Scipio, if we are to believe Polybius (3.70.3ff.), advised him to wait.

Hannibal, too, was anxious to fight before his fickle Gallic allies began to lose their enthusiasm, and while the Roman troops were still comparatively inexperienced (Polybius 3.70.9ff.), so he now set out deliberately to lure Sempronius into a trap. He had noticed a flat and treeless area between the two camps, traversed by a water-course with steep banks overgrown with brambles, and here he decided to lay an ambush: as Polybius percipiently remarks (3.71.2-4), the Romans might have been wary of an ambush in wooded country for it was in that sort of terrain that the Gauls habitually lurked, but they were not at all suspicious of an apparently flat and featureless plain. Here he ordered his younger brother, Mago, to conceal himself during the night, with 1000 picked infantry and as many cavalry. It is not possible to determine exactly where the battle was fought, but the area is just as Polybius described it, to this day - a dull, flat plain, seamed with water-courses, and it is not difficult to imagine how Mago and his men escaped detection. Then, when day dawned, Hannibal mustered his Numidian horsemen and sent them across the river to the Roman camp, with orders to try to provoke the enemy to battle. Meanwhile, he ordered the rest of the army to eat a hearty breakfast, to see to their equipment and to rub themselves down with olive oil around the camp fires (Polybius 3.71.10-11).

The time of year was about that of the winter solstice, according to Polybius (3.72.3), that is to say about December 22nd or 23rd by our calendar (and the Roman calendar seems to have been about in step with our own, at this time), and it was a cold and snowy day. But, if we are to believe our sources, the sight of the Numidians riding right up to his camp was too much for Sempronius, and he ordered first his cavalry, then 6000 skirmishers, and finally his whole army out, most of them without any breakfast (Polybius 3.72.1-3). Nor was he content merely to drive the Numidians off, for the whole Roman army proceeded to cross the Trebbia, swollen breast high, and began to form for battle on the left bank.

Polybius says the Roman army contained 16,000 Roman and 20,000 allied foot, and 4000 cavalry (3.72.11-13); Livy (21.55.4) says the Roman infantry numbered 18,000, which is probably a slip, describes the 20,000 allied foot-soldiers as Latins, and adds a contingent from the Cenomani, the only Gallic tribe in northern Italy to remain loyal - he omits any mention of the Roman cavalry. Sempronius, who was in sole command owing to Scipio's wound, drew his infantry up in the usual three lines (Polybius 3.72.11), presumably each legion with its attached allied cohorts alongside it, and with the cavalry on either flank. Hannibal deployed his army in a similar fashion, about 1400 metres in front of his camp (Polybius 3.72.8), his 20,000 infantry of the line, Spaniards, Celts and Africans, in a single line, with the Celts in the centre, and his 10,000 cavalry equally divided on each flank. Both armies, as usual, had a skirmishing screen in front, 8000 spearmen and slingers on the Carthaginian side, presumably about 4000 *velites,* and an additional 2000 men drawn either from the allies, or from the Cenomani, making up the 6000 skirmishers (cf. Polybius 3.72.2) on the Roman side. If the figures given for Hannibal's army are correct, and if Mago's 2000 men are to be added to the total, the Carthaginian army had been swelled by over 14,000 Celts - 9000 infantry, and 5000 cavalry   - for it had entered Italy with only 20,000 infantry and 6000 cavalry (Polybius 3.56.4). Finally, Hannibal also divided his elephants, and probably stationed them in front of the two wings of his infantry line - this seems to be what Polybius meant (3.72.9) - not, as Livy thought (21.55.2), outside his cavalry, nor, as Appian thought (*Hannibalic War* 7), in front of his cavalry. If this interpretation of

Polybius' statement is right, Hannibal probably intended the elephants to act both as a deterrent to any move the more numerous Roman infantry might make towards out-flanking his own infantry line, and also for use against the flanks of the Roman infantry if opportunity arose. [13]

The battle opened with the usual exchanges between the skirmishers of both sides, the Romans apparently armed mainly with throwing-spears, the Carthaginians possibly armed with stabbing-spears (see above, pp. 14-5), and aided by slingers from the Balearic Islands. In these exchanges, the Carthaginians came off best since they were more highly trained (cf. Polybius 3.73.2), and the Roman skirmishers had in any case already been engaged with Hannibal's Numidian cavalry - presumably these had been recalled to take their place on one or other flank of Hannibal's line, before the battle began. Thus, when the skirmishers fell back through the gaps between the companies of line-infantry, the Carthaginians were ready to take advantage of the swift success of their numerically superior cavalry, which advanced and drove the Roman cavalry from the field, thus exposing the flanks of their infantry. At once the Carthaginian skirmishers, who had apparently reformed behind their own infantry of the line, sallied out and fell upon the flanks of the Roman infantry, accompanied by what Polybius calls "the mass ($\pi\lambda\tilde{\eta}\theta o\varsigma$) of the Numidians" (3.73.7). This presumably refers to the Numidian cavalry, and suggests that on being recalled, they had taken station on either flank behind the heavier cavalry of the Celts and Spaniards, and had not been involved in the charge of the latter two bodies.

Meanwhile the infantry lines had closed, and when they were locked in furious combat, Mago, timing his attack to a nicety, charged into the rear of the Roman lines, throwing their whole army into confusion (Polybius 3.74.1). The flanks of the Roman infantry, assailed in front by the elephants, and in flank by the Carthaginian skirmishers and the Numidians, began to crumble: attacks on the flanks can only be met by the flank units facing outwards, and this the inexperienced Roman soldiers were incapable of doing in the heat of battle. Inevitably they broke, and fled towards the river in their rear (Polybius 3.74.2). In the centre, however, it was a different story, and Hannibal here learned for the first time just how formidable Roman infantry could be in head-on attack: 10,000 of them, their flanks disintegrating and with Mago in their rear, broke through the Celts in the centre of Hannibal's infantry line, and part of the Africans. But realising that since their flanks had fled, they could be of no help to them, and despairing of being able to withdraw to their camp, with both Hannibal's cavalry and the swollen river in their way, they retired in good order to Placentia, presumably wheeling round behind the position Hannibal's left wing had occupied at the outset of the battle (Polybius 3.74.3-6). Of the remainder of the Roman army, the majority were killed along the river by Hannibal's elephants and cavalry, but the few infantry who got away, and most of the cavalry, also made their way to Placentia, where they were joined by Scipio and the force which had remained behind with him to guard the camp (Polybius 3.74.7-8; cf. Livy 21.56.8-9). [14] Hannibal's losses were mainly among his Celtic infantry which had borne the brunt of the Roman thrust in the centre, but, sadly, accord-ing to Polybius (3.74.11), all but one of his remaining elephants, and many men and horses, perished from the rain and snow which followed the battle - Livy (21.56.6) says that "nearly all" the elephants died now, and seven more later in the winter (21.58.11), leaving only one alive.

The battle of the Trebbia illustrates many facets of Hannibal's military genius - his psychological insight into the minds of his opponents, his care for his own men, his willingness to try the unexpected, and his ability to use each element in his forces to the best advantage. It is also interesting as the only major battle, apart from Zama, in which he used elephants: in Polybius' account they play a fairly important part in routing the wings of the Roman infantry, and in the pursuit of the fugitives; in Livy's they help to terrify the Roman cavalry-horses which were unaccustomed to their sight and smell (21.55.7), but his remark that they were "on the wings", apparently beyond the cavalry (cf. 21.55.2), conflicts with the most probable explanation of Polybius' statement about their position, and the rest of his account of their activities is hopelessly confused.

Sempronius, for his part, is largely held responsible for the defeat by Polybius and Livy, but we must remember that Polybius was later the protégé of the family to which Sempronius' colleague belonged, and his views may well have been coloured by the Scipionic family tradition. On the face of it, nothing can excuse Sempronius' folly in leading his men into battle across a freezing river, without apparently taking any thought for their well-being. But despite Polybius' apparent approval of Scipio's alleged advice not to fight (cf.3.70.3-5), it is arguable that Sempronius was right not to wait: it is true that his men were inexperienced, but to spend the next few months in winter-quarters would hardly improve the situation, and there was much to be said for attempting to crush Hannibal before his strength grew with fresh accessions from the Celtic population of the region. Sempronius must have known that his army probably outnumbered the enemy in infantry - 36,000 to 29,000 if Polybius' figures are anything like right - and there was some truth in the reported Roman belief (cf. Polybius 3.68.9) that their infantry had not yet been tested. In the ultimate resort, then, Sempronius' mistake may not so much have been in fighting a battle at all, but in fighting it the way he did.

When news of the battle reached Rome, the Senate took energetic measures to protect Sardinia and Sicily, and Tarentum and other places in Italy - all likely targets for the Carthaginian fleet, which had already been raiding Sicily and southern Italy (cf. Livy 21.49-51.5) - and the consuls-designate who were to take office on March 15th, 217, Cn. Servilius Geminus and C. Flaminius, began to raise levies (see below) and to establish supply-depots at Ariminum and in Etruria. Help was also obtained from King Hiero of Syracuse in the form of 500 Cretan archers and 1000 light infantry (Polybius 3.75), though Livy seems to have thought that they did not arrive until early in 216 (22.37.8). Although Polybius does not say so, it appears from Livy (21.57.3-4) that Sempronius had himself audaciously made his way to Rome to preside at the elections, before returning to Placentia.

In the sources, one of the consuls-designate, C. Flaminius, appears as something of a popular demagogue, and it is often said that his election represented a criticism by "the People" of the Senate's conduct of the war. [15] It is not clear, however, what is meant by "the People". in this context: Flaminius, like all consuls in normal circum-

58

stances, would have been elected by the *comitia centuriata,* presided over, in this case, as we know from Livy, by Sempronius Longus, and we have already seen (above, p. 3) that the structure of this assembly gave most weight to the votes of the wealthier section of the community, and that in general the nature of Roman politics, with its emphasis on personal ties and the patron-client relationship, made it virtually impossible for any-one who was really opposed by the overwhelming majority of the *nobiles,* as Flaminius is alleged to have been, ever to succeed in being elected. We must assume, therefore, despite the tradition that portrays him as a lonely figure at odds with his fellow Senators, that he had the backing of powerful elements in the Senate, backing which they were, perhaps, later glad to deny after his defeat and death at Lake Trasimene.

Attempts to link him with one or other of the powerful *gentes* are not conclusive,[16] but his colleague in his previous consulship in 223, P. Furius Philus, had associations with the Aemilii, and he was censor in 220 with an Aemilius, L. Aemilius Papus. If the Aemilii were among his supporters, we can probably assume that so too were the Cornelii, and if that is the case, his election to a second consulship for 217/6, far from represent-ing any desire for change in the conduct of the war, will rather have been a case of the mixture as before, particularly since his patrician colleague, Cn. Servilius Geminus, probably also had the support of the Aemilian and Cornelian groups. But it may well be true that the conduct of the war hitherto had come under criticism, and, if so, Flaminius may have seemed to many to be just the sort of man to restore the situation, since he had had previous military experience. Moreover, if the Cornelii and their friends thought that their enemies among the nobility were sufficiently strong to secure the consulship for one of their own men, Flaminius' popularity with certain sections of the community at large might have appeared a useful asset: as tribune of the plebs in 232, for example, he had carried a measure providing for the distribution of land in the vicinity of Ariminum to individual Roman citizens and as censor in 220 he had been responsible for building the *via Flaminia* from Rome to Ariminum and the Circus Flaminius in the city. As consul, moreover, in 223, he had campaigned against the Insubres and had won a victory over them for which he allegedly celebrated a triumph by popular vote, against the wishes of the Senatorial majority. Thus, as usual, it makes more sense to see in Flaminius' election to his second consulship not a triumph for "the People", but rather the triumph of a senatorial group perhaps using popular support to tilt the balance in its favour, and some parts of the criticism levelled against him in antiquity - for example that he ignored omens and chose to enter upon his consulship at Ariminum rather than in Rome, as was usual - may suggest that here was a man who wanted to get on with the job, rather than the irresponsible demagogue of tradition.

Polybius tells us little about events during the winter months after the battle of the Trebbia, except to record Hannibal's release of his non-Roman prisoners with the declaration we have already noted - that he had not come to Italy to make war on them, but on the Romans (3.77.3-7) - and his use of different wigs and other forms of disguise to guard against assassination (3.78.1-4). Livy, however, records two Carthaginian attacks on Roman supply-depots near Placentia, the first of which they failed to take, Hannibal himself being wounded in the process, and then gives an account of what purports to be a first attempt by the Carthaginian army to cross the Apennines "at the first doubtful signs of spring" (21.58.2). This, he claims, was foiled by the atrocious weather, and was followed by a drawn engagement fought with Sempronius near Placentia. In view of Polybius' silence, it is difficult to believe all this, and in the case of the alleged first attempt to cross the Apennines, in particular, it seems probable that Livy has been misled by two differing accounts of the real crossing into thinking that Hannibal tried to cross the mountains twice. Polybius (3.78.6) dates his departure from winter quarters, somewhat vaguely, to "when the weather began to change", which suggests April. But he would probably not have tried to cross the Apennines before the snow had cleared from the passes, and before there was sufficient forage for his cavalry, and this means May. Moreover, a date in early May fits in well with Ovid's date for the battle of Lake Trasimene, June 21st (*Fasti* 6.767-8).[17]

When he eventually moved, Hannibal, broadly speaking, had three choices open to him: he could strike more or less directly south by one of the routes leading into Liguria; he could march southeastwards down the Po to the vicinity of Bologna, and then southwards by one of the routes leading into Etruria; or, finally, he could march on down towards Rimini, and then follow the coastal route. There was no point, however, in the first alternative, and much danger to be feared in the wild Ligurian hills, and the tradition recorded by Livy (21.59.10) of a move into Liguria during the winter, countered by a move by Sempronius to Luca, can probably be ignored.[18] But his attitude to the other alternatives must have been partly conditioned by his long-term strategic plans. His object was not to destroy Rome, but to force her to negotiate on his terms by defeating her armies and breaking up her confederacy in Italy, and to do this he had to strike at peninsular Italy - even his presence in the Po valley was not enough, however many victories he might win there. Potentially, perhaps, the most likely source of support was the south,[19] and this had the advantage of being nearer Carthage itself, by sea. But to march to the south would entail cutting communications with the Po valley and with Spain. To march into Etruria, on the other hand, would leave communications with the Celts of the Po valley, and with Spain, open, and Hannibal may have hoped for support from the Etruscans, who had had friendly relations with Carthage in the past, and whose relations with Rome were not of the best - as recently as 241 Falerii had been at war with Rome, and its citizens had been compelled to abandon their hilltop town (now Civita Castellana) and move down to the site in the plain where the church of Santa Maria di Falleri now stands (Livy *Periocha* Book 20, Zonaras 8.18). There is also some reason to think that a *rendez-vous* had been arranged with the Carthaginian fleet on the coast of Etruria, for in 217 a Carthaginian squadron touched at Pisa, its commander believing that he would meet Hannibal there (Polybius 3.96.9). Finally, to attempt to invade peninsular Italy by the east coast route was virtually bound to lead to a collision with the Roman army in terrain which left little room for manoeuvre, as Hannibal's brother, Hasdrubal, was to find to his cost ten years later, whereas it would be much easier to by-pass or outmanoeuvre any army sent to Etruria, and from there the east coast could still be reached behind Ariminum.

Some such considerations as these may have influenced Hannibal to decide to invade Etruria. He probably used the route now followed by *Strada Statale* 64 from

Bologna to Pistoia via the Porretta pass, [20] and he seems to have had no difficulties until he reached an area of marsh caused by the flooding of the river Arno (Livy 22.2.2), probably between Pistoia and Faesulae (Fiesole). He had taken the precaution of placing his most reliable infantry - the Africans and Spaniards - in the van, with the Celts in the centre of the column, and the cavalry, under his brother, Mago, bringing up the rear, and, as a result, the Spaniards and Africans got through without too much difficulty, but the Celts, though prevented from deserting as he had feared, suffered severely (Polybius 3.78. 6ff., Livy 22.2.1ff.). Most of the pack-animals also perished, although Polybius says (3.79.10) that they rendered one last service to their masters by providing them with somewhere firm to snatch a little sleep, since their bodies were not completely submerged. Many of the horses, too, lost their hooves, and Hannibal himself, riding on the last remaining elephant, was stricken with ophthalmia and lost an eye as a result. [21] The march through the marshes took four days and three nights, if we are to believe Polybius (3.79.8), but eventually the army struggled through, and rested near Faesulae, while Hannibal gathered intelligence about the enemy.

The Romans had taken the obvious precautions to cover the alternatives open to the invader, although it is not possible to disentangle with any certainty the conflicting traditions about the numbers of troops they raised, or what they did with the veterans of Scipio's and Sempronius' army, who had spent the winter in Placentia and Cremona. [22] Probably, however, the veterans were eventually withdrawn to Ariminum and there divided between the new consuls, Flaminius taking Sempronius' old soldiers, as Livy says (21.63.1), and Servilius Scipio's (Appian, *Hannibalic War,* 8). The new consuls' armies would also have been made up with new recruits to the normal strength of two legions each, and this may be why Polybius (3.75.5) talks about Flaminius and Servilius levying troops, and why Livy says (21.63.15) that Flaminius had four legions at Lake Trasimene: he knew of a tradition that Flaminius had taken over Sempronius' old troops, and of another that he had raised new troops, and conflated the two, giving Flaminius twice as many men as he really had, for, according to the figures he himself gives, on the authority of the contemporary historian, Fabius Pictor, for the losses at Trasimene, and for those who survived, Flaminius then had only some 25,000 men (cf.22.7.2-4), and it would be difficult to fit many more into the terrain at Trasimene. It has also been argued that Servilius had more than two legions, on the basis of Polybius' statement (3.86.3) that he had no fewer than 4000 cavalry, but this does not necessarily follow, and it is best to assume that he, too, like Flaminius had a normal consular army of two legions, with additional allied troops.

But the troops commanded by Flaminius and Servilius were not the only forces put into the field by Rome this year. There were already two legions, with the usual allied contingents, serving in Spain under Cn. Cornelius Scipio, elder brother of the outgoing consul of 218/17, and Polybius says legions were despatched to Sicily and Sardinia after the Trebbia (3.75.4) - on the basis of Livy's evidence for their numbers in future years, we may assume that two were sent to Sicily and one to Sardinia; the garrison Polybius also says was sent to Tarentum (ibid.) was probably not of legionary strength. Finally, it has been suggested that the practice of raising two "city legions" (*legiones urbanae*) each year, to act as a garrison for the city of Rome, began this year, [23] and

61

this, if true, means that there were eleven legions in the field early in the year, five more than in 218 - a striking demonstration of Rome's immense manpower reserves.

According to Livy (21.63.1), Flaminius had written to Sempronius before he took over as consul, ordering him to bring his legions to Ariminum by March 15th (217), and himself went there to take command on the first day of his consulship, much to Livy's indignation, and, if we are to believe him, to that of Flaminius' contemporaries. But Flaminius ignored all protests, took over Sempronius' army, and led it into Etruria, where he took up a position at Arretium (Arezzo). Meanwhile, his colleague, Servilius, dutifully performed all that was expected of a new consul in Rome (Livy 22.1.4ff.), and then made his way to Ariminum, where he probably took over Scipio's army, and added to it his new recruits.

It thus fell to Flaminius to try to stop Hannibal, and he made a sorry mess of it, if we are to believe our sources, though they are so hostile to him that it is impossible to be certain how far he should really be held to blame. According to Polybius (3.80), Hannibal knew what sort of a man he faced, and deliberately set out to provoke him: leaving his position near Faesulae, he marched past Flaminius at Arretium,[24] laying waste the beautiful Tuscan countryside, until he came to Lake Trasimene, on the road from Arretium to Perusia (Perugia). Here he proceeded to lay an ambush on a vast scale, but unfortunately it is still not possible to say exactly where. In recent years, Italian scholars have argued that the lake has receded since Roman times, and that in 217 the shore was further north than it is now: they have connected some cremation graves found near the modern village of Sanguineto with the battle, drawing attention also to the name of the village, and have concluded that the battle was fought in the square-shaped valley south of Sanguineto, and west of the village of Tuoro.[25] But it is not by any means certain that their conclusions about the north shore of the lake are relevant, or even sound, and the cremation graves may have nothing to do with the battle at all.

It is possible to reconcile Polybius' and Livy's description of the terrain with the valley south of Sanguineto, but not their accounts of Hannibal's dispositions and of the beginning of the battle. Polybius (3.83.1) says that "on the route there was a flat-bottomed valley, this having along its long sides high and continuous hills, and on its short sides, in front a barren, steep crest, and in the rear the lake, leaving a very narrow way through to the valley along the lower slopes," and to fit this, we could take the "barren, steep crest" to be the hill above Sanguineto, rising to Monte Castelnuovo (595 metres), and the "high and continuous hills" to be the ridges running down to Pieve Confini on the west and to Tuoro on the east. Livy's description is much vaguer, but could also be a description of the same valley - he says it was where "Trasimene comes closest to the mountains of Cortona - there is only a very narrow way in between; then the plain broadens out a little, and on the far side the hills again rise" (22.4.2). Livy probably did think that the battle was fought here, since he says (22.4.4) that it was when he had "passed the narrows, after the column began to spread out into the wider plain" that Flaminius first saw the enemy. But his account seems to be muddled, since he says that Flaminius only saw the enemy forces opposite him (*in adverso*), and this should mean on the hills in front of his line of march, i.e., on the hypothesis we are considering,

*Pl. V:*  *Lake Trasimene:* (top) *From above Toricella; the flat area in the foreground may be Polybius' "valley" where the main part of Flaminius' army was slaughtered, its tail stretching round the lake shore to the right.* (bottom) *From near Piere Confini; Livy possibly places the battle here.*

*Pl. VI:* (top) *Callicula — the saddle towards which Hannibal drove the cattle in his breakout from Campania in 217. Pietravairano is to the left. (bottom) Monte Tifata above ancient Capua, Hannibal's winter quarters.*

near Tuoro, but he then goes on to say (22.4.7) that the Roman column was attacked "on the flanks" before line-of-battle could be formed, although if he was marching towards Tuoro, his right flank must have been protected by the lake: to be attacked "on the flanks" (in the plural), Flaminius would have had to wheel his army left towards Sanguineto, but Livy says nothing of this, and implies that the army was continuing along the same line of march when attacked, by saying that "battle commenced in front and on the flanks, before the line (*acies*) could be adequately formed." [26] Polybius' description of the beginning of the battle is also impossible to reconcile with the valley near Sanguineto, for he says (3.84.1) that it was when most of the column had entered the valley, and the leading units of the enemy were already in contact with him, that Hannibal gave the signal to attack, and this could only mean, if the valley was the one south of Sanguineto, that it was when the head of the Roman column had almost reached Tuoro that it was attacked. But then what becomes of his description of Hannibal's dispositions, which imply that Hannibal with the Africans and Spaniards were on the crest in front of Flaminius' line-of-march, the Baliaric slingers and the spearmen to its right, and the Celts and cavalry to its left and all the way round to the narrow entrance to the valley (3.83.2-4)? Once again this implies that Hannibal with the Africans and Spaniards were on the hill above Sanguineto, on the present hypothesis, the Baliares and spearmen on the hills running south to Tuoro, and the Celts and cavalry on the opposite side of the valley, and Flaminius would have had to have wheeled the column to the left, after entering the valley, and to have been advancing towards Sanguineto for the attack to have begun in the way Polybius describes. If Hannibal and the Africans and Spaniards had been near Tuoro, the Baliares and spearmen would have had to be in the lake to fit Polybius' description. (See Map 6).

The only part of the lake shore which fits both Polybius' description of the terrain, and his account of the Carthaginian dispositions at the outset of the battle, is east of Passignano, where there is only a narrow passage between the hills and the shore of the lake, until, near Torricella, the hills recede a little to leave an area of flat land, surrounded on three sides by hills and on the fourth by the lake itself. The only passage in Polybius' description which does not fit, is his use of the word "αὐλών" (valley or defile) to describe the area of flat land, and his statement that it had "high and continuous hills on its long sides," for it is more square than oblong. But there is not much doubt that this is where Polybius thought the battle was fought, and it is best to follow him.

If, then, we adopt this location for the battle, Hannibal marched past the sites of Passignano and Torricella, and then swung away from the lake up the little valley towards Magione. When he reached the crest of the hill, he camped there with his Spanish and African infantry (Polybius 3.83.2). Polybius' account of the dispositions of the rest of the army (3.83.3-4) is obviously from the point of view of someone facing along the Carthaginian line of march, and Hannibal probably detailed off some of the contingents to occupy their positions as they went along. Thus, the Celts and the cavalry occupied all the hills to the left, stretching back towards the entrance to the narrow passage along the lake shore, west of Passignano, with the cavalry probably near the passage itself, while he brought his slingers and spearmen round to the front, and then placed them under the crest of the slopes to the right of the valley.

Flaminius, meanwhile, had probably learned that the Carthaginian army had last been seen disappearing down the road which led along the north shore of the lake, and decided to follow it. He probably camped for the night between the slopes of Monte Gualandro and the Sanguineto stream, and early next morning led his army on past Passignano, his men strung out in a long line, so that when the head of the column was climbing the slopes towards Hannibal's Africans and Spaniards, its tail would still have been somewhere near Passignano. The morning was misty (Polybius 3.84.1), as often happens at the beginning of summer - the date was about June 21st, as we have seen - and this helped to conceal the Carthaginian army: Hannibal was able to wait until the head of the enemy column was in contact with his African and Spanish infantry, before he gave the signal (Polybius 3.84.1), passing the word along to the troops concealed to his left and right.

Of the sites of Hannibal's three great victories, Lake Trasimene is the most reward-ing to visit, wherever precisely one envisages the battle to have been fought. The beauty of the scenery helps to conjure up a picture of what it must have been like as the doomed Roman army marched along the reed-fringed shore of the lake in the early light of that misty morning, past Passignano, where the hills crowd down to the water, and on into the little valley at Torricella. Here, perhaps, the van caught sight of the outposts of Hannibal's main body of infantry, and pressed on up the slope, possibly thinking that it had only to deal with a rearguard, or even that it might surprise the Carthaginian camp, while behind, the rest of the army could still see nothing for the mist rising from the lake and clinging to the slopes of the hills. Then, out of the mist, came the shouts of Hanni-bal's men as they picked up the word to attack, and in a moment the men themselves, leaping down the hillsides, the Balearic slingers and spearmen to the right, the wild Celts to the left and all along the hills to where the distant sounds of battle told where the Carthaginian cavalry was closing the escape route back beyond Passignano.

It must have been a moment of shattering dismay for Flaminius, and even the well-disciplined Roman troops, many of them veterans of the Trebbia, could not organize themselves in time to put up an effective resistance, their officers not really understand-ing what was happening. Even so, 6000 of those in the valley, brushing aside those immediately opposed to them - possibly the skirmishers to the right, possibly the Celts to the left, for Polybius says they lost most heavily (3.85.5) - but unable to see clearly where they could be of most assistance, made their way to the crest of the hills. Looking back, as the mist cleared, they could see the extent of the disaster, but were now too far away to do anything about it - later on they were to be rounded up by a force of Spanish infantry and skirmishers under Maharbal. Behind them, in the valley, their comrades, "unable," as Polybius says, "either to yield to circumstances or to do anything, but as a result of their training thinking the most important thing not to run away or to leave their ranks," stood and fought it out for three long hours (Livy 22.6.1), most of them probably being killed. Here, too, probably, Flaminius himself was slain, by "certain Celts", according to Polybius (3.84.6), by an Insubrian horseman called Ducarius, according to Livy (22.6.1-4), who recognized the Roman general as the man responsible for the earlier defeat of his people.

Along the lake shore the Roman troops had even less chance: some of them tried to swim for it and were drowned, weighed down by the armour they had no time to discard; others waded out into the lake until only their heads remained above the surface, raising their hands in token of surrender, but were cut down by the Carthaginian cavalry, plunging their horses into the water. Polybius (3.84.7) says that 15,000 Roman soldiers were killed in the valley, but this was probably the total of all who were killed, as Livy says, following Fabius Pictor (22.7.1), and Polybius' total of 15,000 prisoners (3.85.2) is probably also too high - Livy says that 10,000 escaped (22.7.2), but since he says nothing about prisoners, this figure probably included all who survived, and probably most of them were taken prisoner, though no doubt some escaped. Hannibal's losses were about 1500 in all, according to Polybius (3.85.5), most of them Celts; Livy (22.7.3) says 2500 were killed in the battle, and many more died later of their wounds. But whichever was true, it was a small price to pay - in military terms - for the destruction of a Roman army.

We shall never know what possessed Flaminius to walk into the trap, and his failure to reconnoitre properly seems inexcusable. But the Roman army was weak in cavalry, and Hannibal's cavalry may have been able to screen his movements. In any case, Flaminius can perhaps hardly be blamed for walking into such a trap: who would have imagined that an army which must have been well over 60,000 strong - it was still 50,000 strong at Cannae over a year later (Polybius 3.114.5) - could be concealed even in a place "naturally created for ambushes," to use Livy's famous phrase (22.4.2)? It is, indeed, difficult to think of a parallel for an ambush on a scale like that of Trasimene, and once in the trap, of course, Flaminius' army was outnumbered by more than two to one, if he only had some 25,000 men. But even if Flaminius was outwitted tactically, his strategy may not have been as silly as it seems. Polybius twice hints that his colleague Servilius was marching to join him, presumably once it was certain which route Hannibal had taken: he says that, before the battle, Flaminius' officers urged him to wait for his colleague (3.81.4), and after his account of it, he says that Servilius had indeed marched to join him, as soon as he heard Hannibal was in Etruria (3.86.1-3), and that he had sent his cavalry on ahead. This cavalry force, under C. Centenius, was annihilated by a Carthaginian detachment under Maharbal, shortly after the battle, and since the news of this fresh disaster reached Rome three days after the news of Trasimene (Polybius 3.86.3), we may conclude that Centenius' cavalry was only about three days away at the time of the battle, and since it was probably defeated at the so-called "Umbrian lake" (*lacus Umber*), near Assisi,[27] it is possible that Servilius was marching down the *via Flaminia*. Thus Flaminius may have thought that it was Hannibal who was marching into a trap, and that if he pursued him, he might be able to catch him between his own army and that of Servilius, somewhere in the Tiber valley beyond Perusia, just as eight years before, the Gauls at Telamon had been caught between the army of L. Aemilius Papus (Flaminius' colleague in the censorship of 220) and that of his colleague, C. Atilius Regulus, returning providentially from Sardinia by way of Pisa.

After his victory, Hannibal assembled his prisoners, and once again released those of them who were not Roman citizens, with the declaration that he had no quarrel with them (Polybius 3.85.1-4). Then, when he learned of the approach of Servilius' cavalry, he sent Maharbal off to deal with it, giving him his highly trained spearmen and some of the cavalry,and soon had the additional satisfaction of hearing that the enemy force had been destroyed. According to Polybius (3.86.5), Maharbal and his men killed about half their opponents at the first attack, then pursued the rest to a hill where they surrendered next day. The rout of his cavalry will, no doubt, have checked Servilius' advance - he is next heard of fighting the Gauls (Livy 22.9.6) - and so no immediate enemy confronted the victorious Carthaginians as Hannibal pondered his next move.

Perhaps his intention had always been to march to the south, and he had taken the route through Etruria to avoid confrontation with a Roman army near Ariminum, in terrain where there would have been less possibility of manoeuvre; perhaps his decision to turn and fight Flaminius had been reached on the spur of the moment, when he realised the opportunity for an ambush which the route round Lake Trasimene offered. Alternatively, he may have originally planned to make Etruria his base for further operations, and have only decided to make for the south as a result of the ease of his victory: Livy says later (22.13.2) that among his prisoners had been three Campanian knights who had been seduced by his promises and gifts into trying to win over their fellow-countrymen to his cause, and it is possible that also among his prisoners had been some Cretan archers who could have told him something about the anti-Roman attitude of the son of King Hiero of Syracuse, who had sent them to serve the Romans (cf. Livy 23.30.11). Livy certainly mentions these Cretans later (24.30.13) as having fought at Trasimene and been captured by Hannibal there, although he never mentions them in his account of Trasimene itself, and in one passage (22.37.8) implies that they did not reach Rome until 216 - Polybius, however, could be taken to imply that they were despatched a year earlier (3.75.7). Thus, some of his prisoners may have convinced Hannibal that his best chance of winning allies lay after all in the south.

Whatever his reasons, Hannibal did decide to march to the south. Polybius (3.86.9) says laconically that having marched through Umbria and Picenum, he reached the Adriatic on the tenth day - that is, presumably, on the tenth day after he left the battle-field, which would have been some three or four days after the battle on June 21st. He would, thus, have reached the Adriatic during the first week of July. Livy, however, has a different story: according to him (22.9.1-3), Hannibal marched through Umbria to Spoletium (Spoleto), and only after failing to take it, swung aside to Picenum and the Adriatic coast. Although there is no direct conflict with Polybius here, a march from Lake Trasimene to the Adriatic via Spoletium is well nigh impossible to reconcile with Polybius' statement that Hannibal reached the sea on the tenth day, and Livy's account should probably be rejected: possibly some Carthaginian raiders ranged as far as Spoletium and were beaten off, and Roman tradition magnified the incident to suggest that Hannibal had been marching on Rome, and had only been deterred by the valiant resistance of this one town. But even if the story were true, it would not necessarily mean that Hannibal had intended to march on Rome, for Spoletium was a Latin colony, and he may have wished to do no more than test the reactions of a Latin state to his repeated release of Latin prisoners, some of whom may well have come from Spoletium. Thus, it would not have been so much that he could not take the place that deterred him, as that it resisted at all. At all events, sooner or later he did reach the Adriatic, and there he was able to give his men a much-needed holiday, building up their strength - they were suffering from scurvy - with good food and the olive-oil they needed to keep their bodies in good condition, and bathing the cavalry horses in old wine to get rid of mange (Polybius 3.87.1-3). He also rearmed his African infantry with captured Roman equipment, and took the opportunity of sending the news of his victories to Carthage by sea, having presumably commandeered a ship in one of the ports on the Adriatic coast. By annihilating one consular army, and cutting across Italy behind the other, he had broken free of the containing enemy forces and could now virtually march where he willed.

At Rome, meanwhile, the news of the defeat at Lake Trasimene had been received with consternation, despite the studied calm of the praetor's announcement that "we have been defeated in a great battle" (Livy 22.7.8), and when, three days later, the news came of the defeat of Servilius' cavalry, even the Senate's confidence was shaken. Recourse was had to the archaic device of appointing a *dictator* with overriding powers, to co-ordinate operations against the enemy, but there was a constitutional difficulty in that a dictator had to be nominated by a consul on Roman soil (cf. Livy 22.8.5ff., and 27.5.15), and now one consul was dead, and the other apparently cut off from Rome by Hannibal's march to the Adriatic. So, according to Livy, for the first time in Roman history, appointment to the dictatorship was left to popular election, and the choice fell on Q. Fabius Maximus, the consul of 233/2 and 228/7. But despite Livy's later assertion (22.31.8-11) that he was only elected "acting dictator" (*pro dictatore*), inscriptions prove that he was a full dictator. [28] Nevertheless, if Livy is right, Fabius was not allowed to nominate his own *magister equitum* ("Master of Horse"), to act as his lieutenant, and this office was also filled by election on this occasion, the choice falling on M. Minucius Rufus, consul of 221/0.

Behind these constitutional oddities we can possibly detect a political wrangle between powerful *nobiles*, for as Livy notes (22.8.5, cf. 22.31.9), the right to nominate a dictator properly belonged to the surviving consul, and although he says that it was impossible to contact him, one wonders whether this was true: if Sempronius Longus could get away after the Trebbia to preside over the elections at Rome, surely some way could have been found to enable Servilius to perform his constitutional duties, since he did not have to come to Rome to nominate a dictator (cf. Livy 25.2.3, 27.33.6, 29.10.1-2). It is possible, then, that Fabius himself engineered the election, assuming that if the choice fell to Servilius, he would not be nominated. But this left him open to the constitutional argument that since he had been elected, his Master of Horse should be too, and thus he found himself saddled with a political opponent as his lieutenant. In Polybius and Livy Minucius Rufus is portrayed as another "popular hero", and some modern scholars have seen in his appointment another assertion of the "popular will".[29] But, as we have seen, the Roman political system in practice left little if any scope for any such assertion of the popular will, and it is much more likely that Minucius owed his election to the continuing influence of the Scipios and their friends - it is significant that his colleague in his previous consulship had been a Cornelius Scipio.

Minucius' subsequent opposition to Fabius' strategy of refusing to engage Hannibal in pitched battle, the strategy which was to earn him the nickname "Cunctator" (the Delayer), is put down in the sources to Minucius' personality, but it is, perhaps, more likely that behind the constitutional wrangling which led to his appointment, we should see a deep-seated conflict between those who, like Fabius, thought that Hannibal could be gradually worn down by dogging his footsteps without risking any full-scale engagement, and those who, like Minucius, thought that he could still be overwhelmed on the field of battle. This conflict was to be fatally resolved by the election of C. Terentius Varro and L. Aemilius Paullus, certainly a political ally of the Scipios, to the consulship of 216/5, and the determination to fight Hannibal again which led to the field of Cannae.

But for the moment Fabius had his way, and there is no doubt that in the circumstances he was right: as Polybius sagely remarks (3.89.8-9), in refusing to be drawn into pitched battles, Fabius was falling back on the factors in which Rome had the advantage - inexhaustible supplies of provisions and men. Orders were immediately given for the raising of two new legions, to replace those lost at Trasimene, and Minucius was perhaps commanded to assemble the *legiones urbanae* at Tibur (Tivoli) on a given day; [30] inhabitants of unfortified towns were commanded to move to places of safety, and all those who lived in areas likely to be traversed by Hannibal, were ordered to leave, having first destroyed all buildings and supplies (Livy 22.11.1ff.) This "scorched earth" policy was, however, probably never fully implemented, for Livy himself remarks on the immense booty seized by Hannibal this same summer in the *ager Falernus,* which was Roman territory (cf. 22.13.9-10 and 22.16.7-8). But the tradition also recorded by Livy (22.32.3, 22.40.7-9), that Hannibal suffered from severe shortages of supplies at the end of 217 and the beginning of 216, if true, perhaps indicates that Fabius' edict was not without effect.

After issuing his orders, Fabius himself set off up the Tiber valley to meet Servilius and his army, now marching down the *via Flaminia* towards Rome. The meeting took place at Ocriculum according to Livy (22.11.5) - Polybius (3.88.8) says Narnia, which is a few kilometres further north - and the Roman author also notes Fabius' strict attention to constitutional niceties in ordering the consul to present himself without his lictors in deference to the dictator's superior *imperium.* Servilius was sent posthaste to Rome to man all available warships and deal with a Carthaginian fleet which had captured some merchant vessels carrying supplies, off Cosa - it was this fleet which had been hoping to meet Hannibal at Pisa. Fabius himself took over command of Servilius' army, and after marching through the Sabine country to Tibur, led the combined armies of himself and Minucius via Praeneste and side-roads to the *via Latina* (Livy 22.12.1-2), and then on to Arpi in Apulia - Polybius (3.88.9) says Aecae (Troia) - where intelligence reports must have indicated Hannibal to be. After restoring the health of his army in Picenum, Hannibal had marched down the coastal plain to Apulia, devastating the countryside as he went (Polybius 3.88.3). Livy (22.9.5) says that he also ravaged the territory of the Marsi and Paeligni, but it seems unlikely that his troops really ventured so far into the hills. (See Map 7).

When he learned of Fabius' approach, Hannibal immediately led his forces out in an attempt to provoke a battle, but Fabius refused to be drawn, and there then began a game of cat-and-mouse, with Fabius always marching parallel to the Carthaginian army, occupying advantageous positions, and while not allowing his men to straggle far from camp, continually harassing the Carthaginian foraging parties. Such warfare was not at all to Hannibal's liking, and it was typical of his generalship that he should break away and thus try to change the situation. Marching up into the Samnite hills, he descended upon the territory of Beneventum (Benevento), and seized an unwalled town Polybius calls "Venusia" (3.90.8), and Livy (22.13.1) "Telesia". Since no unwalled town called Venusia is known in Samnium - it was clearly not the Latin colony of that name (now Venosa) - it is tempting to think that Livy was right, but Telesia (Telese) was a mountain town, difficult to attack, and it is possible that Livy or his source simply guessed that this was the place, because he could not identify a Venusia in Samnium. [31]

From Telesia, if that was the town he had taken, Hannibal came sweeping down on the *ager Falernus,* Roman territory north of the Volturnus (Volturno), and the source of the famous wine which was later to gladden Horace's heart. Polybius (3.90.11) says that his object was either to bring the Roman army to battle, or to show everyone that he was in complete control and that the Romans were abandoning the open country to him - Campania was to be like a theatre to demonstrate the enemy's timidity (3.91.10). Livy (22.13.2-3) says that the three Campanian knights taken prisoner at Trasimene had given him reason to believe that Capua might come over to him. Unfortunately, it is not certain by which route the Carthaginian army entered Campania: Polybius (3.92.2) says that it marched through the pass by the hill called "Eribianos", and camped along the Volturnus; Livy (22.13.5ff.) has a splendid story that Hannibal told his guide to lead him to "Casinum" (now Cassino), but because his pronunciation of Latin was so bad, the guide thought he had said "Casilinum", and led him down "through the territory of Allifae, Calatia and Cales, to the plain of Stella." However, there is something wrong with Livy's story, since Allifae (Alife) lay twenty kilometres northwest of Telesia, Calatia over twenty kilometres southwest of Telesia, and Cales about thirty kilometres due west - even the obvious emendation "Caiatia" (now Caiazzo) for "Calatia" (Caserta), does not really help. But it looks as though Livy's source said that Hannibal marched down the river Calor from Beneventum to its junction with the Volturnus, then turned up the latter to Allifae, and so over the hills to Cales, past some place the name of which is now concealed beneath the "Calatia" of our text of Livy, but which might lie behind the "Callicula mons" he mentions later (22.15.4 - see below), and even the name of the modern hamlet of Vairano Caianello. But however he came, once in the "plain of Stella" which lies between Cales (Calvi) and the lower Volturnus, Hannibal let loose his raiders, gathering an immense store of booty, and ravaging as far as Sinuessa on the coast (Polybius 3.92.1; Livy 22.13.9). This was *ager Romanus,* the first the Carthaginians had come to since leaving Picenum, and they clearly made the most of their opportunity to do as much damage as they could, in the hope of provoking Fabius to battle.

But Fabius, although he had followed Hannibal into Campania, despite constant pressure from Minucius and other officers, refused to be drawn off the slopes of Monte Massico to the north of the *ager Falernus.* (Livy 22.14.1ff.; cf. Polybius 3.92.6). Here he was in a position to cover both the *via Appia* and the *via Latina* should the enemy show the slightest sign of advancing on Rome. He was banking on Hannibal's having to withdraw in time to find suitable winter quarters back on the other side of the Apennines, and was hoping to be able to block the pass by which he would have to leave. When he was satisfied that the enemy intended to retreat by the same route as he had used to reach the *ager Falernus,* he sent small detachments to occupy Casilinum (now confusingly called Capua), which guarded the point at which the *via Appia* crossed the Volturnus, thus effectively blocking a possible escape-route up that river, and what Livy calls the "Callicula mons" (22.15.4); he then followed the Carthaginians as they began to withdraw towards Cales, keeping to the same ridges by which he had come, and sending out a force of 400 cavalry under L. Hostilius Mancinus to reconnoitre - this was lured by the sight of marauding Numidians into trying conclusions with the Carthaginian cavalry under Carthalo, and was cut to pieces with the loss of its commander (Livy 22.15.5ff.).

But Fabius' informed guess about the route Hannibal would choose to use, proved correct, and he was able to occupy the pass itself, with a detachment of 4000 men, himself taking up a position on a hill overlooking the pass on the right (Polybius 3.92.10-11). Since Polybius says that he had guessed that Hannibal would retire by the same pass by which he had come, the hill Fabius occupied may well have been the hill called "Eribianos" which he mentions in his account of Hannibal's entry into the ager Falernus (3.92.1), and this may also be the "mons Callicula" which Livy says he had earlier occupied. There is considerable doubt about the identification of Eribianos-Callicula, but one plausible theory is that it is the hill behind the modern village of Pietravairano, west of the pass of Borgo St. Antonio. [32] If this was Fabius' position, he was also covering the *via Latina,* which ran past the hill on the west. Either here or earlier, the dictator was joined by Minucius who had been sent off to garrison the pass above Terracina through which the *via Appia* ran to Rome (Livy 22.15.11). (See Map 8).

Hannibal camped in the level ground below the hill on which Fabius had taken up his position, and after trying in vain to lure the dictator down to battle (Livy 22.16.1ff.), realised that he would have to try to break through the pass - here called by Livy (22.16.5) the "iugum Calliculae". But once again he was equal to the occasion : in effect, he worked out a plan to trick the 4000 Roman troops guarding the pass from their position. He ordered Hasdrubal, here described by Polybius (3.92.4) as the officer in charge of "services", to collect as much dry wood as possible and bind it into bundles, and to assemble 2000 of the strongest cattle that had been captured. Then he gathered the army-servants together, and, pointing out a saddle between his camp and the pass, ordered them to be ready to drive the cattle towards it as soon as he gave the word. If the location of this incident adopted above is correct, the saddle will have been the one between Monte Caievola, to the west of which would have been Fabius' camp, and Monte S. Nicola. With his usual care, he finally bade his soldiers have their supper and get some rest (Polybius 3.92.3-6). "As the third part of the night was coming to an end," (Polybius 3.92.7 - i.e. about 3 a.m.), he roused the army-servants and ordered them to tie the bundles of wood to the horns of the cattle, then set light to them and drive the cattle towards the saddle he had pointed out; the faithful spearmen were ordered to accompany the cattle-drive, and to seize and hold the saddle. At the same time, he got the rest of his army in motion, his Africans in the van, then the cavalry and the rest of the captured cattle, and the Spaniards and Celts in the rear, making for the pass. The result was that the Roman force guarding the pass, assuming that the enemy was attempting to break out over the saddle, made for that point, only to be non-plussed by what they found, while Hannibal led his main force through the pass without striking a blow. Fabius, meanwhile, true to his habitual caution, remained where he was rather than be drawn into some trap. Next day, Hannibal's Spaniards returned to relieve the spearmen, and safely brought them through, killing about 1000 of the Roman force in the process. The whole episode was a triumph, not only for Hannibal's ingenuity, but for the disciplined expertise of his army.

Having escaped from the *ager Falernus,* the Carthaginian army camped in the territory of Allifae (Livy 22.17.7), and then, according to Livy (22.18.6-7), returned to Apulia by way of the Paeligni, feinting as though to attack Rome, while Fabius continued to dog its march, keeping his army interposed between the enemy and the city. Polybius, however, says that Hannibal marched past "Mount Liburnos" (3.100.2), and this is probably a mistake for "Tiburnos" - i.e. what the Romans called "Mons Tifernus" (now Matese). [33] If this is right, the Carthaginian army probably marched round the northern end of these hills by way of Aesernia (Isernia), and back to Apulia by way of Bovianum (Boiano) - a much more likely route than Livy's for an army encumbered with cattle. Probably about the beginning of September, Hannibal reached a place called Gerunium, which was 200 stades (35.5 kilometres) from Luceria (Lucera: Polybius 3.100.3), and lay somewhere between Dragonara and Casalnuovo Monterotaro; the Roman army took up a position nearby at Larinum (Larino). At this point, according to Livy (22.18.8-10), Fabius was recalled to Rome, ostensibly to perform certain sacrifices, but probably in reality to answer growing criticism of his conduct of the war, leaving his Master of Horse with strict instructions not to engage the enemy. However, Polybius is probably right to imply (3.94.8ff.) that Fabius had returned to Rome earlier, before Hannibal had completed his march past Mount Tifernus to Gerunium, and when Fabius himself was much nearer the city.

Hannibal took Gerunium fairly easily, according to Polybius (3.100.4), slaughtering its inhabitants - he had offered them terms before the assault - but leaving the houses standing to act as granaries: he fortified a camp outside the walls. Livy, however, says the inhabitants had fled, following the collapse of part of the walls (22.18.7). The Carthaginians now began to forage far and wide in preparation for the winter, Hannibal retaining only a third of his army to guard his base. But when Minucius approached, he halved his foragers and advanced towards the Roman position with two-thirds of his forces. Between the two armies there was a hill which Hannibal occupied with 2000 of his spearmen, but Minucius promptly captured the position, and moved his camp to it. This induced Hannibal to keep his men together for a few days, but eventually he was forced to send out foraging parties again, and Minucius now moved up close to his camp and began to harass the foragers. The result was that Hannibal had to abandon his forward position and fall back to Gerunium, having had some difficulty in defending his forward camp, and having lost a considerable number of foragers (Polybius 3.101-2). This was about the only time in the war that Hannibal allowed himself to be drawn into small-scale skirmishing, and let an enemy general seize the initiative. He seems to have been more concerned to protect his foragers than to provoke Minucius to battle - indeed, without his full strength, he could hardly risk a full-scale engagement.

The news of Minucius' success was naturally received with elation at Rome, and his authority was now in some way apparently made equal to that of Fabius. Polybius (3.103.4) seems to have thought that he was actually appointed dictator like Fabius, but this would not only have been quite unprecedented, as Polybius indeed stresses, but would also have been contrary to the whole idea of the dictatorship, the essence of which was precisely that it was a unique office. Livy (22.25-6) has a long and circumstantial debate on the matter, in which he alleges that a tribune of the plebs called "Metellus" carried a bill providing that the *imperium* of the Master of Horse should be made equal to that of the dictator, and this although it amounts to the same thing as Polybius' version, would at least have preserved the uniqueness of the dictatorship in a technical sense. Plutarch, however, in his life of Fabius (8.3ff.), calls the tribune "Metilius" and this is probably correct, for whereas it is easy to understand how an unusual name like this could have been corrupted to the better known "Metellus" in the tradition, it is difficult to see how the reverse could have happened. This is a pity, because a tribune called "Metellus" would presumably have been a member of the well-known family of the Caecilii Metelli, who figure among the supporters of the younger Scipio later (cf., e.g. Livy 29.20, etc.), and thus support from one of their number for Minucius in 217, would have been readily intelligible. Livy also says that the tribune compelled Fabius to hold an election to appoint a *consul suffectus* in place of the dead Flaminius (22.25.11), though the election of M. Atilius Regulus, consul in 227/6, and probably a political ally, cannot have been too unwelcome, and Fabius may himself have suggested the election to obviate the growing demand for Minucius' *imperium* to be made equal to his own - if so, it failed to have the desired effect.

Fabius thus had to return to the front in Apulia with the unwelcome knowledge that Minucius was now technically his equal, and in order to get round what might have proved a difficult situation, he offered Minucius a choice between each of them commanding the whole army on alternate days and dividing the army between them - Minucius chose the latter alternative, no doubt to Fabius' relief, and removed his troops to a new camp about two kilometres away, perhaps occupying the site he had recently obliged Hannibal to vacate (Polybius 3.103.7-8). Hannibal, who seems, as usual, to have been well-informed about what was going on, now set out to tempt Minucius into a trap: once again there was a hill between their two positions, and this he ostentatiously occupied, guessing that Minucius would not be able to resist trying to repeat his former success. But this time, as at the Trebbia, he made use of the apparently flat nature of the terrain to send out, during the night, small parties of troops to occupy any irregularities and hollows they could find. On his side, when Minucius observed that Carthaginian skirmishers had occupied the hill, he sent his own *velites* against them, following these with his cavalry, and eventually with his legions in close order of battle. Hannibal, too, reinforced the men on the hill, and brought up his cavalry and infantry of the line in support. The arrival of the Carthaginian cavalry was the signal for a brisk cavalry engagement, and soon the superiority of the Carthaginians began to tell: the Roman cavalry was dispersed and the *velites* sent reeling back onto the main body, throwing it into confusion. At this moment, the concealed Carthaginian troops also emerged from their hiding-places, and swarmed into the attack from all directions. For a moment it looked as though Minucius' army would be destroyed, but Fabius managed to bring his army up in support, and Hannibal broke off the engagement, though not before Minucius' forces had been severely mauled. Minucius had been taught a lesson, and henceforth the two Roman generals combined their forces again, Fabius assuming effective command, though Minucius remained technically his equal (Polybius 3.103.6-105.11). Both sides now settled down to make preparations for the coming winter.

Probably in December, Fabius and Minucius laid down their commands, their six months term of office being nearly completed, as Livy says (22.31.7), and their armies were taken over by M. Atilius Regulus and Cn. Servilius Geminus respectively. Servilius Geminus, Flaminius' surviving colleague, who had been ordered to take command of the fleet after Trasimene (see above, p. 63), had just returned from chasing the Carthaginian fleet away from Sardinia, and from a daring raid on Africa. Fabius was to perform other sterling services for Rome later in the war, but he owes his fame, rightly, to what he did as dictator in 217. Although his own strategic insight should not be over-praised, and it is clear that Minucius' foolhardiness has been exaggerated in the tradition by way of contrast, it is perhaps not going too far to say that Fabius took over at a time when the war could almost have been lost in a morning, and by his deliberate refusal to be drawn, gave Rome the breathing-space she needed. He certainly deserved the tribute paid him by the contemporary poet, Ennius, who in a famous line described him as "the man who on his own by 'delaying' restored the situation for us" (*unus qui nobis cunctando restituit rem*) a line which received the accolade of being quoted by Vergil (*Aeneid* 6.846).

It was now time for the elections at Rome, and after a considerable amount of constitutional wrangling, which Livy faithfully records (22.33.9-34.1), they were apparently held under the auspices of an *interrex,* presumably after the current consular year had come to an end on March 14th, 216, which meant that there was no consul left in office to hold the elections himself, or to nominate a dictator to hold them in his stead. [34] Reading between the lines, what may have happened is that Cn. Servilius Geminus, as the senior consul of 217/6, after having had his suggestion that the elections should be delayed until after the end of the consular year and then be held under an *interrex,* turned down, nominated L. Veturius Philo, consul of 220/19, as dictator to hold the elections, but that Fabius who was opposed to this man, used his influence with the college of Augurs to have the appointment declared invalid, possibly on the ground that he had not been nominated on Roman soil. Fabius may have been content to see the matter go to an *interregnum,* since *interreges* could only be appointed from among the patricians, and he may have hoped to secure the appointment of one of his friends to hold the elections: Livy later records (27.6.7) that after the death of Flaminius, earlier in the year, the Senate had prevailed upon the People to pass a bill providing for re-election to the consulship of any previous consul as often as the People wished, and it seems probable that Fabius was hoping to be re-elected under the auspices of a friendly *interrex.* If so, he was disappointed, for first C. Claudius Centho, consul 240/39, was appointed, and he in turn nominated P. Cornelius Scipio Asina, consul 221/0, under whom the elections were held. Since he belonged to a rival group, it is not surprising that Fabius failed to be elected.

It is probable that what was really at issue behind these intrigues was, once again, a question of strategy: Fabius would clearly have advocated a continuation of his own defensive policy, his opponents a renewed offensive, and certainly, once the new consuls had been elected, they proceeded to implement an offensive strategy. But the most interesting question concerns the place of one of the new consuls in the factional politics surrounding the elections - C. Terentius Varro. In the tradition Varro is portrayed as an out-and-out demagogue, the son of a butcher according to one story recorded by Livy (22.25.19). But it is clear that the tradition has distorted Varro's position: apart from the fact that no butcher's son could ever have become consul - and it looks as though even Livy did not believe the story - Varro's career does not suggest that he was, in any sense, a revolutionary. He had been quaestor, plebeian and curule aedile, and praetor, and there is no record that he had ever been tribune of the plebs, let alone that he had either initiated or supported any "popular" measures, apart from some vague remarks by Livy (22.26.1-4), until he supported the proposal that Minucius' authority should be made equal to that of Fabius (Livy 22.25.18). Moreover, even after the disastrous defeat at Cannae, for which the tradition holds him mainly responsible, he seems to have continued to enjoy the confidence of the Senate: not merely was he met by a deputation of all classes when he returned to Rome, and solemnly thanked "because he had not despaired of the Republic" (Livy 22.61.14-5), but his authority was renewed each year until 213 - a point made by a spokesman of the remnants of the Cannae legions in 212, if we are to believe Livy (25.6.7). Subsequently, he commanded an army in Etruria in 208 and 207, and led an embassy to Philip V of Macedonia in 203, and another to Africa in 200.

The key to his political allegiance is, possibly, that he supported the tribune Metilius (or Metellus) in his proposal to equate Minucius' authority with Fabius', and was in turn supported by the tribune, Q. Baebius Herennius, a relative, in his candidature for the consulship (Livy 22.34.3-11), for although the speech Livy gives Herennius is a splendid attack on Senatorial privilege as a whole, it is probable that the Baebii were supporters of the Scipionic group, and we have already seen that it is plausible to suggest that Minucius and his supporter the tribune Metilius, represented the same group in opposition to Fabius' strategy. If Varro came from a comparatively humble background - hence the story that he was a butcher's son, and he was certainly a *novus homo* - he would have needed the support of powerful patrons among the nobility, and it is not implausible to suggest that they included the Aemilii and Cornelii. It is possible that he had served under L. Aemilius Paullus, consul in 219/8 and soon to be his colleague in 216, during his campaign in Illyria in 219, for the ancient scholar Servius' explanation of his name (in a note on Vergil's *Aeneid* 11.743), suggests that he had served in Illyricum at some time, and if we are to believe Livy (22.35.2), it was he who presided over Aemilius Paullus' election in 216, after having been elected sole consul at the first elections presided over by the interrex, Cornelius Scipio Asina. [35]

In short, the election of Terentius Varro to the consulship was no more a triumph for "the People" than Flaminius' had been - it was a triumph for those members of the

Senate who wanted to abandon Fabius' strategy and to go all-out to defeat Hannibal on the battlefield. Naturally enough, after the disaster at Cannae, and the death of Aemilius Paullus, it was in the interests of the Senate as a whole that blame should be pinned on "that butcher's son", and in the interests of the Aemilii in particular that it should appear that Aemilius Paullus had been opposed to Varro from the beginning, whereas an analysis of the preliminaries to Cannae (see below, pp. 77-8), suggests that the two men were in broad agreement. It must be remembered that Aemilius Paullus' grandson was Polybius' patron.

Once the elections were over, the Romans certainly appear to have begun to make preparations to crush Hannibal by overwhelming force. For the time being the *imperium* of Cn. Servilius Geminus and M. Atilius Regulus was prorogued, and they were instructed not to risk a general engagement but to train their troops in limited operations (Polybius 3.106.2-5). One of the new praetors, L. Postumius Albinus, who had been consul twice before, in 234/3 and 229/8, [36] was given an army of two legions, possibly the *legiones urbanae* ordered to be raised after Trasimene [37] and sent to northern Italy to try to create a diversion among the Gauls of the Po valley (Polybius 3.106.6), and two new *legiones urbanae* were possibly raised to take their place (see below, p. 91, and Livy 23.14.2).

But the most important question concerns the number of legions Varro and Aemilius Paullus eventually had at Cannae. Polybius states quite unequivocally (3.107.9) that it was decided "to maintain the struggle with eight legions, a thing which had never happened among the Romans before, each of the legions having up to 5000 men, apart from the allies," and this, if true, means that it was decided to raise four new legions, each of 5000 men, and to bring the existing four under Servilius and Atilius up to the same strength. He also believed that an equal number of allied infantry was levied, and consistently with this says that the Romans had 80,000 infantry at Cannae (3.113.5). These figures have been doubted, [38] because Livy (22.36.1-4), although he reports this tradition, also records a variant one - that only 10,000 fresh troops were raised - and it is argued that the smaller total is to be preferred *a priori,* and that Hannibal's tactics at Cannae are unintelligible if he was really outnumbered by nearly 2:1 in infantry. But the *a priori* argument is not necessarily to be accepted - it is very difficult, for example, to accept the lowest of the three estimates Livy gives (29.25.1-4) for the army Scipio took to Africa in 204, and some scholars would accept the highest. [39] But a more serious objection to accepting the tradition that only 10,000 fresh troops were raised for the Cannae campaign, is that this would have only given the Romans a slight numerical advantage, even if the four existing legions under Servilius and Atilius were strengthened to 5000 men, and that as many allied soldiers were levied as Roman. For even if we accept that all the 10,000 were citizen soldiers, that would still only have meant 30,000 citizen troops in all, with 30,000 allied infantry in addition. But Hannibal had 40,000 infantry (3.114.5), and some of the Roman infantry were bound to be left to guard the camp on any day of battle - Polybius indeed believed that 10,000 were left to guard the larger of the two camps, and Appian (*Hannibalic War* 4.26) mentions 5000 in the smaller, for what it is worth. Thus Varro and Paullus, we are being asked to believe, were left to face Hannibal's 40,000 infantry with possibly as few as 45,000 of their own, while their 6000 cavalry (3.113.5) were actually outnumbered by Hannibal's 10,000 (Polybius 3.114.5). If this was the case, the Romans had certainly learnt nothing from the Trebbia, for there they had tried to fight Hannibal with a slight numerical superiority in infantry, and with fewer cavalry, and they had lost. Moreover, it might be argued that Hannibal's tactics, far from being unintelligible if he were really outnumbered by something like 2:1 in infantry, would be unintelligible if his infantry on the field was nearly as numerous as the enemy's.

Finally, it is perhaps significant that Livy's circumstantial account of the Roman losses at Cannae, and of those taken prisoner or who escaped, presupposes the higher total: if the lower total is correct, no tradition of the corresponding numbers killed, taken prisoner and escaped, seems to have survived. In other words, Livy's figures for the Roman killed, and for those who survived whether as prisoners or fugitives, support Polybius' figures for the size of the Roman army, and it cannot be too strongly stressed that Polybius is quite emphatic about his figures, though he obviously realised that they were unusually high. In what follows, then, it will be assumed that the Romans raised four new legions of 5000 foot and 300 cavalry, and brought the existing four up to the same strength, raising the same number of allied foot-soldiers, man for man, and three allied cavalrymen for every two Roman.

The raising of these new troops would have taken time, and this too is borne out by Polybius' narrative, for it appears from this that the consuls only joined Servilius about a week before the battle (i.e. about July 26th, by the Roman calendar: see below, p. 77). The latter part of the winter, and the spring of 216, had been taken up by skirmishing around the bases of the two opposing armies in Apulia, and it was evidently not until the crops had ripened sufficiently to supply his army - i.e. in June - that Hannibal broke away, and with his usual boldness and speed, struck southwards at the Roman supply-base of Cannae (now Canne della Battaglia), on the river Aufidus (Ofanto), about 100 kilometres away (Polybius 3.107.1-3).

According to Livy (22.40.4 - 43), the new consuls had already brought their new forces to join the army watching Hannibal, before the latter moved to Cannae, and he describes an elaborate plan Hannibal devised to lure them to destruction: it was only after the failure of this plan, according to the Roman historian, that Hannibal, faced with discontent among his soldiers, especially the Spaniards, was virtually compelled to move to Cannae, after contemplating making a dash for Gaul with his cavalry, leaving his infantry to its fate. But all this seems improbable in itself, and, in view of Polybius' silence, must be viewed with the greatest suspicion. According to Polybius, it was the Senate's reaction to the report of Hannibal's departure which led to the despatch of the consuls to the front (3.107.7). But although he says that the Senate ordered Servilius to wait, it appears from his narrative later (cf. 3.108.2 and 110.1ff.), that the new consuls only joined Servilius about three or four days' march away from Cannae, and this should mean that Servilius had moved after Hannibal, though keeping his distance, and that the consuls joined him somewhere between his winter-quarters and Cannae, perhaps near Arpi.

From the place at which the armies linked up, according to Polybius (3.110.1), the Romans advanced towards Cannae for two days (July 27th-28th: see below ) and camped about nine kilometres away, probably a little east of Trinitapoli. Here, if we are to believe Polybius (3.110.2-7), Aemilius Paullus became worried about the flat and treeless terrain, so suitable for the Carthaginian cavalry, and proposed that they try to draw the enemy away to ground more suitable to them - possibly he advocated marching due south to the area around the modern San Ferdinando di Puglia. But Varro would have none of it, and the next day (July 29th) being his day of command - the consuls were taking it in turn to exercise overall authority - led the army on eastwards towards the enemy. Hannibal attacked while the Roman army was in line of march, but could not make much headway with his cavalry and light troops against the legions, and broke off the engagement at nightfall. Next day (July 30th), Aemilius Paullus, who was now in command, ordered a further advance, and that night the Roman army camped on the bank - i.e. the left bank (see below) - of the Aufidus. Polybius (3.110.8) says that Aemilius could not now have safely withdrawn, and modern commentators have accepted this. [40] But it is by no means certain that Hannibal could have forced the Romans to stand and fight, and Aemilius' continuation of the advance made the previous day on Varro's orders, suggests that they were in full agreement. Aemilius also sent a third of the army across the river to construct a fortified camp on its right bank, both to cover his own foragers, and to harass those of the enemy (Polybius 3.110.8-11), and this seems rather provocative if he really wanted to avoid battle. Thus the stage was set for the greatest land battle yet fought between Rome and Carthage. (See Map 9).

There is the usual controversy about where exactly it was fought, and in particular on which side of the river, [41] but Polybius' view is quite clearly stated, and there is no good reason to doubt him. If we assume that he thought that the river flowed from south to north - actually it flows from southwest to northeast - it is clear that he thought that the battle was fought east of the river, i.e. on its right bank. Thus he says (3.110.10) that Aemilius Paullus constructed the smaller of the two Roman camps "to the east of the ford", and that on the morning of the battle Varro crossed the river and deployed the troops from the larger camp alongside those from the smaller camp, the whole army then facing south (3.113.2), with its right wing resting on the river (3.113.3) - conversely, he says that the Carthaginian left flank rested on the river (3.113.7). Finally, he says that since the Roman army was facing south and the Carthaginian north, neither was inconvenienced by the rising sun (3.114.8), and this would be true, since, if the battle was fought early in August - the date in the Roman calendar was August 2nd (Aulus Gellius 5.17.5; Macrobius *Saturnalia* 1.16.26) and there is no reason to doubt that it was running roughly true at the time - the sun would have risen a little north of east. Even the tradition recorded by Livy (22.46.9) and other, later sources, that the Romans were troubled by the Volturnus - a south-east wind - blowing in their faces, would fit, since such a wind would certainly have troubled an army facing roughly south more than one facing roughly north, and the tradition may be authentic, because a surviving fragment of the contemporary poet, Ennius, appears to refer to the dust at Cannae (fr. 282 Vahlen).

There is thus absolutely no reason to doubt that the battle was fought on the right bank of the Aufidus, and it could hardly have been fought upstream from Cannae, since the ground rises fairly steeply towards the southwest, and there is really no suitable terrain in the area. The site of the town of Cannae itself is certain - it lay on the hill on the right bank of the river about eight kilometres upstream from the sea, on which now rises a column commemorating the Roman dead. The visitor can reach it easily by following the signs for "Canne della Battaglia" off the old coast road (*Strada Statale* 16), and will obtain the best view of the battlefield by standing on the hill of Cannae and looking towards the sea. The new autostrada, running down to Bari, passes to the south of the battlefield, but a nice touch inspired the construction of an *Area di Servizio* in the appropriate place, called "Canne della Battaglia".

The Roman army thus occupied two camps astride the Aufidus, the larger on the left bank, the smaller on the right. Hannibal's original position will have been near the hill of Cannae itself, but when he realised that the greater part of the Roman army had remained across the river on ground more suitable for his cavalry, he too crossed to the left bank, and established a new camp southwest of the larger Roman camp, thus blocking any possibility of a Roman move to more broken country in that direction (Polybius 3.111.11) [42] Next day - July 31st by the Roman calendar - he ordered his troops to see to their accoutrements and prepare for battle, and the Romans, too, remained quiet (Polybius 3.112.1): this would have been Varro's day of command again, and his refusal to order a general engagement shows that he was just as willing to wait as Aemilius Paullus, who on the following day (August 1st), when Hannibal drew his army out, on the left bank, and offered battle, also refused the challenge (Polybius 3.112.2). Here Polybius remarks that Aemilius was not happy with the ground, and this is a good example of the bias of the tradition, for it appears later that Varro also did not care for it. Thus the day passed with Hannibal's Numidians harassing the Roman watering-parties from the smaller camp, and sometimes riding up to its very palisades (Polybius 3.112.3ff.).

But on August 2nd, just after sunrise (Polybius 3.113.1), Varro ordered the forces in both Roman camps to deploy for battle, leading those from the larger camp across the river to join those from the smaller (Polybius 3.113.2). Polybius offers no explanation for this sudden decision, and Livy merely puts it down to Varro's pique at the harassing by the Numidians (22.45.1-5). But it seems clear that the Roman intention from the beginning of the campaign had been to bring about a battle at a suitable opportunity, and if this was so, there was little or no point in waiting much longer: the morale of the Roman army was more likely to decline if the harassing by the Numidians was allowed to continue, and it was difficult to put a stop to it with inadequate cavalry. The feeding of these huge armies would also have been increasingly a problem, particularly for the Romans, if their forces were as numerous as Polybius believed, and here again Hannibal's superiority in cavalry will have made foraging easier for the Carthaginians.

Moreover, although the sources constantly stress the suitability of the terrain for the Carthaginian cavalry, they seem to forget that the Roman infantry also required reasonably level ground: the Roman tactics were, evidently, to try to smash through Hannibal's line by sheer weight of numbers, and what had happened at the Trebbia must have given them some hope that their infantry could win the battle for them. Neither

*Pl. VII: Cannae:* (top) *the site of the ancient town.* (bottom) *the view from the site of the ancient town across the Aufidius in the middle - ground, towards the sea.*

Polybius nor Livy explains why Varro chose to fight on the right bank of the river, after both he and Aemilius had declined to fight on its left bank and most modern commentators also offer no explanation. But since the manoeuvre involved getting two-thirds of the army across the river before it could deploy, it calls for some explanation. It is probably quite simple: on the left bank the ground is very flat, not rising above the 20-metre contour for about ten kilometres from the coast - perfect cavalry country, as Hannibal is alleged to have remarked to his troops (Polybius 3.111.2). But on the right bank the ground rises steadily from the sea, with a ridge along the river bank, where the town of Cannae lay on one knoll, and where the smaller Roman camp was probably situated on another knoll further downstream. Thus, although it was still suitable country for cavalry, it provided more hope for the infantry than the terrain on the left bank, and Varro deserves credit for spotting it. There is, then, no reason to believe Livy's statement that Varro ordered the army to deploy for battle without consulting his colleague, and that Aemilius Paullus was more or less compelled to follow (22.45.5).

Polybius, as we have seen, believed that the Roman army, including the contingents of the allies, numbered about 80,000 foot, and a little more than 6000 horse (3.113.5), made up of eight legions of 5000 citizen infantry and 300 citizen cavalry each (3.107.9-11), and, presumably, about the same number of allied foot and a larger number of allied cavalry - rather more than 3600 to make up the total of more than 6000. But of these, if we are to believe Polybius (3.117.8), 10,000 foot had been left in the larger camp by Aemilius Paullus, both to guard it, and, if possible to capture Hannibal's: we are not told who these troops were, but it is a natural assumption that they comprised one Roman legion with its complement of allied cohorts. Livy says nothing of any men left to guard the larger camp, but his statement that after the battle 10,000 men fled to it (22.49.13), provides some confirmation for Polybius' view. In the same passage, however, Livy also says that 7000 men fled to the smaller camp, and this raises the question whether any men were left to guard that - it was certainly normal Roman practice to leave men to guard a camp, even during a battle, and, for what it is worth, Appian (*Hannibalic War* 4.26), mentions 5000 men in the smaller camp - perhaps half a legion with some allied cohorts.

There is, thus, some doubt about the actual number of men on the field on the Roman side, and we should almost certainly assume that at most they had a paper-strength of 70,000 infantry, although the probability is that all their cavalry was present. We also cannot be certain what proportion of the Roman army counted as infantry of the line: Polybius (6.21.9-10) says that when the number of men in each legion was more than the usual 4200, as was the case at Cannae, the number of *triarii* remained the same at 600, but the number of *principes, hastati* and *velites* was equally increased from the usual 1200. This would imply that the number of *velites* in each Roman legion at Cannae was, on paper, 1466, and that the total for all seven legions brought into the field - unless we suppose part of a legion was left in the smaller camp - was over 10,000. The proportion of skirmishers in a cohort of allied infantry may have been the same, but at the Trebbia Sempronius Longus seems only to have had 6000 skirmishers (Polybius 3.72.2), and since his four legions, even if depleted, should have provided him with something like 4000 *velites,* it is possible that the proportion of skirmishers in allied cohorts was considerably less than the proportion of *velites* in a Roman legion. If we assume, then, that the allied cohorts at Cannae provided about 5000 skirmishers between them, the Roman infantry of the line, including the allied heavy infantry, will have numbered at most about 55,000 men, and the skirmishers, including *velites,* about 15,000.

Varro stationed his Roman cavalry - about 2400 in all - on his right flank next to the river; then came the foot, the skirmishers out in front as usual, the maniples of the line-infantry closer together than was usual, and within each maniple the number of files apparently reduced, and the number of ranks increased, so that the depth of each maniple was greater than its front, as Polybius says (3.113.3). We do not know exactly how this worked out, but it has been estimated that the depth of all three lines can hardly have been less than 50 men, [43] giving a front of about 1100 men. Allowing one metre per man, and for a gap of half a maniple's width between each of the front line maniples, each Roman legion would have had a front of perhaps about 100 metres, and the whole infantry line, including the cohorts of the allies, would have stretched for something like a kilometre and a half.

Polybius does not say where the allied infantry was placed, but although Livy (22.45.7) says that it was on the left of the infantry line, it seems more likely that each legion of citizen troops was flanked by the allied cohorts usually attached to it, and this would also have meant that each of the four Roman commanders could have commanded his own original forces. Thus Aemilius Paullus, commanding the right wing (Polybius 3.114.6), would have had under him the Roman cavalry (cf. Polybius 3.116.1), and one legion of citizen troops and 5000 allied troops (? ten cohorts), assuming that the 10,000 men left in the larger camp had come from his consular army (cf. Polybius 3.117.8). Next, according to Polybius (3.114.6), commanding the centre, came M. Atilius Regulus, the *consul suffectus* of 217/6, and Cn. Servilius Geminus, Flaminius' original colleague. But Livy (22.40.6) says that Atilius had been sent back to Rome because of his age - his sympathy with Fabius' strategy may have been the real reason - and Polybius may have confused this Marcus with Marcus Minucius Rufus, Fabius' Master of Horse, who fell in the battle, according to Livy (22.49.16). It would have been only natural if Servilius had continued to command the soldiers he had led since December, 217, and that Minucius should have been given command of Atilius' forces, and in this case, the centre of the Roman line would have been filled by the veterans who had fought against Hannibal in Apulia and Campania, and some of whom had served under the elder Scipio in 218. Finally, on the left, Varro, who was also in overall charge, would have had under his personal command his own two new consular legions, with their complement of allied troops, and, on the extreme left, the 3600 allied cavalry. In this way, the most seasoned troops in the Roman army would have been in the centre, where they hoped to win the battle, and the new levies on either flank of the infantry line - which may help to explain the success of Hannibal's enveloping tactics.

Hannibal, when he realised that the Romans were at last deploying for battle across the river, immediately ordered his own skirmishers across to cover the main body, and then led the whole of the rest of his army across by two fords, except for a force left to guard his camp (Polybius 3.113.6). To confront the formidable Roman array now marshalling against him, he had over 40,000 infantry and about 10,000 cavalry (Polybius 3.114.5), but unfortunately no detailed figures are given for the individual contingents. We can, however, make an informed guess at some of them: at the Trebbia he had had 8000 skirmishers and 20,000 infantry in the main line-of-battle (Polybius 3.72.7-8), excluding Mago's force, and although his infantry strength had been considerably augmented since the Trebbia, entirely by Celts, if roughly the same proportion of skirmishers to line-infantry had been retained, he would now have had something like 11,400 skirmishers, and nearly 28,600 infantry of the line. On the other hand, his skirmishers - his "spearmen" (λογχοφόροι) as Polybius calls them - seem to have been highly-trained, specialist troops, as we have seen, and perhaps he would not have wished to mix too many of the Celts in with them. However, we can probably assume that some of the skirmishers at Cannae were Celts, as indeed some must have been at the Trebbia. His original army of 12,000 Africans and 8000 Spanish infantry must have been whittled down since it had entered Italy, but the brunt of the losses at the Trebbia, in the marshes of the Arno, and at Trasimene, had been borne by the Celts, so he perhaps had something like 10,000 Africans and 6000 Spaniards left. Of these, the Africans had been armed with captured Roman equipment after Trasimene (Polybius 3.87.3 and 3.114.1), and were now, presumably, all stationed in the main line of battle, but of the Spaniards at least the Balearic slingers will have been among the skirmishers, and some of the other Spaniards, too, must have been among the spearmen.

Hannibal had considerably fewer infantry than the Romans, though even if we accept Polybius' figures for the Roman numbers, Aemilius Paullus was exaggerating when he declared that they outnumbered the Carthaginians by more than two to one (Polybius 3.109.4). Hannibal's response to the disparity in numbers, according to Plutarch (*Fabius* 15.2-3), was a jest: when one of his officers called Gisgo remarked upon it, he put on a serious look and said, "another thing which has escaped your notice, Gisgo, is even more amazing - that although there are so many of them, there is not one among them called  Gisgo ." But his problem was how to contain and defeat the massed ranks of the Roman infantry. At the Trebbia and at Trasimene he had done it partly by surprise, and in the former battle by using his elephants and skirmishers to crumble the flanks of the Roman infantry line, after they had been exposed by the dispersal of the Roman cavalry. But now he had no elephants left, and although he still retained superiority in cavalry, he was faced by vastly more numerous infantry.

One method he could have used would have been to refuse his centre, as Scipio was to do at Ilipa (see below, p. 147ff.). But he could not win the battle with cavalry alone, and any infantry he advanced would be terribly exposed. The method he devised was a stroke of genius: he seems to have decided, in effect, to use the very strength of the enemy infantry to defeat it, deliberately inviting it to press home its attack on the centre of his line. To this end he divided his Africans into two divisions and placed them at either end of his infantry line. If we are right to assume that there were now about 10,000 of them, they would roughly have covered the equivalent of two Roman legions, assuming that they were drawn up in about the same depth - and since they were to be the jaws of the trap he was planning, he may have arranged them in a somewhat deeper formation than usual. This would have left the Celts and Spaniards to cover the equivalent of the remaining five Roman legions and of the cohorts of allied infantry, a front of over 900 men, and this would have meant their having a depth only about half as great as that of the enemy.

But this was not all, for Hannibal was not merely content to range his Celts and Spaniards in a relatively thin line and leave them to resist the Roman advance as long as they could. When he had ranged his whole army in line, he proceeded to carry out the most extraordinary manoeuvre of the whole battle: "taking the centre companies of Spaniards and Celts," says Polybius (3.113.8-9), "he led them forward, and ranged the remaining companies in rank beside them to suit his plan, making the whole bulge crescent-shaped, and thinning the formation of these latter (i.e. the flanking companies), wishing to keep the Africans as a line of reserve for them in the battle, and to open the action with the Spaniards and Celts." Thus it appears, however we interpret Polybius exactly, that far from refusing his centre, Hannibal actually flung it forward, which involved thinning its depth even further (cf. Polybius 3.113.8 and 115.6), since it would have had more ground to cover. [44] It has been suggested that what really happened was that, in the advance, the centre companies got ahead of the wings, but Polybius evidently believed Hannibal planned the manoeuvre, and we should rather seek to explain its purpose. The most obvious explanation is that he was deliberately tempting the Romans to attack his centre, but possibly he was also trying to buy time: the further the Romans had to push back the Carthaginian centre, the more their impetus would be slowed, particularly since the companies of Celts and Spaniards would tend to bunch as they were pressed back.

Finally, Hannibal seems to have taken equal care with the deployment of his cavalry, for if Polybius is right (3.117.7), he did not divide it equally between his two wings. Polybius says that he placed his Spanish and Celtic cavalry, under Hasdrubal (presumably the commander of the Service Corps), on the left along the river, and the Numidians on the right, under Hanno (probably the man who had led the sortie across the Rhône). But this must have meant that he had more cavalry on the left than on the right, for the Numidians had originally only formed part of the body of 6000 cavalry with which he had arrived in Italy, the rest being Spanish, and even if they had originally amounted to two thirds of the whole cavalry force, their numbers must have been considerably less now. Thus we can probably assume that there were only something like 3500 Numidians on the right to face the 3600 allied cavalry, and this means that there were something like 6500 Spanish and Celtic horsemen opposite the 2400 Roman cavalry.

At first sight this looks odd, for we might have expected the more numerous body of cavalry to be on the open flank, away from the river, where the more numerous part of the Roman cavalry was stationed. But the Numidians could be guaranteed to give a good account of themselves, and at least to hold the allied cavalry in play, while Hasdrubal's force could equally be relied upon to sweep the numerically far inferior Roman cavalry off the field, and it would then be available for further manoeuvres, as turned out to be the case.

The battle opened with the usual skirmishing between the light troops of both sides, neither achieving any great advantage, though the Carthaginians must have been inferior in numbers. Then Hannibal launched his cavalry on the left wing head-on against the Roman cavalry: in the confined space along the river, there was no room for manoeuvre, and Polybius says that after the first charge, most of the troopers dismounted and fought it out hand-to-hand. But the Romans were heavily outnumbered, and in the end the Carthaginians got the upper hand, killing most of the enemy in the mêlée, and chasing the survivors along the river bank (3.115.1-4). By this time the skirmishers on both sides must have withdrawn through the gaps between the companies of the infantry of the line, and Polybius says no more about them: the Roman *velites* seem never to have been very effective once the main battle had been joined, and presumably they were now withdrawn to the rear and played no further part. But Hannibal's skirmishers had played a prominent part in the rout of the Roman infantry at the Trebbia, and they must, surely, now either have supported the Celts and Spaniards, or have been withdrawn behind the Africans and have later played a part in their flank attack.

Now it was the turn of the infantry of the line, and the Romans must have made a magnificent show as they moved steadily forward to engage. But it was the Carthaginians who evidently caught the imagination of the sources, the Africans looking for all the world like Romans, the Celts fighting naked, with their long, slashing swords, in alternating companies with the Spaniards wearing their national dress, short tunics with purple borders, and wielding the short, deadly, cut-and-thrust sword which the Romans had adopted (Polybius 3.114.1-4). For a time the exposed Celts and Spaniards fiercely held their own, but gradually they were pushed back by weight of numbers, breaking up the crescent formation (Polybius 3.115.5). The Roman maniples pressed on, crowding in towards the centre where it appeared victory was to be won, and eventually broke clean through the thin line opposed to them (Polybius 3.115.6).

But the Roman infantry, as it crowded towards the centre in pursuit of the retreating Celts and Spaniards, had now advanced so far that they had the two solid blocks of African infantry on their flanks (Polybius 3.116.8), and these, with perfect discipline, faced left and right respectively, dressed ranks, and fell on the Roman flanks. The technical terms Polybius here uses (3.116.9-10) make it clear that the manoeuvre was carried out by each individual African turning to left or right, not by the whole units wheeling to left or right, something which could hardly have been done in the heat of battle. [45] The Roman troops tried desperately to face about to deal with this new threat, but their formation was breaking up, and only isolated groups managed a manoeuvre which required training and experience - as we saw, it is possible that the new levies of 216 were on the Roman wings, and this may have now proved fatal. It was at this point, according to Polybius (3.116.1-4), that Aemilius Paullus, who had taken part in the cavalry action on the Roman right - Livy (22.49.1) says that he had been wounded by a sling-stone at the start - rode to the centre of the field, while Hannibal, who had been there all along, with his brother Mago (cf. Polybius 3.114.7), also encouraged his men. We can probably assume, though Polybius does not say so, that now that the Roman infantry had been attacked in flank, its impetus would have been checked, and the Celtic and Spanish infantry would thus have had time to reform.

Meanwhile, on the Carthaginian right, the Numidians had been holding the allied cavalry in check with what Polybius (3.116.5) calls "their own peculiar method of fighting": on this side of the battlefield there was plenty of room for manoeuvre, and the Numidians were past masters at this kind of fighting, wheeling in and dashing away before the enemy could close. Livy (22.48.1-4) says that 500 of them even pretended to surrender, but after being led to the rear, at a crucial moment whipped out concealed swords, and, picking up their shields, fell upon the allied cavalry from the rear. But it is hard to believe the details of this story, and since the Romans were fond of accusing the Carthaginians of bad faith - *Punica fides* - and Polybius says nothing of any such incident, it is probably completely untrue: it may have been the sudden and unexpected appearance of Hasdrubal's cavalry on this side of the battle-field which gave rise to the story. For whether it is true or not, the situation on this side of the battle now changed dramatically: after his defeat of the Roman cavalry by the river, Hasdrubal must have kept his men superbly under control, for he now appeared on the Roman left, having either ridden right round the Roman army, or, less probably, having ridden behind his own. His appearance was too much for the allied cavalry, which promptly broke and fled, presumably carrying with it the consul, Terentius Varro (Polybius 3.116.6). Seeing this, Hasdrubal, as a good cavalry commander should, kept his men well in hand, and sending the Numidians off in pursuit, led his own force to attack the Roman rear, delivering repeated charges at numerous points simultaneously (Polybius 3.116.8). Hasdrubal's brilliant handling of his cavalry may have been due to his own initiative, but if it is true, as suggested above, that he had originally been given the more numerous and heavier cavalry force, it is likely that Hannibal had planned his manoeuvres.

The Roman infantry were now virtually surrounded: the shock of their advance had been absorbed by the flexible line of Spaniards and Celts, the Africans held them like a vice on either flank, and now the Celtic and Spanish horse were crashing into their rear. The result was a massacre: Polybius (3.117.1-4) says that of the infantry that had actually taken part in the battle, only about 3000 escaped, leaving about 70,000 dead on the field, and of the cavalry he says only 370 escaped. But there is clearly something wrong with these figures, for according to Polybius himself, 10,000 infantry had been left in the larger camp, where 8000 of them were captured after the battle, the rest having been killed (3.117.7-11), and unless these were in addition to the 80,000, which is contrary to what Polybius said earlier about the numbers put into the field by Rome on this occasion (cf. 3.107.9), then, according to him, only 70,000 infantry actually took part in the battle, and if there were 3000 survivors, only 67,000 can have been killed. It is inconceivable, moreover, that no prisoners were taken on the battlefield, particularly from among the allied soldiers whose lives Hannibal would have wanted to save for propaganda purposes.

Livy's more convincing and detailed figures are, then, to be preferred, though they are scattered about in his narrative, and sometimes difficult to interpret: he says that 47,500 infantry and 2700 cavalry were killed (22.49.15), and from various passages it appears that altogether 19,300 prisoners were taken - 4500 on the field (22.49.18), 2000 who had fled to Cannae (22.49.13), and 12,800 in the two camps (22.49.13, cf. 50.11 and 52.3-4). Finally, he says that 14,550 escaped - 50 with Varro immediately after the battle (22.50.3), who were later joined by 4500 more at Venusia (22.54.1), and eventually 10,000 to Canusium (22.54.4). Casualties among high-ranking Romans were also very high: of the four chief commanders, Polybius and Livy are agreed that Aemilius Paullus and Servilius Geminus were killed, Livy telling the affecting story of how a military tribune called Lentulus found Aemilius sitting on a rock, bleeding profusely, and offered him his horse, only to be refused and to be carried away by his horse's bolting, as a party of Numidians came up (22.49.6-12). But although Polybius (3.116.11) says that M. Atilius Regulus also perished, in reality he lived to be censor in 214/3 (Livy 24.11.6), and, as we have seen, Polybius probably confused him with M. Minucius Rufus, who was killed according to Livy (22.49.16). Both the consuls' quaestors were also killed, twenty-nine military tribunes, out of forty-eight, and no fewer than eighty men who were either already senators or who could have expected to become senators in virtue of having held high office. Later, in a dramatic scene, Hannibal's brother, Mago, was to pour out on the floor of the Carthaginian senate house the gold rings taken from the hands of dead senators and Knights, most of whom had died at Cannae (Livy 23.12.1-2). Hannibal's losses, according to Polybius (3.117.6) were about 4000 Celts, 1500 Spaniards and Africans, and 200 cavalry; Livy (22.52.6) says that he lost about 8000 men.

Whatever the true figures for the numbers and casualties on either side, there can be no doubt that Cannae was a shattering defeat for Rome, and from that day to this, if we are to believe Livy, it has been argued by some that Hannibal missed a golden opportunity of marching on Rome immediately and finishing the war off at a stroke. Livy (22.51.5-6) tells the story of how, after the battle, when Hannibal was being congratulated by his other officers and urged both to take some rest himself and give some to his soldiers, Maharbal thought that not a moment was to be lost and declared that in five days Hannibal could be dining on the Capitol. When Hannibal demurred and said he would need time to consider the matter, Maharbal exclaimed, "You know how to win a victory, Hannibal, but you don't know how to use one." "This day's delay," Livy piously concludes, "is generally believed to have been the salvation of the city and the empire."[46] In recent times, no less a general than Field-Marshal Montgomery has written that "Maharbal was right when he told Hannibal after Cannae that he did not know how to use a victory."[47]

The question whether Hannibal could have won the war by marching on Rome is unanswerable, like all hypothetical questions in history, but an examination of the circumstances at the time strongly suggests that he could not. In the first place, Cannae is over 400 kilometres from Rome, so that even marching at twenty kilometres a day, it would have taken Hannibal's army three weeks to get there, ample time for the Romans to organize the defence of the city. Secondly, despite the rhetorical exaggerations of Livy (e.g. 22.54.9), Rome still had some troops left already under arms, to say nothing of the thousands she could raise from her own citizens and those of her allies, given time. Even for the immediate defence of the city, the two city legions, raised at the beginning of the year (Livy 23.14.2), would have been available, as well as the 1500 men Marcellus had at Ostia and the legion of marines he sent to Teanum Sidicinum (Livy 22.57.7-8). Men who lived in the city could very rapidly have been armed and organized into some sort of temporary home-guard, and a considerable force was in fact raised from the slave population (Livy 22.57.11). Thus Hannibal would certainly not have found the city defenceless, and it is very doubtful whether he could have taken it by an immediate assault: the only city of any size he did take quickly during the war, was Tarentum, and that fell by treachery, something which was inconceivable in the case of Rome.

But if he had settled down to besiege the city, it is even less likely that he would ever have taken it. [48] He had, for example, spent eight months on the siege of Saguntum, and if the Romans had been able to hold him off for anything like that length of time, they would have been able to raise overwhelming relief forces: the survivors of Cannae constituted a force of more than two legions in themselves, Postumius and his two legions could have been recalled from Cisalpine Gaul, and, with the aid of continuing superiority at sea, the legions from Sardinia and Sicily, to say nothing of those in Spain, could have been brought home. Thus Hannibal's besieging army would soon have found itself faced by forces at least as large as those he had fought at Cannae, and would have been in increasing danger of being hemmed in, just the kind of warfare he was always anxious to avoid.

If Hannibal had marched on the city after Cannae, moreover, this would have involved a complete reversal of his long-term strategy, for, despite what the Romans no doubt feared, and despite what he may himself have said or implied from time to time when haranguing his men, the destruction of the city probably formed no part of his plans. Even Livy states that after the battle he told his Roman prisoners that "his war with Rome was not to the death, they were striving for honour and for empire" (22.58.3), and this is borne out by the embassy he sent to the city, led by Carthalo, to propose terms (Livy 22.58.7), and by the terms of his treaty with Philip V of Macedonia, concluded in the next year (cf. Polybius 7.9.12-15). What Hannibal hoped to achieve was to win over Rome's Latin and Italian allies, and he would have risked throwing away the psychological effect of his great victory, which was soon to lead to the defection of much of southern Italy, if he marched away from the areas where he might hope to gain support, into the heart-land of the Roman confederacy, largely populated by Roman citizens and by loyal allies. It is significant that the only time he ever did march on the city, in 211, it was for the purely strategic purpose of drawing the Roman armies away from Capua, his most important ally in Italy.

Thus, for Hannibal, Cannae must have seemed not so much the end of the war, to be followed by a triumphant march on the enemy's capital, as the beginning of the end, and the justification for his adherence to his original strategy was precisely that so much of southern Italy did now begin to come over to him. Looking back on it, with the benefit of hind-sight, we can see that Cannae was the high point of his campaign, and that after it the tide began slowly to turn against him, but the years that followed were to be years of continued success, and the real turning-point only came in 212-211. In short, it was not the case that Hannibal "ran out of ideas" after Cannae, as Montgomery claims: the ideas were still there, and were still worked out with the same ingenuity. The question was whether they were, or had ever been, sufficient to bring Rome to her knees. [49]

# CHAPTER FOUR – THE TIDE TURNS

Polybius ends his third book with his account of the battle of Cannae, and unfortunately the rest of his narrative of the war, in Books 7 to 15, survives only in fragments. We are thus dependent on Livy, and on other later writers, for a continuous account of the war after Cannae, though the surviving fragments of Polybius are still immensely valuable. We have already noted a number of places in which Livy appears to have been mistaken, and even without the testimony of Polybius it is clear that there are a number of later passages in which he gets into a muddle - over chronology, for example - or exaggerates Roman successes, or even suppresses Roman defeats. But it is at least some comfort to remember that Livy used earlier sources, directly or indirectly, including, of course, the complete text of Polybius, and that he was evidently not uncritical in his use of them. In any case, if we are not prepared to take Livy at his face value, except where there is good reason to disbelieve him, we might as well abandon any attempt to write a history of the rest of the war, for the accounts of later writers like Appian and Cassius Dio are clearly far inferior to his.

After Cannae, the war widened to include Sardinia, Greece and Sicily, as well as Italy and Spain, and although in this chapter, for clarity's sake, we shall concentrate on the war in Italy and Sicily, the reader should bear in mind that Roman forces were operating in Spain throughout the period, as they had been doing since the first year of the war, and that from 214 onwards, they were also operating in Greece. Certain constant facts about the background to the war in Italy should also be borne in mind. It is clear, for a start, that Hannibal never had enough troops to protect all the communities which sided with him, as Livy later notes (26.38.1-2), and that there was thus a tendency for Rome to recover control of them as soon as his back was turned. He has also been criticized for his failure to press home attacks on towns,[1] and it is true, if Livy is to be trusted, that very few towns were taken by the Carthaginians by assault or longer siege. But this has nothing to do with his lack of a "siege-train": there is plenty of evidence that he could construct all that was necessary to take a fortified place, if and when he wanted to - after all, only a supply of timber was really necessary. Livy, for example, mentions "mantlets" (*vineae*) in his account of the attack on Casilinum in 216 (23.18.8), a huge wooden tower in the attack on Cumae in 215 (23.37.2), and "machines" (*machinationes*) in the attack on the citadel of Tarentum in the winter of 213/12 (25.11.10): in his account of the attack on Locri in 205, he specifically says that although the Carthaginians had brought no siege-equipment with them, they made it there and then (29.7.4ff.).

But even with siege-engines, Hannibal knew well, if only from his own experience at Saguntum, that sieges were liable to be protracted, and any such operations were bound to curtail his freedom of manoeuvre: he probably calculated that success in the field and his demonstrable ability to march at will wherever he wanted, were more likely to impress Italian communities than the capture of a few of their towns - indeed, he probably reasoned that assaulting their towns was hardly the way to win their friendship, and that any town which had to be taken by assault was unlikely to prove a loyal ally. Thus, after his capture of Nuceria and Acerrae in 216, and his assault on Cumae in 215, he seems almost invariably to have waited for overtures from sympathisers before attempting to capture a place. It is clear, too, that his pose as a liberator often fell on stony ground - he and his army were, after all, foreigners in a sense Romans were not, even to Samnites or Greeks. Thus, if we are to believe Livy (23.5.11-13), Varro himself tried to persuade the Capuans to remain loyal to Rome rather than see Italy become "a province of Numidians and Moors," and in 213, when the younger Fabius attacked Arpi in Apulia, the Roman soldiers are said to have asked the people of the town why they, as Italians, were fighting against old allies on behalf of "foreigners and barbarians," and trying to make Italy tributary to Africa (Livy 24.47.5). One must make allowances, of course, for Livy's patriotic rhetoric, but there may be some truth in these incidents.

Another interesting question about the attitude of Italian communities arises from Livy's statements about the sympathy for the Carthaginian cause shown by the lower classes, by contrast with the general loyalty to Rome of the upper classes. Livy first mentions this in connection with Nola in 216 (23.14.7ff.), and later, in connection with Croton, where he says the same class division was apparent, he makes the general point that "it was as though a single disease had afflicted all the communities of Italy, so that the people disagreed with the upper classes, the senate favouring the Romans, while the people inclined towards the Carthaginians" (24.2.8). This may seem a damaging admission to our eyes, but too much should not be made of it, for in the eyes of a historian like Livy, support from the lower classes was not something to boast about, and he may have exaggerated simply to show that the Carthaginian cause was only attractive to people of no account. His own narrative, moreover, does not bear out his statement that such a division of opinion was universal: in Locri, Arpi and Tarentum, for example, the position was apparently reversed, with the commons favouring Rome, the aristocracy Hannibal (cf. Livy 23.30.8, 24.47.6 and 24.13.3), and even in the case of Croton, though Livy alleges that it was the people who admitted Hannibal's allies, the Bruttians, while the aristocracy held the citadel, in the end, rather than allow a Bruttian admixture in the population, the entire citizen-body emigrated to Locri (Livy 24.3.10-15). What is certain is that the majority of Rome's allies remained loyal to her throughout the war, and although fear of either Rome or upper class leaders undoubtedly played some part in this, it would be absurdly cynical to suggest that this was the only factor involved.

According to Livy (22.58.1-8), after the battle of Cannae, Hannibal released his non-Roman prisoners as usual, and this time also offered to let his Roman prisoners be ransomed, sending one of his officers, named Carthalo, to Rome, with a delegation of prisoners, both to discuss the ransom and to tell the Romans his terms, if they were willing to consider peace. This was a crucial moment for his strategy, designed as it was to bring the Romans to the conference table. But the Roman response was immediate and adamant: the newly appointed dictator, M. Iunius Pera, sent a lictor to meet the delegation and to tell Carthalo to leave Roman territory before nightfall (Livy 22.58.9).

88

The Senate's response to the pleas of the prisoners was equally intransigent: after a savage speech by T. Manlius Torquatus, consul in 235/4 and 224/3, Hannibal's offer to allow them to be ransomed was rejected, and one of the delegates, who had sought to get round his oath to return, by returning to Hannibal's camp immediately after the delegation had left, with the excuse that he had forgotten something, was sent back in chains - the other nine returned of their own free will (Polybius 6.58; Livy 22.60): we can well believe Polybius (ibid.) when he says that Hannibal's joy at his victory was shattered by this evidence of Roman steadfastness and high courage.

But in other respects, his strategy at last began to bear fruit: some of the Apulian communities, including Arpi, Salapia, Aecae and Herdonea, seem to have gone over to him immediately after Cannae, and when he advanced into the Samnite hills, most of the Samnites, except the Pentri, proceeded to throw in their lot with him. The attitude of the town of Compsa was probably typical: the principal Roman supporters fled, leaving Statius Trebius to persuade his fellow-citizens to join the victorious Carthaginians (Livy 23.1.1-3). Hannibal left his booty and baggage here, and instructed his brother, Mago, to take over other seceding towns, using force if necessary. He himself descended upon Campania for the second time, while Mago, his task completed, was then despatched to Carthage with the news of Cannae (Livy 23.11.7). He was never to see his brother again. (See Map 7).

Hannibal's first target was Naples, possession of which, as Livy says, would have given him a seaport - and one only some 550 kilometres by sea from Carthage itself. This is of some significance in view of the criticism sometimes voiced against him that he underestimated the importance of seapower.[2] But although he was able to lure the Neapolitan cavalry into an ambush, it was clear that Naples was not prepared to join him, and he decided it would be too difficult to take the city by assault (Livy 23.1.5-10). In any case, he had got wind of a more tempting prize. Capua, the richest and most populous city in Italy after Rome and, perhaps, Tarentum, had been in a turmoil for the better part of a year. Tentative approaches had already been made to Hannibal after Trasimene (above, p. 69) and now the only thing that deterred secession, in Livy's view (23.4.7-8), was the ancient ties of marriage between the Capuan and Roman nobility - the most influential Capuan senator, for example, Pacuvius Calavius, was married to a daughter of Appius Claudius Pulcher, perhaps the consul of 212/11, and his daughter to M. Livius Salinator, consul in 219/8. Besides this, there were Campanians serving in the Roman army, and, in particular, three hundred young men of the noblest families serving in the cavalry in Sicily. The parents and relatives of these young men succeeded in bringing about a decision to send representatives to Varro, ostensibly to protest the loyalty of Capua to Rome. But Varro's gloomy assessment of the situation convinced them that the time had come to break with Rome, particularly since there was every possibility that, as Carthage's ally, Capua could come to occupy very much the same kind of position as that now occupied by Rome - indeed, Hannibal made vague promises to this effect in his first speech to the Capuan senate (Livy 23.10.1-12). Once they had returned home, the Capuan representatives were able to persuade their fellow countrymen to send them on a mission to Hannibal (Livy 23.6.5). Livy records a tradition, which he himself did not accept (23.6.6-8), that before this deputation left Capua, envoys were sent to Rome to demand as the price of continued loyalty that one consul should henceforth be a Campanian, a demand the Senate indignantly rejected. In view of Livy's doubts we can hardly accept this tradition, but it is, perhaps, an indication of the haughty attitude of Capua.[3]

The agreement between Capua and Hannibal was that no Carthaginian should have jurisdiction over Campanian citizens, that no Campanian should be forced to serve the Carthaginian cause against his will, that Capua should retain its own government, and that 300 Roman prisoners should be handed over for the Campanians to use in exchange for their 300 knights in Sicily (Livy 23.7.1-12). These terms throw an interesting side-light on the kind of objections Capua had to Roman rule: as Roman citizens, the citizens of Capua were, of course, subject to the jurisdiction of Roman magistrates, but they were not allowed to vote at Roman elections, let alone to stand for office, since they were *cives sine suffragio*, and military service in the Roman army must have been growing particularly burdensome. The depth of their feelings was demonstrated, according to Livy (23.7.3), by their arresting the Roman officials and other Roman citizens then in Capua, and shutting them up in the bath-house, where they were all suffocated; but Cassius Dio apparently ascribed this atrocity to Hannibal himself after the surrender of Nuceria (15.57.30: Zonaras 9.2). The welcome given to Hannibal, when he entered the city, was correspondingly rapturous, though marred by the handing over to him of Decius Magius, who had continued to maintain his loyalty to Rome: it is good to record that the ship carrying him to Carthage, was driven to Cyrenaica by bad weather, and that he was eventually given asylum by Ptolemy Philopator, King of Egypt, in whose dominions Cyrenaica then lay (Livy 23.10.11-13). The defection of Capua was followed by that of Atella (Aversa), on the road from Capua to Naples, and of Calatia (Caserta), on the *via Appia* between Capua and Beneventum (cf. Livy 22.61.11). But the towns in south-east Campania, like Acerrae (Acerra), Nola and Nuceria (Nocera) remained loyal to Rome, as did Cumae, Puteoli and Naples on the coast, and after his triumphant entry into Capua, Hannibal first made a second and equally fruitless attempt on Naples, and then advanced on Nola, which commands one of the main routes into Samnium (Livy 23.14.5).

The Romans, meanwhile, had been making every effort to repair the situation. Varro had succeeded in scraping together some 14,500 survivors of Cannae at Canusium, and when a despatch from him reached Rome, it was decided to send M. Claudius Marcellus, one of the praetors, to take over at Canusium, and to summon Varro to Rome. Marcellus was a tough and vigorous commander, who as consul in 222/1 had won a victory over the Insubrian Gauls, in which he had killed the opposing chieftain on the field of battle, and so claimed the right to dedicate the *spolia opima* to Jupiter, an honour won only twice before in Roman history. He had been allotted Sicily as his province, but was apparently still at Ostia in command of a fleet. He had already sent a legion of marines to Teanum Sidicinum on the *via Latina* between Capua and Rome, and now sent a further 1500 marines to the city before handing over command of his fleet to his colleague, the *praetor peregrinus,* P. Furius Philus, and hastening to Canusium (Livy 22.57.7-8). A dictator was appointed in the person of M. Iunius Pera, consul in 245/4, and now presumably an old man, but he and his Master of Horse, Ti. Sempronius Gracchus, set about levying troops. Livy says (22.57.9ff.) that by calling up young men of seventeen, and even some who were younger, four legions of citizen troops and 1000 cavalry were raised, but later (23.14.3-4) he says that when the dictator left the city, he took with him the two *legiones urbanae* which had been raised by the consuls at the beginning of the year. The simplest solution is, perhaps, that Livy was mistaken in saying that four new legions were raised, and should have said that two new ones were recruited, making four in all with the *legiones urbanae* already raised - the two new legions will then be the *legiones urbanae* originally to be assigned to the consul of 215/4 elected after the death in battle of the one originally chosen, but eventually placed under the command of Marcellus at Suessula (cf. Livy 23.25.9 and 23.31.3ff.). In addition, urgent messages were sent to the allies to raise new contingents (Livy 22.57.10).

But it would take time to raise the new *legiones urbanae,* and for the contingents of the allies to come in, and troops were desperately needed immediately to confront Hannibal in Campania. The dictator thus turned first to the slave population of the city, and from this source 8000 soldiers were recruited, after each man had allegedly been asked whether he wished to serve (Livy 22.57.11), whence the term *"volones"* (volunteers) later applied to these men. Criminals on capital charges, and debtors, were also released from prison on condition of military service, and a further 6000 men were raised from this source - they were armed, according to Livy, with captured Gallic weapons from Flaminius' triumph (23.14.3-4). It was, then, perhaps, with this scratch force, made up of the two *legiones urbanae* raised earlier in 216, and the slaves, criminals and debtors now recruited, together with some cohorts (? of allied troops) from the *ager Picenus et Gallicus* (Livy 23.14.2), in all amounting to 25,000 troops, that the dictator left the city (Livy 23.14.4).[4] These measures give some indication of the resolution of the Roman people, and their calm fortitude was never better expressed than in the thanks publicly given to the defeated consul, Terentius Varro, when in response to the Senate's summons he eventually made his way to Rome (Livy 22.61.14). But that there was a grim and ugly side to the Roman mood was shown by the burial alive, in the *forum bovarium* of a male and female Gaul, and a male and female Greek, to appease the angry gods (Livy 22.57.6).

Although Livy implies that the dictator had already been nominated, on the authority of the Senate, before Varro came to Rome (cf.22.57.9), it may in reality have been primarily to nominate a dictator that Varro had been summoned. In any case, he seems to have returned almost directly to Apulia, perhaps taking with him the legion of marines Marcellus had sent to Teanum Sidicinum,[5] and this released Marcellus for duty elsewhere, for, when next he is mentioned, he is at Casilinum on the Volturnus "with an army" (Livy 23.14.10). Livy does not say what this "army" was, but later (23.31.4) it transpires that it consisted largely of the survivors from Cannae - the *legiones Cannenses* - which Marcellus must have brought with him from Apulia (cf. Livy 23.31.4). It thus fell to Marcellus to be the first Roman general to cross swords with Hannibal since Cannae, for while at Casilinum he received an appeal from the government of Nola, and determined to hasten to its assistance. Marching up the Volturnus to Caiatia (Caiazzo), he crossed the river there, and then marched through the hills by way of Saticula (Santa Agata dei Goti) and Trebula (?Maddaloni)[6] and above Suessula (Castel di Sessola) to Nola (Livy 23.14.13). But Hannibal, when he heard of the praetor's arrival in Nola, immediately withdrew, and made again for Naples, only to learn that it, too, now had a Roman officer in command. Again he withdrew, and this time marched southeastwards past Vesuvius to Nuceria (Nocera). He seems to have decided to take this place, and eventually forced its surrender through hunger, though by the terms of the surrender its inhabitants were allowed to depart, and none was willing to join him despite the tempting offers he made. The town itself was sacked and burned, after all its valuables had been turned over to the Carthaginian soldiers (Livy 23.15.1-6). Livy apparently knew nothing of the atrocities alleged to have been committed here, and later at Acerrae (Cassius Dio 15.57.30 and 34; Zonaras 9.2).

From Nuceria Hannibal thrust at Nola again, perhaps hoping either that Marcellus had gone, or to catch him off his guard. But although the praetor distrusted the attitude of the majority of the people of Nola, he was not to be caught napping, and after a series of skirmishes before the walls, succeeded in himself surprising Hannibal, if we are to believe Livy, by a daring sortie from the town, although even Livy says he hesitated to accept the figures recorded by some historians for the Carthaginian losses (23.16.15). Nevertheless, as he says (23.16.16), any success was something at a time when it was harder not to be beaten by Hannibal than it was later to beat him.

Never one to throw good money after bad, Hannibal promptly withdrew from Nola, and marching down the valley of the Clanius to Acerrae, sacked and burned it like Nuceria, though Livy says most of its inhabitants escaped (23.17.1-7). Then he marched northwestwards to Casilinum, having learned that the dictator was near the place and fearing a counter-revolution in Capua with the Roman army so near: Casilinum also guarded the point at which the *via Appia* and the *via Latina* crossed the Volturnus, and if Hannibal could have captured it, it would have been more difficult for the Roman forces to enter Campania. But Casilinum was resolutely defended by Latin troops from Praeneste and by a cohort of 460 men from Perusia, and when all attempts to take the place failed, Hannibal withdrew to Capua for the winter. In the course of his account of these operations, Livy mentions an occasion when a sortie from the fortress was almost cut off by Hannibal's elephants (23.18.6), but this is almost certainly unhistorical, for the last of the elephants he had brought with from Spain, except the one that carried him through the marshes of the Arno, had died during the winter of 218/7, and although the Carthaginian government had decided to send more (Livy 23.13.7), these did not reach him until 215 (Livy 23.41.10). Livy possibly also suppressed a defeat inflicted on the dictator, recorded by Frontinus (*Strategemata* 2.25), Polyaenus (6.38.5-6), and Cassius Dio (Zonaras 9.3).

Livy (23.18.10-16) makes much of the alleged degeneration of the Carthaginian army during its winter sojourn in the rich and luxurious city of Capua - even having Marcellus later declare (23.45.3) that Capua was Hannibal's Cannae. But probably only a small part of the army was actually quartered in Capua: much of it must already have been scattered about in southern Italy, and even the field-army under Hannibal's personal command was too large for him to have risked the resentment which would have been caused if it had been quartered in a friendly city. Probably it was mainly quartered on the *Mons Tifata* (Monte Virgo), northeast of Capua, which was certainly used later by Hannibal as his main base in Campania. Its broad summit provided an ideal camping ground, with good pasture for the horses and pack-animals, and commanded both the Capuan plain and the route up the Volturnus into Samnium.

Hannibal was probably far more worried by his failure to take a port in Campania, or even to capture inland towns like Nola, than by any lowering of morale among his troops. The Romans were also clearly recovering fast: they had held the line of the Volturnus, and the fortress of Casilinum barred the way to the *ager Romanus* by either the *via Appia* or the *via Latina,* while Marcellus' army, now on the hill (Monte Cancello) above Suessula, in what came to be called the "Claudian camp" after him, was only some twenty kilometres away to the southeast, and guarded southeastern Campania and the routes to the south. On the other hand, the Carthaginian commander could be well-satisfied with the overall achievements of the year now drawing to a close: he had started it in command of an army isolated in a hostile land, but now he had a solid base of support in southern Italy from which to launch the next round.

When the weather grew warmer, early in 215, Hannibal launched a second attack on Casilinum, and this time, despite the efforts of the Master of Horse, Ti. Sempronius Gracchus, who commanded the Roman field-army in the area in the absence of the dictator, and who ingeniously floated grain down the Volturnus to the beleagured garrison in watertight jars, it was eventually compelled to surrender on terms (Livy 23.19). The fortress was handed over to the Campanians with an additional force of 700 men from the Carthaginian army. Livy says (23.19.13-18) that the garrison had been reduced to eating roots and grass from the bank outside the walls, and that when the Carthaginians ploughed this up, they sowed turnip-seed - causing Hannibal to exclaim, in exasperated admiration, "have I to sit before Casilinum until that comes up?" But he allowed the survivors of the garrison to be ransomed, and Livy believed that they were eventually released, rejecting a tradition that they were massacred by the Carthaginian cavalry, and referring to the statue set up by the commander of the Praenestine contingent, Marcus Anicius, as evidence. He also says that in addition to other rewards, the Senate offered the Praenestine soldiers the citizenship, though they refused it (23.20.2), and this is interesting in view of the Senate's subsequent indignant rejection of a proposal that the citizenship should be granted to two senators from each Latin state so that from them the Roman Senate might elect new members to make up its own depleted ranks (Livy 23.22.1-9). Sadly, Livy could find no record of the fate of the soldiers from Perusia, who had also formed part of the garrison of Casilinum, but presumably they too were ransomed.

It was at about this time that Rome also began to experience serious financial difficulties. According to Livy (23.21.1ff.), appeals reached the Senate from both Lilybaeum in Sicily, and from Sardinia, for money and supplies, and the Senate was forced to reply that none was available. For the time being, the Roman commanders in both islands were able to obtain local help, but on the motion of M. Minucius, a tribune of the plebs, a finance commission was appointed in Rome, and at its first meeting after the new consuls had taken office on March 15th, 215, the Senate voted that the tax paid by Roman citizens - the *tributum* - should be doubled (Livy 23.31.2). The normal tax was to be collected immediately and used for paying the soldiers, except for the disgraced survivors of Cannae. But by the end of the summer, we find the commanders in Spain appealing for cash and supplies (Livy 23.48.4ff.). The evidence of surviving Roman coins indicates a deliberate debasement of silver coins, which is perhaps referred to by Zonaras (8.26.14) under the year 217, but not precisely dated, and a drastic reduction in the weight standard of bronze coins.[7] But Pliny the Elder's statement (*NH* 33.45) that the *denarius* was retariffed at 16 *asses* instead of 10 in the dictatorship of Q. Fabius Maximus, is impossible, since the *denarius* had not then been introduced (see p. 168 below), and although a passage in Festus (s.v. '*Sesterti notam*') can be restored to refer the retariffing to a *lex Flaminia,* this cannot be held to support Pliny's date since C. Flaminius was dead before Fabius became dictator. The retariffing, and the *lex Flaminia* which authorized it, probably belong to the mid-second century.[8] But it was perhaps during these grim years, partly to restore confidence in the finances, partly as a call on the loyalty of Rome's allies, that the gold coins depicting an oath-scene were issued.[9]

Meanwhile, at Rome, the elections for 215/4 had been held, and the successful candidates for the consulship had been L. Postumius Albinus, consul in 234/3 and 229/8, and at that time commanding an army as praetor against the Gauls in northern Italy, and Ti. Sempronius Gracchus, the Master of Horse to the dictator appointed after Cannae. However, before Postumius could enter upon his consulship, he was defeated and killed by the Gauls: Livy adds the grim detail that the Gauls cut off his head, cleaned out and gilded the skull, and used it as a libation-vessel in the holiest of their shrines (23.24.11-12). His death necessitated a by-election, and at this Marcellus was elected by an overwhelming majority. But when he took up his new office, on March 15th, 215, a clap of thunder was heard, and on the augurs being consulted, his election was pronounced invalid on technical grounds, and he was compelled to abdicate. At a further by-election, Q. Fabius Maximus was elected to replace him (Livy 23.31.12-14).

There seems no doubt that the whole bizarre incident was another example of Fabius' manipulation of the state religion for his own purposes, but it is puzzling that he should have used it against Marcellus, since at the next elections - for 214/3 - as we shall see, a different piece of manipulation by the same man ended in the election of Marcellus. On this occasion, in 215, according to Livy (23.31.13), the Senate spread a rumour that the gods were angry because the election of Marcellus meant that two plebeians had been elected consuls for the first time in Roman history, and it has been suggested that the whole charade was manufactured by Fabius, in collusion with Marcellus, to "put the people in its place". [10] But this is far-fetched, and presupposes that plebeian consuls were still, in some sense, representatives of the people, which is absurd in the case of powerful *nobiles* like Ti. Sempronius Gracchus and M. Claudius Marcellus. On the face of it, the object of the exercise was to do Marcellus out of a consulship, and suspicion inevitably falls on Fabius. Perhaps he was disquieted by Marcellus' tendency to go out and fight Hannibal, and feared another Cannae, and perhaps it is a mistake to think that at the next elections he tried to secure the consulship for Marcellus (see below, p. 99). At all events, Fabius' election to the consulship of 215/4 marks the beginning of a three-year period in which he and his family were to dominate the political scene, he himself being consul again in 214/3, his son praetor in 214/3 and consul in 213/2, and in which the strategy he had advocated since Trasimene was to be given full rein.

The two by-elections for the second consulship seem to have led to a certain amount of reshuffling of commands at the beginning of the new consular year, but eventually the main armies were assigned as follows (Livy 23.31.3ff., 32.1-2): Fabius himself took over most of the army previously commanded by the dictator, M. Iunius Pera, at Teanum Sidicinum; Ti. Gracchus took command of the *volones* who had previously been serving with this army, and, if we are to believe Livy, 25,000 allied troops, although this total is impossibly high; Marcellus, who had been granted the *imperium pro consule,* perhaps as some consolation for his loss of the consulship, despite the fact that he had only been praetor the previous year, was given command of two *legiones urbanae* - probably the ones ordered to be raised after Cannae (see above, p. 91) - and ordered to take them to the Claudian Camp above Suessula: the survivors of Cannae who had previously been there, were now ordered to Sicily, and the two legions already in Sicily were ordered back to Italy, and assigned to the *praetor peregrinus,* M Valerius Laevinus, who was apparently given overall command in Apulia, Lucania and Calabria; the force Varro had commanded in Apulia was apparently sent to Tarentum (Livy 23.32.16 cf. 23.38.9), and Varro himself, his *imperium* prorogued for a further year, was sent to Picenum to raise recruits (Livy 23.32.19). Livy (23.25.6) maintains that it was decided not to replace the two legions cut to pieces with Postumius Albinus in Cisalpine Gaul, but it is possible that this is a mistake, or that the decision was later rescinded, for in his summary of the dispositions made the following year (214), Livy says that the *imperium* of M. Pomponius Matho was prorogued in the *ager Gallicus,* which implies that he had held it in 215, and that he retained the two legions he already commanded (24.10.3, 24.11.2). [11] But if this is right, it is possible that Livy's statements (24.11.2 and 4) that in 214 there were 18 legions in the field and that to produce this number six new legions had to be enrolled, require modification (see below, p. 100), since if Pomponius already commanded two legions in the *ager Gallicus* in 215, there were already sixteen legions in the field in that year, indeed, there may already have been eighteen, for an extra legion was sent to Sardinia later in the year, according to Livy (23.34.10ff.), and by 214 Varro had also apparently raised a legion in Picenum (cf. Livy 24.11.3). [12]

Even if the legions later commanded by Pomponius Matho and Varro, and the extra legion sent to Sardinia, were raised later in the year, the Romans were clearly making strenuous efforts to mobilize their available manpower in 215, with fourteen legions in the field, and, if we are to believe Livy (23.32.14-5), Fabius also tried to reintroduce his "scorched earth" policy by issuing a decree that all crops were to be harvested and conveyed to fortified cities before June 1st, threatening personally to ravage any fields not so harvested, and to sell any slaves he found on them and burn the owners' villas. Of the fourteen legions immediately available, no fewer than seven were concentrated in Campania and the south, where the immediate danger lay. Here, during the summer, the gallant town of Petelia fell to the Carthaginians after a siege of eleven months (Polybius 7.1; Livy 23.30.1-5), and its fall was followed by the surrender of Consentia (Cosenza), the storming of Croton (Crotone), and the secession of Locri (Livy 23.30.5-8, 24.1-4). Thus most of Bruttium passed into Carthaginian control, although Rhegium, commanding the Italian side of the straits of Messina, remained in Roman hands. Much of Lucania was also now under Carthaginian control, although, if Livy is right (23.37.10-11), on at least one occasion, Carthaginian forces here suffered a defeat at the hands of Ti. Sempronius Longus, the consul of 218/7 defeated at the Trebbia, presumably now serving under Valerius Laevinus. [13] Laevinus himself stormed three small towns of the Samnite Hirpini (Livy 23.37.12-3).

In Campania, Hannibal had a frustrating year. He was still anxious to secure a port, and he evidently had hopes of winning over Cumae through the good offices of his Capuan allies. The Capuans first tried to persuade Cumae to secede from the Roman alliance, but, when this failed, resorted to treachery. All Campanians were accustomed to observe a regular religious ceremony at a place called Hamae, about four and a half kilometres from Cumae, and to this place the Capuan senate asked the Cumaean senate to come so that they could talk the matter over, promising that Campanian troops would be there to guard against any hostile move by either Romans or Carthaginians. But the Cumaeans, suspecting treachery, informed the consul Gracchus, then at Liternum (now Patria), north of the mouth of the river of the same name, and only a few kilometres from Cumae. Gracchus immediately ordered the people of Cumae to convey themselves and their movable property inside the walls of their city, and, on the eve of the festival, entered it himself with his whole army. The ceremony took place at night, and Gracchus took the opportunity to fall on the carelessly guarded Campanian camp, killing 2000 of the enemy, before withdrawing to the safety of Cumae (Livy 23.35). Hannibal responded by attacking Cumae, but was beaten off and compelled to retire to his base on Mt. Tifata (Livy 23.36.1-8, 37.1-9).

Fabius, meanwhile, now based at Cales (Calvi), had failed to support Gracchus, allegedly because of bad omens (Livy 23.36.9-10), though in Fabius' case, one suspects that the omens were used to cloak habitual caution. But after Hannibal had withdrawn from Cumae, he recaptured three small towns east of Cales which had gone over to the Carthaginians, and then crossed the Volturnus, marching between Capua and Hannibal's base, if we are to believe Livy (23.39.8), to the Claudian Camp on Monte Cancello near Suessula, whence he sent Marcellus to Nola. From there Marcellus made a series of destructive raids into the territory of the Hirpini and of the Caudine Samnites, until they were forced to appeal to Hannibal (Livy 23.41.13ff.). This episode illustrates the difficulties Hannibal must have had to face continually in trying to protect his allies. His response, now, was typical: instead of wasting time by trying to help the wretched Samnites, he decided to try to nip the nuisance in the bud by attacking Marcellus' base at Nola. Here he was joined by his general, Hanno, from Bruttium, bringing the first - and indeed the only - reinforcements to reach him from outside Italy, including elephants (Livy 23.43.5-6: see below, p. 98). Acting on Hannibal's instructions, Hanno tried to induce the people of Nola to abandon the Roman cause, but when arguments and threats were of no avail, Hannibal invested the town. Marcellus promptly sortied, as he had done the previous year, but the engagement was cut short by a thunderstorm (Livy

23.43.6-44.5). Two days later, however, according to Livy (23.44.6ff.), Marcellus actually drew up his troops outside the town and won a considerable victory, followed, even more ominously for Hannibal, by the desertion of 272 Spanish and Numidian cavalrymen. Since he was able to add the detail that these deserters were, after the war, rewarded with grants of land in their own countries (23.46.6-7), Livy would appear to have had good evidence for his assertions, but it is likely that the Roman success was considerably exaggerated. Plutarch (*Marcellus* 12.2-3) says that Marcellus, after declining battle, attacked Hannibal's forces when they were dispersed to forage - a version which also appears in Zonaras (9.3), and seems more plausible in itself. Nevertheless, Hannibal withdrew, this time to a position near Arpi in Apulia, for the winter, sending Hanno and his forces back to Bruttium (Livy 23.46.8).

When he heard that Hannibal had withdrawn to Apulia, Fabius strengthened and supplied the Claudian Camp, and then moved back to a position near Capua from which he was able to ravage the countryside round the city. As winter approached, he ordered Marcellus to leave an adequate garrison in Nola, and send the rest of his soldiers back to Rome to save expense (Livy 23.48.2); he himself seems to have left his own troops in winter quarters at the *Castra Claudiana* (ibid.). Gracchus, meanwhile, had moved from Cumae to Luceria (Lucera) in Apulia, to watch Hannibal, and this released the praetor, M. Valerius Laevinus, for duty at Brundisium (Livy 23.48.3). Laevinus' instructions were to defend the coast in that area, and, in particular, to take precautions against any hostile move by Philip V, King of Macedonia.

Earlier in the year, an embassy had made its way from Philip to Hannibal's camp, and a treaty had been concluded by which Philip was to undertake to help Hannibal in return for an undertaking that Rome, once defeated, should no longer be permitted to exercise control over any territory in western Illyria (Albania). This is the version of the treaty in Polybius (7.9), but Livy (23.33.10-11) says the terms included a precise under-taking by Philip to come to Hannibal's aid in Italy with the largest fleet he could raise, in return for which Hannibal promised to go to Philip's aid in Greece, once the war with Rome was over. However, Polybius is here actually quoting the terms of the treaty, and his version, with its vaguer references to a general alliance, is preferable to that of Livy.[14] Both parties must have known that there was little or nothing Philip could do to aid Hannibal directly until the overwhelming strength of the Roman navy was destroyed or diverted, and the most Hannibal can have hoped from the alliance was that Philip's belligerent attitude would draw off some of Rome's forces. The Romans were, however, rapidly made fully aware of what was going on by the capture of Philip's envoys on their return, off the Calabrian coast, with three Carthaginian representatives in their company (Livy 23.34.1-9), and this meant that Philip had to send a second embassy to make sure that an agreement had been reached (Livy 23.39.1-4). Thus the Romans were able to make preparations before Philip moved (see below, p. 160).

Another Carthaginian effort to dissipate Rome's strength during the year, was even less successful. A Sardinian delegation had made its way secretly to Carthage and had succeeded in persuading the Carthaginian government that the island was ripe for revolt. A Carthaginian fleet was despatched under Hasdrubal, nicknamed 'the Bald', but was forced to run for the Balearic Islands by bad weather (Livy 23.32.8-12, 34.16-7). While it was being repaired, the Romans were able to reinforce their forces on the island with a second legion under T. Manlius Torquatus, who, as consul in 235, had already served there (Livy 23.34.10-15). The result was that when Hasdrubal the Bald landed, he was swiftly defeated and captured, and the rebellion collapsed (Livy 23.40-41. 7). Hasdrubal's fleet, meanwhile, returning to Carthage, was caught at sea by the Roman squadron based in western Sicily and commanded by Fabius' nephew-by-marriage, T. Otacilius Crassus. The latter had been raiding Africa when he had intelligence of a Carthaginian fleet operating near Sardinia, and had sailed to meet it, capturing seven of its ships (Livy 23.41.8-9). However, one good thing for the Carthaginians may have emerged from the Sardinian fiasco, for it is possible that it was Otacilius' absence from his normal base at Lilybaeum (Marsala), at the western end of Sicily, which enabled another Carthaginian fleet, under Bomilcar, to slip safely through to Locri in southern Italy, with troops, elephants and supplies for Hannibal's army (Livy 23.41.10). [15] But Bomilcar's exploit shows how much more the Carthaginian navy could have done, even in the face of Roman naval superiority, if it had been more boldly handled.

The year 215, uneventful in comparison with the crowded first three years of the war, was now drawing to a close. It was a year in which Hannibal had consolidated his gains in southern Italy, but had been frustrated in other respects, although it is difficult to see what else he could have done, and his plans had been partly thwarted by events in Spain over which he had no control: he had sent his brother, Mago, home after Cannae, and despite opposition in the Carthaginian senate, it had been persuaded to send a considerable force under him to join Hannibal in Italy (Livy 23.11.7ff.). But troops for this force were not immediately available, and so Mago had been sent to Spain to hire them, and by the time he was ready to leave Carthage for Italy, news arrived that Hannibal's other brother, Hasdrubal, had been defeated at the mouth of the Ebro (Livy 23.32.5-6). The result was that Mago was sent back to Spain instead of being sent to Italy (Livy 23.32.11), and although Bomilcar was sent to Italy, as we have seen, he did not bring anything like the forces Mago had raised. The defeat of Hasdrubal had also, naturally, prevented him from marching to Italy, as he had been instructed to do, according to Livy (23.27.9, cf.29.16). Thus Hannibal may have been expecting reinforcements from both north and south which would have greatly augmented his strength, and perhaps enabled him both to protect his Italian allies more effectively, and to mount a new offensive.

The Romans, for their part, had certainly made a considerable recovery after the disaster at Cannae, and although still pursuing Fabius' cautious strategy, had made some gains, and, above all, had not lost a further major battle. Their financial difficulties were, however, becoming alarming. Money sent to Ap. Claudius, the praetor in charge of Sicily, to repay the loan made by Hiero, King of Syracuse, had already been diverted instead to the upkeep of the fleet set to watch the east coast (Livy 23.38.12), and by the end of the year, there was no money available to send to Spain to pay the troops there (Livy 23.48.4ff.). Livy notes that such expenses could only be met by the property tax on individuals, and that the numbers of those eligible to pay it had been seriously reduced by the losses at Trasimene and Cannae. Thus doubling the tax had not produced the desired result. It was therefore decided that the *praetor urbanus,* Q. Fulvius Flaccus, should make a public statement about the nation's financial plight, and urge the state's creditors to give it time to pay. Nevertheless, there were still groups of financiers willing to accept contracts to supply the army in Spain, though they stipulated that they should be exempted from military service during the term of the contract, and, secondly, that the state should, in effect, insure goods sent by sea against loss by storm or enemy action. Thus, as Livy unctuously observes (23.49.3), "the business of the state was administered through private funds - such were the standards of conduct and such the love of country which ran through all classes like a single current." But when he goes on to remark that the contracts were honestly fulfilled, he omits to mention that only some two years later they were the subject of a considerable scandal!

The elections for the consulship of 214/3, held probably towards the end of 215, or the beginning of 214, under the presidency of Q. Fabius Maximus, were remarkable for another display of Fabius' skill in manipulating the machinery of politics. According to Livy (24.7.11ff.), after the *centuria praerogativa* had recorded its votes for T. Otacilius Crassus and M. Aemilius Regillus, both of whom had probably been praetors in 217/6, [16] Fabius made use of his powers as presiding consul to make the electors a speech reminding them of the many problems which faced the Republic, and arguing that the two men for whom the first votes had been cast, were unsuitable. Then he bade the *centuria praerogativa* vote again, and it meekly complied, this time casting its votes for Fabius himself and for M. Claudius Marcellus, whereupon the succeeding centuries followed suit until they had secured the necessary majority.

It is even more difficult to understand these extraordinary proceedings since both the ultimately successful candidates were related to Otacilius Crassus, whose election Fabius refused to allow, Fabius himself being his uncle by marriage (Livy 24.8.11), and Marcellus his half-brother (Plutarch, *Marcellus,* 2.1). There can be little doubt that Fabius' main object was to secure the consulship for himself, but other questions remain - in particular, why did he really object to Otacilius Crassus and Aemilius Regillus, and did he intend to secure the consulship for Marcellus as well as for himself? There may, of course, be some truth in his reported objection to Aemilius Regillus - that his religious duties as *flamen Quirinalis* would prevent him from leaving Rome (Livy 24.8.10) [17] - but it seems hardly likely that Fabius really accused Otacilius Crassus of having failed to prevent reinforcements reaching Hannibal (cf. Livy 24.8.13ff.), particularly since he was re-elected praetor and given the same command of the fleet based on Sicily (Livy 24.10.5). It is possible that his main objection was to Aemilius Regillus, perhaps for the religious reason Livy gives, perhaps because he feared a swing to the Aemilii and their friends - and that he then had also to argue for the rejection of Otacilius since, for technical reasons, the vote for him could not stand, if the vote for Aemilius Regillus was changed. Similarly, at the elections for 210/9, if we are to believe Livy (26.22.2-13), the objections voiced by Manlius Torquatus to his own election, appear to have meant that the vote of the *centuria praerogativa* for the unfortunate Otacilius Crassus on that occasion, could not stand. In the case of the elections for 214/3, it is significant that after Fabius' intervention at the consular elections, Otacilius was re-elected to the praetorship, whereas Aemilius Regillus got nothing.

As for Marcellus, we have already seen reason to believe (above, p. 94) that Fabius had deliberately worked the state religion to deprive him of the consulship the previous year, and although he had co-operated with him in Campania, one wonders whether he would really have wanted Marcellus to be elected consul now - Marcellus' readiness to challenge Hannibal to battle, if true, was hardly in line with Fabius' own strategy, and Fabius' orders to him to send his troops back to Rome at the end of 215, may have been intended to remove any reason for even his proconsular authority's being renewed. Perhaps, then, having secured his main object in preventing Aemilius Regillus from being elected, Fabius was unable to prevent Marcellus' recent exploits from carrying him to the consulship, however much he might have wished it otherwise.

The disposition of commands followed much the same pattern as in the previous year: Fabius himself returned to Campania, and Marcellus, apparently, to his old camp near Suessula (cf. Livy 24.13.9-11), each in command of two legions, with their usual allied complement. Tiberius Gracchus had his *imperium* prorogued and was assigned to command the two legions of *volones,* first at Luceria (Livy 24.11.3), but later at Beneventum (Livy 24.12.6). Fabius' son, elected praetor this year, was assigned two legions in Apulia (24.11.3), and later took Gracchus' place at Luceria. Varro continued in Picenum with one legion, and M. Pomponius Matho is also said to have retained command of two legions in the adjacent part of Cisalpine Gaul (Livy 24.10.3 and 11.2). Valerius Laevinus remained in command of a fleet and one legion based on Brundisium. Sardinia and Sicily were to be held by two legions each, as before, and Otacilius was sent back to command the fleet based at Lilybaeum in western Sicily. Finally, two new *legiones urbanae* were assigned to the protection of the city of Rome, and although Livy omits mention of them, we should not forget the army of two legions still commanded by the Scipios in Spain.

With the two legions in Spain, and including the two of *volones,* the total number of legions in the field this year thus comes to twenty, of which two - the *legiones urbanae* - were newly raised. Livy, however, says that the total was eighteen (24.11.2), and that six were newly raised (24.11.4). The probable explanation of the first discrepancy is that he has omitted the two legions in Spain, as he often does; [18] alternatively, he may have omitted the *volones* from the count of legions, though they are certainly not omitted from the account of dispositions (24.10.3). It is more difficult to explain why he says that six new legions were raised this year, but it is possible that he simply arrived at this figure by comparing a source which recorded that there were twelve in the field at the beginning of 215, with his source for his statement that it was decided to put eighteen into the field in 214, forgetting that later in 215, a second legion had been raised and sent to Sardinia (Livy 23.34.13), that Varro had also raised his legion in Picenum during that year, and, possibly, that the two legions assigned to M. Pomponius Matho in the *ager Gallicus,* had also been subsequently raised. [19]

It has recently been suggested that in order to raise new legions in 214, the property qualification of those liable to service in the legions was lowered from 11,000 to 4000 *asses.* [20] There seems to be little doubt that the qualification for *assidui* was so lowered at some point between a period before that of Fabius Pictor and Polybius' time, for Livy, presumably following Fabius Pictor, attributes the qualification of 11,000 *asses* to King Servius Tullius, and this must mean that it had been at that figure as far back as Fabius Pictor could trace, but Polybius (6.19.2) gives it as 400 *drachmai,* which is probably the equivalent of 4000 *asses.* The period of the Hannibalic War, when Rome found it necessary to raise more citizen soldiers than ever before, is clearly a likely time for the reduction to have been effected, but it is possible that it was in the year 215, or even in 216, when, if we accept Polybius' total for the numbers of legions raised for the Cannae campaign, no fewer than eight new legions were raised - six, including the *legiones urbanae,* before Cannae, and two (the new *legiones urbanae*) after it.

Paradoxically, one effect of lowering the qualification for legionary service may have been to make it more difficult to find sufficient *proletarii* to man the fleet, for some of these would now have qualified as *assidui* and thus have been called up for the legions. In order to make up the crews, Livy tells us (24.11.7-9), the consuls issued an edict that citizens whose property had been rated above certain levels at the last census (in 220/19), were to provide sailors and their pay in proportion to their assets - Senators, for example, providing eight sailors with a year's pay. When Livy goes on to say that the sailors raised in this way were armed and equipped by their "masters" (*dominis:* 24.11 9), he indicates that they were slaves, despite his concluding remark that this was the first time that a Roman fleet was manned by "naval allies" (*sociis navalibus:* 24.11.9) at private expense. [21]

Livy (24.11.5) says that the consuls of 214/3 were ordered to commission 150 warships, including the 50 already under M. Valerius Laevinus at Brundisium, and later (24.11.6), that 100 new ships were built. But in addition to the 35 based on Spain, which he omits, there were later 100 at Syracuse (Polybius 8.1.7; Livy 24.27.5), and these were joined by 30 more in 213 (see below, p. 107). The old fleet based on Ostia now seems to have disappeared, as did Otacilius' old Lilybaeum squadron, but Otacilius probably retained 30 of his old ships, and added 70 of the new ones to them, to make up the 100 operating off Syracuse; the 30 which later joined this fleet, will then be the remaining 30 new ships built this year. [22]

The year's campaigning opened with Hannibal moving back to his old base on Mt. Tifata near Capua, in response to an appeal from that city, and then marching down to Lake Avernus, east of Cumae, ostensibly to sacrifice at this traditional entrance to the underworld, but in reality so as to be in a position to make an attempt on Puteoli (Pozzuoli), in pursuance of his long-standing objective of capturing a port (Livy 24.12. 1-4). Fabius, who had strengthened the defences of Puteoli the year before (Livy 24.7. 10), immediately left Rome to join his army, ordering Gracchus to move to Beneventum, and his son to take Gracchus' place at Luceria. Hannibal probed the defences of Puteoli for three days, but, unable to take the place, moved on to ravage the territory of Naples. His proximity roused Roman fears for Nola once more, but Marcellus forestalled any possibility of treachery by a rapid march to Suessula, sending a substantial force to strengthen the garrison of Nola. At this point, Livy records yet another battle between Marcellus and Hannibal in which, he claims, Hannibal only escaped annihilation because of the failure of Marcellus' cavalry to take up its position in time (Livy 24.17.1-7). But Hannibal was, in any case, after larger game: while at Lake Avernus he had been approached by five young noblemen of Tarentum who had been taken prisoner either at Trasimene or Cannae, and been released in accordance with Hannibal's normal policy towards prisoners from states allied to Rome; now they undertook to deliver the great port into his hands (Livy 24.13.1-5). This suggests that Hannibal's confrontation with Marcellus was merely a piece of bluff to focus Roman attention on Nola. But, if so, the bluff failed, for when he slipped away from Marcellus and marched for Tarentum, he found that its garrison had been reinforced and that there was no hope of taking the city (Livy 24.17.8, 20.9-14). From Tarentum he withdrew to Salapia (Salpi) in Apulia, and began to send his cavalry out to collect forage for the winter.

Meanwhile, Hanno had been ordered up from Bruttium, and his army and that of Gracchus had collided on the river Calor, near Beneventum. It was presumably because he feared the arrival of Hanno that Fabius had ordered Gracchus to Beneventum in the first place, for with Naples, Nola and Beneventum firmly held, the routes between Bruttium and Lucania and Campania were effectively barred. According to Livy (24.15.2), Hanno had 17,000 infantry, mostly Bruttians and Lucanians, and 1200 cavalry, mostly Numidians and Moors. Gracchus' army consisted largely of the *volones,* who, inspired by the offer of freedom, fought fanatically and routed Hanno's army, Hanno himself escaping with a mere 2000 men, mostly cavalry (Livy 24.14-16). He later partially retrieved the situation by annihilating a force of loyal Lucanians sent by Gracchus to raid parts of Lucania which sided with Carthage (Livy 24.20.1-2), but his defeat at Beneventum was not the end of Carthaginian defeats this year, for Fabius and Marcellus combined to launch a determined assault on Casilinum, and succeeded in recapturing it (Livy 24.19), and Fabius then invaded Samnium, devastating the region round Caudium, and recovering a number of towns, including Telesia and Compsa; if we are to believe Livy (24.20.3-6), his operations extended as far as Blanda (now Maratea) in Lucania, and Aecae (Troia) in Apulia, though since the latter lay only eighteen kilometres south of his son's base at Luceria, it was more probably taken by the son. Thus Hannibal had been thwarted at every turn, and the Romans had begun to recover some of the ground lost in 216 and 215.

But the overall situation was changed dramatically, once again, by the defection of Syracuse from the Roman alliance. The old king, Hiero, Rome's faithful ally since the early days of the First Punic War, had died sometime in the spring or early summer of 215 (Livy 24.4.1), and had been succeeded by his grandson, Hieronymos, then only some fifteen years old. Hieronymos' father, Hiero's son, Gelo, if we are to believe Livy (23.30.10-12), had already been inclined to espouse the Carthaginian cause after Cannae, but had died before his father, and if this is true, it would not be surprising if his son had imbibed something of the same attitude. But according to Livy (24.5-6), it was the revelation of a plot against his life, in which the leader of the pro-Roman faction in Syracuse was allegedly implicated, which finally turned the young king against Rome. Envoys were sent to Hannibal, and he sent back a young Carthaginian nobleman, also called Hannibal, accompanied by two Syracusan brothers, Hippocrates and Epicydes, who had been born in Carthage of a Carthaginian mother, but whose grandfather had been a prominent citizen of Syracuse (Polybius 7.2.1-4; Livy 24.6.1-2). The result was that when the Roman praetor governing western Sicily, Ap. Claudius Pulcher, sent to renew the treaty between Rome and Syracuse, his envoys met with nothing but rudeness from the young king, who in his turn sent representatives to Carthage to negotiate a treaty on the basis of dividing Sicily between them at the river Himera. Later, his vanity flattered by Hippocrates and Epicydes, Hieronymos actually proposed that he should have the whole of Sicily in return for joining Carthage - a proposal Polybius says the Carthaginians were happy to accept, for the time being (7.3-4). (See Map 10).

The situation in Syracuse was, however, extremely complicated: not only were there pro-Roman and pro-Carthaginian factions, but there were also elements hostile to the monarchy, whether for their own purposes or for ideological reasons, and the usual plotting to secure influence over the king to which his youth and inexperience inevitably gave rise. The result was that after a reign of only thirteen months (Polybius 7.7.3), Hieronymos was assassinated at Leontinoi, sometime in the early summer of 214. Livy (24.4-7.9) compresses all the events in Sicily from the death of Hiero to the murder of his successor into his narrative of the consular year 215/4, but the evidence of Polybius leaves little doubt that he should have dated the murder of Hieronymos to the consular year 214/3. [23] The young king's death made the situation even more complicated: in Livy's view (24.21.1ff.), the assassins had been primarily motivated by the desire to overthrow the monarchy, and they were able to prevail upon Hieronymos' uncle-by-marriage, Adranodoros, to join them. Elections were held, and Adranodoros himself and some of the principal conspirators were elected magistrates of a new republic of Syracuse.

But the Carthaginian agents, Hippocrates and Epicydes, were still at large, and they were able to persuade many of the soldiers, particularly the mercenaries, and also considerable numbers of ordinary citizens, that their leaders were only interested in personal power, and were preparing to hand the city over to Rome in order to ensure its continuation. A further complication was that Adranodoros and other members of the old royal family were suspected of plotting to restore the monarchy. Eventually, the atmosphere of plot and counter-plot exploded in violence, and Adranodoros and the royal family, including Hiero's daughters and grand-daughters, were murdered amidst scenes of revolting cruelty. For the moment it looked as though, in the end, the old alliance with Rome would be renewed, and envoys were sent to Ap. Claudius Pulcher, who was apparently still exercising propraetorian authority in western Sicily (cf. Polybius 8.3.1), although one of the praetors of 214/3 had been appointed to Sicily. The first Syracusan delegation to Appius Claudius secured a ten days' truce, which brought to an end the desultory hostilities begun on the borders between Syracusan and Roman territory under Hieronymos, and then a second delegation was sent to renew the old treaty. It was at this point, according to Livy (24.27.6), that Marcellus arrived in Sicily: he had apparently been ill at Nola after his third encounter with Hannibal (Livy 24.20.7), but had now recovered, and had been sent to Sicily in view of the dangerous developments on the island. Thus it was to him that Appius Claudius sent the second Syracusan delegation, and he in turn sent representatives to Syracuse to discuss the renewal of the treaty.

But meanwhile Hippocrates and Epicydes had made use of their popularity, first with the ordinary citizens of Syracuse to secure election to the offices left vacant by the deaths of Adranodoros and Hieronymos' brother-in-law, Themistos, and then with the mercenaries and deserters from the Roman army to spread the rumour that Syracuse was being betrayed to the Romans. Here their propaganda was greatly aided when Appius Claudius sent warships to lie off the harbour of Syracuse, after news had arrived that a Carthaginian fleet had reached Cape Pachynon. Numbers of Syracusans actually flocked down to the shore to repel a Roman landing, but a well-argued speech by one of the leading citizens, Apollonides, momentarily succeeded in inducing a calmer atmosphere, and it was decided to send a delegation to ratify the treaty with Rome (Livy 24.27.7-28.9). Then the pro-Roman faction made a mistake: thinking that it would be a good idea to remove the mercenaries and deserters from the city, they sent 4000 of them, under Hippocrates, to Leontinoi, following a request for protection, and alleged attacks by this force on the border territories of the Roman province, and upon Roman troops sent to protect them, led Marcellus to demand the expulsion of Hippocrates and Epicydes. Epicydes, however, simply left Syracuse to join his brother at Leontinoi, and there they so worked on the feelings of the populace, that when the Syracusan authorities demanded their expulsion, the people of Leontinoi promptly declared their independence.

The Syracusan government, now desperate to avoid a calamity, was reduced to informing Marcellus that it no longer had any control over Leontinoi, and that it was thus powerless to secure the expulsion of the Carthaginian agents: it even offered to help him to capture the town, provided that he undertook to hand it back to Syracuse, if he took it (Livy 24.29). Marcellus and Appius Claudius promptly assaulted Leontinoi, and took it without difficulty, but Hippocrates and Epicydes managed to make their escape to Herbessos. Shortly afterwards, a Syracusan column, 8000 strong, reached the river Mylas on its way to Leontinoi, and there heard alarming reports of Roman brutality at Leontinoi, reports which Livy, naturally, says were untrue (24.30.3-4). Although the Syracusan officers in command were eventually able to persuade their troops to march on to Herbessos, Hippocrates and Epicydes daringly rode out to meet them, and, as luck would have it, found that the leading unit was a force of 600 Cretan archers, who had served under them, and had, moreover, Livy says (24.30.13), been freed by Hannibal áfter the battle of Lake Trasimene, in which they had taken part on the Roman side. This tradition is somewhat dubious, because there is no record of any such unit at Trasimene, and Livy (22.37.8) dates the arrival of the troops sent to Rome's aid by Hiero, after Trasimene. But Polybius (3.75.7) says that the Romans asked Hiero for help after the Trebbia, and that he sent them 500 Cretans and 1000 'peltasts'. By implication this was before Trasimene, and it is thus just possible that the Cretan archers had taken part in that battle.

At all events, the Cretan archers seem to have been sympathetically disposed towards Hippocrates and Epicydes, whatever their reason, and the rest was relatively plain sailing. Hippocrates concocted a letter which he claimed to have intercepted, and which purported to be from the Syracusan officers to Marcellus, condoning his atrocities at Leontinoi, and urging him to take steps to eliminate the mercenary troops still left in

Syracusan service. In the resulting uproar, the Syracusan officers were forced to flee for their lives, and Hippocrates and Epicydes then led the now mutinous troops on Syracuse. Here similar rumours had been going around, with the consequence that even sober citizens of standing had been inflamed against Rome, as Livy admits (24.32.1), and although the authorities attempted to close the gates against the mutinous army, it was too late: Hippocrates and Epicydes forced their way in, and in the confused fighting that followed, most of the magistrates and Syracusan officers were killed, and the two Carthaginian agents were triumphantly elected generals. Livy has nothing but contempt for them: "thus" he remarks (24.32.9), "Syracuse, after freedom had shone upon the city for a brief moment, relapsed into its old slavery"; and there can be little doubt that their activities ultimately brought nothing but hardship to the city of their origin. But it is difficult to withold admiration from the way in which they had so skilfully manipulated events to the advantage of Carthage: Hannibal had certainly picked his men well.

In Livy's account, the beginning of the Roman siege of Syracuse follows immediately after the election of Hippocrates and Epicydes to office (24.33.1ff.), but it is almost certain that in reality Marcellus did not attack the city until the spring of 213. This is apparent from Livy's own statement (24.39.12) that at the end of the first phase of the siege, Ap. Claudius Pulcher left Syracuse to stand for election to the consulship, for he was certainly elected consul for 212/11, and would thus have left Syracuse towards the end of 213, and not towards the end of 214, as Livy implies. In short, Livy has misplaced his account of the first year's operations against Syracuse - it should have come about ten chapters later. We must remember, therefore, that while the events leading to the final secession of Syracuse had been taking place, the war in Italy had come to the usual lull for the winter of 214/3, with Hannibal taking up winter quarters at Salapia in Apulia, and Fabius returning to Rome to hold the elections.

The elections for 213/2  resulted in the elevation to the consulship of Fabius' son, also called Quintus Fabius Maximus, and of Ti. Sempronius Gracchus, the consul of 215. Roman dispositions were much the same as for the previous year: the younger Fabius was to command against Hannibal in Apulia with the two legions previously commanded by his father, while one of the new praetors, M. Aemilius Lepidus, took over the two legions based on Luceria previously commanded by himself. Gracchus was to continue in command of his old army in Lucania, but Marcellus' old force, based on the Claudian Camp, was assigned to another of the new praetors, Cn. Fulvius Centumalus. The only other changes were the replacement of Pomponius Matho in Cisalpine Gaul by yet another of the new praetors, P. Sempronius Tuditanus, and the raising of two new *legiones urbanae* (Livy 24.44.1-6).

Clearly the influence of Fabius was still paramount, and it was not to be expected that there would be any radical departures in Roman strategy. Hardly any operations are, indeed, recorded in the Italian theatre during this year, except for the recapture of Arpi in Apulia by the younger Fabius (Livy 24.45-47.11), and this is chiefly interesting, if what Livy says is true, for the desertion of 1000 Spanish soldiers of the Carthaginian garrison, on condition that the rest of the garrison was allowed to depart, a condition that was scrupulously fulfilled (24.47.8-9). This is the second desertion from Hannibal's army which Livy records, the other having been at Nola in 215 (Livy 23.46.6), and if it is authentic, it may indicate that the virtual stalemate in Italy, with few chances of booty, was having its effect on the morale of Hannibal's army.

But stalemate in Italy could have been broken by victory in Sicily, as Hannibal must have calculated: with Sicily in Carthaginian hands, the precarious communications he had been maintaining with Carthage could be established on a firm footing, and it would at last be possible for him to receive a steady stream of reinforcements. For even if Rome retained her domination at sea, western Sicily was far nearer to Carthage than any seaport in Italy - it is only 210 kilometres by sea from Carthage to Lilybaeum - and Carthaginian troops once landed in Sicily would be safe from the Roman fleet, and would then only have the straits of Messina to cross. Thus the struggle for Syracuse was crucial, and the Romans once more showed their tenacious grasp of long-term strategy by persisting in the siege, probably for nearly two years, despite their commitments in Italy, Spain, and now also in Greece. It has been argued that Carthage wasted her efforts in Sicily, and would have been better advised to send the considerable forces she raised for the Sicilian campaign, direct to Hannibal in Italy. [24] There is something in this, but these forces would still have had to be conveyed to Italy, and this would undoubtedly have been made easier if Sicily could have been brought under Carthaginian control.

Marcellus probably commenced operations against Syracuse in the spring of 213, as we have seen. He began with an all-out assault by land and sea, concentrating on the area of the Hexapyloi Gate by land, and on the Stoa Skytike (Shoemakers' Colonnade) in the Achradina quarter, where the city walls reached down to the quayside, by sea (Polybius 8.3.2). At this date, the fortifications of the city enclosed an area roughly triangular in shape, with its base on the sea, and its apex at the western end of the plateau known as Epipolai. At the southeastern corner lay the quarter called 'The Island' or Ortygia, originally an island where the first Greek colonists had settled over five hundred years before, but now a peninsula joined to the mainland by a causeway. To the west and southwest of Ortygia stretched the great bay which formed the Grand Harbour, and to the north the smaller bay known as the Little Harbour. The Hexapyloi Gate was certainly in the north wall of the city built by the tyrant Dionysius I early in the fourth century, probably at the spot now known as Scala Graeca (Greek Stairs), where the main road to the north ran down from Epipolai. [25] The Achradina quarter used to be thought to include the whole eastern part of the city north of the island, but is now thought to have been only the area immediately adjoining Ortygia, in the low land to southeast of Epipolai. [26] Thus the Roman assault by land was evidently designed to break into the Epipolai plateau at its northeast corner, and the attack from the sea was most probably on the north side of the Little Harbour, and intended to capture the Achradina quarter which was shut off from the Epipolai by its own fortifications. [27] (See Map 11).

The seaward assault was under the personal command of Marcellus himself, though contrary to what Polybius implies (8.3.1), he would also have been in overall command of the whole operation, with Ap. Claudius Pulcher commanding the land forces under

*Pl. VIII: Syracuse:* (top) *the Grand Harbour from Epipolai.* (centre) *the walls of Dionysius I near Scala Graeca.* (bottom) *the Euryalos Fort at the western end of the Epipolai plateau.*

his direction. Marcellus had removed the port oars from four quinqueremes, and the starboard oars from four more, then lashed them together two by two, erecting on the bows huge scaling-ladders, protected by wicker-work screens, which could be lowered by pulleys attached to the masts - the complete contraptions were known as "*sambucae*" (harps) from their shape. But the Romans had reckoned without the ingenuity of the defenders, inspired by the great scientist, Archimedes. He had not only constructed a series of throwing-machines designed to hurl stones and other missiles to various ranges, which caused severe casualties as the Roman ships approached, but had also prepared huge beams, which swung over the walls to drop stones and lumps of lead onto the *sambucae,* or let down an "iron hand" on a chain, which seized the prows of the ships, lifted them into the air, and then let them fall with disastrous effect (Polybius 8.4-6.6) - later tradition even credited him with concentrating the sun's rays by means of huge lenses to set fire to the Roman ships (Diodorus 26.18, Zonaras 9.4). Similar devices also helped to beat off Appius Claudius' land attack with heavy losses, and the Romans were forced to abandon the idea of taking the city by assault, and to concentrate on reducing it by starvation. Appius Claudius was left in command of the blockade with two-thirds of the Roman forces, while Marcellus took the remaining third to try to recover some of the other towns in Sicily which had gone over to Carthage (Polybius 8.7.12).

Marcellus rapidly recovered Heloros, on the east coast south of Syracuse, and Herbessos between Syracuse and Leontinoi, and took Megara Hyblaea, on the coast north of Syracuse, by storm, sacking it as an object lesson to the rest of Sicily. But at this point a Carthaginian army, reputedly of 25,000 foot, 3000 horse, and 12 elephants, under Himilco, landed on the south coast near Heraclea Minoa (Livy 24.35.1-3). Heraclea itself swiftly fell to the Carthaginians, and then Agrigentum, about thirty kilometres to the east, forestalling Marcellus' march to its relief. However, on his way back to Syracuse, Marcellus encountered a Syracusan army under Hippocrates which had been sent out to link up with Himilco, and took most of the infantry prisoner, although Hippocrates and the cavalry managed to escape (Livy 24.35.6-36.1). But Marcellus was sufficiently alarmed by the Carthaginian landing to fall back on Syracuse, and a few days after his defeat, Hippocrates was joined by Himilco at Akrai (Palazzolo Acreide), and their combined forces then advanced to the river Anapos, just south of Syracuse. Shortly afterwards, a Carthaginian fleet of 55 quinqueremes, under Bomilcar, managed to reach the Grand Harbour (Livy 24.36.3), and it began to look as though Syracuse would now swiftly be relieved. But at this point the Roman besiegers were also reinforced: Livy (24.36.4ff.) says that a fleet of thirty quinqueremes landed a legion at Panormus (Palermo), and then escorted it by a coastal route to meet Appius Claudius at "Pachynum" while Himilco failed to intercept it, because he took an inland route. This can hardly be right, because the Roman legion could not have marched from Panormus all the way round the west end of the island and along its south coast, past the Carthaginian bases at Heraclea Minoa and Agrigentum, and if it marched east from Panormus along the north coast, as it must have done, it would not have had to march down as far as Cape Pachynon to meet the other Roman forces. But the arrival of an extra legion certainly brought Marcellus' strength up to three legions, making a total of something like 25,000 men, including the allied contingents, and probably brought it up to four: before Marcellus' arrival on the island, the Roman forces there had consisted of the two legions made up of the survivors from Cannae (the *legiones Cannenses*), and it seems probable that Marcellus had brought some troops with him. According to Livy, when dispositions were made at the beginning of the consular year 213/2, it was decided that the praetor, Cn. Fulvius Centumalus, who was given command of Marcellus' old post at Suessula, should take there the *legiones urbanae* - (Livy 24.44.3: i.e., presumably, those raised the previous year, leaving the new *legiones urbanae* of 213 as garrison for Rome). But if Fulvius Centumalus had to take new troops to Suessula, this implies that the forces previously there had gone. Perhaps Marcellus had taken one legion to Sicily with him in 214, and the second was the one landed at Panormus. [28]

If this was the truth of the matter, Himilco's relieving army was now probably outnumbered, and the Carthaginian general evidently decided that there was likely to be more profit in keeping his army mobile than in attempting to defeat the Roman forces besieging Syracuse. Accordingly, he withdrew from Syracuse, and his strategy was swiftly justified by the revolt of Murgantia (or Morgantina), a Roman supply-depot which has now been plausibly identified with the ancient site at Serra Orlando, near Aidone, about eight-five kilometres northwest of Syracuse. [29] Murgantia's example was followed by other communities. At Henna, however, in the centre of the island, the Roman garrison-commander, Lucius Pinarius, anticipating trouble, surprised and massacred the townspeople (Livy 24.38-39.7). Marcellus condoned this brutality, hoping that the other Sicilians would be deterred from revolt, but the news that a town famous throughout Sicily for its shrine of Proserpine, had been treated in this way, had the opposite effect, and now even communities which had been wavering, went over to the Carthaginian side (Livy 24.39.8-9). But by now winter was approaching, and while Hippocrates withdrew to Murgantia and Himilco to Agrigentum, Marcellus constructed a winter camp at Leon, some seven kilometres north of the Hexapyloi Gate, placing his new lieutenant, T. Quinctius Crispinus, in charge of the fleet and the old camp at the Olympium, about two kilometres to the south of the city (Livy 24.39.12-3, cf. 33.3).

We have already seen that it must have been towards the end of 213, and not 214 as Livy thought (24.39.12), that Marcellus' old lieutenant, Ap. Claudius Pulcher, left Syracuse for Rome to stand for the consulship, since he certainly became consul on March 15th, 212. The elections at which he was successful, were presided over by a dictator, C. Claudius Centho, nominated by Ti. Sempronius Gracchus, one of the consuls of 213/2, instead of by Gracchus himself or by his colleague, the younger Fabius, as would have been normal, and although Livy (25.2.3) says that this was because it was considered unwise to call one of the consuls away from the front, this seems a weak excuse. It seems more likely that the nomination of a dictator to hold the elections was yet another example of the political wire-pulling we have noted before, and certainly the elections appear to have resulted in the eclipse of Fabius and his supporters, and in the coming to power of a different group, with a different approach to strategy. It is possible, then, that the nomination of a dictator to preside at the elections, was intended to prevent the younger Fabius from exercising any influence as presiding consul, for as the senior consul of 213/2 - his name appears above that of Gracchus in the *fasti* - he would normally have presided.

The man chosen to be dictator, C. Claudius Centho, consul in 240/39, had been one of the *interreges* in 216, whose appointment led ultimately to the election of C. Terentius Varro as consul (see above, p. 73),, and he now chose as his Master of Horse, Q. Fulvius Flaccus, consul in 237/6 and 224/3. At the elections, Fulvius Flaccus himself was chosen, as was only to be expected, since it was usual for a dictator to recommend his Master of Horse to the electors, and Ap. Claudius Pulcher, the dictator's nephew, was chosen as his colleague, a clear indication of the influence the presiding magistrate could exert. The same *gentes* also won two of the four praetorships for C. Claudius Nero and Cn. Fulvius Flaccus, brother of the new consul, Q. Fulvius Flaccus, but Fabius and his family and supporters were conspicuous by their absence. It is also noticeable that all the commands in Italy were changed, with the exception of those of Ti. Sempronius Gracchus in Lucania, and of P. Sempronius Tuditanus, a member of the same *gens,* in Cisalpine Gaul (Livy 25.2.3-5, 3.1-5). Commands outside Italy were left in the same hands, but this was largely to be expected, since changes would have been more difficult to accomplish, and the commanders in Sicily and Spain, in particular, were proving successful. It is, moreover, probable that the Cornelii and their supporters co-operated with the Claudii and Fulvii at the elections, for one of the other praetors was a P. Cornelius Sulla, an ancestor of Sulla Felix, the dictator, and the other, M. Iunius Silanus, belonged to a family which had links with the Aemilii. [30] It was also in this year that the young P. Cornelius Scipio was elected to the curule aedileship, his colleague being another member of the *gens Cornelia,* M. Cornelius Cethegus (Livy 25.2.6).

Dispositions remained much as they had been in previous years, the only changes being that the *legiones urbanae* of 213 were assigned to the new praetor, M. Iunius Silanus, to form the nucleus of a new army in Etruria (Livy 25.3.4) - clearly the Senate was anticipating trouble there - and that the army in Picenum, now transferred to the praetor, C. Claudius Nero, from Terentius Varro, was also two legions strong (Livy, ibid.). This represents an increase of three legions over the previous year, with the raising of two new *legiones urbanae* (Livy 25.3.7), bringing the total up to an unprecedented twenty-five legions, and a new vigour appeared in the conduct of the war in Italy,with the investment of Capua later in the year. Elsewhere, too, there seems to have been a new urgency on the Roman side: Marcellus took the Epipolai heights overlooking Syracuse, during the spring, and probably brought the siege to a triumphant conclusion with the capture of the city by the end of the year (see below, p. 115); the Scipios in Spain may have recovered Saguntum this year (below, p. 129), and in Greece negotiations were opened with the Aetolian League which either this year or the next, resulted in an alliance between the League and Rome (below, p. 161). Thus the eclipse of the Fabii would certainly seem to have had an effect on the Roman war-effort.

The domestic scene was enlivened by the uncovering of a scandal involving several of the contractors responsible for supplying the Roman armies in Spain and elsewhere. The state had undertaken to insure ships and cargoes engaged in this traffic, against risks by storm or enemy action, and some of the contractors had been loading worthless cargoes into old, leaky vessels, and sinking them at sea, after taking the crews off, then exaggerating the value of their losses. The scandal had been reported to one of the praetors of the previous year, [31] but the Senate had chosen to ignore the matter for fear of offending the contractors. Now, however, the matter was taken up by two tribunes of the plebs, who proposed to fine the principal offender, Marcus Postumius of Pyrge. But Postumius had the right to appeal to the *concilium plebis,* and when the day for the hearing came, his fellow contractors first tried to get another tribune to veto the proceedings, and then, when they saw that he was hesitant, broke the assembly up by violence. The consuls next brought the matter before the Senate, denouncing the actions of Postumius and his supporters in the strongest terms, and the two tribunes who had proposed to fine him, now dropped the idea of a fine, and charged him instead with treason. It appears that in the end Postumius went into exile and was outlawed, and that the same fate overtook many of his associates (Livy 25.3.8-4.11). The whole episode throws an interesting sidelight on the "patriotism" of some Romans, and also, surely, indicates that the vessels carrying supplies were not normally escorted by warships, which makes the Carthaginian navy's failure to interrupt such supplies all the more culpable. [32]

It was at about the time this scandal broke, or a few months earlier, that Hannibal finally took Tarentum. Livy (25.11.20) says that he found disagreement in his sources between the consular years 213/2 and 212/1, but that the majority, and those nearer in time to the event, favoured 212/1, and so he, too, places it in that year. However, he also implies that it took place during the winter, since he says (ibid.) that Hannibal returned to winter quarters after taking the city, and this is confirmed by Polybius (8.34.13), and it is impossible that it occurred in the winter of 212/1 - the winter of 213/2 must be the one to which the sources refer. Thus, if Livy and the sources he followed were right to date the capture of the city to the consular year 212/1, it must have taken place after March 15th, 212, but before Hannibal moved from winter quarters. This is not impossible, since, as we have seen, Hannibal often did not leave his winter base until about May, when there began to be forage for his army, and since Livy goes on to say (25.12.1) that the new consuls were detained in Rome until April 26th, it is possible that the fall of Tarentum should be dated to between March 15th and the end of April.

Hannibal had had high hopes of winning over the city during the autumn of 214, when he had been approached by some Tarentine nobles while near Lake Avernus (Livy 24.13.1-5), but although he had marched on the city, no move in his favour had materialized. Now the execution of some Tarentine hostages who had escaped, inflamed the nobility of Tarentum, particularly the relatives of the dead men, and thirteen of them formed a conspiracy under the leadership of two men called Niko and Philomenos (Livy 25.7.10-8.3). Pretending that they were going out hunting, they left the city and made their way to Hannibal's camp, where they had the first of several meetings with the Carthaginian general, under the guise of leaving the city to hunt or raid, and after they had obtained Hannibal's assurance that the Tarentines would continue to govern themselves, keep all their possessions, pay no tribute to Carthage, and not be forced to have a Carthaginian garrison, plans were concerted for letting the Carthaginians into the city. Philomenos took to going out regularly at night, posing as a fanatical huntsman, until the guards became used to opening the gate at his whistle. The gate he habitually used is described by Polybius (8.25.7) as "the gateway (or gate-tower) below the so-called Temenid Gate," and the Temenid Gate has been identified with the one in the eastern wall of the city, in the neighbourhood of Masseria Collepazzo, north of the modern *via di Lecce*: Philomenos' gate, then, probably lay south of this, in the Marzullo property. [33] The conspirators waited until they learnt that on a certain day the commandant of the Roman garrison - Caius Livius, according to Polybius (8.25.7), Marcus Livius, according to Livy (26.39.1, etc.) - was going to an all-day party in the Museum, near the market-place, and well over in the western part of the city, and agreed with Hannibal to make the attempt that night. It is amusing to note that Livy does not mention the garrison-commander's name, which was the same as his own, in connection with the taking of the city, but only later, when he had courageously held the citadel for a number of years.

Hannibal's winter base lay three days' march from Tarentum (Polybius 8.26.2), and for some time he had been pretending to be sick to avoid arousing any suspicions about his reasons for staying in the neighbourhood. Now he got ready a force of 8000 infantry and 2000 cavalry, and ordering them to take four days' rations, set out for the city, throwing out a screen of Numidian cavalry about five kilometres in advance of the main column, so that anyone who escaped them, would simply announce that a raiding-party of Numidian horsemen was approaching. About 21 kilometres from the city he halted for supper, and issued instructions to his officers to keep their men together and do nothing on their own initiative. Then, just after dusk, he set off again, with Philomenos as a guide. As had been foreseen, Livius had been feasting since early in the day, and when, at sunset, as the drinking was at its height, news was brought that a raiding-party of Numidians was in the neighbourhood, he merely gave orders for a cavalry sortie in the morning. When the party eventually broke up, some of the conspirators escorted Livius to his quarters, and then posted themselves at strategic points to prevent any further intelligence reaching him. Then, when all was quiet, they proceeded to put the plan they had agreed with Hannibal into operation. The plan was for Hannibal to approach the Temenid Gate, and to light a fire on the mound called the Tomb of Hyakinthos, or the Tomb of Apollo Hyakinthos, which local tradition now identifies with the *Erto di Cicalone,* a hill about 1300 metres east of the ancient city wall. [34] When the conspirators in the city saw the signal, they answered it by lighting a torch of their own, and then seized the gate, killing the guards and sawing through the bars which secured the gate, since they did not have the right hook for drawing out the bolts which fastened them. Once the gate was open, Hannibal led the main body of his infantry through and marched swiftly for the market-place, probably along the shore of the *mare Piccolo* which formed the ancient harbour, [35] leaving his cavalry outside the wall to deal with any emergencies. Meanwhile Philomenos had made his way to the gate he normally used, accompanied by 1000 African troops: at his whistle, a guard came down and opened a postern-gate, and Philomenos walked in, accompanied by an African dressed as a shepherd, and carrying, with two others, a wild boar on a stretcher. As the guard was examining the boar, he was cut down, and then the four admitted through the postern-gate about thirty more Africans, who killed the other guards, and opened the main gate for the rest of the force; then they proceeded to the market-place to join Hannibal. Hannibal now divided his force, keeping most of it under his control, but sending some 2000 Celts, in three detachments, with some of the conspirators, to seize the approaches to the market-place. The conspirators were to protect any Tarentine citizens they encountered, and to warn the others to stay where they were - all Romans were to be put to the sword (Polybius 8.26-30.4). (See Map 12).

When he heard that the enemy was in the city, the Roman commander at least had the wit to make for the citadel, but Philomenos and his companions had got hold of Roman bugles and trumpeters who knew how to use them, so when the Romans living in the city heard the call to arms, they came running up in scattered groups and fell an easy prey to the Carthaginians. When it was fully day, Hannibal summoned the Tarentines to assemble in the market-square, and since those who favoured Rome, had already prudently taken refuge in the citadel, he was well received: he bade all Tarentine citizens write "Tarentine" on the doors of their houses, and then selected officers to supervise the pillaging of houses not so inscribed (Polybius 8.30.5-31). The following day, after another assembly, Hannibal decided to shut the citadel off from the town by constructing a palisade with a moat in front of it, and succeeded in doing so after beating off a sortie from the citadel: Hannibal's palisade and ditch probably followed roughly the line of the present canal built by Ferdinand of Aragon in A.D. 1480. [36] Later, he constructed a more elaborate system of fortifications, although at one point he did prepare siege-works for assaulting the citadel. Finally, he suggested to the Tarentines a plan for dragging their ships on wheeled carriages across from the inner harbour where they were bottled up by the Roman-held citadel, to the outer bay, using a street running parallel to the eastern fortifications of the citadel, along the line of the present *Corso due Mari*.[37] He then returned to his winter-quarters at three days' march from Tarentum (Polybius 8.34). The capture of this great port shows that Hannibal had lost none of his skill as a commander, and that his army was still an effic-ient fighting-machine. Its fall was followed, later in 212, by the defection of Metapon-tum, the garrison of which had gone to join the garrison at Tarentum, and of Thurii (Livy 25.15.7): Appian (*Hannibalic War* 6.35) says that Heraclea also defected at this time. Thus the whole coastline of the "instep" of Italy passed into Carthaginian control.

Elsewhere in Italy, however, things did not go nearly so well for the Carthaginians. The crucial front was still in Campania, and here, once the weather made it possible, Hannibal tried to relieve the food-shortage in Capua. The presence of Roman forces in the vicinity had prevented the Capuans from sowing their crops, and they had requested him to have grain conveyed to them before the consuls arrived and invested the city, as they were expected to do. Hannibal ordered Hanno up from Bruttium, and after march-ing to within some four kilometres of Beneventum, the latter began to collect grain from the neighbouring communities, telling the Capuans to assemble all the farm-carts and draught-animals they could, and to meet him on a given day. But the Capuan response was so lethargic that he was forced to defer the date for collecting most of the grain, and this gave the people of Beneventum ample time to inform the consuls, then near Bovianum, about what was happening. The result was that Q. Fulvius Flaccus marched to Beneventum, and on learning that Hanno had gone off with most of his troops to forage, decided to attack his camp in his absence. Hanno had sited the camp carefully on a hill, and for a time its defenders were able to resist all attacks, causing the consul, if Livy is to be believed (25.14.2), to contemplate withdrawal, But then the heroism of the prefect of a cohort of Paeligni shamed the Romans into making a renewed effort, and the camp was taken. Hanno made his way back to Bruttium with the survivors of the disaster (Livy 25.13-4).

Meanwhile, Ap. Claudius Pulcher had joined his colleague at Beneventum, and the people of Capua sent a second frantic appeal to Hannibal (Livy 25.15.1-3). His response was to send them a force of 2000 cavalry to provide some protection against the devastation of their lands, but the consuls had decided to invest the city, not merely to devastate the surrounding countryside, an indication of the new aggressive strategy now in favour with the leaders of Rome. At first, indeed, the consuls tended to be over-bold and allowed themselves to be surprised by the Carthaginian cavalry. Then Hannibal at last came marching to the relief of his allies. His one chance of removing the threat from Capua, without himself becoming entangled in its defence, was to bring the Roman army to battle, and to inflict another crushing defeat upon it, and there is no reason to doubt Livy's statement (25.19.1-2) that he offered battle soon after his arrival. It would also be in keeping with the new aggressive spirit of the Romans, that they should have been prepared to accept the challenge. But there is something suspicious about Livy's account of the way in which the battle came to be broken off - he says a new body of troops was seen approaching, and that neither side was sure of its identity. But it is clear that Hannibal was unable to force a decisive result (Livy 25.15.18-19.5).

The troops seen approaching turned out to belong to the army of the proconsul, Ti. Sempronius Gracchus, who had been ordered to bring his cavalry and light infantry from Lucania to join the consuls, but who had been killed before he could do so (Livy 25.16-7). Livy knew of two versions of Gracchus' death: according to one, he was lured into an ambush through the treachery of a Lucanian, at a place known as the "Old Plains" in Lucania; according to the other, he was surprised while bathing in the river Calor near Beneventum. These conflicting traditions about Gracchus' death, which could not be suppressed, perhaps obscure a defeat, as is suggested by the dispersal of the *volones* who had served him so faithfully (Livy 25.20.4). (See Map 11).

Hannibal's intervention in Campania made the investment of Capua much more difficult, if not impossible, and the consuls were anxious to draw him away. So, during the night following the inconclusive engagement near the city, Fulvius Flaccus marched away towards Cumae, and Appius Claudius towards Lucania. Hannibal, when informed that the Roman camp was deserted, decided to follow Appius Claudius, but if Livy is to be believed (25.19.8), the consul simply led his pursuer in circles, and returned to Capua by a different route. However, Livy follows his account of Claudius' successful manoeuvre by describing the destruction of a force of nearly 16,000 men, allegedly under the command of a mere senior centurion, in Lucania (25.19.9-17), and although it is perfectly possible that Hannibal was, for once, out-foxed, and the details of Livy's story of the annihilation of M. Centenius Paenula's force are scarcely credible, it is possible that Hannibal knew what he was doing, and saw his chance to inflict one of his devastating blows on an isolated Roman force, when the Roman high command thought he was following Claudius.

Hannibal, in any case, probably reasoned that there was little he could do directly to prevent the Romans' investing Capua, if they were determined to do so, and thought that there was always the possibility that his presence elsewhere might induce them to abandon the siege - he was to pursue the same strategy even more spectacularly in 211 (see below, p. 121ff.). Now, although he must soon have learnt that both consuls had returned to Capua, he himself did not return, but instead swooped on Apulia. The Roman army here was commanded by the praetor, Cn. Fulvius Flaccus, brother of the consul Q. Fulvius Flaccus, and had been successful in reducing a number of towns which had defected to the Carthaginians: it was now near Herdonea (Ordona), a town of some strategic importance, commanding the route from Beneventum to Brundisium near the coast. But the praetor's success had bred a certain carelessness in himself and his army, if Livy is to be believed (25.20.6-7), and Hannibal decided to seize his opportunity. Concealing some 3000 skirmishers among the farms and in the woodland and scrub, and throwing out 2000 cavalry as a screen to cover all possible routes of escape, he fell upon the praetor's army, and the result was a massacre: if we are to believe Livy (25.21.9-10), the praetor himself fled the field with 200 horsemen, but of the remaining 18,000 men in his army, not more than 2000 escaped.

Livy's account of this disaster has inevitably attracted suspicion because of the similar defeat of the proconsul, Cn. Fulvius Centumalus, also alleged to have taken place at Herdonea, in 210 (Livy 27.1.4-15). [38] But although there are similarities between Livy's accounts of the two defeats, and the coincidence of place and of the names of the Roman commanders suggest confusion, in a war like this, there was inevitably a tendency for engagements often to occur in the same place (cf. the battles outside Nola), and many of Rome's leaders had similar names, for obvious reasons. Finally, although it has been argued that the death of the proconsul in 210 must be historical, and that therefore the battle in which he was killed must also be historical, it is equally difficult to account for the charge of *perduellio* (treason) brought against the praetor, Cn. Fulvius Flaccus (Livy 26.2.7ff.), if his defeat is dismissed as unhistorical. [39] It therefore seems likely that the first battle of Herdonea, in 212, is also historical.

If the first battle of Herdonea is historical, it was Hannibal's greatest victory in the field since Cannae, but his departure from Campania enabled the Romans to concentrate seriously on the siege of Capua: grain was stored in Casilinum, in a new fort built at the mouth of the Volturnus, and at Puteoli, and all necessary equipment for the siege was made ready. Reinforcements were also summoned, the praetor, C. Claudius Nero, being ordered to bring his forces from the Claudian Camp near Suessula (Livy 25.22.7): at the beginning of the year, he had been assigned to command the two legions in Picenum, previously commanded by Terentius Varro, and then transferred to Suessula (Livy 25.3.4). Thus no fewer than three armies, consisting of six legions and, presumably, the usual allied contingents, in all, perhaps, 40-50,000 men, took station around Capua, and began the work of constructing a continuous ditch and palisade. Before these works were completed, the Capuans managed to send off yet another appeal to Hannibal, then once more in the neighbourhood of Tarentum, and the Romans also tried to sow disunity in the city by offering to allow anyone who left before March 15th (211), freedom and security of possession - an offer which Livy says the Capuans treated with contempt

(25.22.11-13). But their delegation to Hannibal had to be content with a vague promise that the consuls would not resist his coming, and only just managed to get back into the city before it was completely surrounded by a double ditch and rampart (Livy 25.22.15-6).

It was at about the time that the circumvallation of Capua was completed - i.e. in the autumn of 212 - that the siege of Syracuse came to an end, according to Livy (25.23.1), and although this has been disputed, there is no good reason to believe that Livy was wrong here. The argument that he was rests on the assumption that the gap in his narrative between Book 25, Chapter 31, which describes the fall of Syracuse, and Book 25, Chapter 40, which describes mopping-up operations in Sicily, is artificial, and that both passages should refer to the same consular year. Hence, it is argued, since the deaths of the Scipios in Spain, described by Livy in 25.32-39, actually happened in 211, although Livy assigned them to 212, the fall of Syracuse also properly belongs to 211.[40] But all this is very tenuous, and would mean that the events described by Livy in 25.23-31 would have to be stretched to cover a year or more. It seems best, then, to keep to Livy's chronology, and to accept that all the events described in 25.23-31, up to and including the fall of Syracuse, belong to the year 212 (i.e. the consular year 212/11), beginning in the spring, as Livy says (25.23.2), and as is confirmed by Polybius' reference to the spring festival in honour of Artemis (8.37.2). [41]

It is probably not going too far to say that even the threat to Capua was not so important to Hannibal's chances of success in Italy as the threat to Syracuse: the whole of the Greek south of Italy was now in his hands, except for Rhegium, as well as Bruttium and much of Lucania, and, if Sicily could have been won, he might have been able to establish secure communications with Carthage, and to open a "second front" in Italy. One has only to reflect what this might have meant, to realise that a Carthaginian success in Sicily, even if it had not brought ultimate victory to Carthage, could have greatly prolonged the war, particularly since the Scipios were defeated in Spain in 211, and could have left Rome as she was in the 270s, before her conquest of southern Italy. Success for Rome at Syracuse, moreover, came largely by accident, as we shall see, and only after Carthage, for the first time in the war, had begun to make a real effort at sea. In many ways, then, the fall of Syracuse was the turning point of the war.

According to Livy (25.23.2), at the beginning of spring, 212, Marcellus was uncertain whether to carry the war to Himilco and Hippocrates in Agrigentum, or to press on with the siege of Syracuse. He tried to bring about the betrayal of the city through Roman sympathisers, exiled at the time of the defection of the city, but this came to nothing when the plot was discovered. Then, shortly afterwards, the question of the ransom of a Spartan named Damippos, who had been captured by Roman warships while attempting to leave Syracuse on a mission to Philip of Macedonia, led to a series of parleys at what Livy calls "the harbour of Trogili" (*portus Trogilorum*), near a tower called "Galeagra" (25.23.10). The Harbour of Trogili has been plausibly identified with the inlet northeast of Scala Graeca now called Santa Panayia, [42] and the Galeagra Tower was probably one of the towers in the wall built by Dionysius I, somewhere in the section where it turns south, west of Panayia, to climb the slope towards Scala Graeca. This was where the Romans had attacked the year before, and they must have been familiar with the fortifications, but now a member of the Roman party at one of the parleys estimated the height of the tower, according to Polybius (8.37.1) - the wall according to Livy (25.23.11-2) - by counting the courses of masonry, which were even at this point, and found that it was lower than the Romans had thought.

The observation was reported to Marcellus, but there did not seem to be any way of making use of it until a deserter brought the information that the Syracusans were celebrating the festival of Artemis, and that although food was scarce, plenty of wine had been provided by the authorities. Immediately Marcellus called to mind what he had been told about the height of the fortifications, and determined to try to scale them at night. Picking his men with care, he sent men carrying made-to-measure ladders off first, escorted by a single maniple under a tribune, and then followed them with further maniples, one at a time, up to about 1000 men, while he himself, with the main force, moved on the Hexapyloi Gate. The scaling party got to the top of the wall without being spotted, since the guards were congregated in the towers celebrating the festival, and making their way along it, took the guards in the first two towers completely by surprise. When they reached the Hexapyloi Gate, they climbed down and smashed open a postern-gate, while a signal was made to Marcellus from the Gate. All attempt at concealment now abandoned, the Romans swarmed in to attack the wall, and, once inside, fought their way up onto the Epipolai heights. By dawn the Hexapyloi Gate was firmly in Roman hands, and Marcellus and his army were inside (Polybius 8.37). Epicydes led a desperate sortie from the Island of Ortygia, but once he realised that the Epipolai had fallen, withdrew into the Achradina quarter, which was shut off from the outer city by its own fortifications (Livy 25.24.8-10).

Marcellus knew that it would still be a difficult task to take the rest of the city, and decided first to try to persuade its defenders to surrender, using the Syracusan exiles present with his forces. However, this approach failed, as at first did a similar attempt to induce the surrender of the Euryalos fort, at the extreme western end of the Epipolai defences. But after the Roman troops had been allowed to plunder the captured quarters of the city, although Livy assures us that no lives were taken (25.25.9), the commander of Euryalos agreed to give up the fort on condition that he and his men were given safe conduct to Achradina. This meant that at least Marcellus no longer had to fear that relieving forces might get into Epipolai through the fort, and he proceeded to invest Achradina.

It was at this point that Himilco and Hippocrates arrived with their forces from Agrigentum to attempt to relieve the city. Hippocrates established himself on the shore of the Grand Harbour, and having signalled to Achradina, attacked what Livy calls (25.26.4) "the old Roman camp" - by which he probably means the camp at the Olympeum, south of the city (cf.24.33.3), rather than the winter camp at Leon north of the city, which was nowhere near the Grand Harbour. At the same time, Epicydes sallied from Achradina, and the Carthaginian fleet moved in close to the shore to prevent Marcellus from sending aid to his old camp. But the Carthaginian attacks were beaten off with some ease, if Livy is to be believed (25.26.5), and then tragedy struck their army: it was now autumn (Livy 25.26.7), and the heat and humidity combined to spread disease in both armies, but affected the Carthaginians more, probably not so much because it was unused to the climate, as Livy alleges, as because it was encamped near the marshes of the Anapos, whereas most of the Roman troops were now occupying the comparatively healthier heights of the Epipolai plateau. The Sicilians in the Carthaginian army dispersed to various towns in the neighbourhood, but the Carthaginian troops were virtually wiped out, and both Himilco and Hippocrates perished.

The only real hope for the Syracusans now lay in the Carthaginian fleet, which could at least get supplies into the beleagured city, and for the first time in the war, the Carthaginian navy made a real effort. A Carthaginian squadron under Bomilcar had entered the Grand Harbour in 213 (see above), only to leave again, shortly afterwards, unable to effect anything because of the numerical superiority of the Roman fleet (Livy 24.36.3 and 7): Livy says that the Roman fleet was easily twice the size of the Carthaginian squadron, and both he and Polybius mention a Roman fleet of 100 warships operating in Sicilian waters (Livy 24.27.5; Polybius 8.15), later reinforced by 30 more (Livy 24.36.4). But Bomilcar was back early in 212, this time with 90 ships, and at the time of the fall of Epipolai, left for Carthage with 35, leaving 55 behind to help the Syracusans: it is interesting that Livy says he slipped out of harbour when it was blowing so hard that the Roman blockading ships could not ride at anchor in the open sea (25.25.11), which suggests that in actual seamanship the Carthaginian seamen were still superior to the Roman, although Bomilcar's mission was desperate  and he may have been prepared to take a risk to get away. The Carthaginians responded to his news by manning a further 65 warships, and with these, making his total 100 in all, he returned within a matter of days to Syracuse (Livy 25.25.13), to take part in the attacks on Marcellus' positions.

Shortly after the outbreak of disease, Bomilcar had returned to Carthage again, probably, although Livy does not say so, to avoid contagion spreading to his crews. He may have left some of his warships at Syracuse, perhaps as many as 55 as before, but this time he was able to persuade his fellow-countrymen to send him back with no fewer than 130 warships, escorting as many as 700 merchant vessels loaded with supplies (Livy 25.27.2-4). Livy says that the wind was favourable for his crossing from Carthage to Sicily, but prevented him from rounding Cape Pachynon, so when the news of his approach reached Syracuse, Epicydes himself sailed to meet him, fearing that if the wind continued to blow from the east for many more days, he would return to Africa. According to Livy (25.27.8), further, Bomilcar was not so much afraid of the strength of the Roman fleet - actually he now had superior numbers - as of the fact that the wind was more favourable to the Romans than to himself, though in battle, of course, the ships of both fleets would have been rowed, not sailed. But, in the end, Epicydes persuaded him to try the fortunes of battle, and Marcellus, too, fearing to be pent up in a hostile city and attacked by land and sea, decided to stake everything on a naval battle, even with a numerically inferior fleet, and sailed south to Cape Pachynon.

For a few days the hostile fleets lay on either side of the cape while the wind blew itself out. When it subsided, Bomilcar was the first to move, standing out to sea apparently to round the cape more easily. It was, perhaps, the supreme moment of the war: Marcellus should have had about the same number of ships as Bomilcar, but had probably been forced to leave some behind to cover the Syracusan fleet and any Carthaginian warships there may have been at Syracuse, so that, for the first time, the Carthaginian fleet actually outnumbered the Roman. If Bomilcar had fought and won, the immediate effect would at least have been that Syracuse would have received ample supplies, and if his victory had been at all decisive, there would have been every chance of raising the siege, and perhaps recovering the situation in Sicily as a whole. But says Livy (25.27.12), when the Carthaginian admiral saw the Roman ships bearing down on him, "overcome by some sudden misgiving - it is uncertain what it was - he hoisted sail and stood out to sea, and having sent messages to Heraclea to order the transports back to Africa, himself sailed past Sicily and made for Tarentum." Perhaps he remembered the day, twenty-nine years before, when a Carthaginian fleet similarly bringing supplies to Lilybaeum, had gone down to defeat off the Aegates Islands and so lost the first war. But, whatever his reasons, the chance was gone.

Epicydes immediately seems to have given up hope, and sailed away to Agrigentum, and when this news reached the Sicilian troops gathering in towns near Syracuse, they too apparently at once decided that it was hopeless to continue the struggle. After discussing the matter with the besieged forces in Syracuse, they sent envoys to Marcellus to discuss terms of surrender, and these were agreed upon without difficulty. A delegation was then sent to lay them before the Syracusans, and there too things seemed to go well: the officers whom Epicydes had left in command, were swiftly eliminated, and after an assembly had been held to elect new magistrates, some of them were sent to Marcellus. But the army in Syracuse consisted largely of mercenaries and deserters, who thought that they had more to fear from Roman vengeance than the ordinary citizens, and these attacked the new magistrates and started an indiscriminate massacre of the civilian population (Livy 25.28-9).

The return of the delegation sent to Marcellus, however, drove a wedge between the deserters and the mercenaries, when the latter realised that they would be included in the terms offered, and at the same time Marcellus sent an agent, a Spanish auxiliary soldier, back with the Syracusan envoys, to sound out one of the six officers now in charge of the defences, a Spaniard like himself, named Moericus. Moericus responded favourably, and concocted a plan with Marcellus to let the Romans in through the section of walls he commanded, from the Fountain of Arethusa round to the mouth of the Grand Harbour. [43] On the agreed night, Marcellus ordered a quadrireme to tow a merchant-ship, loaded with soldiers, to Ortygia, where they were to be landed near the gate by the Fountain of Arethusa, while at the same time he made a feint attack on the Achradina defences. Moericus played his part according to plan, admitting the Roman troops through the gate near which they had landed, and as more and more of the defenders hurried out of Ortygia to beat off the attack on Achradina, more Roman troops were landed to seize the now lightly-guarded defences of Ortygia. When Marcellus learned that Ortygia and part of Achradina were in his hands, he called off his attack to give the Syracusans a chance to realise that they had no hope left (Livy 25.30. 7-12), and he judged the situation shrewdly, for the gates of Achradina were soon opened, and representatives sent to him, asking now for nothing more than that the lives of the citizens of Syracuse should be spared. The long siege was over.

Livy probably plays down the loss of life which followed Marcellus' decision to allow his troops to pillage the city, although he admits that some brutalities were committed (25.31.9). But the presence of Syracusan exiles, loyal to Rome, with the Roman army, probably checked some of the worst excesses, and there was certainly no question of the city's being destroyed, as was to happen to Corinth and Carthage itself, in the next century. It would be nice to record that Archimedes survived to live out an honoured old age, but despite Marcellus' orders, he was killed during the sack, intent upon a geometrical problem he was working out in the dust, according to Livy (25.31. 9-10). Plutarch, in his life of Marcellus (19.4-6), preserves three traditions about his end - that a soldier, sent by Marcellus, ordered him to accompany him to the general, and killed him when he refused to come until he had worked out his problem; that he was simply killed by a soldier when he refused to give up working on the problem; and that he was carrying some of his mathematical instruments to Marcellus, when some soldiers set upon him, thinking that he had valuables in the box. At all events, Archimedes did not survive to place his talents at the service of Rome, like some modern rocket expert.

Syracuse fell to Rome, probably, towards the end of 212, and although there still remained some Carthaginian forces in Sicily, and a number of towns which still sided with them, the chances of their being anything more than a minor irritant were now remote. Marcellus' authority was, however, certainly prolonged into 211 (Livy 26.1.6), and it is probably to this year that we should assign the mopping-up operations described by Livy in 25.40-1, since, as we shall see (below, p. 130), the defeat of the Scipios described in 25.32-9, although assigned by Livy to 212, almost certainly properly belongs to 211. After the fall of Syracuse, the main Carthaginian forces were concentrated on Agrigentum under Epicydes, Hanno, and a new general, called Mottones, [44] sent to Sicily by Hannibal. Mottones' successes in command of a force of Numidians encouraged the Carthaginians to advance to the river Himera, east of Agrigentum, and thither Marcellus also marched, taking up a position about six kilometres away (Livy 25.40.9). Here, too, Mottones had some success in skirmishes, but when he was called away to deal with a mutiny, Hanno and Epicydes, jealous of his success, gave battle with disastrous results, largely because of the desertion of their Numidian cavalry. The Carthaginian army was all but annihilated, and the remnants withdrew precipitately to Agrigentum. But Marcellus did not follow up his victory, perhaps because it was late in the year, and he wished to return to Rome in time for the elections, at which he intended to stand for the consulship (of 210/9).

Meanwhile, the elections for 211/10 had been held, probably soon after the fall of Syracuse, and Cn. Fulvius Centumalus and P. Sulpicius Galba had been elected consul, the latter despite his not having previously held any curule office (Livy 25.41.11). It is clear from the election of Fulvius Centumalus, that the same families which had come to power at the elections of 212/11, still held the ascendancy, and Galba probably owed his remarkable rise to the highest magistracy as much to his connections with the Fulvii and their supporters as to his high lineage - the family was said to be descended from Jupiter himself. But it is possible that the increasing importance of Greece at this time - (it was either in 212 or in 211 that the alliance was concluded with the Aetolian League) - also had something to do with Galba's election, for the Sulpicii had long had connections with Greece, [45] and towards the end of his year of office, Galba was assigned to the command in Greece, the first time this theatre of the war had been put under a man of consular rank.

But that there was no change in the direction of the war was shown when the Senate came to discuss the dispositions for 211, for it was agreed that the consuls of 212/11 should continue in command of the forces investing Capua, as well as C. Claudius Nero, one of the praetors of that year, and Marcellus was continued in his command in Sicily. Indeed, there were only two minor changes: C. Sulpicius, one of the new praetors, and possibly a relative of the consul Sulpicius Galba, took over from P. Cornelius Lentulus in western Sicily, and L. Cornelius Lentulus, another of the new praetors, took over from Q. Mucius Scaevola in Sardinia. Unfortunately, Livy's list of the legions in service this year (26.1.2ff.) is incomplete, for although he says that the total was to be twenty-three (26.1.13), he only actually mentions fifteen, and of these the two he assigns to the fleet commanded by T. Otacilius Crassus in Sicilian waters, appear here mysteriously for the first time (26.1.12). We can, however, easily see where six of the missing legions were to be found: two of them were those commanded by C. Claudius Nero at Capua which Livy omits here, but mentions later on (26.5.8), and two of them were under the command of Marcellus in Sicily - Livy merely says that Marcellus was to continue in command of the "army" which he had (26.1.6), and was to reinforce his army from the legions commanded by P. Cornelius Lentulus, who was now to be superseded by C. Sulpicius (26.1.7-9). But Livy must be wrong to separate Cornelius Lentulus' legions from those of Marcellus - all four will have taken part in the siege of Syracuse and other operations - and also wrong to imply that Marcellus had not used the *legiones Cannenses*, whose punishment was now to be shared by the disgraced survivors of the first battle of Herdonea (26.1.8-9). [46] Livy also omits the new *legiones urbanae* presumably raised this year, as they had been every year since 217. But even with these, the total only comes to nineteen, assuming that the statement that Otacilius commanded two with the fleet, is incorrect, and that the Spanish legions are also omitted: as we have seen, Livy never seems to have included these in his totals, and in any case, he now - wrongly - believed them to have been destroyed. But the two *legiones urbanae* of 212 would now have been ready for service in the field, and the addition of these two, brings the total to twenty-one.

There are, perhaps, three ways in which this total can be harmonized with that of Livy: firstly, it is possible that he was here drawing on a different source from the one he usually followed, and that his new source correctly gave the total as twenty-three, including the two legions in Spain, though Livy, who believed those legions to have been destroyed, did not realise this. Secondly, the total may include the two legions allegedly destroyed at the first battle of Herdonea, and may thus be evidence that no such battle had taken place - however, if the arguments above (see p. 114) are accepted, the balance of probability is in favour of the historicity of that battle. Thirdly, Livy may, after all, be correct in assigning Otacilius Crassus' fleet two legions for the first time: normally Roman warships only had 40 marines on board, but these could be increased to as many as 120, and it is possible that the renewed activity of the Carthaginian navy in Sicilian waters had induced the Senate to raise additional marines for the Roman fleet there, and that the total number of marines was now regarded as of a strength equivalent to two legions.

But whatever the truth of the matter, half or nearly half the legions stationed in Italy were still assigned to the siege of Capua, and it is clear that this was to be Rome's principal objective this year. Little attempt was made to take the city by assault, but a tight net was drawn about it, and lack of food soon became the most pressing problem for the defenders. Occasional sorties were made, however, and for a time the Capuans held their own, particularly in cavalry engagements, until the Romans adopted the practice of mounting infantry skirmishers behind their horsemen (Livy 26.4).[47] Hannibal, meanwhile, was torn between his continuing desire to take the citadel of Tarentum and the obvious necessity of doing something to relieve Capua. But when the desperate situation of Capua became clear to him, he decided to march into Campania, leaving his heavy baggage in Bruttium, and taking only picked troops with him. He apparently reached a position hidden behind Mt. Tifata without the Romans being aware of his presence, and from there concerted plans with the Capuans for a combined assault on the Roman lines. The Capuans were easily beaten back, but for a time it appeared that Hannibal's thrust was not to be denied, a unit of Spaniards, supported by three elephants, actually penetrating the siege-works at one point. But, in the end, the effort came to nothing, and Hannibal broke off the engagement, covering his retreat with his cavalry (Livy 26.5-6).

His dilemma was now acute: he did not want to stay in Campania because the Roman forces had swept the area clean of supplies, and in any case he was afraid of being hemmed in, perhaps remembering what had happened in 216. But he could not just abandon the city of Capua to its fate. His solution was typical in its boldness and simplicity: he would preserve his freedom of manoeuvre, and try to draw the Roman armies away from Capua, by marching on Rome itself. He was careful to let the Capuans know his plans, in case his departure so dispirited them that they were induced to surrender, and then, on the fifth day after his arrival, as Polybius tells us (9.5.7), he slipped away at night, leaving his camp-fires burning. The route he took to Rome has been the subject of much controversy. Polybius (9.5.8) merely says that he made a series of rapid marches "through Samnium", but Livy (26.9.1-3, 11-3) takes him along the *via Latina* until he came to Tusculum, then to Gabii and on into the district called Pupinia where he camped, some twelve kilometres from the city (26.9.12) - later (26.10.3), he says he moved round to the river Anio, and camped some four and a half kilometres from the city, near the Colline Gate. Livy, however, also records (26.11.10-11) a quite different route, which he attributes to Coelius Antipater, and although he tries to reconcile this route with his own by suggesting that Coelius' was the one used by Hannibal when he withdrew, it is likely that Coelius' route is in reality the correct one for the advance on Rome: it agrees with Polybius' vague remark that Hannibal marched "through Samnium", whereas the *via Latina* does not run through Samnium, and also makes more sense than a direct approach along the *via Latina,* since the roundabout route Coelius suggests would have brought the Carthaginian army almost to within sight of the city, before it became apparent that its real objective was Rome. According to Coelius, then, Hannibal left Campania for Samnium, and then marched into the territory of the Paeligni, and on past Sulmo (Sulmona) to that of the Marrucini. From there, he made his way past Alba to the territory of the Marsi, and by way of Amiternum (San Vettorino), Foruli (Civita Tommasa), Cutiliae (on Lago di Contagliano), Reate (Rieti) and Eretum (Grotta Marozza or Rimane), to the temple in the Grove of Feronia, which Livy says all authorities agreed he plundered (26.11.10). The only thing which does not quite make sense in this route, is the reference to the Marrucini, for if Hannibal had really marched into their territory, he would have had to descend the river Aternus (Aterno) towards the Adriatic, and then swing back to Alba (Colle di Albe). It is thus possible that the true reading should be "Marruvini" here, for Marruvium (San Benedetto) was the chief town of the Marsi, and on the route from Sulmo to Alba. The reference to the Marsi after Alba is then a difficulty, but could be explained by supposing that a branch of the Marsi living in the upper Liris valley is meant. [48] (See Map 13).

Hannibal's appearance before the city of Rome naturally caused something of a panic, but Polybius says (9.6.6) that, as luck would have it, the consuls had completed the enrolment of one legion, and were engaged in enrolling another one: probably he is here referring to the new *legiones urbanae* of 211, but the word he uses for the units in question - "στρατόπεδον" - can refer to a consular army of two legions, and he might, therefore, be referring to the old *legiones urbanae* of 212 as well as the new ones of 211; [49] in any case the *legiones urbanae* of 212 may well have also been available. Thus there appear to have been plenty of troops in the city, and when the consuls boldly led them out, Hannibal had to abandon any hope he might have had of taking the city by a *coup de main.* But in all probability, he had never intended any such thing, his ravaging being intended merely to further his primary objective of drawing the army away from Capua. When the consuls actually advanced to within just under two kilometres of his camp, however, he decided that the time had come to leave: sufficient time had elapsed for the Romans to have raised the siege of Capua, if they were going to do so, and it was no part of his plans to become involved in extensive operations in Latium. He had some difficulty in re-crossing the Anio, which he had originally crossed on his arrival before the city (Polybius 9.5.9), because the bridges had been broken down, and the consul, Sulpicius Galba, attacked his army as it was fording the stream. But the Numidians covered the retreat with their usual masterly efficiency, and he managed to break away, marching at speed for five days, perhaps up the valley of the Anio by way of Tibur and Subla-quaeum (Subiaco), in order to avoid the possibility of colliding with Roman forces marching to the relief of the city along the *via Latina.* When, however, he learned that the Roman army before Capua had not moved, he halted and made a surprise night attack on his pursuers. Then he set off again, marching rapidly all the way to Rhegium (Polybius 9.6-7): it was typical of Hannibal that, one gamble having failed, he should immediately try to retrieve the situation by surprise in another place.

This is Polybius' version of the famous march on Rome, but Livy not only has a different version of the route of the Carthaginian army to Rome, but also a different

account of the operations in and around the city: according to him (26.8ff.), the proconsul, Q. Fulvius Flaccus, learned of Hannibal's intentions from deserters, before the
Carthaginian army left Campania, and informed the Senate. Then,when the Senate con-
vened to discuss the situation, P. Cornelius Scipio Asina, consul of 221/0, urged the recall
of every available man and every available general for the defence of Rome, whereas
Q. Fabius Maximus argued that Hannibal was merely trying to lure the Romans from
Capua, and that they should not abandon the siege. Eventually a compromise was
reached, on the motion of P. Valerius Flaccus, probably the consul of 227/6, that the
commanders of the army before Capua be informed of the situation, and the decision
whether to send forces to Rome be left to them. Thereupon, the latter decided that
since Ap. Claudius Pulcher had been severely wounded in repulsing the Capuan attempt
to break through the Roman lines, Q. Fulvius Flaccus should march to the relief of the
city, taking with him picked troops from the three armies surrounding Capua, amounting
in all to 15,000 infantry and 1000 cavalry. Flaccus then marched to Rome along the *via
Appia,* entering the city by the Porta Capena at the time Hannibal was encamped in the
Pupinia district, some twelve kilometres from the city. Finally, in Livy's version, although
the consuls are mentioned, it is Fulvius Flaccus who plays the chief part in the defence of
Rome.

But all this is very dubious: if Fulvius Flaccus did come to Rome, as a mere proconsul, he would certainly have been outranked by the two consuls, and it is possible
that Livy or his source has confused him with Cn. Fulvius Centumalus, one of the two
consuls. On the other hand, it is, perhaps, significant that Polybius in discussing the
reactions of the Roman forces at Capua to the news of Hannibal's march, mentions only
Appius Claudius (9.7.2 and 7), so it is possible that Fulvius Flaccus was summoned to
Rome, as Livy says, and one would like to believe Livy's story (26.11.5ff.) that when
Hannibal was before the city, the land upon which he was encamped, came up for sale
and was sold without any diminution of price because of his presence. Hannibal's
response is said to have been to summon an auctioneer and to have the banks around
the *forum* put up for sale, but it is not recorded that he found any takers.

Hannibal's failure to return to Campania, and the return of Fulvius Flaccus, if he
had ever been away, naturally disheartened the defenders of Capua, and the harsh
punishment of some Numidians who pretended to be deserters in order to get through
to Hannibal with an appeal, finally broke their spirit. The *medix tuticus,* the chief
magistrate of Capua, was compelled to call a meeting of the council, and it voted to
send a delegation to the Roman commanders to surrender the city, despite a savage
speech by one of its members, Vibius Virrius, who afterwards committed suicide, with
about twenty-seven other members who agreed with him, rather than fall into Roman
hands. Next day, by order of the proconsuls, the Jupiter Gate, facing the main Roman
camp, was opened, and a legion, with a detachment of cavalry, entered the city. All
weapons were collected, guards stationed at all the gates, and the Carthaginian garrison
and all remaining senators made prisoners. According to Livy (26.15), the proconsuls
disagreed about what was to be done with the senators, who had been sent to Cales and
Teanum under guard, and Fulvius Flaccus had them executed on his own initiative. But
he also reports a tradition (26.16.1) that Ap. Claudius Pulcher had died before the

surrender. The surrender of Capua was followed by those of Atella and Calatia, and here too about seventy senators were executed, and other leading men imprisoned, but the rest of the population was sold into slavery (Livy 26.16.6). As to the fate of Capua, there was discussion about whether the city itself should be destroyed, but eventually the mass of resident aliens, freedmen, small traders and artisans was allowed to remain. The land and buildings were, however, to become the property of the Roman people, and no independent political organization was to be permitted. (Livy 26.16.7ff.).

It was at this point, according to Livy (26.17.1-3) - i.e., probably, towards the end of 211 - that the Senate passed a decree giving the command in Spain to the propraetor, C. Claudius Nero, and we must here leave the war in Italy to consider what had been happening in Spain since Hannibal's departure seven years before. The war in Italy still had eight years to run, and both sides were still to experience triumph and disaster before Hannibal finally left. But with the capture of Capua, the tide definitely turned against the Carthaginians. Hannibal still held parts of Apulia, Samnium and Lucania, most of the Greek cities of the south, and the whole of Bruttium, and was still very dangerous in the field, as he was to prove on more than one occasion. But he had never been able to shake the loyalty of the Latin states, nor that of the hard core of Rome's allies in the centre of the peninsula, and now that Rome had recovered control of most of Sicily, he must have realised that there was little chance of his ever again receiving reinforcements direct from Carthage. One chance remained to reverse the tide in Italy - if his brothers, Hasdrubal and Mago, could bring or send him help from Spain - and if he soon heard what had happened in Spain in 211, he must have had high hopes that the chance would come. But, as we shall see, it was to be four years before a Carthaginian army reached Italy from Spain, and then it came leaving the Carthaginian cause in Spain sliding to disaster, and was itself destroyed before it could join Hannibal.

## CHAPTER FIVE — THE WAR IN SPAIN

The operations in Spain during the Second Punic War were largely confined to the east and south of the Iberian peninsula. The main areas involved were the valley of the Ebro in the northeast, and that of the Guadalquivir in the south, with the route linking them running through the coastal plains of Valencia and Murcia, and through the mountains by the valleys of the Jucar or Segura to the headwaters of the Guadalquivir. The coastal regions had been partially colonized by both Greeks and Phoenicians, and here there were some towns in the normal Graeco-Roman sense. But they were probably quite small - even in Cartagena, one of the two most important towns in Carthaginian Spain (the other being Gades or Cadiz), Scipio took fewer than 10,000 prisoners (Polybius 10.17.6) - and although the sources talk about "cities" and "towns", they were probably more like fortified villages. Certainly the most significant native political units were tribal in nature, the most important tribes being the Ilergetes in Huesca, the Edetani or Sedetani in Teruel, the Celtiberes in the mountains between the headwaters of the Guadiana and the Tagus and the Ebro valley, the Carpetani or Carpesii around Toledo, in the eastern part of New Castile, and the Turdetani or Turduli in the south. The country, then as later, lent itself to guerilla warfare, and was extremely difficult to conquer or control, and since both sides relied heavily on the support of the local tribes, there was inevitably much changing of sides by the latter, as the balance of victory or defeat inclined now to Rome, now to Carthage. But although there is much talk of "treachery" in the sources, we can hardly blame the Spaniards for looking to their own interests. (See Map 14).

As we have seen (above, p. 50), the Romans originally seem to have assumed that their quarrel with Carthage would be fought out in Spain and Africa, and even after Hannibal had brought the war to Italy, the Senate evidently accepted the decision of the consul assigned to the Spanish front, to send his army there, since it made no move to recall it, and thereafter continually reinforced it until, after thirteen years of bitter warfare, the Carthaginians were driven from the country. The original Roman army landed in the autumn of 218, under the command of Cn. Cornelius Scipio, consul in 222/1, and brother of the consul of 218/7, P. Cornelius Scipio. It consisted of most of Publius Scipio's consular army, less the small force he must have taken back to Italy with him, that is to say, the greater part of two legions with their normal complement of citizen cavalry, together with 14,000 allied infantry, and 1600 allied horse, in all amounting to probably just under 25,000 men (cf. Livy 21.17.8). Gnaeus Scipio's task, according to Livy (21.32.3-4), was to assist the Spanish tribes already on friendly terms with Rome, to win others over to the Roman cause, and, ultimately, to drive the Carthaginians out of Spain. This was the first time a Roman army had ever set foot in a country which was to remain part of the Roman empire, after the war was over, for some six hundred years.

Gnaeus Scipio landed at Emporion (Ampurias), originally a colony of Rome's ally, Marseille, and, using this as a base, rapidly overran the coastal settlements as far south as the Ebro, making full use of his fleet. He then turned his attention to the interior, and, after further successes, defeated the Carthaginian forces left in control by Hannibal, at a place Polybius calls "Kissa" (3.76.7), which was probably either near Tarraco (Tarragona), or may indeed have been the Spanish name for Tarraco.[1] The commander of the Carthaginian forces, Hanno, was captured, as was the baggage left behind by Hannibal, and among the Spaniards taken prisoner was Andobales ('Indibilis' in Livy), chief of the Ilergetes (cf. Polybius 10.18.7), a man described by Polybius (3.76.7) as "τύραννος of the regions of the interior", a description which is confirmed by his apparent ability later to command both Suessetani (Livy 25.34.6) and Lacetani (Livy 28.24.4), both tribes living nearer the coast than his own Ilergetes. Hannibal's brother, Hasdrubal, who had been left in overall command in Spain, hastened to Hanno's aid, but was unable to do anything except cut off the crews of some of Scipio's ships, which were scattered about the countryside, and then withdrew to Cartagena. Gnaeus Scipio, for his part, according to Polybius (3.76.12-3), having punished those responsible for the slack discipline among the marines, gathered all his forces in Tarraco for the winter. But Livy (21.61.5-11) records a second intervention by Hasdrubal, and a further campaign by Scipio against the Ilergetes, Ausetani and Lacetani. Almost certainly Livy has misunderstood his sources here, and thought that two differing accounts of the same campaign were accounts of different campaigns.[2] But even without these further successes, the first round of the war in Spain had definitely gone to Rome: the Roman army was safely ashore, had a secure base, and had overrun much of the territory between the Ebro and the Pyrenees. Above all, Scipio's forces now lay athwart Hannibal's communications with his base.

The following year (217), Hasdrubal seems to have decided, first, to try to destroy Rome's naval superiority off the coast of northeast Spain: by so doing, he could have cut Scipio's communications with Italy, and then overwhelmed him on land in the absence of supplies and reinforcements. Accordingly, he manned 40 quinqueremes, and with his fleet keeping pace with him, advanced to the Ebro (Polybius 3.95.1-3). Scipio, according to Polybius (3.95.4-5), was at first inclined to meet the offensive on both land and sea, but realising that he was liable to be outnumbered on land, decided instead first to meet the naval threat. He should have had a decisive superiority in numbers, since the Roman fleet originally assigned to Spain had consisted of 60 quinqueremes (Polybius 3.41.2), and he evidently had some help from Marseille (cf. Polybius 3.95.6). But he now apparently only had 35 warships in all (Polybius 3.95.5). One explanation that has been offered[3] is that his brother had taken at least thirty, and possibly more, of the original sixty, back to Italy with him from the Rhône, but this seems unlikely since Publius probably only took a small force with him, and it is more likely that Gnaeus was simply unable to man all his ships: his crews had suffered in Hasdrubal's raid the previous year, and, realising his weakness on land, he may well have drafted some of his naval personnel into his army. Nor do we know how many Massiliot warships he had, though the guess that they numbered twenty, and were replaced by the twenty Roman ships Publius Scipio brought to Spain later in 217 (Polybius 3.97.2), may be right.[4] But despite its slight inferiority in numbers, Gnaeus' fleet won a resounding success, perhaps through the Massiliots' nullifying the superior speed and manoeuvrability of the Carthaginian warships by forming a second line, as is suggested by the famous fragment of the historian Sosylos (Jacoby, *FGH* 176 F 1), the man who taught Hannibal Greek, according to Cornelius Nepos (*Hannibal* 13.3). After a brief struggle, the Carthaginian fleet fled to shore, losing six ships in the process, and when the Romans and their allies boldly followed, they succeeded in capturing nineteen more (Polybius 3.96.6). Thus the Carthaginian navy in Spanish waters was halved at a stroke, and Rome's command of the sea off the coast of Spain was never again challenged.

Livy (22.20.4-10) follows his account of the naval battle by describing attacks by the Roman fleet on a place called Onusa, presumably on the coast between the Ebro and Cartagena, although Polyaenus (8.16.6) seems to call Cartagena "Oinussa" ; on Cartagena itself, and on another place called Loguntica, where a great quantity of esparto grass was stored for making ships' ropes: according to the elder Pliny (*Naturalis Historia* 31.8.43.94), Cartagena was once called "Spartaria" because of the esparto grass which grew there, so Loguntica was perhaps also in the area. Finally the Roman fleet is alleged to have attacked Ebusus (Ibiza) in the Balearic group of islands. But Polybius says nothing of all this, nor about the further land campaigns under Gnaeus Scipio which Livy records (22.20.10ff.). According to the latter, Gnaeus' successes persuaded no fewer than 120 Spanish tribes to throw in their lot with Rome, and confident now in his land forces, he advanced to the *"saltus Castulonensis"* (the pass of Castulo), while Hasdrubal withdrew to Lusitania (Portugal) and the Atlantic coast. But the only known Castulo lay on the river Guadelimar, in the modern province of Jaén,[5] and it is inconceivable that Gnaeus could have advanced as far as that. Moreover, when Livy further alleges (22.21.3) that when the Romans had withdrawn from the pass to the coast, the Ilergetes began to raid the land of Rome's allies, he implies that the "pass of Castulo" lay near their territory, which was north of the Ebro. Livy goes on to say that although Scipio sent a punitive expedition which easily crushed the Ilergetes, their rising drew Hasdrubal back across the Ebro to the territory of the Ilergavonenses, a people who apparently lived on the coast near the mouth of the Ebro, while the Roman forces took up a position at "Nova Classis", a place which should also have been on the coast, judging from its name ("New Fleet"). But then the Celtiberes, instigated by Scipio, attacked Carthaginian Spain, and after Hasdrubal had hastened to repel them, twice defeated him. All this is extraordinarily complicated, and since none of it is mentioned by Polybius, one is tempted to reject it out of hand: certainly, if Scipio did fight any campaigns on land, after his naval victory, they were fought north of the Ebro, for Polybius, who passes straight from his account of the naval battle off the Ebro to the arrival of Gnaeus' brother, Publius, states categorically (3.97.4) that up to this time, the Romans had not ventured to cross the Ebro. But apart from the naval operations by the Roman fleet, which make sense, the rest of Gnaeus Scipio's exploits, as recorded by Livy, are probably unhistorical.[6]

According to Polybius (3.97.1), it was the news of Gnaeus Scipio's naval victory which finally prompted the Senate to send his brother, Publius, to Spain, with twenty ships. Livy (22.22.1) appears to have written that he had thirty warships (only two inferior MSS have the figure 20), and adds 8000 men, and a great quantity of supplies.

In Polybius' view, the decision to reinforce the army in Spain was mainly due to fear that if the Carthaginians were allowed to regain control there, they would be able to send reinforcements to Hannibal (3.97.3), and he is surely right. The brothers were now encouraged to cross the Ebro and advance as far as Saguntum, taking up a position near the temple of Aphrodite, about seven kilometres from the city (Polybius 3.97.6): remains of both the temple and of the Scipios' camp have been found in modern times.[7] Here, through the treachery of an influential Spanish chieftain named Abilyx, and the gullibility of the Carthaginian garrison-commander, Bostar, a number of hostages left in Saguntum by Hannibal to ensure the loyalty of their tribes, fell into Roman hands, and were sent back to their homes by the Scipios. This incident is told at inordinate length by Polybius (3.98-9), and its truth has been doubted, partly because it is difficult to see why the hostages were in Saguntum rather than in Cartagena, partly because the younger Scipio later made similar use of the hostages he did find in the latter city (Polybius 10.18.3ff.).[8] But although it is likely that the importance of the incident has been exaggerated, one is reluctant to reject Polybius' testimony in its entirety. In any case, what was significant in this, probably the first Roman foray beyond the Ebro, was the apparent ease with which the Scipios advanced as far as Saguntum: it is clear that the Carthaginian hold on this part of Spain was tenuous. It is possible that it was also now that Iliturgi and Intibili defected to Rome, assuming that the attacks on these places by the Carthaginians two years later (Livy 23.49.5-4) refer to attacks on towns in Catalonia, although the best known Iliturgi certainly lay not in Catalonia but in Andalusia (see below, p. 129).

Any attempt by Hasdrubal to recover the situation in 216 had to be postponed until he received reinforcements, and even when these arrived, he was prevented from taking the offensive by a serious rising among what Livy (23.26.5ff.) calls the Tartesii, but were probably the Turdetani.[9] Even when these were crushed, after some severe fighting, the news that Hasdrubal had been ordered to march to Italy caused further unrest. Hasdrubal wrote to the Carthaginian senate urging it to send reinforcements to control Spain, if it was serious about his going to Italy, and it was only after the arrival of a considerable force under Himilco, that he finally felt free to set out, either late in 216, which is what Livy implies (23.27.9ff.), or, more probably, early in 215.[10] The Scipios concentrated their forces near a place called Ibera, a town on the south bank of the Ebro near its mouth, and here a decisive battle was fought. Hasdrubal used much the same tactics as his brother had done at Cannae, placing his Spanish infantry in the centre, flanked by what Livy (23.29.4) calls "Poeni" on the right, and Africans and mercenaries on the left, with his cavalry, as usual, on the wings. Since the Poeni are contrasted with the Africans, if Livy or his source was being accurate here, they were probably levies from Carthaginian and other Phoenician settlements in Spain (see above, p. 9). But the Spaniards were not equal to containing the thrust of the Roman infantry in the centre, and although the Poeni and Africans fell on its flanks as it drove forward, it was able to face outwards to left and right and drive apart the jaws of the trap. As a result, the Carthaginian army was almost annihilated, though Hasdrubal himself was able to make his escape. The Roman victory was less important in the context of the Spanish war than in that of the war as a whole, for although it led to no decisive result in Spain, it effectively prevented Hasdrubal from marching to Italy, as Livy remarks

(23.29.17), and also diverted to Spain the reinforcements under Mago originally intended for Hannibal in Italy (Livy 23.32.5-12).

Livy records further Roman successes in Spain during the years 215 to 212, but it is doubtful how far they can be accepted as historical. In his first passage (23.48.4-49. 14), he first mentions an appeal by the Scipios for money to pay their troops and for supplies of all kinds for their army, and goes on to describe how contracts were let to three companies of businessmen (see above, p. 99). Then he gives an account of Roman victories at places called Iliturgi and Intibili, and although a case has been made out for locating these places in Catalonia, rather than in Andalusia where the best known Iliturgi was certainly located, [11] we can, surely, not accept the exaggerated details of Carthaginian losses. In the second passage (24.41-2), Livy says that Mago and Hasdrubal routed large forces of Spaniards, and that "further Spain" (i.e., presumably, at this date, Spain beyond the Ebro) would have defected to the Carthaginians had not Publius Scipio rapidly crossed the Ebro and come to the aid of Rome's allies. He then records operations near *Castrum Album* (White Fort), famous as the place where Hannibal's father, Hamilcar, was killed. This is usually thought to be the same as the "Akra Leuke" (White Cape) of Diodoros (25.10.3), now Alicante, although Diodoros actually says that Hamilcar was killed at Helike, and Livy's *Castrum Album* may have been in the Sierra Morena, near Castulo, which he says defected to Rome soon afterwards (24.41.7). [12] But whether the *Castrum Album* is to be located at Alicante or near Castulo (which lay in Jaén: see below, p. 130) it is hard to believe that Roman forces were operating as far south as this in 214. Next, in Livy's narrative, comes a further Carthaginian attack on Iliturgi (24.41.8-10), which is obviously a doublet of the one discussed above, [13] and on an otherwise unknown place called Bigerra (24.41.11), and then he goes on to describe battles near Munda and Aurinx (24.42.1-8), which are again too far south for the elder Scipios to be winning battles there in 214, assuming that Munda is the famous place of that name (now Monda in Malaga), and that Aurinx is the same as the place called Orongis, attacked by Lucius Scipio in 207 (Livy 28.3.2: see below, p. 144), which is thought to have been situated in Granada. Finally, under this year (214), Livy almost apologetically records the recovery of Saguntum, though since he says (24.42.9) that it was now the eighth year it had been in Carthaginian hands, his source for its recovery almost certainly dated it in 212/11, rather than in 214/3.

In the final passage of his account of the Scipios' activities in Spain, before his description of the operations which led to their deaths, Livy alleges (24.48) that they contacted the Numidian prince, Syphax, in Africa, and formed an alliance with him, whereupon the Carthaginians made use of a rival, Gala, and of his famous son, Masinissa, to defeat him. This episode is reminiscent of the younger Scipio's attempts to win Syphax over in 206 (cf. Livy 28.17.2ff.), and may thus be another doublet. [14] But Livy does give circumstantial details - for example, the name of one of the centurions allegedly sent to help Syphax train his Numidians in infantry tactics - and later (27.4.5ff.) records the sending of envoys by Syphax to Rome in 210. Appian (*History of Spain*, 15) alleges that the Carthaginians recalled Hasdrubal to deal with the threat from Syphax, and then sent him back to Spain, with reinforcements. There may, thus, be some truth in all this, but one would have thought that contact with Syphax implies that the Scipios were far further south than they are really likely to have been.

But even though Livy, or his sources, clearly exaggerated Roman successes in these years, and probably took the Scipios further south than they ever ventured in reality, it is clear that by 212 they had extended Roman influence over many of the tribes lying south of the Ebro, and now felt confident enough to attempt offensives against the main centres of Carthaginian power, the area around Cartagena, and the valley of the Baetis (Guadalquivir). Livy dates the offensive to 212, but it is almost certain that it should be dated to 211. Firstly, Livy himself remarks (25.32.1) that nothing much had happened in Spain for two years before the offensive, whereas, as we have seen, he records considerable operations in 214 (24.41-2). Secondly, he says (25.36.14) that Gnaeus Scipio was killed in his eighth year of command in Spain, and since he first arrived there in 218, this means that he was killed in 211. Finally, according to Livy (26.17.1-3), it was in the autumn of 211, after the capture of Capua, that C. Claudius Nero was sent to Spain to take over command of the remnants of the Scipios' armies. [15]

After their successes in 214, then, we must suppose that the Scipios waited for two years, 213 and 212, before they felt strong enough to begin a further offensive. These were years when much of the Roman war-effort was devoted to Sicily and Campania, and the Scipios may well have found themselves starved of supplies. But by 211 the Carthaginians had considerably reinforced their armies in Spain, and the Scipios were now faced by three generals, Hasdrubal Gisgo, and Hannibal's brothers, Hasdrubal (Barca) and Mago. Perhaps unaware by just how much they were now out-numbered, the Roman commanders decided to divide their own forces in an attempt to crush the enemy simultaneously, Publius taking two-thirds against Hasdrubal Gisgo and Mago, who were acting in conjunction, and Gnaeus one third and the Celtiberian allies, in whom they placed a dangerous confidence, against the other Hasdrubal (Livy 25.32.1-8). The brothers advanced together as far as a place Livy calls "Amtorgis" (25.32.9), the whereabouts of which is unknown, and there Gnaeus left Publius to face Hasdrubal Barca, who was in the vicinity, while he set out to confront the other Carthaginian generals.

Publius was the first to fall: he had perhaps advanced as far as Castulo (near Linares in the province of Jaén), [16] as Appian says (*History of Spain,* 16), though Gnaeus can hardly have got as far as Urso (Orsuna), as Appian alleges in the same passage, when he began to find himself under increasing attack by Numidian cavalry led by Masinissa. Then, hearing that the Spanish chieftain Andobales (Indibilis), who had evidently been released since his capture in 218 (see above, p. 126), was approaching with 7500 Suessetani, he attempted a forced night march to destroy this force before it could join the Carthaginians. But the plan misfired, and finding himself beset by all his foes, he fell fighting with most of his men, apart from a detachment under Tiberius Fonteius, which held the camp (Livy 25.34). Meanwhile Gnaeus had been deserted by his Celtiberian allies (Livy 25.33), and had decided to retreat, but had evidently not got far before Hasdrubal Barca was joined by his fellow-generals, fresh from their triumph over Publius. A swift withdrawal was now vital, but although the Romans were able to slip away at night, next day the Numidians caught up with them, and by continual harassment brought the column to a halt (Livy 25.35). Desperately,

Gnaeus Scipio took his stand on a bare, stony hill, piling the pack-loads around its summit to make some sort of rampart. But the enemy soon swarmed over these improvised defences in overwhelming numbers, and Gnaeus himself was killed, either in the assault, or shortly afterwards in a watch-tower in which he had taken refuge. The place where he met his fate is named as "Ilorci" by the elder Pliny (*Naturalis Historia* 8.3.9.), and this has been plausibly identified with the modern village of Lorqui, some nineteen kilometres north of Murcia, on the river Segura. [17] It was tragic that the two Scipios should perish like this when elsewhere the tide was at last beginning to turn in Rome's favour, for they had nobly maintained the struggle, far from home, for eight long years. Cicero, in his speech on behalf of L. Cornelius Balbus, a citizen from Gades, refers to them as the "thunderbolts of our empire" (*fulmina nostri imperii*: 34), presumably thinking of their brief glory, followed by sudden extinction, though Lucretius (3.1034) and Vergil (*Aeneid* 6.842-3) use a similar image (*fulmen/fulmina belli*) to refer, perhaps, to the swift and destructive power of the younger Scipio and his adoptive grandson, Scipio Aemilianus.

The remnants of the two Roman armies somehow managed to make their way back to the Ebro, under Tiberius Fonteius, who had been left in charge of his camp by Publius Scipio, and Lucius Marcius, a Roman Knight serving in Gnaeus Scipio's army, either as a senior centurion, according to Cicero (*pro Balbo* 34), or as a tribune of the soldiers, according to Valerius Maximus (2.7.15). Livy (25.37.1-6) says that Marcius was unanimously elected general by the remnants of the Roman forces, and set about fortifying a position north of the Ebro. Here he is alleged, first, to have inflicted heavy losses on the Carthaginian army of Hasdrubal Gisgo, by a sudden sortie from his own camp (Livy 25.37.11-5), and then to have surprised the two Carthaginian camps (Livy 25.37.16-39.11). But that these romantic exploits are probably largely unhistorical is revealed by the confusion prevailing among Livy's sources, which he here quotes in some detail (25.39.12-5): Claudius Quadrigarius gave the Carthaginian losses as 37,000 killed and 1830 captured; Valerius Antias said that it was Mago's camp which was captured, with a loss of 7000 men, and that Hasdrubal was then defeated in battle with a loss of 10,000 killed and 4330 captured; and Piso, finally, said that 5000 of Mago's army were ambushed and killed in pursuit of the Roman forces - a version which, apart from the surely still exaggerated losses inflicted on the Carthaginians, seems the most plausible. An analysis of the forces the younger Scipio had at his disposal in 209, bearing in mind that he had brought 10,000 infantry and 1000 cavalry with him (Livy 26.19.10), and that Claudius Nero had previously brought about the same number (see below), shows that Marcius and Fonteius can only have had about 8000 infantry and 1000 cavalry, and with so small a force they must have been compelled to remain on the defensive. But one should not deny all credit to Marcius, for the Romans did manage to hold the line of the Ebro, and Livy records (25.39.17) that a shield, allegedly bearing a portrait of Hasdrubal, and called the "Marcian shield", hung in the temple of Jupiter on the Capitol until the great fire of 83, and if this shield did have something to do with the Lucius Marcius of the Second Punic War, it looks as though he was honoured by his contemporaries.

At all events, whether through the efforts of Marcius and his men, or through their own negligence, the Carthaginians failed to press home their advantage, though it is possible that they did succeed in extending their influence once more even beyond the Ebro, for there were hostages from the Ilergetes, who lived between the Ebro and the Pyrenees, in Cartagena in 209, although they might have been there ever since Hannibal had subdued the Ilergetes in 218. [18] In the late autumn of 211, C. Claudius Nero arrived with reinforcements to take over command of the Roman army. According to Livy (26.17.1), he brought with him 6000 Roman infantry and 300 Roman cavalry, with the same number of Latin infantry and 800 allied cavalry. These figures have been doubted, [19] and the figure of 300 citizen cavalry suggests that Nero had a single legion of citizen troops. If this is right, and the number of his citizen troops was only about 4000, but his Latin infantry did number 6000, we get Appian's figure of 10,000 infantry for his army (*History of Spain,* 17). Appian also gives him 1000 cavalry, which is almost the same as Livy's 1100, but falsely says that Marcellus accompanied him - probably this is due to confusion with Marcius.

Livy asserts (26.17.2ff.) that with these forces, augmented by the *socii navales* from his fleet, Nero marched to join Ti. Fonteius and Marcius at the Ebro, and then, crossing the river, succeeded in trapping Hasdrubal Barca at a pass called "Black Stones" (*Lapides Atri*), in the country of the Ausetani, between Iliturgi and Mentissa. The pass has been identified with the defile still called "Monte Negro" between Cabanes (which may be the Catalonian Iliturgi) and Barriol, [20] but it must remain doubtful whether Nero would really have ventured across the Ebro so soon after the defeat of the Scipios. However, the argument that his associations with Fabian strategy would have made him naturally inclined to stand on the defensive, [21] is misconceived, for in reality he was associated more with the new offensive spirit demonstrated by the relentless siege of Capua, and his actions in 207 (see below, p. 185ff.) hardly stamp him as a "defensive" general: if he did stand on the defensive in Spain, it was because he could do nothing else. If, on the other hand, he did cross the river, as Livy says he did, this too came to nothing, for Hasdrubal is said to have evaded the trap at the Black Stones pass by keeping up his negotiations with the Romans, while his men slipped quietly away to safety. But it is clear that Nero was at least able to hold on to the coastal area north of the Ebro, and thus provide a beach-head for the renewed Roman offensive in 209.

It was almost certainly in 210, and not in 211, as Livy thought, that a new commander was appointed to the Spanish front in the person of the young P. Cornelius Scipio, son and nephew respectively of the Scipios killed in 211. Since Livy believed that the elder Scipios were killed in 212, it was, perhaps, natural for him to date the appointment of the younger to 211, but the relevant fragments of Polybius show that the capture of Cartagena, which Livy dated to 210, actually occurred in 209, and Livy evidently agreed with Polybius that the capture of Cartagena followed Scipio's first winter in Spain (cf. 26.20.1-6 and 26.41.1). In any case, C. Claudius Nero, by Livy's own account, can only have been appointed to the Spanish command late in 211, and the Senate would hardly have appointed yet another commander to supersede him, in the same year. [22] The circumstances of the younger Scipio's appointment to the command were most unusual: he had never held any office higher than that of curule aedile - in 213, not in 217 as Polybius implies (10.4.5 - cf. Livy 25.2.6-8)[23] - and when given *imperium pro consule* to go to Spain, was technically a *privatus,* whereas normally such authority was only granted to an outgoing consul or praetor. There was a recent parallel for the grant of *imperium* to a *privatus* within Scipio's own family, for his uncle, Gnaeus, had apparently held it from 217 to 211,[24] although he had ceased to be consul in 221. But Gnaeus had at least been consul, and the grant of *imperium* to a young man who had never held high office, was certainly unprecedented. We can hardly believe Livy's story (26.18.1ff.) that recourse was had to holding an election for the Spanish command, since there was no agreement on whom to send, and that Scipio offered himself as a candidate when no one else seemed prepared to go - the Romans just did not do things like that - but we can, possibly, accept the detail that the appointment was made by the *comitia centuriata* (cf. Livy 26.18.9): it would have been in keeping with the Roman respect for constitutional forms that when it was a question of conferring *imperium pro consule* on a *privatus,* it was left to the body which elected the consuls. However, it seems more likely that the Senate had already decided to put forward Scipio's name, than that it literally left the choice to the vagaries of popular whim, although if, as seems likely, the proposal was controversial, those in favour of it may well have tried to whip up "popular" support.

But why did anyone think of putting forward so comparatively unknown a candidate for so dangerous a task, when there were tried and experienced commanders available, for example, M. Claudius Marcellus, who had returned from Sicily in 211, and was consul in the very year of Scipio's appointment? Probably the explanation lies, as usual, in the rivalries of differing groups within the Senate: Fabius' influence was still strong, as was to be shown by his re-election to the consulship for 209/8, and many Senators may have been inclined to abandon Spain, at least for the time being, except, perhaps, for a limited holding-operation in the northeast, in favour of concentrating on the war in Italy, and, possibly, in Greece - it was in this year that P. Sulpicius Galba was sent there as proconsul. But the Scipionic faction will still have been immensely influential, despite the deaths of so many of its leading men, and may have been able to persuade a majority in the Senate that it was essential not to neglect Spain. If this was the case, the choice of the young Scipio was, perhaps, not so surprising: he had a good record as a soldier, albeit in minor posts, and there was something to be said for sending a relative of the dead Scipios, for he might be able to take up the ties they had established with some of the Spanish communities. Above all, it must be remembered, he was now the head of the most powerful *gens* among the Roman nobility, and thus a political force to be reckoned with in his own right, nor is it at all inconceivable that his clear-sighted and glamorous personality had already made an impression on contemporaries, as it certainly was to do later.[25]

But whatever the reasons for it, the choice of the younger Scipio was, of course, abundantly justified by results. He landed at Emporion, probably in the summer of 210, with a force of 10,000 infantry and, probably, 1000 cavalry (Livy 26.19.10), bringing the total Roman forces in Spain up to 28,000 infantry and 3000 cavalry (cf. Polybius 10.6.7 and 9.6). From Emporion he marched to Tarraco, and, summoning representatives of the Spanish tribes to meet him there, spoke to them in enthusiastic and encouraging terms. He then made a tour of the areas still under Roman control, congratulating the troops who had so gallantly held on, and doing special honour to

Lucius Marcius (Livy 26.19.10-20.4). He spent the winter of 210/9 at Tarraco, and there he must have begun to plan his campaign for the coming year.

For once we are lucky enough to have, from Polybius, some idea of the actual considerations which governed an ancient general's thinking, for Polybius says (10.9.3) that his account was derived from a letter Scipio himself wrote to Philip of Macedonia, presumably some fifteen or more years later, when Philip had become an ally of Rome. Thus, Polybius tells us (10.7.1), even before he had left Rome, Scipio had come to the conclusion that the defeat of his father and uncle was due to the treachery of their Spanish allies, and their own division of their forces. Now he knew that Rome's allies north of the Ebro had remained loyal, and had learned not only that there was serious disaffection against Carthaginian rule to the south, but that the Carthaginian generals were quarrelling among themselves (Polybius 10.7.3). Their forces were also divided: according to Polybius (10.7.5), Mago was "on this side of the Pillars of Herakles" among the Konioi, but the Konioi (*Conii* in Latin) are usually thought to have lived in the extreme south of what is now Portugal, well outside the Pillars of Herakles (i.e. the Straits of Gibraltar), so perhaps what Polybius actually wrote was "outside" (ἐκτός) the Pillars, "inside" (ἐντός) being a subsequent copyist's error; alternatively, Polybius' Konioi may be the same as Appian's Kouneoi (*History of Spain,* 57-8), who seem to have lived near the lower Baetis.[26] Hasdrubal Gisgo, according to Polybius, was in Lusitania, near the mouth of the Tagus, and Hasdrubal Barca, among the Carpetani (or Carpesii), near the headwaters of the Tagus, in the modern province of Toledo.

Livy (26.20.6) has different dispositions - Hasdrubal Gisgo near Gades, Mago near Castulo, and Hasdrubal Barca in the region of Saguntum - but it is impossible to believe that Hasdrubal Barca was near Saguntum in the winter of 210/9, since, if he had been, Scipio could not have contemplated attacking Cartagena, and there is no reason to doubt that Polybius is also right about the positions of the other two Carthaginian generals at that time. However, it is just possible that the dispositions Livy records for the three Carthaginian armies are correct for the winter of 211/10, which is their purported date in his account, even though he was wrong to believe that Scipio had already arrived in 211. In this case, the Carthaginian armies may have withdrawn from east to west during 210, perhaps in pursuance of a plan to make it possible for Hasdrubal Barca to march to Italy, necessitating the other two generals' standing on the defensive. But by the winter of 210/9, Scipio knew that the Carthaginian armies were widely separated, and at a considerable distance from himself, the nearest being the one commanded by Hasdrubal Barca. He rejected the idea of attacking them separately, because of the risk that if he marched against one of them, the others might be able to combine with it to overwhelm him, if he ran into difficulties (Polybius 10.7.7). But their separation, and the realisation that none lay within ten days' march of Cartagena (Polybius 10.7.5), probably gave him an idea, nothing less than an attack on Cartagena itself.

The city was an obvious prize: it was the only place with a decent harbour on the east coast of Spain and favourably situated for the direct run to Carthage; the Carthaginians kept most of their treasure and war-material there, as well as the hostages from the Spanish tribes, and yet it only had a garrison of 1000 regular soldiers, because the Carthaginians could not conceive that anyone would attack it (Polybius 10.8.2-4). Scipio had learned too, that its position, though strong, was not as strong as it might appear at first sight, for he had been told by fishermen who fished there, that the lagoon which protected the city on the north was shallow and fordable in most places, and that the water in it usually receded towards evening (Polybius 10.8.6-7). Finally, he calculated that if he failed to take the place quickly, by assault, his mastery of the sea would enable him to save his army (Polybius 10.8.9).

Scipio communicated his plan to no one except his friend, Caius Laelius, since obviously, if any inkling of it reached the Carthaginians, they were bound to take steps either to reinforce the garrison, or to move their field-armies nearer to the city. Probably as early in the year (209) as the weather made possible (cf. Livy 26.41.1), so as to anticipate any possible move by any of the three Carthaginian armies, he ordered fleet and army to assemble at the mouth of the Ebro, and joined them there himself with 5000 Spanish troops. [27] He then ordered Laelius to take command of the fleet, and set off himself with the land forces, numbering 25,000 infantry and 2500 cavalry (Polybius 10.9.6), leaving M. Iunius Silanus, praetor in 212/11, and now exercising either proprae-torian or proconsular authority,[28] to guard the Ebro with 3000 foot and 500 horse, according to Polybius (10.6.7), 300 horse, according to Livy (26.42.1). Polybius says (10.9.7) that the march to Cartagena took seven days, and Livy (26.42.6), presumably following him, says the same, but swiftly as Scipio would have wanted to move, no army could have marched 460 kilometres in a week, so we must assume either that Polybius or his source was mistaken, or that the figure in our text of Polybius is corrupt, though in that case, the corruption took place before Livy's time. Alternatively, the seven days could originally have referred to a march from some place much nearer Cartagena, and could have been mistakenly referred by Polybius to the whole march.

Polybius, who says that he writes from his own observation (10.11.4), has left us a careful description of Cartagena as it then was, and this fits what can be seen to this day, provided that we correct Polybius' orientation, which seems to be wrong by at least 45° (thus "north" in Polybius should be "north-east", and so on), and note that the three smaller hills in the city which Polybius implies lay in a line from west to east (10.10.10), actually lay on the points of a triangle: without proper maps, or a compass, such errors in ancient writers are perfectly excusable, though it is curious that Polybius correctly orientates the bay at the head of which the city lies, and then goes on to give it dimensions which are too large (10.10.1).[29] The city lay on a peninsula, joined to the mainland by a narrow neck of land to the east, with an extensive lagoon to the north, connected with the sea on the south by an artificial canal to the west. Within the city, the main features were the five hills: on the south, facing the bay, was the hill on which lay the temple of the god Polybius calls Asklepios (probably Eshmoun to the Carthagin-ians), now Monte Concepcion; to the east, opposite the neck of the peninsula, the hill of Hephaistos (the Carthaginian Kousor), now Castillo de Despeña Perros; to the north, along the shore of the lagoon, the hill of Kronos (the Carthaginian Baal Hammon), now Monte Sacro, and the hill of Aletes - apparently a local Spanish deity - now San José; and on the west, by the canal, the hill on which stood a magnificent palace, said to have built for Hannibal's brother-in-law, Hasdrubal, now Monte Molinete. Scipio's camp was to the east of the neck of the isthmus joining the city to the mainland, with his entrenchments to the west protecting him from attack by relieving forces, and the side facing the city left open to facilitate his assault. Here there was another hill, now called Castillo de los Moros, which Livy (26.44.6) calls the Hill of Mercury: this would have added to the strength of the Roman position, and provided an excellent command-post - it is not mentioned by Polybius. (See Map 15).

When he had taken up his position, and his fleet had arrived, Scipio harangued his men, explaining his reasons for coming to attack the city, and promising rewards to those who first mounted the walls, or displayed conspicuous gallantry in other respects. All this was normal, but then, according to Polybius (10.11.7), Scipio went on to say that the god Poseidon (Neptune to the Romans) had appeared to him in his sleep, and suggested the plan to him, declaring that he would so clearly co-operate with them, when the time for action came, that his services would be manifest to the whole army. There has been considerable speculation about the implications of this story for Scipio's personality. [30] Polybius evidently thought (cf. 10.2-5) that the tradition that Scipio was specially favoured by fortune, had gone too far, and in emphasising the rational calculation on which his success was based, has conjured up a man who deliberately played upon the superstitions of his men, for in this case we have Polybius' word for it, presumably based on Scipio's own letter to Philip of Macedonia, that he already knew about the way in which the water tended to recede from the lagoon towards evening, the natural phenomenon which was later to appear to fulfil Neptune's promise of aid. But there is no need to attribute too cynical an attitude to him, if we suppose that he regarded the phenomenon itself as a sign that the gods favoured his plan - perhaps he learned of it after his dream, which might have been produced by the strain of trying to decide whether the risks attendant upon his plan were worth taking, and the comforting thought that his mastery of the sea could be used to minimise the risks. The combination of rational calculation with genuine religious conviction is, after all, no more difficult to accept in a Scipio than in a Cromwell.

The whole story of the ebb from the lagoon has also been dismissed as fiction, because, it is argued, if Scipio knew that it would occur in the evening, he would not have attacked in the morning (cf. Polybius 10.12.1), and because, if he could learn about it from fishermen, Mago, the commander of the Carthaginian garrison, would also have known about it, and taken the necessary precautions. [31] But Polybius' account, based as it is on the best of evidence, cannot be so lightly dismissed, and some other explanation must be found for the difficulties. The probable explanation lies in the nature of the phenomenon itself. Polybius (10.8.7) says that it usually occurred towards evening, but leaves its nature unclear; Livy (26.45.8) says that it occurred about midday on the day in question, and was due to a combination of tide and a north wind; Appian (*History of Spain,* 21) attributes it simply to the tide, as does Frontinus (*Strategemata* 3.8.1). But although there is a slight tide in the Mediterranean, its effect is negligible at Cartagena, [32] and thus the ebb, if it occurred, must have been due to something else, as is suggested by Polybius' remark that it usually occurred towards evening, since this would not, of course, be true of any effect of the tide. But it is attested that a north or north-east wind can lower the level of the sea near Cartagena by as much as 1.5 metres, [33] and thus Livy's narrative may here preserve the vital clue. If this is correct, what Scipio learned from the fishermen was that sometimes the water receded from the lagoon, leaving it even easier to wade through than it usually was, and that if this occurred, it was usually towards evening. His morning assault, then, would have been intended partly as a cover for his real intentions, since if he waited until evening, and Mago knew about the ebb, then he would quickly realise what the Romans intended, and take steps to guard the walls long the lagoon. But partly, too, the morning assault will have been intended as a real effort to take the city, in case the water-level in the lagoon did not go down and it proved unfordable after all. As for Mago's failure to safeguard against an attack through the lagoon, this may have been a calculated risk, due to the fewness of his troops, particularly if he was convinced by Scipio's attack on the isthmus walls that the Romans were unaware that the lagoon could be forded.

There remains the difficulty that if the phenomenon did not always occur, Scipio could not promise his men Neptune's aid. One way round this difficulty would be to accept Livy's version of the episode (26.45.7-9), for he says that it was only when Scipio received a report that "the tide was receding" that he made his reference to Neptune. But this is not necessary: in Polybius' version, when Scipio refers to his dream about Neptune, he makes no precise reference to the ebbing of the water in the lagoon, but merely to the service Neptune had promised to render. If the ebb did not occur, and the lagoon still proved fordable, as there was every reason to believe it would, from the information of the fishermen (cf. Polybius 10.8.7), then the mere fact that so apparently formidable an obstacle was in reality no obstacle at all, would appear almost miraculous, and this in itself would be enough to encourage men about to embark on a difficult and dangerous enterprise. But if the ebb did occur, then the men would naturally interpret this as due to Neptune's aid.

The accounts of the actual assault in Polybius and Livy are similar, though Livy, as usual, adds details, and, in particular, brings out the importance of the sea-borne assault, which Polybius only mentions at the beginning, and which he seems to have thought was only responsible for long-range bombardment (10.12.1). The attack began with the fleet moving in to encircle all the parts of the city accessible from the sea, while by land 2000 of the strongest Roman soldiers, accompanied by men carrying ladders, advanced to attack the walls across the isthmus, opposite the Roman camp. The Carthaginian commander, Mago, divided his 1000 regulars into two groups, stationing one on the citadel (Monte Molinete), and the other on what Polybius (10.12.2) calls the "eastern" hill, which - correcting his orientation - means Monte Concepcion, on the south side of the city. At the same time, he armed 2000 of the strongest citizens, and stationed them near the gate leading to the isthmus, ordering the rest to do their best to defend the remaining walls. These dispositions have been doubted, because they appear to mean that Mago did not place his best men to ward off Scipio's assault from the landward side, and yet later (10.12.8), Polybius says that both sides had the pick of their men fighting there. [34] But Mago may well have thought, at first, that the attack from the sea was the most dangerous threat, as perhaps Scipio had intended he should, and hence stationed half his regular force on Monte Concepcion, while the 500 on the citadel could both act as a general reserve, and also easily lend a hand in defending the seaward-facing walls running between Monte Concepcion and the citadel. When Polybius says "both sides had picked out their best men" for the fighting at the isthmus, moreover, he is probably referring to the fact that the defenders were the pick of the townspeople, as he has said twice before (10.12.3 and 10.12.7). This is, perhaps, a more likely explanation than that Mago sent his regulars to the isthmus when the assault began, [35] for his initial determination to resist in the citadel, after the walls had been taken (Polybius 10.15.7), suggests that he still had troops there, and Monte Concepcion, too, had to be cleared of defenders, after Scipio's army had entered the city (Polybius 10.15.3).

Whoever the Carthaginian defenders at the isthmus were, at first they gave a good account of themselves, even sallying out and falling upon the attacking force, when Scipio ordered the assault to begin. But they could not maintain the struggle for long, since Scipio deliberately held his men back near his camp, where they could be easily reinforced. Soon numbers told, and the defenders were driven back within the walls, the Romans nearly managing to enter with the fugitives, and, in any case, being able to get their scaling-ladders into position undisturbed (Polybius 10.12.4-11). This Carthaginian sortie, foolish in the circumstances, and evidently launched too soon, might also suggest the ill-disciplined fanaticism of recently-armed civilians rather than the disciplined courage of seasoned troops. But when the Romans began to mount their ladders, they were soon in difficulties because of the height of the wall: some of the ladders broke, and some of those climbing them grew dizzy and fell off, while the defenders threw beams and other heavy objects down on them. Eventually, as the day wore on, Scipio had the signal for withdrawal sounded (Polybius 10.13).

The defenders breathed a sigh of relief, but the time had now come for Scipio to carry out his daring plan of sending men through the lagoon. He gathered a force of 500 men, with ladders, either at the isthmus, from where they could have waded round the walls, or, more probably, on the north side of the lagoon, near the place now called Molino de Truchao, where a headland probably then jutted into the water, and from which a ridge, still visible this century, though the lagoon has dried up, probably ran across to the city walls: an attack from here was far less likely to be spotted, and would have made the receding of the water appear even more miraculous when it happened. [36] At the same time, after giving his troops at the isthmus time to refresh themselves, he launched another all-out assault on the walls facing his camp. Disheartened, the defenders still put up a stubborn resistance, but, at the height of the struggle, the water suddenly began to recede from the edges of the lagoon, a strong current flowing out through the channel at its southwest corner. Immediately, Scipio ordered his assault-party to begin wading across, while the rest of his men, believing that the promise of Neptune's help had been fulfilled, redoubled their efforts. [37] The assault-party raced through the shallow water to the walls, probably somewhere between Monte Molinete and Monte Sacro, and, finding them deserted, set up their scaling-ladders, and seized them without a blow (Polybius 10.14). They then marched along the walls eastwards towards the gate facing the isthmus, sweeping the defenders out of the way as they encountered them. Reaching the gate, some of them descended to cut through the bars, while, at the same time, some of the attackers outside managed to force their way in, and others succeeded in gaining the battlements at last. Those who burst in through the gate immediately occupied Monte Concepcion along the seaward side of the city, after dislodging its defenders, presumably to help the attack from the sea (Polybius 10.15.1-3). Livy (26.48.5ff.) says that later a marine called Sextus Digitius claimed the *corona muralis,* as the first man over the wall, and this suggests that the fleet played a more important part in the capture of the city than is apparent from Polybius' account.

When Scipio thought that a sufficient number of men had entered the city, he loosed most of them on the inhabitants, "as is the Roman custom," Polybius grimly notes (10.15.4-6), ordering them to kill anyone they came across, sparing none, while he himself, with about 1000 men, headed for the citadel. Here, at first, Mago was inclined to continue resistance, but when he saw that the rest of the city was in enemy hands, he sent a message out and surrendered the citadel. Scipio spent the night there, with his 1000 men, after ordering the rest of the troops who had entered the city, to bivouac in the market-place, guarding the booty, and the light infantry to occupy Monte Concepcion (Polybius 10.15.7-11). Next day, the booty was divided up among the victorious soldiers, and Scipio, assembling the prisoners to the number of 10,000, first ordered the citizens, with their wives and children, and the artisans, probably poor men who were not of citizen status [38], to be set aside. The citizens he then dismissed to their homes, after exhorting them to be well-disposed towards Rome. The artisans he told they were now public slaves of the Roman state, but that they could hope for freedom after the war, if they worked willingly. From the rest of the prisoners - presumably, the slaves - he selected the strongest and incorporated them into the crews of his ships, promising them also freedom when the war was over, and was thus able to man the eighteen ships captured in the harbour, and to double the size of his crews (Polybius 10.17.6-16). Mago and the Carthaginians captured with him were handed over to Caius Laelius, who was ordered to pay them due attention - they included two members of the inner Council of Thirty, and members of the Carthaginian senate (Polybius 10.18.1-2). Finally, he turned to the hostages, over three hundred in number, and bade them write to their relations to tell them that they were safe and would be sent home if their tribes chose to side with Rome. He also presented them with gifts, and at the prompting of the wife of Mandonios, brother of Andobales, chief of the Ilergetes, assured the women that they would not be molested (Polybius 10.18.6-15). When some of his young soldiers tried to present him with a young girl, he refused the gift and handed her over to her father (Polybius 10.19.3-7). Typically, Livy elaborates this story by giving the girl a lover to whom Scipio surrendered her (26.50.1-12).

The capture of Cartagena was a stroke of genius on Scipio's part, and marked the beginning of the end for the Carthaginians in Spain. The speed and efficiency with which the assault was carried out, are striking enough in themselves, but still more striking is the sheer daring of marching over 450 kilometres from the Roman bases north of the Ebro to assault one of the two most important cities in Spain, in face of the overwhelming numerical superiority of the three Carthaginian armies in the field. Though the march from the Ebro to Cartagena cannot compare in length or difficulty with Hannibal's march to Italy, it marks Scipio out as a general of the same stamp, bold, resolute and calculating, and the actual capture of the city is in marked contrast to Hannibal's failure to take places like Naples, Nola and Cumae. It is probably also true to say that the capture of Cartagena was the essential preliminary to the expulsion of the Carthaginians from Spain. While it remained in Carthaginian hands, the Roman bases north of the Ebro were always liable to attack, and communications down the east coast by land and sea were also under threat, This would be particularly true if and when the Romans attempted to invade the Baetis valley, and this had to be done, if the Carthaginians were to be driven entirely out of Spain. The elder Scipios seem to have been trying both to invade Baetica and to deal with the Cartagena area, in their last campaign, and had paid the price of this division of objective. Now the younger Scipio had eliminated Cartagena, and could concentrate on the Baetis region, without having continually to look over his shoulder. The capture of the hostages also enabled him to win over many of the Spanish tribes which might otherwise have threatened his communications, and the fall of Cartagena must in any case have created the impression that Rome's was now the winning cause. Finally, the loss of Cartagena meant, for Carthage, the loss of the munitions and treasure stored in the city, and, presumably, of the mines in the area, although this does not seem to have had any marked effect on her ability, for example, to hire mercenaries.

After taking Cartagena, Scipio did not embark on any further operations during the same year, unless we accept the attack on Baria (Vera), about 100 kilometres south-west of Cartagena, recorded by Valerius Maximus (3.7.1). But he allowed no relaxation among his troops: they were put through a rigorous training programme (Polybius 10.20. 1-4), particular attention being paid to their physical fitness - Polybius says that they were ordered to do 30 stades (over five kilometres) with their equipment - and their arms drill; Scipio himself personally visited the workshops where arms were being made. It has been suggested that it was now that the Romans adopted the Spanish sword, and even that the *pilum*, the throwing-spear used by the legionaries, was adapted in some way in imitation of the Spanish *falarica,* but this is not now generally accepted. [39] But Scipio may well have now begun to train his men in the new infantry tactics he was to use at Baecula the following year.

When winter approached, Scipio returned to Tarraco with his main forces and the fleet, leaving an adequate garrison in Cartagena. On his way back, he received a stream of delegations from Spanish tribes, to some of which he gave answers then and there, but he postponed his answers to others until he had reached Terraco, where he had summoned representatives of all Rome's allies, old and new, to meet him (Livy 26.51.10-4). Throughout the winter (209/8) the swing to Rome among the tribes continued, one of the first chiefs to come to Tarraco being Edeco, possibly chief of the Edetani or Sedetani, who lived between the Ebro and the Sucro, [40] and the courteous treatment he received at Scipio's hands so impressed others that all the tribes north of the Ebro now threw in their lot with Rome (Polybius 10.34-35.3). Even Andobales and Mandonios, chiefs of the Ilergetes, who had hitherto been amongst Carthage's most loyal adherents, now withdrew from Hasdrubal Barca's camp, and most of the other Spaniards followed their example (Polybius 10.35.6-8). Aware of this growing disaffection against Carthaginian rule, Hasdrubal now decided to bring Scipio to battle at the first opportunity: if successful, he could then consider what to do next in security, but if defeated, he was determined to cut his losses, and march to join his brother in Italy with every man he could persuade to come with him (Polybius 10.37.4-5). Scipio was also anxious to engage Hasdrubal, whose army was the nearest, before the other two armies could combine with it, and took the precaution of beaching his ships, and adding their crews to his army (Polybius 10.35.5), thus, presumably, more than making up for any losses he had incurred in the taking of Cartagena. So the stage was set for a major confrontation in the field.

Scipio left Tarraco either at the beginning of spring, (Livy 27.17.8), or at the beginning of summer (Livy 27.17.1), 208, [41] and advanced southwards, receiving the accession of Andobales and Mandonios on the march (Polybius 10.37.7ff.; Livy 27.17.9ff.). Hasdrubal Barca was now near a town Polybius (10.38.7) calls "Baikula" (Baecula in Livy 27.18.1), which is probably to be identified with the modern Bailén, about forty kilometres north of Jaén, a good strategic position, barring Scipio's way to the Baetis valley. [42] On hearing of Scipio's approach, Hasdrubal moved to a strong defensive position (Polybius 10.38.8), possibly after a skirmish between his cavalry and the light troops of Scipio's advance-guard, as Livy says (27.18.1-5). Both our principal sources are agreed on the nature of Hasdrubal's new position, but Livy's description (27.18.5-6; cf. Polybius 10.38.8) is fuller: it was a flat-topped hill, protected by a river in the rear, and surrounded in front and on the sides by steep banks; in front, the hill descended to a flat, sloping terrace, ringed with a parapet-like rim. This is usually identified with one or other of the hills to the east of Bailén, perhaps more plausibly with the one between the Arroyo de la Muela and the Arroyo de Cañada Baeza, [43] though it is difficult to see, in either case, what Polybius and Livy meant by saying that the position was protected in the rear by a river, since the nearest river of any size, the Guadiel, flows in front: perhaps the Rio del Rumblar, which flows into the Guadalquivir west of Bailén, is meant, [44] but this would have been some eight kilometres west of Hasdrubal's position, and could hardly be said to protect it. It has also been argued that the defensive nature of Hasdrubal's position gives the lie to Polybius' assertion that he wanted to fight a battle, [45] but if he had really wanted to avoid battle, he could easily have retreated before Scipio's advance, and it is clear that he was hoping to tempt the latter into attacking him in a strong position. (See Map 16).

Scipio probably camped somewhere to the east, perhaps near Tobaruela, and here, according to Polybius (10.38.10), he waited for two days, unwilling to throw himself at Hasdrubal's strong position. According to Livy (27.18.7 and 10), it was on the day after Hasdrubal had moved his position, that Scipio decided to attack, and Livy also adds that he detached two cohorts, one to guard the "jaws" of the valley down which the river, presumably the Guadiel, flowed, perhaps near the place where the modern road from Bailén to Malaga crosses the Guadiel, the other to block the road which led from Baecula into the country "along the slopes of the hill," by which a track running along the line of the modern road from Bailén to Linares may be meant. [46] If Livy is right about these dispositions, and there is no reason to doubt him, despite Polybius' silence, they suggest that Scipio was worried about the possible approach of Hasdrubal's fellow-generals, Mago and Hasdrubal Gisgo, and this is confirmed by Polybius, who says that it was this anxiety which decided him to attack, after he had waited for two days, presumably in the hope that Hasdrubal would come down off his hill (10.38.10).

Scipio began the attack by sending forward his skirmishers and a picked force of infantry of the line to engage the covering force Hasdrubal had stationed on the lower terrace (Polybius 10.39.1) - Livy says it consisted of Numidian cavalry and Balearic and African skirmishers (27.18.7). Livy also implies (27.18.10) that Scipio himself led the initial attack, but this is unlikely, and Polybius' account makes it clear that Scipio did not join the attack until later. At first Hasdrubal waited the outcome of the attack on the lower terrace, but when he saw how hard-pressed his troops there were, he began to deploy his main forces on the forward edge of the higher plateau to support his skirmishers below. Scipio, who had clearly hoped to draw Hasdrubal's main body into the fight with his initial assault forces, now promptly ordered the rest of his skirmishers forward to support them, while he himself led half his infantry of the line round the hill to the right, probably up the Arroyo de la Muela, ordering Laelius to take the other half and attack round the hill to the left, probably up the Arroyo de Cañada Baeza (Polybius 10.39.3-4). Hasdrubal was still deploying his forces, and had not yet occupied the ground on his wings, when Scipio and Laelius fell upon him, and he realized that he had been outmanoeuvred. Immediately, he decided to withdraw, as he had determined to do in the event of defeat, and somehow managed to extricate his treasure, his elephants and perhaps between half and two-thirds of his army, largely by sacrificing his light troops on the lower terrace. With what he could salve from the rout, he made for the Tagus, and eventually for Italy.

The battle of Baecula was Scipio's first experience of command on the field of battle, and is the earliest illustration of his battle-tactics. Particularly interesting is his use of light troops fo focus the enemy's attention on the centre and compel him to commit his forces to that point, while he used his infantry of the line to attack the enemy's wings. He was to use these tactics again, with variations, at Ilipa and the Great Plains. At Baecula, however, Hasdrubal had not committed his main force to the extent that he could not extricate it, and thus he was able to escape annihilation by sacrificing his light troops. Indeed, the tactics only really worked at the Great Plains, their weakness being precisely that the enemy's best troops tended to remain uncommitted and so able to withdraw, though it is possible that Hasdrubal Gisgo's Africans would not have been able to do so at Ilipa, if it had not been for the cloud-burst (see below, p. 150). It would have been interesting to see how Hannibal would have countered them, but at Zama Scipio either chose not to use them, or had no chance to do so.

The immediate effect of the battle of Baecula was to win over the tribes in the neighbourhood to Rome, and thus, ultimately, to pave the way for the invasion of the lower Baetis valley two years later. Polybius (10.40.2ff.), followed by Livy, says that the Spaniards were so impressed by Scipio's achievement that they saluted him as "king", as Edeco and Andobales had done previously, but that Scipio deprecated the title, declaring that they should call him "general" (στρατηγός in the Greek): Livy (27.19.4), perhaps more accurately, says that he declared that the greatest title he could have was that of "*imperator*", already bestowed upon him by his soldiers. This is the first recorded instance of the title being bestowed upon a Roman general after a victory, but this is, perhaps, a coincidence, and in any case, of course, contemporaries would not have seen in the title all the implications it was later to attract.

A more interesting question, from the military point of view, is whether Scipio should have made more effort to stop Hasdrubal getting away with so much of his army intact - his failure to follow up his victory here with a vigorous pursuit is in marked contrast to his annihilating pursuit of Hasdrubal Gisgo's army after Ilipa. If we are to believe Livy (28.42.14-5), his failure to prevent Hasdrubal Barca from marching to Italy was already the subject of criticism by Fabius Maximus three years later. But a precipitate pursuit of Hasdrubal Barca after Baecula might have laid Scipio open to attack by the other Carthaginian armies in Spain, and have undone much of the work of winning the Spanish tribes in the area over to Rome. As for his failure to stop Hasdrubal from marching to Italy, although we can well see how contemporaries might have been surprised that at last reinforcements for Hannibal should have got away from Spain, now that Rome seemed to be winning the war there, it is difficult to see how Scipio could have prevented it, if Hasdrubal was really determined to go: it would have been impossible to hold the whole line of the Pyrenees, and the truth of the matter is that the Carthaginians probably could have sent an army to Italy at any time in the past ten years, if they had been prepared to use a roundabout route. There is also the point that Hasdrubal's arrival in Italy in 207 was not nearly as dangerous as it would have been in the years after Cannae, and Scipio may well have calculated that the Roman forces in Italy were now able to cope with the situation, and that his job was to drive the Carthaginians out of Spain. If he did see the matter in this light, he may even have been glad to see Hasdrubal Barca go. Thus, although it is arguable that he should have done more to pursue Hasdrubal in the short term, once he had got away, there was little that could be done about it.

As it was, Scipio seems to have remained in the vicinity of Baecula for some time, judging by Polybius' statement (10.40.11) that he occupied Hasdrubal's camp, and by the reports of the reactions of the Spaniards to his victory, although Livy (27.20.3) says he returned to Tarraco a few days after the battle. His only move against Hasdrubal Barca was the despatch of a small force to the Pyrenees - to observe his movements, according to Polybius (ibid.), to block his way, according to Livy (27.20.2). Livy also records a conference between Hasdrubal and his fellow-generals (27.20.3-8), at which it was decided that Hasdrubal should proceed to Italy, with his army reinforced by Spanish troops, that Mago should hand over his army to Hasdrubal Gisgo and go to the Balearic Islands to hire more men, while Gisgo retired into Lusitania, and that the Numidian prince, Masinissa, should be given a roving commission to harry Rome's allies with his cavalry. But although there is nothing intrinsically improbable about such a conference, and it might seem unlikely that Hasdrubal Barca should simply have disappeared into the blue without apprising his fellow-generals of his intentions, they were probably already aware that this was what he intended to do, and they could have been given definite information by messenger. It is suspicious that when Livy resumes his narrative of the war in Spain (28.1.1ff.), he says nothing about Mago's mission: he is once more in Celtiberia, and Livy merely says that a general called Hanno had been sent from Carthage to replace Hasdrubal Barca.

The year 207 saw a lull in operations in the Spanish theatre, unless we are to accept the theory that the Ilipa campaign should be dated to this year, [47] and not to

206. The main argument for the theory is that it is difficult to fit all that Scipio is alleged to have done after Ilipa, into the same year, and still leave time for him to return to Rome to stand at the elections for the consulship of 205/4. But Polybius says that Ilipa was fought in the spring (11.20.1), and it is possible to fit the later events into the remaining months of the year, particularly if the elections were delayed, as they frequently were during this war, whereas to date Ilipa to 207 conflicts with Livy, and would make it difficult to accept Polybius' assertion that it was fought in the spring.

The surviving fragments of Polybius' tenth and eleventh books contain no reference to any operations in Spain which can be referred to the time between the battle of Baecula and that of Ilipa, but Livy, although he naturally devotes most of his narrative of 207 to events in Italy, culminating in the defeat of Hasdrubal Barca at the Metaurus, does record some operations in Spain (28.1-4.4), and provides a clue to why Scipio was unable to press home the advantage gained by the Baecula campaign until over a year later. Livy says that the new general sent to replace Hasdrubal Barca, joined Mago and lost no time in carrying out a vigorous recruiting-campaign among the Celtiberi. Scipio responded by despatching a flying-column of 10,000 foot and 500 horse, under M. Iunius Silanus, and with these forces Silanus destroyed the Carthaginian army, capturing the new general, Hanno, although Mago escaped with the cavalry and about 2000 infantry. Scipio himself then marched into Baetica against Hasdrubal Gisgo, but the latter dispersed his forces among the various towns in the southern part of the region, and Scipio withdrew, thinking that to take the towns one by one would be a long and arduous task. He did, however, send his brother, Lucius, to take a town called "Orongis" (Livy 28.3.2), which is probably the same place as the Aurinx mentioned by Livy in an earlier passage (24.42.5), and is thought to have been somewhere near Baza or Huéscar, to the northeast of Granada: [48] such a demonstration was, perhaps, thought necessary in order not to leave the Spaniards with the impression that Scipio was baffled by Hasdrubal Gisgo's strategy. Thus the war in Spain certainly continued during 207, and if no important operations were attempted by either side, this is, perhaps, because both were waiting on events in Italy, although the tradition that Scipio actually sent troops there this year (Livy 27.38.11-2) seems improbable.

Hasdrubal Gisgo's refusal to face Scipio in the field in 207, and his dispersal of his forces among the towns in southern Baetica, suggest that he had decided that he could best serve the Carthaginian cause by trying to prolong the war in Spain. But if this was the case, then something had happened to change his mind before he advanced to meet Scipio at Ilipa in 206. Perhaps he was merely trying to win time in order to gather new forces, after the departure of Hasdrubal Barca and the subsequent dispersal of the troops commanded by Hanno and Mago. But in all probability, he had also heard, by the end of 207, of the defeat of Hasdrubal Barca at the Metaurus, and, if so, he would have realised that there was now little hope of victory in Italy. He may also have heard from Carthage of the increasing Roman naval activity off the coast of Africa in 208 and 207: in 208, Valerius Laevinus had taken 100 ships to Africa, and, after raiding the coast, had encountered a Carthaginian fleet off Clupea, and captured 18 of its ships (Livy 27.29.7-8); then, in 207, he had returned, and again defeated the Carthaginian fleet, this time sinking four ships and capturing a further 17 (Livy 28.4.7).

As it turned out, these operations were followed, in 206, by a reduction in the fleet based on Sicily (Livy 28.10.16), but to the Carthaginian government and to its generals in Spain, the previous two years' operations may well have looked like the prelude to invasion. Thus Hasdrubal Gisgo may have begun to think that a mere prolonging of the war in Spain was now no longer enough: some decisive stroke against Scipio was required, both to recover the situation in Spain itself, and, perhaps, if possible, to enable yet another attempt to be made to reinforce Hannibal.

This, then, is the background to the Ilipa campaign. Hasdrubal Gisgo and Mago succeeded in raising an army estimated by Polybius (11.20.2) at 70,000 foot and 4000 horse, and by Livy (28.12.13-4) at about 50,000 foot and 4500 horse, though he adds that whereas most writers were agreed on the number of cavalry, some said that the infantry numbered 70,000. It has been argued that Livy's lower figure for the infantry is to be accepted, [49] but it is difficult to account for Scipio's manoeuvre of extending his wings to left and right at Ilipa, unless he was considerably outnumbered in infantry, since it was his cavalry and skirmishers who eventually outflanked Hasdrubal's line (cf. Polybius 11.23.5-6), not his infantry of the line, despite their march to the flank; yet, according to Polybius (11.20.8), with his Spaniards, Scipio had 45,000 infantry, and although Livy (28.13.5) makes his whole force, including cavalry, 45,000, this is probably just a mistake. If, then, Scipio had 45,000 infantry to Hasdrubal's 50,000, it would hardly have been worthwhile carrying out his complicated manoeuvre with his infantry of the line, since the Carthaginian forces, when deployed, would barely have extended beyond his own. It seems best, therefore, to accept that something like Polybius' figure of 70,000 infantry is correct for Hasdrubal's army.

Having gathered his forces, Hasdrubal advanced, in spring 206, to a place the manuscripts of Polybius call "Ilinga" or "Elinga" (11.20.1), Livy (28.12.15) "Silpia", but the name of which was probably, in reality, "Ilipa". Appian (*History of Spain*, 25) says Hasdrubal concentrated his forces at "Kareone" or "Karbone" (cf. op. cit., 27), which is probably "Karmone" (now Carmona), about thirty kilometres east of Seville, and evidently thought that the battle was fought there. But although this may represent an earlier stage in the Carthaginian advance towards Ilipa, clearly Polybius and Livy must be preferred for the actual site of the battle. Ilipa has been plausibly located at Alcalá del Rio, fourteen kilometres north of Seville, on the right bank of the Guadalquivir. [50] Scipio, according to Polybius (11.20.3ff.), had sent Iunius Silanus to collect the troops promised by a Spanish chieftain called Kolichas (Culchas in Livy), and himself advanced, with the rest of his forces, to the vicinity of Castulo, which lay a few kilometres south of Linares. [51] Here he was joined by Silanus and Kolichas, and then continued to advance (cf. Polybius 11.20.8), down the right bank of the Guadalquivir, until he came within sight of the enemy. Meanwhile Hasdrubal and Mago, if they had assembled their army near Carmona, must have crossed the Guadalquivir to confront the enemy, since it appears from Livy (28.16.3) that, after the battle, Hasdrubal, who was presumably making for Gades (cf. 28.16.8), was prevented from crossing the Guadalquivir, and this must mean that the battle was fought on its right bank. The Carthaginian camp has been plausibly located on an unnamed hill five kilometres south-west of Pelagos, Scipio's on a hill now called Pelegatos, about six kilometres east of the

145

modern Burguillos, the two positions being from six to 10.5 kilometres north-east of Alcalá del Rio. [52] Livy's account of the Roman advance is similar to Polybius' up to a point, but since he mentions no further advance after Baecula, his version has led some scholars to locate the battle there. [53] But it is clear that Livy's narrative is muddled, since he earlier located the Carthaginians near "Silpia" (28.12.14-5), as we have seen, and Polybius' account leaves no doubt that he believed the Romans continued to advance beyond Castulo and the neighbourhood of Baecula.

While the Roman army was pitching camp, Mago and Masinissa attacked with their cavalry, but Scipio had foreseen the danger and managed to beat the attack off with his own cavalry, which he had concealed behind a hill - perhaps the spur of Pelagatos which sweeps round to the west (Polybius 11.21.1-5). Livy (28.13.6-9) probably exaggerates when he says that first the Roman light infantry and then the infantry of the line joined in the struggle before the Carthaginian cavalry was put to flight. After this preliminary action, the light troops and cavalry of the two armies continued to skirmish for several days, but although the main forces of both armies were deployed each day, no general engagement followed (Polybius 11.21.7). This desultory skirmishing, however, enabled Scipio to note that Hasdrubal always drew out his forces late in the day, and always deployed them in the same order - Africans in the centre, Spanish allies on either wing, with the elephants, of which he had thirty-two, according to Polybius (11.20.2), thirty-six according to Appian (*History of Spain* 25), in front of the Spaniards. He himself habitually deployed his own forces even later in the day, presumably to avoid all possibility of a decisive engagement until he was ready, with his Roman troops in the centre, and his Spanish allies also on the wings.

But presumably when he thought Hasdrubal had got thoroughly used to this daily routine, Scipio issued careful orders to his men to have an early breakfast, and to march out as soon as it was light, sending his cavalry and skirmishers in advance to harass the enemy camp (Polybius 11.22.4-5). Then, just as the sun was rising, he deployed his main forces in the plain between the two camps, but this time with his Spanish allies in the centre, and his Roman troops on either wing (Polybius 11.22.6). Hasdrubal, taken completely by surprise, had to deploy his own army in a hurry, before his men had eaten breakfast, and immediately to order out his own cavalry and skirmishers to engage the corresponding enemy troops; worse still, he had no time to change his normal order of battle, but could only keep to his usual arrangement, thus opposing Scipio's Roman infantry of the line with his own Spanish allies. But even now Scipio did not launch his attack immediately, and the skirmishing between the light infantry and the cavalry of both armies continued for some time: presumably Scipio was waiting for the effects of hunger to take their toll of Carthaginian morale, but one wonders why Hasdrubal did not take the opportunity to re-deploy his main forces. Perhaps he dared not do so in case Scipio launched his attack while his army was in the confusion of redeployment, or perhaps he even thought that he could win the battle by breaking through Scipio's centre, and cutting his army in half, though in that case he should have seized the initiative and attacked.

But in the end, it was Scipio who judged that the time was ripe, and ordering his skirmishers and cavalry to retire through the gaps between the maniples of infantry of the line, and stationing them behind the infantry on either wing, *velites* in front, cavalry behind (Polybius 11.22.10), ordered his whole line to advance. Nor was this to be the end of the subtleties of Scipio's plan of attack, for, when the two armies were some seven hundred metres apart,[54] he bade his Spanish allies in the centre continue to advance, but the Roman troops to their left and right to carry out a series of complicated manoeuvres. Polybius' account of these (11.22.11-23.7), though difficult to understand, is more detailed and technical than Livy's (28.14.14ff.), for although the latter appears to have followed Polybius or some common source, he compresses the narrative to the point of obscurity. (See Map 17).

First, then, Scipio ordered the infantry and cavalry on the right to wheel to the right, and those on the left to wheel to the left (Polybius 11.22.11): this manoeuvre could have been carried out by each individual man or horse turning to right or left, or by each unit of infantry and cavalry wheeling by pivoting on the right or left file leader, but the term used by Polybius (ἐπιστρέφειν) is used by ancient technical military writers to mean the latter, and presumably Polybius here uses it in the same technical sense.[55] Next, Polybius says (11.23.1-2), "(Scipio) himself taking from the right, and Lucius Marcius and Marcus Iunius (Silanus) from the left, the leading three squadrons of horse, and in front of these the usual *velites,* and three maniples - this unit of infantry is called a "cohort" among the Romans - wheeling them to the left in the former case, to the right in the latter, they led them forward straight at the enemy, advancing rapidly, with those next in order always backing up and following the wheel round." Here again, Polybius appears to be using technical terms (περικλάσαντες and περίκλασις) which refer to a column of troops wheeling to right or left.[56]

It is clear that Polybius believed that these manoeuvres were carried out by all the Roman troops on the right and left wings, for, in the passage immediately after the one translated above, he contrasts the Roman troops with the Spaniards in the centre, who, he says, were still some distance from the enemy because they had continued to advance slowly, and the result of the whole manoeuvre, in his words, was that "they (i.e. Scipio and his fellow-commanders) fell simultaneously on both wings of the enemy with the Roman forces in column" (11.23.3). The reason why he only mentions specifically three squadrons of cavalry, with the usual *velites* in front of them, and three maniples of infantry, is that he is referring to the units which would have been leading the extension to right and left - as he actually says in the case of the three squadrons of cavalry - and which now led the wheel to left and right straight at the enemy. The remark about the three maniples being called a "cohort" also becomes clear, if one remembers that the Roman legions would have been ranged in their normal three lines, consisting, from front to rear, of maniples of *hastati, principes* and *triarii,* so that when the lines wheeled into column to right and left, the columns would have been led by a maniple each of *hastati, principes* and *triarii,* and Polybius is correct in saying that a unit consisting of three such maniples was called a cohort. But when he refers to "those next in order always backing up and following the wheel round" (11.23.2), he makes it clear that the whole of each of the three lines followed the leading units round. Livy, however, may have misunderstood him, or a common source, for he talks about "three cohorts of infantry" (28.14.17), and this has led some modern scholars to suppose that

147

this second manoeuvre was carried out by only three cohorts of infantry of the line on either wing, accompanied by three squadrons of cavalry and three units of *velites*. [57] But even Livy says that the others followed (ibid.), and in any case, there cannot be any doubt about what Polybius meant. The only serious objection to believing him is that it is difficult to imagine that all the Roman troops present on the battlefield - perhaps as many as 12,500 one either wing [58] - could have carried out such complicated manoeuvres in the very face of the enemy. But Polybius' account is so circumstantial and detailed that it is best to accept it as it stands.

The third manoeuvre, Polybius says (11.23.4), "by which the rear units, falling into the same straight line as the leading units, were able to engage the enemy in battle, had an opposite direction to each other, both in general the right wing to the left, and in particular the infantry to the cavalry." He goes on to explain (11.23.5-6) that, on the right, the cavalry and *velites* came into line on the right, the infantry on the left, whereas the opposite was the case on the left wing, and that the result was that with the cavalry and *velites* on both wings their right had become their left, whereas, he implies, this was not so of the infantry of the line (see diagram). He also evidently thought (cf.11.23.5) that it was the cavalry and *velites* on either wing that was now in a position to outflank the enemy, not the infantry of the line.

It is, thus, possible to understand what Polybius thought the Roman army did, and once his technical terms are given their precise meaning, everything in his account falls into place, even the detail that at the end of the three manoeuvres, the units which had begun on the left of the cavalry and *velites,* now found themselves on the right, and *vice versa.* But a number of puzzles remain. Firstly, how far did the two wings continue to march to right and left before they wheeled towards the enemy? The answer seems to be that they started their wheel at about the point at which they came opposite the ends of the enemy line, for, as we have seen, Polybius thought that it was the cavalry and *velites,* coming up on the outside of the infantry of the line in each case, which now attempted to outflank the enemy. This also suggests, as was argued above, that the Roman army was considerably outnumbered by the enemy. Secondly, what does Polybius mean when he says (11.23.1) that Scipio and his fellow-commanders took, in addition to the leading three squadrons of cavalry, "the usual *velites* in front of them"? The position of the *velites* is easily explained, for Polybius has already said (11.22.10) that when Scipio withdrew the cavalry and *velites,* he placed the latter in front of the former, and presumably throughout the first and second manoeuvres each squadron of cavalry was preceded by a unit of velites. But to describe the latter as "the usual velites" implies that they were somehow normally attached to *turmae* of cavalry, and this was not the case, for normally the *velites* were attached to maniples of infantry of the line (cf. Polybius 6.24.4). Perhaps, then, what he really meant was that the three units of *velites* usually attached to the three leading *maniples* of infantry of the line, now preced- ed the three leading units of cavalry, and so on. Alternatively, Polybius may be imply- ing that units of *velites* had been trained to co-operate with *turmae* of cavalry, and that now each unit of *velites* preceded its own *turma.* The third puzzle concerns the Carthaginian cavalry and skirmishers: Polybius mentions them in connection with the preliminary skirmishing (11.22.8-9), but never mentions them again, although Livy

(28.15.1) does mention Baliares on the wings. One possibility is that the Carthaginian cavalry, which one would assume to have been deployed on the flanks of the Spanish allies, after being recalled from the skirmishing, were thrown into confusion by the panic-stricken elephants (cf. Polybius 11.24.1), as was to happen at Zama. [59] Another possibility is that both the Carthaginian cavalry and their skirmishers, having withdrawn through the gaps between the units of their infantry of the line, like their Roman counterparts, simply never got back into the battle.

But the most difficult puzzle is the point of Scipio's second and third manoeuvres: if what he wanted to achieve was just to extend his line so as to outflank the enemy with his *velites* and cavalry, all he needed to have done was to order his Roman units to wheel and march to right and left until they overlapped the Carthaginian line, and then to wheel again and advance in line towards the enemy, the *velites* and cavalry delaying their second wheel until they were beyond the infantry of the line, in each case. In short, what was the point of approaching the Carthaginian line with two columns at right angles to it, when this necessitated what must have been the complicated manoeuvre of the rear units coming up again into line alongside the leading units? It has been suggested that the approach-march in column would have exposed fewer men and horses to the enemy's long-distance missiles, for example the sling-stones of the Balearic islanders mentioned by Livy. [60] But we never hear of other Roman armies advancing in line being troubled in this way, and a simpler explanation is that the advance in columns was made in the interests of speed, for a column can advance more quickly than a line, and Scipio was anxious to fall upon the enemy with his Roman troops before there was any possibility of his more unreliable Spanish allies' being engaged by Hasdrubal's Africans. But it is also possible that the advance in column was made precisely to deter Hasdrubal from launching his Africans at the weak centre of the Roman army, the great risk which Scipio's complicated manoeuvres entailed, for if Hasdrubal's Africans had advanced, the Roman infantry of the line would have been on their flanks, and, be it noted, in the correct order of battle, since the *hastati* would have been on the inside of each column, the *principes* in the middle, and the *triarii* on the outside, so that a simple wheel to left or right by each maniple would have brought them into line of battle, indeed, it is just possible that Scipio was rather hoping for such a move on Hasdrubal's part.

To sum up, then, when the Roman and Carthaginian lines were some seven hundred metres apart, Scipio ordered his Spanish allies in the centre to continue to march slowly forward, while his Roman troops to their right and left first wheeled to right and left, and marched in column until the leading units were about opposite the ends of the Carthaginian line, then wheeled to left and right respectively, and advanced, still in column, straight towards the Carthaginian line, finally deploying into line again, just before contact was made with the enemy, with the infantry of the line on the inside, and the cavalry and *velites* on the outside, so that the latter now outflanked the Spanish allies of the Carthaginians. Meanwhile, the Spanish allies in the centre of the Roman line, had continued their slow advance, but had not yet made contact with Hasdrubal's Africans, when the Romans fell on his wings.

The first to suffer were Hasdrubal's elephants. Polybius says (11.22.2) that they had normally been placed "in front of both wings," and it is possible that they had now been

149

moved out to the extremities of the two wings in an attempt to counter Scipio's out-flanking manoeuvre, for they are said to have been hit by the missiles of the *velites* and cavalry and thrown into confusion (Polybius 11.24.1). Galled by the missiles, they began to get out of hand, doing as much damage to their own side as to the enemy, and perhaps, as was suggested above, throwing the Carthaginian cavalry into confusion, though Livy (28.15.5) says that they shifted from the wings to the centre. The Cartha-ginian wings, assailed in front by Scipio's infantry of the line, and in flank by his *velites* and cavalry, put up a gallant fight, but when the heat of the day reached its height, their lack of food, and the fact that they were opposed by Scipio's best troops, began to tell. At first they gave back step by step, but gradually the withdrawal quicken-ed until they had been pressed back to the foot of the hill on which lay the Carthaginian camp, and here one more determined attack by the Romans turned retreat into rout, and they fled to the camp. Meanwhile, Hasdrubal's Africans had stood stolidly where they were, unable to get at Scipio's Spanish allies, but fearing to aid their own allies lest they be attacked by Scipio's (Polybius 11.24.2-3). Scipio's plan had probably been to crush them between his converging wings, though Polybius suggests (11.24.8) that the latter were about to attack the Carthaginian camp, but in the event, a violent thunder-storm broke over the battlefield, and the Roman army withdrew to its own camp: over two thousand years later a similar storm was to save the Austrians at Solferino. [61]

The battle of Ilipa is the most fascinating of all Scipio's battles, and it is a pity that even Polybius' clear and technical account, is not in places more detailed. As it is, although we can understand what he says, a number of problems remain, as we have seen, and it is difficult to grasp how perhaps as many as 25,000 men carried out such complicated manoeuvres. One thing, however, is clear and that is that the Roman army at Ilipa, to say nothing of its commanders, was a very different proposition from the armies which had fought at the Trebbia or at Cannae. The fighting qualities of the Roman soldiers had never been in doubt, but now they had learned to move as units, and had a general who had tactical ideas far beyond those of a Sempronius Longus or a Terentius Varro, even, one suspects, beyond those of Fabius or Marcellus. Once again one notes Scipio's use of his best troops on the wings, with the added refinement, this time, of refusing his centre. From the point of view of the student of military history, it is unfortunate that the battle was not fought to a finish, since we shall never know whether Scipio would have been able to turn his wings inward and annihilate Hasdrubal's centre. As it is, the battle is like the Unfinished Symphony, a classic as far as it goes, but not to be compared with Cannae in the final analysis.

Polybius' account of the Ilipa campaign breaks off at the thunderstorm (11.24.9), but Livy (28.15.12ff.) says that, next day, the Carthaginians prepared themselves to defend their camp, but that desertion amongst his Spanish allies eventually decided Hasdrubal to retreat during the following night. His first task was to cross the Baetis (Guadalquivir), which ran between him and the remaining centres of Carthaginian power, such as Gades, but this was prevented by Scipio's rapid pursuit, which was in marked contrast to his inertia after Baecula. Making use of native guides, Scipio managed to get to the fords first, and Hasdrubal was forced to swing away southwestwards towards the coast. But the pursuit was pressed so closely by the Roman cavalry and light infantry that the Carthaginians were compelled to turn at bay, and in a second battle their army was almost annihilated, Hasdrubal himself escaping with a bare 6000 men to the nearest hills (Livy 28.16.1-6). Here they took up a position on a steep hill and defied all Roman attempts to dislodge them, but surrounded as they were, with no supplies, their situation was hopeless. Hasdrubal managed to get a message through to the coast, asking for ships to meet him, and thus made his escape to Gades, and later the Numidian prince, Masinissa, also escaped, after secret talks with Silanus, who had been left in charge by Scipio when he returned to Tarraco. Finally, Mago also made his way to the coast, where he was taken off by ships sent back by Hasdrubal, and the rest of the Carthaginian army, abandoned by its commanders, either deserted or dispersed. Silanus marched to rejoin Scipio at Tarraco, with the news, as Livy puts it (28.16.15), that the war in Spain was over, though as it turned out, this was somewhat premature.

Scipio himself was certainly not content to rest on his laurels, and was evidently already thinking ahead to the possibility of invading Africa. It may have been on his instructions that Silanus had entered into discussions with Masinissa (cf. Livy 28.16.11-2), and now he sent Laelius to Africa to persuade the powerful king, Syphax, to come over to the Roman cause (Livy 28.17.3ff.). It is possible that the elder Scipios had already been in touch with Syphax in 213 or 212 (see above), and although Carthage had used Masinissa's father, Gala, to drive him from his kingdom (Livy 24.48.13-49.6), he had subsequently recovered it, and in 210 is alleged to have sent envoys to Rome to strengthen relations (Livy 27.4.5-9). But now, although he appeared to listen sympathe- tically to the Roman overtures, he would not enter into any formal agreement, unless Scipio himself came to Africa. This must mean, if we are to accept the tradition of earlier relations between him and Rome as genuine, either that they had never got beyond some informal exchange of friendly gestures, or that Syphax considered that any agreement he had made had been with Scipio's father and uncle, and now wished to renew it with the son. At all events, Scipio seems to have been willing to fall in with his wishes, and, leaving Marcius in charge at Tarraco, according to Livy (28.17.11), he hurried by forced marches to Cartagena, where he left Silanus, and embarked himself and his party on two quinqueremes for the voyage to Africa. However, since when he returned to Cartagena (Livy 28.18.12), it was with Marcius that he co-operated in the punitive operations described below (see p. 152), it is possible that Livy has got these generals the wrong way round, and that it was Silanus who was left at Tarraco, and Marcius at Cartagena. [62]

As luck would have it, according to Livy (28.17.13ff.), Hasdrubal Gisgo had just entered the harbour in Syphax' kingdom to which Scipio was bound, with a squadron of seven quinqueremes, and thus found himself with the chance of eliminating the general who had lately defeated him. But the Roman warships were able to enter the harbour before the Carthaginians could intercept them, and neither side then dared to come to blows for fear of offending Syphax. Thus the hitherto relatively unimportant Numidian king found himself entertaining simultaneously the rival generals of the two most powerful states in the Mediterranean world. [63] According to Livy's account (28.18.6ff.), both he and Hasdrubal were much impressed by Scipio's personality (cf. Polybius 11.24a.4), and Syphax was prevailed upon to conclude a formal treaty with

Rome, whereupon Scipio returned to Cartagena. But in the light of what was to happen, it is clear that Syphax had by no means committed himself wholeheartedly to the Roman cause.

Scipio must, by now, have already been thinking of returning to Rome to stand for the consulship of 205/4, but there was still work for him in Spain, particularly the consolidation of Rome's control of the Spanish tribes. So, while Marcius marched from Tarraco to Castulo, according to Livy (28.19.4) - as was argued above, Marcius may in reality have been in Cartagena - Scipio himself advanced from Cartagena upon a place Livy calls Iliturgi. However, Appian (*History of Spain,* 32) calls the first place "Kastax" and the second "Ilurgia", and since a fragment of Polybius (11.24.10) mentions an "Ilourgia", it is probable that Appian was at least right about the latter. In this case, Ilurgia or Ilourgia is probably the same place as Ilorci (modern Lorqui), the site of Gnaeus Scipio's death (see above, p. 131), as, indeed, is suggested by Livy's statement (28.19.2) that Scipio's motive for attacking "Iliturgi" was that its inhabitants had murdered some of the refugees from that disaster. There is also the point that Livy says that Scipio reached "Iliturgi" in five days' marching from Cartagena, which is impossible if Iliturgi is to be located near Mengibar in Jaén,[64] for that lay 320 kilometres away from Cartagena, through mountainous country; Lorqui lies only 87 kilometres from Cartagena. But wherever the place in question was, Scipio stormed it and massacred its surviving inhabitants as an example to the rest of Spain. He then moved on to Castulo, which lay near Linares,[65] if we accept Livy's version, or to Appian's otherwise unknown Castax - which cannot be the same as Castulo, since Appian elsewhere mentions that place as "Kastolon" (*History of Spain,* 16). Castulo or Castax promptly surrendered, and Scipio then returned to Cartagena, leaving Marcius to continue operations. Crossing the Baetis, the latter received the surrender of two towns not named by Livy (28.22.1), and then moved on to Astapa (now Estepa, near Osuna), where the townspeople massacred their womenfolk and children, and died fighting to the last man in a desperate sortie (Livy 28.22.2-23.5). Other communities in the area then surrendered, and Marcius rejoined his commander-in-chief at Cartagena (Livy 28.23.5). But here deserters came to Scipio from Gades, offering to betray the city to Rome. Mago had established himself there after his escape from Ilipa, and had collected a considerable force, so the prize was a tempting one, and once again the faithful Marcius was sent off with an infantry force, marching light, while Laelius was instructed to take a small squadron of seven triremes and one quinquereme, to act in concert with him (Livy 28.23.6-8).

At this juncture, however, Spain was thrown into a turmoil when Scipio fell ill, and rumour began to exaggerate the danger to his life. Andobales and Mandonios are said (Livy 28.24.3-4) to have roused their "fellow-countrymen", the Lacetani (a people who lived near the site of Barcelona), and to have joined the Celtiberi to raid the lands of Rome's allies the Suessetani and Sedetani. In reality, Andobales was chief of the Ilergetes (cf. Polybius 10.18.7), who lived between Saragossa and Lerida, and Livy later correctly describes the rising as a rebellion of the Ilergetes (28.31.3). But Andobales is said to have had widespread influence in north-east Spain (cf. Polybius 3.76.7), so perhaps we can accept that the Lacetani were also involved in the rising. Worse still, there was a mutiny in a force of 8000 Roman troops stationed at Sucro,

Livy says (28.24.5), to control the tribes living north of the Ebro. However, since Sucro lay on the river of the same name, now the Jucar, some 200 kilometres south of the Ebro, Livy must either have mistaken the location of the force, or its purpose - probably the latter, since the mutiny was dealt with from Cartagena, not Tarraco. According to Livy (28.24.6ff.), the trouble had started before Scipio's illness, and was brought about by idleness and the straitened circumstances of soldiers grown accustomed to booty: now they demanded either to be led to war, or to be sent home, and in any case to be paid. But the news that Scipio was alive and well seems to have caused the rebellious Spanish tribes, apart from the Ilergetes, to return to their allegiance, and the mutiny also petered out. The ring-leaders were arrested and executed, and the remainder overawed by the presence of superior forces, ostensibly collected for a punitive expedition against Andobales and Mandonios (Livy 28.25-9). The names of the chief mutineers are given by Livy (28.24.13) as Caius Albius of Cales and Caius Atrius of Umbria, and although they look suspiciously like invented names - meaning Caius White and Caius Black - if they are authentic, it is interesting that the first would have been a Latin, from one of the twelve Latin colonies which, in 209, had refused to supply their contingents of recruits, partly on the grounds of the long service overseas being required of their men (cf. Livy 27.9.1ff.);the Umbrian was, presumably, an ordinary Italian ally. It is also interesting to compare Livy's version of Scipio's speech to the mutineers (28.27-29.8) with Polybius' much sterner oration (11.28-30).

Marcius, meanwhile, had reached the Baetis on his way to Gades, and had dispersed a force raised by one of Mago's officers (Livy 28.30.1-2). But Mago had learned of the plot to betray Gades and arrested the ring-leaders, and although the ships taking them to Africa were surprised by Laelius' squadron off Carteia, most of them made good their escape, including the quinquereme carrying the prisoners (Livy 28.30.3-12). [66] When Laelius returned to Carteia, he learned that the plot to hand over Gades had been betrayed, and both he and Marcius then withdrew, whereupon Mago, encouraged by their departure, and hearing of the rebellion among the Ilergetes, actually began to dream again of recovering Spain, if we are to believe Livy (28.31.3), and sent to Carthage for reinforcements.

But Scipio, having put down the mutiny by a judicious mixture of force and leniency, now marched against Andobales and Mandonios, and crushed their rebellion in a swift campaign. The site of the final battle cannot be precisely determined, but it lay four days' march up the Ebro (Polybius 11.32.1), and this indicates that the rebellion was a serious business: had it not been swiftly put down, the Roman position in the whole area would have been endangered, and their communications with Italy through Tarraco threatened. It was, thus, essential to bring the enemy to battle as soon as possible, and not to allow them to protract the rebellion by guerilla tactics. To achieve this, Scipio first tempted the Spaniards by driving cattle into a level space between the opposing camps, then sent his *velites* in to attack them when they started to round up the cattle, finally launching his cavalry, which had been concealed behind a spur (Polybius 11.32.2-4). Infuriated, the Spaniards next day deployed for battle, but since the valley was too narrow to hold their whole force, according to Livy (28.33.8), they put two-thirds of their infantry and the whole of their cavalry into line, but held back the remaining infantry at an angle on the hill on which their camp lay. Polybius (11.32.6) at first seems to imply that the whole of their force was deployed on the floor of the valley, but later mentions some of their troops drawn up "on the side of the hill" (11.33.1), and at the end of his account (11.33.6) says that they were light troops who formed a third of the Spanish army, thus confirming Livy.

Scipio was happy to see the Spaniards deploying in the valley, since the confined conditions suited his superior troops, and immediately deployed his own men for battle. Against the Spanish troops drawn up at the foot of the hill, he probably detached his *velites,* though unfortunately there is a gap in the text of Polybius at this point, and advanced on the Spaniards drawn up on the valley floor with a front of four cohorts (Polybius 11.33.1). Meanwhile, Laelius with the cavalry descended the spurs leading from the site of the Roman camp to the valley, and apparently worked his way round to fall on the rear of the enemy cavalry, which seems to have been congregated on the Spanish left wing (Polybius 11.33.2; Livy 28.33.9-11). The result was a massacre: Polybius (11.33.5) says that almost all those who had come down into the valley, both infantry and cavalry, were killed - Livy (28.33.15) says not one survived. The Spanish light troops, however, managed to make good their escape, with Andobales in their company. But Andobales had no heart to continue the fight: sending his brother, Mandonios, to Scipio, he threw himself on the Roman's mercy, and Scipio, rather than provoke desperate resistance, accepted their surrender, demanding neither the handing over of arms nor of hostages.

After this swift success, Scipio left Silanus in charge again at Tarraco, and once more set off to join Marcius in the Baetis valley. Here a meeting was arranged between Scipio and Masinissa, who had persuaded Mago to allow him to cross over to the main-land from the island on which Gades was situated, ostensibly to exercise his cavalry-horses in raiding the surrounding area. Once again Scipio's personality had the desired effect, and Masinissa pledged his support should Scipio come to Africa (Livy 28.34.12-35.12). Scipio then returned to Tarraco and Masinissa to Gades. It was possibly on his return-march on this occasion that Scipio founded the colony of Italica, just west of Seville (Appian, *History of Spain,* 38): as Appian notes, this was later to be the native city of Trajan and Hadrian, who may thus have been descended from some of Scipio's veterans.

By now Mago had come to the conclusion that there was no hope for the Carthaginian cause in Spain, but as he was preparing to withdraw to Africa, instructions reached him from Carthage to take what forces he had to northern Italy, where he was to recruit an army amongst the Ligures and Gauls, and then try to join Hannibal (Livy 28.36.1-2). First, however, he seems to have decided on an attempt to recover Cartagena, though he made the mistake of wringing all he could from the wretched inhabitants of Gades before he left (Livy 28.36.3). Perhaps all he had intended was to try to pick up extra funds from Cartagena, since he can hardly have hoped, at this late stage, to establish a new front in Spain, but the result was that when his surprise attack on Cartagena failed, and he returned to Gades - either because this had been his intention from the first, or because his forces had been too badly mauled to proceed - he found the gates of Gades closed against him. So, after treacherously luring the magistrates of the city to a conference, and killing them, he made off to the island of Pityusa (Ibiza), where he received generous help from the Carthaginian inhabitants, and then proceeded to Majorca. Here, however, he was given a very different reception, and was thus forced to put into Minorca for the winter (Livy 28.36-7). Tradition holds that the main town of the island, now Mahón, was so named after him.

With Mago's departure, Gades finally surrendered to Rome, and thus, although Rome was to be involved in almost continuous warfare in Spain for a generation or more, and the final conquest of the north-west was not to come until the time of Augustus, the last vestige of Carthaginian rule was finally removed. Scipio was at last free to return to Italy, and before a meeting of the Senate held in the Temple of Bellona, outside the city, made his report (Livy 28.38.1-3). But although he had hoped to be allowed to triumph, he did not press the matter, because, as Livy notes (28.38.4), "it was accepted that no one had ever triumphed to that day, who had acted without holding a magistracy." It was, no doubt, some consolation that at the elections, perhaps delayed until his arrival, he was elected consul for the following year (205/4).

His achievement had, of course, been magnificent: in five years he had driven the Carthaginians from Spain, whereas his father and uncle, after eight years, had only met with disaster. Why did he succeed where they had failed? Part of the answer, undoubtedly, lies in his personality, in his ability to train his soldiers to a high pitch of efficiency, and in his tactical skill on the battlefield. But the fundamental reason for his success perhaps lies in his very different conception of the way the war in Spain should be fought. His father and uncle seem to have thought in terms of winning over tribes and gradually acquiring control of territory, but he seems to have thought primarily of striking at the Carthaginians. Thus his immediate capture of Cartagena not only deprived them of the hostages, munitions and treasure kept in the city, but also of the base from which they controlled southeastern Spain: by taking it, Scipio virtually eliminated one area of Carthaginian rule, and gave himself only one target to aim at for the future. Thereafter, it is noticeable that the campaigns of 208, 207, and 206 were all directed specifically at Carthaginian armies, rather than at Spanish tribes, strongholds or territory, until after the victory at Ilipa. The one exception is Lucius Scipio's capture of Orongis in 207, and this, as was noted above (see p. 144), followed Hasdrubal Gisgo's decision to disperse his forces amongst the towns of southern Baetica, and was probably intended as a demonstration to the Spaniards that Scipio's withdrawal was not a sign of weakness or bafflement. Apart from this, it was only after Hasdrubal Barca's defeat in the Ilipa campaign, that there was a series of operations against towns - Ilorci, Castulo (or Kastax) and Astapa, for example - designed to rivet Roman control on the areas from which the Carthaginians had now been expelled, and the final campaign, the one against the Ilergetes in the Ebro valley, was the first against a Spanish tribe which Scipio had conducted. Thus he never allowed himself to become bogged down in the endless guerilla warfare in which the Spaniards were to prove themselves so adept in the next century. His excursion to Africa, and his meeting with Masinissa, finally, show that he always retained firmly in his mind that the primary task was the defeat of Carthage, not the conquest of Spain, though his victories in Spain were, of course, the first steps in that conquest, and there can be little doubt that a man of his evident intelligence would have seen beyond the immediate objective and realised the inevitability of Rome's future role. His foundation of Italica, if nothing else, indicates that he was certain that the Romans had come to stay.

# CHAPTER SIX – MACEDONIA AND THE METAURUS

When Scipio returned to Italy towards the end of 206, the war in Italy had almost come to a close: Hannibal was now confined to Bruttium, where, though watched by both consuls of 206/5, no action had been taken against him since early in 206. But the five years which had elapsed since the surrender of Capua in 211 had not been without incident. Hannibal had marched and counter-marched, and had more than once proved too much for his opponents, although Livy also records a number of defeats inflicted upon him. But no reinforcements had reached him, and when, in 207, his brother, Hasdrubal, had at last arrived in Italy, it had only been to meet defeat and death at the Metaurus. Meanwhile, the war in Sicily had finally come to an end, with the capture of Agrigentum in 210, and the war in Greece had briefly flared with the conclusion of an alliance between Rome and the Aetolian League, probably in the summer of 211. But there, too, fighting was coming to a close by the end of 206, with the conclusion of peace between Philip V of Macedonia and the Aetolian League, though Rome did not finally make peace with the king until 205.

Although the first round of Rome's conflict with Macedonia, the so-called First Macedonian War (215-205) was never more than a side-issue to the greater struggle with Carthage, and is far more significant for its consequences than for itself, it does form part of the history of the Second Punic War, and cannot be ignored. It is a matter of controversy how early the Roman Republic became involved with the Greek world: some of the alleged early contacts between Rome and Greece have been dismissed as unhistorical,[1] and it is worth remembering that Thucydides could devote two whole books of his history of the Peloponnesian War to the Athenian expedition to Sicily in 415-3, when Rome is supposed to have been in existence for more than three hundred years, without once mentioning Rome or Romans. But early in the third century the Greek world had come into contact with Rome with a vengeance, when Pyrrhus, King of Epirus, invaded Italy on behalf of the Greek cities of southern Italy, and in 229 Roman forces had for the first time crossed the Adriatic to deal with the Illyrian pirates of Albania and coastal Yugoslavia. As a result of this war, Rome had established a loose protectorate over what is now southwestern Albania, including some of the off-shore islands, and, in particular, Corcyra (Corfu). Nor is there any reason to doubt Polybius when he says (2.12.4) that one of the Roman commanders, L. Postumius Albinus, consul of 229/8, sent embassies to the Aetolian and Achaean Leagues, and that later the Romans sent envoys to Athens and Corinth (2.12.8).

By this time, of course, the Greek world was very different from the one Thucydides had known, two centuries earlier.[2] Alexander the Great had destroyed the Persian Empire, and in its place, after his death, there had grown up a kaleidoscope of successor states, many of them ruled by descendants of his marshals. These included

Egypt under the Ptolemies, who also ruled part of modern Libya; Syria, comprising modern Israel, Lebanon, Syria, Iraq and Persia; and in western Asia Minor, the kingdoms of Bithynia in the northwest, and Pergamum in the centre. Old Greece, weakened by interminable inter-state wars, had fallen prey to Macedonia in the fourth century, but smaller states still abounded, some owing allegiance to one or other of the great powers, others, like the island republic of Rhodes, maintaining a precarious independence. But in mainland Greece, too, there had been a tendency for larger political entities than the old city-states to develop, though city-states, more or less independent of the larger entities, like Athens and Sparta, still existed. The most important of the powers with which Rome had to deal, at this time, were the Achaean League in the northern and western Peloponnese, the Aetolian League in central Greece, and in the north, the kingdom of Macedonia itself, extending into parts of what are now southern Albania, Yugoslavia and Bulgaria. In 229, the king of Macedonia had died, leaving as his heir a boy of eight, the future Philip V, but for the next eight years, the kingdom had been ruled by a cousin, Antigonos Doson, at first as regent, but for the last seven years as king. It had been Antigonos Doson who had created the "symmachy", a confederation of Greek leagues, including the Achaean League, and others such as the Thessalians, Phocians, Boeotians and Euboeans, under the presidency of the king of Macedonia, which, while in effect it gave Macedonia dominance in Greece, still left the Greek states independent, and also provided them with military protection against the Aetolians, and any other enemies, including, later, the Romans. (See map on end papers).

In the summer of 221, Antigonos Doson died, and the new king, Philip V, now sixteen years old, was immediately faced with trouble from the Aetolian League, leading to the so-called Social War, which was brought to an end, some two months after the battle of Lake Trasimene, by the Treaty of Naupactus.[3] It was at the peace conference leading to this treaty that Agelaos of Naupactus made his celebrated appeal for an end to the quarrels in Greece (Polybius 5.104), warning his fellow-countrymen about the "clouds in the west". But, in Polybius' view, Philip, who had heard of the Roman defeat at Trasimene while attending the Nemean Games in July, had been advised to rid himself of the war with the Aetolian League as soon as possible, so as to be able to interfere in the Roman protectorate in Illyria, and even in Italy (Polybius 5.101.6-8), though for the time being trouble on the northwestern borders of his own kingdom fully occupied his attention (Polybius 5.108). Rome has been accused of having had something to do with stirring up this trouble,[4] but this is very unlikely in view of the desperate situation in Italy, and argues far too long-sighted a policy on Rome's part.

Polybius believed, on the contrary, that the first move came from Philip. During the winter of 217/6 he had constructed 100 of the light Illyrian galleys known as "lemboi", and at the beginning of the following summer (Polybius 5.109.4), he sailed through the Euripos and round Cape Malea to the vicinity of Leukas and Kephallenia. Here he waited anxiously for news of the Roman fleet, according to Polybius (5.109.5) - probably, in particular, the fleet of 75 quinqueremes based on western Sicily (Livy 22.37.13). But when he heard that it was still at Lilybaeum, he put to sea again and proceeded towards Apollonia, on the bay of Valona (Vlone), in modern Albania. This was one of the towns which had come under Rome's protection as a result of the first of her wars against the Illyrian pirates, in 229/8. Rome's protectorate extended from south of Lissus (Lesh) to just north of Phoinike in Epirus, and must have been of some concern to the kings of Macedonia since it had come into being. But hitherto they had scrupulously avoided any conflict with Rome, and even though after Rome's second intervention, in 219, her principal enemy, Demetrios of Pharos, had taken refuge with Philip, there is no reason to believe that he had in any way instigated Demetrios' activities, for these had included an attack on Pylos in Messenia, a member of the Achaean League, and so, nominally, an ally of Philip's, in conjunction with his enemies, the Aetolians (cf. Polybius 4.16.7).[5] Even the allegation that Apollonia was Philip's target in 216 may be due to a false inference from his attack upon the place two years later - his real target in 216 may have been his enemy Scerdilaidas of Illyria,[6] for it was the latter that appealed to Rome (Polybius 5.110.8). In any case, the expedition came to nothing, for when Philip was approaching the mouth of the Aous (Vijose), which flowed past Apollonia, he heard a rumour that some Roman quinqueremes had reached Rhegium on their way to Illyria (Polybius 5.110.1-3), and this was enough to send him scuttling back to Kephallenia, and eventually to Macedonia, although it subsequently transpired that the Roman squadron consisted of only ten warships (Polybius 5.110.8-9) - a striking illustration of the importance of Roman sea-power at this date, even though no direct conflict resulted.

However, even if Philip had not intended to attack Apollonia in the summer of 216, the news of Rome's defeat at Cannae in August of that year, must now finally have convinced him that he had little to fear from the Republic, and everything to gain from an alliance with an apparently victorious Carthage (cf. Livy 23.33.4). Accordingly, in 215, he despatched envoys to Hannibal, led by one Xenophanes of Athens. Livy (23.33. 5, 34.4) alleges that Xenophanes and his party twice fell into Roman hands, but that on the first occasion they were able to convince their captors that their mission was to Rome, not Hannibal, Even if the first capture is not historical,[7] there is certainly no reason to doubt that Xenophanes and his colleagues were captured on their way back to Philip, accompanied by Carthaginian officers - it was the accent of the latter which allegedly betrayed the party, when their ship was intercepted (Livy 23.34.6) - and it is the copy of the treaty captured on this occasion which Polybius quotes (cf. 7.9.1). But there is no reason to believe that it was altered in any substantial way when Philip subsequently sent a second embassy, which succeeded in reaching Hannibal and in returning safely to Macedonia (Livy 23.39), and certainly there is no reason to prefer to Polybius' version the ones recorded by Livy (23.33.10-12), Appian (*History of Macedonia,* 1) and Zonaras (9.4.2-3).[8] The treaty as recorded by Polybius provided for a mutual alliance between Philip and his allies and Carthage and her subjects and allies, against their enemies in general, and against Rome in particular, and laid down that once victory over Rome had been assured, any peace treaty would forbid the Romans to make war against Philip, and provide that "the Romans should no longer be masters of Corcyra, Apollonia, Epidamnos, Pharos, Dimale, the Parthinoi, or Atintania" (Polybius 7.9.13). The treaty makes no mention of any specific undertaking by either side to help the other, and the question must remain open how far either Hannibal envisaged direct help to or from Philip, or Philip to or from Hannibal. In the event, Carthaginian help to Philip was limited to the late and ephemeral appearance of a Carthaginian fleet in

Greek waters (see below, p. 163), and Philip gave no direct help to Carthage, unless there is any truth in the tradition that there were Macedonian troops in Africa in 202 (Livy 30.33.5, see below, p. 222). But both sides were probably content that each would, to some extent, distract Rome from the activities of the other: Philip clearly hoped that Rome's pre-occupation with Hannibal in Italy would leave him a free hand in Illyria, while Hannibal no doubt hoped that some of Rome's forces would be diverted to Greece, and in particular, perhaps, that her naval strength guarding the sea approaches to Sicily and Italy would be dissipated.

But the capture of Philip's first envoys, and the necessity to send others, delayed the beginning of Philip's operations, and Rome, forewarned, was able to take steps to forestall any intervention by Philip in Italy, and to be ready to intervene herself in Illyria. Thus, soon after the capture of the envoys, the fleet based at Tarentum was strengthened to fifty-five ships, and orders were given to its commander, P. Valerius Flaccus, not merely to patrol the coast of Italy, but to go in search of any information which might reveal Philip's intentions (Livy 23.38.9-10). Later in the year (215), the praetor, M. Valerius Laevinus, was ordered to Brundisium with the forces he had been commanding at Luceria, also to defend the coast against possible attack by Philip (Livy 23.48.3). Laevinus' *imperium* was prorogued in 214, for a further year, with similar instructions (Livy 24.10.4), and during the summer (Livy 24.40.1), he was approached by envoys from Oricus, who told him, according to Livy, that Philip had attempted to attack Apollonia with 120 *lemboi,* and had then taken Oricus (Livy 24.40.2ff.). Since Oricus lay at the mouth of the river on which Apollonia also lay, it seems probable that Livy here reverses the order of Philip's operations,[9] but in either case, Laevinus, having taken precautions to safeguard Italy, promptly sailed to Oricus, reaching it in two days, and easily recaptured it, since it was only held by a small garrison of Philip's troops. Next, according to Livy (24.40.7ff.), having received an appeal from Apollonia, he despatched a force under Q. Naevius Crista, Prefect of the Allies, which entered Apollonia secretly during the night, and then carried out a surprise attack on the Macedonian camp, killing or capturing nearly 3000 of the enemy, and returning with catapults and other siege-equipment, while Philip, roused suddenly from his sleep, had to flee ignominiously to his ships, without his clothes. But Laevinus had probably already blocked the mouth of the Aous - though Livy puts it now[10] - and Philip had literally to burn his boats, and retreat over the mountains back to Macedonia. The sources upon which Livy drew probably exaggerated the success of the night attack, even if they did not invent it, but it is clear that Philip had completely miscalculated Rome's ability to spare forces for Illyria: it is perhaps significant that his attack on Oricus and Apollonia apparently came after Hannibal's attempt on Tarentum in this year (cf. Livy 24.20.9ff.), since, if we are to believe Livy (24.20.12), Laevinus was still at Brundisium when that took place. Philip must have been hoping that the threat to Tarentum would prevent any interference across the Adriatic by the Roman forces at Brundisium. But once again Rome's resources, and her complete command of the sea, enabled her to checkmate Philip, without seriously weakening her forces in Italy.

The threat to the Illyrian protectorate, moreover, and probably fears that Philip might yet seek to interfere in Italy, now led to a permanent Roman presence across the

Adriatic, for Laevinus and his squadron wintered (214/3) at Oricus (Livy 24.40.17), and in March, 213, his *imperium* was prorogued again, this time with "Greece and Macedonia" as his province (Livy 24.44.5). However, for two years, Laevinus apparently did nothing, while Philip subdued the hinterland of the Roman protectorate, overrunning Atintania, conquering the Dassaretae and the Parthinoi, capturing Dimale, and even winning a port on the Adriatic by a brilliant surprise attack on Lissus (Polybius 8.13.7). [11] But Laevinus probably calculated that his forces were too few to risk operations at any distance from the coast, and that in view of the worsening situation in Sicily, he could not hope for more. Nevertheless, the mere presence of his fleet virtually precluded any attempt by Philip to cross the Adriatic, and it is very doubtful, whatever the Romans may have believed now or later, that he ever seriously contemplated invading Italy, despite Livy's assertion, for example, that Tarentum - captured by Hannibal early in 212 (see above, p. 110) - would have made a suitable port for him (24.13.5), and the evidence that even Syracuse may have hoped for some sort of aid from him (cf. Livy 25.23.8-9).

In 212, however, Laevinus did make a first cautious approach to the Aetolian League (Livy 25.23.9, 26.24.1), and eventually, in summer 211, a treaty was concluded:[12] a copy of part of the text was discovered in 1949, on an inscription from Acarnania (*SEG* xiii 382). Unnecessary difficulties have been raised about the Roman delay in concluding an alliance which seems so obviously advantageous: the point is, probably, not so much that the Romans were obtuse, as that the Aetolians required convincing that such an alliance was to their advantage - it is significant, if we can trust such a detail in Livy, that in his speech to the Aetolians, Laevinus referred to the fall of Syracuse and Capua as proof that Rome was winning the war with Carthage (Livy 26. 24.2). [13] The treaty laid it down that it should be open to the people of Elis and Sparta, King Attalus of Pergamum, and the Illyrian chieftains, Scerdilaidas and Pleuratus, to join the alliance on the same terms if they so wished; that the Aetolians should begin operations against Philip immediately, and that the Romans should aid them by sea with not less than twenty-five quinqueremes. Of the towns northwards from Aetolia as far as Corcyra, the territory, buildings and walls were to be handed over to the Aetolians, the other booty to belong to Rome, and, in particular, the Romans were to ensure that Acarnania was handed over to the Aetolians. Finally, neither side was to conclude a treaty with Philip which left it open to him to continue to make war on the other (Livy 26.24.8-13). It has been pointed out that the treaty contains a number of clauses foreign to normal Roman treaties, [14] and the probable explanation is that Laevinus was largely responsible for the details, not the Senate, and this probably also explains why there was a further delay of two years before the treaty was ratified by Rome (Livy 26.24.14-5), although the Romans may also have been waiting to see if the Aetolians meant business. (See Map 18).

But the delay in ratification certainly did not delay the beginning of operations: the Aetolians possibly made an immediate raid on Thessaly, [15] and Laevinus took Zakynthos, except for the citadel of the one town on the island, and then Oeniadae, on the coast of Acarnania, and the small island, simply called "Nasos" (Island) in the Gulf of Melite, handing at least the latter two over to the Aetolians as the treaty had specified. Then the Roman fleet retired to Corcyra for the winter (Livy 26.24.15-6).

Philip, who had heard of the treaty while at his capital, Pella (Livy 26.25.1), responded with another attack on Oricus and Apollonia (Livy 26.25.1-2), and then hastened to secure his northern borders, where he seized the strategic town of Sintia (Livy 26.25.3), which probably lay between the modern Prilep and Köprülü, south of Skopje in Yugoslavia. At this point he possibly heard of the Aetolian attack on Thessaly, since he marched rapidly south through Pelagonia, Lyncestis and Bottiaea to the Tempe pass, where he left a general called Perseus, with 4000 men, to guard access into Macedonia by this route, before doubling back to attack the Maedi in Thrace, and to capture their capital at Iamphorynna, which lay somewhere in the southwest corner of what is now Bulgaria (Livy 26.25.4-8). [17] The moment his back was turned, the Aetolians mobilized for an attack on Acarnania, but the resolute defiance of the Acarnanians made them hesitate, and then the news that Philip was on his way caused them to abandon the enterprise. Philip, who had in fact not got beyond Dium, then returned to Pella (Livy 26.25. 9-17; Polybius 9.40.4-6). The campaigns of this year vividly illustrate Philip's problems: if his claims to protect his allies in central and southern Greece were to appear credible, he had to do something to counter Roman and Aetolian attacks upon them, but, at the same time, he had continually to ward off incursions along his northern borders.

Next spring (210), Laevinus and the Aetolians attacked and took Antikyra in Phocis, [18] which lay at modern Aspra Spitia at the head of the bay of the same name, east of the Gulf of Krisa. Their object was probably, partly, to threaten a possible line of communication between Philip and his allies in the Peloponnese. In accordance with the terms of the alliance, the inhabitants of Antikyra were enslaved, and the town handed over to the Aetolians. Despite the disgust felt by many Greeks at what they regarded as the barbarous Roman methods of warfare, the successes of Laevinus and his allies were not without effect: Elis and Messenia seem to have joined the alliance almost immediately, as was allowed for in the first clause of the treaty, and Chlainias of Aetolia was also able to persuade the Spartans to join, in a speech recorded by Polybius (9.28-31.6), despite a passionate plea by the Acarnanian envoy, Lykiskos (Polybius 9.32.3-39.7). Thus Laevinus would have had something to console him during the long illness which delayed his departure for Rome to take up the well-earned consulship for 210/9, to which he had been elected in his absence (Livy 26.26.4). When he eventually did reach Rome, he is said to have told the Senate that the legion which had been serving in Greece could now be withdrawn, and that the fleet was sufficient to keep Philip from Italy (Livy 26.28.2). Thus his successor, P. Sulpicius Galba, consul in 211/10, whose *imperium* was prorogued as proconsul in Greece, was instructed to dismiss all the troops in Greece, except the *socii navales* (Livy 26.28.9), though some Roman troops seem to have been retained, since Livy reports their presence at a later date (209: 27.32.2).

Livy records no operations in Greece in 210, after the capture of Antikyra, but a fragment of Polybius' ninth book (9.41-2) describes Philip's siege of Echinous, on the north shore of the Gulf of Malis (now Akhinos), and the repulse of an Aetolian army commanded by Dorimachos, supported by the Roman fleet under Sulpicius. This episode is possibly to be explained as an attempt by Philip to secure his route south from Thessaly, and another fragment of Polybius (9.45.3), referring to Xyniai, suggests that

Philip's attack on Echinous may have been connected with an attempt to find a way through the hills north of Lamia, along the route now followed by the modern road from Pharsalos to Lamia. Philip probably also now took Phalara, the port of Lamia, which was in his hands next year (Livy 27.30.3). He thus secured his communications with Euboea, and put himself within striking distance of Thermopylae, and of Aetolia, via the Spercheios valley. But the Romans succeeded in taking Aegina (cf. Polybius 9.42. 5-8), and received a welcome accession to their side in the person of Attalus, King of Pergamum: his election to the presidency of the Aetolian League in the autumn (Livy 27.29.10), shows that he was soon expected to arrive in Greece.

The next operations recorded by Livy (27.29-33), are dated by him to the consular year 208/7, but properly belong to 209, as the references to the Nemean Games (27.30.9, 17; 31.9) show. [19] Operations began with an attack on the borders of Philip's allies, the Achaean League, by Machanidas, who is described by Livy as *"tyrannus"* of Sparta, but who was probably, technically, the guardian of Pelops, the infant king (cf. Livy 34.32.1; Diodoros 27.1). Simultaneously, the Aetolians attacked across the narrow strait between Antirhion and Rhion, just west of Naupactos on the Gulf of Corinth. In response to an appeal from the Achaeans, and in view of the rumour that Attalus of Pergamum was about to come to Greece, Philip hastened south, but was confronted at Lamia by an Aetolian force, including an advance-guard from Attalus' army and some troops from the Roman fleet. After twice defeating this force, and driving it back within the walls of Lamia, Philip retired to Phalara to meet ambassadors from the king of Egypt, Rhodes, Athens and Chios, come to attempt to mediate between him and the Aetolians. With them came Amynander, King of Athamania in north-west Greece, representing Aetolian interests. Livy remarks (27.30.5) that the mediators were not so much concerned for the welfare of the Aetolians, as in trying to ensure that Philip did not become too powerful, but it was also in Philip's interests that the war should be brought to an end as soon as possible, and he readily agreed to a thirty-day truce in order to allow for peace negotiations at a general meeting in Achaea.

After these discussions, Philip made his way south to Chalcis in Euboea, which he fortified against the expected arrival of Attalus, and then went on to take part in the celebration of the festival in honour of the goddess Hera at Argos, towards the end of June. After the festival, he proceeded to Aigion, on the Gulf of Corinth, where the peace-conference was to meet (Livy 27.30.7-9). Discussions began on the question of ending the war between Philip and the Aetolians, but they had scarcely started when a rumour that Attalus had reached Aegina, and that the Roman fleet was at Naupactos, encouraged the Aetolians to raise their demands. At this Philip angrily dismissed the conference, declaring that he had never really had any hope of peace, but had wanted to make it clear that it was his enemies who were responsible for the continuation of hostilities. He left 4000 troops to aid the Achaeans, and himself took five of their warships, which, Livy says (27.30.16), he hoped to add to the Carthaginian fleet lately sent to him and to the ships coming from King Prusias of Bithynia, and thus at last to challenge the Roman fleet. The Carthaginian fleet referred to here, had been sent from Tarentum to Corcyra when Philip was preparing to attack the Aetolians (Livy 27.15.7), and the threat it posed possibly explains Sulpicius' apparently late arrival in the Gulf of

Corinth. But after appearing off Corcyra, it vanishes from the record until the following year, possibly returning to Carthage, possibly retiring to Lissus, which was now in Philip's hands.

Philip himself returned to Argos to celebrate the Nemean Games in July, and, if we are to believe Livy (27.31.1), to give himself up to wild debauchery. But when the Roman fleet crossed the Gulf of Corinth from Naupactos, and began to raid the coast between Sikyon and Corinth, he was rapidly at hand to drive the scattered Roman raiders back to their ships, before returning to his pleasures, and a few days after the Nemean Games, he was ready enough to march to Dyme to join the Achaeans in an attempt to expell the Aetolians from Elis. Crossing the river Larissos - where the young Philopoemen gave an earnest of things to come (Plutarch, *Philopoemen*, 7.3ff.) - the combined army advanced confidently on Elis, not knowing that Sulpicius had secretly thrown 4000 troops into the town. When he spotted the Roman troops issuing from Elis with the Aetolians, Philip was at first for withdrawing, but when he saw some of his Illyrian soldiers hard pressed, he gallantly charged the Roman detachment, only to have his horse killed under him, and to be rescued after a desperate struggle. Extricating his army, he withdrew some twenty-two kilometres from Elis, and then, next day, stormed and took a fort probably called "Phyrcus". [20]

At this point, Philip received news that Macedonia itself was again threatened by an incursion of northern tribesmen, so leaving forces to aid the Achaeans, he marched in ten days to Demetrias on the Gulf of Pagasai, where he received worse news - that the Dardanians had invaded Macedonia, encouraged by a rumour of his death. According to Livy (27.33.2ff.), in his attack on the Roman raiders near Sikyon, earlier in the summer, the king's horse had crashed into a tree, and one of the horns which decorated his helmet had broken off on an overhanging branch. This trophy had been found by an Aetolian soldier, and taken to the Illyrian chieftain, Scerdilaidas, who recognized it and spread the story of the king's death. After telling this picturesque story, Livy omits to mention what happened when Philip advanced against the invaders of his kingdom, but a later source (Justin 29.4.6) says they made off, though not without immense booty. Sulpicius, meanwhile, had brought his fleet round to the Saronic Gulf to join Attalus at Aegina, where they spent the winter, while the Achaeans had succeeded in defeating the Aetolians and Eleans in a battle not far from Messene (Livy 27.33.4-5). The year had proved a frustrating one for Philip, and although the Romans had won no decisive success, they had retained their mastery of the sea, due principally to the Carthaginian failure to come to Philip's aid, and now had a new ally in Attalus of Pergamum.

With the coming of spring (208), Philip first ordered his army to assemble at Larisa in Thessaly, and then went to Demetrias to meet representatives of his allies. Here it was made clear that an ominous situation was developing: Machanidas of Sparta was threatening Argos, the Boeotians and Euboeans appealed for protection against the Roman and Pergamene fleet, and requests for aid also came from Acarnania and Epirus since the Illyrians were reported to be on the move in the northwest. In the northeast the Maedi of Thrace were threatening an invasion of Macedonia, and, finally, the Aetolians had strengthened the fortifications of Thermopylae to hinder Philip's communications

*Pl. IX:* (top) *Lamia – view across the acropolis to Mount Oita.* (bottom) *Acrocorinth – one of the "Fetters" held by the Macedonians, with the remains of the later Roman City of Corinth in the foreground.*

with his southern allies. As Polybius says (10.41.7), Philip was like a wild beast, surrounded by danger on all sides. But he promised aid to all his allies, and took vigorous steps to implement his promises: a force was sent to the island of Peparethos to protect it against Attalus, troops were sent to Boeotia, Phocis and Euboea, and he himself marched to join his main field-army at Skotousa, northwest of Pharsalos in Thessaly. Here he heard that Attalus had arrived at Nikaia, east of Thermopylae, and that the officials of the Aetolian League were about to hold a meeting at Herakleia, just to the west of the pass, and hurried south in an attempt to disperse the meeting. Failing in this, he ravaged the shores of what Polybius calls the "Ainian" Gulf (10.42.5), more usually called the Malian Gulf, and returned himself to Demetrias with his royal guard and light troops, ordering his main force back to Skotousa. He then waited for his enemies to attack, sending orders to his officers on Peparethos and in Phocis and Euboea to inform him of any developments by fire-signals to a mountain Polybius calls "Tisaion" (10.42.7), which lay somewhere on the coast of Magnesia opposite Artemision in Euboea. [21] Polybius introduces an elaborate and fascinating excursus on fire-signalling at this point in his narrative (10.43-7), but for future events we have to rely again on Livy, though he evidently drew heavily on the Greek historian.

Livy says (28.5.1ff.) [22] that Sulpicius and Attalus first made for Lemnos with a combined fleet of sixty quinqueremes, and then descended upon Peparethos, ravaging all the land around the main town. From Peparethos they moved to Nikaia, and then attacked Oreos on the north coast of Euboea. There the Macedonian officer in command, Plator, treacherously admitted the Roman forces into the citadel near the sea, presumably the acropolis of the ancient town of Histiaia, and when the inhabitants tried to take refuge in the other citadel, in the centre of the town, they found the gates closed by some of the traitors, and were either killed or taken prisoner. The Macedonian garrison was released by agreement between Plator and Sulpicius, and conveyed by sea to Demetrias; Plator himself joined Attalus. From Oreos, Sulpicius sailed to Chalcis, but found the town resolutely defended by officers loyal to Philip, and so sailed back to Kynos in Locris, the sea-port of Opous, the main town of the Opuntian Locrians, which lay about ten kilometres away (Livy 28.6.8-12). Here Attalus and his forces were probably left to raid Locris, while Sulpicius returned to Oreos (cf. Livy 28.7.4): this division of forces was to prove dangerous, but Livy explains that Sulpicius had granted the concession to Attalus, because the booty from Oreos had gone to the Roman troops.

Philip, meanwhile, had been warned of the Roman attacks on Euboea by fire-signals from Oreos, but these had been deliberately lit too late by the treacherous Plator, and in any case Philip felt it to be too dangerous to attempt to cross to the island in face of the enemy's naval superiority. When he heard about the move against Chalcis, however, he rapidly rejoined his army at Skotousa, and marched to Elatea in Phocis, brushing aside the Aetolian troops at Thermopylae en route. Livy says (28.7.1-3) that he covered the distance - nearly ninety kilometres - in a single day, but it is unlikely that any army could have moved so fast. From Elatea he descended upon Opous, and almost caught Attalus napping - the king of Pergamum was engaged upon the lucrative business of extorting money from the Locrians. But Philip's force was spotted by a band of Cretans who had wandered some distance, foraging, and Attalus was able to escape to his ships just in time. Philip, baulked of his prey, returned to Opous, cursing gods and men, according to Livy (28.7.8), and, more particularly, blaming the Opuntians for giving in so easily. He then withdrew northwestwards to Thronion. Attalus made first for Oreos, but there received news that Prusias of Bithynia had invaded his kingdom, and returned to Asia Minor. Philip, meanwhile, took Thronion, which was under Aetolian control - it lay near the modern hamlet of Pikraki [23] - and then apparently cut southwards through the mountains, probably by the Klisoura pass, past the site of the splendid mediaeval castle of Boudonitza, above the modern village of Mendhenitsa, into the Kephisos valley, for Livy says he took Tithronion and Drymiai there (28.7.9-13). But an attempt to hold Lilaia, near the source of the Kephisos, failed, if we are to believe Pausanias (10.33.3) - this episode is not mentioned by Livy. This brief campaign resulted in what was known as Epicnemidian Locris passing into Philip's hands, and this eased his communications with the south.

After these successes, Philip returned to Elatea to meet ambassadors from Egypt and Rhodes come to renew their attempt to end the war in Greece. However, according to Livy (28.7.14ff.), when the king heard that Machanidas of Sparta was about to attack Elis as its people prepared for the Olympic Games (i.e. about July or August, 208), he decided that he must try to intervene. Marching swiftly through Boeotia to Megara, and thence by way of Corinth, Phlious and Pheneos, he had reached Heraia in Arcadia when he heard that Machanidas had withdrawn, and turned aside to Aigion, on the Gulf of Corinth, where the congress of the Achaean League was in session, and where he hoped, once again, to meet a Carthaginian squadron. Here we can accept Livy's facts, but there is some doubt about his statement that Machanidas was about to attack Elis, since both had been allies of the Aetolians the previous year. One possibility is that Elis had broken with the Aetolians after what had happened that year, but this seems unlikely, because, despite Philip's success at Phyrcus, and the defeat of the Eleans and Aetolians near Messene, Philip had, after all, been beaten off from Elis itself, and in any case, he would surely have gone on to strengthen his position in Elis, after Machanidas' withdrawal, if Elis had now been an actual or potential ally. A more likely explanation is that, after their success against Elis, the Achaeans had usurped control of the Games, and that Machanidas was seeking to recover control on Elis' behalf. [24] Following Machanidas' withdrawal, Philip would thus have felt free to pursue his long-term aim of linking-up with the Carthaginian fleet, and attempting to wrest control of Greek waters from Rome. But once more he was disappointed: the Carthaginians had heard that Attalus and Sulpicius had left Oreos, and were afraid of being caught in the Gulf of Corinth, so they had made off to Acarnania. They probably then made for home, for we hear no more of Carthaginian ships in Greek waters. This was the year of M. Valerius Laevinus' naval victory off Clupea in Africa (see above, p. 144), and this threat to the homeland perhaps explains the Carthaginian fleet's recall from Greece.

But despite his disappointment and his many anxieties, Philip addressed the Achaean leaders in optimistic vein, declaring, with some justification, that he had not failed at any point, but had beaten the enemy wherever they had not given him the slip (Livy 28.8.1-6). Then, taking three quadriremes and three biremes from the Achaeans, he crossed over to a place Livy calls "Anticyra" (28.8.7), but which, presumably must be different from the place captured by Laevinus and the Aetolians in 210 - the present Anticyra must have been in Ozolian Locris. [25] Here he joined a fleet of seven quinqueremes and more than twenty *lemboi* which he had sent into the Gulf of Corinth to join the Carthaginian fleet, the ships having presumably been dragged across the Isthmus. The combined fleet sailed to Erythrai, near Eupalion, and from here the king's forces ranged far and wide in a great cattle-raid, the inhabitants having fled. Returning to the Isthmus, the king then ordered his army to march north through Boeotia, while he himself dragged his ships back across the Isthmus, and boldly sailed from Kenchreai, the port of Corinth on the Saronic Gulf. Skirting the coast of Attica, past Sounion, despite the presence of the Roman fleet at Aegina, the king reached Chalcis, and went on from there to recapture Oreos with some ease. Finally he returned to Demetrias. His successes on land, and perhaps the ease with which he had challenged Rome's superiority at sea, now encouraged him to attempt to match that superiority for, according to Livy (28.8.14), on his return to Demetrias, he gave orders for the laying down of 100 new warships at Cassandreia, before he departed for his north-western frontiers to repel one of the periodic invasions of the Dardanians.

It was probably in the autumn of 208 that the Romans sacked Dyme in Achaea, and enslaved its population - it was later ransomed by Philip (Livy 32.21.28, 22.10; Pausanias 7.17.5), but thereafter the war in Greece seems to have stagnated for some two years (cf. Livy 29.12.1). This was welcome relief for Philip, who was also, to some extent, freed from the necessity to protect his Peloponnesian allies, despite the renewed activity of Machanidas of Sparta (cf. Polybius 11.18.8), by the election of Philopoemen as *strategos* of the Achaean League for 208/7, and his thorough re-organization of the League army (Polybius 11.9ff., Plutarch, *Philopoemen,* 9; Pausanias 8.50.1). But although Philip's recovery of Zakynthos (cf. Livy 36.31.11) is probably to be dated to this year, and although he clearly felt secure enough to reject further attempts by neutral states to mediate (cf. Polybius 11.4-6), he did not press on with the creation of his new navy, partly, perhaps, because of the expense involved, but also, probably, because he still feared to try conclusions with the Roman fleet. When news came of the defeat of Hannibal's brother at the Metaurus early in the summer, he must have begun to fear that Rome would begin seriously to turn her attention towards Greece (cf. Polybius 11.6.1). If he was to face Rome, he had first to deal with Aetolia, and this is the background to his great raid on Aetolia in 207 (cf. Polybius 11.7; Livy 36.31.11). The resolution of the Aetolians must have been severely shaken by this blow, and Rome's allies received a further set-back when Machanidas was defeated and killed at Mantinea by the Achaean "new model" army under Philopoemen: Polybius' description of this battle is one of the best accounts of an ancient battle which has come down to us (11.11-8). Thus when the neutral powers once again tried to mediate, probably in the winter of 207/6, the Aetolians were at last ready to accept Philip's terms, though peace was probably not finally concluded until the autumn of 206. [26]

The peace between Philip and the Aetolians, however, did not include Rome, and although Livy almost certainly exaggerates the promptitude with which Rome responded (29.12.3), there is no doubt that in the spring of 205, the Senate did send a new commander to Greece, with considerable reinforcements. The new commander was P.Sempronius

Tuditanus, and he was granted *imperium pro consule,* even though he had never held the consulship, and had only been praetor as far back as 213/2, another example of an "extraordinary command" during this war. Sempronius brought with him 11,000 men and thirty-five warships (Livy 29.12.2). Probably the Senate had not felt it necessary to take more vigorous measures against Philip before this, because he clearly did not constitute any danger to Italy. But now, with Scipio preparing to invade Africa, and the war in Italy virtually at a standstill, with Hannibal confined to Bruttium, following the defeat of his brother, the last thing Rome wanted was to be distracted by renewed military activity on Philip's part. Sempronius landed at Dyrrachium (Durazzo), and set about besieging Dimale, which had been captured by Philip in 213/2. But when Philip hastened up and began ravaging the territory of Apollonia, Sempronius abandoned the siege of Dimale, and went to Apollonia's relief, though refusing the chance of battle with the Macedonian army. The situation thus rapidly reached stalemate, and when the Epirotes approached the two belligerents with peace proposals, both were more than ready to talk terms. The result was the Peace of Phoinike, by which Philip agreed to surrender the territory of the Parthinoi, Dimale, and the two now unknown towns of Bargyllon and Eugenon, but was allowed to keep Atintania, and probably the greater part of those areas of Illyria which he had overrun in 213 (Livy 29.12.3-16). There is considerable controversy about the list of signatories to the peace, particularly on the Roman side, as recorded by Livy (29.12.14), but this controversy properly concerns the origins of the Second Macedonian War, rather than the Second Punic War.[27]

For the time being there was peace again in Greece, and although the war which now came to an end, may have been a triumph for Philip, in the context of the Balkans, it was no less a triumph for Rome in the context of the struggle with Carthage: with the minimum of effort, she had entirely frustrated any possibility of Philip's directly aiding Hannibal, and although she had not gained anything in Greece, except the dubious and potentially dangerous friendship of certain Greek states, and had indeed lost some parts of her Illyrian protectorate, she had, nevertheless, maintained the essentials of her presence even there. In recent years, it has become fashionable to take Philip's side in the quarrel, and one cannot but admire the speed and boldness of his campaigns, from 211 to 207. But one should not allow one's attitude to Rome's second intervention in Greece, from 200 to 196, to colour one's attitude to the first: Philip had attempted to seize the opportunity of Rome's weakness after Cannae, to stab her in the back, and it is difficult to excuse his intervention on the side of Carthage, unless one is to believe that Rome already cherished long-term plans to conquer Greece, for which there is no evidence, and which the history of the first half of the next century shows to be quite false.

By the time the Peace of Phoinike was concluded, as we have seen, the war in Italy, too, had almost been fought to a finish. But the six years that had passed since the fall of Capua, had seen a continuation of the bitter warfare in southern Italy that had been going on ever since Hannibal arrived in the summer of 217. In many respects, of course, the worst was over, with the fall of Syracuse in 212, followed by the fall of Capua in 211: even the financial situation seems to have improved enough for Rome to issue a new coinage, the *denarius,* probably in 211.[28] But Rome had also suffered further disasters in these years, and the strain of war showed, for example, in 209, when twelve of the thirty Latin colonies refused to supply their quotas of men for the Roman army. There had also been one moment of desperate danger for the Republic, when, in 207, Hannibal's brother, Hasdrubal, had finally crossed the Alps to join him. We must, therefore, now go back to consider what had been happening in the central theatre of the war between the fall of Capua, and the return of Scipio from Spain, on the one hand, and the Peace of Phoinike, on the other.

Towards the end of 211, Marcellus' reputation stood as high as anyone's, after his capture of Syracuse and his further successes in Sicily, and despite the Senate's refusal to grant him a triumph (Livy 26.21.1ff.), mainly on the ground, it appears, that the war in Sicily had not yet come to an end, he was granted the lesser honour of entering the city "in ovation" (Livy 26.21.5), and it is not surprising that he should have been elected to the consulship for 210/9 - his fourth if one counts the consulship to which he was elected for 215/4, but which he was forced to abdicate. Nor, in view of his successes in Greece, is it any more surprising that M. Valerius Laevinus should have been elected, in absence, as his colleague. However, that there was opposition to Marcellus and Laevinus is suggested by Livy's account of the elections (26.22.2ff.), although it clearly cannot be accepted as it stands. According to him, when the *centuria praerogativa* had originally given its vote for T. Manlius Torquatus and T. Otacilius Crassus, Manlius protested that he was too poor-sighted, and asked the presiding consul, Cn. Fulvius Centumalus, to order the century to vote again, whereupon, after consultation with the elder men of the same tribe, the *centuria praerogativa* proceeded to vote for Marcellus and Laevinus, the other centuries, as so often seems to have been the case, following suit. But there is something suspicious about this story, since one must presume that Torquatus had allowed his name to go forward as a candidate, in the first place, and the whole story is suspiciously like the one told about the elections to the consulship of 214/3, when Otacilius Crassus is also said to have been robbed of a consulship after the *centuria praerogativa* had voted for him, and again in favour of Marcellus. Livy also says (26.23.2) that on this occasion Otacilius died soon afterwards, and this suggests that what really happened was that he was elected, but died before he could take office, and that Marcellus was elected to replace him. As for Torquatus, it is possible that the story about his eye-sight stems from objections voiced against his candidature, perhaps by the presiding consul, and that later his family twisted the story to his credit. [29]

Even when he entered office on March 15th, 210, Marcellus had to face severe criticism for his conduct in Sicily, mainly from representatives of the Sicilians themselves, though it is perhaps significant that Manlius Torquatus is alleged to have led the criticism in the Senate (Livy 26.32.1). But it is clear that a majority of the Senators was behind Marcellus (Livy 26.32.6), although when he drew Sicily as his province, he was prevailed upon to change places with Laevinus, and to take up the command against Hannibal instead (Livy 26.29.6-10). Then, when recruiting began, a difficulty arose in finding men for the fleet and money to pay them, and when the consuls issued an edict ordering private individuals to provide sailors as had been done in 214 (cf. Livy 24.11.7-9), there was a roar of protest, which was only stilled when Laevinus suggested that members of the Senate should give a lead by making over the bulk of the gold and silver in their possession (Livy 26.35-6). This loan was repaid in instalments from 204 to 202 (Livy 29.16.1-3), and although Livy probably exaggerates the extent to which leading men in Rome were prepared to surrender their possessions to the state, the whole episode once again shows how strained the primitive finances of the Roman state were as a result of prolonged warfare. The problem of manning the fleet was exacerbated at this time by the continuing demands of the army, since, with the reduction in the qualification for legionary service earlier in the war (see above, pp. 100-1), more of those who had hitherto served in the fleet, would have found themselves called up for the army, for despite the disbanding of four of the six legions which had been serving in Campania,[30] of two of the four legions in Sicily (Livy 26.28.10), and of the legion which had been serving with the fleet in Greece (Livy 26.28.9), two new *legiones urbanae* were raised this year, as was usual (Livy 26.28.13), and the 10,000 foot and 1000 horse taken by Scipio to Spain (Livy 26.19.10), presumably consisted of a legion and its normal allied complement. Thus there were still twenty-one legions serving this year, as compared with twenty-five in 211. The problem of manning the fleet was also made worse by the continuing dis-affection of many of the towns of southern Italy and of Sicily from which the *socii navales* were drawn.

The dispositions for 210 were naturally rather different from those of 211, following the fall of Capua: one of the consuls - as it turned out, Marcellus - was to have the command against Hannibal, and an army of two legions, brought from Etruria, the other to take command in Sicily, where, in addition to the *legiones Cannenses,* he would have a further two legions brought from Gaul, to replace the two which had been discharged (Livy 26.28.3-4). To replace the legions withdrawn from Etruria, C. Calpurnius Piso was given the *legiones urbanae* of 211 (Livy 26.28.4), and the two legions commanded by Sulpicius Galba in 211, were sent to replace the legions with-drawn from Cisalpine Gaul (Livy ibid.). Gnaeus Fulvius Centumalus, consul of 211/10, retained his command of two legions in Apulia, with *imperium pro consule,* as did Q. Fulvius Flaccus at Capua, though his army was reduced to a single legion. In addition, two legions remained in Sardinia, and the army in Spain was brought up to four legions, with the addition of the reinforcements brought by Scipio (see above, p. 133). With the new *legiones urbanae,* this brings the total to the twenty-one recorded by Livy for this year (26.28.13), though in that case it is curious that Livy was now using a source which apparently included the legions in Spain in its totals (see above, p. 100).

Campaigning in Italy opened with an offer from one of the leading citizens of Salapia to betray the place to Marcellus, and although Hannibal was warned, he chose to ignore the warning, and Salapia passed into Roman hands, despite the desperate courage of its garrison of 500 Numidians, of whom only 50 were taken alive (Livy 26.38.6-14). Livy alleges (26.38.14) that from now on Hannibal was never as superior in cavalry as he had hitherto been, but if his own accounts of subsequent fighting are to be trusted, this is an exaggeration. Marcellus went on to storm Marmoreae and Meles in Samnium, annihilating their Carthaginian garrisons, and capturing quantities of wheat and barley (Livy 27.1.1-2). But these Roman successes were outweighed by the destruction of the proconsul Cn. Fulvius Centumalus' army at Herdonea in Apulia (Livy 27.1.3ff.). Fulvius had moved to the vicinity of the town in the hope of recovering control of it, since it was not naturally strong, nor defended by Carthaginian troops, and now that the neighbouring Salapia had defected from Hannibal, he felt that Herdonea's attitude might also be changing. Hannibal was reported to have gone to Bruttium after the fall of Salapia, but was kept informed of the situation by secret messengers, and suddenly fell on the proconsul's army after an approach-march so rapid that he gave hardly any warning of his coming. In the battle that followed, despite Livy's assertions about the growing weakness of the Carthaginian cavalry, it was this arm which Hannibal again used to deliver the decisive blow, part attacking the Roman camp, part charging the rear of Fulvius' line. Fulvius himself died with eleven of the twelve military tribunes who commanded his two legions under him, but Livy says his sources differed on the Roman losses, some saying 13,000, some 7000 (27.1.13). The survivors were, however, scattered and Hannibal took their camp. He went on punish Herdonea severely, executing the leaders who had been secretly in touch with Fulvius, transferring the rest of the population to Metapontum and Thurii, and burning Herdonea itself to the ground. Yet even this was an admission that he could no longer maintain his grip on towns remote from the main areas under his control. (See Map 19).

Marcellus' response to the disaster at Herdonea was characteristic: informing the Senate of what had happened, he moved resolutely to confront Hannibal at Numistro (Muro Lucano) in Lucania, and here, if we are to believe Livy (27.2.1ff.), a ferocious drawn battle was fought, ending with Hannibal, in effect, conceding defeat by slipping away during the night. But it is odd that Livy does not give any figures for losses, and Julius Frontinus, in his book on *Strategems* (2.2.6), credits Hannibal with a victory here. Hannibal's acceptance of battle, followed by a swift withdrawal, is similar to the course of action he pursued at Grumentum three years later (see below, p. 185), and it is possible that his primary concern at Numistro was likewise to throw Marcellus off his track. But, as on the later occasion, he found it difficult to conceal his movements for long, and was soon brought to bay again near Venusia, where indecisive skirmishing and manoeuvring followed for the rest of the year (Livy 27.2.11-2).

This year also saw fighting by land and sea near Tarentum as the Roman garrison still strove to hold out in the citadel. Towards the end of 211, the Carthaginian fleet under Bomilcar which had made for Tarentum after failing to fight Marcellus off Cape Pachynon the previous autumn, had been forced to leave for lack of supplies (Livy 26.20.7-11; cf. Polybius 9.9.11). But when, in 210, the Romans tried to run supplies through to the beleaguered citadel, their escorting squadron of twenty warships was intercepted by a Tarentine squadron of similar size off Sapriportis, about twenty-two kilometres west of Tarentum, and decisively defeated: some of the Roman warships were sunk, some run ashore and captured between Thurii and Metapontum, though most of the supply-vessels managed to make their escape (Livy 26.39.1-19). The Roman garrison in the citadel of Tarentum, however, still showed plenty of spirit, and boldly sallied out to attack foragers from the city, soon after the disappointment (Livy 26.39.20-3). The Roman fleet, however, also failed to prevent a raid on Sardinia by a Carthaginian squadron at the end of this summer (Livy 27.6.13-4), possibly because it was distracted by rumours of an impending Carthaginian naval attack on Sicily (Livy 27.5.13).

The war in Sicily itself was finally brought to an end this year. Since Marcellus' departure at the end of the previous summer (Livy 26.21.1), the Carthaginian forces in the island had been reinforced from Africa by 8000 infantry and 3000 Numidian cavalry, and Mottones had continued his destructive raids on the agricultural land which was so important to Rome. Even now, some towns were ready to defect to Carthage, and the danger was increased by the low morale of the Roman troops on the island, many of whom were survivors of Cannae, and of the first battle of Herdonea, condemned to serve out the war with no prospect of discharge (Livy 25.5.10, 26.1.9-10). For the time being, however, the praetor, M. Cornelius Cethegus, was able to calm the men down and to bring the disloyal communities to heel (Livy 26.21.14-7). Cornelius does not appear to have been on good terms with Marcellus (cf. Livy 26.26.8), and, as we have seen, overall command in Sicily had originally been assigned to Marcelius. But, as a result of the complaints of the Sicilians, Marcellus had been prevailed upon to exchange provinces with Laevinus, so it fell to the latter to complete the conquest of the island; Cethegus was superseded by one of the new praetors of 210/09, L. Cincius Alimentus, one of the historians of the war (Livy 26.28.3 & 11, cf.21.38.3). Laevinus arrived in Sicily towards the end of 210 (Livy 26.40.1), and first restored order to Syracuse, before advancing on the main Carthaginian base at Agrigentum. Here luck played into his hands: due to the jealousy between the Carthaginian commander-in-chief, Hanno, and the successful cavalry leader, Mottones, the latter had been deprived of his command in favour of Hanno's son, and, furious at the insult, entered into secret negotiations with Laevinus. On the agreed day, a party of his Numidians admitted the Roman forces through the gate leading to the sea. Hanno himself managed to make his escape to Africa, with Hannibal's surviving agent, Epicydes, but further resistance was impossible. Laevinus took stern measures with the city: the leading citizens were beheaded, the rest sold into slavery. But this severity at least had the effect of bringing the war in Sicily to an end, although Livy's succinct account of the final pacification reveals how widespread disaffection had been: twenty towns were betrayed to Rome, and forty surrendered voluntarily - six were taken by assault (26.40. 14). He adds that Laevinus took immediate steps to revive Sicilian agriculture, not merely to feed the inhabitants of the island, but also to relieve the food-supply of Rome and Italy (26.40.15-6). Mottones was rewarded with Roman citizenship (Livy 27.5.7), and lived to command Numidian troops for Rome in the war against Antiochus of Syria, twenty years later (Livy 38.41.12ff.). In accordance with Roman custom, he took the name of his patron, Marcus Valerius Laevinus, and it is as "Maarkos Oalerios Mottones" that he appears on an inscription from Delphi honouring him and four of his sons, Publius, Gaius, Marcus and Quintus (*SIG* 585).

The elections for the following year (209/8) provoked the usual political intrigue (Livy 27.4.1-4, 5.14ff.). Marcellus is said to have declared, in a despatch to the Senate, that he could not abandon his close watch on Hannibal to hold the elections, so, instead, the Senate sent for Laevinus, despite his absence from Italy. But while Laevinus was in Rome, he received a despatch from the commander of his fleet, M. Valerius Messala, who was probably his cousin, and whom he had sent to raid Africa. The information Messala had gleaned about Carthaginian preparations to send reinforcements to Spain, and to recover Sicily, so alarmed the Senate, that it decided the consul should

172

not wait to hold the elections, but should name a dictator to preside at them, and return immediately to his province. Laevinus, however, declared that he would nominate his cousin, when he returned to Sicily, and this led to a furore, since a dictator was not supposed to be nominated except on Roman soil. Accordingly, the Senate, on the motion of M. Lucretius, tribune of the plebs, instructed Laevinus to ask the people whom they wished to be nominated, and then to nominate the man of their choice. But this Laevinus flatly refused to do, and forbade the *praetor urbanus* to do so either, an illustration of the *maius imperium* of a consul in comparison with that of a praetor. The result was that the tribunes, who were not subject to the consular veto, had to take the matter up in their own assembly, the *concilium plebis,* and the plebs then declared its preference for Q. Fulvius Flaccus, consul in 237, 224 and 212. But even then Laevinus would not give in, and slipped quietly out of the city at night so as to avoid having to nominate the people's choice. In the end, it was Marcellus, after all, who had to nominate the dictator.

The simplest explanation for all this is that Laevinus was merely letting the usual family loyalties run away with him, or perhaps that he was piqued at not being allowed to preside at the elections himself. But if there was more to it than this, then presumably he was trying to secure the right to preside at the elections for himself, of for someone of his choice, in order to manipulate them in favour of some member of his family or group, and specifically to prevent Fulvius Flaccus presiding and thus doing the same for someone of his choice. Now Fulvius Flaccus chose as his Master of Horse, the young P. Licinius Crassus, who had been elected *Pontifex Maximus* early in 212, when still only a candidate for the aedileship, [31] and who now might have expected to secure the consulship, since it was customary for a dictator to recommend his Master of Horse to the electorate (cf. Livy 23.24.3, 25.2.3-4, 28.10.1-2, 30.39.4): later in the year, having failed to win the consulship, he did secure election to the censorship (Livy 27.6.17), another remarkable feat for a man who had held neither the consulship nor the praetorship, as Livy remarks. Clearly, then, Crassus was a man of influence who enjoyed considerable support among the powerful *nobiles,* and in particular probably had the backing of the Cornelii Scipiones. But in the event, despite the protests of the tribunes Caius and Lucius Arrenius (Livy 27.6.4), Fulvius Flaccus seems to have used his influence as presiding dictator to secure the consulship for himself, and, possibly, for Q. Fabius Maximus, who certainly now won his fifth consulship. Perhaps, behind all this, we should again see a difference of opinion on strategy, for although when the Senate came to distribute commands for the coming year (209), no great changes were made, it was decided that both consuls should command in Italy for the first time since 211, and that Valerius Laevinus, although continued in command in Sicily, should lose thirty of his warships to Fabius for operations against Tarentum, and two of his legions to Fulvius for operations in Lucania and Bruttium (Livy 27.7.7-17) - the latter were to be replaced by the survivors of the second battle of Herdonea. Fabius was a great believer in finishing off the war in Italy before embarking upon operations elsewhere, as his opposition to Scipio's plan to invade Africa was to show (see below, pp. 193-4), and it is possible that he threw his weight behind Fulvius Flaccus' controversial bid to win election for himself, in return for the dictator's help in securing his own election. [32]

With the two new *legiones urbanae* (cf. Livy 27.22.10) balancing out the loss of two legions at Herdonea - for although the survivors were sought out and sent to Sicily, they do not seem to have been regarded as constituting a legion, but rather as reinforcements for the *legiones Cannenses* and the survivors of the first battle of Herdonea (Livy 27.7.12-3) - the same number of legions (twenty-one) was in service as in 209, and there was no essential difference in their disposition. Fabius was to command in the area of Tarentum with the two legions which had been in Etruria, and these were to be replaced by the *legiones urbanae* of 210 (Livy 27.7.9); Fulvius Flaccus was to command in Lucania and Bruttium, with the two legions from Sicily, as has been said, and Marcellus was to retain command of the forces he had led the previous year (Livy 27.7.11). Thus six legions were still congregated in the south, with, in addition, one at Capua, previously commanded by Fulvius Flaccus, now by T. Quinctius Crispinus, one of the new praetors. Elsewhere, although one or two commanders were changed, the forces remained the same.

The transferring of the disgraced survivors of Herdonea to Sicily, however, provoked a serious crisis, for it appears that many of them were Latins or other allies. Amidst increasing complaints about the length of service of their soldiers, and the expense of paying them (Livy 27.9.1-6), twelve out of the thirty Latin colonies now informed the consuls that they were unable to supply their quotas of men. Despite stern warnings, and reminders of their ancestral ties with Rome, the twelve remained adamant, although the remaining eighteen colonies, if we are to believe Livy (27.10.3-4), expressed themselves willing to supply more than their quotas, if necessary. The Senate was clearly anxious to avoid a showdown, and nothing was done to force the recalcitrant colonies to do their duty; Livy remarks (27.10.10) that the Senate merely forbade any mention of them, or anything to be said to their envoys, and that "this silent punishment seemed best to accord with the dignity of the Roman People." But the whole incident is a vivid indication of the strain the communities of Italy were undergoing, and a reminder of Hannibal's object in invading Italy: according to Livy (27.9.3), one of the complaints of the allies was that the soldiers still serving in the Roman army were worse off than those captured by Hannibal; if that happened, they were returned to their homes without ransom, whereas, if it did not, there seemed to be no end to their service. An analysis of the location of the disloyal colonies is also revealing: they included many of the inner ring, remote from the fighting, Ardea, Nepet, Sutrium, Alba, Sora, Circei, Setia, Narnia, Interamna , whereas all the remoter colonies remained loyal, including Placentia and Cremona, isolated since 218, Ariminum in the *ager Gallicus,* Hadria and Firmum in Picenum, and in the south, Luceria, Venusia, Brundisium, Beneventum and Paestum. One obvious explanation could be that the remoter colonies, being in the firing-line, had their hearts in the struggle to an extent not true of those less affected by it. But it is also possible that most of the manpower of the remoter colonies was retained to defend the colonies themselves, whereas the inner ring of colonies was required to supply troops for remoter campaigns, which was one of their complaints (cf. Livy 27.9.3).

Another indication of the effect the war was having was the decision by the Senate to make use of some of the gold reserves kept in what Livy (27.10.11-3) calls "the more sacred treasury", and money was also raised by renting the *ager Campanus,* confiscated after the surrender of Capua (Livy 27.11.8). Livy's sources also evidently made considerable mention of the necessity to ensure adequate food-supplies at this time. He says that Fulvius Flaccus, as proconsul in command at Capua in 210, had exacted grain in lieu of rent for the confiscated lands about the city (27.3.1), and that commissioners were sent to Etruria to buy grain for the garrison at Tarentum. The embassy to Egypt recorded under the consular year 210/09 (Livy 27.4.10) may also have had something to do with the food supply, particularly if it is identical with the embassy mentioned in a fragment of Polybius (9.11a), but this was not the purpose according to Livy. We have already noticed (above, p. 172) how anxious Valerius Laevinus was to get Sicilian farms back into production, and in 209 he was able to send grain to Rome (Livy 27.8.18).

The opening campaigns of 209 seem to have formed parts of a concerted plan to enable Fabius to attempt the recapture of Tarentum. First, the garrison of Rhegium was ordered to raid Bruttium and attack Caulonia. Livy has little good to say of this force, describing the troops who composed it as "men accustomed to living by theft" who had been sent from Agathyrna in Sicily (27.12.4; cf. 26.40.16-8, and Polybius 9.27.11), and Bruttian deserters. But they certainly seem to have entered into the spirit of the thing, spreading their depredations far and wide. Next, Marcellus was ordered out of winter-quarters as soon as foraging became possible, and manoeuvred to engage Hannibal near Canusium. Here, if we believe Livy (27.12.7ff.), he was first defeated by Hannibal, but then turned the tables in a second engagement in which he inflicted 8000 casualties on the enemy. But at least the extent of the victory is probably exaggerated, since, although Hannibal made off for Bruttium the following night, Marcellus is said to have had so many wounded that he was unable to follow, and even the fact of the victory is doubtful, if Livy has reported correctly (27.21.3) that, at the end of the year, Marcellus was criticized for *two* defeats. It seems to have been characteristic of Hannibal, as we have seen, that if he wished to break away from a hostile army, he should first engage it, and then slip away at night: he had done it already to Marcellus after Numistro in 210 (see above, p. 171), and he was to do it again at Grumentum in 207 (see below, p. 185). On this occasion, it transpires, he was making for Caulonia, presumably because he had heard that it was under attack (cf. Livy 27.15.8, 16.9). But even if he had mauled Marcellus more severely than Roman tradition allowed, Fabius' plan was working, for while Hannibal was engaged at Caulonia, Fabius moved on Tarentum, taking Manduria by assault on the way (Livy 27.15.4).

Fabius planned to attack Tarentum by land and sea, since the Carthaginian fleet, which had apparently returned since its departure in 211, had left the city again, this time to aid Philip of Macedonia (Livy 27.15.7: see above, pp. 163-4). But, in the event, treachery came to Fabius' aid: according to the romantic, but not unbelievable story Livy tells (27.15.9ff.), the commander of the Bruttian contingent which formed part of the Carthaginian garrison of Tarentum, was in love with a woman who had a brother serving in Fabius' army, and who wrote to her brother about her lover. Having informed Fabius, the brother entered Tarentum in disguise and with his sister's help, persuaded the Bruttian to betray his trust. A plan was concocted, and on the agreed night, on Fabius' orders, the Roman garrison still holding the citadel, and the Roman ships preparing to assault from the harbour, created as much noise as possible as a diversion, while Fabius himself moved round to the eastern side of the city. There he waited until he knew from the silence along the walls, that most of the guards had been withdrawn to deal with the apparent dangers elsewhere. Then he moved up to the section of the walls where the Bruttian officer had said his men would be on guard. Aided by the Bruttians, the Romans swarmed over the wall, and opened the nearby gate. Meeting with no resistance, the whole force then advanced to the market-place, and there, at dawn, a fierce fight took place, as the Tarentines rallied. But soon all was over: the Tarentine leaders, Niko and Democrates fell fighting, but Philomenos, the man who had betrayed the city to Hannibal, disappeared - his horse was found later, outside the city, but no trace of him was ever discovered. Carthalo, the Carthaginian garrison-commander, was killed, after laying aside his arms, as he tried to find Fabius to recall a family tie of hospitality between them, and his death was typical of the indiscriminate slaughter visited upon the unhappy city. Yet Livy would have us believe that Fabius showed greater magnaminity than Marcellus at the taking of Syracuse - because he spared some statues (27.16.8). An inscription from Brindisi, found in 1950, has been thought to commemorate Fabius' capture of Tarentum, but unfortunately, although the name "Hannibal" appears on the undamaged part of the stone, neither Fabius nor Tarentum does, so it must remain uncertain to what incident it actually refers. [33]

Hannibal, who had compelled the force besieging Caulonia to surrender, marched day and night to prevent the fall of Tarentum, but was too late. The news that the city had already fallen, while he was still on the way, wrung from him the wry comment (Livy 27.16.10) that the Romans appeared to have their Hannibal too. He halted some seven kilometres from the city (Livy 27.16.11), presumably in the hope that he might tempt Fabius out, though Livy says that it was so as not to give the impression of flight. Then, after a few days, he withdrew to Metapontum, where he concocted an elaborate plan to trick Fabius into thinking that Metapontum would also be betrayed to him. But although Fabius is alleged to have swallowed the bait, for once his attention to religious details may have been of some use to him, for Livy says that bad omens warned him that some danger threatened, and he avoided the trap (27.16.12-6).

The summer also saw the surrender to Fulvius Flaccus of the Hirpini in Samnium, of some Lucanian communities, including, Volcei, and even approaches by some leading Bruttians (Livy 27.15.2-3). In Livy's narrative these incidents occur after Marcellus' two battles with Hannibal, and before Fabius took Tarentum, and this suggests that Fulvius Flaccus seized his opportunity when Hannibal was pre-occupied with Caulonia; alternatively, it might have been while Hannibal was engaged with Marcellus. [34] In either case, it is clear that the morale of Hannibal's allies was now beginning to sag, since, according to Livy, the towns which defected at this time even had Carthaginian garrisons.

Marcellus, meanwhile, had apparently still not recovered from his fights with Hannibal, and as the year drew to a close, was bitterly criticized for remaining idle at Venusia. But when he returned to Rome to answer the criticisms, he not only succeeded in defeating a bill to abrogate his *imperium,* but, next day, was elected consul for 208/7. This has been represented as a triumph for Fabius' faction, [35] but Marcellus, whose fifth consulship this was, was surely, in a sense, a "faction" in his own right, and, judging by his repeated willingness to accept battle with Hannibal, by no means saw eye to eye with Fabius on strategy: in the coming year, too, according to Livy (27.25.13-4), he made a joint attempt with his colleague, T. Quinctius Crispinus, to bring about a decisive engagement. It is also worth noting that it was Fulvius Flaccus, not Fabius, who presided at the elections (Livy 27.20.13), and although he may have co-operated with Fabius to secure their joint election for 209/8 (see above, p. 173), Flaccus was earlier associated with the abandoning of Fabius' strategy, marked by the election of himself and Ap. Claudius Pulcher to the consulship of 212/11 (see above, p. 109). There is, indeed, a case for believing that Fulvius Flaccus and Marcellus were political allies, for Fulvius' colleague in 212/11 had been Marcellus' lieutenant in Sicily, just as Marcellus' colleague in 208/7 had been (cf. Livy 24.39.12-3), and it had, in the end, been Marcellus who had nominated Flaccus for the dictatorship to preside at the elections for 209/8 (see above, p. 173). Finally, although the tribune who attacked Marcellus at the end of 209, C. Publicius Bibulus, belonged to a *gens* sometimes associated with the Cornelii,[36] the most famous member of the *gens*, M. Publicius Malleolus, consul in 232/1, was elected at elections probably presided over by Fabius as consul in 233/2, and it would make sense if the tribune in 209 was acting in Fabius' interests, to prevent the election of Marcellus, just as Fabius himself appears to have been instrumental in forcing Marcellus to abdicate the consulship in 215 (see above,   p. 94).

The dispositions for 208 also suggest that Fabius had again been eclipsed, despite his success in recapturing Tarentum, for whereas Fulvius Flaccus' *imperium* was pro-rogued, to take command of the legion at Capua hitherto commanded by the new consul, T. Quinctius Crispinus (Livy 27.22.4), Fabius' *imperium* was not renewed. Otherwise, dispositions were much the same as for 209, except for some reshuffling of commands, and some changes in the composition of some of the fleets: the thirty warships which had been withdrawn from the Sicilian fleet to aid Fabius' attack on Tarentum, were now sent back, restoring the Sicilian fleet to its former strength of 100 warships, under the command of M. Valerius Laevinus. But, in addition, the new *praetor urbanus,* P. Licinius Varus, was given the job of refitting thirty old warships, and building twenty new ones, to provide a fleet of 50 to guard the coast near Rome (Livy 27.22.9 and 12). There were rumours that the Carthaginians were making naval preparations to attack Italy, Sicily and Sardinia, and Scipio in Spain was similarly ordered to send 50 of his eighty ships to Sardinia (Livy 27.22.7). This increase in naval strength possibly partly explains why no new *legiones urbanae* were raised this year (Livy 27.22.10), the total strength of the Roman army thus remaining at 21 legions, of which seven were concentrated in southern Italy, four under the consuls to operate against Hannibal himself, two to guard the area around Tarentum, and one at Capua.

The year opened, however, with ominous reports from Arretium in Etruria: the pro-praetor, C. Calpurnius Piso, in command in the area in 209, had already reported trouble there after the consular elections, and Marcellus, as consul-elect, had been ordered to go to Etruria and report on the matter, with leave to summon his old army from Venusia, if he thought it necessary (Livy 27.21.6-7). Marcellus' presence may have acted as a deterrent, for things seem to have quietened down before he took office on

March 15th, 208. But now the new pro-praetor assigned to Etruria, C. Hostilius Tubulus, reported further unrest, and was ordered to take hostages from Arretium, and hand them over to C. Terentius Varro. The latter, after his defeat at Cannae, had served as proconsul in Picenum from 215 to 213, and was now invested with *imperium* again (Livy 27.24.1ff.) - yet another example of an extraordinary command. On his arrival, Tubulus promptly moved the forces he commanded into Arretium, and handed the hostages over to Varro, after the flight of seven of the leading citizens with their families. Varro then returned to Rome, but gave such alarmist reports that he was ordered back to Arretium with one of the *legiones urbanae* of 209 while Tubulus was instructed to deploy his forces to prevent any outbreak in the rest of Etruria. This was to be the beginning of trouble in Etruria which was to last for a number of years, and to grow worse with the arrival in Italy of Hannibal's brothers, Hasdrubal and Mago.

Meanwhile, one of the consuls, Quinctius Crispinus, had proceeded, with reinforcements, to the army Fulvius Flaccus had commanded in Lucania, while Marcellus was detained in Rome, allegedly by religious scruples, though it is likely that the emphasis on religion in Livy's account of the beginning of this year (27.23.1-4, 25.7-9) owes much to the unexpected fate of the two consuls. Crispinus made an attempt on Locri, but broke off the attack when Hannibal was reported to be at the Lacinian promontory, some 140 kilometres from Locri. Then, on receipt of the news that Marcellus had at last joined his army at Venusia, and had already left, Crispinus marched to join him somewhere between Venusia and Bantia (Banzi). Thither also came Hannibal, having successfully diverted Crispinus from Locri (Livy 27.25.11-3). The stage was thus set for the first full-scale confrontation with Hannibal since Cannae, if, as Livy says (27.25.14), the two consuls really hoped that with their two armies combined, they could fight the war to a finish. But before battle was joined, the consuls were ambushed, Marcellus being killed, Crispinus mortally wounded.

Livy's account of this episode (27.26.7ff.) does not agree with the fragment of Polybius' tenth book (10.32.1-6) dealing with the same episode, and thus cannot be accepted without question. Polybius says that there was a hill between the Carthaginian and Roman camps, which neither side had occupied, but which the consuls wished to reconnoitre; Livy says that Marcellus was moved by grumblings in his camp that the hill ought to be held as a point of vantage, which seems less probable. Accordingly, in Polybius' version, taking two squadrons of cavalry and thirty *velites,* together with their lictors - Livy says 220 cavalry, of whom 40 were from Fregellae (i.e. Latins), the rest Etruscans - Marcellus and Crispinus rode to the top of the hill. But, according to Polybius, unknown to them, a party of Numidians was lurking at the foot of the hill, and when their lookout signalled to them that some men had appeared at the top of the hill above them, they slipped obliquely across the slope and so cut the consuls off from their camp. Livy, however, says that the Numidians had occupied the hill, and that the scout and some of his comrades were concealed at its foot, near a track leading up the hill from a small plain between the Roman camp and the hill. There seems to be no way of reconciling these two versions, but Polybius' is, on the whole, preferable. Finally, Polybius says that Marcellus and some of his men were cut down at the first onset, whereas Livy says that although the Romans were surrounded, they could have fought on if the Etruscans had not broken and run, and that even then the men from Fregellae continued the fight until both consuls were wounded, Marcellus, pierced with a lance, collapsing dying from his horse. Then they, too, fled, taking with them Crispinus, who had been wounded twice, and the consul's son, who had also been wounded. One of the tribunes, A. Manlius, and the Prefect of the Allies, M. Aulius, were killed, as well as forty-three of the troopers and some of the lictors; five of the latter, eighteen troopers, and another Prefect of the Allies, L. Arrenius, were captured. Livy's account of the fight and the losses is circumstantial, and it makes sense that Latins should fight harder than Etruscans, in view of the trouble in Etruria. But it is difficult to reconcile Livy's figures for the numbers of troopers with Polybius' statement that the consuls were escorted by two squadrons (ἴλαι) of cavalry, for Latins would hardly have served in the same units as Etruscans, and yet we cannot believe that one of the squadrons was 40 strong, the other 180.

Polybius (10 32.7ff.) inveighs against the thoughtlessness which had led Marcellus to hazard his person in so minor an operation - a point picked up by Livy. The latter adds (27.27.11) that there were many different versions of the incident, of which no fewer than three were given by Coelius Antipater, based on the traditional story, the funeral speech delivered by Marcellus' son, and on his own researches - an interesting sidelight on the ultimate sources of Livy. Marcellus was clearly not a soldier of Scipio's calibre, nor even, perhaps, of Claudius Nero's, but there can be no doubt about his personal courage, nor about the spirit he displayed in the dark days after Cannae. He was a typical Roman general - one might almost say a typical Roman - brave, hard and competent, and even if his qualities as a commander have been much exaggerated in the Roman tradition, he was not undeserving of the title "the sword of Rome", bestowed upon him by Posidonius, according to Plutarch (*Marcellus* 9.4). .

Hannibal, who had once said that he respected Fabius as a tutor, but Marcellus as an adversary (Plutarch, ibid.), had his enemy's body buried with full military honours (Livy 27.28.2), but was too wily a general not to try to make full use of his stroke of luck: using Marcellus' signet-ring, he sent a letter to Salapia, purporting to be from the consul, saying that he would be at Salapia the following night. But Crispinus, despite his wound, was sufficiently alert to the danger to warn all the neighbouring communities not to trust any message purporting to come from Marcellus, with the result that the citizens of Salapia were not deceived: they sent Hannibal's messenger back, but prepared a trap. Hannibal made his approach at night, the leading units of his army carefully composed of deserters, who, on reaching the gate, called out to the guards in Latin that the consul was approaching. The guards promptly raised the portcullis, but when some 600 of Hannibal's men had entered, let it down with a crash, and fell upon the trapped soldiers (Livy 27.28.4-12; cf. Polybius 10.38.8). But Hannibal himself, unlike Marcellus, had not risked his life in a minor operation, and had no intention of wasting his strength in assaulting the town. Instead, with one of his swift changes of plan, he made off for Locri, which was once more under attack. The assaulting troops were under the command of L. Cincius Alimentus, who had been summoned from Sicily with naval forces (Livy 27.26.4). A considerable force had also been summoned to join the attack from Tarentum, but Hannibal had got wind of this through his allies at Thurii, and had set a trap on the road from Tarentum, near Petelia, in which 2000 of the Roman force were killed and 1500 captured (Livy 27.26 4-6). Now a message from Hannibal that he had sent on the Numidian cavalry, and was following himself with the infantry at all possible speed, encouraged the Carthaginian commander at Locri to sally out upon the besiegers, and this unexpected daring, coupled with the arrival of the Numidians, turned defeat into rout as the Romans scrambled for safety to their ships (Livy 26.28.13-7). It was possibly on this occasion that Cincius Alimentus was taken prisoner by Hannibal (cf. Livy 21.38.3).

Meanwhile, Crispinus divided the consular armies, instructing Marcellus' son, who was serving as *tribunus militum,* to take his father's forces back to Venusia, and himself withdrawing to Capua. From there he wrote to the Senate that his wounds would prevent him from coming to Rome to hold the elections, and in any case that he feared to leave his army in case Hannibal should threaten Tarentum. The Senate sent the younger Fabius to take over the army at Tarentum, though it is not clear with what authority, and appointed a delegation of three senators to discuss the situation with Crispinus (Livy 27.29.1-5).

By the end of the year, the consul was dead of his wounds - Livy (27.33.7) says that this was the first time in Roman history that both consuls had been killed in war - but he was able to name T. Manlius Torquatus dictator to hold the elections, before he died. According to Livy (27.34), there was one obvious choice for consul in C. Claudius Nero, who had been praetor in 212, and as both praetor and propraetor had been one of the successful commanders at the siege of Capua, before being sent temporarily to Spain after the deaths of the elder Scipios; thereafter, he had been one of Marcellus' officers in the fighting around Canusium in 209 (cf. Livy 27.14.14). He was thus a soldier of experience, and although Livy declares (27.34.2) that men considered him perhaps too prompt and keen to match Hannibal, he was to turn out to be one of the best Roman generals of the war. The problem was, in Livy's view, to find a colleague for him, since Fabius, Laevinus and Manlius himself were ruled out because they were patricians like Claudius Nero, and it was unconstitutional to have two patrician consuls - Livy here seems to forget that Manlius was also, presumably, still ruled out because of his poor eye-sight (see above, p. 169). Eventually, if we are to believe Livy, the Senate prevailed upon his namesake, M. Livius Salinator, consul in 219/8, to stand. He had commanded the Roman forces in the Second Illyrian War jointly with L. Aemilius Paullus, killed at Cannae, and had celebrated a triumph. But after his consulship, he had been tried before the people and condemned on a charge, probably of misappropriation of booty (Frontinus, *Strategemata* 4.1.45; *de viris illustribus,* 50.1). The punish-ment was a fine (cf. Suetonius, *Tiberius,* 3.1), but Salinator had taken the disgrace hard, retiring to his estates in the country, and for many years shunning all public life. Marcellus and Laevinus in 210/09 had induced him to return, but he had continued to wear the drab clothes and long hair and beard traditionally associated with mourning, until the censors of the same year, L. Veturius Philo and P. Licinius Crassus, had compelled him to shave, change his clothes and re-enter the Senate. Even then he had hardly uttered a word until the case of his kinsman, M. Livius Macatus, the man who had first lost Tarentum, and then heroically defended the citadel, came up for discussion (Livy 27.34.5-8; cf. 25.3-5).

Behind this well-known story, and the tradition of the personal hostility between Salinator and Claudius Nero (cf. Livy 27.35.7-9), we get another glimpse of the intense rivalries between the Roman *nobiles* and the groups associated with them. In this case, it is fairly clear that Claudius Nero would have enjoyed the support of the groups which had been prominent in the years 212, 211 and, perhaps, 210, and it is somewhat surprising that a man of his background and ability had not reached the consulship sooner after his praetorship. But in 210/09 he had been up against Valerius Laevinus, and in 209/8 the still more influential Fabius Maximus, and in 208/7 Marcellus' support for Quinctius Crispinus may have been decisive; now he was, perhaps, the patrician with clearly the best claims. His colleague, Livius Salinator, almost certainly enjoyed the support of the Aemilii and Cornelii: Livy (27.38.11) even knew of a tradition that the younger Scipio sent him reinforcements from Spain in 207, and although this is unlikely to be true, it perhaps reflects known friendly relations between the two men.[37] Both Claudius Nero and Livius Salinator were thus associated with opponents of the Fabian strategy, and the tradition of animosity between them may derive from the quarrels of their censorship in 204/3 (cf. Livy 29.37): there is no indication that any such animosity interfered with their co-operation in 207, and if we are inclined to put this down to simple patriotism, as Livy was, it is perhaps worth noting that it was Claudius Nero who nominated his colleague dictator to hold the elections (Livy 28.10. 1-5), which was a most unusual thing to have happened when either consul could have presided, and was, perhaps, due to Nero's desire to honour his colleague (see below, p. 191).

The great danger facing the new consuls when they took office on March 15th, 207, was the imminent arrival of Hannibal's brother, Hasdrubal, in northern Italy. Envoys from Marseille had warned the Senate that he had arrived in France, and Roman agents sent back with them, had reported that he intended to cross the Alps in the spring (Livy 27.36.1-4). The dispositions made in Italy reflect the new danger: Salinator was to command against Hasdrubal in the north, and Nero against Hannibal in the south (Livy 27.35.10), and each consul was to have the usual consular army of two legions with their normal complement of allied troops. But, in addition, Terentius Varro and L. Porcius Licinus, one of the praetors of 207, were to command similar armies in Etruria and the *ager Gallicus* respectively, while, in the south, Q. Fulvius Flaccus was to command two legions in Bruttium, Q. Claudius Flamen, one of the praetors of 208, two more in the region of Tarentum, and C. Hostilius Tubulus, one of the praetors of 209, one at Capua. Thus, with the two new *legiones urbanae* raised this year, bringing the total in service to twenty-three, no fewer than fifteen legions were concentrated in Italy, nearly four times the number that had faced Hannibal in 218 (Livy 27.36.10-13). Basically, the problem as far as Hasdrubal was concerned, was the same as had faced the Senate in 218, though now complicated by Hannibal's presence in southern Italy: Hasdrubal, like his brother before him, once he had entered Cisalpine Gaul, could either strike south across the Apennines into Etruria, or could march southeastwards to Ariminum and then follow the coastal route to the south. Thus Terentius Varro was in a position to block the first of these moves, Porcius Licinus to block the second. But now, with extra forces at its disposal, the Senate could afford to hold back a consular army until it was certain which way Hasdrubal was coming, and this is probably the reason for Salinator's delay in leaving Rome, rather than any diffidence he may have had in the forces he was to command (Livy 27.38.6-8).

The first news of Hasdrubal's coming was contained in a despatch from the praetor, Porcius Licinus, who reported that the Carthaginian general had left his winter quarters and was now crossing the Alps (Livy 27.39.1-2). Livy alleges that Licinus also reported that 8000 Ligurians had been recruited for Hasdrubal's army and were preparing to join him, and that he proposed to march against them. But if this is so, Hasdrubal's unexpectedly rapid crossing of the Alps forestalled any such move (cf. Livy 27.39.4ff.). Livy and Appian (*Hannibalic War*, 52) evidently believed that he used the same route as Hannibal,[38] but the scholar, Varro, a contemporary of Cicero, denied it, according to Servius in his commentary on Vergil's *Aeneid* (10.13). However, although Varro was almost certainly wrong to locate Hannibal's pass between the Montgenèvre and the coast,[39] and may thus have been wrong to say that Hasdrubal used a different one, he could, none the less, have been right about the location of Hasdrubal's pass. He evidently believed that it lay between the route used by Pompey in 77 - almost certainly the Montgenèvre - and the Little St. Bernard, and one immediately thinks of the Mt. Cenis: if this was the pass Hasdrubal used, and if Hannibal used the Col de Clapier, then Livy and Appian would have been right to say that Hasdrubal was helped by his brother's having used the same route, since both would have followed the same route for most of the way, with Hannibal only at the end choosing a minor pass out of the valley of the Arc, whereas Hasdrubal chose the easier Mt. Cenis. Varro would also be right in the sense that the actual passes they used were not the same.

At all events, possibly because he used an easier route, and certainly because he set out earlier and from nearer at hand,[40] Hasdrubal reached Italy earlier than anyone had expected, and possibly, as was suggested above, forestalled Porcius Licinus' move against the Ligures. But he then threw away any advantage his early arrival in Italy had given him, Livy says (27.39.11ff.), by laying siege to Placentia. However, there is something in the reason for this given by Livy - that he wished to impress the Celts of the region - for, like Hannibal, he needed to win support from the Celts before he proceeded, and he certainly later had Celts in his army. In any case, he would have wanted to wait until there would be sufficient forage for his army, and particularly for his cavalry, before advancing. But when he found that he could not take Placentia, he began to move south-eastwards down the line of the future *via Aemilia,* sending off six mounted messengers, four Gauls and two Numidians, to carry a letter to Hannibal (Livy 27.43.1).

According to Livy (27.43.8), Hasdrubal said in the letter that he would meet his brother "in Umbria," and this and the subsequent actions of himself and the Romans are the only evidence we have of his intentions. Unfortunately, Umbria was a large area, spanning the Apennines, and including even the *ager Gallicus* in Livy's day, and since the Carthaginian plans were frustrated, we shall never know what Hasdrubal intended for certain. But he clearly did not cross the Apennines into Etruria, as his brother had done, and if he really did march as far down the coast as Sena Gallica (Senigallia), the natural assumption is that he intended to continue on down the coast route. It has been suggested that the references to Sena in the ancient sources imply no more than that he reached the general area of that town, and that really he got no further south than Fanum,[41] but this is very forced, and in view of the unanimity of the ancient sources that the eventual confrontation with Livius Salinator took place at Sena,[42] we should, surely, accept this as a fact, and make what we can of it, rather than reject it and speculate without evidence. (See Map 19).

The main argument for supposing that Hasdrubal did not advance as far as Sena seems to be that Claudius Nero interpreted his message, when intercepted, to mean that he intended to cross the Apennines to meet Hannibal, since he advised the Senate to block the enemy's path at Narnia (Livy 27.43.9). But even if Nero correctly interpreted Hasdrubal's intentions, and Livy has correctly reported both the interpretation and Nero's advice to the Senate, this still does not prove that Hasdrubal cannot have advanced further south than Fanum, for it would have been perfectly possible for him to have crossed the Appenines by a route further south than the *via Flaminia*: there is, for example, a reasonable modern road (*Strada Statale* 76) which leaves the coast a few kilometres north of Ancona, fourteen kilometres from Sena Gallica, and runs up the valley of the Esino (the ancient Aesis), to rejoin the *via Flaminia* forty-six kilometres north of Foligno (ancient Fulginium), and by taking this route, Hasdrubal could have avoided some of the difficulties of the *via Flaminia* - for example, the Gola del Furlo and the 575-metre Colle di Scheggia: the highest point on the other route is 250 metres lower. Nero's own arrangements, moreover, suggest that he expected to join his colleague in confronting the enemy well to the south of Fanum, for his messages to the peoples along his route to prepare for his coming, went no further than the Praetutii (Livy 27.43.10), who lived in the southern part of Picenum, some hundred kilometres south of Ancona. But, in any case, we cannot be sure that Livy correctly records Nero's interpretation of the message or his consequent advice to the Senate, nor, for that matter, can we be sure that Nero correctly interpreted the message.

There is, indeed, another possibility, that the message was intended to mislead the Romans. On the face of it, Hasdrubal was somewhat naive if he really thought that Celtic and Numidian horsemen, who presumably could not speak fluent Latin, could ride the length of Italy looking for Hannibal, without being captured, and he was also, surely, far too sanguine if he really thought that his brother could break loose from the ring of armies confronting him, and march north to Umbria: he must have known that Hannibal had never been anywhere near Umbria since he marched through on his way to the south in 217, apart from his brief march on Rome in 211, and that it was most unlikely that he would have wanted to risk severing his communications with Lucania and Bruttium, the areas still under his control. If, then, Livy had simply stated that the message said that Hasdrubal hoped to meet Hannibal in Umbria, we might have suspected a mistake by him or his source. But Livy's report of Nero's advice to the Senate to send troops to Narnia is circumstantial, and suggests that the message did contain some statement which led Nero to think that Hasdrubal might advance into Umbria, and this may have been exactly what Hasdrubal hoped: if he really intended to advance down the coastal route, as his march to Sena Gallica suggests, his problem was to divert the Roman forces from that route, which could be too easily blocked, and one way to accomplish this would have been to give them the impression that he intended to cross the

Apennines. He would thus have hoped that the Roman forces in the northeast, under Licinus and Salinator, would fall back down the *via Flaminia,* but they did not do so.

Hasdrubal's intentions must remain uncertain, but, as was argued above, there is no good reason to doubt that he did advance as far as Sena Gallica, and that it was there that he was finally confronted by Livius Salinator's army. Presumably Porcius Licinus had fallen back before him, as he advanced, harassing him all the way (cf. Livy 27.46.6), while Livius Salinator, once it was certain that the enemy was not going to invade Etruria, hastened north to join the praetor. One would like to know where the junction took place, but, unfortunately, only Livy of the ancient sources mentions Licinus, and he is vague on the point. The natural assumption would be that the consul marched up the *via Flaminia* to join the praetor at Fanum, or even further north. But if this were so, it is difficult to understand why he then chose to fall back to Sena, before making a stand, since this involved exposing the *via Flaminia,* and although there was less risk in this than in exposing the coast road, since Hasdrubal was hardly likely to attack Rome, the stand might just as well have been made at Fanum in order not to give Hasdrubal the option. It is possible, then, that Licinus had already fallen back beyond Fanum, before the consul joined him, perhaps by the route outlined above, now followed by the *Strada Statale 76.* Alternatively, if the junction of the praetor's and the consul's armies took place at Fanum or north of it, it is possible that the consul decided to accept the risk of exposing the *via Flaminia* in order to draw Hasdrubal further south, and so nearer to his colleague, Nero. This would involve the further assumption that Salinator and Nero had concerted plans, and that Nero's famous march north to join Salinator was part of those plans, but this is not at all impossible. However, in this case, why did Salinator not fall back still further? The answer is, possibly, that if he fell back further than where the route up the Aesis leaves the coast route, fourteen kilometres beyond Sena, he might have found it difficult to get back across the Apennines, if Hasdrubal chose after all to cross them. There is a modern road (*Strada Statale 77*) which leaves the coast road at Loreto some 55 kilometres beyond Sena, but it is difficult, and the next good route is that followed by the *Strada Statale 4,* which leaves the coast 123 kilometres beyond Sena, and runs up the valley of the Tronto (ancient Truentus), past Ascoli Piceno (ancient Asculum) to Rieti (Reate). Thus Salinator may have felt that if he retreated further than Sena, he would be leaving too many alternatives open to Hasdrubal, and might lose him, with disastrous results.

Meanwhile, in the south, Hannibal seems to have tried desperately to break loose from the Roman forces which confronted him, but unfortunately, Livy's account of this southern campaign makes little or no sense as it stands. According to him (27.40.10ff.), before Claudius Nero reached the area assigned to him, C. Hostilius Tubulus fell upon Hannibal as he was "leading his army along the furthest boundary of Larinum into the territory of the Sallentini," and inflicted heavy losses upon him. This news roused Q. Claudius Flamen, who commanded Roman forces among the Sallentini, from winter quarters, and rather than fight two armies, Hannibal withdrew "from the territory of Tarentum" to Bruttium. Thereupon, Q. Claudius returned to his post among the Sallentini, and Hostilius Tubulus went on to Capua, after handing over most of his army to Claudius Nero at Venusia. Next, according to Livy (27.41.1ff.), Hannibal concentrated his forces in Bruttium, and advanced into Lucania, where he encountered Claudius Nero at Grumentum, and after fighting a battle there, slipped away to Apulia, but was caught by the consul near Venusia and forced to fight another battle. He then withdrew towards Metapontum, and after adding the forces of the garrison there to his army, advanced again to Venusia, and on to Canusium, dogged by Nero all the way.

Here it is the beginning of Livy's account which is particularly difficult to accept: how can Hannibal possibly have been as far north as Larinum (Larino) so early in the year, and why, having got so far, was he heading southeastwards towards the territory of the Sallentini, who lived in the heel of Italy, when Hostilius Tubulus attacked him? One suggestion is that Livy has somehow misunderstood his source or sources, and displaced an account of Hannibal's moves later in the campaign to its beginning.[43] But the difficulty with this hypothesis is that by the end of the campaign, C. Hostilius Tubulus should have been commanding at Capua (cf. Livy 28.10.15), whereas, at the beginning, he had been commanding at Tarentum (cf. Livy 27.35.2 and 14) - Tarentum later seems to have come under Q. Claudius' command (cf. Livy 27.43.2). A more plausible reconstruction might be that Hannibal's march to the vicinity of Larinum properly belongs to 208, when he was near Salapia, only about 100 kilometres away (see above, p. 179). Again the difficulty would be the alleged attack upon him by Hostilius Tubulus, who is last heard of in Etruria that year (cf. Livy 27.24.7), but it is possible that he was transferred to Tarentum in 208, when Terentius Varro was sent to Etruria, rather than early in 207.

At all events, we can probably assume that Livy's account of Hannibal's movements in 207 should properly have begun with his statement (27.41.1) that he concentrated his forces in Bruttium, and advanced to Grumentum in Lucania, though this move was probably not prompted merely by the hope of recovering towns in Lucania which had defected, as Livy says. At Grumentum, if we are to believe Livy (27.41.2-42.7), he was confronted by Claudius Nero, and his army savagely mauled, losing 8000 men not to mention four elephants killed, and two captured. But it is fairly clear that the Roman tradition, as so often, magnified the Carthaginian losses, for not only did Hannibal give Nero the slip, but continued his advance towards Apulia. Leaving fires burning and tents up in his camp, and even a few Numidians to show themselves, he slipped quietly away "during the third watch" (Livy 27.42.10), with all his old mastery, and one suspects that he was following his usual practice of accepting battle in order to break away from his opponents. But Nero was not so easily shaken off: when day dawned, he was at first taken in by the appearance of the Numidians Hannibal had left behind, but when they too made off, and the enemy camp appeared deserted, he sent two horsemen to reconnoitre and then ordered his forces to enter. Even then, according to Livy (27.42.13), he was delayed for a whole day by his men scattering to plunder, and only next day set out in pursuit, although it seems more likely that the delay was due more to the losses inflicted on his army in its alleged victory. But it was impossible to conceal all trace of an army as large as Hannibal's, and Nero soon picked up the scent, and by forced marches caught up with the enemy at Venusia. Here, according to Livy (27.42.15), a second scrambling fight took place, in which Hannibal lost a further 2000 men, before he slipped away again at night, by mountain tracks, to Metapontum, on the coast west of Tarentum. This, too, has been doubted,[44] but it is possible that Hannibal, having failed to shake Nero off as he advanced northwards, was now trying to confuse him by apparently doubling back on his tracks; he also picked up useful reinforcements at Metapontum, sending its commander, Hanno, to Bruttium to collect fresh forces. But still Nero dogged his footsteps, summoning the proconsul, Q. Fulvius Flaccus, from Capua into Lucania, when he set off for Metapontum (Livy 27.42.15-7). Finally, Hannibal advanced once more to Venusia, and then swung away northeastwards to Canusium.

It was at this point, according to Livy, that the Romans intercepted Hasdrubal's message: the messengers, having ridden the length of Italy safely, had reached Metapontum, only to find Hannibal gone, and it was in following him that they were picked up by Roman foragers near Tarentum. Taken to the propraetor, Q. Claudius, who now commanded in that area, they at first baffled him with vague answers to questions, but under threat of torture, they told the truth - that the letter they carried was from Hasdrubal to Hannibal. They and the letter, seal unbroken, were promptly sent to the consul, guarded by two squadrons of Samnite cavalry, under a military tribune. At Nero's headquarters the letter was read by an interpreter, and the prisoners questioned further (Livy 27.43.1-5). Then, whether as a result of having concerted plans with his colleague earlier, or on his own initiative, Nero decided to march to join Salinator with a picked force, leaving most of his army behind to watch Hannibal, under a subordinate officer. It was essential to his plans that no hint of his intentions should reach Hannibal, but he could not just disappear, so, first, he sent Hasdrubal's letter to Rome with a despatch in which he revealed his own intentions, and advised that the legion stationed at Capua, now under C. Hostilius Tubulus, be summoned to Rome, that fresh troops be raised in the city, and that the city legions be sent to confront the enemy at Narnia (Livy 27.43.8ff.).

The contents of Nero's despatch to the Senate, as reported by Livy, may suggest that he assumed that it was Hasdrubal's intention to cross the Apennines into Umbria, as has been argued (see above, p. 183), but it is more likely that Nero's advice to the Senate was merely intended to persuade it to take sensible precautions against such a possibility, for he himself evidently had no intention of marching to guard Rome, and appears to have assumed that Hasdrubal was still marching down the coastal route east of the Apennines. The route he intended to take is given by Livy (27.43.10) as through the territory of Larinum, the Marrucini, Frentani and Praetutii, and this may indeed contain a hint that he had expected to meet Salinator further south than Sena, since otherwise one might have expected some reference to Picenum in Livy's report of his proposed line of march. Messengers were sent to these four peoples to prepare provisions for his troops, and to provide horses and mules to pull carts for those who might drop out through fatigue. Then, choosing from the citizen and allied troops in his army, 6000 foot and 1000 horse, and giving out that he was about to attack the nearest Lucanian town, he marched from his camp at night, then swung round and raced for Picenum, leaving the rest of his army under the command of his legate, Q. Catius (Livy 27.43. 6-12). Livy has a marvellous description of the anxiety felt at Rome when the consul's despatch was received, and of the welcome his men received along the route (27.44-45. 11), and we can well believe him, for this was the last great crisis of the war.

186

As he drew near his colleague's position, Nero sent messengers ahead to warn Salinator of his coming, and to consult him as to the best way of combining their forces. Salinator replied that it would be best for Nero to join him secretly, at night, and gave his own men orders to take Nero's into their own tents, so that their presence might be concealed - such precautions were very necessary if Hasdrubal's camp was only some seven hundred metres away, as Livy says (27.46.4). All went according to plan, and next day Salinator, Nero and Licinus conferred. The general opinion, Livy alleges (27.46.7ff.), was that they should wait a few days, while Nero's men recovered, and the enemy position was reconnoitred. But Nero would have none of it, declaring that delay would take away all the advantage his swift march had won for them, and make it more and more dangerous, since Hannibal was bound, sooner or later, to learn of his absence. These arguments convinced his colleagues, and immediately the Roman army deployed for battle.

According to Livy (27.47.1ff.), Hasdrubal, too, was not unwilling to accept the challenge, but when riding forward with a small cavalry escort, noticed some old shields in the enemy ranks he had not seen before, and some unusually stringy horses - the enemy's numbers also seemed greater than they had been. Immediately he had the recall sounded, and sent men down to the river to pick up some prisoners and to see if any of the enemy soldiers had an especially weather-beaten look: the river was probably what is now called the Cesano, which flows into the sea just north of Senigallia.[45] At the same time, other Carthaginian scouts were ordered to ride round the enemy camps to see if they had been extended, and in particular to note if trumpet-calls were sounded once or twice (Livy 27.47.3). Even then the Romans nearly got away with it: there were still two camps, as before, one for Salinator's army, the other for that of Licinus, and neither had been extended. But the trumpet-calls gave the game away to a general of Hasdrubal's experience, for the scouts reported that they had sounded once in the praetor's camp, but twice in the consul's. If this famous story is true, it argues crass stupidity on the Romans' part, after all their efforts to conceal Nero's arrival. But it is just the sort of detail which is apt to give away elaborate deceptions, and the Romans were great sticklers for such proprieties.

Hasdrubal realised at once that he was faced by two consuls, but, if we are to believe Livy (27.47.5), he was not so much worried by the thought that the enemy army had been reinforced, as by the question of how the other consul had managed to get away from Hannibal. If this is true, and one inevitably wonders how Livy could have had access to such information, it may give a clue to Hasdrubal's subsequent intentions, for Livy says that he did not guess the truth, that Nero had simply got away from Hannibal, but assumed that his brother must have suffered some serious reverse, and that he had, after all, come too late. At the same time, Livy adds (27.47.8), he also thought that his letter to Hannibal might have been intercepted, and that Nero might have marched as quickly as possible to overwhelm him. His decision was to retreat that night, but, Livy says (27.47.9-10), one of his guides - presumably local men - slipped away to a hiding-place he had previously marked out for himself, and the other swam the Metaurus, the river twenty-four kilometres northwest of Senigallia, and so, presumably, some twenty kilometres from Hasdrubal's camp. The result was that the

Carthaginian army went astray, and, as it blundered about, men began to fall out through weariness or lack of sleep - we must remember that if the confrontation with Salinator is correctly located at the river Cesano, Hasdrubal's men would have had a twenty-kilometre march before ever they reached the Metaurus. Hasdrubal now gave orders to follow the river bank until it was light enough to find the way, and intended to cross as soon as he could find a suitable place. But due to the windings of the river, the Carthaginian army did not progress very far, and the further up river it went, the higher became the banks and the harder it was to find a ford. Thus the enemy was given time to catch up (Livy 27.47.10-11).

This account creates difficulties, especially for those who believe that Hasdrubal had never crossed the Metaurus, but had been confronted by Salinator at Fanum, for in that case he was trying to find a way up the *left* bank of the Metaurus, and this should not have presented any difficulties since the *via Flaminia* itself followed the left bank of the river. If, on the other hand, we follow the ancient authorities and locate the confrontation at Sena, it is argued,[46] Hasdrubal should have found it easy enough to find his way back across the Metaurus by the way he must have come in the first place, even if the ford did lie some distance upstream to avoid the marshes mentioned by Appian (*Hannibalic War,* 52). But this argument presupposes that Hasdrubal was simply trying to retreat by the quickest and easiest route up the coast, and this may not have been the case: even if he did assume that Hannibal had been defeated, as Livy suggests, he may have wanted to avoid the coastal route in order to throw the inevitable pursuit off the scent. He could, for example, have been trying to make his way across the Appennines by some such route as Hannibal must have followed on his march from Lake Trasimene to the sea in 217, hoping to reach Etruria, where, later in the year, the Senate ordered Salinator to make enquiries into which communities had been planning to go over to Hasdrubal or had, indeed, already give him help (Livy 28.10.4-5). Alternatively, if he still had hopes of joining Hannibal, he may have been trying to reach the *via Flaminia* southwest of Fanum, in order to march round the Roman armies at Sena. In either case, he might well have preferred to avoid the normal ford across the Metaurus, and to cross the river higher up, and this could be why he had provided himself with guides - he would hardly have needed them, after all, if he was just trying to find the ford he had used on his way south. But, whatever his intentions, it is much easier to understand how he could have gone astray up the *right* bank of the Metaurus, and since there is little doubt that this is what the ancient sources thought happened, we should accept that this is what occurred.

As it turned out, however, Hasdrubal failed to shake off the pursuit, and, as day dawned, soon found himself under attack, first by Claudius Nero and the cavalry, and then by Porcius Licinus and the Roman light infantry. Desperately he tried to lay out a camp on a hill overlooking the river bank, but soon Livius Salinator came in sight with the Roman infantry of the line, already deploying for battle, and he knew that he must fight (Livy 27.48.1-3). Unfortunately it is not possible to locate the site of this crucial battle with any certainty, even if we reject all suggested locations north of the river: at least six locations south of the river have been proposed,[47] and all we can probably say is that it was fought somewhere between Fano and Fosombrone, but across the river from the *via Flaminia* (the modern *Strada Statale* 3). The date was possibly June 22nd, by the Roman calendar, for Ovid (*Fasti* 6.770) says that on this day "Hasdrubal fell by his own sword," and although Hasdrubal is not said to have committed suicide, it is quite clear that he deliberately sought death in battle when he realised that he had been decisively defeated. [48]

For the battle itself we are fortunate to have Polybius' account (11.1.2-3.6), which differs somewhat from Livy's (27.48.4ff.), but is not without its own problems. According to Polybius, Hasdrubal drew up his Spaniards and Celts in depth on a narrow front, placing his ten elephants in front of the centre of his line, and attacked the Roman left. It subsequently transpires that his Spanish troops were on his right (cf. 11.1.8-9), and this makes sense, since it is clear that he was happy merely to hold the Roman right with his left, where the ground was difficult (cf. 11.1.5), and he would naturally have wanted his best troops on his right, where he planned to attack. But Polybius' statements that Claudius Nero, when he had moved round to the Roman left, "attacked the Carthaginians in flank against the elephants," and that the elephants "threw both the Roman and the Spanish ranks into confusion" (11.1.7 and 9), imply that the elephants were not in front of the Carthaginian centre, but in front of the right wing of the Spaniards, at the extreme right of the line, and this too makes sense, since Hasdrubal will have been hoping that the elephants would help the attack of the Spaniards on his right. Livy (27. 48.5-7) says the Gauls were on the Carthaginian left, protected by a hill, the Spaniards on the right, and the Ligurians in the centre behind the elephants, but although what he says about the hill may be accepted, since it is confirmed by what Polybius says about the difficult ground on the Carthaginian left, Polybius says nothing about any Ligurians in Hasdrubal's army, and Livy is probably also wrong about the position of the elephants, for the reasons given above.

The truth is, then, probably, that Hasdrubal left the Celts on the hill where he had started to lay out his camp - many of them were later butchered drunk in their beds (Polybius 11.3.1) - and massed his faithful Spaniards on the right, with the elephants in front of their right wing, hoping to win the battle by smashing the Roman left, while the Roman right could not make effective headway against the Celts up the hill. Livy (27.48.4) says Salinator commanded the Roman left, Claudius Nero the right, and Porcius Licinus the centre, and this is borne out by Polybius, although he does not mention the praetor. Thus, while Salinator strove to withstand the attack of Hasdrubal's Spaniards, Nero was faced with the prospect of advancing uphill against the Celts, and once again he showed a touch of originality: finding it impossible to advance and outflank the enemy opposite him because of the difficult terrain, he apparently withdrew some of his men from the rear ranks of the right wing, and marching them round to the left of the Roman line, fell upon the Carthaginian flank (Polybius 11.1.7). Hitherto the struggle there had been even, with the elephants wreaking impartial havoc to both sides (Polybius 11.1.9), but Nero's attack was decisive: his force seems to have curled right round the Carthaginian right so that the Spaniards found themselves attacked from front and rear (Polybius 11.1.10). Most of them were killed on the field, and of the elephants six were also killed, with their mahouts, and the remaining four, having burst through the Roman line, were later captured, wandering alone without their drivers. Hasdrubal himself, having done all that a good general should, as Polybius emphasises (11.2), fell in the thick of the fight. Finally, the Romans overran the Carthaginian camp, and slaughtered many of the Celts sleeping, drunk, on their litters "like sacrificial victims."

According to Polybius (11.3.2), no fewer than 10,000 Carthaginians (i.e. Spaniards and Africans) and Celts fell in the battle, for 2000 Romans, and the sale of the prisoners fetched 300 talents - this has been calculated to mean that there were about 10,000 of them;[49] Livy, however, despite his grossly exaggerated total for the Carthaginian losses (56,000), says that there were only 5400 prisoners (27.49.6). In addition, some of Hasdrubal's men must have escaped (cf. Livy 27.49.8-9), and some may never have reached the battlefield at all, if there is any truth in Livy's story of men flinging themselves down to sleep during the wanderings of the previous night (27.47.9, cf. 49.8). Rejecting Livy's figure for the Carthaginian dead, Hasdrubal's army would thus appear to have been between 20,000 and 30,000 strong, and this is confirmed by his apparent willingness to accept battle with the forces of Salinator and Licinus (cf. Livy 27.47.1), but not once he suspected that those forces had been further increased: Salinator's army would have been a full consular army of two legions and allied contingents, totalling, perhaps 20 - 25,000 men, but although Licinus also had two legions (cf. Livy 27.36.12), his army is specifically described as "weak" ("invalidus" - Livy 27.39.2), and may not have contained more than about 12 - 15,000 men. Thus Hasdrubal would have thought that he could fight a combined army of 30 - 40,000 men, but not when reinforced by Nero's 7000. [50]

Immediately after the battle - Livy (27.50.1) says during the night following it - Claudius Nero set out to return to his army in the south, and, marching even more rapidly than he had come, is alleged to have reached the camp "on the sixth day" (Livy ibid.). But since the distance he had to cover was more than 472 kilometres, assuming the Roman position to have been near Canusium, where Hannibal was last reported (Livy 27.42.16) - 362 kilometres even if Hannibal was now near Larinum (see above, p. 185) - it is very difficult to believe this, and certainly, if Nero's force, after fighting a hard battle, kept up an average speed of sixty-eighty kilometres a-day for six days, it was one of the greatest marches in history. The last grim scene was played out before Hannibal's outposts: his brother's head, carefully preserved, was flung at their feet, and captured Africans - probably officers of Hasdrubal's army - were paraded in chains, two being released to carry to Hannibal details of what had happened (Livy 27.50.11). Hannibal must have realised, at once, that he had at last come to the end of the road: he is said to have declared that he recognized in his brother's dead face, the fate of Carthage (Livy 27.51.12), and even if he made no such remark, he immediately broke camp, and began to concentrate in Bruttium all the outlying garrisons he could now no longer hope to protect, transporting the entire population of Metapontum and of the Lucanian towns still under his control, to the same area (Livy 27.50.13).

The relief at Rome was correspondingly great: first came a rumour that two cavalrymen from Narnia, who had taken part in the battle, had ridden into the camp at what Livy (27.50.6) calls the "jaws of Umbria" - presumably he means the camp of the two *legiones urbanae* at their home town (cf. 27.43.9) - with the news that the

Carthaginian army had been cut to pieces, though there was, naturally, some hesitation in believing this, because the battle was said to have taken place only two days before they reached the camp, some two hundred kilometres from the Metaurus. Next came a letter from the camp's commander, L. Manlius Acidinus, about the arrival of the cavalrymen, but even then there were some who refused to believe the news. But finally came three official envoys from Livius Salinator, and at last the city could give full rein to its joy (Livy 27.50.6-51.10). Later, at the end of the summer, the two victorious generals were summoned to Rome, to celebrate the first triumph allowed to any general for a victory in this war, Salinator with the army which had formed the principal part of the victorious forces. The two consuls agreed to meet at Praeneste and proceed from there, and their progress was a triumph in itself. Then came the solemn entry into the city, Livius Salinator borne in the traditional four-horse chariot, followed by his soldiers, because the battle had been fought in his province, and technically under his command, but with Nero, riding alone, attracting the greater attention (Livy 28.9.1-5). For the first time in nearly twelve years of war a decisive victory had been won on Italian soil.

The elections followed soon afterwards, and although both consuls were present in Rome, it was decided that a dictator should be nominated to hold them, and Nero nominated his colleague, he in turn choosing Q. Caecilius Metellus as his Master of Horse (Livy 28.10.1). This unusual procedure has prompted speculation, but it is not at all clear what lay behind it. One obvious possibility is that certain elements in the Senate wished to prevent either Claudius Nero or Livius Salinator from presiding at the elections, and so forced a decision to appoint a dictator, whereupon Claudius Nero turned the tables by nominating his colleague as dictator. But a more attractive hypothesis is that Nero, who would probably normally have presided at the elections as senior consul - his name appears first in the *fasti* - chose this method of honouring his colleague, under whose auspices the battle of the Metaurus had been won, or, possibly, was forced to do so.[51] The gainers, in the first instance, were L. Veturius Philo and Q. Caecilius Metellus, who were duly elected consuls for 206/5: both had been among the three envoys sent to Rome by Salinator with the official news of his victory (Livy 27.51.3), and both had been commended to the electors by the *Equites* and by their former commander-in-chief (Livy 28.9.10-20). Caecilius Metellus had the added commendation of having been chosen Salinator's Master of Horse. But, in the long run, it was, perhaps, the Cornelii who gained, since both the new consuls were political allies - Caecilius Metellus, for example, later championed Scipio's cause in the Senate (cf. Livy 29.20.1ff.).

After the elections, but before the end of the consular year 207/6, Salinator was sent to Etruria to inquire into reports that certain Etruscan and Umbrian communities had been planning to go over to Hasdrubal, and that some had even sent him aid (Livy 28.10.4-5). In the following March, when the Senate made its dispositions for the following year, Salinator's *imperium* was prorogued, and he took over command of the two legions which Terentius Varro had previously commanded in Etruria (Livy 28.10. 11).[52] For the rest dispositions were much the same as for the previous year, except that both consuls were assigned to Bruttium (Livy 28.10.8), each with an army of two legions, and that one of the new praetors, Q. Mamilius Turrinus, was to take over

Porcius Licinus' army, and carry out reprisals against the Celtic tribes which had aided Hasdrubal (Livy 28.10.12). The total number of legions was, however, reduced from twenty-three to twenty, the two legions which had garrisoned Sardinia for a number of years being brought home and, presumably, disbanded - they were to be replaced by a single new legion (Livy 28.10.14) - and Salinator's army probably also being disbanded, as a reward for its part in the victory at the Metaurus. But what was of more significance for Roman confidence that the war had now swung decisively in their favour, was that the consuls were instructed to get people back to their land, and in particular issued an edict that former colonists of Placentia and Cremona should return to their colonies by a given day, the praetor, Mamilius, being instructed to protect them from the Gauls (Livy 28.11.8ff.).

At the beginning of spring, 206 (Livy 28.11.11), the two new consuls took the field, and proceeded to ravage the territory of Consentia in Bruttium. But, after being ambushed in a defile, they withdrew and contented themselves with re-subjugating Lucania. "With Hannibal," Livy remarks (28.12.1), "nothing of moment was attempted this year, since he avoided all confrontation, in a time of such public and private disaster, and the Romans did not dare to disturb the calm, such was the power they thought resided in this one general, although everything else about him was crashing in ruin." Livy goes on to pay Rome's greatest enemy a remarkable tribute (28.12.2-9), echoing one of the surviving fragments of Polybius' eleventh book. Thus, for the time being, there was a lull in the war in Italy and elsewhere: only in Spain did this year see the decisive battle of Ilipa and the final elimination of Carthaginian forces in the country. At the end of the year, Scipio returned to stand for the consulship of 205/4 at elections possibly postponed until he could be there, [53] and presided over by the friendly L. Veturius Philo (Livy 28.38.6).

# CHAPTER SEVEN – THE INVASION OF AFRICA

After his successes in Spain, it was, perhaps, inevitable that Scipio should be elected consul for 205/6, though we may doubt whether the unanimity of the electors was quite as absolute as Livy says (28.38.6), in view of the evident opposition there had been to Scipio's desire for a triumph (cf. Livy 28.38.4). The presiding consul, L. Veturius Philo, was probably friendly, as was his colleague, Q. Caecilius Metellus, and most of those elected with Scipio were also, probably, political allies, including his fellow-consul, P. Licinius Crassus, the *pontifex maximus*.[1] The election of the latter also meant that when the Senate decided that Sicily and Bruttium should be the consular provinces for the year, it was inevitable that Sicily should go to Scipio, since Crassus' religious duties precluded him from leaving Italy (Livy 28.38.12). But Livy's bald statement to this effect probably conceals considerable debate in the Senate, for, on the face of it, there was no reason for one of the consuls to be assigned to Sicily, where there had been no serious fighting since 210, and even if Hannibal in Bruttium hardly required two consuls, there were obvious reasons why Scipio should have been assigned to that theatre. The decision to make Sicily a consular province, as everyone knew, really meant that the first decision had been taken towards the invasion of Africa, and, judging by the opposition later, this must have occasioned debate.

The first business before the Senate, after the new consuls had taken office, was uncontroversial: on Scipio's motion, the Senate voted that he should celebrate the games he had vowed during the mutiny in Spain out of the money he himself had brought into the treasury, and envoys from Saguntum were also graciously received and rewarded (Livy 28.38.14ff.). But then the question of Scipio's plans for Africa was raised, and feelings were exacerbated by his grandiloquent declaration that he would not merely carry on the war, but finish it, and that this could only be accomplished if he took an army to Africa; what made matters worse was his threat to put his plan to the People, if the Senate opposed it. Unfortunately, we cannot be certain that the tradition Livy records here (28.40.1-2) has not been coloured by later events, for the question whether it was the Senate or the People which decided on consular commands was to become a vital issue in the last hundred years of the Republic. Nor can we be certain how far Livy's versions of the speeches delivered by Fabius Maximus and by Scipio at the subsequent debate (28.40.3-44.18) reproduce what was actually said. But that there was a debate can hardly be doubted, and we also have no reason to doubt that Fabius was Scipio's principal antagonist.

According to Livy, then, Fabius first tried to play upon the natural resentment of his audience by suggesting that Scipio was assuming the issue had been settled, before the Senate made its decision. He next tried to obviate the suspicion that he might be jealous of Scipio, and then argued that Scipio's real task should be the defeat of

Hannibal, maintaining that the Republic could not support campaigns in both Italy and Africa, that Hannibal was still formidable, that experience showed that invading Africa was risky, and that the possibility of Mago's coming to join his brother could not be ignored: "I myself think," he ended, "that P. Cornelius was made consul for the sake of the Republic and of us, not for his own private gain, and that the armies are enrolled to guard the city and Italy, not that consuls, like kings in their arrogance, may transport them anywhere in the world they wish." Fabius' speech, even if not authentic, is extremely interesting, since it so exactly expresses the essential isolationism of Rome's foreign policy, and also hints that many Senators were disturbed by rumours of the regal acclamations accorded to Scipio in Spain.

Scipio, for his part, is alleged to have begun by hinting that Fabius' motivation was jealousy, and went on to argue that no one had talked of his ambition or of the dangers when he was sent to Spain: the dangers of invading Africa were no greater. Hannibal's own example had shown the value of taking the offensive, and there was more likelihood of Carthage's allies rebelling against her than there had been of Rome's allies joining Hannibal. But without allies, Carthage would find herself without troops, since she had no citizen soldiers. The invasion of Africa, finally, would inevitably compel Hannibal to return, so that he, Scipio, would be fighting the main enemy after all, and would be fighting him in his own country, which could now be made to suffer as Italy had suffered.

We can infer from the outcome that Scipio had the support of a majority in the Senate, but he still had one crucial hurdle to overcome, the suspicion that he intended to by-pass the Senate if its decision went against him. Thus, after he and Fabius had delivered their speeches, the much-respected Q. Fulvius Flaccus, four times consul, asked Scipio, point-blank, if he would abide by the Senate's decision. Scipio tried to evade the question by declaring that he would do what was in the interests of the state, but Fulvius then turned to the tribunes and asked if they would intervene on his behalf, if he refused to express an opinion in the debate. This raised further constitutional issues, but the tribunes ruled that if Scipio allowed the Senate to decide, he must abide by that decision, and that they would not allow a bill on the matter to be put before the people; if, on the other hand, he refused to allow the Senate to decide, they would protect any Senator, like Fulvius, who refused to express an opinion. The tribunes' ruling was a compromise, but it must have shown Scipio that if he did try to by-pass the Senate, he would not have an easy passage, and, after asking for a day's grace, he decided that he would, after all, abide by the Senate's decision. This probably satisfied a sufficient number of those Senators, who, although basically on Scipio's side, resented his high-handed attitude, and eventually the Senate's decision was that Scipio should have Sicily as his province, with permission to cross to Africa if he judged it to be in the public interest (Livy 28.45.1-8).

This debate is interesting because it is one of the very few on questions of policy which Livy reports in his account of the Hannibalic War. But some modern scholars perhaps make too much of it, when they see the decision as crucial to the whole future history of Rome,[2] for although the invasion of Africa can be seen, with the benefit of hindsight, to have been an important step along the road towards Rome's eventual domination of the Mediterranean, this would not have been how contemporaries saw it - to them the question was one of strategy, not foreign policy. Even in the long term, the decision to send an army to Spain in 218, was more important than the decision to allow Scipio to proceed to Africa, since although the latter led to the defeat of Carthage, it did not immediately result in a permanent Roman presence in Africa. Scipio, too, appears to have had strictly limited aims, as his willingness to negotiate with Carthage indicates.

According to Livy's account (28.45.13), even though the Senate decided to allow Scipio to implement his plans, its support was somewhat grudging: Scipio was not allowed to levy new troops in Italy, although he could call for volunteers, and accept what help he could get from Rome's Italian allies towards the building of new ships, and the equipping of them and the rest of his forces. This tradition seems designed to enhance the popularity of Scipio, and its details may well be untrue, or, at least, exaggerated.[3] In particular, the Senate's attitude to Scipio's need for troops was probably not as grudging as Livy seems to have thought, for there were probably already considerable numbers of troops in Sicily - the remnants from Cannae and the two battles of Herdonea (see above, p. 174) - and with the 7000 volunteers Scipio is alleged to have taken to Sicily with him (Livy 28.46.1), the forces congregated in Sicily seem to have reached a strength at least equivalent to four legions (see below, pp. 202-3). The Senate, after all, still had to maintain a considerable army in southern Italy; four legions to watch Hannibal in Bruttium, with probably two more at Tarentum, and one at Capua - and there were additional commitments this year: Sempronius Tuditanus is alleged to have taken 10,000 foot and 1000 horse to Greece (Livy 29.12.2: presumably a legion together with its complement of allies), and Mago's landing in Liguria necessitated moving the army hitherto stationed in Etruria, into Cisalpine Gaul, and its replacement with the *legiones urbanae* originally raised in 207, which had remained as a garrison for Rome itself, apart from moving up to Narnia under the threat of Hasdrubal's advance (cf. Livy 28.46.13). In general, although there only appear to have been eighteen legions in service this year, or twenty if we regard the addition of Scipio's volunteers as bringing the army in Sicily up to the equivalent of four legions: this followed nine years in which the legionary total had never fallen below twenty, and had twice risen to twenty-five, once to twenty-three, and we must also remember that twelve of the Latin colonies were still not supplying their quotas. It is, thus, clear that it might have been difficult to raise extra regular forces for Scipio.

Unfortunately, we do not know when Scipio arrived in Sicily, but he did not take office until March 15th, by the Roman calendar, and we must, presumably, allow at least a month or two for his preparations, so he probably did not get to Sicily before the end of May or the beginning of June. Then he had to select and train his forces for the invasion, and again we may, perhaps, allow a month or two for this. Nevertheless, he should have been ready by about August, and yet we know that he did not embark for Africa until the following year. A natural assumption would be that, by the time he was ready, he felt that it was too late to accomplish anything in Africa before the onset of winter, but judging by the strategy he pursued in 204, when eventually he did land, he would have been quite content just to establish himself ashore before the winter, in 205, and the delay could have been disastrous, partly because he could have found himself superseded, and partly because the longer he delayed, on any rational calculation, the better prepared the Carthaginians should have been. Perhaps, however, the preparations took longer than we suppose, and additional delays may have been imposed by the Pleminius affair (see below, p. 199ff.), the establishing of communications with the Numidians in Africa, and, in particular, the necessity to clarify Syphax' attitude, and, finally, by Mago's landing in Liguria.

Mago had spent the winter of 206/5 in Minorca, and crossed to Liguria in the summer of 205 (Livy 28.46.7), with an army of 12,000 foot and about 2000 horse, escorted by thirty warships. He seized Genoa, and then used his fleet to stir up trouble on the coast of the Ligurian Alps, using Savona as his base. The Senate was informed of all this in despatches from Sp. Lucretius, the praetor who had been assigned to Cisalpine Gaul, and steps were taken to reinforce his army with troops from Etruria, under the command of the proconsul, M. Livius Salinator, and to replace these in Etruria with the *legiones urbanae* (Livy 28.46.13). With memories of Hasdrubal's invasion in mind, this might have had the effect of delaying Scipio's plans, particularly when it became apparent that the Carthaginian navy was stirring from its normal lethargy. According to Livy (28.46.10), Mago had sent twenty of his thirty warships home to Africa to protect it from Scipio's impending invasion, and although Livy's motive can hardly be the right one - it is more likely that the warships were sent to ask for reinforcements, and to help escort them if they were forthcoming[4] - we have no reason to doubt Livy when he says (29.4.6) that the Carthaginian government responded by sending 6000 foot, 800 horse, and even seven elephants, with funds to hire more troops, all escorted by twenty-five warships. That these reinforcements reached Mago (Livy 29.5.2) is a striking illustration of how much more the Carthaginian navy could have done to reinforce Hannibal, who was much nearer, although it must be admitted that the Roman fleet based on Sicily, upon which the prevention of such operations was mainly bound to devolve, had been greatly reduced in 206 (Livy 28.10.16). Livy also says (28.46.14) that some eighty Carthaginian merchantmen were captured off Sardinia during 205, and that, of his sources, Coelius Antipater said they were carrying supplies to Hannibal, whereas Valerius Antias said they were transporting Mago's booty to Africa. Appian (*Hannibalic War*, 54) supports Coelius, and adds the details that the whole fleet was 100 strong, and that 20 ships were sunk, 60 captured and the rest scattered back to Africa. But although Valerius Antias can hardly be right,[5] it is possible that the ships were really on their way to Mago, and that their presence off Sardinia diverted the Roman squadron based there from the fleet which did get through to Mago, for on the face of it, it seems improbable that even merchant-vessels entirely dependent on sails, as Appian says, could have been blown to Sardinia if they were making for Hannibal in Bruttium from Carthage.

The only direct step taken by Scipio during his consulship to further the invasion of Africa, was to send Laelius off to raid the coast, with the thirty ships already based on Sicily when he arrived - the thirty new ships brought with him, Livy alleges (29.1.14), had to be hauled ashore at Panormus because their timbers were still green, and needed to be dried out.[6] Laelius' raid, even if on a small scale, was the last of many such raids carried out by the Roman navy during the war - a great contrast with the Carthaginian navy's inactivity in this respect. The Roman navy had raided Africa, or the islands lying between Sicily and Africa, every year from 218 to 215 (cf. Livy 21.51.1-2; 22.31.1ff.; 23.21.2; 23.41.8), and although there had been a lull from 214 to 211, probably because of the concentration of all available naval forces on Sicily in those years, in 210, after the capture of Agrigentum, a squadron of 50 ships had been despatched under M. Valerius Messala to raid Africa, and, as Livy puts it (27.5.1), "to see what the Carthaginians were doing and preparing to do." Messala's squadron had landed near Utica, and after ravaging far and wide, had returned to Lilybaeum in less than a fortnight with booty and prisoners, from whom the information had been extracted that numerous forces were being raised to join Hasdrubal in Spain, and that a huge fleet was being prepared to attempt the recovery of Sicily (Livy 27.5.8-13). In the event, the only Carthaginian naval activity Livy reports that year had been a raid on Sardinia by 40 ships (27.6.13-4). In 209, as we have seen (above, p. 173), thirty ships had been detached from the Roman fleet based on Sicily to aid Fabius against Tarentum, and although Valerius Laevinus had been left 70 to raid Africa if he chose, he had retained them to protect the island, probably because of the rumours of Carthaginian naval preparations (Livy 27.7.15-6, 8.17). But further such rumours had caused the Senate, in 208, to increase the number of warships in commission to 281, the largest total of the war, and the Sicilian fleet had been restored to its strength of 100 warships (Livy 27.22.9). With these Valerius Laevinus had raided Africa again, landing near Clupea (Kelibia) on the east side of the promontory ending in Cape Bon, and for the first time in the war this had actually brought the Carthaginian fleet out to face the challenge: 83 Carthaginian warships had encountered Laevinus' 100 off Clupea in the largest naval engagement of the war, but the Romans had captured eighteen of the enemy, and driven the rest off in flight (Livy 27.29.7-8). In 207, too, Laevinus had raided Africa, ravaging the territory of both Utica and of Carthage itself, and on its way back to Sicily, he had again encountered a Carthaginian fleet, this time 70 strong, and had captured a further 17 vessels and sunk 4. Livy remarks, in connection with this second naval victory, that "from then on the sea became safe, enemy ships having been driven off it, and great supplies of corn were brought to Rome" (28.4.5-7). But these successes had, perhaps, bred too much complacency, for, as we have seen, the Sicilian squadron had been reduced to 30 ships in 206 (Livy 28.10.16), and this may have resulted in reinforcements reaching Mago. (See Map 20).

Laelius' raid on Africa, then, was necessarily on a small scale. He landed near Hippo Regius (Bône, Annaba) and spread devastation far and wide in an area not yet affected by the war (Livy 29.3.7ff.). Something like panic gripped the Carthaginians, who thought that Scipio himself had landed. Immediate steps were taken to levy troops in the city of Carthage - (Livy 29.4.2: presumably these would have been Carthaginian citizens) - and to hire soldiers from amongst the Africans; the fortifications of the city were repaired, supplies brought in, arms got ready, and ships manned. Then came news that the enemy was not Scipio and his army, but merely a raiding-party under Laelius, and Carthage breathed again. The strategy now was to take steps to ensure the loyalty of the Numidian chieftains, particularly Syphax, and at the same time to seek to divert Scipio: Livy alleges (29.4.4) that envoys were sent to Philip of Macedonia to promise him 200 talents if he transported troops to Sicily or Italy, but this seems improbable, although a bribe to try to induce the king to continue the struggle in Greece is, perhaps, not unlikely. Reinforcements were sent to Mago, as we have seen, and envoys were sent to both him and Hannibal to do all they could to keep Scipio in Sicily.

Meanwhile, to Laelius, busy gathering in booty from the surrounding countryside, came the Numidian prince, Masinissa, with a few horsemen - and many a complaint at Scipio's delay (Livy 29.4.7-9). The Numidian had been leading an adventurous life since his meeting with Scipio near Gades in 206. While still in Spain, his father, Gala, had died, and the crown had passed, according to Numidian custom, to Gala's eldest brother, Oezalces. But Oezalces, too, had shortly died, and his eldest son, Capussa, had succeeded to the throne, only to be defeated and killed by another, more distant relative, Mazaetullus, who seized power ostensibly on behalf of Capussa's younger brother, Lacumazes, and who married no less a person than Hannibal's niece, widow of the dead king, Oezalces (Livy 29.29.6-13). Learning all this, Masinissa had crossed to Mauretania from Spain, begged help of Baga, King of the Moors, and ridden boldly for his father's kingdom, where he had been rapidly joined by 500 of his fellow-tribesmen. Next, falling in with the young king, Lacumazes, on his way to Syphax, he had driven the boy's forces into a place Livy (29.30.6) calls "Thapsus", though it can hardly be the famous place of that name on the east coast of modern Tunisia (now Rass Dimasse), since that lay in Carthaginian territory. Masinissa had captured the town, wherever it was, but Lacumazes escaped. These successes, however, had roused the Numidians to Masinissa's support, and though faced with a numerically superior army, under Mazaetullus, reinforced by troops sent with Lacumazes by Syphax, he had won a decisive victory. He had, then, induced Mazaetullus and Lacumazes, who had escaped from their defeat to Carthaginian territory, to throw in their lot with him, thus hoping to remove a focus of trouble, knowing that he would probably have to deal with Syphax (Livy 29.30.7-12).

Syphax, if we are to believe Livy (29.31.1ff.), had not originally been much concerned whether Lacumazes or Masinissa ruled the Maesulian Numidians, but Hasdrubal Gisgo, who had been at his court, had persuaded him that Masinissa was a danger both to him and to Carthage. Roused at last, Syphax had invaded Maesulian territory, and routed Masinissa's army, but Masinissa had taken to the hills and carried on successful guerilla operations, until Syphax deputed an officer named Bucar to hunt him down. Bucar had eventually brought him to bay, allegedly near Clupea (Livy 29. 32.6), but Masinissa had again escaped, though with only four horsemen: pursued by five of Bucar's men, they had plunged into a river, and two had been drowned, but Masinissa and the other two had crawled out amongst the reeds on the farther bank. Bucar had returned to Syphax with the news that Masinissa was dead, but that worthy had hidden in a cave until his wound was healed, and then had boldly made his way back to his ancestral lands, where he had rapidly gathered 6000 foot and 4000 horse, and begun again to raid Carthaginian territory and that of Syphax' tribe, the Masaesulii. Syphax had gathered his forces again, and between Cirta and Hippo had trapped Masinissa between his own troops and those of his son, Vermina. But Masinissa had still managed to fight his way out of the trap, and had made his way to the Lesser Syrtis, where he had taken refuge between what Livy (29.33.9) calls the "Punic Emporia" (which was the district around the modern Qabes or Gabes) and the Garamantes of the Fezzan, until Laelius' arrival.

But despite Masinissa's pleas, and the eagerness of his army, fired by the sight of the booty Laelius had brought back with him, Scipio still delayed and a note of criticism even sounds in Livy's narrative when he remarks that the "greater plan was interrupted by a lesser one, the possibility of recapturing Locri" (29.6.1). Locri had defected to the Carthaginians in 215 (Livy 23.30.8, 24.1), but some prisoners from it, captured by Roman raiding parties from Rhegium, had been recognized by Locrian exiles who had fled to Rhegium when their town went over to Hannibal, and, as luck would have it, they included a number of men who had worked on the citadel. These now undertook to betray Locri to the Romans if they were ransomed and returned, and, after doing this, the Locrian exiles laid the plan before Scipio in Syracuse. Scipio promptly ordered a force of 3000 men from Rhegium, under an officer named Q. Pleminius, to co-operate with the exiles (Livy 29.6.2-9).

Up to a point, all went well, and the main citadel was taken by the Romans, but many of the Carthaginian garrison, under their commander, Hamilcar, were able to take refuge in the other citadel, where they managed to hold out, and even to make things difficult for the Roman troops in the main citadel, despite the fact that the townspeople took the Roman side (Livy 29.6.10ff.). Scipio, informed that the situation was critical, and that Hannibal himself was approaching, left his brother, Lucius, in charge in Sicily, and set sail for Locri with a small squadron. Hannibal halted for the night at the river Bulotus - probably the river which flows into the sea near the modern Gioiosa Marina - and sent forward a messenger with orders to Hamilcar to create a diversion next day (Livy 29.7.3). But when fighting began at dawn, according to Livy (29.7.4), he was unwilling to enter the citadel held by his men, and could not begin to assault the rest of the town until ladders and other siege-equipment had been prepared. This gave Scipio the chance to slip into the town, and when, next day, Hannibal's army moved up to the assault, he boldly sortied and threw the Carthaginian assault troops into confusion. Hannibal immediately withdrew, and ordered the garrison to decide for itself what to do, whereupon Hamilcar and his men fired the houses in which they were living, and escaped to the safety of Hannibal's army in the confusion. Livy (29.7.8-10) makes the most of this first encounter between Hannibal and Scipio, alleging that it was when Hannibal learnt of Scipio's presence that he decided to withdraw, and that the Carthaginian garrison ran like men in flight. But it is possible that Hannibal's sole concern was really the safety of the men who formed the garrison - at this stage in the war men must have been far more important to him than the retention of hostile towns - and if this is so, the whole episode can be regarded as a successful little operation for the Carthaginians.

There then followed an ugly episode which threatened Scipio's career and reflects no credit on his judgement of men. According to Livy (29.8-9.7), Pleminius and his men behaved with such brutality, after Scipio's departure, that even the two military tribunes who had shared the command with Pleminius, were driven to protest, and this led to riots between their men and Pleminius' in the course of which, first, the tribunes were flogged at Pleminius' orders, and then Pleminius himself assaulted and gravely wounded.

Scipio returned to Locri to investigate the matter, and acquitted Pleminius, leaving him still in command, but ordered the military tribunes to be arrested and sent to Rome (Livy 29.9.8). Here we can, perhaps, grant that Scipio felt that discipline had to be upheld, and hence that Pleminius, as the senior officer, had to be supported. But it is extraordinary that he did not at least replace Pleminius at Locri, in view of the allegations about his behaviour towards the townspeople, which had nothing to do with the point of discipline. In the event, Pleminius was furious at what he regarded as Scipio's lenient treatment of the tribunes, and, once his commander-in-chief had departed, vented his wrath upon the hapless officers and upon the leading Locrians who had complained to Scipio.

Eventually, complaints about these happenings were to reach the ears of the Senate, but for the time being attention at Rome was focussed on other things, in particular, if Livy is to be believed (29.10.4ff.), on a prophecy discovered in the Sibylline Books to the effect that if a foreign enemy should bring war to Italy, he could be driven from Italy and defeated if the Idaean Mother were brought from Pessinus to Rome. This led to the despatch of an embassy to King Attalus of Pergamum, in whose realm Pessinus lay, and a signal honour for Scipio's family, when his cousin, P. Cornelius Scipio Nasica, was chosen, in accordance with Delphi's injunction, as "the best man in Rome", to receive the image of the goddess on its arrival. These extraordinary proceedings, unless they merely reflect the atmosphere of superstition which Hannibal's presence in Italy still engendered, possibly reflect continued arguments about the proper strategy to pursue, for if people could be persuaded that the Gods would bring about Hannibal's removal through the agency of the Idaean Mother, there would, clearly, be no point in Scipio's invading Africa. But if so, Scipio's family and supporters neatly turned the affair to their own ends.

More importantly, when the time for the elections for 204/3 came round, Scipio's colleague and friend, Licinius Crassus, who was ill, was able to secure the nomination of Q. Caecilius Metellus as dictator to hold the elections, and under his auspices yet another member of the *gens Cornelia,* M. Cornelius Cethegus, was elected consul (Livy 29.11.9ff.). His colleague was to be P. Sempronius Tuditanus, who was elected in his absence: he had been appointed to the command in Greece earlier in the year, and had, possibly, brought the war in Greece to an end by the Peace of Phoinike in time to influence the electors on his behalf. Scipio, who would not have wanted operations in Greece to distract attention from his own plans, may have lent Tuditanus his support.[7] At the same time, two of the four praetors were also likely to be friendly - one, M. Pomponius Matho, was Scipio's cousin, the other, M. Marcius Ralla, later served on his staff in Africa (cf. Livy 30.38.4).

Thus, when the new consuls took office on March 15th, 204, there seems to have been no opposition to the prorogation of Scipio's *imperium* for a further year (Livy 29.13.3). Most of the other commands remained the same, except that Q. Caecilius Metellus was withdrawn from Bruttium, and his two legions discharged. His place was to be taken by Sempronius Tuditanus in command of two new legions; the other consul, Cornelius Cethegus, was assigned to command in Etruria, and this, and the fact that

Livius Salinator and Sp. Lucretius were continued in command of four legions in Cisalpine Gaul, indicates that Mago was now regarded as the main threat (Livy 29.13.1ff.). After dealing with these matters, and the reception of the Idaean Mother (Livy 29.14. 1-14), the Senate turned to the question of the twelve recalcitrant Latin colonies, which, for five years, had not supplied their quotas of soldiers. It was decided to demand extra troops from them, as well as an annual tax (Livy 29.15), and this argues a considerable return of confidence in the Senate, which had clearly been reluctant to proceed to extremes with the colonies in the years since they had first refused to honour their obligations. A further return to confidence was marked by the decision to begin refunding the loans made to the state in 210 (Livy 29.16.1-3).

But all this paled into insignificance when envoys arrived from Locri to complain of the doings of Pleminius and his men, since, as Livy implies (29.16.5), the matter clearly touched Scipio's whole position. As might have been expected, it was Fabius who brought this aspect of the matter into the open, when, after the Locrians had had their say, he asked whether they had laid the matter before Scipio. They replied that they had indeed done so, but that Scipio was too busy, and in any case had indicated his attitude by leaving Pleminius in charge (Livy 29.19.1-2). This gave Fabius the opportunity to deliver a blistering attack upon Scipio, and to propose that Pleminius should be arrested and brought to Rome to stand trial, that Scipio should be recalled for leaving his province without the Senate's authority and that arrangements should be made with the tribunes of the people to introduce a bill for the abrogation of his command, and that everything should be done to restore the situation in Locri, in particular by replacing the Roman soldiers there with four cohorts of Latins (Livy 29.19. 3-9). Fabius was supported by a number of Senators, who inveighed against the un-Roman behaviour of Scipio and his staff at Syracuse - walking in the Gymnasium in cloak and sandals and the like - and the slack discipline of his troops (Livy 29.19.11-3): Plutarch, in his life of Cato the Censor (3.5ff.), says that Fabius was supported by Cato, who had served under Fabius at the capture of Tarentum, but who was now Scipio's Quaestor. However, Scipio was ably defended by Q. Caecilius Metellus, the consul of 206/5, who, although supporting Fabius in other respects, pointed out how unfair it would be to take the action proposed by Fabius against Scipio himself, when it was admitted that he had not even been present when the crimes were committed. Metellus' sober speech had its effect, and it was decided that the praetor recently allotted Sicily, M. Pomponius Matho, should proceed to Sicily to hold an inquiry, accompanied by ten commissioners chosen from the Senate by the consuls, two tribunes of the people and one aedile. Once Metellus' proposal had been accepted, the result was a foregone con-clusion, for the praetor in charge of the enquiry was Scipio's cousin, as has been said, and the predominance of men friendly to the Scipio's at the recent elections probably ensured that a majority of the senatorial commissioners were sympathetic - according to one of the sources used by Livy (cf.29.21.1), they even included Metellus himself.

On their way to Locri, the commissioners either encountered Pleminius on his way into voluntary exile at Naples, and arrested him, or found that Scipio had already had him and his principal associates arrested at Locri - Livy found both versions in his sources (29.21.1-2). In either case, the prisoners were conveyed to Rhegium in the first instance. At Locri the commissioners first made sure that the treasures plundered from the famous temple of Proserpine were restored, and then saw to it that restitution was made to individual citizens. Later, before an assembly of the Locrians, the praetor bade those who wished to bring charges against Pleminius go to Rhegium - if they wished to charge Scipio they were to send a delegation to Messina, where he and his ten commissioners would hold an enquiry. In reply, the Locrians said they would bring charges against Pleminius, but tactfully excused Scipio on the ground that what had happened had not been at his orders or with his consent (Livy 29.21.7-11). The praetor and the commissioners were thus relieved of the troublesome duty of examining Scipio's conduct. But Pleminius and thirty-two of his associates were found guilty, and sent in chains to Rome, where, according to the source Livy followed, Pleminius died in prison before proceedings against him had ended (29.22.7-9). But Livy also quotes a tradition from the historian Clodius Licinus, according to which Pleminius was still alive in Scipio's second consulship in 194/3: he was said to have attempted to escape from prison by bribing accomplices to set fire to the city in various places, but was detected and sent to the Tullianum, where, presumably, he was executed (Livy 29.22.10). When finally, the praetor and commissioners arrived in Sicily to investigate the charges of slackness against Scipio and his army, Scipio put his army and navy through their paces to such good effect that the board of enquiry not merely bade him sail for Africa as soon as possible, but later extolled his efforts in the Senate. Thus the danger to Scipio's plans from his enemies in the Senate evaporated.

But the delay had, in other respects, created a dangerous situation. In particular, the Carthaginians were now fully alerted, and steps had been taken to re-establish friendly relations with Syphax, the powerful king of the Masaesulian Numidians, and now, following his defeat of Masinissa, ruler also of the Maesulii. The Carthaginian general, Hasdrubal Gisgo, had established a strong personal friendship with Syphax, beginning at the time of his famous meeting with Scipio at Syphax' court, and this was now strengthened by Syphax' marriage to Hasdrubal's daughter, Sophonisba. Thus Syphax was induced to conclude a treaty of alliance with Carthage (Livy 29.23.1-5), and Hasdrubal also shrewdly persuaded him to send envoys to Scipio to warn him that if he invaded Africa, he (Syphax) would feel bound to support Carthage (Livy 29.23.6-10). Scipio tried to dissuade the Numidian king, sending envoys of his own to Africa, but in his heart of hearts he must have known that it was useless, and he was worried that a rumour of Syphax' hostility might leak out owing to the presence of Numidian envoys at Syracuse. So he gave out that they had come to urge him to hasten the invasion, as Masinissa had done, and to lend credibility to this story, ordered his forces to concentrate at Lilybaeum.

It was only now, according to Livy (29.24.7ff.), that Scipio made his choice of forces to take with him to Africa, though in all probability he had already picked his men, since they would have needed to train together (cf. 29.1.1ff.). The forces in Sicily, from which the choice was made, included the survivors from Cannae and the two battles of Herdonea, all apparently referred to in Livy's sources as the *legiones Cannenses*, as well as the men Scipio had brought with him the previous year, and although Livy says (29.13.6) that the *Cannensis exercitus* had been assigned to the praetor, M. Pomponius Matho, at the beginning of the year, there is no reason to doubt that soldiers from these legions formed the majority of Scipio's force: as Livy remarks (29.24.13), they were the most experienced soldiers in the Roman army, and Scipio knew that Cannae had not really been lost through any cowardice of their's - having served with them at that battle, he may well have had a fellow-feeling for them. There is also no reason to doubt that he weeded out those he did not think were suitable, and made the numbers up from the troops he had brought with him to Sicily (Livy 29.24.13). But Livy's statement (29.24.14) that he made his legions up to 6200 foot and 300 foot, is doubtful, since, if it was true, these would have been the largest legions to serve in the Roman army before the Third Macedonian War, over thirty years later.

It is not possible to be certain how many men Scipio finally took with him to Africa.[8] We can almost certainly assume that his army consisted of two legions and the usual contingents of allies, and this means that the lowest of the three totals reported by Livy (29.25.1-2) for the infantry - 10,000 - must be rejected as it stands, though it is curious that this tradition recorded so high a total for the cavalry - 2200. The highest of Livy's three totals - 35,000 for infantry and cavalry combined - must also probably be rejected, since even if the Roman troops numbered 13,000, this would still mean that the army included 22,000 allied troops, and that is far too high a proportion. This leaves the middle total - 16,000 infantry and 1600 cavalry - and this may be right, although this would mean that the legions were barely of normal strength - 4200 foot - and the allied contingents, if anything, slightly less strong, which would be unusual, particularly since, judging by the fuss made by the allies in 209 (cf. Livy 27.9.1ff.), there were plenty of allied troops serving in Sicily when Scipio arrived, and he had brought more with him (cf. Livy 28.45.19-20).

It is, thus, possible that none of the totals recorded by Livy is correct as it stands, but that the true total was somewhere between 17,600 and 35,000, for infantry and cavalry combined. It is probably idle to juggle with the figures as given, but it seems possible that Livy's lowest total is correct for the *Roman* infantry, i.e. represents two legions of 5000 men each, for it would make sense to suppose that Scipio wanted to take two strong legions, and we have both Polybius' and Livy's word for it that 5000 was a possible total for legions at this date (cf. Polybius 3.107.9ff., and Livy 22.36.3). It is also possible that this tradition records the true total of the cavalry, i.e. represents 600 Roman cavalry and 1600 allied cavalry, and if this is the case, then it is further possible that the second of Livy's totals - 16,000 infantry and 1600 cavalry - is true of the *allied* contingents. In short, the truth may be that Scipio's army contained 10,000 Roman infantry, 600 Roman cavalry, 16,000 allied infantry, and 1600 allied cavalry, making 28,200 men in all. In any case, it seems far more likely that the army's total strength was of this order, than either 17,600 or 35,000.

Livy (29.25.5-13) gives an interesting account of the preparations for the voyage - rations for 45 days, cooked food for 15, warships to carry one light, transports (of which there were 400) two - but impressive as it all sounds, there is one astonishing detail upon which Livy does not comment - that the invasion fleet was to be escorted by a mere 40 warships. Of course, we do not know how many ships the Carthaginians had at this stage of the war - though one tradition Livy reports (30.43.12) held that they had 500 of all types left at the end. But Scipio must at least have heard of Laevinus' encounters with Carthaginian fleets 83 and 70 strong in 208 and 207, and although 39 of these had either been sunk or captured, one would have thought that any intelligent estimate of the number of ships they might put into the water, would have been between 50 and 100. To make matters worse, even if he had to rely exclusively on the warships based on Sicily, Scipio had sixty available, if we are to believe Livy (cf. 28.10.16 and 46.1), and it was folly to add to the risks of invasion by not taking every available warship. But it was, possibly, the difficulty of manning more that kept the number down to forty, and Scipio may have thought the risk worth taking in view of the poor showing of the Carthaginian navy: after all, Laelius had only the previous year got to Africa and back safely, with only thirty warships (Livy 29.1.14). At all events, when all was ready, the invasion fleet sailed, Scipio and his brother, Lucius, commanding twenty warships on the right, Laelius and Scipio's Quaestor, M. Porcius Cato, the twenty on the left (Livy 29.25.10). Unfortunately, Livy does not give any indication of the time of year, but we may guess that it was the late spring or early summer (June-July, 204: cf. Livy 29.34.7).

According to Livy (29.25.12), Scipio ordered his pilots to steer for Emporia, which, as we have seen, lay in the region of the modern Gabes, since the area was fertile, its population unwarlike, and it was hoped that it could be rapidly overrun before help arrived from Carthage some three hundred kilometres to the north. A good wind rapidly carried the fleet away from Sicily, but about midday the wind dropped and fog came down, lasting all through the following night. However, at dawn, when the fog dispersed before a rising wind, land was soon sighted which Scipio's pilot declared to be the "Promontory of Mercury" (i.e. Cape Bon), and Scipio ordered him to steer for a landing-place further down the coast - which should mean further down the east coast, beyond Cape Bon, if the intention really was to land at Emporia. But again the wind dropped and the fog came down, as on the previous day, and when darkness fell, orders were given to anchor to avoid the dangers of collision or running aground. If Livy's account so far is true, the Roman fleet should now have been somewhere off the east coast of Tunisia, south of Cape Bon, but he goes on to say (29.27.12) that when the fog dispersed once more at dawn, the nearest land in sight was the "Promontory of the Beautiful One" (now Cap Farina or Rass Sidi Ali el Mekki), the promontory *west* of Cape Bon, and Scipio ordered the pilots to steer for this and disembarked his forces (Livy 29.27.13). (See Map 20).

On the face of it, it seems improbable that Scipio thus allowed his plans to be altered, and landed in a totally different place from the one intended - the alleged original landing-place at Emporia, moreover, was twice as far from Lilybaeum as the actual landing-place, and would have involved additional risks of the Carthaginians' cutting communications with Sicily. Most scholars, therefore, assume that Livy was mistaken about the original orders, and that Scipio had intended to land where he did land, from the first. This is probably correct, but it is just possible that Scipio had originally intended to land near Emporia, not merely because of the reasons Livy gives, but because he believed Masinissa to be in that area, for although Livy believed that Masinissa's flight to Emporia had taken place before Laelius' raid in 205 (cf.29.33. 8-9), this would mean that Masinissa would have had to make his way from Emporia to Bône - only about 100 kilometres from Syphax' capital at Cirta (Constantine) - to meet Laelius, and then find some refuge until Scipio's arrival. But before his last defeat at Syphax' hands, Masinissa had been in the hills between Hippo (Bône) and Cirta (Livy 29.32.14), and this may have been when he met Laelius. If, then, Scipio had subsequently learnt of Masinissa's defeat and flight to the region of Emporia, he might have thought it important enough to join up with the Numidian to land near Emporia, but not important enough to risk his fleet any further once the fog had thrown his original plans into disarray.

But there is no reason to doubt that the Roman expeditionary force did eventually land near Cap Farina, about twenty kilometres north of Utica. The landing was, as usual, unopposed, and, after sending his warships to reconnoitre Utica, Scipio occupied some low hills a short distance inland. Here the first engagement of the African war took place when a force of 500 cavalry, sent from Carthage under an officer called Hanno to spy out the Roman position and attack foragers, collided with the Roman outposts, with the result that Hanno himself was killed and his men dispersed (Livy 29.28.10ff.). Scipio followed up this success by ravaging the surrounding countryside, and taking the nearest township, after which he loaded his booty and prisoners onto the transports, and sent them back to Sicily. Shortly afterwards, the Roman forces were greatly cheered by the arrival of Masinissa, either from the region of Emporia, or from some refuge he had occupied nearer at hand, since meeting Laelius at Hippo. He had with him a force of cavalry which some of Livy's sources put at a mere 200 men, though the majority put it at 2000 (Livy 29.29.4) - Livy, after telling the story of Masinissa's adventures since leaving Spain, sapiently remarks that the lower figure is more consistent with the low ebb of Masinissa's fortunes.

Meanwhile the Carthaginians, undeterred by the defeat of the original Hanno's cavalry-force, had raised another under an officer of the same name - a circumstance which has inevitably roused the suspicion that one of these two early engagements is a doublet of the other. But in this particular instance Livy shows himself to be aware of the possibility of confusion (cf. 29.35.2), and since he decided that there really were two engagements, it seems best to believe him. [10] Urgent messages were also sent to Hasdrubal Gisgo and Syphax, but in the meantime, Hanno, having raised as many men as he could, particularly Numidians, seized a town Livy calls Salaeca, some twenty-two kilometres from the Roman camp, which was now on the hills about a kilometre and a half southwest of Utica (Livy 29.34.1-6). Scipio, affecting to scorn Hanno's ability as a cavalry leader, since he had quartered his men in a town during the summer, ordered Masinissa to ride up to the town and try to lure the Carthaginians out in pursuit. The plan worked perfectly: Hanno and his men pursued Masinissa past the hills where Scipio lay concealed, and were taken in the flank as Masinissa wheeled his force back to charge them in front. Hanno fell with a thousand of his men at the head of the column, the rest scattered in flight, hotly pursued by their enemies, and lost a further thousand men. The topographical indications of Livy (29.34.7-17) and Appian (*History of Libya,* 14) have led to the identification of the battlefield as being south of the saddle joining the hills running southwest from Utica, now called the Djebel Menzel Roul, to the Djebel Doumis. [12]

On the day this skirmish took place, the transports which had carried the first booty to Sicily, returned loaded with provisions. Scipio, having rewarded those who had distinguished themselves in the recent engagement, placed a strong garrison in Salaeca, and set out on a week-long foray into the interior, returning to load fresh spoils onto the transports and send them back to Sicily (Livy 29.35.3-5). He then set about the siege of Utica, hoping to use it as a base for the remainder of the campaign. But despite the siege-equipment he had brought with him, or had been brought by the transports on their return, he could not take the city, and after forty days, with winter drawing on, and Carthaginian forces under Hasdrubal Gisgo and Syphax beginning to mass in considerable numbers, he was forced to abandon the siege and look about for a suitable site for winter-quarters. The place he chose was about three kilometres east of Utica, on the hill on the northern end of which now lies the village of Kalaat el Andelous - the site was still known as the "*Castra Cornelia*" in Caesar's time, over 150 years later (cf. Caesar, *Civil Wars,* 2.24). The hill was a peninsula in Scipio's day, but the sea has now receded to the west. [13] Livy (29.36.1-3) notes that Scipio's army was well-provisioned, with supplies gathered from the surrounding countryside, and brought by sea from Sicily, Italy and Sardinia - not to mention 1200 togas and 12,000 tunics from the latter island.

Although he had established himself ashore, and beaten off all the forces sent against him, Scipio was now in a precarious position, without a proper base and forced to winter on a barren headland, cut off from home by the winter weather and faced by enemy forces which probably outnumbered his own, though it is difficult to accept Polybius' estimate (14.1.14, cf. Livy 29.35.10-11) that they numbered 80,000 foot and 13,000 horse. One wonders why he had not acted to prevent the concentration of these forces, as he acted the following year, when he marched to confront the enemy at the Great Plains. But he probably feared to cut his communications with the coast until he had estimated the enemy strength, knowing full well that the forces sent against him under the two Hannos did not represent anything like the strength the Carthaginians could put into the field. His caution contrasts strongly with Hannibal's boldness when he arrived in Italy, and must have caused disappointment at home after his grandiloquent promises at the beginning of his consulship, over eighteen months before. Nevertheless, when the new consuls, Cn. Servilius Caepio and C. Servilius Geminus, took office on March 15th, 203, there seems to have been no question of Scipio's *imperium* not being renewed - indeed, if Livy is to be believed (30.1.10), a decree was passed proroguing his *imperium* "until such time as he should bring the war in Africa to an end."

During the winter, Scipio had tried to induce Syphax to abandon his alliance with Carthage, and it was the information brought back by his envoys that the huts occupied by the Carthaginian and Numidian soldiers were built of wood or reeds, which gave him the idea of surprising the enemy camps and setting fire to them. In Polybius' account of this episode (14.1.1ff.), the initiative seems to come from Scipio himself, and he deliberately sets out to protract the negotiations by hinting that he might accept Syphax' proposal that the Carthaginians should evacuate Italy, in return for a Roman evacuation of Africa (cf. 14.1.8-10), and this is the version Livy accepts (30.3.4-7), explicitly rejecting Valerius Antias' statement that Syphax himself paid a visit to the Roman camp; Appian (*History of Libya*, 17) and Cassius Dio (17.72; Zonaras 9.12) seem to have believed that Syphax began the negotiations, though they do not mention any visit by him to the Roman camp. It would seem that some Roman historians found something distasteful in Scipio's conduct on this occasion - as well they might - but there seems little doubt that he deliberately exploited the negotiations to gain information about the Carthaginian positions. According to Polybius (14.1.13), as time went on, he began to send men of tried experience, including some of his officers, among the envoys, disguised as servants. The Carthaginians occupied two camps, one with Hasdrubal and his forces, the other with Syphax and his Numidians, ten stades (i.e. about 1.75 kilometres) apart (Polybius 14.1.14), and both lying about sixty stades (i.e. about 10.5 kilometres) from Castra Cornelia. They have been plausibly located, the one on the hill now occupied by the village of Douar Touba, the other some three kilometres to the west on a hill called Koudiat el Mabtouha. [14] They were thus both within striking distance of the Roman army, and sufficiently far apart to make it possible to launch separate attacks upon them.

At the first hint of spring (Polybius 14.2.1: i.e. the end of March or the beginning of April, 203), Scipio launched his ships, and began to construct siege-engines upon them as though about to attack Utica from the sea, and at the same time occupied the hill overlooking the city with 2000 men, partly to reinforce the impression that he was intent upon taking the place, and partly to guard against any sudden sortie from it against his camp. He also sent a further delegation to Syphax to ask if the proposed terms would be agreeable to Carthage, assuming that Syphax approved of them - the delegation was not to return until a definite answer was forthcoming. Syphax, who was genuinely delighted with what he took to be the successful outcome of his efforts to secure peace, if Polybius is to be believed (14.2.7), immediately sent word to Hasdrubal, and when he learned that the Carthaginian response was also favourable, sent Scipio's envoys back to him with the news. Thereupon Scipio sent a final delegation to tell Syphax that he personally approved and was eager for peace, but that the members of his council disagreed. He did this, Polybius says (14.2.13-4), "so that he might not appear to have broken the truce, if, while formal negotiations between them about a peace-treaty were still continuing, he should commit any act of war. But having made this declaration he considered that whatever happened, his conduct would not be open to blame."

Scipio evidently had certain qualms about his intentions, and technically put himself in the right by suggesting that his staff was not satisfied. But it appears to have been little short of a barefaced lie to give the Carthaginians the impression that he was himself satisfied, and his conduct on this occasion puts an entirely new complexion on Roman criticisms of "Punic faith". At the same time, however, Polybius does imply that Syphax and Hasdrubal were now aware that negotiations had broken down, because he says that although they were far from suspecting Scipio's true intentions, they did begin to think of ways of recommencing hostilities (14.3.3). Livy (30.4.8) goes further and says that the Carthaginians envoys who went to Scipio before his last message was sent, made some totally unacceptable demands, which gave Scipio the excuse he needed: he also makes Scipio's rejection of the terms far more explicit, and says that it was only now that he began to make overt moves against Utica (30.4.9-12). Appian (*History of*

*Libya,* 17) even alleges a treacherous attempt by Syphax to kill Masinissa, and this tradition is also recorded by Zonaras (9.12). But most of this is probably to be rejected as a Roman attempt to justify Scipio's conduct.

According to Polybius (14.3.4ff.), Scipio gave the impression of being about to attack Utica, but communicated his secret plan to his most able and trustworthy officers, bidding them lead the legions out when the bugles sounded the signal for setting the night-watches, at supper time. He also made careful enquiries of the spies he had sent to the enemy camps, and gave Masinissa overall direction of the operation. At the end of the first watch (i.e. about 9 or 10 p.m.), leaving sufficient troops to guard the camp, he advanced with the rest towards the enemy, dividing his forces into two when they drew near: Laelius and Masinissa were given half the Roman troops and all the Numidians to attack Syphax' camp, while Scipio himself took the other half of the Roman troops to attack Hasdrubal, advancing slowly so that Laelius and Masinissa would be in position to attack first. The plan worked to perfection: Laelius sent men forward to fire the huts, while keeping the main body of his troops together to cover the operation - Masinissa covered the exits from the camp. The fire spread rapidly, and the wretched Numidians, thinking it accidental, were either burnt in their huts, or trampled to death as they rushed to get clear; those who did, were cut down as they tried to escape from the camp. Meanwhile, the Carthaginian troops in the other camp, also thinking the fire in the Numidian camp accidental, rushed out, some to help, some simply to watch in growing alarm. Scipio then fell upon those who had come out, killing some and driving the others back into the camp, to which he immediately set fire, with horrifying results. Hasdrubal, at last realising that the fire in the other camp was no accident, decided to escape at all costs, and managed to get away, as did Syphax, with a few horsemen; the rest of their armies perished. Polybius gives no figures for the losses, though he may have done so in a passage lost at the end of the fifth chapter of Book 14. Livy (30.6.8) says 40,000 of the enemy were killed, and 5000 taken prisoner; Appian (*History of Libya,* 23) says 30,000 were killed, 2400 taken prisoner. But none of these figures is at all likely unless one is prepared to accept the surely exaggerated total of 93,000 men for the combined forces of Syphax and Hasdrubal, given by Polybius and Livy. Livy (30.7.1) says that Hasdrubal first made for the nearest township, with a few Africans, and was joined there by the survivors of the disaster, and this is confirmed by Polybius (14.6.2), who says that Hasdrubal first thought of defending the place, but that when he saw that the inhabitants were dismayed at the prospect of being attacked, fled with the survivors, amounting to less than 500 horse, and about 2000 foot. The town was then surrendered to Scipio, and spared by him, though he allowed his soldiers to plunder two neighbouring towns before returning to Castra Cornelia.

The Carthaginians, naturally, were dismayed by the disaster, since it left them with no forces to check Scipio should he seek to advance against Carthage itself, and when the senate met, some suggested that Hannibal should be immediately recalled, others that envoys should be sent to Scipio to ask for a truce and begin negotiations for peace. But, in the end, the more courageous decision was taken to communicate with Syphax, who had retreated to a place called Abba, and to collect the survivors of the disaster (Polybius 14.6.6-12). This decision may have been prompted by Scipio's failure to advance on Carthage as had been feared - instead, presumably thinking that the possession of a secure base was more important than a premature attack on the enemy capital or chasing after the remnants of the disaster, he recommenced the siege of Utica. Syphax, meanwhile, was heartened by the arrival of 4000 Celtiberian mercenaries at Abba, and further encouraged to remain faithful to the Carthaginian cause by his wife, while exaggerated reports of the numbers of the Celtiberians also encouraged the Carthaginians to redouble their efforts to raise more troops. Thus, within thirty days, if Polybius is to be believed (14.7.9- i.e. about the end of April, or the beginning of May, 203), an army of 30,000 Carthaginian, Numidian and Celtiberian troops had been gathered at the "Great Plains", probably the plain of Souk el Kremis, near Bou Salem, where the river Medjerda (the ancient Bagradas) is joined by four tributaries, about 110 kilometres southwest of Utica. [15] It has been argued that Polybius' figure for the Carthaginian forces is too large, since his account of the battle which followed suggests that all but the 4000 Celtiberians were routed by Scipio's cavalry. [16] But it has been pointed out that since both Syphax and Hasdrubal Gisgo were there, the implication is that most of the available Carthaginian forces had been sent to join Syphax, and that this is confirmed by the distress caused at Carthage by the subsequent defeat; Scipio, moreover, would hardly have dared to divide his forces in the way he is said to have done, if the main Carthaginian forces had still been concentrated near Carthage. [17] It is, finally, possible that Polybius' account of the battle, which as usual omits all reference to allied contingents on the Roman side, should be interpreted to mean that literally only Roman citizen troops were engaged with the Celtiberians (see below).

When the news of the enemy concentration at the Great Plains reached Scipio, he immediately left his naval forces and part of his army to cover Utica, and set out with the rest, in light marching order, to confront Syphax and Hasdrubal. This is the first time that he had ventured into the interior, and he clearly thought that the time had come to destroy the Carthaginian army in the field, before its numbers grew too large, and, if possible, as the pursuit after the battle was to show, to eliminate Syphax. Unfortunately, neither Polybius nor Livy gives any figures for his army, but both imply that he took most of it with him, and the important part played by cavalry in the battle, suggests that virtually all the cavalry was present - in any case, it would have been more use in the field than in the siege. Assuming, then, that he had originally had something in excess of 25,000 men, and that any losses he had incurred had been made up by accessions to Masinissa's force, we can probably suppose that he had with him something like 20,000 men.

He reached the Great Plains in five days, and camped on a hill within thirty stades (5.5 kilometres) of the enemy. Next day, he moved down from the hill, and, throwing out a cavalry screen, advanced to within seven stades (1200 metres) of the enemy position, where he formed a second camp. Desultory skirmishing took place on the two following days, and then, on the fourth, the two armies deployed for battle (Polybius 14.8.1-4). There are a number of puzzles in Polybius' account of the battle (14.8.5ff.), which is closely followed by Livy (30.8.5ff.): they both say that Scipio drew up his

Roman forces in the usual three-line formation, *hastati* in front, *principes* in the middle, and *triarii* in the rear, with the Italian cavalry, under Laelius, on the right, and Masinissa's Numidians on the left, and that Syphax and Hasdrubal placed their Celtiberians in the centre, with Syphax' Numidians on the left, and the Carthaginians on the right. But if it is true that the whole Carthaginian army numbered 30,000 men, and that the Celtiberians were only 4000 strong, the Roman infantry must have overlapped the Celtiberians to a considerable extent on either flank,[18] and it is certainly impossible to believe, as Polybius and Livy imply, that the Italian cavalry and Masinissa's Numidians, by themselves, were able to rout some 26,000 men, since Laelius cannot have had more than about 2000 men at most (see above, p. 203), and Masinissa, even allowing for accessions, hardly as many. In any case, a good proportion of Syphax' Numidians and the Carthaginians must have been infantry, and it would have been most unusual for cavalry to rout infantry in the manner suggested. (See Map 21).

In short, we must assume that the charge of Laelius' and Masinissa's cavalry was primarily directed against the Numidian and Carthaginian cavalry opposite them, and that the Numidian and Carthaginian infantry was mainly routed by the Roman infantry. But this still leaves the problem of what happened to the Celtiberians. Polybius (14.8.7) says that they had been placed "opposite the Roman maniples," and that, at first, they held out staunchly against "the Romans" (14.8.9). "But" he goes on (14.8.11), "at the same time as those on their wings were routed, they were swiftly surrounded by the *principes* and *triarii,* and cut to pieces on the spot, all but a few." The implication of this is that while the Celtiberians were held by the *hastati* in front, the *principes* and *triarii* were moved out to left and right and fell upon their flanks, which had been exposed by the flight of Syphax' Numidians and the Carthaginians. But this implies that the *hastati* had roughly the same frontage as the Celtiberi, and that this is why it was necessary to bring the *principes* and *triarii* up on either flank - in other words, that the Roman units belonged to a single legion of roughly the same strength as the Celtiberi, and that not all the Roman troops on the battlefield were involved.

A possible answer to the problem is that Syphax' Numidians on the Carthaginian left were roughly as numerous as the Celtiberians and Carthaginians combined - which is not at all improbable in itself - so that when Scipio drew up his forces in what was probably the normal Roman manner (see above, p. 80), with a legion on the right, then its attached allied cohorts, then his second legion, and the remaining allied cohorts on the left, the right-hand legion and its allied cohorts roughly stretched along the front of Syphax' Numidians, the left-hand legion came opposite the Celtiberians, and its attached allied cohorts and Masinissa's Numidians were left to confront the Carthaginian troops, both infantry and cavalry, on the Carthaginian right. Thus, after the rout of Syphax' Numidians and the Carthaginians, the Celtiberians were confronted by a single Roman legion, and it was the *hastati, principes* and *triarii* from this who were involved in their destruction. If this is correct, the manoeuvre carried out by this legion, though on a relatively small scale, represented another tactical innovation on Scipio's part - presuming him to have been responsible for it: instead of refusing his centre as at Ilipa, he here used his *hastati* to pin the enemy centre, while bringing up his *principes* and *triarii* to attack the enemy flanks. The danger was that the *hastati,* who would have been outnumbered, would give way before the *principes* and *triarii* could complete their manoeuvre, but the Celtiberians were, presumably, already dispirited by the flight of their Numidian and Carthaginian allies, and although fighting with the courage of despair, could not break the *hastati* before being taken in flank and rear.

The courageous fight put up by the Celtiberians nevertheless enabled Syphax and his cavalry to make their way back to their own land, while Hasdrubal and the Carthaginian survivors fled to Carthage. But by his bold march to the Great Plains, Scipio had effectively driven a wedge between the Numidians and Carthage, and he now set about exploiting the situation. After deliberations with his council, he himself decided to remain in the region of the Great Plains to overrun the many small towns and villages in the neighbourhood, while Masinissa and Laelius, with the Numidians and part of the Roman forces, should pursue Syphax (Polybius 14.9.1-5). Meanwhile, there was renewed consternation at Carthage, but, in the end, the advice of the more courageous members of the senate was again accepted - to launch the fleet against the Roman forces besieging Utica, and to recall Hannibal. At the same time, however, steps were to be taken to put the city into readiness to stand a siege, and consideration given to the sort of terms they would be prepared to accept in order to bring the war to an end (Polybius 14.9.5-11).

While the Carthaginians proceeded to act upon their decisions, Scipio withdrew from the Great Plains, his army laden with plunder. The time had clearly now come to bring direct pressure to bear on Carthage, so Scipio sent his plunder on to Castra Cornelia, and himself led his victorious army on Tunis, occupying the town on the flight of its garrison: Tunis lies only about 120 stades (i.e. just over 21 kilometres) from Carthage, at the base of the peninsula on which Carthage itself lay, so that Scipio now effectively cut Carthage off from her own hinterland. But hardly had he occupied Tunis when the Carthaginian fleet was observed putting to sea, and he had to hurry back to Utica in case his forces there were taken by surprise. His problem was that his warships were now equipped with various siege-engines for the assault on Utica, and were there- fore in no state to fight the Carthaginian fleet. His solution was to create a wall of ships to withstand the Carthaginian attack, by anchoring his warships in a line and surrounding them with transports three and four deep: masts and yards were lowered and used to lash the ships together (Polybius 14.10.2-12). At this point Polybius' narrative breaks off, but Livy (30.10.7) adds that 1000 picked men were stationed on the transports with a large supply of missiles.

Meanwhile, the Carthaginian fleet, far from hurrying to take the Romans by surprise, spent a whole day in getting from Carthage to a port Livy says the Africans called "Rusucmon" (30.10.9), which probably lay near the modern Porto Farina. Next day, at dawn, they put to sea and drew up their ships in battle array, expecting the Romans to come out and fight, and only when they realised that they were not going to do so did they proceed to attack the transports. Here, too, they made little headway at first, since the Roman merchantmen were higher than their warships, but at last they managed to grapple the ships in the first line with iron hooks fastened on poles, and were able to drag some sixty transports off in triumph, the Roman defenders just managing to scramble back onto their second line of transports in time. As Livy remarks, the joy at Carthage was greater than the success warranted, but the more grateful since here was a success at last after so many disasters (30.10.20-1). But the success really only serves to emphasise how totally the Carthaginian navy had hitherto failed to do any damage to Scipio.

Any dismay the Romans may have felt at the threat now posed by the Carthaginian navy was, in any case, soon dissipated by the arrival of Syphax as a prisoner. After the battle of the Great Plains, Laelius and Masinissa had pursued him into Numidia, the Maesulii joyfully welcoming Masinissa as king, and rapidly ejecting Syphax' officers and garrisons. But Syphax' own people, the Masaesulii, did not desert him, and he had soon gathered fresh forces, which, Livy says (30.11.5), were as numerous as those he had previously had at his disposal, though now composed of raw and untrained troops. With these he confronted Laelius and Masinissa, and a scrambling cavalry-skirmish took place, in which, at first, the superior numbers of the Masaesulii told. But when Roman infantry - presumably light infantry since they seem to be contrasted with the legions in Livy's account (30.11.6ff.) - was thrown into the gaps between their own cavalry squadrons, the balance began to swing in their favour, and at the approach of the infantry of the line, the Masaesulii fled. Syphax, riding up to the Roman line, either in despair, or in a last effort to shame his own men into standing and fighting, had his horse wounded under him, and was overpowered.

Immediately, after the victory, Masinissa rode hard for Syphax' capital, Cirta, taking the captured Syphax with him to demonstrate the completeness of his triumph, while Laelius followed more slowly with the infantry, and at the sight of their king in chains, the leading men of Cirta surrendered the town without a fight. At the doors of the palace, according to Livy (30.12.11), Masinissa was met by Sophonisba, who begged him not to let her fall into Roman hands, and Masinissa was so taken with her youth and beauty, as to go through a ceremony of marriage with her, much to the annoyance of Laelius, who wished to include her among the other prisoners. But in the end Masinissa persuaded him to refer the matter to Scipio. The latter, when the prisoners reached his camp near Utica, greeted Syphax courteously, but when Masinissa and Laelius arrived some time later, pointed out to the former that Sophonisba was technically Rome's prisoner, even if she had not been Hasdrubal's daughter (Livy 30. 14.4ff.). Thereupon Masinissa is said to have sent a slave to Sophonisba with poison, which she promptly took (Livy 30.15.1ff.). This romantic story has been doubted, [19] but there is nothing intrinsically improbable in it, and it may be true. Scipio is also alleged (Livy 30.15.11ff.) to have paraded his troops, and in their presence addressed Masinissa as king, presenting him with a number of honorific gifts, including an ivory staff. Later, when Laelius reached Rome with Syphax and the other prisoners, and envoys from Masinissa, the Senate is said to have approved Scipio's use of the title "king" and the giving of gifts (Livy 30.17.12). All this, too, has been doubted, [20] but it finds some confirmation in a bronze coin bearing Masinissa's name, with a staff or sceptre behind the image of the king's head. [21] The ivory sceptre presented to Masinissa was, no doubt, primarily intended as a symbol of royalty, but it must also have been pointed out to the king, if he did not know it already, that the Latin word for a staff or sceptre - *scipio* - was the word from which Scipio's family derived its name, allegedly because an ancestor had led his blind father about as though he was the blind man's staff (Macrobius, *Saturae* 1.6.26).

The news of Syphax' defeat and capture had a profound effect upon Carthage, and finally tilted the balance in its senate against those who had advocated a continuation of the war: even if they exaggerate the numbers involved, it is clear from Polybius and Livy that Carthage had come increasingly to rely upon Numidian support, and the Carthaginian leaders seem to have felt that continued resistance, without such support, was futile. The result was that the thirty senators who formed the inner council, were sent to Scipio's camp, now apparently once more at Tunis (cf. Polybius 15.1.6), to sue for peace (Livy 30.16.1ff.). Here they blamed Hannibal and his supporters for the war, which has suggested to some that we should see in them representatives of the land-owning interests of Carthage, long alleged to have been opposed to Hannibal's family. [22] There may be some truth in this, but even if it is not true, to place the blame for the war on Hannibal was an obvious move to placate the Roman general. Scipio's reply was that he was willing to consider terms, and he proposed that Carthage hand over all prisoners, deserters and runaway slaves, withdraw her armies from Italy and Cisalpine Gaul, cease to interfere in Spain, evacuate all the islands between Italy and Africa, surrender all save twenty warships, and agree to supply the Roman army with 500,000 measures of wheat and 300,000 measures of barley (Livy 30.16.10-11). In addition, he demanded an indemnity, though Livy found that his sources conflicted on the sum, some saying 5000 talents, some 5000 pounds of silver, some double pay for the Roman troops in Africa (Livy 30.16.12). Appian (*History of Libya,* 32) adds clauses forbidding the Carthaginians to recruit mercenaries, restricting their territory to the land within what were called the "Phoenician trenches" (see below, p. 228), and granting Masinissa both his own ancestral dominion and that of Syphax. Scipio gave the Carthaginians three days to decide whether to accept or reject these terms, and they promptly accepted them, partly, Livy suggests (30.16.14-5), to allow time for Hannibal to cross from Italy. An armistice was then concluded, and envoys sent to Rome, taking with them, Livy says, a few prisoners, deserters and runaway slaves, for the sake of appearances.

It is unfortunate that we do not have Polybius' account of these negotiations with Scipio and of subsequent events up to the alleged capture by the Carthaginians of transports carrying supplies to Scipio's army, probably early in 202. Livy (30.21.11ff.) says that when the Carthaginian envoys reached Rome and were given audience by the Senate in the temple of Bellona, they too tried to shift the whole burden of guilt for the war onto Hannibal's shoulders, even arguing that the senate and people of Carthage had never broken the treaty with Rome, and asking that the terms of the treaty concluded with C. Lutatius Catulus at the end of the First Punic War, should stand! But when members of the Senate began to question them about this treaty, they claimed that they were too young to remember it. This caused an outburst of indignation, and when the Carthaginian envoys had withdrawn, after M. Livius Salinator had proposed that debate be deferred until the consul, C. Servilius Geminus, could be present, and Q. Caecilius Metellus that the decision should be left to Scipio, M. Valerius Laevinus proposed that the envoys should be ordered to depart, and that written instructions should be sent to

Scipio not to slacken his war efforts. Laelius and Q. Fulvius Gillo, one of Scipio's officers who had escorted the Carthaginian envoys to Rome, added their influence to the view that the peace-terms should be rejected, by arguing that Scipio's hopes of peace had been based on the assumption that Hannibal and Mago would not be recalled to Africa - as it was, they alleged, the Carthaginians were only waiting for the arrival of the brothers to renew the war. Thus, in the end, Livy says (30.23.8), Laevinus' proposal was carried.

But Livy's version of what happened can hardly stand against Polybius' explicit assertions (15.1.3-4) that the Senate and People of Rome did ratify the peace-terms, and is clearly the product of a Roman tradition designed to allay any possible suspicion that Rome was guilty of renewing the war after a solemn treaty had been concluded. Appian (*History of Libya,* 31-2) says that the Senate decided to leave the decision to Scipio, that he concluded peace along the lines Livy says he had originally proposed, though, as we have seen, with some additions, and that it was while both sides were waiting for the exchange of oaths ratifying the treaty that the violation by Carthage took place. Cassius Dio (17.74) says that the Romans would not receive the Carthaginian envoys sent to discuss the terms put to them by Scipio, until Hannibal and Mago had left Italy, that when they did grant the envoys an audience after Hannibal and Mago had departed, there was still considerable debate, but that in the end they did ratify the treaty on the terms Scipio had proposed. Finally, a second century papyrus has been found (*Rylands Papyri* iii no. 491), containing a fragment of a contemporary or near-contemporary account of the Second Punic War, which bears upon these negotiations, but does nothing to resolve the problems: the author was clearly more pro-Carthaginian than our other sources, but his omission of any reference to the alleged violation of the truce by the Carthaginians, can hardly be used to prove that no such violation took place, against the tradition recorded by Polybius (cf.15.1.1), and the other sources. [23]

It is impossible to reconcile these conflicting accounts, but we should probably accept Polybius' and Cassius Dio's plain statements that the peace-treaty was ratified, and it is possible that Cassius Dio is right when he says that ratification was delayed until Hannibal and Mago had left Italy - Livy, indeed, seems to have believed that the Carthaginian envoys did not even arrive until after news had reached Rome of the departure of Hannibal and Mago (cf. 30.21.1 and 11). Certainly, the most important consequence of the negotiations, whether or not a peace-treaty was formally concluded, was the final departure of the Carthaginian armies from Italy. Mago had landed near Genoa in 205, as we have seen (above, p. 196), and had set about recruiting troops, apart from receiving reinforcements from Carthage. But although Livy (29.36.10-12) says that much of Etruria was ready to go over to him, it was not until 203 that he had evidently felt strong enough to advance, and then he had been brought to battle in the territory of the Insubres by the proconsul, M. Cornelius Cethegus, and the praetor, P. Quinctilius Varus, and heavily defeated (Livy 30.18). The details of the battle have been questioned, [24] but that there was a battle can hardly be doubted. Striving to rally his men, Mago was wounded in the thigh, and when his troops saw him being carried from the field, their retreat turned into a rout. Nevertheless, Mago had been able to extricate much of his army, and to make his way back to the coast, and it was here that he was met by envoys from Carthage, summoning him back to Africa. Livy believed that Mago himself died of his wound on the return voyage, and that some of his ships were captured by the Roman fleet based on Sardinia (30.19.5-6), but it would appear that most of his forces reached Africa in safety.

Hannibal, meanwhile, had also received his summons to return. Since his encounter with Scipio before Locri in 205, he had found his freedom of action even in Bruttium severely limited, although no real attempt had been made to bring him to battle. In 204 he had defeated the consul, P. Sempronius Tuditanus, in a running fight near Croton, but Livy alleges that when Tuditanus was joined by the proconsul, P. Licinius Crassus, their combined forces had been able to defeat Hannibal in turn (29.36.4-9). Later that same year, according to Livy (29.38.1), Tuditanus had gone on to storm Clampetia, on the west coast of Bruttium, now Amantea, and Consentia (Cosenza), Pandosia (near Mendocino), and other small towns in the area had surrendered to Rome. But since he also reports the surrender of Consentia and Clampetia, among other places, to the consul, Cn .Servilius Caepio, in 203 (30.19.10), some confusion must have arisen, and this casts doubts on his further statement (30.19.11) that Caepio won a battle near Croton - he admits that "reports of the battle are obscure," and hints that Valerius Antias may have invented it. Nevertheless, from a purely military point of view, Hannibal cannot have found his recall as unwelcome as Livy rhetorically alleges (30.20. 1-4), though we may well believe that his departure was tinged with sadness, and even that he wondered whether he had not, after all, made a mistake in not marching on Rome after Cannae (Livy 30.20.5-9). Livy also claims that he abandoned what he calls the "useless crowd" of his soldiers, distributing them among the few Bruttian towns which remained loyal to him, and butchered Italians who refused to go, in the temple of Juno Lacinia where they had taken refuge (30.20.5-6). Appian (*Hannibalic War*, 58-9) has even more lurid tales to tell of the prelude to Hannibal's departure, but may preserve a fragment of truth when he says that he slaughtered about 4000 horses and a large number of pack-animals, for these would have been difficult to transport by sea. Unfortunately, we do not know how many men Hannibal took to Africa with him, but his dispositions at Zama suggest that there may have been about 12,000 of them.

Hannibal and Mago probably left Italy in the autumn of 203, and Hannibal himself had almost certainly landed - at Leptis Minor (now Lamta), between Hadrumentum and Thapsus (Livy 30.25.11) - before the incidents which led to the renewal of war, and this goes far to explain why the Carthaginians acted as they did. According to Livy (30.24. 5ff.), a convoy of 200 transports, escorted by 30 warships, under the propraetor, Cn. Octavius, crossing to Africa from Sicily, was first held up by adverse winds, and then scattered when the wind changed and started to blow towards Africa: the warships managed to reach the promontory of Apollo (i.e. the cape elsewhere called the "promontory of the Beautiful One", now Cap Farina), but most of the transports, which would not have had oars to help them, were blown to the island of Aegimurus (now Djeziret Djamur), some to the *Calidae Aquae* (Warm Springs, now Korbous) on the west coast of Cap Bon. All this took place in full sight of Carthage and caused great excitement: people flocked into the main square of the city, and when the magistrates summoned a meeting of the senate, demanded that this prize should not be let slip. Presumably, there was a food shortage in the city, caused partly by the presence of the Roman army at Tunis, partly by the necessity to furnish Scipio with the enormous quantities of wheat and barley he had demanded. The upshot was that the Carthaginian senate, yielding to popular demand, ordered Hasdrubal to take fifty warships and collect the scattered transports (probably early in 202).

It is at this point that the surviving fragments of Polybius take up the story again: according to him (15.1.1ff.), Scipio was seriously disturbed both by the loss of supplies to his own forces and the consequent gain to Carthage, but also at the threat to peace. His immediate response was to send three envoys to Carthage to discuss what had happened, and to inform the Carthaginians that the Senate and People of Rome had ratified the peace treaty, despatches to this effect having lately reached him. The Roman envoys first addressed the Carthaginian senate, and were then brought before the popular assembly: here they expressed amazement that the Carthaginians, who had sued for peace, should now break the treaty, and warned them against relying on Hannibal and his army. According to Livy (30.25.3), the envoys only escaped molestation by the populace by appealing to the magistrates, but Polybius (15.2.4) says merely that the assembly voted to dismiss them without an answer. Polybius goes on to say that the plot to attack the envoys on their return to Castra Cornelia was the work of those among Carthage's politicians who were determined to renew the conflict at all costs, and who sent a messenger to Hasdrubal, then commanding the Carthaginian fleet near Utica, to attack the envoys' ship. But Livy (30.25.5) says that the Carthaginian admiral either acted on secret orders from Carthage, or on his own initiative. But both go on to tell much the same story. The quinquereme bearing the Roman envoys was given an escort of two Carthaginian triremes, which were ordered, according to Polybius (15.2.8), to return as soon as they passed the mouth of the river Macar (i.e. the Bagradas). Then, as the Roman quinquereme continued on its way, three Carthaginian triremes - quadriremes, according to Livy (30.25.5) - suddenly bore down upon her. The quinquereme managed to avoid their rams, and her crew gallantly fought off attempts at boarding, eventually managing to beach her where they could see Roman foragers running down to the shore to their assistance, though not before many on board had been killed. Polybius (15.2.15) says the envoys themselves miraculuously survived, but Appian (*History of Libya,* 34), probably following a later Roman source, claims that some were killed.

Hostilities now commenced again, with even greater bitterness, Scipio, in particular, marching into the interior and taking town after town, refusing to allow surrender, and selling the inhabitants as slaves, though when Laelius and Fulvius Gillo returned from Rome, escorting the Carthaginian ambassadors, he ordered them to be returned, unharmed, to Carthage (Polybius 15.4.5ff.). Anxiety about his own position may have added to Scipio's bitter mood: according to Livy (30.24.1-3), Cn. Servilius Caepio, one of the consuls of 203/2, had actually crossed to Sicily towards the end of his year of office, with the intention of invading Africa, and had only been stopped by the appointment of a dictator to restrain him. This story has been doubted because the *fasti Capitolini* record that the dictator, P. Sulpicius Galba, was appointed to hold the elections, and some of Livy's sources apparently said the same (cf. 30.26.12). [25] But although it is most improbable that Galba was appointed simply to restrain Servilius Caepio, it is not inconceivable that, having been appointed to hold the elections, he did make use of his *imperium maius* to restrain the consul. Then, after the new consuls, M. Servilius Geminus and Ti. Claudius Nero, had taken office on March 15th, 202, they raised the question of the consular commands in the Senate, both hoping to be assigned to Africa, and although due to the efforts of Q. Caecilius Metellus, the decision was left to the people, and they decided for Scipio, the Senate nevertheless decreed that the consuls should draw lots for Africa: according to Livy (30.27.5), Ti. Claudius Nero was the lucky man, and he was assigned a fleet of fifty quinqueremes to take to Africa, there to act with an authority equal to that of Scipio. The details of this story are again unlikely to be true, since the Senate had already decided, at the beginning of 203, if we are to believe Livy (30.1.10), that Scipio's *imperium* should be prorogued until he brought the war in Africa to a conclusion, and therefore had no need to refer the matter to the people; and if we can believe that opposition to Scipio in the Senate was such that Metellus and Scipio's other supporters decided to try to engineer a popular vote in his favour, then we can hardly believe that the Senate decided to ignore it.[26] On the other hand, the story does hang together, after a fashion, on the assumption that a small majority in the Senate was opposed to Scipio. However, it is, perhaps, more likely that the decision to appoint Ti. Claudius Nero to assist Scipio in command of a fleet, was not so much aimed at diminishing Scipio's power as prompted by the renewal of hostilities, and, in particular, the increased activity of the Carthaginian navy, which seems, at this time, to have taken up a station near Utica (cf. Polybius 15.2.7), from which it could threaten Scipio's supply lines. In the event, in any case, Claudius Nero was so slow in making his preparations (Livy 30.38.7), and, when he did set out, was so delayed by storms, that winter was upon him - that of 202/1 - before ever he got to Africa: when his *imperium* expired on March 14th, 201, it was not renewed (Livy 30.39.1-3), and by that time, of course, Zama had been fought and won.

Scipio was probably made well aware of at least some of this by Laelius, when the latter returned to Africa, and his campaign of terror and destruction in the hinterland of Carthage may have been partly designed to provoke the Carthaginians into giving battle to him. On the other hand, however, he was unwilling to face Hannibal until rejoined by Masinissa and his forces, particularly his splendid cavalry, and sent a constant stream of appeals to the Numidian king (Polybius 15.4.3). Masinissa, at this time, was engaged in trying to secure control of his father's kingdom and as much of Syphax' dominion as he could win, with the aid of a small Roman force. But Hannibal, too, was having difficulty in raising cavalry - difficulty which would have been all the more acute if, as Appian says (*Hannibalic War,* 59), he had been forced to dispose of most of his cavalry horses before leaving Italy. Eventually, according to Polybius (15.3.5-7), he prevailed upon a relative of Syphax, one Tychaios, reputed to command the best cavalry in Africa, to join him. Appian (*History of Libya,* 33) may refer to Tychaios when he says that Hannibal allied himself to the chief of a tribe called the "Areakidai", but it is very improbable that Hannibal had 4000 cavalrymen shot as deserters from Syphax' army, and handed their horses over to his own troops, even though this would have provided exactly the same number of mounts as Appian says he had destroyed! Appian, however, may be right in saying that Hannibal was also joined by "Mesotylos" who is presumably the usurper

Mazaetullus mentioned by Livy in his account of Masinissa's earlier adventures (29.29. 8ff.), but although Appian adds Syphax' son, Vermina, to Hannibal's allies at this time, Livy (30.36.7) seems to have believed that he only came to Carthage's aid after the battle of Zama.

Eventually the constant appeals from Carthage, provoked by Scipio's whirlwind campaign, forced Hannibal to move from Hadrumentum (Sousse), which he had made his base, and advance to a place Polybius calls Zama (15.5.3), lying five days' march west (i.e. southwest) of Carthage. Unfortunately, there seem to have been at least three, if not four, places in ancient Tunisia called Zama, but it seems likely that the one referred to here lay at Seba Biar, about thirteen kilometres east of Zanfour. [27] In any case, although Cornelius Nepos (*Hannibal* 6.3) says the subsequent battle was fought "at Zama" (*apud Zamam*), and this name is now so traditionally associated with it that it would be mere pedantry to give it another name (e.g., Margaron or Naraggara), it is clear from Polybius' narrative that the battle was not fought there, but some distance away, and within about 30 stades (i.e. about five kilometres) of Scipio's camp. It is, thus, the site of Scipio's camp which fixes the site of the battlefield, not Hannibal's camp at Zama. But, unfortunately, the site of Scipio's camp is also uncertain. The manuscripts of Polybius say it was at a place called "Margaron" (15.5.4), which is otherwise unknown, but Livy (30.29.9) says it was at Naraggara, which is known, and which is usually located at the modern Sidi Youssef. Modern commentators are of the opinion that Naraggara is probably what Polybius also wrote, [28] but this creates the difficulty that the area around Sidi Youssef is too hilly to fit the requirements of the battle. There are, basically, two ways round the problem, neither wholly satisfactory: one is that Scipio's camp was located at a place called Naraggara, but that this was not at Sidi Youssef; the other is that the camp really did lie at the otherwise unknown Margaron, and that Livy or his sources assimilated this to the slightly better known Naraggara. It is, thus, not possible to locate the site of this decisive battle with any certainty, but a plausible hypothesis is that it was fought in the plain of Draa el Metnan, a little south of the road (P5) from Sidi Youssef to El Kef (the ancient Sicca Veneria) and near its junction with the road from Kasserine to El Kef (P 17). [29] The difficulty with this is that the site is some twenty-seven kilometres from Sidi Youssef, and so cannot be reconciled with Polybius' statement that Scipio's camp before the battle was at Margaron (15.5.4), if Margaron was at Sidi Youssef, but, as was argued above, this was not necessarily the case. (See Map 20).

However, assuming that the battle was fought somewhere near El Kef, the general strategy of the campaign is clear. Following the breakdown of the peace-negotiations, Scipio had advanced up the Bagradas, past the site of his victory at the Great Plains, partly to provoke Hannibal to battle, but mainly to safeguard his communications with Masinissa, and to ensure that Hannibal did not interpose himself between the Roman army and its Numidian allies. Hannibal's advance westward to Zama may have been designed to suggest that he intended to place his army between Scipio and his bases on the coast, and thus either induce him to retreat to the coast, in which case Hannibal could then have turned upon Masinissa and dealt with him separately, or to force him to fight before Masinissa joined him. But, if so, why did Hannibal then continue to advance westwards towards Scipio and by taking up a position only some five kilometres away (Polybius 15.6.2), virtually ensure that a battle would take place?

The answer may be that Hannibal had reason to believe that Scipio was still without Numidian support, though, as it turned out, he was wrong. For, according to Polybius (15.5.4ff.), from his camp at Zama, Hannibal had sent three spies to ascertain Scipio's whereabouts - he had not yet moved to "Margaron" - and to reconnoitre his camp. These men had been captured, but instead of executing them, Scipio had ordered them to be shown round his camp, and then to be sent back to Hannibal under escort. This story has been doubted, [30] because it is told so often of ancient commanders, beginning with Xerxes in 481 (Herodotus 7.146.7). But the stories could be true, in many instances, when, as was the case with Xerxes, the commander in question wanted to impress his enemies with the magnitude of his forces, and the story could be true of Scipio, though for a different reason: if he had reason to believe that Masinissa would soon join him - as indeed he did - he might have been quite willing for Hannibal's spies to make careful note of the absence of Numidians in his camp. It is less easy to believe that Hannibal was so struck by Scipio's action that he conceived the idea of arranging a meeting with his opponent, and sent a herald to his camp to propose it. But if Hannibal now thought that he had an opportunity to bring Scipio to battle before Masinissa arrived, he might well have proposed the meeting as a cover for his plans.

Scipio's response to the proposal, according to Polybius (15.5.10), was to send the herald back with a message that he would shortly inform Hannibal of a suitable place and time, and it was only on the day after the herald had left, if Polybius is to be trusted (15.5.12), that Masinissa at last arrived. It is true that Livy (30.29.4) says that the captured spies had already reported Masinissa's arrival to Hannibal, but Polybius' narrative is, as so often, precise, detailed and clear, and should be preferred - if it is true, even after the return of his herald, Hannibal still did not know of Masinissa's arrival. It is thus not surprising that when he received the promised further message from Scipio saying that he was now ready for the meeting, he should have broken camp, and advanced from Zama towards Scipio's new position at "Margaron" (Polybius 15.6.1-2).

With the arrival of Masinissa, Scipio must now have been confident that he could meet Hannibal on something like equal terms: Polybius says (15.5.12) that Masinissa brought with him 6000 foot and 6000 horse, but Livy (30.29.4) says 4000 horse, and this is probably what Polybius wrote. These reinforcements probably brought his numbers up to over 30,000 men in all, and it was now, according to Polybius (15.5.14), that he advanced to Margaron, and camped there in a suitable place, within a javelin's throw of water, perhaps on the hill now called Koudiat el Behaina, which has a spring on its southern slope. [31] Hannibal's position, thirty stades away (Polybius 15.6.2), could then have been on the hill of Koudiat Bougrine, about five and a half kilometres south-east of Koudiat el Behaina: Polybius says that Hannibal's position had the disadvantage of not being within easy reach of water, and this is true of Koudiat Bougrine. [32]

It was between the two camps that the famous meeting between the two generals took place, only an interpreter being present (Polybius 15.6.3). This detail has been thought to cast doubt on the story, [33] since both Scipio and Hannibal spoke Greek, and Hannibal also perhaps spoke Latin, albeit badly (cf. Livy 22.13.6, Zonaras 8.24). But both men would have wanted to make sure, on this occasion, that they were not misunderstood, and each would probably have preferred to speak in his own language. Hannibal, in Polybius' version - which possibly derived from the Scipionic family tradition - spoke first, saying that he wished their two countries had never gone to war, and that now they ought to try to make peace; he adjured Scipio not to be too confident, citing his own case as an example of how rapidly fortunes could change, and ended by saying that Rome should retain Sicily, Sardinia and Spain, and have in addition all the islands between Italy and Africa, and that on this basis they should make peace (Polybius 15.6.4-7.9). Scipio countered by asserting that Carthage was responsible for both wars, and that no one was more aware than he of the fickleness of fortune. But as to the terms Hannibal proposed, he declared that although they might have been acceptable if Hannibal had left Italy before the Romans invaded Africa, they were not so now when he and his army controlled most of the country. He also pointed out that Hannibal had omitted all mention of conditions like the return of prisoners, the surrender of warships and the payment of an indemnity, which the Carthaginians had agreed upon before their treacherous violation of the peace: why, after that, should he be prepared to accept less onerous terms? He ended by demanding that the Carthaginians be prepared to place themselves at Rome's mercy, or to fight (Polybius 15.8).

Apart from the somewhat conventional references by both men to the variability of fortune, there is nothing here to excite disquiet, and both men may have gone to the meeting with a genuine desire to avoid further bloodshed, even if they really believed that a battle was inevitable. Hannibal, who by now must have known that Scipio had, after all, been joined by Masinissa, may still have thought that it was worth trying to secure more favourable terms than those agreed upon after the capture of Syphax, assuming that Scipio would be anxious to avoid the hazards of fighting a pitched battle with a general of his reputation. Equally, Scipio may, indeed, have been prepared to avoid a battle if he could secure the Carthaginian's agreement to the same sort of terms as had been offered before, for these amounted to virtual surrender, and were, essentially, the terms upon which peace was concluded after Zama. Thus, although neither man appears to have been willing to give way on essentials, each might have had his reasons for thinking that peace could be made without a battle. At the same time, we must, surely, make some allowance for natural curiosity, and even if both really believed that a battle was inevitable, they might each have been anxious to size up the other. But as they had, probably, both expected, the meeting came to nothing, and next day, at daybreak, they led their forces out to battle (Polybius 15.9.2).

It is not possible to determine exactly how large the opposing armies were, since Polybius does not say. But he does say that more than 20,000 were killed on the Carthaginian side, not many fewer than this taken prisoner (15.14.9), and that very few escaped (15.14.9), and this means that he believed that Hannibal had, in all, something like 40,000 men. Elsewhere (15.11.1), he says that there were 12,000 infantry in his first line, and, on the assumption that the three lines were of approximately equal strength, this would mean that the Carthaginian army consisted of 36,000 infantry and 4000 cavalry. Appian (*History of Libya*, 40) gives Hannibal 50,000 men in all, but neither Livy, nor Cassius Dio (Zonaras) gives any figures. It is even more difficult to determine the size of the Roman army, since Polybius does not give any figures for it, except for the statement that Masinissa had brought 6000 foot and 4000 horse, assuming that is what he wrote (15.5.12: see above, p. 219). But Appian (*History of Libya*, 41) gives Scipio 23,000 Roman and Italian foot, and 1500 horse, and this may well be right - it would fit with what we concluded to be the likely total for his forces when he left Sicily (see above, p. 203). A difficulty is that Polybius implies that at the beginning of the final stage of the battle, Hannibal's third line was about equivalent in strength to Scipio's remaining Roman and Italian infantry (15.14.6). But we may suppose that he was reckoning without the *velites,* and we must allow for fairly heavy losses among the *hastati.* Thus the Roman and Italian infantry may, by then, have been only about 16,000 strong, and although we have suggested that Hannibal's third line had originally consisted of some 12,000 men, like the first, it may have contained more, and, in any case, he may be presumed to have been able to rally some of his defeated first and second lines, and to have placed them on either wing of his veterans (cf. Polybius 15.13.9-10). If, then, Scipio did have 23,000 Roman and Italian infantry at the beginning of the battle, and 1500 Roman and Italian cavalry, Masinissa's force would have brought the infantry total up to 29,000, the cavalry to 5500, and we should probably add the 600 horse said by Appian (*History of Libya,* 41) to have been brought by another Numidian chieftain named Dacamas. Thus Scipio would have been outnumbered in infantry (29,000 to 36,000), but would have had a substantial superiority in cavalry (6100 to 4000), and this is borne out by the important part cavalry played in his victory.

Scipio drew up his Roman troops - and it must be assumed that when Polybius refers to "Romans" here, as elsewhere, he includes the allied contingents - in the usual three-line formation. But instead of placing the maniples of *principes* behind the gaps between the maniples of *hastati,* he placed them directly behind the maniples of *hastati,* thus leaving corridors right through his lines, since the maniples of *triarii* were, as usual, directly behind those of the *hastati* (Polybius 15.9.7). The intervals between the maniples of *hastati,* in the front line, were filled with what Polybius (15.9.9) calls the "*speirai*" of *velites*: this is the term he usually uses of maniples, and this is, roughly, the meaning here, for, although the *velites* were not divided into maniples, they were attached, in equal numbers, to the maniples of *hastati, principes* and *triarii.* Thus, in the standard legion (cf. Polybius 6.21.9), there were 40 *velites* attached to each maniple. Presumably, then, Polybius means that at Zama the three detachments of *velites* belonging to each of the groups of three maniples placed one behind the other - i.e. to each cohort (see above, p. 147)- were stationed together in the intervals between the maniples of *hastati.* This would make sense, for, in the standard legion, the *velites* of each cohort would have been of the same strength as a maniple of *principes,* and we may assume that the gaps left between the maniples of *hastati* were such that they could be filled by the maniples of *principes,* when the legion was drawn up in the checker-board formation. Scipio's legions at Zama would not, of course, have been any longer of standard strength, but it is to be presumed that the relative strengths of the various units remained roughly the same. In this instance, too, the normal checker-board formation was abandoned, apparently to provide corridors down which it was hoped to usher Hannibal's elephants, and the *velités* were ordered, if forced back by the elephants, to retire to the rear along these corridors, if they had time - if not, to withdraw sideways between the lines (Polybius 15.9.10). Finally, on the right wing Scipio stationed all the Numidians Masinissa had brought with him (Polybius 15.9.8), presumably with the cavalry outside the infantry, and Laelius and the Italian cavalry were placed on the left wing. We do not know where Dacamas and his force of Numidian cavalry was stationed: it would have been natural to put them with Masinissa's cavalry, but possibly they were placed with Laelius' Italian cavalry, since otherwise the cavalry on the left would have been far less numerous than that on the right.

Hannibal also drew up his army in three lines, the first composed of 12,000 Ligurian, Celtic, Balearic and Moorish mercenaries (Polybius 15.11.1). Of these the Balearic islanders and the Moors were usually used as skirmishers, armed with slings and throwing-spears, and Appian (*History of Libya,* 40) speaks of Celts and Ligurians mixed with "archers and slingers, Moors and Baliares." It is, thus, possible that we should regard the first line as a mixture of skirmishers and infantry of the line, for the view that Hannibal had trained the Baliares and Moors as ordinary infantry of the line, [34] is most improbable, and yet Polybius does speak of this first line as though it was not simply a skirmishing line (cf. 15.12.7-8). Though none of our sources say so, most of the Ligurians and Celts in this line must have belonged to Mago's army, and presumably some of the Baliares had too, though they also may have included the 2000 sent to Carthage by Mago in 206 (Livy 28.37.9). Behind this first line, according to Polybius (15.11.2), Hannibal placed his "Libyans" and "Carthaginians", i.e. levies from the native population of the Carthaginian hinterland and from Carthage itself. Livy (30.23.5) says that the second line also included what he calls "a legion of Macedonians," presumably the 4000 soldiers under Sopater he mentions earlier (30.26.3), and whom he later alleges were captured by the Romans (30.42.4-5). But in view of Polybius' silence, we can probably exclude them from the reckoning: the tradition about their presence at Zama probably derives from Roman propaganda against Philip V of Macedonia. Hannibal's third line consisted of the soldiers who had come with him from Italy, a stade (i.e. 178 metres) behind the second line (Polybius 15.11.2). Livy (30.33.6) and Appian (*History of Libya,* 40) make these troops mainly Bruttians, but they clearly included all the survivors of his Italian army, even, presumably, some of the Africans, Numidians and Spaniards who had marched with him from Cartagena, and the Celts who had joined him in the Po valley - as Polybius says later (15.16.4), they were his best troops. On his left Hannibal placed his Numidian cavalry, opposite Masinissa's Numidians, on his right the Carthaginian cavalry, opposite Laelius and the Roman and Italian horse: we do not know how numerous Hannibal's cavalry was, but it possibly numbered about 4000 in all (see above, pp. 220-1), and we can probably assume that there were more Numidians than Carthaginians. Finally, in front of his whole force, Hannibal placed his elephants, eighty in number (Polybius 15.11.1). Both generals addressed their troops - in Polybius' versions (15.10 and 15.11.7-12), somewhat platitudinously, though he does add the surely authentic detail that Hannibal had to rely on the mercenary officers to address their men in their own languages, while he himself concentrated on reminding his veterans of all they had done together, even pointing out to them that Scipio's army included men from the army they had beaten at Cannae.

The battle opened with desultory skirmishing between the opposing forces of Numidians, but the first crucial move came when Hannibal ordered his elephants to charge: he had never had so many under his command before, and it is certain that no soldier in Scipio's army had ever faced anything like a massed charge of eighty elephants. Hannibal's hope must have been that they would, at least, disrupt Scipio's front line, and cause some losses in it, so that his own infantry would start off with an advantage. But, as so often was the case, they proved more of a liability than a devastating weapon: some of them, terrified by the scream of trumpets and horns, wheeled back on the Numidians on the Carthaginian left, and at that moment, Masinissa charged home, driving these Numidians off the field, thus exposing the Carthaginian left flank (Polybius 15.12.2). Other elephants did charge the Roman *velites,* and inflicted severe losses upon them, but suffered equally severely themselves, until they eventually broke right through the Roman lines along the corridors Scipio had left, and disappeared off the field (Polybius 15.12.3-4). Others again broke out to the right and were driven off by showers of javelins, whereupon Laelius, too, seized this moment of confusion to charge the Carthaginian cavalry on Hannibal's right, which broke and fled (Polybius 15.12.5). It has been suggested that Hannibal, knowing his weakness in cavalry, deliberately used his own to lure the enemy cavalry off the field,[35] and this would certainly explain the ease of the Roman victory in this part of the battle, and why the Roman cavalry only returned at a late stage in the battle. But it must remain no more than a conjecture, and if Hannibal's plan was for his cavalry deliberately to retreat, he was taking a great risk, since not only did he expose his flanks, but he could not guarantee that the Roman cavalry would not return in time to take his army in the rear. For the time being, however, the cavalry of both sides disappeared from the field, Masinissa and Laelius pressing the pursuit closely (Polybius 15.12.6).

The infantry lines now closed, except for Hannibal's veterans, who stayed where they were, the Romans shouting their war-cry and clashing their spears on their shields, Hannibal's mercenaries screaming a babble of different languages (Polybius 15.12.8-9). Unfortunately, there is some corruption at this point in Polybius' text (15.13.1): what the manuscripts say is that "as the whole battle was hand to hand and man to man, since the antagonists did not use spears or swords, the mercenaries at first had the upper hand through their skill and daring." But this hardly makes sense, although Livy does describe the Roman soldiers as advancing "pushing with their shield-bosses" (30.34.3). The simplest solution is to suppose that what Polybius really wrote was " . . . since the antagonists did not use spears but swords" (διὰ τὸ μὴ δόρασι ξίφεσι δὲ χρῆσθαι τοὺς ἀγωνι ζομένους instead of διὰ τὸ μὴ δόρασι μηδὲ ξίφεσι χρῆσθαι τοὺς ἀγωνι ζομένους ), but the corruption may be more serious and conceal some reference to long-range weapons like the slings of the Balearic islanders. But, for whatever reason, the Romans continued to advance, their order and the superiority of their arms giving them the advantage (Polybius 15.13.2), while the men behind the front line gave close support and shouted their encouragement, unlike the Carthaginian second line, if Polybius is to be believed (15.13.3), which gave the mercenaries no support or encouragement. Eventually, the mercenaries gave way, and, according to Polybius (15. 13.4), actually started to attack the Carthaginians in the second line, feeling that they had been let down by them. Later Polybius says that Hannibal had deliberately placed the Carthaginian troops in the second line so that they would be compelled to stand and fight (15.16.3), and this confirms what he says about their cowardice earlier (15.13.3). But although we may well believe that these Carthaginian levies were not very good - and the same may be true of the Africans stationed with them in the second line (cf. Polybius 15.11.2) - it really makes no sense to suggest, as Polybius does (15.13.5), that it was the attack of the mercenaries which compelled the Carthaginians to stand and fight - it would probably have had the opposite effect. A more likely explanation is that Hannibal had ordered the second line not to admit the remnants of the first into its ranks, for obvious reasons, just as later he would not allow his third line to admit remnants of the first two (cf. Polybius 15.13.9), and that this caused some fighting between the mercenaries and the men in the second line.

As it turned out, indeed, Hannibal's second line, composed of Carthaginians and Africans, though Polybius only mentions the Carthaginians in his account of the actual battle, seems, even in his view, to have given a good account of itself: "fighting fanatically and in an extraordinary manner," he says (15.13.6), these allegedly cowardly soldiers threw the maniples of *hastati,* already depleted by their struggle with the mercenaries, into confusion. Hannibal must have been hoping that as many as possible of the Roman troops would be drawn into the struggle with his first two lines, so that he could use his third line, composed of his best troops, to deliver a devastating blow before the Roman cavalry returned. But so far, if we are to believe Polybius, only the *hastati* had been involved, and even now, he says (15.13.7), although the officers of the *principes* could see what had happened in front of them, they "checked their ranks" ($\dot{\epsilon}\pi\dot{\epsilon}\sigma\tau\eta\sigma\alpha\nu$ $\tau\grave{\alpha}\varsigma$ $\alpha\dot{\upsilon}\tau\tilde{\omega}\nu$ $\tau\dot{\alpha}\xi\epsilon\iota\varsigma$), i.e., refused to allow their men to be drawn into the confusion in front. Some commentators, however, believe that the phrase used here by Polybius means "brought up their ranks to assist" - i.e., that the *principes* were now drawn into the struggle. [36] But this does not seem to be the real meaning of the Greek, and it is noticeable that Polybius goes on to say (15.13.8) that "the greater part of the mercenaries and the Carthaginians were cut down on the spot, some by their own men, some by the *hastati*" - he does not mention the *principes* as being involved - and later (15.14.3) it is the *hastati* whom Scipio recalls from the sursuit. Nevertheless, it is difficult to believe that the *hastati,* numbering, perhaps, about 6500 men, actually succeeded in defeating Hannibal's first two lines, numbering, presumably, over 20,000 men, and the *principes* may have been involved.

Hannibal, as we have seen, refused to allow the broken remnants of his first two lines into his third line, but ordered his veterans to level spears, thus compelling the survivors to make their way to the wings, where, presumably, some would have rallied, and formed up alongside the veterans. The space between the opposing lines was now covered in the carnage of the preceding struggle: Polybius says (15.14.2) that the heaps of bloody corpses made the ground slippery, and this, combined with the litter of arms haphazardly thrown away among the bodies, made any advance difficult for men marching in rank. This was the second crucial moment of the battle, for Hannibal had, presumably, held his veterans back (cf. Polybius 15.12.7), partly as a general reserve to counter any enveloping tactics that Scipio might attempt, but partly to administer the *coup de grâce* as Scipio's men emerged weary and in some confusion from their struggle with the first two Carthaginian lines. But he must have hoped that at least the *principes* would have been drawn into the struggle, leaving at most the *triarii*, who numbered only half as many men as either *principes* or *hastati*, fresh and uncommitted. But even though Polybius may be wrong to imply that the *principes* had not been drawn into the fighting at all, we can probably assume that they had remained largely uncommitted, and this probably explains why Hannibal did not launch his third line at the *hastati* as they emerged victorious but in some disarray from their struggle with his second line: if his last line became locked in combat with the *hastati* alone, this would give Scipio just the chance he needed, to repeat his favourite tactics of pinning the enemy's centre with part of his army, while using the rest of it to envelop his flanks.

So Scipio was given time to reorganize: the wounded were conveyed to the rear, the *hastati* recalled and reformed opposite the centre of Hannibal's line - presumably they had lost fairly heavily, and now closed up to form a shorter front, partly by lessening the intervals between the maniples, for the *principes* and *triarii* now closed up on either wing, almost certainly half of each to left and right, since there were fewer *triarii* (Polybius 15.14.3-4). As usual, Polybius says nothing about the Latin and Italian cohorts, but we may suppose that his remarks about the new deployment of *hastati*, *principes* and *triarii* refer to the allied contingents as well as the Roman. However, we can probably assume that neither the *velites*, including the allied skirmishers, if there were any, nor Masinissa's Numidian infantry, were involved. Thus, as Polybius says (15.14.6), the Roman troops were nearly equal in numbers to Hannibal's third line, which may, as suggested above, have included some of his first and second line troops, on either wing.

When the reorganization was complete, Scipio gave the order to advance through the ground strewn with the carnage of the previous fighting, and the two lines closed. The resulting fight - one of the most crucial in the history of Europe - must have been a grim business, since, as Polybius points out (15.14.6), the antagonists were equal in spirit and courage, and had the same sort of arms - many of Hannibal's veterans, of course, being armed with captured Roman equipment. But at this critical moment, Masinissa and Laelius returned from their pursuit of Hannibal's cavalry, and fell upon his rear: most of the veterans fought and died where they stood, and very few of those who tried to get away, managed to escape, since the Roman cavalry was already in their rear, and the country was open (Polybius 15.14.7-8). Hannibal, having done all that a general could, fled the field with a few horsemen, and never drew rein till he reached Hadrumentum: perhaps he should have stayed and died with his men, but it is clear from his subsequent actions that he thought that he still had a task to perform, both in bringing the war to an end, and in rebuilding Carthage after it was over. Scipio pursued the enemy as far as their camp, which he plundered, and then returned to his own (Polybius 15.15.2). According to Polybius (15.14.9), the Romans had lost more than 1500 killed, but the Carthaginians more than 20,000, with not many fewer taken prisoner. Appian, however, says that the Roman losses were 2500, and those of Masinissa rather more, whereas he gives the Carthaginian killed as 25,000, but the number of prisoners as only 8500 - these figures may be nearer the truth.

Polybius appends to his account of the battle a brief assessment of Hannibal's handling of it (15.15.3ff.), and concludes that although he had done all that a good general should have done, "good man as he was, he met another better" (Polybius 15.6.6 - the quotation is from *Iliad* 4.300). But although this judgement has been accepted by some modern commentators, [37] Scipio's victory at Zama must not be held to prove the point. Both generals were undoubtedly superb handlers of the set-piece battle, and if Scipio appears to have learnt something from Hannibal's tactics, he was certainly no slavish imitator. There was, indeed, a considerable difference between the ways the two men used particularly their infantry: Scipio tended to use it as a striking force, to attack the enemy flanks, whereas, of all the world's great generals, Hannibal is remarkable in being essentially defensive in his use of infantry: at Cannae, for example, the only really offensive move carried out by his infantry was the turn to left and right executed by his Africans in the final stages of the battle. At Zama, too, Hannibal's infantry appear to have waited for the Romans to come at them, particularly the veterans, but Scipio was either unwilling or unable to use his enveloping tactics with his infantry, and, indeed, it is clear from Polybius' account (cf. 15.15.6-8) that Scipio won by the superior organization and fighting-qualities of his troops, not by superior tactics - the story might have been very different if Hannibal had been able to match Scipio's cavalry in numbers and quality, and if he had not had to rely, for a third of his infantry strength, on hastily raised levies.

Scipio's successful assault of Cartagena also stands in apparent contrast to Hannibal's failure to take places like Naples and Cumae, but although one would not wish to detract from Scipio's achievement at Cartagena, the overall circumstances must be borne in mind: apart from the particular weaknesses in the Carthaginian position in Spain at this time, it should also be remembered that Cartagena was an enemy town against which Scipio could use any method he cared to adopt, whereas Hannibal was always hoping that the towns in Italy would come over to him, and may not have wanted to risk incurring hostility by an all-out assault, followed, inevitably, by massacre and pillage.

As strategists, too, both men were clear-sighted and bold, but it is astonishing that anyone should rate Scipio higher in this respect, for although his strategy in Spain was skilful and successful, the problems he had to face there were as nothing compared to the problems Hannibal had to face in Italy: Scipio's task, essentially, was to defeat the forces of an alien power, and he could rely on the actual or potential support of most of the indigenous population, once he had won some successes. But Hannibal not only had to contend with the immense manpower resources of the Roman commonwealth itself, but had to win over a population all of which had been under Roman control for some two generations, and much of which no longer regarded the Romans as alien in the sense that he and his soldiers were. As for Scipio's invasion of Africa, it appears obvious and pedestrian compared to Hannibal's breathtaking boldness in invading Italy: the Romans had, after all, already invaded Africa during the First Punic War, and it had been their original plan in 218, as Polybius makes clear (3.40.2), but no one, least of all the Romans, had imagined that the war could be carried into Italy. Scipio's slowness in implementing his plan is also in marked contrast to Hannibal's speed: assuming that Scipio eventually landed in Africa in the late spring or early summer of 204, he had already been planning the invasion for over a year, and it took him nearly another year even to break out of his original bridgehead to win the battle of the Great Plains, whereas within just over two years of his departure from Cartagena, Hannibal had marched thousands of kilometres, to carry the war into the heart of enemy territory, had shattered three Roman armies, and was on the point of overrunning much of southern Italy. Again, the success of Scipio's strategy in Spain and Africa,as compared to the ultimate failure of Hannibal's in Italy, is not the only criterion one should adopt in assessing their relative merits as strategists: no other strategy could have brought Carthage as near success, and it is this that is the measure of Hannibal's quality, not his ultimate failure.

Nothing, finally, that Scipio ever did can compare with Hannibal's ability to maintain himself in a hostile land for fifteen years, faced with overwhelming resources in manpower, and when one compares him with that other great general who lost in the end, Napoleon, it is worth remembering that the latter would have had to prolong the war to 1820 or thereabouts to match Hannibal's ability to maintain a losing struggle. There is a story (Livy 35.14.5ff., cf. Plutarch, *Flamininus,* 21.3) that years after Zama, Hannibal met Scipio again at Ephesus, and when Scipio asked who he considered to be the greatest generals, Hannibal named Alexander, Pyrrhus and himself, in that order. But when Scipio smilingly asked what would have been his opinion if he had won the battle of Zama, Hannibal replied that in that case he would have put himself first. This, while a graceful compliment, in a way, to his old antagonist, is more subtle than appears at first sight: if Hannibal had won at Zama, who would ever have rated Scipio higher than him?

There is a gap in Polybius' narrative after his account of the battle of Zama, and the next surviving fragment (15.17) describes a meeting between Scipio and Carthaginian ambassadors sent to sue for peace. Livy (30.35.10-11) says that Hannibal was summoned immediately to Carthage from Hadrumentum, thus seeing his native city for the first time since he had left it as a boy, thirty-six years before. In the senate he forthrightly declared that he had not merely been beaten in a battle, but in a war, and that there was no hope left save in suing for peace. Scipio, having plundered the enemy camp immediately after the battle, had meanwhile returned to the coast, on receipt of a message that the propraetor, P. Cornelius Lentulus, had arrived at Utica with 50 warships and 100 transports, carrying all kinds of supplies. Thinking the time had now come to drive home the lesson of his victory, he sent Laelius off to Rome with the news, and then ordered Cn. Octavius to take command of the land-forces and march on Carthage, while he took command of the combined fleets of himself and Lentulus, and made for Carthage by sea (Livy 30.36.1-3). Not far from the harbour, he was met by a Carthaginian ship wreathed in fillets and olive branches, and bearing ten of the leading men of Carthage, sent at Hannibal's suggestion to sue for peace. But Scipio returned no answer to their supplications, save that they should meet him at Tunis, to which he was about to move his camp. Then, having made a demonstration before the harbour of Carthage, he returned to Utica, recalling Octavius (Livy 30.36.4-6). On the march to Tunis, intelligence was received that Syphax' son, Vermina, was on his way to Carthage's aid with a force composed mainly of cavalry, but this was easily routed, with heavy loss, by the Roman cavalry supported by some infantry, on the first day of the festival of the Saturnalia (Livy 30.36.8), i.e. on 12th December, 202, by the Roman calendar, in what was to prove the last battle of the Second Punic War.

227

At Tunis, thirty Carthaginian envoys waited upon Scipio - presumably they were the senators who formed the Council of Thirty. Livy (30.36.10) alleges that the officers who composed Scipio's staff, were eager to destroy Carthage, because of the "just anger" the Romans felt. However, when they considered how great a task it would be, and how long the siege of so well-fortified and strong a city would last, they were inclined to make peace, and Scipio, who was troubled by the thought that a successor might come and reap the reward for all his labours, felt the same way. This statement about Scipio's motives has been challenged, [38] largely on the ground that Scipio would not have been superseded, even if the war had continued. This may be true, but he would only have been human had he felt some anxiety on the score, in view of what had been happening since 203 (see above, pp. 216-7). However, the point is an academic one, since, in the end, the decision was taken to attempt to negotiate a peace, and undoubtedly the main consideration was the sheer difficulty and cost of trying to take Carthage. The principal conditions proposed by the Romans were, according to Polybius (15.18), that Carthage should retain all the possessions in Africa (i.e. Tunisia) which she had held before the beginning of the war, should suffer no further injury, be governed by her own laws and customs, and not have to accept a garrison of Roman troops. In return, she was to make reparation for all injuries done the Romans during the earlier truce, hand over prisoners of war and runaway slaves, and surrender all warships, except ten triremes, and all her remaining elephants. For the future, the Carthaginians were not to make war on any nation outside Africa, and on no nation in Africa without Rome's approval. In particular, they were to restore to Masinissa, within the boundaries subsequently to be delimitated, all houses, lands, cities and other property which had belonged to him or his ancestors. For the present, they were to furnish the Roman army with sufficient provisions for three months, and pay the soldiers until a reply came from Rome about the treaty; subsequently, they were to pay 10,000 talents of silver over a period of fifty years, at the rate of 200 Euboeic talents each year, and, finally, as surety, they were to hand over 100 hostages, to be chosen by the Roman general, from their young men between the ages of fourteen and thirty.

These are clearly the terms Scipio proposed, not the final treaty, since some of the clauses - for example the one specifying provisions and pay for the Roman army - are inappropriate to the final treaty. But it is unlikely that the variations in other authors are due to their quoting the final treaty, but at least in some cases, to their having had access to a more accurate version of the proposed terms. Thus Appian (*History of Libya*, 54) says that the Carthaginian dominions were defined as lying "within the Phoenician trenches": where exactly these ran is not known, but they certainly existed in 202, as is shown by the reference to them by the contemporary author Eumachos of Naples (Jacoby *FGH* 178 F2) - they probably ran from somewhere near the mouth of the river Tucca, on the north coast, where now the frontier between modern Algeria and Tunisia begins, to the east coast of Tunisia in the neighbourhood of the Lesser Syrtis. [39] Appian also says that the time-limit for determining the possessions of Carthage was to be Scipio's crossing to Africa, not the beginning of the war, and this, too, may be right, though it is more doubtful that the proposed terms required Carthage to withdraw all troops from places "beyond the Phoenician trenches", as Appian says - in his text this clause is appended to one requiring Mago to withdraw from Liguria, and this had already happened the previous year. [40] Polybius' clause about the handing over of prisoners and runaway slaves clearly omits deserters, who are mentioned by Livy (30. 37.3) and Appian, and Livy is also probably right that it was specified that the Carthaginians should not tame any more elephants, Appian that they should not recruit any more mercenaries amongst the Celts or Ligurians (cf. Cassius Dio 17.82). Appian's version of the clause limiting Carthage's freedom to make war expressly forbids her to make war on any ally of Rome, particularly Masinissa, and this seems to be implied by a later passage in Livy (42.23.3-4), reporting a speech by Carthaginian envoys in 172, but cannot be accepted with any certainty;[41] more acceptable is Appian's clause requiring the Carthaginians to be friends and allies of the Romans by land and sea, which is confirmed by the help given by Carthage to Rome in her wars against Philip V, Antiochus and Philip's son, Perseus, in the second century (cf. Livy 31.19.2, 36.4.7-9, 36.44.5ff., 42.35, 43.3, 43.6.). Appian may also record a genuine detail when he says that originally 150 hostages were required: 50 may have been handed back when the treaty was finally concluded, and the remaining hundred retained until the indemnity was paid in full - later references in Livy (32.2.3-4. 40.34.14, 45.14.5) show that Carthaginian hostages were still being held at Rome until at least 168, and, as was usual, that their personnel was changed from time to time. Finally, Appian is probably right that Rome was to withdraw her forces from Carthaginian territory in Africa within 150 days of the conclusion of peace.

As was only to be expected, the proposed new terms were harsher than those proposed and accepted in 203, in particular in limiting Carthage's freedom of action: even if Appian is wrong to say that the new terms forbade her to wage war on any ally of Rome, Polybius' version - that she was forbidden to wage war in Africa without Rome's permission - left her extremely vulnerable to possible aggression by Masinissa, and the clause requiring the Carthaginians to be friends and allies of the Romans, recorded by Appian, also put them in a new position of subservience. In addition, the indemnity was doubled, and the size of the fleet allowed the defeated city, halved. The clause demanding the surrender of her elephants and forbidding the taming of any more, was also new, and perhaps owed something to the formidable number Hannibal had been able to bring into the field at Zama.

The terms were conveyed to their fellow-countrymen by the thirty Carthaginian envoys, and when, at a meeting of the Carthaginian senate, a member of either the senate or the Council of Thirty, attempted to speak in favour of rejecting the terms, Hannibal strode forward and forcibly dragged him from the rostrum. At this there was a murmur of indignation, but Hannibal, while admitting that he might have acted contrary to normal custom - he had left Carthage at the age of nine, he pointed out, so they must forgive him - nevertheless strongly maintained that it was only love for his country which made him act like this: it seemed amazing and extraordinary to him, he declared, that there was any Carthaginian alive who did not thank his lucky stars to get such lenient terms when they were at Rome's mercy. This speech, coming from such a source, carried the day, and the senate immediately despatched envoys to accept the terms (Polybius 15.19.2-9). Livy (30.37.7) says that the senator who tried to oppose accepting the terms, was called Gisgo, and, if this is true, it is a nice thought that this may have been that Gisgo who expressed disquiet at the disparity in numbers at Cannae, now determined to show his old general, in totally different and inappropriate circumstances, that he could be as resolute as anyone.

When the Carthaginian envoys returned to Scipio's camp, the first task was to put a value on the ships and cargoes seized by the Carthaginians during the truce. When this had been done, and 25,000 lbs. of silver paid over, a three-months armistice was concluded, the Carthaginians being forbidden, in the meantime, to send envoys to any state except Rome, or to receive any without informing the Roman general. Then the Carthaginian envoys were sent on to Rome, escorted by three of Scipio's officers, including his brother, Lucius (Livy 30.38.1-4). At Rome, the consular year had ended, on March 14th, 201, by the Roman calendar, without new officials having been elected - Livy says bad weather had prevented the elections (30.39.5). Thus, when the Carthaginian envoys arrived, with their escort, the Republic was without regular magistrates. However, a dictator had been nominated by one of the outgoing consuls, to hold the elections, and he was apparently still in office - he celebrated the festival of Ceres on April 19th (Livy 30.39.8). So it was, presumably, this dictator, C. Servilius Geminus, who summoned a meeting of the Senate at the Temple of Bellona to hear the report of Scipio's officers. Before a joyful house, it fell to L. Veturius Philo to declare that the last battle the Carthaginians would ever fight, had been fought with Hannibal, and at long last an end put to the war - for good measure he added that Vermina, too, had been defeated. The glad news was then given to an assembly of the people (Livy 30.40. 1-4).

The Carthaginian ambassadors were, however, denied an audience until new consuls were elected. Under the auspices, presumably, of the dictator, the elections were then held, and Cn. Cornelius Lentulus and P. Aelius Paetus, the dictator's Master of Horse, chosen consuls. But at the first meeting of the Senate after the elections, a problem immediately arose since the new consul, Lentulus, like his predecessor, Ti. Claudius Nero, thought he saw a chance either of an easy victory, if peace was not made, or of the honour of concluding the peace-treaty as consul. He therefore declared that he would not allow any other business to be transacted until he was decreed Africa as his province, his colleague, Aelius Paetus, weakly giving way (Livy 30.40.7-8). At this two tribunes of the plebs protested that the matter had already been settled the previous year when the people had been asked who they wished to command in Africa, and had voted overwhelmingly for Scipio. Eventually, the decision was left to the Senate, and it decided on a compromise: one of the consuls, to be decided by lot or mutual agreement, was to take command of a fleet of fifty quinqueremes and proceed to Sicily; if it proved impossible to conclude peace, he was to cross to Africa and take command at sea, while Scipio continued to command on land; if peace was concluded, the tribunes were to ask the people whether Scipio or the consul should be left to complete its ratification, and bring the victorious army home; if the people decided it should be Scipio, the consul was not to cross to Africa (Livy 30.40.9ff.).

This shameful bickering at Rome's moment of triumph shows just how bitter were the rivalries amongst her leading men, and how jealous his peers were of Scipio's success - it is significant that the consul, Cornelius Lentulus, even belonged to the same *gens* as Scipio, though to a different family, and that his colleague, Aelius Paetus, belonged to a family which is often thought to have supported the Cornelii. It is also clear, if Livy's accounts of this affair is to be trusted, that Scipio's support in the Senate was not sufficient to end the matter there. Presumably, as usual ,we should interpret the part played by the people's tribunes and the people itself not as an example of popular initiative, but as an example of the use which could be made, by the *nobiles,* of "popular support" - the two tribunes involved, for example, Q. Minucius Thermus and M? Acilius Glabrio, although the latter certainly, and the former probably, were *novi homines,* are both likely to have been protégés of the Cornelii Scipiones. But although we can assume that Scipio never harboured any thoughts of revolution, even such use of popular support as he made, was ominous for the future. [42]

Even after these internal squabbles had been resolved, the Carthaginian ambassadors were kept waiting while envoys from Philip V, King of Macedonia, were given audience: the situation in Greece was already looking ugly, and was soon to deteriorate into a renewal of war between Rome and Macedonia. Then, at last, audience was given to the ambassadors from Carthage (Livy 30.42.11ff.). In Livy's account, their main spokesman was one Hasdrubal, nicknamed "the Kid", long an enemy of Hannibal's family, and all the old ground was gone over - how the war was the responsibility of a few, not of the Carthaginians as a whole. One would not have thought that this kind of argument would have had much effect, and Rome certainly made no move to demand the extradition of Hannibal, for example. But, in any case, if Livy is to be believed, a majority of the Senate was in favour of making peace, and there can, in reality, have been few Romans who wanted a renewal of war, when peace was now so near. Thus, although the consul, Lentulus, refused to allow the Senate to pass a decree, he could not prevent the tribunes putting before the people the questions whether it was their wish that the Senate should decree that peace be made, and who should conclude the peace and bring the army home, and the people voted that the Senate should so decree, and that Scipio should have the responsibility of making the final arrangements (Livy 30.43.3). Accordingly, the Senate decreed that Scipio should conclude peace on such terms as he thought fit and in accordance with the views of the senatorial commissioners to be appointed for the purpose. At the request of the Carthaginian ambassadors that they be allowed to visit the Carthaginian prisoners in Rome, the Senate even agreed to allow 200 of them, chosen by the ambassadors, to be released without ransom, if peace was made. Finally, steps were taken to ensure that the priests responsible for the solemnities attending the making of peace, were provided with all that was necessary (Livy 30.43.4-9).

Returning to Africa, the Carthaginian ambassadors concluded peace with Scipio on the terms previously specified. Carthage then handed over the warships, elephants, deserters, runaway slaves, and 4000 prisoners. The warships Scipio ordered to be taken out to sea and burnt - Livy says (30.43.11) that some of his sources said there were 500 of them, of all types, and if this is anything like the truth, it finally goes to show how much more the Carthaginian fleet could have done: Livy adds that the sight of the warships burning was as sad for the Carthaginians as if their city itself was in flames. The

231

collection of the first instalment of the indemnity caused a further outburst of misery in the Carthaginian senate - provoking Hannibal to declare scornfully that it took a money loss to make them weep, when the loss of their arms and ships had not raised a tear (Livy 30.44.4-12). Scipio, having rewarded Masinissa with the grant of Cirta and other towns and lands which had once belonged to Syphax, embarked his army and returned to celebrate the most magnificent triumph the city of Rome had ever seen (Polybius 16.23; Livy 30.45.2ff.), and to assume the cognomen "Africanus" - the first Roman general to be known by a name derived from the scene of his victories, though Livy says he could not discover who had first conferred it. It is also in connection with Scipio's triumph that Livy makes his only reference to his great Greek predecessor, for Livy believed that Syphax had died before the triumph, but dutifully reports that "Polybius, an authority by no means to be despised, records that this king was led in the triumph" (30.45.5, cf. Polybius 16.23.6).

Thus, some seventeen years after it had broken out, the great war finally came officially to an end. Although the peace-treaty contained within it the germs of future trouble, and we, with the benefit of hindsight, cannot help but think of the destruction of Carthage fifty-five years later, it was an honourable peace, in the circumstances. Carthage was left intact, with wide dominions in Africa, and rapidly recovered her prosperity - within ten years she was offering to pay off several instalments of the indemnity in advance, though the offer was refused (Livy 36.4.7-9) - and it is to the credit of Scipio and his advisers, and of the Senate and people of Rome as a whole, that they did not push matters to extremes, after all they had suffered. The conduct of their generation stands in marked contrast to that of their grandsons, and it is nice to think, if the story is true, [43] that years later Scipio and Hannibal could meet, and talk, and smile at each other, though lesser men of both their nations had already driven the one into exile, and were soon to drag down the other.

The comparative ease with which Scipio defeated Carthage in the end, with forces which probably amounted to no more than about a tenth of those mobilized by Rome at the time, emphasizes the real relative strength of the two powers, for although by then Carthage's strength had been much reduced, Rome too had suffered severely. But because of Hannibal's strategy, the war had really been not so much a trial of strength between Rome and Carthage, as a trial of strength between Rome and Africans, Spaniards, Celts, Italians, Sicilians and Greeks - indeed, in the main theatre of the war, for most of its duration, Rome had found herself repeating the struggles of the previous century to impose her control on southern Italy. Thus, as Polybius saw, the Hannibalic War was far more than just the second round in the struggle with Carthage - it was, rather, the crucial stage in Rome's rise to dominion over the Mediterranean world. By the end of it, the "clouds in the west" spoken of by Agelaos at its beginning, had already begun to overshadow most of his world, and Rome had emerged not merely as the dominant power in Italy, with overseas dominions in Sardinia, Corsica and western Sicily, but as the ruler of the whole of Sicily and of eastern and southern Spain, and through her newly acquired allies, or recently defeated foes, now dominated much of Algeria and Tunisia, central and southern Greece, the Aegean, and even western Asia Minor. In terms of the Mediterranean world, in short, Rome had emerged as a "super power" and it was soon to be made clear that she had no rival.

This was, indeed, the first and most important consequence of the Hannibalic War - that it revealed the latent power of the Roman Republic, just as the Second World War revealed that of the United States and the Soviet Union. In the case of these modern "super powers" we tend to think, first, of their industrial and technological capacity, but in Rome's case it was, above all, her capacity to produce men that counted. Most of her previous wars had been fought with an army of four legions and their complement of allied contingents, and Polybius says that when eight legions were mobilized for the Cannae campaign, this had never before been done (3.107.9). But if Polybius is right in stating that there were eight legions at Cannae, Rome had already mobilized a total of ten, since there were already two in Spain, and by 211 there were twenty-five in the field, which, taking the allied contingents and the men serving at sea into consideration, represented something like a quarter of a million men.[1] It is true that there are signs that even Rome's resources in manpower were strained: the property qualification for legionary service had probably been lowered some years before (see above, pp. 100-1), and there were difficulties in manning the fleet in 214 (Livy 24.11.7ff.), and in finding recruits for the legions in 212 (Livy 25.5.5ff.). But the men were found, and even if legions were under strength and ships undermanned, there is no evidence that any theatre of the war was unduly neglected because of a shortage of men. Similarly, although by 209 the strain on allied manpower was such that even Latin colonies were refusing to fulfil their obligations, there is no evidence that there was any serious falling off in the total number of allied soldiers serving with the Roman forces, despite the defection of much of southern Italy and of Sicily.

Rome's total citizen population was already enormous in 218 - it has been estimated that there were then 325,000 adult males, of whom about 240,000 would have been available for military service in some form or other.[2] This was largely due to Rome's policy of absorbing citizens of other states, including manumitted slaves, into her own citizen-body, and this comparative generosity - noticed by Philip V of Macedonia in his letter to the people of Larisa in Thessaly ($SIG^3$ No. 543) - paid dividends in the Hannibalic War, and not merely in giving the Republic a huge reservoir of citizen manpower: Hannibal's plan in invading Italy had been based on the hope that Rome's Latin and Italian allies would join him, as his repeated declarations to his non-Roman prisoners show, but not a single Latin state ever went over to him, and probably a majority of even the non-Latin allies refused to join him. Undoubtedly fear of the consequences was partly the reason - in Etruria, for example - but it would be absurd to suggest that this was the only reason. A more fundamental explanation lies in the complexity of the relations between Rome and her allies: though there was much in common between citizens without the vote, Latins, and other allies, there were also considerable differences which stood in the way of their making common cause, and within individual states there were also class differences (see above, p. 88). There is also no reason to doubt that many of the allies had a genuine fellow-feeling for the Romans, particularly in comparison with Hannibal and his soldiers, who were aliens in a different sense: many Latins were, after all, descended from Roman citizens, spoke the same language, worshipped the same gods, and had the same or similar customs and institutions, and even among the non-Latin allies, to some of whom the Romans were, perhaps, as "foreign" as Celts or Spaniards or Africans, there must have been some who hoped for Roman citizenship and many who had developed personal ties, if only through fighting alongside citizen troops - the Indian Mutiny provides many an illustration of how strong such ties could be.[3]

By contrast, Carthage had no such reservoir of citizen manpower - citizens were probably not called up for service in her armies until Scipio invaded Africa, and even some of the officers in both her army and navy were foreigners - and although her mercenaries fought well and on the whole proved loyal, they were necessarily limited in number, and there was no machinery for mobilizing the manpower of her allies such as Rome had in Italy. Thus, in the end, just as many Spaniards were probably fighting for Rome as for Carthage, and even in Africa, although Utica, for example, surprisingly stayed loyal despite being under intermittent siege for more than two years, and although we hear of no disaffection among the native population of the Carthaginian hinterland, it is clear that Carthage had to rely heavily on Numidian support, until this, too, was lost through the defeat of Syphax. The war, indeed, revealed that the Carthaginian "empire" was a very loose and ramshackle affair by comparison with the Roman confederacy: the Spaniards changed sides at will, the Numidians wavered, even before Scipio's landing, and in the end Gades opened its gates without a fight, although its people were of Phoenician descent like the Carthaginians themselves; Polybius' account of the aftermath of Scipio's capture of Carthage's own colony, Cartagena, hardly suggests that the flame of Carthaginian patriotism burned very high even amongst its inhabitants. Carthage was only able to maintain the struggle for so long because of the new allies Hannibal's strategy won for her, and it was probably typical of the attitude of many of them that the Capuans should insist on complete independence, including the right not to serve in the Carthaginian forces against their will.

Rome's resources in manpower are the main reason for her victory over Carthage and her rise to dominion over the Mediterranean world, but there are other reasons, and one of the most important is her naval power. If ever there was a "Silent Service" it was the Roman navy - only once in the Hannibalic War did it voice its opinion, when the marine, Sextus Digitius, claimed the *corona muralis* for having been the first over the wall at Cartagena (Livy 26.48.6-13) - yet because there were no great sea-battles in the Second Punic War and in the conflicts of the second century, it is all too easy to overlook how large a part Rome's command of the sea played in her victory over Carthage and in her subsequent conquests. The Mediterranean world, after all, bordered upon a sea, and communications in antiquity were often easier by sea than by land. If the Carthaginian navy had continued to dominate the western Mediterranean, as it had done before the First Punic War, Carthage might still not have been able to defeat Rome in Italy, although Hannibal's task would have been made immeasurably easier, but there could hardly have been any question of Rome's taking the offensive in Sicily, Spain, Africa or Greece, or acquiring and retaining control of overseas possessions. As it was, the reverse was the case: Rome was able to convey her forces to all theatres by sea, at will, and continually to reinforce and supply them, whereas Hannibal was largely cut off from his bases. Roman sea-power after the First Punic War is, indeed, a classic illustration of the importance of a fleet in being, as is shown by the panic-stricken flight of Philip V from Apollonia in 216 (cf. Polybius 5.110), and the general ineffectiveness of the Carthaginian navy throughout the Hannibalic War. The last serious challenge to Roman sea-power was made during the war with Antiochus, in 191 and 190, and it is doubtful whether Rome would have been able to take the offensive in Asia Minor, and so win the decisive battle of Magnesia, if her navy, aided superbly by ships of Rhodes, had not previously won a series of victories, culminating in the battle of Myonnesos in September, 190.[4]

The complexities of the naval side of the Hannibalic War are also a vivid reminder of how complicated and far-flung the Second Punic War was, as a whole, and there can be no doubt that another reason why Rome won was the generally sound and sensible way in which the Senate managed the whole war-effort, and this, too, is a factor to be borne in mind in considering Rome's rise to dominion over the Mediterranean. The initial surprise achieved by Hannibal, and the apparent incompetence of some senatorial generals, should not blind our eyes to the achievement of the Senate in fighting a war on a scale never before seen in the ancient world. No one could have anticipated Hannibal's march to Italy, but the Romans reacted sensibly to the crisis, and although the decision to persist with the offensive in Spain may have been the elder Scipio's own, the Senate certainly sanctioned it, and thereafter retained an army in Spain, despite all disasters at home, thus effectively severing Hannibal's communications with his base. Elsewhere, too, the Senate hardly made a mistake in strategy, for it was strategically sound to confront

Hannibal almost immediately, in northern Italy, with what should have been adequate forces, and neither the Trebbia nor Trasimene was due to mistakes of strategy. It is arguable that after Trasimene, Fabius' ideas of fighting a war of attrition should have been rigidly adhered to and thus the culminating disaster at Cannae avoided, but this would probably not have prevented the defection of southern Italy and so a long drawn-out war, and there was something to be said for drawing upon the immense resources in manpower which Rome had at her disposal, to concentrate what should have been overwhelming forces against Hannibal in one last effort to defeat him decisively in the field.

Thereafter, we may feel that while adhering to Fabian caution where Hannibal himself was concerned, Rome could have reacted more swiftly to crush the Campanian revolt, since she had fifteen legions in the field in 215, twenty in 214, and twenty-two in 213, but although concentration on Capua did not necessarily involve fighting a pitched battle with Hannibal, as events were to prove, some allowance must be made for the natural reluctance to avoid even the possibility of such confrontation, after the disasters of the first three years of the war. But it was, surely, right to react swiftly to the defection of Syracuse, as Rome did, thus denying Carthage her bridge to Italy, and the siege of Capua, continued despite Hannibal's march on Rome, shows that the Senate had a firm grasp of priorities, and was not to be panicked into allowing its strategy to be dictated by the enemy. From 211 onwards, indeed, it is difficult to find fault with the Senate's handling of the war. The continuing importance of the Spanish front was understood, as is shown by the despatch of, first, C. Claudius Nero, and, then, the younger Scipio, both with reinforcements. It may have been a mistake to react to the potential threat posed by Philip V of Macedonia even to the extent that Rome did, since his reaction to the news that a Roman war-fleet was approaching, in 216, to which reference has already been made, shows that Roman sea-power was enough by itself to deter him from intervening in Italy. But by 211 Rome could well afford the limited forces she sent to Greece, and however ludicrous one may think the manner in which Sulpicius Galba dashed about the place, with no decisive result, Rome's handling of the situation, both militarily and diplomatically, was really masterly in the context of the Hannibalic War as a whole. The handling of the situation in 207, similarly, shows that the Senate had learnt by its experience ten years before, and although the problem was now complicated by Hannibal's presence in southern Italy, exactly the right dispositions were made to check him, and to crush his brother, before the two could unite, even if we may allow the persona. initiative of Claudius Nero to have been ultimately responsible for the victory at the Metaurus. Scipio's invasion of Africa, finally, although opposed by many senators, and often credited to Scipio's strategic genius, was, ultimately, sanctioned by the Senate, and was no more than a reversion to the strategy originally adopted by that body in 218.

Within this broad framework one must also admire the Senate's handling of details: in the absence of a war-cabinet or a General Staff, it was, after all, the Senate which decided where the armies and fleets were to operate, how many troops and ships they were to comprise, who was to command them, and how they were to be supplied and, if need be, reinforced. As far as we know, no Roman forces failed because they were inadequate for the task set them, or because they were inadequately supplied or reinforced. It is possible that the disaster in Spain, in 211, was due to the inadequacy of the forces at the disposal of the elder Scipios, and they also had problems of supply (cf. Livy 23.49.4-5), but one has the distinct impression that it was not so much because he had larger forces that the younger Scipio succeeded where they had failed, as because he set about his task in a different way (see above, p. 155). Other commanders also grumbled about supplies from time to time (cf., e.g., Livy 23.21.1ff.), but on the whole the absence of reference to such problems is probably not wholly due to the nature of the sources, for they do not entirely ignore this aspect of the war (cf., e.g., Livy 22.11.6; 25.20.2ff; 29.35.1, 36.1-3; 30.3.1-2, 24.5ff.). Overall, given the primitive machinery of government and finance in the Roman Republic, it is astonishing that it managed so well with a war on this scale, and it is clear that the chief credit must go to the Senate, as Livy's impressive accounts of the annual dispositions of commands and forces make clear.

Behind the Senate's successful handling of the war, we must also recognize the stability of Rome's political institutions, as Polybius saw (cf. 3.118.7-9). Despite the intrigues we have noted, no bloodshed was ever involved, no revolution, no suspension of the constitution or of the rights of citizens, no dictatorship, except in the technical, Roman sense. It is true that normal constitutional custom was modified in three important respects: repeated consulships were expressly sanctioned by a plebiscite passed in 217 (Livy 27.6.7), a number of men were elevated to the consulship before they had held the praetorship, and, most significantly for the future, there are several examples of *imperium* being granted to private individuals, not merely by prorogation. But what is far more striking is the predominantly normal way in which political life went on: elections continued to be held, assemblies to meet, policy to be debated in the Senate. We hear of opposition to the established order, but we have seen that most, if not all, the alleged "popular" agitation should be put down to the intense rivalries between the *nobiles,* rather than to real opposition to them as a class, and nobody seems to have suggested that the system should be changed, or that, for example, one man should be appointed to co-ordinate the war-effort, or even to command continuously on one front - the nearest approach to this was the decision to prorogue Scipio's *imperium* until he had brought the war in Africa to a successful conclusion, and even this was questioned. Of course, we do not know how ordinary Romans, let alone ordinary Latins or Italians, felt about how the war was run, but it would be as absurd to argue from the lack of evidence that the Senate and the magistrates did not have the support of the majority of the population, as it would be to argue the reverse, though the reverse is much more likely to be nearer the truth.

Particularly striking is the absence of anything that can be called a peace-party, even in the darkest hours after Cannae: Livy may be guilty of patriotic exaggeration, but there is no reason to doubt him when he says (22.58.9) that Hannibal's envoy, Carthalo, was not even allowed to remain on Roman territory, and in the absence of any evidence to the contrary, we have to accept that no one spoke up in favour of hearing the Carthaginian proposals - instead, Livy reserves his criticisms for men like L. Caecilius Metellus, who allegedly advocated flight from Italy (22.53.5). Ultimately, this was the rock upon which Hannibal's hopes foundered, for it seems probable that the kind of victory he envisaged was precisely one in which the Romans would be forced to accept his terms, not one which would end with the destruction of Rome (cf. Polybius 7.9.12ff.). But he does not seem to have realised that this was an impossible dream: Rome was prepared to negotiate peace-treaties on something like equal terms, as the treaty with Philip shows, but she would never have negotiated such a peace with an enemy on Italian soil, nor from a position of weakness. In short, there was no alternative to destroying her, and this was something which Hannibal, for all his victories, was either unable or, perhaps, unwilling to achieve, as his refusal to march on the city after Cannae indicates.

Any nation that goes through a conflict of the length and magnitude of the Second Punic War, is bound to be affected by it, and the Roman Republic was no exception. The strain the war inflicted on the Romans who lived through it is perhaps most vividly shown by what Livy has to say about the religious life of the Republic during the conflict, for his source here must ultimately be the contemporary priestly records, collated by the *pontifex maximus,* P. Mucius Scaevola, in the last half of the second century. Livy reports an increasing number of prodigies, and the Senate evidently took extraordinary measures to allay public fears, even resorting to human sacrifice after Cannae (22.57.6). It is also significant how the various festivals tended to increase in number, length and lavishness, and how external religious centres were looked to for advice and comfort: in 216, for example, envoys were sent to Delphi, including one of the earliest historians of the war, Q. Fabius Pictor (Livy 22.57.5), and in 205 the Magna Mater of Pessinus in Asia Minor was welcomed with elaborate pomp and ceremony (Livy 29.10.4ff.), though the Senate took steps to ensure that the most extravagant aspects of the ceremonies associated with her worship, were avoided.

But there is no reason to doubt that if the conclusion of peace with Carthage had been followed by a period of general peace, the Roman Republic would have recovered, just as Carthage appears to have done, judging by her willingness to pay off the war-indemnity, in a lump sum, within ten years, despite the loss of her overseas dominions and the encroachments of Masinissa on her African territory (cf. Livy 36.4.5-9). The end of the struggle with Carthage, however, did not bring peace to the Republic, for warfare was still going on in northern Italy and in Spain, and, within a year, Rome was also committed to a renewal of the conflict with Philip of Macedonia. The wars of the second century, moreover, tended to be either lengthy, or fought at a considerable distance, or both, unlike Rome's earlier wars, apart from the two great conflicts with Carthage.

As far as northern Italy was concerned, although Carthage herself was no longer directly involved, Livy does allege (30.10.1ff.) that an officer from the army of either Hasdrubal or Mago was still active in the region of Placentia and Cremona in 200, and that according to one tradition, he was not finally captured until 197 (32.30.12). In any case, it was inevitable that Rome should seek to remove the threat posed by the Celtic tribes which had supported both Hannibal and Hasdrubal, and by the Ligures who had joined Mago, and in every year from 201 to 188, except in 189 when both consuls commanded in the east, one or both of them were assigned to Gaul or Liguria, and frequently a praetor was also sent to northern Italy. The gradual spread of Roman control can be seen in the foundation of new colonies - Bononia (Bologna) and Aquileia, both Latin colonies, in 189 and 183, and Mutina (Modena) and Parma, both citizen colonies, in 183 - the reinforcement of the existing Latin colonies at Placentia and Cremona, the distribution of land to individual settlers, and the building of roads, of which the most notable were the *via Aemilia* from Ariminum through Bononia to Placentia, and the new *via Flaminia* from Arretium to Bononia, both constructed under the consuls of 187/6, one of whom was the ill-fated Flaminius' son.

The Ligures proved more difficult to subdue than the Celts, and we hear of almost continuous fighting against them down to 154, though the resistance of the main tribes - the Ingauni north and west of Genoa, and the Apuani above Luna (Spezia) - was broken by the 170s, when a new Latin colony was probably established at Luca,[5] and a Roman citizen colony at Luna. Thereafter, although fighting continued, one has the impression that it was at least partly due to the ambitions of Roman generals, eager for what they took to be easy glory, although further problems arose from the western Ligurians when Rome began to look for a land-route to Marseille. Probably in 148, the *via Postumia* was built from Genoa to Cremona and on to Aquileia. In the long term, of course, this conquest of northern Italy looks forward to the conquest of Gaul by Julius Caesar, and of the Alpine regions up to the Danube, under Augustus, and in a sense Hannibal's march through southern France to Italy can be seen to have drawn Rome's attention to this whole region - after all, the elder Scipio's landing at the mouth of the Rhône in 218 was the first time a Roman army had ever set foot in France.[6]

In Spain, too, Rome inherited a legacy from the Hannibalic War, and although an independent Spain posed no direct threat to the Republic, and it would have been theoretically possible to withdraw the Roman forces once the Carthaginians had been eliminated, it would be naive to suggest that Rome had any real alternative to maintaining a permanent presence in the country. Hardly had Scipio left, in 206, before his successors had to subdue a revolt, and nearly all governors down to 178 fought campaigns. We first hear of the division of the country into "Nearer" and "Farther" Spain, in 199 (Livy 31.50.11, cf. 33.27.1-4), and from 197 onwards two extra praetors were regularly elected to govern the two provinces. Such a subdivision had been foreshadowed by Scipio's campaigns in 206, when he tended to leave one of his subordinates in Tarraco and one in Cartagena (see above, p. 151ff.), although at this stage what was later to form the "Farther" province was not yet finally under Roman control - the divison was mainly due to the difficulty of communication between the two areas. Nearer Spain included the Ebro valley region and the east coast down to - probably - the river Almanzora, north east of Baria, i.e., in modern terms, most of Aragon, Catalonia, Valencia and Murcia; Farther Spain comprised the Baetis region, south of the Sierra Morena, i.e., roughly, Andalusia. The Roman government tried to work through the existing tribal organization, although there were some towns, and some of these, for example Emporium and Gades, were singled out for especially favoured treatment, having separate treaties and issuing their own coins. The reasons for the constant warfare are hard to determine, since we only have the Roman side of it, but although there was probably no systematic exploitation, the Spanish "allies" were certainly obliged to pay tribute both in cash and in kind, and Livy constantly refers to the quantities of bullion brought home by Roman governors. But perhaps the most oppressive feature of Roman rule was the levying of auxiliary troops. There can be no doubt, too, that many Roman governors were brutal and rapacious, and the Senate virtually recognized this when, in 171, it set up a special commission to enquire into the activities of some of them, and passed a decree setting down guide-lines for future governors (Livy 43.2.3ff.). That some sort of accommodation could be reached with the Spaniards, despite their fierce spirit of independence, was shown in 178 by the famous governorship of Ti. Sempronius Gracchus, son of the consul of 215/4, and father of the revolutionary tribunes of 133 and 123, which, with the corresponding governorship of L. Postumius Albinus in Farther Spain in the same year, ushered in a period of comparative peace which lasted a quarter of a century.[7]

It is more difficult to assess Rome's increasing involvement in eastern affairs after the Hannibalic War, although Polybius' natural interest in the subject, and the preservation of substantial fragments of his work, and of virtually the whole of Livy's account of the period from 201 to 167 - the year in which, for Polybius, Rome's dominion over "nearly the whole inhabited world" began - make it possible to follow the shifts and turns of Rome's policy in some detail.[8] It is obvious that Rome had been willing to conclude the Peace of Phoinike with Philip of Macedonia, in 205, mainly because with the departure of Attalus of Pergamum from Greece in 208, and the conclusion of a separate peace by the Aetolian League two years later, it would have fallen to Rome to shoulder the whole burden of the war against Philip, if she had wanted to continue it, at a time when the struggle with Carthage was reaching its climax. But it would not be surprising if the Senate kept a wary eye on Philip, and there is little reason to doubt Livy when he says (30.26.2-4) that at the end of the consular year 203/2, three envoys, including Terentius Varro, were sent to Greece to protest at alleged violations of the Peace of Phoinike by Philip's officers, against Rome's erstwhile allies, although we may take leave to doubt the accusation made by them, according to Livy, that Philip had sent troops to Carthage's aid at the end of 203.[9] Nor is the reality of this embassy called in question by the Senate's refusal to listen to the appeal of the Aetolians about Philip's attacks upon their allies on the coast of the Propontis in 202 (cf. Livy 31.29.4), for its attention was then firmly fixed on the situation in Africa, and it may have been more than willing, in any case, to make this calculated rebuff to the Aetolians for making their separate peace with Philip in 206. But, if Livy is to be believed (31.3.2-3), by early in 201, the Senate was sufficiently alarmed to invest M. Valerius Laevinus with *imperium* and send him to Greece with a fleet, and the election to the consulship of 200/199 of P. Sulpicius Galba, who had commanded the Roman forces in Greece from 210 to 206, must mean that by then the renewal of war with Philip was regarded as almost inevitable.

It would be beyond the scope of this book to examine the tangled and controversial problem of the rights and wrongs of Rome's declaration of war upon Philip in March/April 200, by the Roman calendar (probably December/January 201/200, in reality), and, in any case, a more important question is the reason for Rome's attitude. One possibility is that the Romans, or some of them, had never regarded the Peace of Phoinike as anything more than a temporary pause in their quarrel with Philip, and had been determined to seek their revenge, once the war with Carthage was over - this would explain the haste with which the Republic embarked upon this new war so soon after the end of the war with Carthage, and we must certainly make due allowance for the natural hostility many Romans must have continued to feel towards Philip, after his alliance with Hannibal. Livy's account of the rejection of Galba's original war-motion by the *comitia centuriata* (31.6.3) also suggests that there was a difference of opinion among the *nobiles,* for although he says that the reason was general war-weariness, combined with "popular" hostility towards the Senate, whipped up by the tribune, Q. Baebius, it is difficult to believe that popular sentiment could have swayed the *comitia centuriata,* of all bodies, if the *nobiles* had been united in their desire for war. Perhaps the truth of the matter is that Sulpicius Galba and his supporters were eager for a war which might give them the chance to win glory to offset that of Scipio, and that Baebius was really acting in the latter's interest.

But, in the end, the *comitia centuriata* passed the motion for war, and this must mean that a majority of the Senate had become convinced that it was either necessary, or desirable, or both, and basically the reason for this must have been the fear that Philip, if left unchecked, would eliminate Rome's friends, actual or potential, in the Greek world, and that a Macedonia unhampered by enemies nearer home, would be a threat to the Republic's interests, particularly in Illyria. If this is the case, the question whether Rome's ally, Attalus of Pergamum, was in the right or in the wrong in his quarrel with Philip, is of no more importance than the question whether Rhodes and Athens were or were not allies of Rome at the time, or whether Philip had or had not attacked Rome's protectorate in Illyria (cf. Polybius 17.1.14 and Livy 32.33.3). Nor is it really of any importance whether Macedonia was actually a threat or not: it was certainly a threat to Rome's interests in Illyria, and although no precautions were taken to guard against a Macedonian attack upon Italy, such as had been taken in 215/4, and were later to be taken against Antiochus, which suggests that the Senate did not literally fear for the safety of Italy, Philip had been making increasing use of his navy in the Aegean in recent years, and rumours of his notorious pact with Antiochus, whether or not it is historical, may have suggested that he could call upon the aid of Antiochus' still more formidable navy.

But whether it was a desire for revenge, or fear of Philip's aggressive ambitions, or even a genuine concern for the rights of her allies, which primarily motivated the Romans, it is at least clear that it was not "imperialism" in the sense of a desire for territorial expansion, for the peace terms negotiated with Philip after Flamininus' victory at Kynoskephalai in 197, left Philip as king, with at least Macedonia proper intact, and however cynical one may feel about the "freedom of the Greeks" proclaimed by Flamininus at the Isthmian Games in the summer of 196 (cf. Polybius 18.46), [10] Rome did eventually withdraw her forces from Greece, even from the so-called "fetters" - the great fortresses of Demetrias, Chalcis and Acrocorinth. Of course, "freedom" for the Greek states, interpreted as meaning independence for states which could make out a case for having been independent at some time in the past, exactly suited Rome's purposes, which were to prevent the growth of any power-bloc such had Philip had threatened to create. But there is no reason to doubt that it also suited many Greeks, and they could certainly have fared far worse at Rome's hands, as the future was to show.

241

The new Roman policy, however, contained within it the germs of future trouble, since it immediately disappointed Aetolian hopes of aggrandizement at Philip's expense (cf. Polybius 18.45), and it also raised the question whether it applied to Greek states in Thrace and Asia Minor, which had long been a bone of contention between the successors of Alexander, and to which Antiochus of Syria was even now laying claim: immediately after the Isthmian proclamation, Antiochus' envoys were informed that their master should withdraw from those he had already taken, and refrain from molesting the others (Polybius 18.47.1). But again the fundamental reason for Rome's attitude to Antiochus seems to have been apprehension of his coming to dominate Greece, as was later made clear by Flamininus' cynical offer to allow him a free hand in Asia, provided that he kept out of Europe (cf. Livy 34.57.4-59.8). [11] In this case, too, Rome's fears were immensely increased when - in 195 - the Syrian king was joined by no less a person than Hannibal: he had been denounced to Rome by his political enemies for alleged dealings with Antiochus, and had fled from Carthage following the arrival of a Roman embassy sent, despite the protests of Scipio Africanus, ostensibly to mediate between Carthage and Masinissa, but which Hannibal believed was really directed at himself (Livy 33.45.6ff.). Reports that he had joined Antiochus were probably enough to secure Scipio his second consulship - for 194/3 - and fears of a possible attack upon Italy may have been responsible for the founding of maritime colonies at Sipontum (Siponto), Thurii, Croton, in Bruttium, and at Tempsa, in 194. [12] But even then Roman fears were allayed, for their army was withdrawn from Greece and the Fetters handed over to Greek control, and a peaceful compromise with Antiochus might have been reached, but for the absurdly over-confident truculence displayed by the Aetolians - exemplified by the grandiloquent declaration of their *strategos* that he would hand Flamininus a copy of their invitation to Antiochus to come and liberate Greece and adjudicate between them and the Romans, on the banks of the Tiber (Livy 35.33.8-10).

However much the Romans may have been in the wrong in the diplomatic exchanges with Antiochus, they cannot reasonably be expected to have been prepared to tolerate a Syrian military presence in Greece itself, for, apart from anything else, their dispositions in 191 show that they did fear an attack upon Italy (cf. Livy 36.2.7), and Antiochus' considerable navy gave more point to such fears in his case than in that of Philip: in the spring of 197 he had put to sea with 100 decked warships and 200 lighter vessels (Livy 33.19.10), of which 40 and 60, respectively, accompanied him to Greece in the autumn of 192 (Livy 35.43.3); by the summer of 190 it has been calculated that the total Syrian fleet amounted to 136 or 137 decked vessels and a large number of lighter ships. [13] It is true that Antiochus may never have had any intention even of seeking a permanent military presence in Greece, let alone of attacking Italy, but this does not mean that Roman fears may not have been perfectly genuine: despite its obvious rhetorical exaggeration, something of contemporary Roman alarm may survive in the speech of advice Livy puts into Hannibal's mouth at Antiochus' council of war at Demetrias (36.7.2-21), and it is easy to believe, as Livy has Hannibal say, that the thing the Romans most feared was to hear that Hannibal was in Italy again. But it is sad to recall that the great general fought his last battle at sea, when he was defeated off Side in mid-summer 190 (Livy 37.23-4): one wonders what might have happened if he had been in command of Antiochus' army at Magnesia, some months later.

The Second Macedonian War and the war with Antiochus can thus be seen to have had direct links with the Hannibalic War, even if Rome's involvement in the east was not as inevitable as her commitments in northern Italy and in Spain, and it can certainly be argued that but for Philip's fatal alliance with Hannibal in 215, Rome's empire would at least have been far slower to extend eastwards across the Adriatic, for it is clear that her statesmen were very reluctant to take over direct control in the Greek world, whereas they showed no such reluctance in the west. Once committed to intervention in the Greek world, however, they were not prepared to ignore the rise of any one state to a position of power, and at the same time were subjected to increasing pressures to intervene in the interminable quarrels to which the Greeks were prone - some idea of the complexities faced by the Senate is given by the presence in Rome, in just one year - 184 - of no fewer that four delegations from Sparta alone, each representing a different faction (Polybius 23.4). Thus the apparent resurgence of Macedonian power after Philip's death, and the attempts of his son, Perseus, to secure the friendship of states with which his father had not been on good terms, were bound to arouse Rome's suspicions, which were fanned by the enmity of the new king of Pergamum, Eumenes. This led to the outbreak of the Third Macedonian War in 171, and the partition of Macedonia into four self-governing republics, after Aemilius Paullus' victory at Pydna in 168.

When Aemilius Paullus celebrated his magnificent triumph over King Perseus and the Macedonians, the Republic could look back on forty years of almost unbroken success, beginning with the defeat of Hasdrubal Barca at the Metaurus. There were still problems - in northern Italy, for example - but the main resistance had been broken even in Liguria, Spain was quiescent for the time being, Antiochus of Syria had been humbled and excluded from interference in the west by the treaty of Apamea, and now the kingdom of Macedonia had finally been crushed. There followed some thirteen years of comparative peace, broken only by relatively minor operations in northern Italy, Corsica and Sardinia, and Dalmatia. But in 154 the governor of Farther Spain was defeated by the Lusitani, and this disaster ushered in a further period of twenty years of almost continuous warfare in Spain, north Africa and Greece. In the case of Spain, the bitter conflicts were a direct legacy of the Hannibalic War, and were virtually bound to continue until the whole country was conquered, which did not happen until Augustus' grim marshal, Agrippa, took the matter in hand. In Greece, too, it was really inevitable that Rome should, sooner or later, annex Macedonia, particularly because of its strategic importance in guarding against the barbarians of Yugoslavia and Bulgaria, and it is worth remembering that the Achaean League, with which Rome went to war after the defeat of the pretender to the Macedonian throne in 148, had been Philip's ally in his first war with Rome, and after the dismemberment of the Aetolian League between 191 and 187, and the break-up of the Macedonian kingdom in 167, had remained the most powerful state in Greece: it was on the question of Sparta's right to secede from the League, significantly, that war broke out in 146.

There is also, of course, a certain inevitability about the final conflict between Rome and Carthage, and, looking back from this distance in time, it is tempting to see it as a final legacy from Hannibal to both nations, though he had been dead for over thirty years before it broke out. [14] Moreover, although there is no doubt that Rome

243

could have avoided the final show-down, since there was no basic conflict of interest between the two powers, [15] there was always a danger inherent in the position occupied by the energetic and ambitious Masinissa, whose power had been deliberately enhanced as a counter-weight to that of Carthage. There were evidently disputes between him and Carthage, leading to the despatch of Roman embassies, in 195 (cf. Livy 33.47.8), 193 - when one of the Roman envoys was Scipio Africanus himself (Livy 34.62.16-8) - and in 174 (Livy 41.22.1-3), and it was because of a similar dispute that the most famous embassy was sent in 153. This returned frustrated because the Carthaginians, in effect, had denied its competence by appealing to the peace-treaty of 201, and alarmed at what they had seen of the growing prosperity and power of their ancient enemies. According to Appian (*History of Libya*, 69), the Senate was determined on war from this moment on and was only waiting for a pretext, and this is confirmed by a surviving fragment of Polybius' thirty-sixth book. One of the members of the embassy had been the ageing M. Porcius Cato, who had served under Fabius Maximus at the capture of Tarentum in 209, and had jointly commanded the escorting squadron on the left of Scipio's invasion fleet in 204, and it was no doubt partly memories of the earlier struggle which drove the old man on to demand the destruction of Carthage. But even now the saner and perhaps more generous counsels of Cato's opponent, Scipio Nasica - who all those years before had been declared the best man in Rome - might have prevailed, had not the Carthaginians, provoked beyond endurance by Masinissa's encroachments, used force to resist him, contrary to the peace-treaty of 201. This was the pretext for which the "hawks" in the Senate had been waiting, and despite all efforts by the Carthaginians to placate them, the situation rapidly degenerated into a war which Carthage could not hope to win, and which ended, in 146, with the destruction of the city by Scipio Aemilianus, grandson of the Aemilius Paullus killed at Cannae, and grandson by adoption of Scipio Africanus. Polybius, who was with him at the end, heard him quote from the *Iliad* (6.448-9) the lines in which Hector foretells the destruction of Troy, and on asking him what he meant, was told that the Roman general feared a similar fate for Rome (cf. Appian, *History of Libya,* 132).

The same year that saw the destruction of Carthage, also saw that of Corinth, and the end of the war in Greece, but the war in Spain raged on for another thirteen years, and by the time that country had again been temporarily pacified, the Republic had been plunged into the first of a series of internal upheavals which were eventually to destroy it, and it has been suggested that these too were ultimately a consequence of the Hannibalic War - indeed, that its after-effects doomed the Roman Empire to be short-lived, and can still be discerned in the southern Italy of to-day. [16] This is, surely, going too far, but the view that the Hannibalic War and its aftermath put a cumulative strain on the Roman Republic, and so were ultimately responsible for its collapse, is worthy of more serious consideration. In particular, it has been argued that the devastation of Italy during the war, and the prolonged absence of men from their farms both during the war, and, more especially, during the overseas wars of the second century, led to the expropriation of small farms by capitalist landowners who could afford to exploit new agricultural methods and cheap slave labour, to create large estates - later known as *latifundia.* The result was what has been termed the "deracination" of the Roman peasant-farmers upon whom the Republic depended for the soldiers to man its legions, and Tiberius Gracchus' attempt, as tribune in 133, to resettle landless citizens, with all the dire consequences which were to follow. [17] But, in the first place, the effects of the Hannibalic War upon Italian agriculture, and, in particular, upon the *ager Romanus,* have been much exaggerated: after 217 the war hardly affected Roman territory at all, except, briefly, in 211, and in any case, Campania, the scene of much fighting from 217 to 211, certainly recovered. [18] Secondly, the spread of *latifundia* has probably also been exaggerated: it is worth noting that the word does not appear in Latin before the time of Seneca and Petronius, in the first century A.D., and the evidence, both literary and archaeological, can be interpreted to show that there was no marked change in the pattern of Italian agriculture in the second century. [19]

It is possible, too, that the decline in the number of those qualified for legionary service, in the second century, has also been exaggerated, not least, perhaps, by the Gracchi themselves. The view that there was such a decline rests partly on Appian's statements that Tiberius Gracchus' object was to produce more such men (cf. *Civil Wars,* 1.7.30, 9.35, 10.40, 11.43 and 46), partly on evidence that the Roman authorities experienced increasing difficulties in recruiting for the legions between 200 and 133. [20] But Appian's views have been questioned, [21] and Tiberius Gracchus' primary concern, in so far as it was not personal pique and the desire to further his own ambitions, may have been simply to improve the lot of the landless proletariat, not necessarily in order to produce more men for the legions, though he may have used some such argument to convince his opponents. The earlier difficulties in recruiting certainly do not, by themselves, prove that there was any shortage of qualified men, only that there were increasing objections to military service from those qualified, and this is really not so very surprising seeing that so much military service was now overseas and of long duration, particularly in Spain. In 169, for example, when the consuls found it difficult to raise men, the praetors, C. Sulpicius Galus and M. Claudius Marcellus, are said by Livy (43.14.2ff.) to have declared that "the levy was not difficult for consuls, only for consuls with over-ambitious plans," and that they - the praetors - could raise all the men that were needed - this they subsequently did, within eleven days. Again, in 151, the objections were to the harsh methods employed by the consuls (Livy, Epitome of Book 48). If there was a further reduction in the qualification for legionary service, as has been suggested, this would, of course, be good evidence for a decline in the number of those already qualified to serve, but the suggestion rests on dubious evidence, [22] and one would have thought that it was precisely those who owned the smaller farms who were suffering the most, if "deracination" was really taking place.

There is better evidence for a decline in the numbers of men available for military service in the Latin states, and this, too, has been interpreted as symptomatic of the general decline of the Italian peasantry. [23] In 193, for example, the consul, Q. Minucius Thermus, is already said to have raised Latin contingents "in accordance with the number of men of military age available in each state" (*pro numero cuiusque iuniorum* - Livy 34.56.6 - i.e., not according to the quotas demanded by treaty), and six years later, in response to an appeal from the Latin authorities, the *praetor peregrinus* ordered the repatriation of 12,000 Latins who either themselves, or whose fathers, had been citizens of Latin states in 204 or later (Livy 39.3.4-6); in 177, the Senate again acceded to

Latin demands, this time that the laws governing emigration should be strictly enforced (Livy 41.8.6ff.). It is also possible that the abandoning of the policy of founding Latin colonies [24] was also partly due to the difficulty of finding enough Latin colonists, but is more likely to have been due to the unwillingness of Roman citizens any longer to be drafted into Latin colonies, as is suggested by the founding of new-style, larger Roman colonies.

Clearly, however, the Latin states were experiencing manpower difficulties, but it is not at all certain that this was due to any "deracination" of Latin peasants, for, in the first place, there is reason to believe that the Roman government was making disproportionate demands upon allied manpower, particularly in the period 200 to 180, [25] and this would have tended to fall most heavily upon the Latins. This, too, has been interpreted as indicating a decline in the number of citizens available for service, but could equally well be due to the increasing unwillingness of citizens to serve. In the second place, the appeals of the Latin authorities in 187 and 177 suggest that their problem was mainly that an increasing number of their citizens were emigrating to Roman territory and thereby becoming Roman citizens, and although this could have been due to their experiencing difficulties in making a living as farmers, the natural conclusion is, simply, that they were finding the prospect of becoming Roman citizens increasingly attractive. Certainly the archaeological evidence does not suggest any more significant change in the pattern of farming in allied territory, than in Roman territory, during the second century. [26]

It is not difficult to see why Latins should have become increasingly anxious to become Roman citizens during the second century. As Roman power expanded, the very idea of becoming a citizen of the most powerful state in the world must have become more attractive, apart from any concrete benefits that might accrue, and undoubtedly there were also concrete benefits. The abandoning of the policy of founding Latin colonies, for example, may have been a blow to Latins who had hoped for the chance of a new life in the rich lands of Cisalpine Gaul which some of them had helped to win, and to become a Roman citizen and thus be able to join one of the new citizen colonies was now their only chance. Even when, in 173, unoccupied land in Cisalpine Gaul and Liguria, which had been annexed by the Roman state, was assigned to individual settlers, including Latins, they only received three *iugera* (0.8 hectares or just under two acres), whereas Roman citizens received ten (Livy 42.4.4.). Worse still, at the triumph of C. Claudius Pulcher for his victory over the Istri and Ligures in 177, allied troops received only half what citizen soldiers received from the booty: Livy remarks (41.13.8) that - not surprisingly - the allied soldiers followed their commander's triumphal chariot in an angry silence. Allied states may also have resented the way in which Rome sought to apply Roman laws throughout Italy, without extending the privileges of citizenship: by a tribunician law of 193, for example, the Roman law on usury was applied to all Latins and Italians in their dealings with Roman citizens (Livy 35.7.4-5), and the steps taken to suppress the worship of Bacchus in the 180s also seem to have applied throughout Italy (cf. Livy 39.14.7ff.) - a copy of the Senatorial decree was unearthed at Tiriolo in Bruttium, though the district may have been *ager Romanus* at this date. [27] Latin states would certainly have resented incidents like the one in 173 when the consul, L. Postumius Albinus, demanded entertainment of Praeneste when he passed through the town (Livy 42.1.6ff.).

There can certainly be no doubt that by 125 there was sufficient demand for the citizenship among Rome's allies for it to be worthwhile for Roman statesmen to take up their cause, for in that year the consul, M. Fulvius Flaccus, proposed the granting of the citizenship, apparently to all the Italians (Valerius Maximus 9.5.1; Appian, *Civil Wars,* 1.21), and the desperate rebellion of the Latin town of Fregellae (Ceperano), when Flaccus' proposal was circumvented, shows that it was the Latins who were principally concerned. Allied resentment may have been exacerbated at this time by the activities of the Gracchan land commissioners, but Flaccus' alternative proposal - to grant the allies the right of appeal against the authority of Roman magistrates (*ius provocationis* - Valerius Maximus, loc. cit.) - suggests that the resentment was more deep seated, and that basically what the allies wanted was the same kind of protection against the arbitrary use of *imperium* by Roman magistrates, which Roman citizens enjoyed. This is borne out by some of the things alleged to have been said by Gaius Gracchus in advocating the extension of the citizenship to the Latins, and of Latin rights to the Italians, in 122 (cf. Plutarch, *Gaius Gracchus,* 12, and the fragments of Gracchus' speeches in *ORF*$^2$ 190-2), and, more significantly, by the counter-proposal of Livius Drusus to exempt Latins from arbitrary punishment by Roman officers (Plutarch, op. cit., 9).

If this sort of thing was the root-cause of allied disaffection, we may suspect that it had been going on for some time, and before Roman statesmen became interested in the allied cause, emigration to Roman territory may have seemed the only way out for the Latins, since it must have become depressingly clear, as time went on, that there was little likelihood of their communities being enfranchised as a whole. It is true that all the *cives sine suffragio* except the rebellious Campanians, seem to hava acquired the full citizenship before 90, though we only know the date - 188 - in the case of three such states (Arpinum, Formiae and Fundi: Livy 38.37.6ff.), and that even the Campanians seem to have been readmitted to their former status in the censorship of 189/8 (Livy 38.36.5-6). But apart from these examples of limited generosity, there had been no grants of the citizenship to communities since before Hannibal's invasion, and after 188 there were no further grants to communities of either the full citizenship or even the *civitas sine suffragio,* until Rome's hand was forced by the great revolt of the allies in 91.

It is, of course, possible that Rome's attitude towards her allies in the second century was partly conditioned by distrust, arising from allied disloyalty during the Hannibalic War. Naturally those who had been actively disloyal, were punished, mainly by confiscation of parts of their territory, though the Bruttii seem also to have been degraded to carrying out purely menial duties for the army. [28] The twelve Latin colonies which had refused to supply their quotas of men in 209, in addition to being required to supply extra troops in 204, were commanded to make census-returns to Rome according to instructions received from the Roman authorities, and to levy a tax on their citizens at the same rate as that levied on Roman citizens, to ensure that they would have enough to pay for their troops (Livy 29.15.9). But these punishments were not excessively harsh, and the readmission of the Campanians to their former status, within less than twenty years of the end of the war, does not suggest that Rome harboured any particular grudge against them. Rather it looks as though Rome's leaders simply saw nó reason to change the status of the allies, for the admission of *cives sine suffragio* to the full citizenship was hardly a great step forward, and if this was the case, it would be typical of their attitude towards so many of the problems that came crowding in upon them in the second century.

For Hannibal's most potent legacy to Rome may have been this largely negative one - to reinforce existing attitudes among the nobility, at a time when Rome's changing role in the world cried out for her leaders to adapt. There can, at all events, be no doubt that Rome's leaders maintained a quite extraordinary complacency in the face of the changes around them, and this may well have been bred of a feeling that the system which had defeated Hannibal, needed no alteration. This emerges in Polybius' famous excursus on the Roman constitution and military system in his sixth book, which must have been written under the influence of his noble friends, and where he specifically declares (6.11.1) that the constitution "was both at its best and perfect in Hannibal's time." It is still more extraordinary that he praises the military system, since one might have thought that if the Romans had learned anything from their experiences during the Hannibalic War, it would have been that a militia army, commanded for a year at a time by men who ultimately owed their position to election to office largely on the basis of their family and connections, was not always likely to be successful in complicated, long drawn-out campaigns. But it is notable that the second century saw, if anything, a return to pre-war practice rather than a development along the lines suggested by the war, when, as we have seen, re-iterated consulships, long tenure of command, and even grants of *imperium* to *privati,* had all been permitted. Thus, in the thirty-four years from 200 to 167, no fewer than thirty-three consuls commanded in Liguria, and twenty in various parts of Cisalpine Gaul. In Spain annual tenure of command in the two provinces became normal with the election of two extra praetors from 197, and it is significant that although a law was passed in 180 providing that only four praetors should be elected in alternate years, so that the governors of the two Spains would have two years in their provinces (Livy 40.44.2), this law was certainly repealed by 173, and probably by 175.[29] Even in the great wars in the east, we find three commanders appointed in succession against Philip V, although the last of these, T. Quinctius Flamininus, having gone to Greece as consul in 198, then retained his *imperium* as proconsul until 194. Four men subsequently commanded against Philip's son, Perseus, from 171 to 168, and, still more remarkably, three men commanded in succession against Antiochus, despite the success of the first, M.' Acilius Glabrio, the consul of 191/0 - but then he was a *novus homo.*

The success of Scipio Africanus in Spain and Africa, and, to a lesser extent, that of Flamininus in Greece, showed that what was required was an able general, with time enough to complete the task before him, and this was to be demonstrated again in the case of Scipio Aemilianus in Africa and in Spain, and, pre-eminently, in that of Marius in Africa and the north, at the end of the second century. But such lengthy tenures of command were contrary to the whole *ethos* of the *nobiles,* and it is probable that the apparent insistence upon annual tenure of command, as a normal rule, in the second century, was due to the jealousy felt by the *nobiles* as a class against men like Scipio Africanus - it is significant that he had to wait until 194 for a second consulship, and was virtually hounded out of public life in the 180s. This may also be the background to the law carried by the tribune, L. Villius, in 180, laying down strict rules about the ages at which men could stand for office, and the effect of Villius' bill can be discerned in the elevation to the consulship in the 170s of a number of men who although strictly not *novi homines,* nevertheless came from families which had not produced a consul for many years - M. Iunius Brutus in 178/7, Q. Petillius Spurinus in 176/5, P. and Q. Mucius Scaevola in 175/4 and 174/3, M. and C. Popillius Laenas in 173/2 and 172/1, C. Cassius Longinus in 171/0, and A. Hostilius Mancinus in 170/69. But it is important to stress that if there were objections to the elevation of individuals above their fellows, the objections came from the class of *nobiles* as a whole: there was no suggestion that the class should be widened, or, if there was, it had little effect, since between 200 and 146 only four men reached the consulship who are known to have come from families which had never before achieved curule office (M. Porcius Cato in 195/4, M.' Acilius Glabrio in 191/0, Cn. Octavius in 165/4, and L. Mummius in 146). It is also worth noting that the rise of these men to positions of influence did not have any appreciable effect on the attitudes of the *nobiles* as a whole, judging by the behaviour of the Popillii Laenates, for example (see below).

It is not until we have the writings of Cicero and Sallust that we catch a glimpse of the attitude of the *nobiles* as a class to outsiders, but the attitude of individuals in the second century speaks for itself: in 200, for example, the young patrician, M. Aemilius Lepidus, was so rude to King Philip of Macedonia at Abydos, that the king was driven to remark that he forgave him for three reasons, firstly because he was young and inexperienced, secondly because he was the handsomest man of his day, and thirdly - and most significantly - because he was a Roman (Polybius 16.34.6). The incident which led to Postumius Albinus' demand on Praeneste as consul in 173, is probably also typical: Livy says that his quarrel with the Praenestines arose from an occasion when he had visited their town as a private citizen to perform a sacrifice in the temple of Fortune, and had not been honoured with any public or private ceremony (42.1.7.). But the most famous example of Roman arrogance was provided by C. Popillius Laenas, the consul of 172/1, when on a mission to Egypt in 168: asked by King Antiochus IV of Syria for time to consider an ultimatum, Popillius simply drew a line round the king with his staff and bade him answer before he stepped outside it (Polybius 29.27).

If Roman *nobiles* behaved in this kind of way towards kings when on diplomatic missions, we can assume that their attitude to those of their own countrymen they felt to be beneath them, was no better: Cato, for example, is said to have been regarded as not worthy of the censorship, despite his having held the consulship (Plutarch, *Cato the Elder,* 16.3ff.), and it was perhaps partly sneers at his origins which provoked his hostility to the patrician Scipios (cf. Plutarch, op. cit., 11). We can probably assume that ordinary Romans did not aspire to challenge the *nobiles'* virtual monopoly of office, but there must have been many men, like Cato, who were comparatively well off and who resented their exclusion from positions of power, since most of them were not lucky enough to find a patron like Cato's friend, Valerius Flaccus. In particular, there was a growing business-class for whom the spread of Roman influence in the second century must have opened up many opportunities. [30] Such men had already made their

249

mark during the Hannibalic War when they had contracted to supply the armies in Spain (Livy 23.49.1-4), and in 212 had given a striking demonstration of their power when they had succeeded in breaking up a meeting of the *concilium plebis* engaged on voting on the fining of some of their number for alleged fraud in connection with the Spanish supplies (Livy 25.3.8ff.). One might have expected such men to be natural allies of the *nobiles* since they belonged to the same social class, and must have provided the few recruits there were to the governing oligarchy, particularly in the lower ranks of the Senate. But the *nobiles* affected to despise those who were in business or trade, and relations between the Senate and the businessmen were not cordial: there was trouble over contracts in 184 and 169, for example (Livy 39.44.8 and 43.16.2ff.), the former largely du to the attitude of Cato, who, as censor, in the the typical fashion of the parvenu, seems to have tried to be more noble than the *nobiles,* and in 167, Livy says (45.18.3-4), the mines in Macedonia were deliberately closed down to avoid having to lease them to *publicani.* Livy also notes that censors often offended the whole class of which the *equites* were the cream, by removing them from the eighteen centuries in which the *equites* voted (43.16.1ff.). Thus, in the end, it was natural for the revolutionary tribune, Gaius Gracchus, to try to win the support of the *equites,* opening a breach between them and the Senate which was to cause endless trouble in the next century.

Polybius also believed that there was a decline in standards among the *nobiles* during the second century, and that particularly after the victory over Perseus, the old Roman character was undermined by the spread of luxury and extravagance (cf. 31.25. 2ff. Loeb, and 18.35.1-3). Polybius cites a speech of Cato in this connection, and it was Cato who became identified in the tradition with an attempt to stem the spread of Greek culture, and restore the old Roman virtues. But although there can be no doubt that the growth of Roman power, particularly in the east, did bring with it a spread of wealth and luxury, at least for the few, one must not go too far in accepting the picture painted by Cato and Polybius: for one thing, if the Romans did start to degenerate in the second century, they were remarkable in being able to continue the process for several hundred years, while not only holding on to the empire they had won in Cato's day, but immensely expanding it. But it is doubtful whether there really ever had been any "brave days of old" when sturdy peasants were summoned from the plough to become dictator, like L. Quinctius Cincinnatus, or were discovered by Samnite ambassadors eating boiled turnips before the fire, like M.'Curius Dentatus: if there was less corruption and vice before the second century, it was mainly because there was less opportunity for them, and it is worth noting that the first law against corrupt practices at elections was passed in 358/7 (Livy 7.15.12), and that as early as 275 an ex-consul, P. Cornelius Rufinus, was allegedly expelled from the Senate for extravagance (Dionysius of Halicarnassus 20.13). We must remember that the picture Livy paints of early Rome in Books 1 to 10 is an idealised one - nobody really knew what the Romans of the fifth and fourth centuries had been like - and that owing mainly to the loss of Livy's Books 11 to 20, we have far less detail about Rome from 292 to 218, than we have for the period from 218 to 167. [31]

As for Cato's view that it was contact with Greek civilization that ruined the Roman character, this too became part of Roman mythology, which liked to depict the inhabitants of the eastern Mediterranean as "wily orientals" who corrupted the simple

Romans with whom they came into contact. [32] But although there is no doubt that Greek culture had a profound effect upon the Romans - the earliest Roman historians, for example, Q. Fabius Pictor and L. Cincius Alimentus, wrote in Greek, as did the unfortunate consul of 151, A. Postumius Albinus, who was taken to task by Cato for apologizing for his bad Greek (Polybius 39.1) - Cato himself knew perfectly well that Greek culture did not necessarily corrupt anyone, for although he affected to despise men like Postumius Albinus, he himself could certainly understand and speak Greek, and knew something of Greek history and literature: he knew about the famous out-flanking march made by the Persians to turn Leonidas' defences at Thermopylae, for example, and used his knowledge to carry out a similar manoeuvre against Antiochus' army in 191 (Plutarch, *Cato the Elder,* 13), and he twice at least quoted Homer's *Odyssey* to good effect (cf. Polybius 35.6; Plutarch, op. cit., 27).

To accept the view that the Romans degenerated after the Hannibalic War is not only mistaken, but is to fall into the same error as Roman writers like Cicero and Livy, who evidently believed that there was nothing fundamentally wrong with the Roman Republic which the elimination of a few corrupt practices and evil men would not put right. But there *was* something fundamentally wrong with the Roman Republic - quite simply, the system which Polybius so much admired, while perhaps admirably adapted to the needs of a city-state, was no longer adequate when Rome ceased to be a city-state. The problem was, essentially, that whereas the Romans had learned the secret of creating a nation in Italy, by their comparative generosity in extending their citizenship to other communities, and in the Italian confederacy had created a stable and flexible system which had stood the test of Hannibal's invasion, Roman institutions had remained those of a city-state - for example, requiring citizens to be present in Rome to exercise their voting-rights, when they were scattered the length and breadth of Italy - and, at its heart, the ruling nobility remained a narrow oligarchy, which persisted in thinking in city-state terms - in terms, for example, of family politics, the patron-client relationship, the competence of amateur "gentlemen" to command armies and govern provinces, the adequacy of militia armies to fight long-distance wars, lasting for many years. But as the empire expanded, so the problems multiplied, until in the end the *nobiles* were overwhelmed - indeed, virtually exterminated in the series of civil wars which started with Sulla's march on Rome in 88.

But it is important to realise that the Hannibalic War created neither the attitudes of mind which eventually doomed the *nobiles*, nor the problems they had to face. Roman *nobiles* had always been narrow-minded and arrogant - they could hardly be anything else, given the nature of their upbringing and the deep-seated Roman respect for the *mos maiorum* (the custom of their ancestors), and as for the problems, although it is true that most of them were the inevitable consequences of the expansion of the Roman empire, and that it was the widespread nature of the Second Punic War which finally and irrevocably set Rome on her imperial path, the possibility, even the probability, of such a development was there long before Hannibal set foot in Italy. After all, the Roman confederacy in Italy was an empire in itself, despite the theoretical sovereignty of Rome's allies, and Rome had already embarked upon the conquest of the region between the Apennines and the Alps before the Celtic tribes of the area threw in their lot with the Carthaginians. In Sicily, and in Sardinia and Corsica, moreover, Rome had already acquired overseas provinces, paying tribute, before the Hannibalic War, and the two Illyrian Wars, leading to the establishment of the loose protectorate over western Albania, marked the true beginning of her involvement in the east. In the west, too, she had long had relations with Marseille, and although her interest in Spain was probably primarily due to suspicion of Carthaginian activities there, it certainly antedated the Second Punic War - even Africa had seen a Roman army as long ago as 256.

The wars fought by Rome down to 218 had, in general, been neither long nor fought at a distance, and the one great exception - the first war with Carthage - had borne more heavily on those liable for service in the navy, the *proletarii* and the *socii navales,* than on those liable for legionary service. But any war that is not a mere border-skirmish, is bound to put a strain on a militia-system and on the people from whom the militia is drawn, and in so far as there is any truth in the theory of the "deracination" of the Italian peasantry, it had probably begun before the Hannibalic War: C. Flaminius himself, after all, had as tribune in 232 carried a *plebiscitum* assigning individual allotments to Roman citizens in the *ager Gallicus et Picenus,* and the language Polybius uses of this measure (2.21.8), suggests that it was viewed in the same light as the similar measure of Tiberius Gracchus a century later. There are also indications that some Romans owned large estates remote from Rome, by the time of the Second Punic War: Hannibal is said (Livy 22.23.4), for example, to have spared an estate belonging to Fabius near Gerunium, in order to rouse ill-feeling against him, [33] and Fabius' edict of 215, as reported by Livy (23.32.15), refers to *villae* and to slaves. Specialist farming seems already to have appeared in Campania before Hannibal invaded it in 217 (cf. Livy 22.15.2), and the "capitalists" who are alleged to have exploited the new opportunities of the second century, and whose differences with the *nobiles* Gaius Gracchus was to exploit, did not suddenly spring into being as a result of the Hannibalic War: they were already powerful enough for the Senate to be wary of offending them over the scandal of the supply-contracts for the Spanish armies in 213 (Livy 25.3.12), and to disrupt a public assembly in 212 (Livy 25.3.14ff.).

It is also, surely, a mistake to think that Rome's relations with her allies only began to go sour as a result of the Hannibalic War. It seems hardly likely that the wave of disaffection which broke over southern Italy after Cannae was simply the result of Hannibal's victory there: one may reasonably doubt whether most of the Samnites, Lucanians and Bruttians had ever entertained very friendly feelings towards the Republic, and Livy alleges that at least three Campanian noblemen had been won over after Trasimene (22.13.2ff.), and also some nobles from Tarentum, before Hannibal entered southern Italy. The revolt of Falerii in 241 shows that there was some hostility to Rome in Etruria long before the outbreak of the Second Punic War, and although it was only in 212 that the first sign of disaffection during the war appeared (Livy 25.3.4), it is not impossible that Hannibal's invasion of Etruria in 217 - which may have been planned far enough in advance for a *rendez-vous* with the Carthaginian fleet to have been arranged (cf. Polybius 3.96.9) - was based on the assumption that the Etruscans were a likely source of support. Even the Latins may have begun to resent the continual demands made upon their manpower, before the trouble in 209, particularly if, in practice, the majority of the allied contingents in the Roman army were drawn from Latin states (see above, p. 12), and although the treachery of the Brundisian, Dasius (cf. Livy 21.48.9), was an isolated phenomenon, there may have been some kind of pressure from the Latins behind the proposal of Sp. Carvilius, in 216, that two senators from each Latin state should be granted Roman citizenship and adlected into the Roman Senate (Livy 23.22.4ff.) - nor will the indignant outburst of a short-sighted senator like T. Manlius Torquatus, if it is historical (cf. Livy 23.22.7), have gone unnoticed by the Latins.

Other developments which may seem to have originated in the Hannibalic War, can also be seen, on examination, to have begun before it. Thus, although the war saw the first extraordinary commands, foreshadowing the rise of the great army commanders from Marius to Caesar, the possibility had been there ever since the first prorogation of *imperium* in 326, and, on the other hand, it is clear that there had already grown up among the *nobiles* strongly-held views against any one of their number achieving pre-eminence: this emerges from the objections voiced at the elections for 209/8 against reiteration of the consulship (Livy 27.6.4), and from the relatively normal way in which men continued to progress to the consulship, despite the crisis - only twice were both consuls men who had held the office before (in 214/3 and 210/9), only four men actually held repeated consulships during the war (Q. Fabius Maximus, M. Claudius Marcellus, Ti. Sempronius Gracchus and Q. Fulvius Flaccus), and only one man (Q. Fabius Maximus, inevitably) held the consulship in successive years. Nor did the war prevent the usual small crop of *novi homines* from reaching the highest office in the state: C. Flaminius was a special case, since he had already held the consulship before, but there was also C. Terentius Varro in 216/5 and P. Licinius Crassus in 205/4. The arrogance displayed by the *nobiles* in the second century, moreover, although it may have been enhanced by the feeling that it was they who had overcome Hannibal, was no new thing, judging by the behaviour of P. Claudius Pulcher, the consul of 249/8, and, still more, of his sister, who on being caught in a crowd returning from the games, was heard to remark that she wished her brother were still alive and could lose another Roman fleet (Livy, Periocha Book 19). Despite what Polybius believed, there is no reason to suppose that the *nobiles* did degenerate in the second century, and Cato's bug-bear, Greek culture, had certainly begun to pervade all walks of Roman life long before the great wars in the east: there is, for example, a close parallel for the sending to Pessinus for the image of the *Magna Mater* in 205, in the sending to Epidaurus for the serpent of Asclepius in 292 (Valerius Maximus 1.8.2), the first Greek plays were performed in Rome in 240 (cf. Cicero, *Brutus,* 72), and, presumably, Fabius Pictor had learned his Greek long before he was sent to Delphi in 216, and settled down to write his history of the war in that language.

Thus the Hannibalic War should not be looked upon as a catastrophe which wrenched the Republic from its true path and set it on the road to ruin, but at most as a catalyst which accelerated processes that had already begun. It was a turning-point in the history of Rome and of the Mediterranean world, but only in the sense that it is the point at which Rome clearly and irrevocably emerges as the most powerful state in the Mediterranean world, not in the sense that during it Rome literally turned from one path to another. The process which led to Rome's establishment of her empire had really begun long before - when the assembly voted to accept the alliance with the Mamertines, or when the first great extension of the citizenship to the Latins took place, or even when Romulus founded the city, or the first settlers squatted on the Palatine Hill.

To say this may appear to diminish the importance of the subject of this book, but history is only worth studying for its own sake, and to dwell too long on the consequences of the Hannibalic War, to the exclusion of the war itself, is to deny the Romans what was, in some ways, their finest hour. They show up at their worst in resorting to the primitive rites of human sacrifice after Cannae, in the brutal excesses of the sacks of Agrigentum and Tarentum, and in some of their other behaviour in Italy, Sicily, Greece and Spain. But one cannot deny them courage and resolution, and, above all, competence: their generals come out badly in comparison with Hannibal in the first three years of the war, and from time to time thereafter, but in general they were far more efficient than their enemies. There is also a certain magnanimity about the Romans, which, despite occasional lapses, like the quite unnecessary intransigence displayed towards Carthage in the middle of the second century, goes far towards explaining their success in welding together the diverse peoples of the Mediterranean world into a coherent empire. It would, after all, have been relatively easy to destroy such places as Syracuse or Capua, as Carthage and Corinth were destroyed in 146, and to sell their populations into slavery. But savagely as they punished some of their enemies, they did not indulge in any orgy of revenge after the Hannibalic War: the cities they took, survived, as did the peoples they conquered - Samnites, Lucanians and Bruttians remained allies, the Capuans were even readmitted to the citizenship within a quarter of a century of their surrender. It was this willingness to treat defeated foes as human beings, to recognize their separate existence as city-states, tribes or nations, which is the hall-mark of Rome as an imperial power. It says volumes, too, for their political maturity and respect for constitutional forms that the complicated machinery of government continued to function even amidst disaster - there are few states in the ancient world in which a general who had lost a battle like Cannae would have dared to remain, let alone would have continued to be treated respectfully as head of state.

Of course, when one speaks of "Roman" harshness or magnanimity, brutality or courage, one is bound to speak almost exclusively about the upper classes, since we have no evidence about the feelings or attitudes of ordinary men and women. But here and there we catch a glimpse which suggests that the stereotyped image of the courageous, stubborn, disciplined Roman of tradition, is not too far from the truth, as when Polybius tells us of the way Sempronius Longus' men were put on their honour to be in Ariminum "on a certain day at bedtime" (3.61.10), or when Livy says (24.18.15) that cavalrymen and centurions refused their pay, or describes how when moneys held in trust for widows and orphans had been made over to the treasury, any necessities they required were paid for by a promissory note from the quaestor (24.18.13-4). The story that the land on which Hannibal was encamped outside Rome in 211, fetched a good price in the Roman market, may not be true, but could well be, exemplifying as it does not only the supreme confidence felt by the Romans in ultimate victory, but also the way in which something like normal life continued.

But one cannot leave the war, which, since Polybius' time (cf. 1.3.2), "most people call the Hannibalic," without a final word about the great general himself. The author of a recent study of his march to Italy has written that he "scents an aura like Hitler's round Hannibal, rather than any glamour," [34] presumably referring to his share of responsibility for the war, the curious hold he must have had on those around him, and, perhaps, the blitzkrieg-like quality of the planning and execution of his invasion of Italy. But even if he was motivated by a desire for revenge - which is by no means certain - there is no evidence that he entertained any fantasies about a master-race or envisaged a "final solution" to the Roman problem, and the first is virtually precluded by the heterogeneous nature of his army, the last by the terms of his treaty with Philip of Macedonia. Nor, at the end, did he have visions of a final Götterdämerung, but rather showed a resolute willingness to face reality.

Apart from what we can glean from his actions, we really do not know what sort of a person Hannibal was. Polybius, the nearest in time of the extant sources, says that "some consider him to have been cruel to excess, some avaricious" (9.22.8). But the Greek historian himself seems to have thought that any cruelty Hannibal displayed was the result of circumstances, and in his main narrative records few atrocities committed by him or his army. It also emerges (cf. 9.26.11) that it was among the Romans that Hannibal had a reputation for cruelty, and the accusation comes oddly from such a source. As for avarice, although Polybius seems to have accepted this because it derived from the Carthaginians themselves, we must remember that these were presumably contemporary Carthaginians, talking about the man their fathers had exiled, and it is also suspicious that Polybius mentions Masinissa in this connection (9.25.4). Livy also accuses Hannibal of cruelty and avarice, in a passage probably based on the Polybian (26.38.3), and, inevitably, of a "more than Punic perfidy" (21.4.9). But he, too, records few actual atrocities, or, indeed, examples of treachery, and certainly nothing to compare with Scipio's behaviour before the burning of the camps, As against these generalised accusations we may set Hannibal's chivalrous attitude towards dead foes (cf. Livy 22. 7.5, 52.6; 27.28.2), although it has been pointed out that "chivalry is not inconsistent with acts of cruelty." [35] A possibly authentic trait, since it has survived despite the conventionalized portrait of the grim avenger, is the wry sense of humour which lies behind many of the anecdotes told about Hannibal (cf. Livy 21.30.8, 22.30.10. 23.19.4, 27.16.10, 30.44.4ff.; Plutarch, *Fabius,* 15.2-3). Since this sort of epigrammatic utterance was commonly attributed to ancient generals - Plutarch wrote an essay about them (*Apophthegms of Kings and Generals*) - we cannot be certain that they are authentic, but if they are, Hannibal would share the trait with many other great commanders, and it would help to explain the hold he had on his men.

But it is as a general that Hannibal really comes alive. Because it failed in the end, the astonishing strategic insight that lay behind his march to Italy is all too easy to overlook, yet few generals in history would even have dreamed of such a plan, let alone have put it into operation - perhaps Marlborough's march to Blenheim offers a parallel in brilliance of conception and boldness of execution, but Marlborough was not marching into the unknown as Hannibal was, nor did he have to march anything like as far or to face such odds. Few would deny that Hannibal's conduct of the war down to

Cannae was masterly, and if Rome had accepted his offer of peace after the battle, the invasion of Italy would have ranked as one of the most conclusive examples of the military art. But although Hannibal's conduct of the war after Cannae has been criticized, it is too easy to forget the strategic skill, tactical ingenuity and sheer force of personality that must have gone into maintaining the struggle, against increasing odds, for the next thirteen years: the achievements of other great generals fighting a losing cause - Napoleon after Moscow, for example, or Robert E. Lee in the American Civil War - seem pale by comparison - and it is worth remembering how the situation in Italy could have changed again, almost overnight, even as late as 207, if Hasdrubal had succeeded in breaking through to the south. Indeed, it is arguable that these last thirteen years, far from being a mere anticlimax after the brilliance of the first three, are Hannibal's greatest claim to fame, as Polybius seems to have thought (cf. 8.19.1-2), and even the last campaign, in 202, shows that Hannibal had lost none of his boldness and skill.

In the day-to-day conduct of operations there are few generals to compare with Hannibal: from his use of Hanno's outflanking force at the crossing of the Rhône, to his retention of his third line as a reserve, and, possibly, his use of his cavalry as a decoy, at Zama, he showed a consistent sureness of touch, an ability to assess any situation and to arrive at a solution, often involving a departure from normal methods and considerable boldness. He was clearly a master of what amounted to psychological warfare, and of all the tricks a general needs to deceive the enemy: it is easy to admire the planning of the ambush at Trasimene, but easy also to forget how unique an ambush on such a scale is in the annals of warfare, and even the Carthaginian dispositions at Cannae, made in full view of the enemy, actually constituted a gigantic trap. He started with the advantage that he had a highly-trained and experienced army, but he showed a striking ability to make the best use of its different components. His use of cavalry is the most obvious example: the heavier, Celtic and Spanish cavalry, for instance, was used as a striking-force at Cannae, but not the Numidians - the latter, whether used to screen an advance, as on the approach-march to Tarentum (Polybius 8.26.4), as a harassing force to provoke an engagement, as at the Trebbia (Polybius 3.71.10ff.) or at Cannae (Polybius 3.112.3-4), as a holding force, as at Cannae again (Polybius 3.116.5), or to cover a withdrawal, as on the retreat from Rome in 211 (Polybius 9.7.5), were never thrown away by being asked to do something they were not capable of doing. But it was not only cavalry that was used with such precision - various types of infantry were also used with a similar regard for their capabilities, for example the skirmishers at the Trebbia (Polybius 3.73.1ff.), or in the break-out from the *ager Falernus* (Polybius 3.92.9ff.), the Spaniards and Celts at Cannae, with the Africans ranged on either wing ready to deliver the decisive blow. Even elephants were used at the Trebbia with some success (Polybius 3.74.2 and 7), and if they failed at Zama, to use them in such numbers as a shock-force was certainly worth a try. Hannibal's tactics at Zama, indeed, sometimes criticized, [36] really reveal that the master had not lost his touch, as Polybius saw (15.15.3ff.): his use of his third line of veterans as a reserve was possibly the first example of the use of a true reserve in ancient warfare, and proved an effective counter to Scipio's favourite enveloping tactics. Scipio won in the end, not through superior skill, but because he had the better army (cf. Polybius 15.13.2 and 15.15.7-8), and even then it was touch and go (cf. Polybius 15.14.6).

Despite Roman claims, it is clear that Hannibal never lost a major battle until he was defeated at Zama (cf. Polybius 15.16.5), and only once does he appear to have fumbled - when drawn into the series of scrambling fights with Minucius in 217 (Polybius 3.101-2). But even then he rapidly cut his losses, and later retrieved the situation, and this is his hall-mark as a general - he never allowed the enemy to pin him down for long, never squandered his men in useless engagements, never tried crudely to batter his way through a check or a difficulty, but always kept his options open. Like a boxer faced by a heavier opponent he feinted, weaved and dodged, and kept out of range - but his punch was devastating when he saw his chance.

But, in the end, it is, perhaps, almost an impertinence for an armchair historian who has never experienced a battle, and never commanded anything more than a patrol of Scouts, to assess one of the great commanders of history, [37] and Hannibal himself is said to have had little patience with amateur critics. According to Cicero (*de Oratore,* 2.75), the great general, when in exile at Ephesus, was once invited to attend a lecture by one Phormio, and after being treated to a lengthy discourse on the commander's art, was asked by his friends what he thought of it. "I have seen many old drivellers," he replied, "on more than one occasion, but I have seen no one who drivelled more than Phormio." I cannot help but wonder what he would have thought of this book.

# APPENDIX I  —  The Sources

No contemporary evidence for the Hannibalic War survives, except for a few coins and a limited amount of archaeological material, such as the remains of buildings, camps and fortifications. But we are fortunate to have, in the writings of the Greek historian, Polybius, a near contemporary account of the war, although it does not survive complete. Polybius was born at an uncertain date, probably in the last decade of the third century, and appears to have lived until at least about 118 - an ancient essay on "Long Lives" attributed to the second century A.D. writer, Lucian, states that he died from a fall from his horse at the age of 82. He was born into an influential family of Megalopolis in Arcadia, being the son of Lykortas, who was president (*strategos*) of the Achaean League in 182/1, and himself rose to be vice-president of the League (*hipparchos*) in 170/69, during Rome's war with King Perseus of Macedonia. In 167, after the defeat of Perseus, he was summoned to Rome, with a thousand other prominent Achaeans, ostensibly for an examination of their conduct during the late war, and was detained there for some sixteen years. But Polybius was probably more fortunate than most of his fellow-country-men in attracting the attention of prominent Romans, in particular the eighteen-year old Scipio Aemilianus, son of the Roman general who had defeated Perseus at Pydna, and grandson of the consul, L. Aemilius Paullus, killed at Cannae in 216, but who had been adopted by the son of no less a person than Scipio Africanus, the conqueror of Hannibal himself. Polybius probably accompanied Scipio Aemilianus to Spain in 151, when he served on the staff of the consul, Lucullus, and was certainly at his side when he took Carthage in 146.

Polybius was thus in a position to talk to eye-witnesses of the Hannibalic War, including men who had taken part on the Carthaginian side, and sometimes claims to have done so (e.g. 3.48.12, and cf. 4.2.2.). He also had access to documentary evidence now lost, such as the copies of the treaties between Rome and Carthage (cf. 3.22-7), the inscription set up by Hannibal himself on the Lacinian promontory (now Capo Colonne), recording details of his forces (cf. 3.33.18, 56.4), and Scipio Africanus' letter to Philip V of Macedonia, setting out his reasons for attacking Cartagena (10.9.3). Polybius was also a great believer in seeing things for himself, and had travelled extensively in "Africa, Spain and Gaul and on the sea bordering those countries in the west," as he himself says (3.59.7): it was typical of him to have followed Hannibal's route through the Alps (3.48.12).

Naturally, too, Polybius made use of earlier historians of the Hannibalic War, whose works have now almost completely perished, including Q. Fabius Pictor (cf.3.8.1), a Roman senator who was one of the three envoys sent to Delphi in 216 (Livy 22.57.5, 23.11.1-6), and Sosylos of Sparta, who is said to have taught Hannibal Greek, and to have accompanied him on his march (Cornelius Nepos, *Hannibal*, 13.3), though

Polybius appears to have had little but contempt for him (cf. 3.20.5). Others whose works he probably used, though he does not mention them, included Silenos of Kaleakte in Spain, who is also said to have accompanied Hannibal (Nepos, loc. cit.), and the Roman L. Cincius Alimentus, who was praetor in Sicily in 210/9, and was taken prisoner by Hannibal (Livy 21.38.3). But Polybius himself makes it clear that for recent and contemporary history, in his view, the most important thing was to question people who had taken part (12.4c.2-5), and we must remember that oral evidence was, for the most part, the only substitute available to the ancient historian for the kind of records and documents to which we are now accustomed.

Polybius is not the most exciting historian to read, his style being often flat and dull, his manner pedantic. But anyone who works with him must soon develop a considerable respect for the precision and good sense of his writing, his wide knowledge and his insight into the way men think and act; his accounts of military operations, and particularly of set-piece battles are the best which have survived from antiquity. He sometimes makes mistakes, for example in describing L. Cornelius Scipio, the consul of 190/89, as the *elder* brother of Scipio Africanus (10.4.1), or in his orientation of Cartagena (10.9.7ff.), and he clearly had his prejudices, like everyone else, for example against the Aetolians or the pro-Roman politicians of the Achaean League. But it is usually very difficult to argue that he is wrong, and where he differs from other sources, it seems best, in principle, to follow him: he is the nearest in time to the events, and had the better opportunities for research into the original evidence, including the oral evidence of eyewitnesses. Of course, later writers like Livy also had access, through Polybius himself and his written sources, to some of the original evidence, but it is clear that as time went on the evidence became contaminated by later traditions - for example, Roman attempts to justify their intervention on Saguntum's behalf.

A more difficult problem is how far we should accept the evidence of later writers where they give additional information which does not conflict directly with Polybius, for it is clear that he did not include everything in his narrative - for example, he says almost nothing about Roman politics during the war - and, of course, his narrative is in any case fragmentary after his account of Cannae. Here one can only use one's judgement, but in general the case is obviously different for the years 218-16, where Polybius' narrative survives intact, from the period after 216: I would, for example, be inclined to reject much of Livy's narrative of events during the winter of 218/7, which are not recorded by Polybius (see pp. 59-60 above), and of Gnaeus Scipio's campaigns in 218/17 (see pp. 126-7 above), where at least we have Polybius' explicit denial that the Romans crossed the Ebro before the arrival of Gnaeus' brother, Publius. But where Polybius' narrative does not survive, we can do nothing else but to follow the later sources, particularly Livy, and I do not myself believe that there is any reason to doubt that we can thereby arrive at something like the truth.

Livy is by far the most important of the other ancient historians who wrote about the Hannibalic War, and whose work has survived. He was born at Padua (ancient Patavium), probably in 64, and died probably in A.D.12, and wrote a voluminous history of Rome from its origins to 9 B.C., in 142 books, of which thirty-five survive intact, including Books 21 to 30, which contain his account of the Hannibalic War. Unlike Polybius, Livy was thus unable to question people who had taken part in the war, but he, too, like Polybius, would have had access to a wealth of material now lost to us, including the writings of contemporary or near-contemporary authors, such as Polybius himself, and official records of one kind or another. But it is doubtful how far he actually consulted the original evidence for himself: although, for example, he includes Polybius' figures for the numbers in Hannibal's army when he reached Italy, among a number of other versions (21.38.2-5), he does not mention Hannibal's own version in the Lacinian inscription, on which Polybius based his figure, although he knew of the existence of the inscription (cf. 28.46.16), and himself preferred one of the other versions. He refers to some of the contemporary writers by name, for example Fabius Pictor (22.7.4), Cincius Alimentus (21.38.3-5), and Silenos (26.49.3), but he appears to regard them as on a par with later historians like L. Coelius Antipater, a younger contemporary of Polybius, who was possibly his principal source (cf. 21.38.6, 22.31.8ff., 23.6.8, 26.11.10, 27.27.13, 28.46.14, 29.27.14, 29.35.2), and Valerius Antias, who wrote in the first century, and who, although criticized by Livy for exaggerating numbers (26.49.3), is cited elsewhere four times in Books 21-30 (25.39.14, 29.35.2, 30.19.11, 30.29.7). Polybius , though clearly used extensively, as far as we can judge by comparing Livy's account with the surviving fragments, is only mentioned once by name, and that right at the end (30.45.5).

It is natural to develop an affection for Livy, for the elegance and vividness of his writing, and too easy to be critical of him: he had not had the experience of military or political affairs that Polybius judged to be so important - but then no more have most of the historians who presume to take him to task - and he clearly glamourised the past and was biased both in favour of Rome, and of the Roman establishment. But although he could have done more original research - for example by visiting some of the terrain over which the war was fought - he was certainly not uncritical of what he read. He was, for example, aware that Roman sources sometimes exaggerated Roman successes (cf. 26. 49.3), and even of the danger of producing the "doublets" for which he has been so much criticized, when two sources gave differing accounts of the same event (cf. 29.35.2). But what is particularly noteworthy is that he says far more about his sources than any other ancient writer on the Hannibalic War, including Polybius, and that where he discusses his sources, as he frequently does, he approaches more nearly to modern conceptions of the way history should be written than any other ancient historian. In the ultimate resort, he is not only invaluable in filling in the gaps where Polybius' narrative is lost, but in adding details to the somewhat jejune account Polybius wrote: sometimes these additional details seem of dubious worth, but it is Livy who tells us most of what we know, for example, about Roman dispositions and the Roman political scene. If, where Polybius fails us, we reject Livy's account of the war, we must abandon any attempt to write a history of it, and it is reasonable to accept what he says as true - or as near the truth as we shall ever get - unless it is obviously wrong, or improbable.

Apart from Polybius and Livy, the three most important sources for the war are Plutarch, Appian and Cassius Dio. Of these, Appian is the most useful, particularly on numbers, where he is often surprisingly sane, but one is bound to be a little wary of a man who apparently thought that the Ebro flows into the Atlantic (*History of Spain, 6*), and whose account of the battle of Cannae, for example, bears little or no resemblance to those of Polybius or Livy, and hardly makes sense in itself. Unfortunately, the account of the Hannibalic War by Cassius Dio, in Books 13-17 of his monumental history of Rome, survives only in excerpts and in the Annals of the 12th century A.D. Byzantine historian, Zonaras, who appears to have followed Dio closely, though perhaps carelessly. Plutarch, whose lives of Fabius, Marcellus, Cato the Elder, and Philopoemen, are relevant, is useful and interesting in places, but adds little of importance.

On the sources of Polybius see Walbank, *Commentary I,* 26-35, and on those of Livy P. G. Walsh, *Livy: his Historical Aims and Methods* (Cambridge, 1961), 110-37. The most readily available translation of Polybius is the one by W. R. Paton in the Loeb Classical Library; of Livy the one in the Penguin Classics by Aubrey de Sélincourt.

The following is a list of - I hope - all the ancient writers mentioned in the text, apart from Polybius and Livy.

| | |
|---|---|
| *Acilius,* Gaius | Roman historian who wrote a history of Rome in Greek, now lost, probably published in 142: one of Livy's sources, though perhaps indirectly (cf. 25.39.12). |
| *Ammianus Marcellinus* | Roman historian of the 4th century A.D., who wrote a history of Rome from A.D.96 to A.D.378. |
| *Appian* (Appianus) | 2nd century A.D. Greek historian who wrote a history of Rome divided partly by subject matter (e.g. the *Hannibalic War*), partly geographically (e.g. *History of Spain*) - the latter works are often referred to by their Greek or Roman titles, e.g. the *History of Spain* as "*Iberike*" or "*Iberica*" or "*Hispana*". There is a translation of all Appian's works in the Loeb Classical Library. |
| *Aristotle* | Greek philosopher and scientist, lived 383-22. |
| *Cato* (M. Porcius Cato) | Roman statesman (c.232-147), consul in 195/4 and censor 184/3, wrote history of Rome, entitled "*Origines*", now mostly lost, which was possibly used by Polybius, and a treatise on agriculture (*de re rustica*) which has survived. |
| *Cicero,* M. Tullius | Roman statesman and barrister, lived 106-43. |
| *Cincius Alimentus,* L. | one of Polybius' and Livy's sources, praetor in 210/9, wrote history of Rome, now lost, in Greek. |
| *Claudius Quadrigarius,* Q. | Roman annalist of the first century, whose work, now largely lost, was used extensively by Livy. |
| *Coelius Antipater,* L. | a younger contemporary of Polybius, one of Livy's most important sources, work now mostly lost. |
| *Cassius Dio* | Roman senator of Bithynian origin (consul in A.D. 220 and 229), who wrote a history of Rome, in Greek, from its origins to his own day (translation of relevant surviving portions in volume II of the Loeb Classical Library edition). |

| | |
|---|---|
| *Diodoros* | Sicilian historian (hence often referred to as Diodorus Siculus - i.e. Diodorus the Sicilian), of the first century; wrote universal history, of which books 25 to 27 contained an account of the Hannibalic War, but survive only in fragments. |
| *Dionysius of Halicarnassus* | wrote history of Rome to 264, in Greek, most of which survives. |
| *Ennius, Q.* | Roman poet contemporary with the Hannibalic War (lived 239-169), wrote epic poem entitled *Annals,* on the history of Rome from its origins, including two books (9 and 10), on the Hannibalic War, fragments of which survive. |
| *Eumachos of Naples* | Greek historian of the second century, whose work is now lost. |
| *Eutropius* | wrote a brief history of Rome from its foundation to his own day (4th century A.D.). |
| *Festus,* Sextus Pompeius | 4th century A.D. grammarian who abridged a dictionary or glossary of Latin words and phrases written by M. Verrius Flaccus in the time of Augustus. |
| *Fabius Pictor, Q.* | Roman senator, contemporary with the Hannibalic War, wrote a history of Rome, in Greek, now lost, which was one of the most important sources for Polybius and Livy. |
| *Florus,* L. Annaeus | wrote a brief history of Rome down to the time of Augustus, during the reigns of Trajan and Hadrian. |
| *Frontinus,* Sextus Julius | Roman senator and soldier (governor of Britain 75-78 A.D.), who wrote a book on *Strategems.* |
| *Gellius,* Aulus | second century A.D. author of a miscellany on history, antiquities, philosophy and philology, entitled "Noctes Atticae" (Attic Nights). |
| *Horace* (Q. Horatius Flaccus) | Roman poet (65 to 8). |
| *Justin* (Justinus) | Roman historian of uncertain date who wrote an epitome of the history of the Macedonian monarchy by the Augustan historian Pompeius Trogus, now lost. |
| *Macrobius* | fourth century A.D. author of a book on history, mythology and antiquarian research entitled "Saturnalium Conviviorum Libri VII" (Seven Books on the Christmas Dinner Party). |
| *Cornelius Nepos* | 1st century author of a number of works now lost, and of a series of lives of which those of Cicero's friend Atticus, and of Cato the Elder, are certainly by him, but the rest, including that of Hannibal, are attributed by some MSS to the 4th century A.D. Aemilius Probus. |
| *Orosius,* Paulus | Christian historian of the fifth century A.D., who wrote a history of the world from its creation to A.D. 417 - in seven books. |
| *Ovid* (P. Ovidius Naso): | Roman poet of Augustus' time (43 B.C. - A.D. 18) who wrote, among other works, a long poem on the Roman calendar (*Fasti*). |

| | |
|---|---|
| *Pausanias:* | Greek traveller and topographer of 2nd century A.D., wrote *Itinerary of Greece* (Periegesis) in 10 books. |
| *Philinus:* | 3rd century Sicilian historian from Agrigentum, who wrote history of 1st Punic War from Carthaginian standpoint, now lost. |
| *Piso,* L. Calpurnius: | Roman annalist of 2nd century (consul 133), one of Livy's sources, work now lost. |
| *Pliny the Elder* (C. Plinius Secundus): | 1st century A.D. (23-79 A.D.) administrator and scholar who wrote voluminous work entitled *Historia Naturalis* in 37 books, on every subject under the sun, and perished in the eruption of Vesuvius. |
| *Plutarch:* | c.46-120 A.D., wrote parallel lives of prominent Greeks and Romans, as well as considerable number of treatises on other works, usually collectively known as *Moralia* (Moral Works). |
| *Polyaenus:* | Greek rhetorician of 2nd century A.D. who wrote book on *Strategems,* dedicated to the emperor, M. Aurelius, and his colleague L. Aurelius Verus. |
| *Posidonius:* | Stoic philosopher from Apamea in Syria, who lived from c.135 to c.50, and, among others, taught Cicero. |
| *Postumius Albinus,* A.: | Roman historian of 2nd century, criticized by Cato, for apologizing for his bad Greek, but probably used as a source by Polybius. |
| *Servius* (Servius Maurus or Marius Honoratus): | Roman scholar of 4th century A.D., who wrote commentary on Vergil which is extant, though probably contaminated by later hands. |
| *Silenos:* | Greek historian from Kaleakte in Spain, accompanied Hannibal, and wrote history of war, now lost, which was probably one of Polybius' sources. |
| *Silius Italicus:* | 1st century A.D. poet (consul A.D.68), wrote epic poem on 2nd Punic War, which has been described as "by common consent the longest and worst poem in the whole range of Latin literature" (Everyman Classical Dictionary, s.v.). |
| *Sosylos* | Greek historian from Sparta, who accompanied Hannibal, and whose work was used by Polybius, though now lost. |
| *Strabo* | contemporary of Augustus (c.54 B.C. - c.A.D.24), who wrote on the geography of the Graeco-Roman world. |
| *Thucydides* | 5th century Athenian historian |
| *Timagenes of Alexandria* | Greek rhetorician and historian of the first century, whose work is now lost, but was used by Strabo, and, possibly, by Livy. |
| *Tzetzes* (Joannes) | Greek grammarian of the 12th century A.D., who wrote an extraordinary historical poem, including some strange remarks about the Hannibalic War, allegedly drawing upon the histories of Dionysius of Halicarnassus, Diodoros and Cassius Dio. |

| | |
|---|---|
| *Valerius Antias* | Roman historian of the first century, whose work is now lost, but was used extensively by Livy. |
| *Valerius Maximus* | Roman historian of the first century A.D. |
| *Varro*, C. Terentius | Roman scholar and antiquarian of the first century. |
| *Vergil* (P. Vergilius Maro) | Roman poet of the first century (70-19). |
| *de viris illustribus*: | an anonymous work on famous Romans, once attributed to Aurelius Victor of the 4th century A.D. |
| *Zonaras* | Byzantine historian of the 12th century A.D., who appears, in effect, to have epitomised Cassius Dio. |

# APPENDIX II — Glossary of Latin and other technical terms

A.  abbreviation for Roman first-name (*praenomen*) Aulus.

*acies*  line-of-battle (as opposed to *agmen* - line-of-march).

aedile (*aedilis*)  title of four of the annual Roman magistrates. There were two curule aediles (*aediles curules*) in charge of public works and buildings, markets, weights and measures, and of festivals and shows, elected from the patricians in 'odd' years by the Julian calendar, plebeians in 'even' years. Plebeian aediles, of whom there were also two each year, were elected by the *concilium plebis,* and were always plebeians: they had much the same functions as curule aediles, but with less prestige.

*ager*  land or territory - e.g., *ager Romanus,* Roman territory.

*agmen*  line-of-march.

*asses*  small Roman copper coins, of which there were ten to the *denarius* (q.v.).

*auctoritas*  authority in the sense of influence or prestige - not the authority to act (which was *imperium* q.v.): a man derived *auctoritas* from his family background, the offices he had held, the campaigns he had fought, and so on - thus, e.g., an ex-consul had more *auctoritas* than an ex-praetor - and the auctoritas of a body like the Senate (q.v.) was the collective *auctoritas* of all its members, and something more, in view of its antiquity and permanence.

augurs (*augures*)  members of a college of priests, made up of patricians and plebeians, whose function it was to interpret the signs and portents (*auspicia* - see below). Note that augurs were men from the leading families, following a normal career, not professional priests.

*auspicia*  auspices, natural phenomena such as thunder or the flight of birds, thought to reveal the will of the gods. Certain magistrates, particularly consuls, were entitled to "take the auspices" (i.e. to ask for an interpretation of such signs), and hence were said to act "under their own auspices" (*suis auspiciis*).

C.  abbreviation for first name Gaius or Caius.

*campus Martius*  the Field of Mars, outside the original boundary of the city (the *pomerium*), where the *comitia centuriata* (q.v.) met.

*censor*  title of a pair of Roman magistrates, normally elected every five years, for a term of eighteen months, during which they held a census, assigning men to their class and/or century in

|  |  |
|---|---|
| | the *comitia centuriata*, tribe in the *comitia tributa*, chose members of the Senate, and let out state contracts for public buildings and works, the collection of taxes, etc. |
| *centuria praerogativa* | the first century to vote in the *comitia centuriata*, chosen by lot from the thirty-five centuries of *iuniores* (q.v.) in the First Class. |
| centurion (*centurio*) | Roman officer in command of one of the two centuries which made up a maniple (q.v.). |
| century (*centuria*) | either half a maniple (see above, under centurion), or a voting unit in the *comitia centuriata* (originally the same thing, since the *comitia centuriata* was, in origin, the people under arms, and hence met in the campus Martius). |
| Cisalpine Gaul (*Gallia Cisalpina*) | Gaul on this side of the Alps, i.e. northern Italy. (Note that Polybius called the inhabitants of most of this part of Italy, and the inhabitants of France, Celts (Κελτοί), whereas the Romans called them Gauls (*Galli*). |
| *civitas sine suffragio* | citizenship without the vote, a special status granted to certain states in Campania, Picenum and the Sabine country, bringing with it all the privileges and duties of Roman citizenship, but not the right to vote or stand at elections. |
| client(s) (*cliens, clientes*) | a term used by the Romans of men dependent in some way upon a *patronus* (i.e. patron). A man's clients could be, e.g., the small farmers or labourers who lived on or near his estates, citizens whom he had defended in the law courts or whose interests he had otherwise promoted, soldiers he had commanded, foreigners he had protected or even conquered. The relationship was often passed on from generation to generation, and clients were, above all, expected to support their *patronus* in politics. |
| Cn. | abbreviation for first-name Gnaeus. |
| cohort (*cohors*) | unit in the Roman army - in a legion consisting of a maniple each of *hastati, principes* and *triarii* (qq.vv.); also used of a contingent of infantry from an allied state, or, more loosely, of any infantry force. |
| colony (*colonia*) | an urban settlement founded by the Roman state, consisting either of Roman citizens (*colonia civium Romanorum*), or of a mixture of Latins and Roman citizens (*colonia Latina*). (N.B. the Romans did not use the term *colonia*, as we use 'colony', to refer to territory outside Italy conquered by Rome - such territories they called *provinciae*, i.e. provinces). |
| *comitia centuriata* | the Assembly in Centuries, which elected consuls, praetors and censors, voted on the issue of peace or war, and on charges of *perduellio* (high treason). |
| *comitia tributa* | the Assembly in Tribes (q.v.), which elected some of the lesser magistrates, e.g. quaestors (q.v.), and voted on legislation. |

| | |
|---|---|
| *concilium plebis* | the Council of the Plebs, virtually identical to the above, except that patricians (q.v.) were excluded; elected tribunes of the plebs (q.v.) and plebeian aediles, and passed bills technically known as *plebiscita* (i.e. plebiscites), though often referred to as *leges* (i.e. laws). |
| *consul* | title of the chief magistrates of the Roman Republic, of whom there were two, usually elected towards the end of the year to take office on the following March 15th, for a term of one year. (From 153 the consuls took office on January 1st.) |
| *consul suffectus* | a consul elected to replace another who died in office, or who abdicated. |
| *corona muralis* | the "wall crown" awarded to the first man over the wall of a captured city. (One must presume that it usually went to the first man who lived to tell the tale!) |
| curule (*curulis*) | term used to describe certain higher magistracies (consulship, praetorship, curule aedileship), derived from the chair of office on which such magistrates sat (*sella curulis*). |
| D. | abbreviation for first-name Decimus. |
| *denarius* | Roman silver coin, probably introduced in 211, and worth ten asses; probably equivalent to one Greek *drachma.* |
| *dictator* | title of a Roman magistrate appointed in an emergency, normally on the nomination of a consul, without a colleague, for a maximum term of six months. During his term of office, a dictator's *imperium* (q.v.) was greater (*maius*) than that of all other magistrates, as was symbolized by his twenty-four lictors (q.v.). Dictators were appointed for a variety of reasons, the commonest being to hold the elections (*comitiorum habendorum causa*), but the Hannibalic War saw the last dictators appointed in effect to take over the running of the state (*rei gerendae causa*), before the civil wars of the first century, in Q. Fabius Maximus and M. Iunius Pera. |
| *eques* (plural *equites*) | meaning, generally, "horseman (men)," this term was used in a narrow sense of the wealthy Romans, probably mostly of senatorial family at the time of the Hannibalic War, who were assigned to the eighteen centuries of *equites* in the *comitia centuriata,* and to whom the state granted a horse for service in the cavalry - hence *equites equo publico*. In the third century the censors began to add to the *equites equo publico* other men whose incomes were sufficient to enable them to serve in the cavalry, and eventually there grew up a class of rich non-senators to whom the term '*equites*' was applied, though it was probably not used in this sense before the 1st century. Thus much of what Livy, e.g., says about the import-ance of the *publicani* among the *equites* is probably anachronistic. |

| | |
|---|---|
| *fabri tignarii* | literally "workers on beams or logs" (i.e. carpenters, or, perhaps, builders), the term was used of the citizens belonging to one of the five odd centuries in the *comitia centuriata,* which apparently voted before the centuries of the Second Class, and so probably contained fairly wealthy citizens. |
| *fasces* | bundles of canes, with an axe tied in with them, borne by the lictors who attended Roman magistrates, and symbolizing their authority to flog and execute. |
| *fasti* | a calendar or almanac, setting out the days of the year, with festivals, other events, and, particularly, the magistrates. Parts of several such almanacs have been preserved in inscriptions on stone - hence *fasti Capitolini* (the Capitol *fasti*), *fasti Praenestini* (the *fasti* from Praeneste). |
| *flamen* | a priest, in particular the *flamen Dialis* (priest of Jupiter), *flamen Martialis* (priest of Mars), and *flamen Quirinalis* (priest of Quirinus); usually, as in the case of *pontifices* (q.v.), men of noble birth, but in this case appointed to serve a particular deity, and subject to more religious taboos - a *flamen,* for example, could not leave Rome, and hence could not hold an office which might take him out of Rome. |
| *gens* (plural *gentes*) | a clan, i.e. a group of families sharing a common name and certain religious rites - thus the *gens Cornelia* included a number of leading families (e.g. Cornelii Scipiones, Cornelii Lentuli and Cornelii Cethegi). A Roman's second name (*nomen*) was that of his *gens,* and it was probably only if more than one family within the *gens* achieved distinction that they acquired distinctive names (*cognomina*) - thus C. Flaminius, but P. Cornelius Scipio. *Cognomina* were often opprobrious (e.g. Flaccus means "flap-eared"), but not necessarily so (e.g. Maximus means "the greatest"), and could be shared by families belonging to different *gentes* - e.g. Crassus ("thick") by the Otacilii and the Licinii. |
| *gladius* | the short, cut-and-thrust sword of the Roman legionary, possibly originally adopted from the Samnites, possibly from the Spaniards, whence the term *gladius Hispaniensis* (Spanish sword). |
| *hasta* | the thrusting-spear from which the *hastati* (see below) derived their name, but probably only still used by the *triarii* (q.v.) during the Hannibalic War. |
| *hastati* | the first-line troops of a legion when drawn up in battle formation. The term originally meant "armed with a *hasta*", but by Hannibal's time the *hastati* were almost certainly armed with the *pilum* (q.v.). In the standard legion, according to Polybius, there were ten maniples (q.v.) of *hastati,* each consisting of 120 men, to whom 40 *velites* (q.v.) were attached; each maniple consisted of two centuries of 60 *hastati* and 20 *velites,* each commanded by a centurion. |

*ilai* (ἴλαι) Polybius' Greek term for cavalry squadrons in the Roman army (= *turmae,* q.v.), or, generally, for any units of cavalry.

*hipparchos* (ἵππαρχος) literally "leader of the cavalry" - the title of the vice-president of some Greek leagues, e.g. the Achaean League, but also used for actual commanders of cavalry.

*imperator* a term used to mean, generally, a commander-in-chief, but, more specifically, a title accorded to a victorious Roman general by his troops, on the field of battle, and then used as an honorary title after the name, e.g. in Cicero's correspondence. But Caesar used it almost as a *praenomen* - "Imperator Caesar" - and this practice was followed by Augustus and his successors, so that the title came to mean something like "emperor", though always with a military connotation. It was allegedly used for the first time of Scipio after Baecula, but was in reality, I suspect, very ancient.

*imperium* the almost mystical power or authority held by certain Roman magistrates, during their term of office. The Romans appear to have believed that *imperium* belonged to the Roman People as a whole, and in particular to the *patres* (the fathers - strictly, the patrician members of the Senate), and hence the term could be used of the "empire". Even the kings were held to have been, in some sense, elective, their *imperium* reverting to the *patres* at death, and, similarly, under the Republic, the *imperium* of magistrates who possessed it, was absolute and all-embracing during their term of office, subject only to certain rights belonging to all Roman citizens, and they could not be deposed or prosecuted while they held it.

*imperium pro consule/praetore* literally "*imperium* instead of, or on behalf of, a consul/ praetor", i.e. authority granted to a man, usually at the end of a year of office as consul or praetor - but occasionally to others - so that he could continue to act in addition to the new magistrates. (Note that Romans of the republican period did not use the nouns *proconsul* or *propraetor,* though it is convenient to adopt later Roman practice and refer to a man with *imperium pro consule,* e.g., as a proconsul).

*interrex* (plural *interreges*) title given to officials appointed from the patrician members of the Senate, to hold office for five days at a time each, if no curule magistrates had been elected by the end of a consular year, primarily to hold the elections, each *interrex* nominating his successor until the elections were held. The title - "king for an interval" - is another reminder of the continuity of *imperium* from the monarchy to the Republic.

*iuniores* adult, male Roman citizens of military age (17 to 46), in particular those belonging to the thirty-five centuries of *iuniores* of the First Class in the *comitia centuriata.*

269

*ius* (plural *iura*)      right or law, particularly the rights of Roman citizens and their allies: *ius provocationis,* the right of Roman citizens to appeal to the People against a magistrate's decision; *ius commercii,* the right of citizens of certain allied states to enter into contracts with Roman citizens which would be recognized as valid by Roman law; *ius conubii,* the right of citizens of certain allied states to enter into a legal marriage with Roman citizens; *ius migrandi,* the right of citizens of Latin states to emigrate to Roman territory and so become Roman citizens.

L.      abbreviation of first-name Lucius.

Latin      the language spoken by the Romans and their neighbours in the district of Latium, or a citizen of a Latin state.

legate (*legatus*)      an envoy or commissioner appointed by the Senate, or a staff-officer serving under a general with *imperium.*

legion (*legio,* plural *legiones*) the principal unit of the Roman army, with a normal paper-strength of 4200 men, made up of 1200 *velites,* 1200 *hastati,* 1200 *principes,* and 600 *triarii,* usually with 300 citizen cavalry attached. Polybius uses the Greek word "στρατόπεδον" to mean a legion - e.g. 10.16.4, but also, confusingly, other bodies of men, e.g. the allied units attached to a legion - ibid. - and a consular army of two legions + allied contingents, as at 11.26.6; in a non-technical sense, the word just means "army".

*lemboi* (Greek λέμβοι, Latin *lembi*) light, undecked warships, used particularly by the Illyrians.

*lex*      a law of the Roman state, strictly speaking passed by the *comitia centuriata* or the *comitia tributa* (see above, on *concilium plebis*).

*lictor*      attendant on certain Roman magistrates - dictators had twenty-four, consuls twelve and praetors six.

M.      abbreviation for first-name Marcus.

M'.      abbreviation for first-name Manius.

*magister equitum*      Master of the Horse - title of the lieutenant of a dictator, usually nominated by him.

magistrate (*magistratus*)      the Roman term for an official of state, not necessarily with judicial functions, though any magistrate with *imperium* could exercise a judicial function.

*maius*      literally "greater" - especially in the phrase *imperium maius:* for example, a dictator had *imperium maius* as compared to a consul.

maniple (*manipulus*)      literally "handful" - the basic sub-unit of the legion at the time of the Hannibalic War. There were 10 maniples each of *hastati, principes* and *triarii,* and the 1200 *velites* were divided equally among the resulting 30 maniples. Hence the maniples varied in size: a maniple of *hastati* or *principes,* with its

| | |
|---|---|
| | attached *velites,* consisted of 160 men, but a maniple of *triarii* with its *velites* contained only 100 men. |
| *nobilis* (plural *nobiles*) | a noble, a man one of whose ancestors in the direct male line had achieved high office, probably, strictly, the consulship, but possibly, more widely, any curule office (see below on *novus homo*). |
| *nomen Latinum* | literally "the Latin Name": a collective term for Rome's Latin allies, also called "*socii nominis Latini*" (allies of the Latin Name). |
| *novus homo* (plural *novi homines*) | a "new man", a man who achieved high office, in particular the consulship, and none of whose ancestors in the direct male line had achieved such office before him. |
| ovation (*ovatio*) | the lesser triumph (q.v.): the general honoured with an ovation entered the city on horseback or on foot, with his soldiers, not in the four-horse chariot reserved for triumphs. |
| P. | abbreviation for first-name Publius. |
| *patres* | literally "fathers": term used particularly of the patrician (see below) members of the Senate, but also of Senators in general, for example when addressing them. |
| patrician (*patricius*) | a member of certain Roman gentes, of which the most important, in Hannibal's time, were the Aemilii, Claudii (but note that the Claudii Marcelli were plebeians), Cornelii, Fabii, Valerii, Manlii, Postumii, Quinctii, Servilii (but note that some Servilii were plebeians, e.g. C. Servilius Geminus, consul 203/2), Sulpicii and Veturii. The origin of the patrician *gentes* was unclear even to the Romans, but it is important to realise that they did not use the term "patrician" vaguely to mean "noble" or "upper class", and, in particular, that the terms "patrician" and "*nobilis*" were not synonymous: almost all patricians were, no doubt, *nobiles,* but by no means all *nobiles* were patricians. |
| patron (patronus) | (see above, on clients): someone who looked after the interests of others, whether individuals or other states. |
| *pilum* | the throwing-spear used by the *hastati* and *principes.* |
| plebeians (*plebs*) | all Roman citizens, except those belonging to patrician *gentes,* were known as the *plebs* (a singular, collective noun). By the time of the Hannibalic War, some plebeian families - e.g. the Caecilli Metelli, Claudii Marcelli, Fulvii Flacci and Sempronii Gracchi - were almost as influential as even the greatest patrician families, and it is a great mistake to think that to describe such men as "plebeians" means anything like "men of the people", though the word *plebs* can, of course, be used of the "common people" of Rome and elsewhere. |
| *plebiscitum* | a decree of the plebeian assembly, the *concilium plebis,* made binding on the whole Roman people by the *lex Hortensia* of 287, and often referred to as *leges* (see above, under *lex*). |

*pontifex (pontifices* in the plural)    a member of an important college of priests, usually drawn from the leading *nobiles,* both patrician and plebeian. As in the case of the *augures* (see above), the *pontifices* were not professional priests.

*pontifex maximus*    the head of the college of *pontifices.*

*praetor*    title of certain Roman magistrates, and of the magistrates of some other Latin states. At Rome, in Hannibal's time, four praetors were elected each year: the *praetor urbanus* (city praetor), whose function, originally, was to take over the judicial functions of the consuls, but who, in virtue of his *imperium,* could command in war - in the absence of the consuls, the *praetor urbanus* was the senior magistrate, and, e.g., presided in the Senate; the *praetor peregrinus* (foreign praetor) was originally in charge of legal issues involving foreigners (*peregrini*), but, again, could command in war. The other two praetors were the governors of Sardinia and Corsica, and of Sicily.

prefect (*praefectus*)    title of various Roman officials, either in charge of certain districts in Italy - e.g. Capua after 211 - or officers in the army, particularly the *praefecti socium* (prefects of the allies), apparently Roman officers in command of allied soldiers, and presumably superior to the native officers.

*princeps Senatus*    literally "leading man in the Senate", the title of the man whose name the censors placed first on the list of senators; a great honour, the title conferred no power or official position - the *princeps Senatus* did not, for example, preside in the Senate. (Something like the 'Father of the House' in the British House of Commons).

*principes*    soldiers of the second line in the legionary order-of-battle, though the name means "leading men"; organized in exactly the same way as the *hastati* (q.v.).

*privatus*    term used of a man holding no magistracy - thus Scipio was a *privatus* when *imperium pro consule* (see above) was conferred on him to take over the command in Spain.

*proletarii*    technically citizens too poor, or otherwise unqualified to belong to any other century in the *comitia centuriata,* except the single century of the *proletarii.*

prorogue    technical term (from the Latin *prorogare*) used of prolonging the *imperium* of a magistrate after his term of office had ended - (not used in the sense of "to prorogue Parliament", i.e. to discontinue a session of Parliament without dissolving it).

*provincia*    originally the sphere in which a magistrate exercised *imperium,* hence the area, and so a "province".

*publicani*    although familiar in the New Testament as "publicans", the *publicani* of Hannibal's day were wealthy businessmen who

|  |  |
|---|---|
|  | contracted with the Roman state for public works, the collection of taxes, and so on. |
| Q. | abbreviation of the first-name Quintus. |
| quadrireme (Greek τετρήρης, Latin *quadriremis*) | a ship with an oar-power ratio of 4:3 compared to a trireme (q.v.), probably not produced by an extra bank of oars, but by increasing the number of rowers on certain oars. |
| *quaestor* | title of a Roman magistrate, originally of the two lieutenants of the consuls in charge of the treasury; later there were quaestors in charge of the fleet, Ostia, and to act as the lieutenants of men with *imperium*. Election to the quaestorship was the first important step in a man's career, and from the 80s onwards, entitled him to a seat in the Senate. |
| quinquereme (Greek πεντήρης, Latin *quinqueremis*) | a ship with an oar-power ratio of 5:3 compared to a trireme. It is very unlikely that a quinquereme had five banks of oars, but it is not certain how many banks it had, nor how many men rowed each oar. It was the standard battleship of both the Roman and the Carthaginian navies. |
| Senate (*Senatus*) | the supreme deliberative council of the Roman state, the Senate was, theoretically, a body of leading men upon whom magistrates with *imperium*, and, particularly, the consuls, could call upon for advice, but was, in practice, the government of Rome, as is indicated by the phrase "The Senate and People of Rome" (*Senatus Populusque Romanus* - SPQR), used of the Republic as an active entity. |
| *senatus consultum* | a decree of the Senate (meaning, literally, something like "the result of a consultation of the Senate"); in order to take effect, such a decree had to be enforced by a magistrate holding *imperium.* |
| Serv. | abbreviation for the first-name Servius. |
| Sex. | abbreviation for the first-name Sextus. |
| Sibylline Books | a collection of prophecies sold to King Tarquinius Priscus by the Sibyl of Cumae, according to legend, and preserved on the Capitol Hill, for consultation by the Senate. |
| *socius* (plural *socii*) | an ally, especially the allies of Rome in Italy - hence the term "Social War" (i.e. "War of the Allies") used of the great rebellion of the allies in 91. |
| *strategos (στρατηγός)* | either a general, or, more particularly, the president of certain Greek leagues, especially the Achaean and Aetolian Leagues. Polybius also uses the term to mean "consul" (e.g. 1.7.12), sometimes with the addition of the adjective "ὕπατος", i.e. "highest" (e.g. 1.52.5), which can also mean "consul" by itself (e.g. 6.12.1); a *strategos hexapelekus* (στρατηγὸς ἐξαπέλεκυς, i.e. 'six-axed strategos') in Polybius means a praetor. |

| | |
|---|---|
| T. | abbreviation for the first-name Titus. |
| talent (Greek τάλαντον, Latin *talentum*) | originally a measure of weight, but hence the sum of money represented by that weight of gold or silver. The weight varied from system to system, but the Euboeic-Attic talent used by, e.g., Polybius, weighed 26.196 kilograms. |
| Ti. | abbreviation for the first-name Tiberius. |
| *triarii* | the soldiers of the third line in the legionary order-of-battle, 600 men strong in the standard legion. The *triarii,* who consisted of the older men in a legion, possibly retained the *hasta* or thrusting-spear, after the first two lines had abandoned it in favour of the throwing-spear (*pilum*). |
| tribe (*tribus*) | as a technical term, a geographical subdivision of the Roman people - citizens were registered in the tribe in which their property lay. By Hannibal's time there were thirty-five tribes, four urban and thirty-one rural. |
| tribune (*tribunus,* plural *tribuni*) | title of Roman officials of two distinct types: (i) *tribuni militum* - tribunes of the soldiers - the six officers attached to each legion, usually young men of senatorial rank aspiring to a political career; (ii) *tribuni plebis* - tribunes of the *plebs* - originally elected by the *plebs* to represent its interests and to protect the rights of plebeians against patricians, they had the power to 'veto' (meaning, literally, "I forbid") the acts of magistrates. By the time of the Hannibalic War, they had become part of the regular machinery of the state, and were often used by the Senate, for example, to sound out public opinion by laying matters before the *concilium plebis.* They became regular members of the Senate in 149, or, possibly, in 196. |
| *tributum* | the direct tax paid by Roman citizens (abolished in 167), or, generally, tribute paid by subjects. |
| trireme (Greek τριήρης, Latin *triremis*) | in classical Greece certainly a warship rowed by three banks of oars, each oar being rowed by a single man, though the term was possibly used later of a warship with an oar-power of 3 - e.g. with a single bank, each oar rowed by three men, or some other combination. |
| triumph (*triumphus*) | the parade through the streets of Rome by a victorious general and his men - an honour normally granted by the Senate, but exceptionally, it is alleged, by the people. |
| *turma* | a squadron of cavalry, with a paper-strength of 30. |
| *velites* | the light-infantry or skirmishers attached to a legion, 1200 strong in the standard legion, divided equally, for organizational purposes, among the 30 maniples of the infantry of the line. |

For the sake of convenience, I have assumed that Hannibal reached the top of the final pass on November 1st (see p. 33 above and n. 5 on p. 286). This means, of course, that all the other absolute dates are arbitrary. But the intervals between them should be about right for the period up to the day the army left the sea to march to the crossing of the Rhône, and almost exact thereafter.

I have also assumed an average day's march was 80 stades (14.2 kilometres) long. This is what is implied by Polybius' statement (3.50.1) that Hannibal marched 800 stades "along the river" in ten days, but it is, of course, possible that along other parts of the route the army marched slower or faster (see Proctor, 26-34). Polybius also tells us about some rest-days, and I have assumed that on the long stretches of the route from Cartagena to the Rhône, a rest-day was allowed once a week. From the Rhône onwards rest-days seem to have been allowed as and when circumstances permitted, as was only natural. The longest continuous marches appear to have been the ten days' march "along the river", and the nine days' march from the site of the battle in the gorge to the summit of the final pass. But the former followed a period of rest on the "island" for which I have allowed four days, but which could well have been longer, and in the latter case, Hannibal could well have been deliberately forcing the pace, as his wait for stragglers at the summit of the pass suggests (cf. Polybius 3.53.9). If, however, the location of the battle in the gorge between Pontcharra and La Rochette is correct, the army could have marched from there to the Col de Clapier in about eight days at the average speed of 14.2 kilometres a day. Thus, once he had got some distance beyond the gorge, Hannibal could have allowed a rest-day - for example, at Aiguebelle, about one day's march from the gorge - leaving about 100 kilometres to march to the summit of the Col de Clapier in the remaining seven days.

| | | |
|---|---|---|
| June 8th | : | departure from Cartagena |
| July 15th | : | arrival at the Ebro (distance 2600 stades - Polybius 3.39.6 - i.e. 32½ days marching + five rest-days). |
| July 16th | : | march to Emporion (Ampurias) and subjugation of tribes |
| August 28th | | north of Ebro. (This is the most variable part of the diary: the actual distance from the Ebro to Emporion was 1600 stades - Polybius 3.39.7 - i.e. 20 days marching + three rest-days, but we have no means of telling how long it took to subdue the tribes or to re-organize the army.) |
| August 29th | : | departure from Emporion (this date is arrived at by calculating back from the arrival at the summit of the pass on November 1st, and assuming that the march from Emporion to the Rhône took 23 days). |

| | | |
|---|---|---|
| September 17th | : | army leaves the sea to march to the crossing-place. |
| September 20th | : | arrival at crossing-place, four days' march from sea (Polybius 3.42.1). (Distance from Emporion to crossing-place 1600 stades - Polybius 3.39.8, cf. Walbank I, 371 - i.e. 20 days marching (the last four from the sea to the Rhône crossing) + three rest-days). |
| September 21st-22nd | : | two days spent collecting boats, etc., for crossing Rhône (Polybius 3.42.6). |
| Night of September 22nd/23rd | : | Hanno sets off up Rhône "on the third night" (Polybius 3.42.6). |
| September 23rd | : | main army waits at crossing-place; Hanno waits for darkness to cover his crossing (?). |
| Night of September 23rd/24th | : | Hanno crosses river under cover of darkness (?). |
| September 24th | : | main army continues to wait at crossing; Hanno rests in strong position on left bank (Polybius 3.42.9). |
| Night of September 24th/25th | : | Hanno moves back down river "on the fifth night at dawn" (Polybius 3.43.1). |
| September 25th | : | forcing of the crossing. |
| September 26th | : | "next day" (Polybius 3.44.3), assembly of troops, skirmish between Numidian and Roman cavalry. |
| September 27th | : | "on the day after the assembly" (Polybius 3.45.5), Hannibal sends cavalry towards sea to cover rear, infantry up river, while elephants brought across. After elephants have crossed, sets off up river with them and cavalry (Polybius 3.47.1). |
| September 27th-30th | : | four days march to "island" (Polybius 3.49.5). (Distance Tarascon-Aygues = c.58 kilometres). |
| September 30th - October 4th | : | days spent on "island" helping Braneus to oust brother and refitting army. |
| October 5th-14th | : | ten days march "along the river" (Polybius 3.50.1: distance 800 stades - 142 kilometres - Aygues-?St. Nazaire-en-Royans). |
| October 14th | : | beginning of "the ascent towards the Alps" (Polybius 3.50.1). Hannibal camps "near the pass" (Polybius 3.50.5); Gallic scouts report departure of Allobroges after nightfall. |
| October 15th | : | Hannibal advances openly and camps again near enemy positions commanding difficult part of route (Polybius 3.50.8). |
| Night of October 15th/16th | : | Hannibal occupies positions vacated by Allobroges (Polybius 3.50.9). |
| October 16th | : | battle with Allobroges, ending in capture of town (Polybius 3.51: distance from Tarascon-Villard-de-Lans 236 kilometres =? Polybius' 1400 stades - 248 kilometres - from crossing to "ascent of the Alps". |

| | | |
|---|---|---|
| October 17th | : | army rests in captured town (Polybius 3.52.1). |
| October 18th-21st | : | four days' march ends in meeting with treacherous Gauls (Polybius 3.52.2: distance Villard-de-Lans-Tencin = 57 kilometres). |
| October 22nd-23rd | : | two days further advance under guidance of treacherous Gauls, ending in ambush in gorge (Polybius 3.52.8ff.: distance Tencin-Pontcharra = 14 kilometres). |
| Night of October 23rd/24th | : | Hannibal spends night with infantry at "bare rock" while cavalry and pack-train struggles through gorge (Polybius 3.53.5). |
| October 24th | : | Hannibal and infantry rejoin cavalry and pack-train, and advance "towards the highest pass of the Alps" (Polybius 3.53.6). |
| November 1st | : | army reaches top of pass "on the ninth day" and waits for two days (i.e. ? that day and next: Polybius 3.53.9: distance La Rochette-Col de Clapier c. 112 kilometres). |
| November 2nd | : | wait on pass for stragglers (Polybius 3.53.9-10). |
| November 3rd | : | first day of descent, ending in camp on ridge (Polybius 3.55.6). |
| November 4th | : | day spent repairing track for horses and pack-animals, ending in camp where snow had cleared (Polybius 3.55.7). |
| November 5th-6th | : | two further days spent repairing track for elephants, making three days work on track in all (Polybius 3.55.8). |
| November 7th-8th | : | whole army continues descent and reaches plains "on the third day" (Polybius 3.56.1: assuming that this is counted from last day of work on track). |
| November 8th | : | army reaches plains five months after leaving Cartagena (Polybius 3.56.3), having spent fifteen days on "the crossing of the Alps" (i.e. on march from site of battle in gorge to plains, ? excluding day spent on summit of pass). |

# CHRONOLOGICAL OUTLINE

| | ITALY | SICILY | AFRICA | SPAIN | GREECE etc. |
|---|---|---|---|---|---|
| 264/3 | Ap.Claudius Caudex M.Fulvius Flaccus — Rome accepts appeal of Mamertini | Claudius Caudex takes first Roman army to Sicily | | | |
| 256/5 | L.Manlius Vulso Longus Q.Caedicius | Battle of Ecnomus | Roman invasion of Africa (defeated 255) | | |
| 247/6 | L.Caecilius Metellus N.Fabius Buteo | Hamilcar appointed to command Carthaginian forces | Hannibal born | | |
| 242/1 | C.Lutatius Catulus A.Postumius Albinus (1) | B. of Aegates Is. (March 10, 241); 1st Punic War ends | Mutiny of mercenaries begins | | |
| 238/7 | Ti.Sempronius Gracchus P.Valerius Falto — Rome annexes Sardinia | | end of Mercenary War | Hamilcar takes command of Carthaginian forces | |
| 231/0 | M.Pomponius Matho C.Papirius Maso | | | Roman embassy to Hamilcar | |
| 229/8 | L.Postumius Albinus (2) Cn.Fulvius Centumalus | | | Death of Hamilcar | 1st Illyrian War |

| Year / Consuls | Italy | Carthaginian raids / Africa | Declaration of war | Spain / Mediterranean |
|---|---|---|---|---|
| 226/5<br>M.Valerius Messalla<br>L.Apustius Fullo | | | | Ebro agreement with Hasdrubal (?) |
| 225/4<br>L.Aemilius Papus<br>C.Atilius Regulus | Gallic invasion defeated at Telamon in Etruria | | | |
| 221/0<br>P.Cornelius Scipio Asina<br>M.Minucius Rufus | | | | Death of Hasdrubal; accession of Philip V; Hannibal succeeds to command |
| 220/19<br>C.Lutatius Catulus<br>L.Veturius Philo | | | | Hannibal's campaign against Vaccaei; first Roman ultimatum |
| 219/8<br>L.Aemilius Paullus (1)<br>M.Livius Salinator (1) | | | | Siege of Saguntum   2nd Illyrian War |
| 218/7<br>P.Cornelius Scipio<br>Ti.Sempronius Longus | Hannibal arrives in Italy; b.of Ticinus; b. of Trebbia | Carthaginian naval raids | Fabius Buteo's declaration of war | Hannibal leaves for Italy (June); Cn. Scipio lands (autumn) |
| 217/6<br>Cn.Servilius Geminus<br>C.Flaminius (2) | B. of L. Trasimene; Hannibal invades Campania and breaks out at Callicula; skirmishes near Gerunium | Servilius raids Africa | | Cn. Scipio's naval victory off Ebro; P.Scipio arrives; Romans advance to Saguntum |

| | ITALY | SICILY | AFRICA | SPAIN | GREECE etc. |
|---|---|---|---|---|---|
| **216/5**<br>C.Terentius Varro<br>L.Aemilius Paullus (2) | B. of Cannae; Capua defects; Hannibal attacks Naples and Nola, takes Nuceria and Acerrae, and begins siege of Casilinum | | P.Furius Philus raids Africa | Hasdrubal defeated near mouth of Ebro (early 215) | |
| **215/4**<br>Ti.Sempronius Gracchus (1)<br>Q.Fabius Maximus (3) | Hannibal takes Casilinum, & attacks Cumae; 3rd b. at Nola; Bomilcar lands reinforcements at Locri | Death of King Hiero of Syracuse | T.Otacilius Crassus raids Africa | Scipios defeat Hasdrubal before Iliturgi and Intibili (?) | alliance between Philip & Hannibal |
| **214/3**<br>Q.Fabius Maximus (4)<br>M.Claudius Marcellus (3) | Romans recapture Casilinum; Hannibal attacks Puteoli; Gracchus defeats Hanno on R.Calor; 4th b. at Nola; Hannibal fails at Tarentum | Death of Hieronymos; Marcellus arrives & takes Leontinoi; defection of Syracuse | | alleged Roman victories near Castulo, Munda and Aurinx | Valerius Laevinus defeats Philip near Apollonia, and winters at Corcyra |
| **213/2**<br>Q.Fabius Maximus (the son)<br>Ti.Sempronius Gracchus (2) | Fabius recaptures Arpi | unsuccessful assaults on Syracuse; Carthaginian army lands at Heraclea | | recapture of Saguntum (?); alleged negotiations with Syphax | |

| Year / Consuls | Italy | Sicily | Africa | Spain | Greece |
|---|---|---|---|---|---|
| 212/1<br>Q.Fulvius Flaccus (3)<br>Ap.Claudius Pulcher | Hannibal takes Tarentum (early); Romans begin siege of Capua; Hanno defeated near Beneventum; Gracchus killed; 1st b. of Herdonea | Marcellus takes Epipolai (spring), beats off land and sea relief forces, frightens Bomilcar off C.Pachynon, & takes Syracuse (late autumn) | | | Laevinus begins negotiations with Aetolian League |
| 211/10<br>Cn.Fulvius Centumalus<br>P.Sulpicius Galba | Hannibal's march on Rome; surrender of Capua | Marcellus' mopping-up operations | | defeat and deaths of elder Scipios; Claudius Nero takes over | Alliance between Rome and Aetolian League; minor operations in NW; Galba takes over |
| 210/09<br>M.Claudius Marcellus (4)<br>M.Valerius Laevinus | Recapture of Salapia 2nd b. of Herdonea; b. of Numistro | Laevinus captures Agrigentum, and pacifies Sicily | Valerius Messala raids Africa | the younger Scipio takes command | Philip takes Echinous; Galba takes Aegina |
| 209/8<br>Q.Fabius Maximus (5)<br>Q.Fulvius Flaccus (4) | 12 Latin colonies refuse troops; Fabius recaptures Tarentum | | | Scipio captures Cartagena | Philip defeats Aetolians at Lamia & attacks Elis; Carthaginian fleet in Greek waters |
| 208/7<br>M.Claudius Marcellus (5)<br>T.Quinctius Crispinus | consuls killed in ambush | | Valerius Laevinus raids Africa and defeats Carthaginian fleet off Clupea | B. of Baecula | Operations in Euboea & Locris; Carthaginian fleet leaves Greece |

| | ITALY | SICILY | AFRICA | SPAIN | GREECE etc. |
|---|---|---|---|---|---|
| **207/6**<br>C.Claudius Nero<br>M.Livius Salinator (2) | Metaurus campaign | | Valerius Laevinus raids Africa and defeats Carthaginian fleet for second time | Iunius Silanus disperses Carthaginian recruits; L.Scipio takes Orongis | Philip raids Aetolia; Machanidas killed at Mantinea |
| **206/5**<br>L. Veturius Philo<br>Q.Caecilius Metallus | Minor operations in Bruttium | | | B.of Ilipa (spring); suppression of mutiny and Ilergetes; Scipio visits Syphax; Mago leaves for Balearic Is. | Philip concludes peace with Aetolians; Sempronius Tuditanus takes over |
| **205/4**<br>P.Cornelius Scipio<br>P.Licinius Crassus Dives | capture of Locri; Pleminius incident; Mago lands at Genoa | | Laelius raids Africa | | Peace of Phoinike |
| **204/3**<br>M.Cornelius Cethegus<br>P.Sempronius Tuditanus | Minor operations in Bruttium | Scipio organizes army for invasion of Africa | Scipio lands (June ?) defeats Carthaginian cavalry forces, begins siege of Utica, and winters at Castra Cornelia; burning of the camps (winter) | | |
| **203/2**<br>Cn.Servilius Caepio<br>C.Servilius Geminus | Caepio campaigns in Bruttium, Geminus against Mago; Mago & Hannibal withdraw | | B. of the Great Plains (June ?); Carthage sues for peace; capture of Roman convoy (winter) | | |

202/1
M.Servilius Pulex
  Geminus
Ti.Claudius Nero

Battle of Zama
(October ?); defeat
of Vermina (December
12th)

201/0
Cn.Cornelius
  Lentulus
P.Aelius Paetus

Formal conclusion
of peace

# NOTES TO CHAPTER I

1.   for Polybius and other ancient writers see Appendix I, 258-64.
    All translations are my own, although I inevitably owe many felicities to others. Note that where Polybius or Livy is the primary source for something in the text, I do not usually cite any secondary sources.
2.   all dates are B.C., unless otherwise specified or obviously not. Since at this time the consuls took office on March 15th, and held it until the following March 14th, consular years will be expressed in the form, e.g., 218/7.
3.   cf. Gibbon, *Decline and Fall of the Roman Empire* (Everyman Edition), ch. XXXI, 217ff.
4.   for a brief explanation of these and other technical terms see Appendix II,
5.   cf., e.g., E. S. Staveley, *Greek and Roman Voting and Elections* (London 1972), 123-132, and notes, 246-7.
6.   see, e.g., M. Gelzer, *Die Nobilität der römische Republik* (first published Stuttgart 1922), now translated into English by R. Seager under the title *The Roman Nobility* (Oxford 1969), 3-139; H. H. Scullard, *Roman Politics 220-150 B.C.* (second edition Oxford 1973), 1-38.
7.   cf., e.g., Scullard *Roman Politics* 44-5. For politics during the war, in general, see Scullard, op. cit., 39-88; F. Cassola, *I Gruppi Politici Romani nel III Secolo A.C.* (Trieste 1962), 259-427.
8.   cf. *Commentariolum Petitionis* (A Pamphlet on Electioneering), 53, and compare 5 and 51.
9.   Aristotle *Politics* 1272b24f.; Diodoros 13.43 and 14.45. On Carthage and the Carthaginians see B.H. Warmington, *Carthage* (London 1964); A. J. Toynbee, *Hannibal's Legacy* (London 1965), I, 28-38; G. C. & C. Picard, *The Life and Death of Carthage* (London 1968).
10.   cf., e.g., T. Frank, *CP* 1926, 313-4; *CAH* 7.689; T. A. Dorey & D. R. Dudley, *Rome Against Carthage* (London 1971), 29-30.
11.   I can think of only three - Livy 23.46.6 (272 Numidian and Spanish horsemen), 24.47.8-9 (1000 Spaniards) Livy 26.40.3ff. (Mottones). Livy also says that 3000 Carpetani deserted during the crossing of the Pyrenees (21.24.4ff.), but Polybius says nothing of this, and in any case, these would be levies.
12.   the Greeks called these people "Phoinikes", whence the Latin "Poeni" and the English "Punic". But as late as the fifth century A.D. St. Augustine says that if one asked peasants in the old territory of Carthage who they were, they would reply "Chanani" (i.e. Canaanites - *Epistolae ad Romanos inchoata expositio,* 13; cf. D. Harden, *The Phoenicians* (London 1963), 20ff., and 219 n.5.
13.   in fact they were probably of Berber stock, cf. S. Gsell, *Histoire ancienne de l'Afrique du Nord* (Paris 1912ff.), i 309ff.
14.   Brunt *IM* 391 n.1.
15.   Brunt *IM* 17-21.
16.   Brunt *IM* 44ff.
17.   see Table IVb, Brunt *IM* 45.
18.   cf. A.N. Sherwin-White, *The Roman Citizenship* (second edition Oxford 1973), 96ff; Toynbee *HL* I, 249-257.
19.   E. Badian, *Foreign Clientelae* (Oxford 1958), 25-8.
20.   Sherwin-White, op.cit., 123ff., and see p. 60 above.
21.   Brunt *IM,* Appendix 6, 545-8.
22.   Brunt *IM,* Appendix 26, 677-86.
23.   the *velites* may originally have been called *rorarii* (cf. Livy 8.8.8, 8.9.4), but cf. Walbank's note on Polybius 6.21.7 (I, 701-2). Despite Livy's statement that the *velites* first appeared in 211 (24.4.10), he mentions them at the Trebbia in 218 (21.55.11): I shall use the term of Roman skirmishers throughout, but see E. Gabba, *Republican Rome: the Army and the Allies* (trans. P. J. Cuff, Oxford 1976), 5-6.
24.   on Roman arms see P. Couissin, *Les Armes Romaines* (Paris 1926); J. Kromayer & G. Veith, *Heerwesen und Kriegführung der Griechen und Römer* (Munich 1928), 261ff.; E. Mayer, *Kleine Schriften* (Halle 1910-24), II 198ff.; Schulten *RE* s.v. 'pilum'.
25.   ἀκοντισταί: 3.65.5, 3.65.7 cf. 10; 3.69.8, 11; 3.72.2.
    γροσφομάχοι: 6.21.7; 11.22.10; 15.9.9; 15.12.3.

26. on elephants see Gavin de Beer, *Hannibal* (London 1974), 191 and 100-7, and in general H.H. Scullard, *The Elephant in the Greek and Roman World* (London 1974).
27. J. Kromayer, *Philologus* 1897, 485ff.
28. on Roman and Carthaginian warships see R. C. Anderson, *Oared Fighting Ships* (London 1962), 21-30; on the crews of Roman ships see Brunt *IM* 65, 421-2; on the use of slaves Livy 24.11.7ff., 26.35; prisoners of war Polybius 10.17.11.
29. cf. Brunt *IM* 279ff.
30. Walbank I, 337ff.
31. although the tradition is dismissed as a Roman fabrication by some scholars (e.g. Beloch, *Griechische Geschichte*, IV i 642), it is possible that some move by the Carthaginian fleet had aroused Roman suspicions.
32. see Walbank I, 314-5.
33. presumably the Carthaginians called this place "Kart Hadasht" like their own city. The Romans called it "Nova Carthago" - which is like saying "New Newcastle" - but Polybius says it was called either "Karchedon" (i.e. Carthage), or "Kaine Polis" (New City) (2.13.1), and in fact uses both names himself - cf., e.g., 3.13.7 and 10.6.8. For convenience I shall call it by its modern name - Cartagena.
34. cf. Walbank I, 317.
35. G. V. Sumner, *Harvard Studies in Classical Philology*, 72 (1967), 216.
36. Walbank I, 319, and references there.
37. see particularly 3.39.6 where the distances given for between Cartagena and the "Iber" and between the "Iber" and Ampurias only make sense if the "Iber" is the Ebro.
38. cf., e.g., H. H. Scullard, *A History of the Roman World 753-146 B.C.* (third edition London 1961), 184-5; E. Badian, *Foreign Clientelae*, 47ff.
39. Scullard, op. cit., 179; Walbank I, 170.
40. cf. Sumner, op. cit. n. 35 above, 222-32 - Ebo or Girona; J. Carcopino, *Revue des études anciennes*, 1953, 258-93 - Jucar.
41. E. Taubler, *Die Vorgeschichte des zweiten punischen Kriegs* (Berlin 1921), 44; F. R. Kramer, *American Journal of Philology*, 69 (1948), 1ff.; Scullard, op. cit., 178; Walbank I, 168.
42. see Badian, *Foreign Clientelae*, 48.
43. for the controversy surrounding the exact relationship between Rome and Saguntum see Walbank I, 321 and 357, and Badian, op. cit., 49ff. It is, in my view, certain that there was no formal *foedus* between the two states, since, if there had been, Polybius would have mentioned it.
44. Sumner, op. cit., 236.
45. Appian may simply have confused the name "Torboletai" with "Turbuli", another name for Livy's "Turdetani" (cf. 28.39.8 & 11).
46. Sumner, op .cit. , 235.
47. on Saguntum see Walbank I, 319-20, and references there.
48. but see Sumner, op.cit., 238-41.
49. Walbank I, 320.
50. Sir Denis Proctor, *Hannibal's March in History* (Oxford 1971), 48-51.
51. Broughton, *MRR* I, 241 n. 7; Munzer, *RE* s.v. 'Fabius' no. 116, col. 116f. On the conditional nature of declaration of war by the *comitia centuriata* see Walbank I, 334.
52. see F. R. Kramer, *AJP*, 1948, 1-26.

# NOTES TO CHAPTER II

1.    cf. Proctor, 22-4.
2.    Walbank, I, 363.
3.    Silius Italicus (3.65ff.) says that Hannibal also sent his wife, Imilce, and the son born to them during the siege of Saguntum, back to Carthage, before leaving for Italy. But since no other writer records his wife's name - Silius Italicus constantly invents names, both Carthaginian and Roman - or that Hannibal had any children, we can hardly accept these statements.
4.    cf., e.g., Scullard, *History*, 187 ("at the end of April"); Dorey and Dudley, *Rome Against Carthage*, 38 ("towards the end of April").
5.    see now Proctor, 40-5.
6.    Proctor shows - 15ff. - that when Polybius says (3.34.6) that Hannibal brought his stroops out of winter quarters "ὑπὸ τὴν ἐαρινὴν ὥραν", he does not mean "in the early spring" (as the Loeb translation, e.g., has it), but at most "in spring" - and, strictly speaking, summer begins on June 21st/22nd. For a tentative reconstruction of the diary of the march see Appendix III.
7.    e.g., L. Cottrell, *Enemy of Rome* (London 1960), 37; de Beer, *Hannibal* (London 1969), 120. Valerius Maximus (8.3.2) does, however, say that Hamilcar had four sons, whom he called his "lion cubs" (*catuli leonini*).
8.    for the length of Polybius' *stadion* - 177.55 metres - see Proctor, 10. As Walbank points out (I 371), it is unnecessary to insert 600 stadioi here, as many editors do.
9.    See G.C. & C. Picard, *The Life and Death of Carthage*. 248 and 250.
10.   the literature is voluminous, but in my view by far the best discussion is now Sir Denis Proctor's *Hannibal's March in History* (Oxford 1971). To his bibliography and the references in Walbank may be added: A. Guillaume, *Annibal franchit les Alpes, 218 av. J.-C.* (La Touche-Montfleury Edition des Cahiers de l'Alpe, 1967); P. Marquion, *L'itinéraire d'Hannibal. Essai d'identification du point ou il aborda les Alpes, Cahiers d'Histoire* (published by the universities of Clermont-Lyon-Grenoble. Lyon, Faculté des Lettres), 17 (1972), 105-19; E. de Saint-Denis, *Encore l'itinéraire transalpin d'Hannibal, Revue des études Latines,* 51 (1973), 122-49.
11.   see Walbank I, 382, on Polybius 3.48.12.
12.   Proctor, 103-17.
13.   Proctor, 89-96
14.   de Beer, *Hannibal's March* (London 1967), 35-47; Procter, 122-53.
15.   e.g. by Walbank I, 387.
16.   e.g. Walbank, ibid.
17.   Proctor, 166-9.
18.   de Beer (*Hannibal's March,* 64) locates the Tricorii in the vicinity of Gap on the basis of mediaeval diocese boundaries. If this is correct, we should have to give up the attempt to understand Livy's - and Timagenes of Alexandria's - references to the three tribes, Tricastini, Vocontii and Tricorii.
19.   Proctor, 165ff. It is worth noting that if Livy misplaced an account of the crossing of the Durance in one of his sources, the source in question presumably had Hannibal cross the Rhône *below* the Durance.
20.   Gavin de Beer, originally in *Alps and Elephants* (London 1955), more recently in *Hannibal's March* (London 1967), and in *Hannibal* (London 1969), 120-82.
21.   as de Beer himself argues, *Hannibal's March,* 64, *Hannibal,* 149.
22.   cf. Proctor, 171-4. De Beer's calculations about the flow of water in various parts of the river at various times of the year, are really irrelevant.
23.   cf., e.g., Walbank I, 383ff. Where I differ from Walbank is that, in my view, only the actual account of the crossing of the Durance has been misplaced - i.e. from 21.31.9 " . . . haud usquam impedita via" to 21.31.12 " . . . incertis clamoribus turbarentur." Is it possible, indeed, that the whole difficulty is due to some copyist's error, rather than Livy's? - note "quartis castris ad Insulam *pervenit*" (21.31.4), " . . . priusquam ad Druentiam flumen *pervenit*" (21.31.9), " . . . ab Druentia campestri maxime itinere *ad Alpis* cum bona pace incolentium ea loca Gallorum *pervenit*" (21.32.6); and note also " . . . non quia *rectior ad*

*Alpis* via esset" (21.31.2), and "cum iam *Alpes* peteret, non *recta* regione iter instituit."

24.  Walbank I, 384.
25.  cf. Proctor, 155ff. Proctor thinks that the Carthaginians may have cut across the extreme northern tip of the Vercors from some point on RN 532 in the 20 kilometres before one comes to St. Quentin, but the route suggested in the text above is the obvious one.
26.  cf. Proctor, 150-1.
27.  Proctor, 157. Cularo was renamed Gratianopolis in honour of the emperor Gratian in the 4th century A.D. - whence Grenoble.
28.  unfortunately de Beer's neat identification of the "Cremonis iugum" with the Col de Grimone on RN 539 between Chatillon-en-Diois and la Croix Haute (*Hannibal's March*, 67-8) must be rejected, since - for the reasons given above - it is nowhere near the route suggested by Polybius' account, or by Livy's statement that Hannibal marched "along the farthest frontier of the Vocontii" for that matter.
29.  de Beer, *Hannibal,* 165; but cf. Proctor, 205-6.
30.  Walbank (I, 391) argues that these two days are the last two of the four implied by Polybius 3.52.2 ("τεταρταῖος"), but I can see no reason for this, unless with Walbank we suppose that the fifteen days the army is said to have spent on "the crossing of the Alps" (ἡ τῶν ᾽Αλπεων ὑπερβολή: Polybius 3.56.3), are to be counted from the day upon which Hannibal "began the ascent towards the Alps" (Polybius 3.50.1), which is impossible - see above.
31.  John Hoyte in his amusing book *Trunk Road for Hannibal* (London 1960) locates the first ambush here, but this is based on the erroneous view that the "island" lay between the Rhône and the Isère.
32.  this vitiates de Beer's identification with the rock of Chateau Queyras (*Hannibal's March,* 95-6), which is in any case, as we have seen, on the wrong route. De Beer seems completely to have misunderstood Polybius' account here.
33.  e.g. by Walbank I, 391.
34.  J.F.T. de Montholon, *Memoires... à Sainte-Hélène* (1905 edition), Vol. IV, 277-81.
35.  Proctor, 191-6. A variation of the col de Clapier route was proposed by M. A. de Lavis - Trafford in 1956 (*Bulletin commémorant le centenaire de la Société d'Histoire et d'Archéologie de Maurienne.* Tome XIII, 1956, 109-200).
36.  cf. Walbank I, 392.
37.  cf. de Beer, *Hannibal's March,* 112-3.
38.  e.g. by Walbank I, 391-2.
39.  cf. Walbank, ibid., and n.30 above.
40.  in reality, it was at least a whole day's march more, for, as we saw (above,    ), the point at which Hannibal "began the ascent towards the Alps", is *not* the same as the point from which the earlier calculation of 1200 stades (3.39.9-10) was made, but some distance before it.
41.  I take "ἡ τῶν ᾽Αλπεων ὑπερβολή" in 3.49.13 to refer to the same thing as "αἱ τῶν ᾽Αλπεων ὑπερβολαί" in 3.39.10, and to include the "ὑπερβολαί" of 3.50.5 - (also called "δυσχωρίαι" in 3.50.3 and 8) - and the "ὑπερβολαί αἱ ἀνωτάτω τῶν ᾽Αλπεων" in 3.53.6. But I do not think that "ἡ τῶν ᾽Αλπεων ὑπερβολή" in 3.56.3 can refer to the same thing, but must refer only to the nine days' march from the battle in the gorge to the summit of the pass, and to the six days of the descent, for the reasons given above.

Another alternative is to take "the ninth day" on which the army reached the top of the pass, to mean the ninth day from the departure from the captured town (as does R.L. Dunbabin, *CR,* 1931, 52-7 and 121-5). This has the merit of making "on the ninth day" refer back to the same point as "on the fourth day" in 3.52.2, but would still mean that the expression was used in a different way from the similar expressions in 3.52.2 and 3.56.1, and would also mean that the army marched all the way from the captured town to the summit of the pass in nine days, although the distance cannot have been much less than the 1200 stades Polybius gives for the distance between "the ascent of the Alps" and the plains (3.49.10), whereas we would only expect the army to have marched something like 720 stades in nine days, particularly when it had to fight the battle in the gorge on the way. This alternative still also involves juggling with Polybius' timing of the descent as do the others.

One final possibility is that the fifteen days are the six days march to the site of the ambush in the gorge, added to the nine days march from there to the summit of the pass. This has the merit of not involving any juggling with Polybius' timing, but there seems to be no good reason why Polybius should have referred to this part of the march as "the crossing of the Alps" - this phrase surely implies that the descent was included.

42.  see Appendix III.
43.  it is typical of Livy's attitude to his sources that although he cites Polybius' figures in his own discussion of the numbers in Hannibal's army when it reached Italy (21.38.2ff.), without naming him, he appears to have paid no attention to the evidence Polybius in turn cites for his figures, but seems inclined to prefer those of L. Cincius Alimentus.

# NOTES TO CHAPTER III

1. W. Hoffmann, *Rheinisches Museum für Philologie,* 1951, 77ff.
2. cf. Proctor, 49-51.
3. e.g. Proctor, 47-8.
4. de Sanctis (III ii 4ff.) argues that it had been decided to try to stop Hannibal in southern France, but although this is accepted by, e.g., Scullard (*History,* 186), there is no reason to doubt the ancient evidence.
5. Walbank I, 375-7; for a slightly different explanation see Brunt, 646-7.
6. Livy (21.32.5) says first that he returned to Genoa, but then contradicts himself and agrees with Polybius (21.39.3).
7. Walbank I, 399.
8. the tradition has been doubted - e.g. by E. Wölfllin, *Hermes,* 1888, 307-10, 479-80; E. Meyer, *Kleine Schriften* ii 430 - on the ground that if it had been true, the alternative tradition attributed to Coelius Antipater by Livy (21.46.10), that the consul's life was saved by a Ligurian slave, would never have arisen. But Polybius cites the younger Scipio's friend, C. Laelius, as his authority, and the alternative tradition may go back to the campaign of vilification later directed against Scipio Africanus (cf. de Sanctis, III ii 25-6 n. 39).
9. Livy rightly rejected the version of Coelius Antipater here (cf. 21.47.4-5) - it held that Mago immediately crossed the Po with the cavalry and the Spanish infantry, while Hannibal crossed by a ford higher up, using the elephants to break the force of the current. Livy says that anyone who knows the Po, finds this, hard to believe - one of the few occasions when he appears to draw on his own experience.
10. see J. Kromayer, *Antike Schlachtfelder,* iii.1.47ff.; B.L. Hallward, *CAH* VIII, 709 and 726; de Sanctis III ii 92ff. The only difficulty is that both Polybius (3.74.4) and Livy (21.56.2-3) are agreed that at the battle, 10,000 Roman troops broke through the Carthaginian line and got away to Placentia. This suggests that the Romans were facing towards Placentia in the battle and had thus crossed the Trebbia from west to east before it. If the view adopted in the text above is accepted, we have to suppose that the 10,000 went round the Carthaginian left wing to get away.
11. Walbank I, 402.
12. Proctor, 63-70.
13. I can find no evidence for the assertion by G.C. & C. Picard (*Life and Death of Carthage,* 250) that Hannibal only had three elephants left after crossing the Alps, and it is certainly contradicted by the part they played at the Trebbia. As for the numbers on the Roman side at the battle - see Walbank I, 405-6 - I can see little point in speculating: in general I shall reproduce what the sources say about numbers, without constantly reiterating that they are probably too high. Their numbers for the Romans, at least, would in any case at best be based on paper-strengths.
14. Livy, consistently with his view that the Roman camp was to the west of the Trebbia, says that Scipio and his men crossed the river on rafts during the night after the battle.
15. cf., e.g., Scullard, *History,* 190, and *Roman Politics,* 44; Dorey & Dudley, *Rome Against Carthage,* 50.
16. in particular, I find it hard to accept Cassola's theory (*Gruppi Politici,* 261ff.) that Flaminius was linked to Fabius Maximus. For possible links between Flaminius and the Aemilii see Scullard, *Roman Politics,* 53-4.
17. see Walbank I, 412-3.
18. Walbank I, 411.
19. G.C. & C. Picard (*Life and Death of Carthage,* 239-41) argue on the basis of numismatic and archaeological evidence that Capua, Tarentum, and other Greek cities of the south felt threatened by the development of industry at Rome and Praeneste, and that Hannibal must have known this. Considering the primitive nature of ancient industry, this seems far-fetched, but Hannibal will certainly have known that Tarentum and the other Greek cities of the south had been the last places in peninsular Italy to succumb to Rome, and may have known or suspected something of Capua's attitude.

20. J. Kromayer, *Antike Schlachtfelder*, iii.1.104-47; de Sanctis III ii 104-9.
21. for an interesting study of the implications of Hannibal's loss of an eye, see T.W. Africa, *Historia* 19 (1970), 528-38.
22. Walbank I, 410-11; Brunt, 418-9 and 647-8.
23. Brunt, 648.
24. Livy (22.3.6) says that Hannibal "having left the enemy on his left and making for Faesulae *(Faesulas petens)*, advanced to ravage the middle lands of Etruria," but, as it stands, this is nonsense, since Faesulae was eighty kilometres behind him when he passed Flaminius at Arretium. Livy's text has been emended to read, e.g., *"Faesulas praeteriens"* (passing by Faesulae: Conway) or *"Cortonam petens"* (making for Cortona: Dunbabin), but Livy may himself have made a mistake through misunderstanding his sources.
25. G. Susini, *Ricerche sulla battaglia del Trasimeno (Annuario dell' Accademia etrusca di Cortona*, 11, 1959-60), and *Studi annibalici: Atti del convegno svoltosi a Cortona-Tuoro sul Trasimeno-Perugia*, 1961 (Cortona 1964), 132-6. For criticisms see Walbank *JRS* 1961, 232-4, and see also P.G. Walsh, *CR* 1962, 99.
26. for a defence of Livy's account see T.A. Dorey, *Euphrosyne* 1961, 213-5.
27. de Sanctis III ii 122-4; Walbank I, 420-1.
28. see Broughton, *MRR* I, 245-6, n.2. G.V. Sumner, *Phoenix* 29 (1975), 250-9, attempts to defend the statement of the *Fasti Capitolini* that Fabius was elected *"interregni causa"*, but as Broughton points out, Fabius acted as though he had been appointed *"rei gerendae causa"*, and with Servilius still alive, there could be no *interregnum* - unless he was believed to be dead. See, further, n.34 below.
29. cf., e.g., Scullard, *Roman Politics*, 46. It may not even be true, as has been claimed (Dorey & Dudley, *Rome Against Carthage*, 54) that Minucius was "a man of humble origin," for although he was not a member of the patrician *gens Minucia*, there had been a plebeian consul called Minucius as far back as 305 (Broughton *MRR* I, 166).
30. see above, p. 61, and n. 23. Brunt's suggestion would explain the speed with which Minucius was apparently able to assemble the new army, although Livy believed it consisted of new troops (22.11.3), and also why Appian *(Hannibalic War*, 8) says that Rome put 13 legions into the field this year: they would be the two in Spain, two under Flaminius, two under Servilius, two in Sicily, 1 in Sardinia, the two *legiones urbanae* (which formed, with Servilius' two, the four legions which later fought under Fabius and Minucius - Livy 22.27.10), and the two ordered to be raised by Fabius on becoming dictator. Polybius, on the other hand, appears to have given Fabius four legions before he took over Servilius' army (3.88.7) - on which see Walbank *ad loc.*
31. Walbank I, 424.
32. Walbank I, 427-8.
33. H. Nissen, *Italische Landeskunde* (Berlin 1883-1902), ii 786 n.2; Walbank I, 433.
34. I believe that this is the only possible explanation, if it is true, as Livy says (22.34.1), that the elections were held under an *interrex*, since an *interregnum* could only occur if the consular year ended without new consuls' having been elected. Presumably when the consuls wrote to the Senate that "it was better that the elections should be held under an *interrex* than that either consul should be called away from the war" (Livy 22.33.10), they did not mean that the elections should be held immediately, but that they should be delayed until the consular year ended, and presumably also, they preferred this to appointing a dictator since even that would have meant one or other of them returning to Roman soil - the nearest being at Aufidena or Allifae some 200 kilometres away. Possibly when the Senate replied that it preferred a dictator, one of the consuls nominated him where he was, and this is why he was declared "vitio creatus".

G. V. Sumner (*art. cit.* n.28 above) has argued that Livy's whole account of these elections is untrue, mainly on the ground that the *fasti* do not record that L. Veturius Philo abdicated *vitio creatus*, and that Fabius' dictatorship is described as *interregni causa*. But it seems cavalier to dismiss Livy's circumstantial story on the basis of the admittedly not always complete and accurate record of the *fasti*, and the detail that Terentius Varro was elected sole consul, may be true - see n. 35 below. See also Scullard, *Roman Politics*, 49ff.
35. this may have been normal procedure when elections to the consulship were held under an *interrex*, for Plutarch (*Marcellus*, 6.1) records the same procedure when Marcellus was elected in 222, and it would have been in keeping with Roman attitudes that since the elections were irregular, they should try to return to normality - i.e. to elections presided over by a consul - as soon as possible.
36. Livy (22.36.7) notes that of the consuls and praetors elected this year, none except Varro was elected to an office he had not held before. (On the identity of the praetor, M. Pomponius Matho, see Broughton, *MRR* I, 246, n.4.)

37. see n.30 above.
38. e.g., by de Sanctis III ii 131-5; Brunt, 419 n.2, 672. But cf. Walbank I, 439-40, for a defence of Polybius' figures.
39. see Brunt, 673-4, for arguments in favour of the middle estimate, and Scullard, *SASPW*, 318ff., for the higher estimate.
40. e.g. Kromayer, *Antike Schlachtfelder*, iii 1.303 n.2; Walbank I, 442; but cf. Scullard, *Roman Politics*, 52 n.4.
41. for summaries see Scullard, *History*, 437-8, and Walbank I, 435-8.
42. Livy, who says that Hannibal originally placed his camp "near" Cannae (*prope eum vicum* - 22.43.10 - i.e., presumably, on the same side of the river), omits to note this move to the left bank, merely remarking later (22.44.3) that the Romans from the smaller camp found it easier to obtain water from the river "because the farther bank held no force of the enemy."
43. Walbank I, 444.
44. this is decisive against the view of Kromayer (op.cit., III i 314-5) that the manoeuvre resulted in a formation *en echelon* - see Walbank I, 445. For the view that the centre companies simply got ahead of their wings in the advance, see de Sanctis III ii 162.
45. Polybius' words for the manoeuvre of the right-hand division of Africans are "κλίναντες ἐπ' ἀσπίδα" (turning to the shield-side), and for the left-hand division "ἐπὶ δόρυ ποιούμενοι τὴν κλίσιν" (making their turn to the spear-side), and the terms κλίνω/κλίσις are used by Greek technical writers for an individual turning, as opposed to terms like "ἐπιστρέφειν" for a unit (cf. Polybius 11.22.11) - see Asklepiodotos 10.2 and 10.4.
46. it does not matter for the purposes of the argument whether the incident is historical or not, but it is worth noting that although Polybius mentions Maharbal in his account of Trasimene and its aftermath (3.84.14, 86.4), he implies that the commander of the Numidians at Cannae was Hanno (3.114.7), not Maharbal as Livy says (22.46.7).
47. *A History of Warfare* (London 1968), 97.
48. not because he lacked a siege-train, as is sometimes said (e.g. Dorey & Dudley, *Rome Against Carthage*, 67-8): he had presumably had a siege-train - whatever that may mean in an ancient context - at Saguntum, and still required eight months to take the town. In reality, he could easily and rapidly have constructed anything he wanted - ladders, mantlets, siege-towers, battering-rams, even catapults - see p. 87 above.
49. later, Livy twice says that Hannibal expressed regret for not having marched on Rome after Cannae (26.7.3ff., 30.20.8), but even if this is true, it would be understandable in view of the later ruin of his hopes. What is important is his strategy in 216, not his later regrets.

# NOTES TO CHAPTER IV

1. e.g. by Scullard, *History,* 206; Dorey & Dudley, *Rome Against Carthage,* 70; Montgomery, *History of Warfare,* 97.
2. e.g., Montgomery, loc. cit.
3. for the view that Capua's attitude was partly determined by economic considerations, see p. 288 above, n. 19.
4. for a slightly different interpretation see Brunt, 648-51. The cohorts from the *ager Picenus et Gallicus* could have been of Roman citizens, but would then, perhaps, not have been referred to as "cohorts" - the troops later recruited by Varro in Picenum (cf. Livy 23.32.19) are later referred to as a legion (cf. 24.11.3). There were allied communities in Picenum - Ancona, Firmum (Latin), and Asculum - and Ariminum, too, was a Latin colony.
5. cf. Brunt, 649.
6. the MSS of Livy have "per agrum . . . Trebianumque" here, but Trebia (Trevi) was in Umbria: Livy must have written "Trebulanumque".
7. cf. Festus s.v. *'Sexantari asses',* and M.H. Crawford, *Roman Republican Coinage* (Cambridge 1974), 43, 596, 611-2, 615.
8. Crawford, op.cit., 612-4.
9. Crawford, op.cit., 46 and 715.
10. Scullard, *Roman Politics,* 58.
11. Broughton, *MRR* I, 256.
12. 2 under Fabius, 2 (*volones*) under Gracchus, 2 (*legiones urbanae*) under Marcellus, 2 (ex Sicily) under Laevinus + 1 (Marcellus' old *legio classica*) at Tarentum, 2 in Sicily (*legiones Cannenses*), 2 in the *ager Gallicus* under Pomponius, 1 in Picenum under Varro, 2 in Sardinia, and 2 in Spain.
13. the episode has been doubted, e.g., by H. Hesselbarth, *Historisch-kritische Untersuchungen zur dritten Dekade des Livius* (Halle, 1889), 472, n.1 - see Broughton, *MRR* I, 258 n.7.
14. Walbank II, 42ff.
15. J. H. Thiel, *Studies on the History of Roman Sea-power in Republican Times* (Amsterdam, 1946), 70-1.
16. Broughton, *MRR* I, 246 n.5.
17. Livy records Fabius as describing him as *flamen Quirinalis* on this occasion (24.8.10), but when he mentions the creation of a successor in 204, after his death the previous year, he describes him as *flamen Martialis* (29.38.6). There were precedents for a *flamen's* being prevented from leaving Rome: e.g., in 242, the consul, A. Postumius Albinus, then the *flamen Martialis,* was forbidden to leave the city by the *Pontifex Maximus,* L. Caecilius Metellus (Livy *Periocha* Book 19, cf. 37.51.1-2).
18. cf. de Sanctis III ii 258 n. 115.
19. Brunt, who apparently did not see the difficulty arising from Livy's statements about Pomponius Matho and his army, thinks that only five new legions had to be raised in 214, or four if Varro had already raised his before the end of the previous year (cf. Brunt, 650).
20. Brunt, 66, 75, 403ff.
21. at first sight Livy's description of the new sailors as *"socii navales"* contradicts his implication that they were slaves: perhaps all he means is that the slaves took the place of the usual *socii navales* - they were, as he says, *"socii navales* produced at private expense", instead of being paid for by the state. It must be remembered, of course, that many of the states from whom *socii navales* were normally drawn, had either defected, or were in the process of defecting.
22. Thiel, op. cit., 74ff.
23. Walbank II, 2.
24. cf., e.g., de Beer, *Hannibal,* 233 and 240.
25. P. Orsi, *Notizie degli Scavi di Antichità,* 1893, 171; E. A. Freeman, *The History of Sicily from the Earliest Times* (Oxford, 1891-4), iv, 501-3; A. Holm, *Geschichte Siciliens in Altertum* (Leipzig, 1870-98), iii, 359-60; H.W. Parke, *JHS* 1944, 100; K. Fabricius, *Das Antike Syrakus* (*Klio,* Beiheft **38,** Leipzig 1932), illustrations 1 & **34.**
26. Fabricius, op. cit., 20-30.
27. cf. Walbank II, 70.

28.  for a discussion of Marcellus' forces see Walbank II, 77-8, and references there.
29.  E. Krim, *American Journal of Archaeology,* 1958, 79-90; the site has been excavated by the University of Princeton. Livy (24.27.5) implies that Murgantia was on the coast, but in *RE* 16, cols. 299-301, s.v.'Morgantina' it is suggested that "Megara" should be read at this point in his text.
30.  Scullard, *Roman Politics,* 35-6; on the elections for 212/1 see Scullard, op. cit., 61-2. For Roman dispositions this year see Livy 25.3: apart from the changes in command in all but two of the armies in Italy, the only new departure was the stationing of an army in Etruria.
31.  it is not certain which one, because the MSS of Livy have "*Aemilio praetori urb.* (or urb)" here (25.1.11), and the *praetor urbanus* in 213/2 was M. Atilius Regulus, not M. Aemilius Lepidus. It would seem more appropriate to report such a scandal to the *praetor urbanus,* so probably we should read "*Atilio praetori urb.*" - see Broughton *MRR* I, 266 n.2.
32.  G.C. & C. Picard (*Life and Death of Carthage,* 59-60) suggest that this episode represents an attack on Roman businessmen by "those in power", and even that the downfall of Postumius of Pyrge and his associate, Pomponius of Veii, led to the defeat of the Scipios in Spain, whose armies they had been supplying. This seems very far-fetched.
33.  G. B. dal Lago, *Rivista di storia antica,* I, fasc. 4, 1895-9, 5ff.; Oehler, *RE* s.v. 'Tarentum (I)', col. 2308; Walbank II, 103.
34.  Oehler, op. cit., col. 2312.
35.  Walbank II, 105-6.
36.  Walbank II, 107.
37.  Walbank II, 109.
38.  de Sanctis III ii 459, n. 28; but cf. Toynbee II, 48 & 524ff.
39.  cf. Broughton, *MRR* I, 271 n.2; Toynbee II, 48-9.
40.  de Sanctis III ii 331-4.
41.  cf. Walbank II, 6-8.
42.  H.W. Parke, *JHS* 1944, 100-2.
43.  for the location of the Fountain of Arethusa see Margaret Guido, *Syracuse: a Handbook to its History and Principal Monuments* (London 1958), No. 6 on map at beginning. The fountain lies about half-way down the west side of Ortygia.
44.  Livy (25.40.5) says the "*populares*" called him Muttines, and this is the form he uses elsewhere (e.g. 25.40.8, 10 and 13): Polybius (9.22.4) calls him "Muttonos", but he is Muttones on a contemporary inscription from Delphi (Dittenberger, *SIG,* 585).
45.  one of them, for example, had been sent to Greece to study the laws of Athens and other cities as long ago as 454: Livy 3.31.7-8, Dionysius of Halicarnassus 10.52.3.
46.  cf. Brunt, 652.
47.  on Livy's statement that this occasion marked the introduction of *velites* into the Roman army (26.4.9), see above, p. 284, n. 23.
48.  cf. Walbank II, 121-4.
49.  cf. Walbank II, 126.

# NOTES TO CHAPTER V

1. near Tarraco according to Hübner, *Hermes* 1866, 77ff., 337ff.; *RE* s.v. 'Cessetani', col. 1995; the same as Tarraco according to J. Vallejo, *Tito Livio, Libro XXI, edición, estudio preliminar y commentario* (Madrid 1946), xlviiiff.
2. de Sanctis III ii 240-1, n. 59; Scullard, *SAPW,* 46 n.2; Walbank I, 409. *
3. Thiel, 40-2.
4. Thiel, ibid.
5. Scullard, *SASP,* 257 n.52.
6. de Sanctis III ii 242-3 n. 62.
7. A. Schulten, *Jahrbuch des deutschen ärchaologischen Instituts* 1927, 232-5.
8. K. J. Beloch, *Hermes* 1915, 361; de Sanctis III ii 243-4 n. 65.
9. Scullard, *SAPW,* 47.
10. de Sanctis III ii 246, n. 71.
11. A. Schulten, *Hermes* 1928. 288ff. The best known Iliturgi has now been located by an inscription near Mengibar in Jaén: *Archivo Español di Arqueologia,* 1960, 193ff.
12. cf. G. V. Sumner, *HSCP,* 1967.
13. de Sanctis III ii 247-8 n. 76.
14. U. Kahrstedt, vol. iii of Meltzer's *Geschichte der Carthager* (Berlin 1913), 254-5, 513 n.2; S. Gsell, *Histoire ancienne de l'Afrique du Nord* (Paris 1913-20), iii 181; M. Holleaux, *Rome, la Grèce et les monarchies Hellénistiques au III$^e$ siecle av. J.-C,* 171 n.2.
15. cf. de Sanctis III ii 446-7, n.4; Scullard, *SAPW,* 50-1 n.1, 304.
16. see n.5 above.
17. Scullard, *SAPW,* 50-1, n.1.
18. cf. de Sanctis III ii 450.
19. Scullard, *SAPW,* 53-4, n.4.
20. Scullard, *SAPW,* 55 n.1.
21. Scullard, *SASP,* 38.
22. cf. de Sanctis III ii 454 n. 18, 468 n. 38; A. Klotz, *Hermes,* 1952, 340. This readjustment of Livy's chronology also means that his date for the Baecula campaign is wrong: he should have dated it to 208, not 209.
23. Polybius is also wrong to say (10.4.1) that Scipio's brother, Lucius, was the elder, and that the brothers were aediles in the same year: Lucius was, in reality, the younger and probably held the aedileship in 195 - see Broughton, *MRR* I, 267 n.4, and 340; Walbank II, 199-200.
24. Broughton, *MRR* I, 247 n.10.
25. cf. Scullard, *Roman Politics,* 66-7. But I am dubious about Scullard's assertion that "the People . . . seeing the opportunity for more spoils in overseas campaigns, wanted an offensive to be renewed in Spain": recent experiences in Spain hardly suggested that spoils would be easily forthcoming!
26. the location of the Konioi in southern Portugal depends upon their identification with the Kynetes of, e.g., Herodotus 2.33 - cf. Hübner, *RE* s.v. 'Cynetes' cols. 1906-8; Schweighäuser proposed the emendation "ἐκτός" for "ἐντός" in his edition of Polybius (Leipzig 1789-95). W. Brewitz, *Scipio Africanus Maior in Spanien* (Diss. Tübingen 1914), 210-6, and de Sanctis III ii 464 n.34, reject the identification of the Konioi with the Kynetes, but as Walbank says, in his note on Polybius 10.7.5, to say that Mago was "outside" the Pillars has more point than to say that he was "inside" - it is Mago's distance from Cartagena which is in question.
27. so Livy 26.41.2, assuming that "sociorum" here refers to Spaniards. Polybius says nothing of Spanish allies in Scipio's forces at Cartagena, however (cf.10.9.6), and Scipio is said to have attributed his father's and uncle's fall to their reliance upon Spanish allies (10.6.2). If we wish to reconcile Livy and Polybius here, we could suppose that the Spanish allies were left with Silanus at the Ebro, where they would be most useful, defending their own homes. I assume here, and in my calculations of the numbers left to Fonteius and Marcius after the disaster in 211 (above, p. 131), that Scipio's army of 25,000 foot and 2500 horse at Cartagena, did not include any Spaniards: cf. Scullard, *SAPW,* 66 n.2.
28. Broughton, *MRR* I, 284 n.4.

29.    cf. Walbank II, 205-12; Scullard, *SAPW*, 289-99, *SASP*, 48-52.
30.    cf. Walbank II, 191-6, for references, and add Scullard, *SASP*, 48ff.
31.    cf. Walbank II, 192-6, and references there.
32.    cf. *The Mediterranean Pilot* (6th edition) i 68-9.
33.    ibid.
34.    cf. R. Laqueur, *Hermes,* 1921, 161-2.
35.    as is suggested by Scullard, *SAPW*, 83, and accepted by Walbank II, 214.
36.    Scullard, *SAPW*, 298.
37.    the Penguin translation of Livy 26.46 gives the impression that Scipio himself led the 500 (p. 416, line 6: "the 500 with Scipio"), but the words "with Scipio" are not in Livy's text, and it is most improbable that Scipio would have risked his life on such an enterprise.
38.    Walbank II, 216.
39.    Polybius (fr. 179) says that the Spanish sword was adopted at the time of Hannibal, but it is possible that both this weapon and the *pilum* were adopted from Spanish mercenaries during the First Punic War: see G. Veith in J. Kromayer and G. Veith, *Heerwesen und Kriegfuhrung der Griechen und Römer* (Munich 1928), 325; J. Marquardt, *Römische Staatsverwaltung* (Leipzig 1881-5), 139ff., 220ff.; E. Meyer, *Kleine Schriften,* ii 200 n.1; A. Schulten, *Numantia* (Munich 1914), i 209ff.; *RE* s.v. 'pilum' col. 1344.
40.    see Walbank II, 245-6, on Polybius 10.34.2
41.    see n. 22 above.
42.    Scullard, *SAPW*, 300-1.
43.    Scullard, loc.cit., and *SASP*, 258-60 n. 54, with photographs 28-9 on 79-80.
44.    as Walbank (II, 250) suggests, following Scullard, *SAPW*, 300ff., cf. *SASP*, 71 and n. 54 on 258-60. Could the "river" be the Arroyo del Jarosa?
45.    de Sanctis III ii 478.
46.    Scullard, *SASP*, 72.
47.    de Sanctis III ii 496-7 n. 84; Scullard, *SAPW*, 304-9, and Walbank II, 17-8, argue convincingly for retaining the date 206 for Ilipa.
48.    E. Meyer, *Kleine Schriften,* ii 405.
49.    Scullard, *SAPW*, 125 n.1; Walbank II, 297.
50.    Scullard, *SASP,* n. 63 on 262-3, and photographs 30-2 on 145.
51.    see n. 5 above.
52.    Scullard, *SASP* n. 63 on 262-3.
53.    e.g. Th. Mommsen, *Römische Geschichte* (Berlin 1874) I, 634.
54.    the MSS of Polybius 11.22.11 actually have the words "περί στάδιον" ("about a stade", i.e. about 178 metres, but Livy (28.14.13) says "not more than 500 paces," which would mean about 740 metres, so the text of Polybius is usually emended to read "περί τετραστάδιον" ("about four stades", or 710 metres): it is difficult to believe that Scipio would have dared to carry out the manoeuvres Polybius describes, if less than 200 metres separated him from the enemy.
55.    cf. Asklepiodotos 10.4; κλίνω and κλίσις are used of individuals (cf. n. 45 on p. 290).
56.    cf. Polybius 10.23.6 and Walbank's note and loc.
57.    e.g. G. Veith, *Antike Schlachtfelder,* iv 523; F. Taeger, *Klio,* 1931, 342.
58.    if Scipio's total force amounted to just under 50,000 men, he would presumably not have wanted his Roman forces to be outnumbered by the Spaniards. In 209, he seems to have had 28,000 foot and 3000 horse (Polybius 10.9.6 and 6.7, cf. p. 135 above, and n. 27). Throughout the discussion, I assume that when Polybius says "Romans", he means "Romans and Italian allies" as appears to have been his custom, and I have adopted the same usage. Livy (28.15.1) mentions Latin troops on the Roman side, and "Carthaginienses" on the Carthaginian (28.14.4): this should mean "Carthaginian citizens", but perhaps Livy should have said "Poeni" as at 23.29.4 - see above, pp. 9 & 128.
59.    cf. Scullard, *SAPW*, 134-6.
60.    Walbank II, 304.
61.    cf. Edward Crankshaw, *The Fall of the House of Hapsburg* (London 1970), 171-2.
62.    this may help to explain how Scipio was able to get through so much between Ilipa and his departure for Rome - see Scullard, *SAPW*, 304-9; note also Livy's references to the forced marches from Tarraco to Cartagena (*itineribus magnis:* 28.17.11). Scullard (loc.cit.) supposes that he had gone from Ilipa straight to Cartagena, not to Tarraco as Livy says, but this is, perhaps, unnecessary - see Broughton, *MRR* I, 301 n. 4.
63.    the scene of the meeting was probably at Siga (modern Takembrit), west of Oran: see Walbank II, 306, on Polybius 11.24a.4.
64.    see n. 11 above.
65.    see n. 5 above.
66.    Livy seems to have misplaced Carteia in this passage - it lay east of the straits, not west as he implies (28.30.3).

# NOTES TO CHAPTER VI

1. see, e.g., M. Holleaux, *Rome, la Grèce et les monarchies hellénistiques au III<sup>e</sup> siecle av. J.-C.* (Paris 1931), 1-96.
2. for a concise survey see Toynbee, *Hannibal's Legacy*, I 39-83.
3. Walbank, *Philip V of Macedon* (Cambridge 1940), 20ff.
4. Holleaux, op. cit., 166, and *CAH* vii 855.
5. cf. J. V. A. Fine, *JRS*, 1936, 24-39.
6. cf. E. Badian, *BSR*, 1952, 89.
7. cf. W. Boguth, *M. Valerius Laevinus. Ein Beitrag zur Geschichte des zweiten punischen Krieges* (Progr. Krems, 1892), 8; Holleaux, *Rome, la Grèce*, 183 n. 2.
8. on the treaty see Walbank II, 42-56; A. H. McDonald, *JRS* 1956, 153-7; E. Badian, *Latomus* 1958, 197-211.
9. F. A. Scott, *Macedonien und Rom während des hannibalischen Krieges* (Diss. Leipzig. 1873), 190 n.5; Holleaux, op. cit., 191 nn. 3 & 4.
10. Scott, loc. cit., Holleaux, loc. cit.
11. it is not possible to date these operations of Philip precisely - we learn of them from subsequent references by Livy (27.30.13, 29.12.3ff., cf. Polybius 8.38).
12. on the chronology of the Aetolian alliance see Walbank, *Philip*, 301-4.
13. cf. J. P. V. D. Balsdon, *JRS*, 1954, 31.
14. cf. Walbank, *Philip*, 83-4 and n. 8.
15. B. Niese, *Geschichte der griechischen und makedonischen Staaten seit der Schlacht bei Chaeronea* (Gotha 1893-1903), ii 478.
16. Niese, op. cit., ii 478 n. 3; de Sanctis III ii 418 n. 54.
17. de Sanctis III ii 418 n. 55.
18. Walbank II, 179 on Polybius 9.39.2.
19. Walbank, *Philip*, 304-5. Similarly, the election of Attalus to the Aetolian *strategia* (Livy 27.29.10) must refer to that of 210/09.
20. most of the MSS of Livy have "Pyrgum" at 27.32.7, but one has "Phyrcum" and since there was such a place in Elis - cf. Thucydides 5.49.1 - this, the more difficult reading, is probably to be preferred here.
21. Walbank II, 258.
22. Livy dates these events to 207, but the reference to the Olympic Games in 28.7.14 shows that they should have been dated to 208, since, then as now, the Games were held in even years - cf. n. 19 above.
23. cf. *CIL* ii 533; Oldfather, *RE* 6a, col. 609f.
24. Walbank, *Philip*, 96 and 304 n. 5.
25. But L. Lerat (*Revue de philologie, de littérature et d'histoire anciennes*, 1947, 12-18, cf. *Les Locriens de l'Ouest*, Paris 1952, i 54-9) has argued that no Antikyra in Locris ever existed, so there may be some corruption in Livy's text, unless we are to suppose that, after all, Antikyra in Phocis is meant (cf. n. 18 above), and that Philip had retaken it since 210.
26. Walbank, *Philip*, 99-102, and Appendix III, 305-6.
27. Walbank, *Philip*, 103-4.
28. cf. Crawford, *Roman Republican Coinage*, 28-35.
29. Scullard, *Roman Politics*, 64-5.
30. C. Claudius Nero appears to have formed a single legion out of the two he had commanded, to take to Spain (Livy 26.17.1: see p. 132 above), and Q. Fulvius Flaccus was, in 210, ordered to form a single legion out of his two at Capua (Livy 26.18.6-8). Nothing more is heard of the two legions Ap. Claudius Pulcher had commanded at Capua, so presumably they were discharged. I do not understand Brunt, 418 note (d), when he says that "a single legion was formed from the six hitherto in Campania, the other legionaries being discharged," though it amounts to the same thing when he goes on to note that the survivors of the two legions in Spain were brought up to four (i.e., presumably, one brought by Claudius Nero, the other by Scipio).
31. see Broughton, *MRR* I, 271 n. 3. Another complication is that one of Crassus' rivals for the supreme pontificate was Q. Fulvius Flaccus himself (Livy 25.5.3).

32.  cf. Scullard, *Roman Politics*, 68-9. Flaccus may have been at one with Fabius in thinking that it was desirable to concentrate on Italy, but have differed from him in approving Marcellus' plan, in 208, to try to defeat Hannibal in pitched battle - see above, 177-8.
33.  the inscription was published by F. Ribbezo, *Il Carrocio del Sud*, S. ii, vol. 4.2, February 1951. G. Vitucci, *Rivista di filologia e d'istruzzione classica*, 1953, 43-61, considers it an *elogium* of Fabius Cunctator, but Broughton, *MRR* II, Additions and Corrections, 2-3, prefers to accept the view of Gabba (*Athenaeum*, 1958, 90-105) that it honours a local magistrate of Brundisium. But de Beer is, in any case, incorrect to say (*Hannibal*, 259, under a photograph of the inscription) that it contains "the only known contemporary mention of Hannibal by name," since the lettering of the inscription is of the 1st century A.D.
34.  Walbank II, 189.
35.  Scullard, *Roman Politics*, 20-1.
36.  Scullard, op. cit., 35 and 53.
37.  Scullard, op. cit., 72-3 and n. 3 on 72.
38.  Proctor, 198, denies that there was any disagreement between Livy and Varro, but when Livy says (27.39.2) that Hasdrubal *"per munita pleraque transitu fratris, quae antea invia fuerant, ducebat,"* we must surely take him to mean that Hasdrubal followed the same general route as Hannibal.
39.  cf. Proctor, 193-4, for Varro's location of the passes used by Hannibal, Hasdrubal and Pompey.
40.  G.C. & C. Picard, *Life and Death of Carthage*, 260, suggest that Hasdrubal also picked up the Punic garrisons they believe Hannibal had left in southern France - see above     n.
41.  Walbank II, 268-9.
42.  in addition to Livy (27.46.4), see Cicero, *Brutus*, 73; Silius Italicus 15.552; Appian, *Hannibalic War*, 52; *de viris illustribus*, 4.8.2; Eutropius 3.18.2; Zonaras, 9.9.
43.  de Sanctis III ii 567-9.
44.  de Sanctis, ibid.
45.  cf. Dorey & Dudley, *Rome Against Carthage*, 84.
46.  cf. Walbank II, 269.
47.  Scullard, *History*, 439; Walbank II, 270.
48.  cf. de Sanctis III ii 574-5; Scullard, *SAPW*, 324-5.
49.  cf. Walbank II, 273.
50.  Appian's figures of 48,000 foot and 8000 horse for Hasdrubal's army at the beginning of the campaign (*Hannibalic War* 52) may derive from Livy's figure for the Carthaginian dead at the Metaurus, and, in any case, can hardly be accepted. Livy's total for the Roman and allied dead - 8000 (27.49.8) - could be reconciled with Polybius' total of 2000 *Roman* dead, but it is most unlikely that the allies suffered casualties so out of proportion to those of the Roman citizens, and since Polybius never mentions allies in his accounts of battles, his figures must be presumed to include allied dead.

   It is interesting that Appian should say that Hasdrubal had 56,000 men when he entered "Tyrrhenia" (i.e., Etruria: *Hannibalic War*, 52), for this suggests that Hasdrubal had followed the same route as Hannibal, and there is some confirmation in Livy's report of help given to him by Etruscan communities (28.10.4-5). But in that case, he would have encountered Terentius Varro, not Porcius Licinus, in the first instance (cf. Livy 27.36.11-2), so it is probable that Appian simply made a mistake. As for the alleged help from Etruscan communities, Hasdrubal might have had some contact with northern Etruscans as he marched southeast through Cisalpine Gaul.
51.  cf. Broughton, *MRR* I, 298 n. 1; Scullard, *Roman Politics*, 73-4.
52.  Livy here describes these legions as being composed of the *volones* disbanded in 211, and this means, presumably, that the nineteenth and twentieth legions into which the *volones* had been drafted at the beginning of the year (Livy 27.38.10), were the legions then stationed in Etruria, and that soldiers from these legions were then drafted elsewhere, and perhaps, in particular, into Livius Salinator's army (cf. Livy 27.38.7ff.): originally, they had been recruited into the *legiones urbanae* of 210, which had been sent to Etruria in 209 (Livy 27.7.9), and retained there in 208 (Livy 27.22.5).
53.  see pp. 143-4 above, and n. 47 on p. 294.

# NOTES TO CHAPTER VII

1. Scullard, *Roman Politics,* 75.
2. cf., e.g., Scullard, *SAPW,* 161ff., and *History,* 220-1.
3. on the tradition about Scipio's preparations see de Sanctis III ii 645ff.; U. Kahrstedt, *Geschichte der Karthager,* iii 328f., 539; M. Gelzer, *Kleine Schriften* iii (1964), 245ff.; Brunt, 656 and n. 1.
4. Thiel, 148 n. 389.
5. Thiel, 151 nn. 401 and 404.
6. Thiel, 146, doubts the story since Rome already had some 200 ships available, of which over half had been built during the war.
7. Scullard, *Roman Politics,* 76-7.
8. see Scullard, *SAPW,* 318-9, and Brunt, 672-4. Brunt suggests that the figure 35,000 adopted by Livy, is derived from the size of Scipio's army at Zama, which also included Masinissa's Numidians - see p. 221 above.
9. see Scullard, *SAPW,* 183ff.
10. Scullard, op. cit., 189ff.
11. Scullard, *SASP,* 121.
12. Scullard, loc. cit.
13. Scullard, *SASP,* 123 and fig. 10 on 121.
14. Scullard, op. cit., 124-5 and 121 fig. 10.
15. Walbank II, 432.
16. G. Veith, *Antike Schlachtfelder* (Berlin 1903-31), iii.2.591-2, *Schlachtenatlas zur antiken Kriegsgeschichte* (Gotha 1922ff.), Röm. Abt. 8, col. 36; de Sanctis III ii 584.
17. Scullard, *SAPW,* 321-3.
18. e.g. Walbank II, 433, on Polybius 14.8.7.
19. e.g. by de Sanctis III ii 532 n. 137.
20. e.g. by E. Badian, *Foreign Clientelae,* 295.
21. J. Mazard, *Corpus Nummorum Numidiae,* 1950, 30; cf. Scullard, *SASP,* 268-9 n. 97.
22. e.g. Scullard, *SASP,* 134.
23. cf. Walbank II, 441-2.
24. e.g. by V. Ehrenberg, *RE* s.v. 'Mago' no. 5; de Sanctis III ii 540f., n. 150.
25. Broughton, *MRR,* i 314-5 n. 2.
26. Scullard, *Roman Politics,* 79-80.
27. Walbank II, 447; Scullard, *SASP,* 271-2 n. 104.
28. e.g. Walbank II, 447.
29. Walbank II, 447; Scullard, *SASP,* 273.
30. e.g. by K. Lehmann, *Neue Jahrbücher für Philologie und Pädagogik,* Suppl.-B.21, 1894, 556-9; de Sanctis III ii 594.
31. G. Veith, *Schlachtenatlas,* Röm. Abt. 8, col. 6. The map in Scullard *SASP,* 161, implies that Masinissa joined Scipio at Margaron, but this is not what Polybius says.
32. Veith, ibid.
33. e.g. by E. Groag, *Hannibal als Politiker* (Vienna 1929), 99 n.2.
34. as Veith, *Antike Schlachtfelder,* iii.2.678-9, and de Sanctis, III ii 607-8, suggest.
35. K. Lehmann, op. cit., 589f.; Veith, *Antike Schlachtfelder,* iii.2.655-6; Scullard, *SASP,* 150.
36. cf. W. R. Paton in the Loeb Classical Library edition of Polybius, vol. iv, 495. For the view adopted in the text see Walbank II, 460 ad loc.
37. e.g. B.H. Liddell Hart, *A Greater than Napoleon: Scipio Africanus* (London 1926). Montgomery (*A History of Warfare,* 96-7) accepts the view that Scipio was the greatest strategist.
38. e.g. by Scullard, *SAPW,* 251-3, *SASP,* 155-6.
39. cf. Walbank II, 467.
40. cf. Scullard, *SASP,* 158.
41. cf. Badian, *Foreign Clientelae,* 125-6 and 126 n.1.
42. cf. Scullard, *Roman Politics,* 80ff.
43. see M. Holleaux, *Hermes* 48 (1913), 75-98; P. Fraccaro, *Opuscula* (Pavia 1956/7), 349; Scullard, *SASP,* 198 and 285-6 n. 163.

# NOTES TO CHAPTER VIII

1. Brunt, 419-22. I would regard Brunt's estimate of the total number of men serving in the legions - 75,000 - as too low, even though many of the legions may well have been under strength: 80-90,000 would probably be a more accurate estimate.
2. Brunt, 62.
3. see Philip Mason, *A Matter of Honour* (London 1974), 219-312.
4. Thiel, 255-372.
5. Toynbee II, 533ff.
6. on the subjugation of northern Italy see Toynbee II, 252-85. In general see R. M. Errington, *The Dawn of Empire* (London, 1971).
7. on Roman rule in Spain during the second century see the *Cambridge Ancient History*, vol. viii (1930), 306-25; C.H.V. Sutherland, *The Romans in Spain* (London, 1939).
8. see Walbank, *Philip V,* 108-37; Badian, *Foreign Clientelae,* 55ff.
9. Badian, op. cit., 61, and refs. in n.3.
10. Badian, op. cit., 69ff.
11. Badian, op. cit., 75ff.
12. E. T. Salmon, *JRS* 1936, 51ff.
13. Thiel, 273-6.
14. Hannibal committed suicide, probably in 183, at the court of King Prusias of Bithynia, whither he had fled after the defeat of Antiochus, rather than be handed over to Rome (Livy 39.51). On the date see de Sanctis IV i 243.
15. Badian, *Foreign Clientelae,* 125-40.
16. Toynbee II, 9 and 35. For "deracination" see 9 et al.
17. on the Gracchan Revolution see now Keith Richardson, *Daggers in the Forum* (London, 1976).
18. Brunt, 269-77.
19. Martin W. Frederiksen, *Dialoghi di Archeologia,* 1970/1 (Rome 1972), 330-67. I owe this reference to my colleague, Mr. J. J. Paterson.
20. cf., e.g., Toynbee II, 87ff.; Brunt, 75ff.
21. e.g. by Gelzer, *Gnomon* 1929, 299ff., Badian, *Foreign Clientelae,* 169ff.
22. see Brunt, 404ff.: the suggestion rests on the statement Cicero puts into Scipio Aemilianus' mouth in the *de Republica* (2.40) that under the constitution of King Servius Tullius those whose census-rating was under 1500 *asses* were classed as *proletarii.* This, it is argued, must in reality refer to a time subsequent to the one referred to by Polybius when he says (6.19.2) that the qualification for legionary service was 400 *drachmai* (i.e., 400 *denarii* or 4000 *asses*). But it is impossible to be certain of the date at which Cicero's figure was actually the dividing line between *assidui* and *proletarii,* if indeed it ever was.
23. Toynbee II, 136ff.
24. with the possible exception of Luca - see Toynbee II, 143ff. - Aquileia, founded in 183, was the last Latin colony founded in Italy.
25. Toynbee II, 128-35; Brunt, 681ff.
26. see the article cited in n. 19 above.
27. Toynbee II, 120 n. 6 and 397 n. 3.
28. Toynbee II, 117ff.
29. Broughton, *MRR* I, 403 n. 3.
30. Toynbee II, 341ff.
31. cf. A. W. Lintott, *Historia,* 1972, 626-38.
32. see Alan Wardman, *Rome's Debt to Greece* (London, 1976), 1-13.
33. the incident is, perhaps, dubious, because of earlier parallels - for example, in 431, Perikles is said to have made over an estate to the Athenian state in case King Archidamos of Sparta spared it (Thucydides 2.13.1) - but not necessarily to be dismissed solely for that reason: history has a habit of repeating itself.
34. Proctor, *Hannibal's March in History* (Oxford, 1971), 5. More recently, David Irving (*The Trail of the Fox,* London, 1977, pp. 410-11) has drawn the obvious comparison between Hannibal and Rommel - but Mr. Irving should note that it was not Hannibal's African *cavalry* which encircled the Romans at Cannae.
35. Walbank II, 153.
36. e.g. by G. C. & C. Picard, *Life and Death of Carthage,* 265.
37. It is perhaps almost equally impertinent for generals who have little or no first-hand knowledge of the ancient evidence, to pronounce upon ancient warfare!

**MAPS**

MAP 1

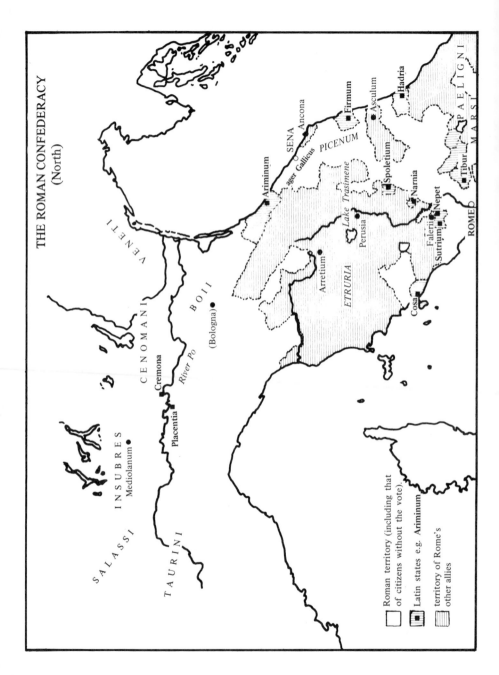

THE ROMAN CONFEDERACY
(North)

VENETI

CENOMANI

INSUBRES
Mediolanum

SALASSI

TAURINI

Cremona

Placentia

River Po

BOII
(Bologna)

ager Gallicus

SENA
Ancona

PICENUM

Firmum

Asculum

Hadria

PAELIGNI

MARSI

Ariminum

Lake Trasimene

Perusia

Arretium

ETRURIA

Spoletium

Narnia

Nepet

Falerii
Sutrium

Tibur

ROME

Cosa

Roman territory (including that
of citizens without the vote).

Latin states e.g. Ariminum

territory of Rome's
other allies

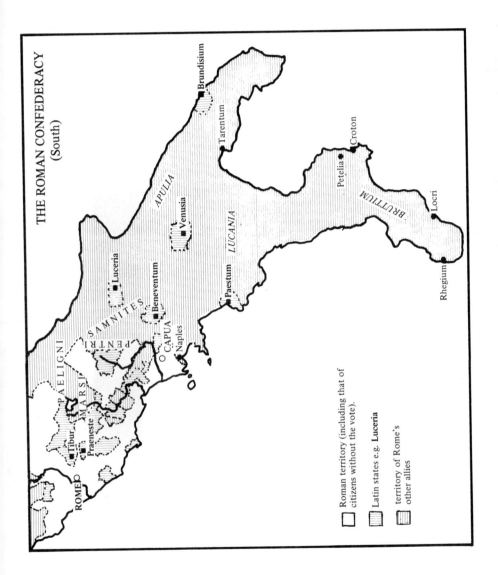

MAP 2

THE ROMAN CONFEDERACY
(South)

Brundisium

Tarentum

Croton

Petelia

BRUTTIUM

Locri

APULIA

Venusia

LUCANIA

Rhegium

Luceria

Paestum

SAMNITES

Beneventum

CAPUA

Naples

PENTRI

PAELIGNI

MARSI

Tibur

Praeneste

ROME

☐ Roman territory (including that of
citizens without the vote).

▨ Latin states e.g. **Luceria**

▦ territory of Rome's
other allies

MAP 3

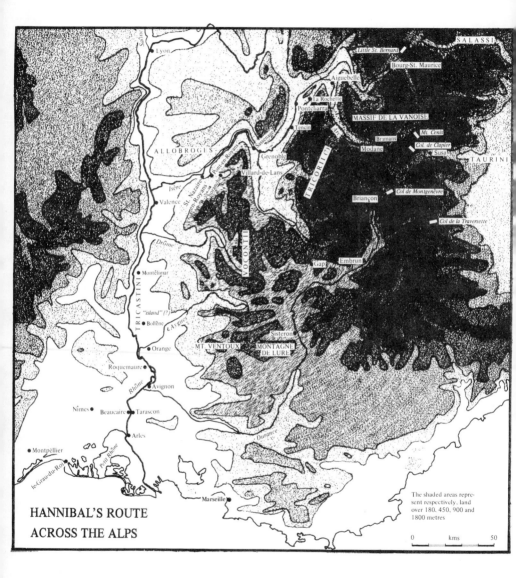

**HANNIBAL'S ROUTE ACROSS THE ALPS**

The shaded areas represent respectively, land over 180, 450, 900 and 1800 metres

0        kms        50

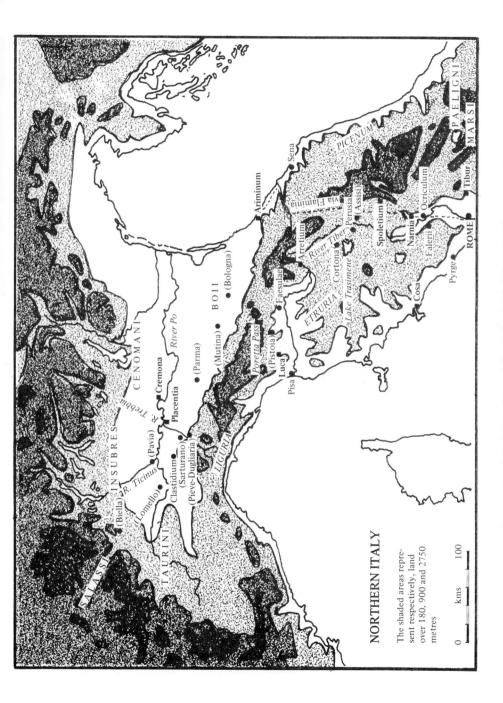

MAP 4

MAP 5

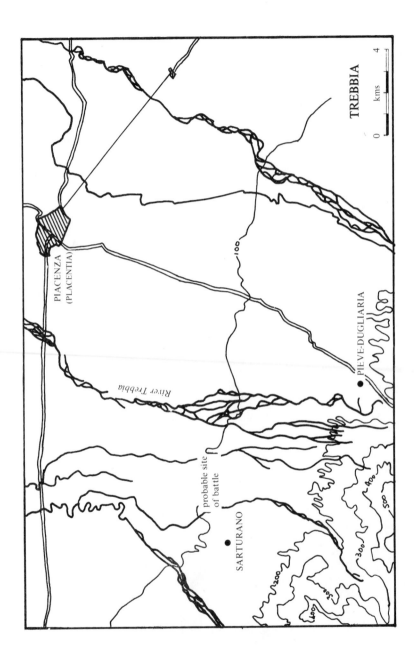

TREBBIA

MAP 6

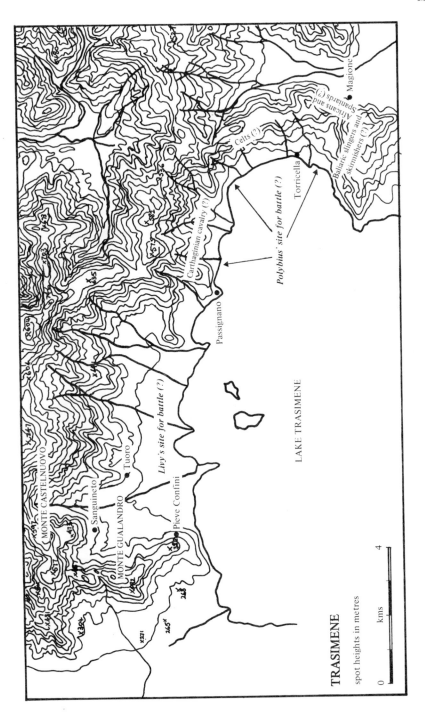

TRASIMENE

spot heights in metres

LAKE TRASIMENE

Passignano

Torricella

Magione

Celts (?)

Africans and Spaniards (?)

Balearic slingers and skirmishers (?)

Carthaginian cavalry (?)

Polybius' site for battle (?)

Livy's site for battle (?)

MONTE CASTELNUOVO

Sanguineto

MONTE GUALANDRO

Tuoro

Pieve Confini

0    kms    4

MAP 7

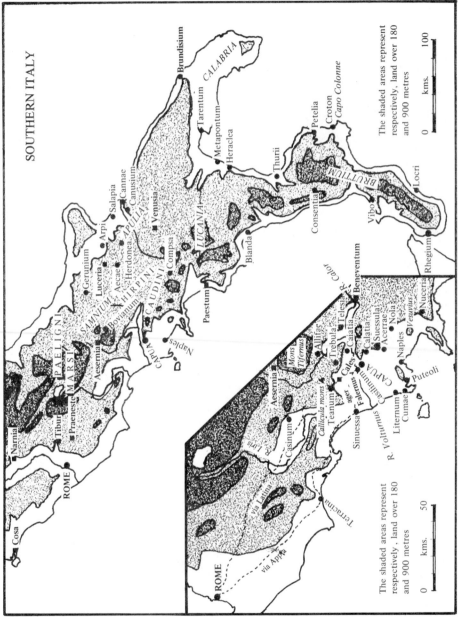

SOUTHERN ITALY

The shaded areas represent respectively, land over 180 and 900 metres

0   kms.   100

The shaded areas represent respectively, land over 180 and 900 metres

0   kms.   50

MAP 8

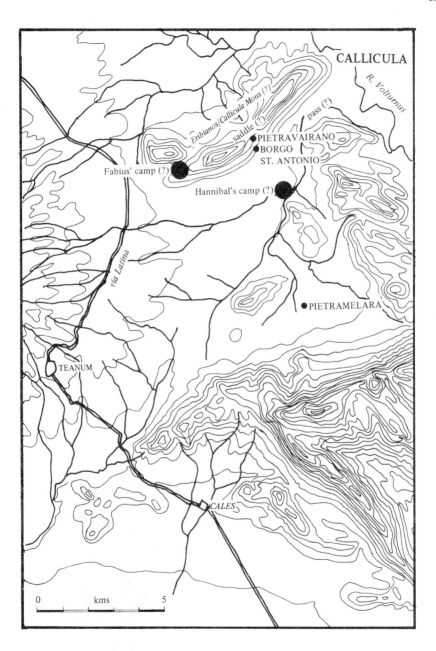

CALLICULA

R. Volturnus

Eribianos/Callicula Mons (?)

saddle (?)

pass (?)

PIETRAVAIRANO

BORGO
ST. ANTONIO

Fabius' camp (?)

Hannibal's camp (?)

PIETRAMELARA

via Latina

TEANUM

CALES

0      kms      5

MAP 9

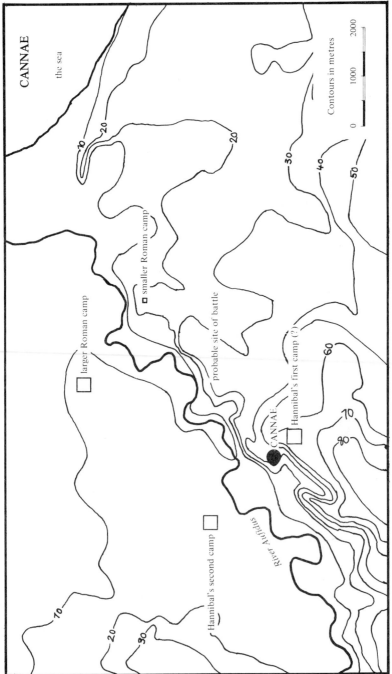

CANNAE

the sea

smaller Roman camp

larger Roman camp

probable site of battle

CANNAE

Hannibal's first camp (?)

Hannibal's second camp

River Aufidus

Contours in metres

0    1000    2000

MAP 10

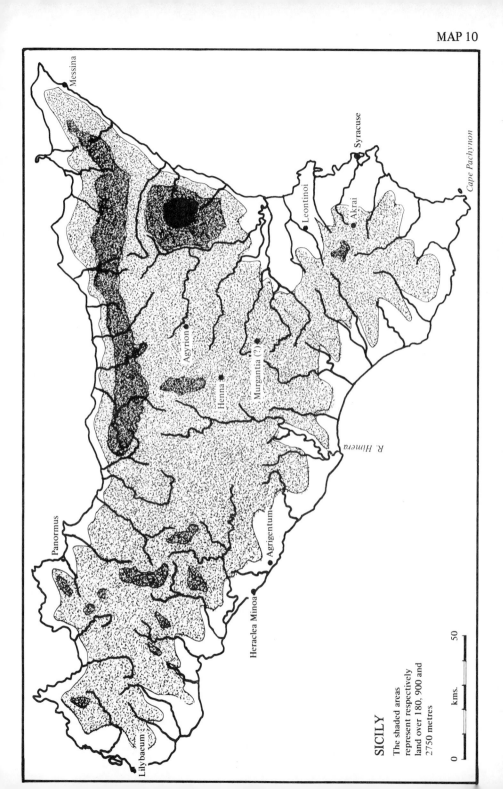

SICILY

The shaded areas
represent respectively
land over 180, 900 and
2750 metres

0    kms.    50

**MAP 11**

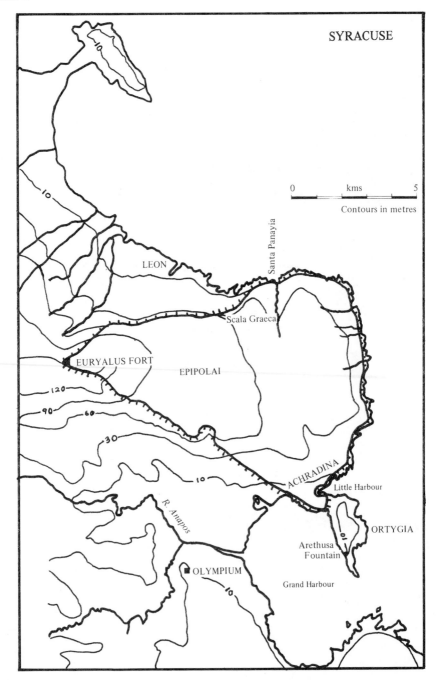

SYRACUSE

0    kms    5

Contours in metres

LEON

Santa Panayia

Scala Graeca

EURYALUS FORT

EPIPOLAI

120

90    60

30

10

ACHRADINA

Little Harbour

R. Anapos

ORTYGIA

Arethusa
Fountain

OLYMPIUM

Grand Harbour

10

**MAP 12**

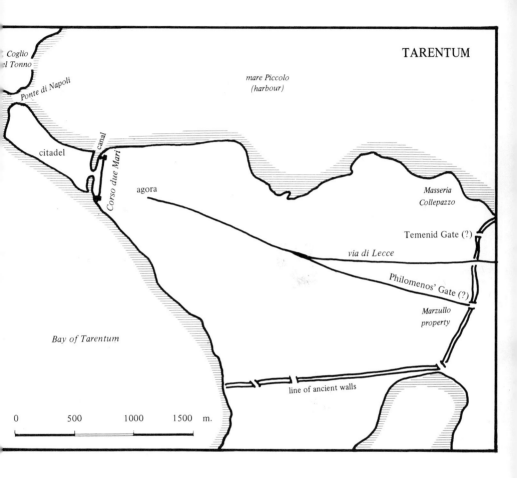

**TARENTUM**

*Coglio el Tonno*

*Ponte di Napoli*

*mare Piccolo
(harbour)*

citadel

*canal*

*Corso due Mari*

agora

*Masseria
Collepazzo*

Temenid Gate (?)

*via di Lecce*

Philomenos' Gate (?)

*Marzullo
property*

*Bay of Tarentum*

line of ancient walls

| 0 | 500 | 1000 | 1500 | m. |

MAP 13

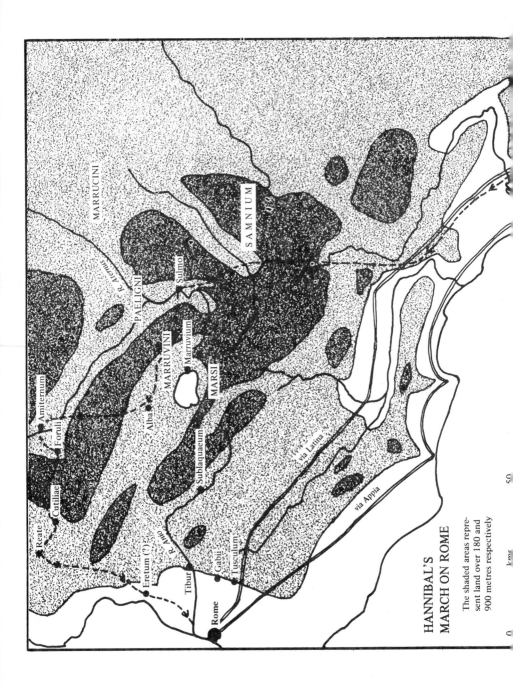

HANNIBAL'S
MARCH ON ROME

The shaded areas repre-
sent land over 180 and
900 metres respectively

MAP 14

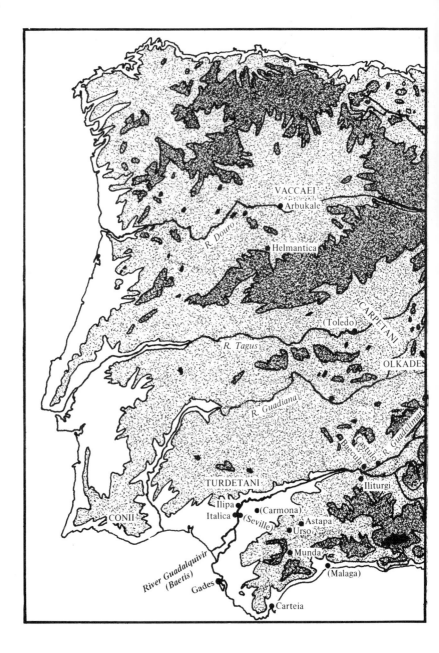

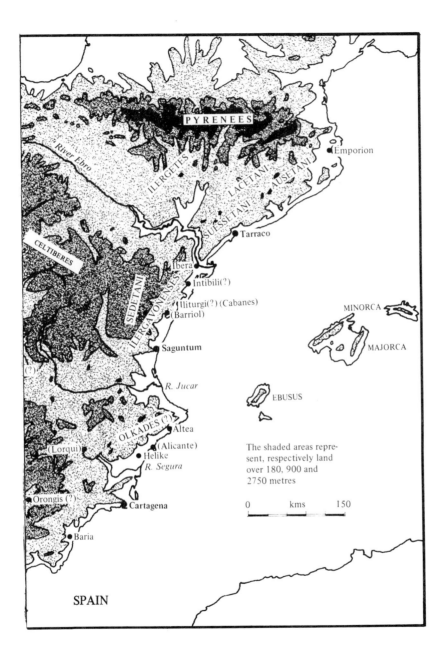

PYRENEES

Emporion

River Ebro

ILERGETES

LACETANI

AUSETANI

SUESSETANI

Tarraco

CELTIBERES

Ibera

Intibili(?)

SEDETANI

Iliturgi(?) (Cabanes)

(Barriol)

MINORCA

ILERCAVONENSES

MAJORCA

Saguntum

(?)

R. Jucar

EBUSUS

OLKADES (?)

Altea

(Lorqui)

(Alicante)

Helike

R. Segura

The shaded areas repre-
sent, respectively land
over 180, 900 and
2750 metres

Orongis (?)

Cartagena

0        kms      150

Baria

SPAIN

MAP 15

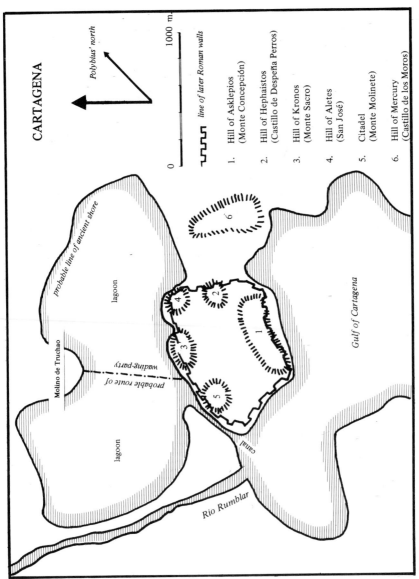

CARTAGENA

*Polybius' north*

1000 m.

0

⊓⊔⊓ line of later Roman walls

1.  Hill of Asklepios
    (Monte Concepción)

2.  Hill of Hephaistos
    (Castillo de Despeña Perros)

3.  Hill of Kronos
    (Monte Sacro)

4.  Hill of Aletes
    (San José)

5.  Citadel
    (Monte Molinete)

6.  Hill of Mercury
    (Castillo de los Moros)

*probable line of ancient shore*

lagoon

Molino de Truchao

*probable route of wading-party*

lagoon

canal

*Rio Rumblar*

*Gulf of Cartagena*

**MAP 16**

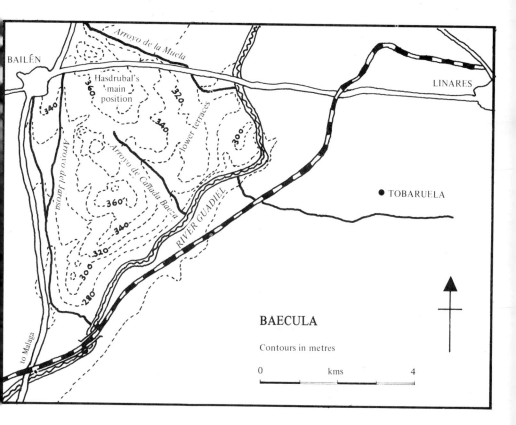

BAILÉN

LINARES

Arroyo de la Muela

Hasdrubal's main position

360

340

320

340

lower terraces

300

Arroyo del Jarosa

Arroyo de Cañada Baeza

RIVER GUADIEL

360

340

320

306

280

to Malaga

● TOBARUELA

**BAECULA**

Contours in metres

0        kms        4

MAP 17

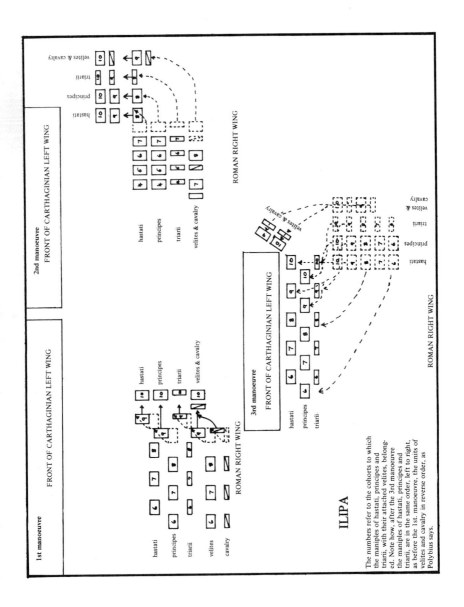

**1st manoeuvre**

FRONT OF CARTHAGINIAN LEFT WING

hastati
principes
triarii
velites
cavalry

ROMAN RIGHT WING

**2nd manoeuvre**

FRONT OF CARTHAGINIAN LEFT WING

hastati
principes
triarii
velites & cavalry

ROMAN RIGHT WING

**3rd manoeuvre**

FRONT OF CARTHAGINIAN LEFT WING

hastati
principes
triarii
velites & cavalry

ROMAN RIGHT WING

## ILIPA

The numbers refer to the cohorts to which the maniples of hastati, principes and triarii, with their attached velites, belonged. Note how, after the 3rd manoeuvre the maniples of hastati, principes and triarii, are in the same order, left to right, as before the 1st manoeuvre, the units of velites and cavalry in reverse order, as Polybius says.

MAP 18

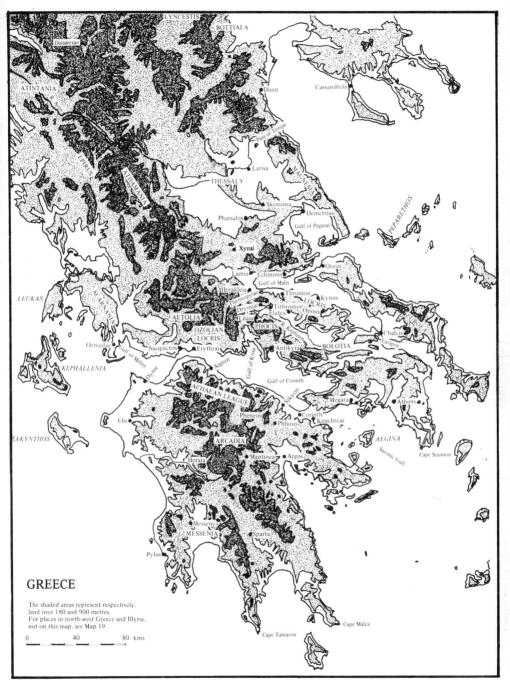

LYNCESTIS

BOTTIAEA

*Dassaretae*

ATINTANIA

Dium

Cassandreia

EPIRUS

TYMPHAIA

Pass of Tempe

Larisa

THESSALY

MAGNESIA

PREPARETHOS

Skotousa

Pharsalos

Demetrias

Gulf of Pagasai

**Xynai**

LEUKAS

ACARNANIA

Lamia

Echinous

Oreos

Herakleia

Gulf of Malis

Thermopylae

Thronion

LOCRIS

Kynos

Drymia

Tithronion

EUBOEA

AETOLIA

Lilaia

Elatea

Opous

OZOLIAN

LOCRIS

PHOCIS

R. Kephisos

Chalcis

Oeniadae

Gulf of Melite

Naupactos

Erythrai

Antikyra

BOEOTIA

Euripos

KEPHALLENIA

Dyme

Aigion

Gulf of Krisa

Gulf of Corinth

ACHAEAN LEAGUE

Sikyon

Megara

Athens

Pheneos

Corinth

Kenchreai

Elis

Phlious

ZAKYNTHOS

AEGINA

ARCADIA

Saronic Gulf

Cape Sounion

Heraia

Mantinea

Argos

Messene

MESSENIA

Sparta

Pylos

# GREECE

The shaded areas represent respectively,
land over 180 and 900 metres.
For places in north-west Greece and Illyria,
not on this map, see Map 19.

0        40        80  kms

Cape Malea

Cape Tainaron

MAP 19

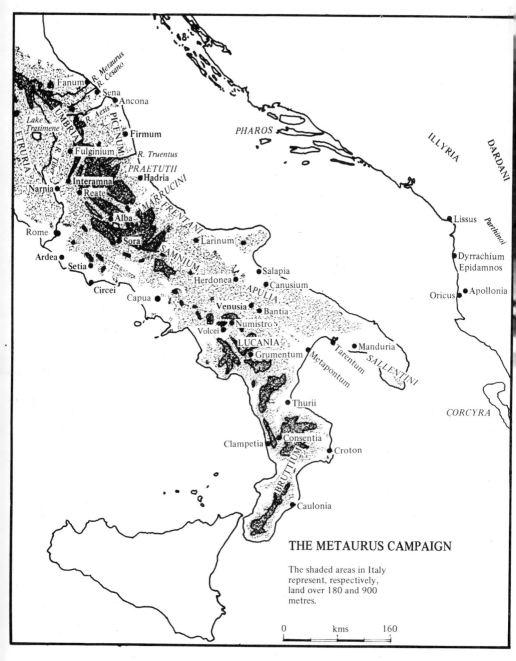

THE METAURUS CAMPAIGN

The shaded areas in Italy represent, respectively, land over 180 and 900 metres.

0    kms    160

MAP 20

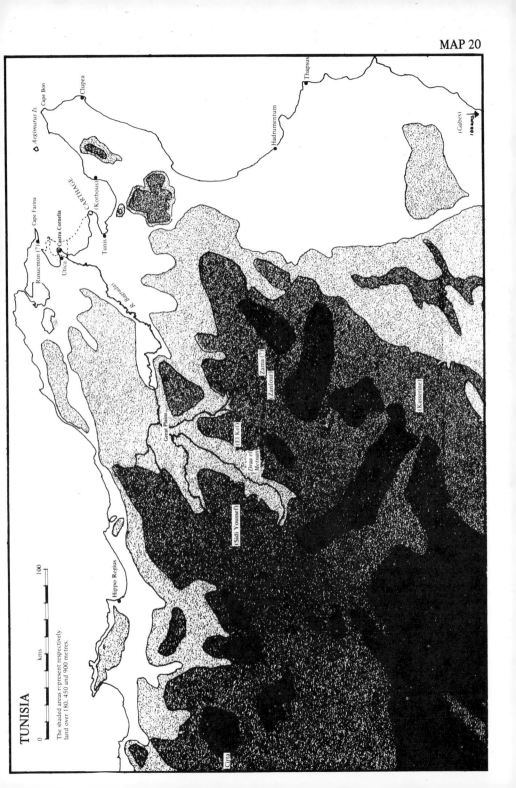

# TUNISIA

The shaded areas represent respectively
land over 180, 450 and 900 metres.

0    kms    100

Agimurus Is.

Cape Bon

Clupea

Thapsus

Hadrumentum

(Gabes)

Cape Farina

CARTHAGE

(Korbous)

Rusucmon (?)

Castra Cornelia

Utica

Tunis

R. Bagradus

Zama (?)

Zanfour)

El Kef

Draa e
Metnan

Kasserin

Great Plains

(Sidi Youssef)

Hippo Regius

Cirta

MAP 21

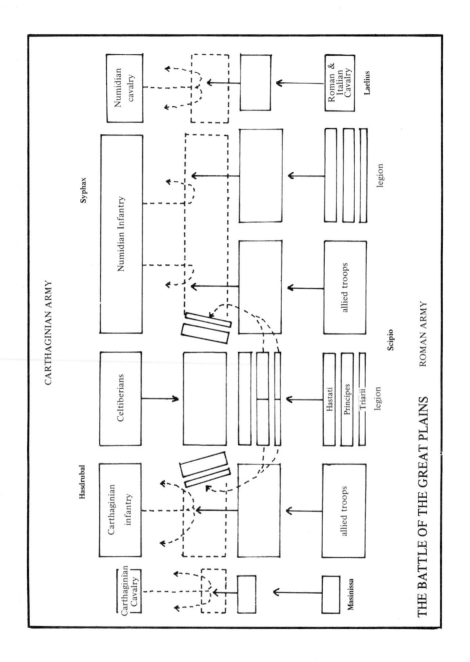

THE BATTLE OF THE GREAT PLAINS

# INDEX

(Romans are mostly listed under their *nomina* - i.e. their second names - and identified, where appropriate, by offices held - cos. = consul, pr. = praetor, tr.pl. = tribune of the *plebs,* dict. = dictator. For further information see T. R. S. Broughton, *The Magistrates of the Roman Republic*).

Alexander the Great: 157, 227, 242.
Algeria: 8, 228, 233.
allied contingents (Roman), organization of: 12-3.
Allifae: 69, 71.
Allobroges: 39, 41, 42, 43, 45, 48.
Almanzora, river: 239.
Alps: 15, 23, 29-35, 37, 38, 40-3, 45-8, 52, 169, 181, 182, 239, 251, 258.
Althaia (Altea): 22.
Ambin, river: 46.
Amiternum (San Vettorino): 122.
Ammianus Marcellinus: 40; Appendix I, 261.
Amtorgis: 130.
Amynander: 163.
Anapos, river: 107, 117.
Ancona: 11, 193.
Andalusia: 8, 128, 129, 239.
Andobales (Indibilis): 126, 130, 139-42, 152-4.
Anicius, Marcus: 13, 93.
Anio, river: 121, 122.
Antigonos Doson: 158.
Antikyra in Phocis: 162.
Antikyra (in Ozolian Locris?): 166, 167, 295 n. 25.
Antiochus III, King of Syria: 20, 172, 229, 235, 241-3, 248, 251.
Antiochus IV, King of Syria: 249.
Antirhion: 163.
Aous (Vijose), river: 159, 160.
Apamea, treaty of: 243.
Apennines: 11, 54, 60, 70, 181-4, 186, 188, 251.
Aphrodite, temple of (at Saguntum): 128.
Apollo, promontory of: 215.
Apollonia: 158-60, 162, 168, 235.
Apollonides: 104.
Appian: 20, 21, 23, 28, 33, 56, 61, 75, 79, 87, 112, 129, 130, 132, 134, 136, 145, 146, 152, 154, 159, 182, 188, 196, 205, 206, 207, 208, 213, 214, 215, 216, 217, 218, 221, 222, 225, 228, 229, 244, 245, 247; Appendix I, 260-1.
Apuani: 239.
Apulia: 68, 71, 72, 76, 80, 88, 91, 95, 97, 100, 102, 105, 114, 124, 170, 185.

Aquileia: 239, 298 n. 24.
Aragon: 239.
Arar (Saône), river: 38.
Arbukale (Toro): 22.
Arc, river: 45, 46, 182.
Arcadia: 166.
Archimedes: 107, 119.
Ardea: 26, 174.
Areakidai: 217.
Arethusa, Fountain of: 118, 292 n. 43.
Argos: 163, 164.
Ariminum (Rimini): 11, 51, 54, 55, 58-62, 66, 174, 181, 239, 254.
Aristotle: 1; Appendix I, 261.
Arno; river: 15, 61, 92.
Arpi: 68, 76, 88, 89, 97, 105.
Arpinum: 247.
Arrenius, Gaius, tr.pl. 210: 173.
Arrenius, Lucius, tr.pl. 210: 173, 179?.
Arroyo de Cañada Baeza: 141, 142.
Arroyo de la Muela: 141, 142.
Artemis, Festival of: 115, 116.
Artemision: 165.
Asculum (Ascoli Piceno): 11, 184.
Asia Minor: 158, 166, 233, 235, 238, 242.
Asklepios (Eshmoun), temple of: 135; image of: 253.
Aspra Spitia: 162.
Assisi: 65.
Astapa (Estepa): 152, 155.
Atella (Aversa): 90, 124.
Aternus, river: 122.
Athamania: 163.
Athens: 157-9, 163, 241.
Atintania: 159, 161, 168.
Atilius:

C. Atilius Regulus, cos. 225/4: 31, 65.
M. Atilius Regulus, cos. suff. 217/6: 72, 73, 75, 80, 85.
C. Atilius Serranus, pr. 218/7: 51.

Atlantic: 23, 127, 261.
Atrius, Caius: 153.
Attalus of Pergamum: 161, 163-6, 200, 240, 241.
Attica: 167.
Aufidus (Ofanto), river: 76-8.

Augustus: 155, 239, 243.
Aulius, Marcus: 179.
Aurinx: 128.
Ausetani: 126, 132.
Avernus, Lake: 101, 102, 110.
Avignon: 35-7, 40.
Aygues, river: 38-41.

Bacchus, worship of: 246.

Baebius:

Q. Baebius, tr.pl.200: 241.
Q. Baebius Herennius, tr.pl. 216: 74.

Baecula (Baikula, Bailén): 140-2, 143, 144, 150, 293 n. 22.
Baetis (Guadalquivir), river and region (Baetica): 21, 25, 125, 130, 134, 140-2, 144, 145, 150, 152-5, 239.
Baga: 198.
Bagradas (Medjerda), river: 209, 218.
Balearic Islands, islanders: 8, 14, 32, 57, 63, 64, 81, 127, 142, 143, 149, 222, 223.
Bantia (Banzi): 178.
Barcelona: 152.
Bargyllon: 168.
Bari: 78.
Baria (Vera): 140, 239.
Barriol: 132.
Baza: 144.
Beaucaire: 36-8, 40.
"Beautiful One", promontory of the (Cap Farina): 204, 205.
Bellona, Temple of: 155, 213, 230.
Beneventum (Benevento): 12, 18, 69, 90, 100-2, 112, 113, 174.
Benghazi: 9.
Biella: 53.
Bigerra: 129.
biremes: 166.
Bithynia: 158, 163, 166.
"Black Stones" (*Lapides Atri*), pass: 132.
Blanda (Maratea): 102.
Blenheim, battle of: 255.
Boeotia, Boeotians: 158, 164-7.
Boii: 29, 31, 32, 51, 54.
Bollène: 40.
Bologna (Bononia): 11, 29, 60, 61, 239.

Bomilcar: 16, 31, 98, 107, 117, 118, 171.
Bon, Cape: 204, 215.
Bône: see Hippo Regius.
Borgo St. Antonio: 70.
Bostar: 128.
Bottiaea: 162.
Boudonitza: 166.
Bourg-St. Maurice: 43.
Bou Salem: 209.
Bovianum (Boiano): 71, 112.
Bramans: 46.
Braneus: 39.
Briançon: 37.
Brundisium (Brindisi): 10, 12, 55, 97, 100, 101, 160, 174, 176.
Bruttium, Bruttii, Bruttians: 12, 88, 96, 97, 102, 112, 113, 115, 121, 124, 157, 168, 171, 173-6, 181, 183-6, 190-3, 195, 196, 200, 215, 222, 242, 246, 247, 252, 254.
Bucar: 198.
Bulgaria: 158, 162, 243.
Bulotus, river: 199.
Burguillos: 146.

Cabanes: 132.
Caecilius:

L. Caecilius Metellus: 237.
Q. Caecilius Metellus, cos. 206/5: 191, 193, 200, 201, 213, 217

Caesar: 30, 206, 239, 253.
Caiatia (Caiazzo): 69, 91.
Calabria: 95, 97.
Calatia (Caserta): 69, 90, 124.
Cales (Calvi): 69, 96, 153.
*Calidae Aquae* (Korbous): 215.
*Callicula mons:* 69, 70.
Calor, river: 69, 102, 113.
Calpurnius:

C. Calpurnius Piso, praetor 211/10: 170, 177.
L. Calpurnius Piso, cos. 133: 131; Appendix I, 263.

Camerinum: 11, 12.
Campania, Campanians: 10, 12, 19, 31, 66, 69, 80, 89-93, 95, 96, 100, 102,

112-114, 121-3, 170, 175, 236, 244, 247, 252.

Cannae: 1, 6, 10, 12, 14, 15, 30, 48, 65, 68, 74, 75, 76, 77-85, 86-9, 91, 92, 94, 95, 98, 101, 102, 114, 128, 143, 150, 159, 168, 172, 178, 179, 180, 202, 203, 215, 222, 226, 230, 233, 236, 237, 239, 252, 254, 256, 259, 261.

Canusium: 85, 90, 175, 180, 185, 186, 190.

Capua, Capuans: 3, 6, 12, 15, 17, 69, 86, 87, 89, 90, 92, 93, 96, 97, 101, 109, 112-5, 120-4, 130, 132, 157, 161, 168-70, 174, 175, 177, 180, 184-6, 195, 235, 236, 254, 288 n. 19.

Capussa: 198.

Cartagena (New Carthage): 9, 21, 22, 23, 25, 29, 32-4, 47-9, 125-8, 130, 132, 134-40, 141, 151-5, 222, 226, 234, 239, 258, 259, 285 n. 33.

Carpesii (Carpetani): 22, 125, 134, 284 n. 11.

Carteia: 153, 294 n. 66.

Carthage: *passim.*

Carthaginian army: 14-5.

Carthaginian fleet: 16, 18, 58, 60, 68, 97, 98, 107, 110, 117, 118, 144, 159, 163, 166, 167, 171, 175, 196, 197, 204, 211, 216, 217, 231, 235.

Carthaginian politics: 4-5, 22, 26, 98, 208-9, 211, 213, 215-6, 229-30, 231, 242.

Carthalo: 70, 86, 88, 176?, 237.

Carvilius, Sp., cos.I 234/3?: 253.

Casale Montferrato: 53.

Casalnuovo Monterotaro: 71.

Casilinum (now Capua): 12, 13, 69, 70, 87, 91, 92, 93, 102, 114.

Casinum (Cassino): 69.

Cassandreia: 167.

Cassius Dio: 22, 23, 87, 90, 92, 206, 214, 221, 229; Appendix I, 260-1.

Cassius:

C. Cassius Longinus, cos.171/0: 249.

Castillo de Despeña Perros: 135.

Castillo de los Moros: 136.

*castra Claudiana* (Claudian Camp) : 93, 95-7, 100, 105, 114.

*castra Cornelia:* 206-8, 211, 216.

*Castrum Album:* 129.

Castulo: 17, 127, 129, 130, 134, 145, 146, 152, 155.

Catalonia: 128, 129, 239.

Catius, Q.: 186.

Cato: see under Porcius.

Caudini (Samnites): 96.

Caudium: 102.

Caulonia: 175, 176.

Celtiberia, Celtiberes (i): 125, 127, 130, 143, 144, 152, 209-11.

Celts (Gauls): 11, 14, 15, 23, 29, 31, 32, 36, 49, 54, 56, 57, 60, 61, 63-5, 71, 81, 82, 84, 85, 112, 182, 183, 189, 190, 192, 222, 229, 238-9, 251, 256.

Cenomani: 11, 56.

Centenius, C.: 65.

Centenius:

M. Centenius Paenula: 113.

Ceres, festival of: 230.

Cesano, river: 187, 188.

Chalcis: 163, 165, 167, 241.

Chios: 163.

Chlainias of Aetolia: 162.

Choranche: 42.

Cicero: see under Tullius.

Cincius:

L. Cincius Alimentus, pr. 210/09: 172, 179, 180, 251; Appendix I, 259-61; 287 n. 43.

Circei: 174.

*Circus Flaminius:* 59.

Cirta (Constantine): 8, 198, 205, 212, 232.

Cisalpine Gaul (see also Celts, Po): 32, 50, 51, 86, 95, 100, 105, 109, 170, 181, 195, 196, 201, 213, 238-9, 246, 248; Appendix II, 266.

Clampetia (Amantea): 215.

Clanius, river: 92.

Clapier, Col de: 46, 47, 182.

Clastidium: 55.

Claudii: 109.

326

Claudius:

C. Claudius Centho, cos. 240/39: 73, 108, 109.
Q. Claudius Flamen, pr. 208/7: 181, 184-6.
M. Claudius Marcellus, cos. I 222/1: 6, 85, 90-7, 100-9, 115-20, 132, 133, 150, 169-179, 181, 253, 289 n. 35.
M. Claudius Marcellus, pr. 169/68: 245.
C. Claudius Nero, cos. 207/6: 109, 114, 120, 124, 130-32, 179-81, 183-91, 236.
Ti. Claudius Nero, cos. 203/2: 217, 230.
P. Claudius Pulcher, cos. 249/8: 253.
Ap. Claudius Pulcher, cos. 212/11: 89?, 98, 103-9, 113, 123, 177.
C. Claudius Pulcher, cos. 177/6: 246.
Q. Claudius Quadrigarius: 131; Appendix I, 261.
Clodius Licinus: 202.
Clupea (Kelibia): 144, 166, 197, 198.
Coelius:

L. Coelius Antipater: 43, 45, 121, 122, 179, 196; Appendix I, 260-1; 288 nn. 8 & 9.

Colle di Scheggia: 183.
Colline Gate: 121.
Compsa: 89, 102.
Consentia (Cosenza): 96, 192, 215.
Contestani: 21.
Corcyra (Corfu): 157, 159, 161, 163, 164.
Corinth: 119, 157, 164, 166, 167, 244, 254.
Corinth, Gulf of: 163, 164, 166, 167.
Cornelii, Cornelian group: 4, 59, 67, 72, 74, 109, 133, 177, 181, 191, 231.

Cornelius:

L. Cornelius Balbus: 131.
M. Cornelius Cethegus, cos. 204/3: 109, 172, 200, 214.
L. Cornelius Lentulus, cos. 237/6: 26.
P. Cornelius Lentulus, pr. 214/3: 120.
L. Cornelius Lentulus, pr. 211/10: 120.
P. Cornelius Lentulus, pr. 203/2: 227.
Cn. Cornelius Lentulus, cos. 202/1: 85, 230, 231.

Cornelius Nepos: 127, 218; Appendix I, 258, 259, 262.
P. Cornelius Rufinus, cos.I 290/89: 250.

Cn. Cornelius Scipio, cos. 222/1: 6, 51, 61, 100, 109, 114, 115, 125-33, 140, 151, 152, 155, 180, 237, 239, 259.
P. Cornelius Scipio, cos. 218/7: 6, 31, 35, 37, 39, 50-3, 55, 57, 58, 61, 62, 100, 109, 114, 115, 125-32, 140, 151, 180, 237, 259.

P. Cornelius Scipio (Africanus), cos. I 205/4: 4-8, 12, 13, 16, 30, 53, 72, 75, 81, 109, 129, 131, 132-56, 157, 169, 170, 173, 177, 179, 181, 191, 192, 193-232, 233, 236, 237, 239, 241, 242, 244, 248, 256, 258, 259, 294 n. 37.

comparison with Hannibal: 226-7.
strategy; 134-5, 139-40, 143, 144, 151, 155-6, 193-4, 206, 208-9, 211, 217, 218-9, 297 n. 37.
tactics: 141-2, 146-50, 153-4, 205, 210-11, 294 n. 54.

L. Cornelius Scipio, cos. 190/89: 129, 144, 155, 199, 204, 230, 259, 293 n. 23.
P. Cornelius Scipio Aemilianus, cos. I 147: 131, 244, 248, 258.
P. Cornelius Scipio Asina, cos. 221/0: 73, 74, 123
P. Cornelius Scipio Nasica, cos. 191/90: 200, 244.
P. Cornelius Sulla, pr. 212/1: 109.
L. Cornelius Sulla (Felix), dict.81-79: 109, 251.

Corsica: 1, 7, 22, 233, 243, 251.
Corso due Mari: 112.
Cortona: 62.
Cosa: 11, 68.
Cremona: 10, 11, 31, 51, 61, 174, 192, 238, 239.
Cremonis iugum: 43.
Cretan mercenaries: 58, 66, 104, 165.
Cromwell, Oliver: 136.
Croton: 32, 88, 96, 215, 242.

Grumentum: 171, 175, 185.
Guadalquivir, river: see Baetis.
Guadelimar, river: 127.
Guadiana, river: 125.
Guadiel, river: 141.

Hadria: 11, 12, 174.
Hadrian: 154.
Hadrumentum (Sousse): 215, 218, 227.
Hamae: 96.
Hamilcar Barca: 7, 19, 20, 21, 22, 24, 129.
Hamilcar (Carthaginian officer): 199.
Hannibal the Rhodian: 17.

Hannibal: *passim.*

assessment of, as general: 255-7.
cavalry, use of: 15, 30, 32-4, 36, 37, 44,
   48, 53-5, 56-8, 61, 62-5, 67, 70, 72,
   83-4, 93, 111, 113, 114, 121, 122,
   170-1, 180, 217, 222-3, 256.
comparison with Scipio: 226-7.
humour: 37, 81, 93, 176, 179.
strategy: 29-32, 60, 66, 69, 85-6, 88-9,
   92, 96, 98, 102, 106, 113-5, 121,
   122, 171, 174, 175, 190, 218-9, 290
   n. 49.
tactics: 53, 55, 58, 71, 72, 81-2, 111-2,
   114, 171, 185, 199, 223ff.

Hannibal (envoy to Syracuse): 102.
Hanno (political opponent of Hannibal):
   5, 26.
Hanno (Hannibal's deputy in northern
   Spain): 34, 126.
Hanno, son of Bomilcar: 36.
Hanno (commander of right wing at Cannae
   - same as above?): 82, 290 n. 46.
Hanno (Hannibal's general in Bruttium -
   same as above?): 96, 97, 102, 112, 113,
   186, 256.
Hanno (Carthaginian general in Sicily):
   119, 172.
Hanno (Carthaginian general in Spain):
   143, 144.
Hanno (Carthaginian cavalry commander
   in Africa): 205, 206.
Hanno, son of Hamilcar: 205, 206.

Hasdrubal the 'Kid': 5, 231.
Hasdrubal Barca (Hannibal's brother): 6,
   32, 52, 60, 98, 124, 126-30, 131?, 132,
   134, 141-4, 157, 167-9, 178, 181-4,
   186-92, 195-7, 236, 238, 243, 296 n.38.
Hasdrubal (Hannibal's brother-in-law): 20-5,
   135.
Hasdrubal (general in Hannibal's army):
   53, 70, 82, 84.
Hasdrubal the 'Bald': 97, 98.
Hasdrubal Gisgo: 130, 131, 134, 141-6,
   149-51, 155, 198, 202, 205-9, 211,
   212, 229-30?
Hasdrubal (Carthaginian admiral - same as
   above?): 216.

*hastati:* 13, 79, 147, 149, 210, 221, 224,
   225; Appendix II, 268.

Hector: 244.
Helike (in Spain): 129.
Helmantica (Salamanca): 22.
Heloros: 107.
Hemeroskopeion (Denia): 23.
Henna (Enna): 108.
Hephaistos (Vulcan, Kousor); hill of: 135.
Hera, festival of: 163
Heraclea (in Italy): 112
Heraclea Minoa: 107, 118.
Heraia: 166.
Herakleia (in Greece): 165.
Herbessos: 104, 107.
Herdonea (Ordona): 89, 114, 120, 170-4,
   195, 202.
Herodotus: 219.
Hexapyloi Gate: 106, 108, 116.
Hiero, King of Syracuse: 12, 19, 58, 66,
   98, 102, 103, 104.
Hieronymos, King of Syracuse: 102, 103.
Himera (Salso), river: 103, 119.
Himilco (Carthaginian general in Spain):
   128.
Himilco (Carthaginian general in Sicily):
   107, 108, 115-7.
Hippocrates: 102-5, 107, 115-7.
Hippo Regius (Bône, Annaba): 197, 198,
   205.

Lacumazes: 198.

*lacus Umber:* 65.

Laelius, Caius: 135, 139, 142, 151-4, 196-9, 204, 205, 208, 210-12, 214, 216, 217, 222, 223, 225, 227, 288 n.8.

Laevinus: see under Valerius.

Lamia: 163.

Languedoc: 32.

Larinum (Larino): 71, 184-6, 190.

Larisa: 164, 234.

Larissos, river: 164.

La Rochette: 44, 46.

Latins: 10-12, 55, 56, 66, 92, 153, 169, 174, 178, 179, 195, 201, 225, 233-4, 239, 245-7, 252-3, 254.

Lebanon: 8, 9, 158.

Lee, Robert E.: 256.

*legiones Cannenses:* 91, 95, 108, 120, 170, 172, 174, 195, 202.

*legiones urbanae:* 61, 68, 75, 91, 100, 101, 105, 108, 109, 120, 122, 170, 174, 177, 178, 181, 186, 190, 195, 196.

*lemboi (lembi):* 158, 160, 167; Appendix II, 270.

Lemnos: 165.

Lentulus: see under Valerius.

Leon: 108.

Leonidas: 251.

Leontinoi: 103, 104, 107.

Leptis Minor (Lamta): 215.

Lérida: 152.

Leukas: 158

Liburnos, mount: see *Mons Tifernus.*

Libya, Libyans: 8, 9, 158, 222; (see also Africa, Africans).

Licinius:

P. Licinius Crassus, cos. 205/4: 173, 180, 193, 200, 215, 253, 295 n.31.

P. Licinius Varus, pr. 208/7: 177.

Licinus: see under Porcius.

Liguria, Ligurians: 21, 22, 30, 32, 60, 154, 182, 189, 195, 196, 222, 228, 229, 238-9, 243, 246, 248.

Lilaia: 166.

Lilybaeum (Marsala): 55, 98, 100, 101, 106, 118, 158, 197, 202, 204.

Linares: 130, 141, 145, 152.

Liris, river: 122.

Lissus (Lesh): 159, 161, 164.

Liternum (Patria): 96.

Little St. Bernard pass: 39, 43, 45, 182.

Livius:

M. Livius Drusus, tr.pl. 122: 247.

C. *or* M. Livius (Macatus): 111, 180.

M. Livius Salinator, cos. I 219/8: 89, 180-4, 186-92, 196, 201, 213.

Livy: *passim* - see esp. Appendix I, 259-60.

Locri: 30, 31, 87, 88, 96, 98, 178-80, 199-202, 215.

Locris (Opuntian): 165.

Loguntica: 127.

Lomello: 53.

Loreto: 184.

Lorqui: 131, 152.

Luca (Lucca): 60, 239, 298 n. 24.

Lucania, Lucani, Lucanians: 12, 95, 96, 102, 105, 109, 113, 115, 124, 171, 173, 174, 176, 178, 183, 185, 186, 190, 192, 252, 254.

Luceria (Lucera): 12, 71, 97, 100-2, 105, 160, 174.

Lucretius, Marcus (tr.pl. 210): 173

Lucretius, Spurius (pr. 205/4): 196, 201.

Lucretius (T. Lucretius Carus, the poet): 131.

Luna (La Spezia): 239.

Lusitania, Lusitani (Portugal): 22, 127, 134, 143, 243.

Lutatius:

C. Lutatius Catulus, cos. 242/1: 213.

Lykiskos of Acarnania: 1, 162.

Lyncestis: 162.

Lyon: 38, 40.

Machanidas: 163, 164, 166, 167.

Macrobius: 77, 213; Appendix I, 262.

Madrid: 22.

Maedi: 162, 164.

Maesuli: 198, 202, 212.
Magilos: 29, 37, 42.
Magione: 63.
Magnesia (district in Greece): 165; (in Asia Minor): 235, 242.
Mago (Hannibal's brother): 15, 30, 52, 56, 57, 81, 83, 85, 89, 98, 124, 129, 130, 131, 134, 141, 143-6, 151-4, 178, 194-8, 201, 214, 215, 222, 228, 238, 288 n.9.
Mago (Carthaginian commander at Cartagena): 136-9.
Maharbal: 64-6, 85, 290 n. 46.
Mahón: 155.
Majorca: 155.
Malaga: 129, 141.
Malis, Gulf of: 162, 165.
Malea, Cape: 158.
Malta: 9.
Mamertini: 18, 19, 254.
Mamilius:

Q. Mamilius Turrinus, pr. 206/5: 191, 192.

Mandonios: 139-41, 152-4.
Manduria: 175.

Manlius:

A. Manlius, tr.mil. 208: 179.
L. Manlius Acidinus, pr. 210/09: 191,
T. Manlius Torquatus, cos. I 235/4: 89, 98, 99, 169, 180, 253.
L. Manlius Vulso, pr. 218/7: 50, 51.

Mantinea: 167.
Marcellus: see under Claudius.
Marcius, Lucius: 131-3, 147, 152-4.

Marcius:

M. Marcius Ralla, pr. 204/3: 200.

Margaron: 218, 219, 297 n. 31.
Marius, Gaius: 248, 253.
Marlborough, Duke of: 255.
Marmoreae: 170.
Marrucini: 122, 186.
Marruvini: 122.
Marruvium (San Benedetto): 122.
Marseille: 23, 26, 28, 32, 126, 181, 239, 251.

Marsi: 11, 68, 122.
Masaesuli: 198, 202, 212.
Masinissa: 129, 130, 143, 146, 151, 154, 155, 198, 199, 202, 204, 205, 208-13, 217-23, 225, 228, 229, 232, 238, 242, 244, 255.
Masseria Collepazzo: 111.
Massif de la Vanoise: 46.
Maurienne: 46.
Mazaetullus: 198, 218.
Mediolanum (Milan): 31.
Megara: 166.
Megara Hyblaea: 107.
Meles: 170.
Melite, Gulf of: 161.
Mendhenitsa: 166.
Mengibar: 152.
Mentissa: 132.
Mercury, Hill of: 136.
Mercury, Promontory of: see Bon, Cape.
Messene: 164, 166.
Messenia: 159, 162.
Messina: 18, 19, 25, 55, 96, 202.
Metagonia: 32.
Metapontum: 112, 171, 176, 185, 186, 190.
Metaurus, river: 6, 144, 157, 167, <u>182-90</u>, 191, 192, 236, 243.
Metilius, Marcus (tr.pl. 217): 72, 74.
Minorca: 30, 155, 196.

Minucius:

M. Minucius, tr.pl. 216: 93.
M. Minucius Rufus, cos. 221/0: 3, 4, 67-74, 80, 85, 257, 289 n. 29.
Q. Minucius Thermus, tr.pl. 201: 231, 245.

Modane: 46.
Moericus: 118.
Molino de Truchao: 138.
*Mons Tifata* (Monte Virgo): 93, 96, 101, 121.

*Mons Tifernus* (Tiburnos, Matese): 71.

Montagne de Lure: 40.
Mont Cenis, Col du: 37, 182.
Monte Caievola: 70.

Pontcharra: 44, 46.
Pont-en-Royans: 42.
Popillius:

M. Popullius Laenas, cos. 173/2: 249.
C. Popillius Laenas, cos. 172/1: 249.

Populonia: 17.
Porcius:

M. Porcius Cato, cos. 195/4: 16, 201, 204, 244, 249-51, 253; Appendix I, 261.
L. Porcius Licinus, pr. 207/6: 181, 182, 184, 187-91.

Porretta pass: 61.
*Porta Capena:* 123.

Porto Farina: 211.
Portugal: see Lusitania, Lusitani.
Poseidon: see Neptune.
Posidonius: 179; Appendix I, 263.

Postumius:

M. Postumius (of Pyrge): 110, 292 n.32.
L. Postumius Albinus, cos.I 229/8: 75, 86, 94, 95, 157.
L. Postumius Albinus, cos. 173/2: 240, 246, 249.
A. Postumius Albinus, cos. 151: 251; Appendix I, 263.

Praeneste (Palestrina): 10, 13, 68, 92, 93, 191, 246, 249, 288 n.19.
Praetutii: 183, 186.
Prilep: 162.
*principes:* 13, 79, 147, 149, 210, 211, 221, 224, 225; Appendix II, 272.

*proletarii:* 3, 17, 101, 252; Appendix II, 272; 298 n. 22.

Propontis (Sea of Marmara): 240.
Proserpine, shrine of (at Henna): 108; temple of (at Locri): 202.
Prusias, King of Bithynia: 163, 166, 298 n. 14.
Ptolemy Philopator: 90.

Publicius:

C. Publicius Bibulus, tr.pl. 209: 177.
M. Publicius Malleolus, cos. 232/1: 177.

Pupinia: 121, 123.
Pydna, battle of: 243, 258.
Pylos: 159.
Pyrenees: 23, 34, 48, 50, 51, 126, 132, 143.
Pyrrhus, King of Epirus: 18, 157, 227.

Qabes: see Gabes.
quadriremes: 118, 166, 216; Appendix II, 273.
Quinctius:

L. Quinctius Cincinnatus, dict. 248: 250.
T. Quinctius Crispinus, cos. 208/7: 108, 174, 176, 178-81.
T. Quinctius Flamininus, cos. 198/7: 241, 242, 248.

Quinctilius:

P. Quinctilius Varus, pr. 204/3: 214.

quinqueremes: 16, 31, 32, 50, 55, 107, 126, 151, 152, 153, 158, 159, 161, 165, 167, 216, 217, 230; Appendix II, 273.

Reate (Rieti): 122, 184.
Rhegium (Reggio di Calabria): 55, 96, 115, 122, 159, 175, 199, 201, 202.
Rhion: 163.
Rhode (Rosas): 23.
Rhodes: 158, 163, 166, 235, 241.
Rhône, river: 23, 29, 31, 34-42, 45, 48, 50, 51, 82, 126, 239, 256.
Rimini: see Ariminum.
Rome, Romans: *passim.*

Roman allies: *passim,* but see esp. 10-13.
Roman army, organization of: 10-14.
Roman cavalry: 10, 13, 14, 37, 50, 51, 53, 54, 56-8, 61, 62-5, 66, 70, 72, 76, 80, 83-4, 102, 121, 125, 132, 133, 135, 144, 145, 146-50, 150-1,

153-4, 170, 173, 178-9, 181, 186, 188, 190, 195, 203, 205, 209-10, 212, 221, 225.

dispositions: 50-1, 54-6, 61-2, 68, 75-6, 91, 95, 100, 105, 107-8, 109, 114, 120-1, 125, 127, 132, 133, 135, 162, 168, 170, 173-4, 177, 181-2, 191-2, 195, 200-1, 202-3, 233-4, 289 n.30, 291 n.4.

elections and politics: 1-4, 58-9, 67-8, 72, 73-5, 88-9, 94-5, 99-100, 105, 108-9, 119-20, 132-3, 169, 172-3, 176-7, 180-1, 191, 193-5, 200, 216-7, 230-1, 237-8, 241.

finances: 93-4, 98-9, 100-1, 168, 169-70, 174-5, 201.

fleet: 16, 31, 73, 98, 101, 107, 117-8, 121, 126-7, 144-5, 158, 160, 162, 163, 167, 171, 172, 177, 196-7, 203-4, 211, 217, 235.

manpower: 10, 68, 234, 298 n. 1.

Romulus: 254.
Roquemaure: 35.
Rubicon, river: 33.
Rumblar, river: 141.
Ruscino: see Perpignan.
Rusucmon: 211.

Saguntum: 22-29, 32, 49, 87, 109, 128, 129, 134, 193, 259, 285 nn. 43 & 47.
St. Nazaire-en-Royans: 41, 42.
Salaeca: 205, 206.
Salapia (Salpi): 89, 102, 105, 170, 171, 179, 185.
Salassi: 43.
Salinator: see under Livius.
Sallentini: 184, 185.
Sallust (C. Sallustius Crispus): 249.
*sambucae:* 107.
Samnium, Samnites: 12, 69, 88-90, 93, 96, 102, 121, 122, 124, 170, 176, 186, 252, 254.
San Ferdinando di Puglia: 77.
Sanguineto: 62-4.

San José: 135.
Santa Panayia: 115.
Saône, river: 38.
Sapriportis: 171.
Saragossa: 152.
Sardinia: 1, 7, 21, 22, 27, 31, 58, 61, 65, 73, 86, 87, 95, 97, 98, 100, 120, 170, 177, 192, 196, 197, 206, 215, 219, 233, 243, 251.
Saronic Gulf: 164, 167.
Sassenage: 42.
Savona: 196.
Sarturano: 54.
Saticula: 91.
Saturnalia: 227.
Scala Graeca: 106, 115.
Scerdilaidas: 159, 161, 164.
Scipio: see under Cornelius.
Seba Biar: 218.
Sedetani: see Edetani.
Segura, river: 125, 131.
Sempronius:

Ti. Sempronius Gracchus, cos. 238/7: 21.
Ti. Sempronius Gracchus, cos.I 215/4: 90-7, 100-2, 105, 108, 109, 113, 253.
Ti. Sempronius Gracchus, cos. 177/6: 240.
Ti. Sempronius Gracchus, tr.pl. 133: 245, 252.
C. Sempronius Gracchus, tr.pl. 123, 122: 247, 250, 252.
Ti. Sempronius Longus, cos. 218/7: 31, 50, 51, 54-6, 58-62, 67, 79, 96, 150, 254.
P. Sempronius Tuditanus, cos. 204/3: 105, 109, 167, 168, 195, 200, 215.

Sena Gallica (Senigallia): 11, 182-4, 186-8.

Senate, the (Roman): *passim,* but see esp. 235-7 and Appendix II, 273.

Seneca: 245.
Senones: 11.
Servilius:

Cn. Servilius Caepio, cos. 204/3: 206, 215-7.

61, 86-9, 95, 102, 110-12, 114, 118,
121, 160, 161, 163, 171, 173, 174,
175-6, 177, 179, 180, 181, 184, 185,
186, 195, 197, 244, 252, 254, 256,
288, n. 19.
Tarraco (Tarragona): 126, 133, 134, 140,
141, 143, 151-4, 239.
Tartesii: 128.
Taurini: 32, 43, 49, 52.
Teanum Sidicinom: 85, 90, 91, 95.
Telamon: 23, 31, 65.
Telesia: 69, 102.
Temenid Gate: 111.
Tempe pass: 162.
Tempsa: 242.
Tencin: 44.

Terentius:

    C. Terentius Varro, cos. 216/5: 3, 4, 7,
    68, 74, 75, 77-80, 84, 88-91, 95, 100
    109, 114, 150, 178, 181, 185, 191,
    240, 253.
    C. Teretius Varro (the scholar): 182;
    Appendix I, 264.

Terracina: 70.
Teruel: 125.
Thapsus (Rass Dimasse): 198?, 215.
Themistos: 104.
Thermopylae: 163-5, 251.
Thessaly, Thessalians: 158, 161, 162, 164,
165, 234.
Thrace: 162, 164, 242.
Thronion: 166.
Thucydides: 157; Appendix I, 263; 298
n. 33.
Thurii: 112, 171, 179, 242.
Tiber, river: 11, 65, 68, 242.
Tibur (Tivoli): 68, 122.
Ticinus (Ticino), river: 6, 15, 52, 53, 55.
Timagenes of Alexandria: 40, 41;
Appendix I, 263.
Tiriolo: 246.
Tisaion, mount: 165.
Tithronion: 166.
Tobaruela: 141.
Toledo: 22, 125, 134.

Torboletai: 25, 285 n. 45.
Torricella: 63, 64.
Trajan: 154.
Trasimene, Lake: 6, 7, 12, 15, 30, 48, 59,
60, 61, 62-5, 66, 67, 69, 75, 81, 89, 95,
98, 102, 104, 158, 188, 236, 252, 256.
Trebbia, river: 6, 12, 15, 30, 48, 52, 54,
55-8, 59, 61, 64, 67, 76, 78, 79, 81, 83,
96, 104, 150, 236, 256, 288 nn. 10 & 14.
Trebula: 91, 291 n. 6.
*triarii*: 13, 79, 147, 149, 210, 211, 221,
225; Appendix II, 274.
Tricastini, Tricastin: 40.
Tricorii: 40, 286 n. 18.
Trinitapoli: 77.
triremes: 16, 152, 216, 228; Appendix II,
274.
Trogili: 115.
Troy: 244.
Truentus (Tronto), river: 184.
Tucca, river: 228.
Tullius:
    M. Tullius Cicero, cos. 63: 3, 43, 131,
    182, 249, 251, 253, 257; Appendix I,
    261.
Tunis: 211, 213, 216, 227, 228.
Tunisia: 8, 17, 198, 204, 218, 228, 233.
Tuoro: 62, 63.
Turdetani (Turduli): 25, 125, 128, 285
n.45.
Turin: 32, 45, 49.
Tusculum: 121.
Tychaios: 217.
Tzetzes: 23; Appendix I, 263.

Umbria: 11, 66, 153, 182, 183, 186, 190,
191.
United States, the: 233.
Urso (Orsuna): 130.
Utica: 8, 9, 21, 197, 205-9, 211, 212, 216,
217, 227, 234.

Vaccaei: 22.
Vairano Caianello: 69.
Val d'Aosta: 43, 45.

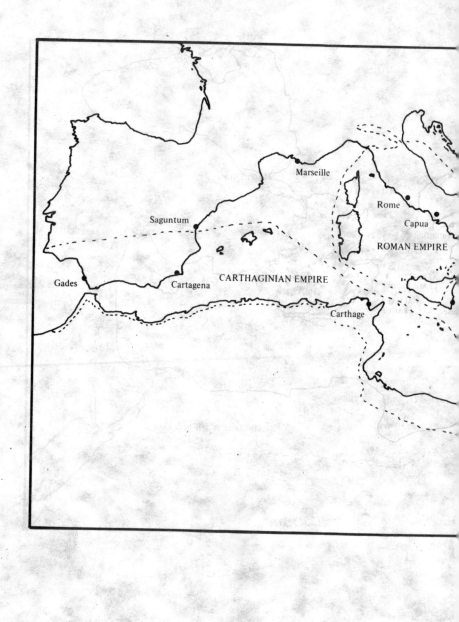